WORLD HISTORY

AN ILLUSTRATED

TIMELINE

WORLD HISTORY
AN ILLUSTRATED TIMELINE

Grange
BOOKS

Published 2007 by Grange Books
an imprint of Grange Books Ltd
The Grange
Kingsnorth Industrial Estate
Hoo, Near Rochester
Kent ME3 9ND
www.Grangebooks.co.uk

The Brown Reference Group plc
(incorporating Andromeda Oxford Limited)
8 Chapel Place
Rivington Street
London
EC2A 3DQ
www.brownreference.com

ISBN: 978-1-84013-920-4

Printed and bound in Thailand

Picture Credits

(t = top, b = bottom, c = center, l = left, r = right)

Cover

Row I : **Daimler Chrysler; PhotoDisc:** Glen Allison; **Digital Vision:** Jeremy Woodhouse;
The Brown Reference Group
Row II: **Phillip Baird:** www.anthroarcheart.org; **NASA; The Brown Reference Group;
Photos.com; NASA; Hamill Gallery of African Art, Boston, M.A.**
Row III: **National Archives; The Brown Reference Group; Photos.com; PhotoDisc:** Mark
Downey
Row IV: **The Brown Reference Group; PhotoDisc:** Tim Hall; **NASA; PhotoDisc:** David
Buffington

AKG-images: 57b, 89c, 153, 213, 218c, 225, 227t, 236, 237t, 244t, 246l, 255c, 255cr, 260r, 261,
281tr, 281b, 287t, 300, 301tl, 307c, 308t, 327c, 344b; British Library 90b; Erich Lessing 34b,
249r, 275b, 369b; Jean-Luis Nou 210b; Robert O'Dea 45; Rabatti-Dominge 207l, 217;
Ancient Art & Architecture Collection Ltd: 174b; **Arizona Office of Tourism:** 157t; **The Art
Archive:** 242b, 266t; Bodleian Library, Oxford 223r; Marco Polo Gallery 294b; Musee des
Arts Africains et Oceaniens 270cr; Natural Science Academy, Kiev 43; Rodriguez Figueroa
Collection, Lima 305; School of Oriental & African Studies/Eileen Tweedy 348b; **Bridgeman
Art Library:** Archives Charmet 287b; Art Museum of Tomsk, Russia 284tl; Biblioteca
Estense, Modena, Italy 212; British Library 268c, 353; Christie's Images, London 218b, 270t;
Giraudon 227b; Giraudon/lauros 197; Giraudon/Topkapi Palace Istanbul 232r, 291l;
Hermitage, St. Petersburg, Russia 238b; Johnny van Haeften Gallery, London 247b; Musee
des Arts Africains et Oceaniens 298c; Museu Nacional de Soares dos Reis, Porto,
Portugal/Giraudon 265; Museum of Fine Arts, Houston, Texas, USA 238t; Natural History
Museum, London 303c, Private Collection 258b; Private Collection/Paul Freeman 303b,
337b; Pro-File Photo Library, Hong Kong 362b; Stapleton Collection 262, 266c, 295, 310cr;
Victoria & Albert Museum, London 222b, 323b; **British Library:** 155; **Christie's Images:**
202b; **Corbis:** 62t, 108b, 205t, 279t, 290t, 345; Paul Almasy 160-161, 252b, 349b; James L.
Amos 229b; Archivo Iconografico, S.A. 10, 75c, 90t, 92t, 94t, 94b, 95, 96t, 103, 110t, 124c,
129b, 137c, 140, 167b, 168-169, 194r, 196, 205b, 208r, 247t, 263c, 279c, 297, 301tr, 314t, 338c,
349t, 362tr; Arte Immagini srl 222c; Asian Art & Archaelogy, Inc 176; Austrian Archives
128; Bettmann 55t, 63, 66t, 102t, 124b, 151b, 177, 204r, 254t, 320b, 327t, 339t, 369t, 379t,
382r, 383b, 388t, 389t, 396, 397b, 411; Stefano Bianchetti 226; Bohemian Nomad
Picturemakers 374; Barnabus Bosshart 209; Bowers Museum of Cultural Art 46; Kevin
Burke 166; Burstein Collection 49, 135b, 214t, 132; Christie's Images 107, 219; Elio Ciol 162;
Richard A.Cooke 42, 163t; Gianni Dagli Orti 11b, 22, 29, 136t, 142, 144r, 184c, 214b, 224,
328b; De Selva Leonard 315b; Nicole Duplaix 183; Macduff Everton 104t, 161; Eye
Ubiquitos/Hugh Rooney 82t; Randy Faris 99; Jack Field 58c; Raymond Gehman 242t;

Georgia Lowell 93, 304; Christel Gerstenberg 169t; Gianni Giansanti/Immaginazione 211;
Todd A. Gipstein 269; Tony Hamblin/Frank Lane Agency 19; Peter Harholdt 310t; Lindsay
Hebberd 187c; Chris Hellier 87t, 112t, 139, 233; John Heseltine 225t, 277; Jon Hicks 286c;
Historical Picture Archive 248t, 338b, 343; Jeremy Horner 148/149; H.H. Huey 220t;
Hulton-Deutsch Collection 363, 390, 397c; James Davis/Eye Ubiquitous 129c; Andrew
Jemola 135t; Dewitt Jones 70t; Wolfgang Kaehler 51, 180, 280, 284c; Layne Kennedy 368;
Richard Klune 308b; David Lees 44; Danny Lehman 41r; Charles & Josette Lenars 117b,
147b; Liu Ligun 66b; Frances G. Mayer 117t, 230t, 283t; Kevin R. Morris 120b, 148b;
Museum of the City of New York 257t; Michael Nicholson 145, 272t; North Carolina
Museum of Art 41l, 302r; Richard T. Nowitz 108t; Christine Osborne 163b, 173, 192, 271;
David Reed, 216b; Reuters 410bl; Roger de la Harpe/Gallo Images 344c; Galen Rowell 165c;
Royal Ontario Museum 78b, 97b, 146, 188t, 189b; Sakamoto Photo Research Laboratory 64,
159; Kevin Schafer 109c; Seattle Art Museum 111t, 299b; Jon Spaull 193; Stapleton
Collection 121t, 181b, 210t, 285, 314b, 325, 337t, 342c, 351; Sygma/EPIX 275t; Sygma/Maher
Attar 106c; Sygma/Thomas Johnson 205c; The Mariner's Museum 243t; Arthur Thevenant
318/319; Gustavo Tomsich 37b; Peter Turnley 408b; Underwood & Underwood 204l;
Ruggero Vanni 115; Sandro Vannini 207r, 296b; Brian A. Vikander 100b, 234b; Werner
Forman Archive 333b; Nik Wheeler 181t; Jane Wishnetsky 96b; Roger Wood 37t, 106t, 109b,
130b, 141b, 246r; Adam Woolfitt 121c, 158, 178b, 272b; Alison Wright 200b; Michael S.
Yamashita 111b, 182b; **Daimler-Chrysler:** 364t; **David Robertson Photography:** 174t;
Department of Defense: 409b; **DigitalVision:** 120t, 126/127; **Easyinternetcafe Ltd:** 407;
Edgar Fah Smith Collection, University of Pennsylvania: 289cl, 361; **Getty Images:** 329,
330b, 333t, 348t, 359, 367, 372tl, 373b, 375t, 375b, 377bl, 378, 379b, 380tr, 381b, 384t, 385b,
392r, 394r, 399t, 399b, 402t; MPI 296c, 313; Time Life Pictures 370, 397t, 402b, 404; Time
Life Pictures/Mansell 358c, 350c; **Hamill Gallery of African Art, Boston, M.A.:** 125, 190;
IBM: 406tl; **Kenoyer, J.M.,Courtesy Dept. of Archaeology and Museums, Govt. of
Pakistan:** 25; **Kobal Collection:** 380tl; **Mary Evans Picture Library:** 274, 282cl, 288cr, 299c,
312, 317t, 324c, 355b, 372tr; **NARA:** 321, 356c, 357, 387, 398; Franklin D. Roosevelt Library
381t; **NASA:** 409t; Marshall Space Flight Center 400t, 401t, 401b; **Network Photographers:**
Georg Gerster 110c; **Otago Museum, Dunedin:** 116; **Otis Elevator Company:** 350t; **PA
Photos:** EPA 127t; **Peter Langer:** 101, 175, 199r, 230b, 195; **Philip Baird:**
www.anthroarcheart.org 87b, 113, 125t, 154b; **Photodisc:** 147t, 203, 251b, 263b, 267b; Larry
Brownstein 342t; David Buffington 365t; Jeremy Woodhouse 385t; **Charles Kerry Studio,
Tyrrell Collection. Courtesy of the Powerhouse Museum, Sydney:** 364b; **Photos.com:**
105, 244c, 251, 286t, 393t; **Photos12.com:** 278, 318t; ARJ 168t, 170c, 198, 220c, 222/223, 306t,
311t, 322; Pierre Jean Chalencon 335t; Collection Cinema 382l, 383r; Fondation Napoleon
335b; Hachade 276; Keystone-Pressedienst 371t; Oasis 165r, 183, 186b, 221, 229t, 234t, 243c,
259, 282cr, 286b, 292, 389b; Serge Sautereau 315t; Snark Archives 354; **Popperfoto.co.uk:**
376; **Rex Features Ltd:** 386b; Pacific Press Service 102b; Sipa Press 403, 405c, 410b, 411t;
Jacques Witt 408t; **Robert Harding Picture Library:** Robert Frerck 98; ImageState 60c;
P.Koch 22/25; J.H.C. Wilson 81; **Robert Hunt Library:** 341, 358t, 387b; **Science & Society:**
Science Museum 339c, 360t, 360b, 362tl, 302c; **Science Photo Library:** A. Barrington Brown
392l; **Skyscan:** 248/249; **South American Pictures:** Tony Morrison 34/35, 118b; Chris Sharp
170/171; **Syojoukouji Possession:** 179b; **TopFoto.co.uk:** 17c, 131, 186t, 191c, 202t, 206t, 235,
238/239, 239b, 240, 250l, 252t, 258t, 267t, 307t, 321, 317b, 318b, 319tr, 323c, 324t, 332t, 344t,
346cl, 350b, 386c, 388c, 393b, 394l, 395, 406tr; Ann Ronan Picture Library 365c; Ann Ronan
Picture Library/HIP 228, 291t, 326c; Ann Ronan Picture Library/James Naysmith 346cr; AP
391t, 391b; ARPL 194l; British Library/HIP 171c, 178t, 179c, 231,306c, 311b, 316, 331b,
332b, 336; British Museum/HIP 172, 182t, 187t; Fotomas 293t; HIP 62b, 232l, 244b, 250r,
254b, 273; HIP/National Railway Museum, York 331t; Image Works 326t; Image
Works/David Frazier 112b; Museum of London/HIP 298t; NASA/Image Works 405t;
National Archives 323t; Novosti 167r, 293b, 400b; UPPA 13b; Derrick Whitty 330t;
Woodmansterne 154t, 294t, 334; **Travel Ink:** David Toase 237b; **TravelChinaGuide.com:**
279b; **U.S.Library of Medicine:** 289cr; **Utah Museum:** 191t; **Werner Forman Archive:** 126t,
129c, 199l, 206b, 215, 216t, 290c; Arizona State Museum 130t; David Bernstein Collection,
New York 151t; Maxwell Museum of Anthropology, Alberquerque 138t; Museum fur
Volkerkunde, Berlin 97t; Noh Theatre Collection, Kongo School, Kyoto 191b; Otago
Museum, Dunedin 16l; **Yves Traynard:** 141t; **Zev Radovan:** 77

CONTENTS

PEOPLING THE EARTH

ANY QUESTIONS REMAIN UNANSWERED *about how and when humans first appeared on Earth. But the evidence of ancient skeletons, whose age can be estimated by techniques such as radiometric dating, suggests the first modern humans—known to science as the species* Homo sapiens, *Latin for "wise man"—were living in Africa at least 160,000 years ago. At the time there were other human groups, all of which subsequently died out. The last to go were the Neanderthals, a stockily built people with brains as big as those of modern humans, who survived until about 28,000 years ago.*

▲ Hand axes, flaked from larger blocks of stone, were early humans' most common tools up to about 250,000 years ago, after which more specialized implements came into use.

Early humans fed themselves by hunting game and fish and by gathering fruits, nuts, berries, and (if they lived near the coast) shellfish. They were skillful toolmakers, using the materials at hand—mostly stone, wood, and animal bones—to make axes, scrapers for cleaning animal skins, fishhooks, and a variety of weapons, including spears and bows and arrows. They lived in small bands, typically of 25 to 30 people, that occasionally linked up with neighboring groups in tribes or clans a few hundred strong.

Coping with the cold was a major problem, since the Earth was in the grip of the last Ice Age. Caves provided natural shelters, particularly when warmed by fires. Otherwise the bands had to fashion huts out

of whatever materials they could find; in eastern Europe they sometimes used the bones of mammoths (giant elephants that have since gone extinct), covering a bone frame with the animals' hairy hides. They also used animal skins to make clothes.

Moving out from Africa, modern humans reached the Near East between 100,000 and 70,000 years ago, and then spread to the east and west, replacing the existing Neanderthal populations. They had found their way to Australia by 45,000 B.C.; the last stage of that particular migration must have involved a sea journey of at least 55 miles (90 km).

America was almost certainly the last continent to be peopled. Scholars believe the first settlers came

---

✦ **c.6.8 m.y.a.** Date of earliest known hominid (human ancestor) remains, found in Chad, Africa, and named *Sahelanthropus tchadensis*.

✦ **c.6.0 m.y.a.** Estimated date of *Orrorin tugenensis*, discovered in Kenya. The find was nicknamed "Millennium Man" because it was made in the year 2000.

✦ **c.3.6 m.y.a.** Fossil footprints found at Laetoli, Tanzania, indicate that hominids were walking on two feet by this date.

✦ **c.3.5 m.y.a.** "Lucy," a female hominid of the species *Australopithecus afarensis*, lived in what is now Ethiopia. Her remains were the oldest yet known when they were discovered in 1974.

✦ **c.2.4 m.y.a.** Oldest known stone tools, found at Hadar in Ethiopia.

✦ **c.2.4 m.y.a.** First appearance of *Homo rudolfensis* and *Homo habilis*, currently thought to be the first direct human ancestors.

✦ **c.1.8 m.y.a.** First appearance of *Homo erectus*, with a brain size about two-thirds that of modern humans.

✦ **c.1 m.y.a.** *Homo erectus* reaches Europe and Asia.

✦ **c.400,000 B.C.** Earliest surviving wooden tool, a spear found at Schoningen (Germany).

✦ **c.160,000** Earliest remains of *Homo sapiens*—the modern human race—found in the Afar region of Ethiopia.

✦ **c.120,000** Neanderthals living in Europe.

✦ **c.100,000** *Homo sapiens* moves out of Africa.

Cave Art

From about 32,000 years B.C. prehistoric cave dwellers in France and Spain started drawing images of big-game animals on the walls of the caverns in which they lived. Similar rock art has also been found in North Africa (from a later date) and in Australia. The artists used charcoal to draw black lines, coloring in the outlines with natural pigments ground to a powder and mixed with water. Some scholars have suggested that the drawings may have had magical significance, helping hunters kill the animals represented, although they may also have been sketched simply for pleasure. Only Homo sapiens—the modern human line—is known to have ever produced art. One of the most famous cave-painting sites is at Lascaux, in the Dordogne region of southern France. Dating back about 16,000 to 17,000 years, paintings like those from the Hall of the Bulls (right) show the animals that inhabited the region at the time, including some, like the aurochs (wild ox), that are now extinct.

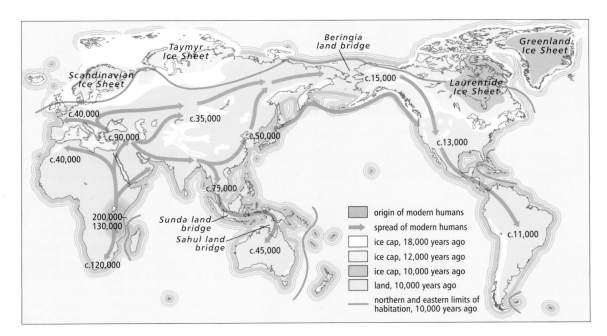

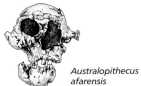

Australopithecus afarensis

Homo habilis

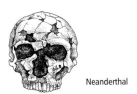

Neanderthal

Homo sapiens

from Asia, but disagree as to the date. Most think they arrived about 15,000 years ago over a land bridge linking Siberia and Alaska at the time; but a few claim that they came as much as 40,000 years ago. Here as elsewhere in prehistory the evidence is incomplete; opinions may change as new finds fill out the picture.

▲ Current evidence suggests that modern humans originated in East Africa at least 160,000 years ago and then spread out from Africa to people most of the world.

▶ The size of the cranium (braincase) increased steadily in early hominids up to Neanderthals and Homo sapiens (modern humans), who had similarly sized brains.

⊕ **c. 90,000** Modern humans living at Qafzeh (Israel).

⊕ **c. 75,000** Modern humans living in Southeast Asia.

⊕ **c. 45,000** Modern humans reach Australia.

📖 **c.45,000** Date of earliest known musical instrument—a flute found in North Africa.

⊕ **c. 40,000** Modern humans move into Europe, living alongside the existing Neanderthal populations.

⊕ **c. 28,000** Last surviving Neanderthal population, living in southern Spain, becomes extinct.

⊕ **c. 15,000** Likely date for first settlement of America. Some scholars, however, think people could have arrived as early as 40,000 B.C.

THE AGRICULTURAL REVOLUTION

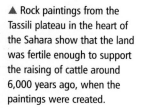

STARTING ABOUT 13,000 YEARS AGO, *people made the major advance of cultivating plants and domesticating (taming) animals. This great shift occurred independently in West and East Asia, the Americas, and Africa. Although revolutionary in its effects, the change from nomadic foraging to settled agriculture was a gradual one that took several thousand years. Recent research suggests that farming did not necessarily go hand in hand with the development of towns, as formerly thought.*

People first began to raise plants for food as the climate became warmer and wetter at the end of the last Ice Age. In the Fertile Crescent, a swath of land across West Asia, early farmers grew wheat and barley from wild grass seeds. In China the first agriculturalists cultivated wild millet in the north and wild rice in the south. Early inhabitants of Ecuador may have grown squash as long as 10,000 years ago.

The cultivation of plants was accompanied by the domestication of animals—sheep, goats, and cattle in Asia, the pig in both Europe and China. Although there were no mammals suitable for domestication in North and Central America, natives of Peru in South America domesticated the guinea pig about 8,000 years ago and the llama some 2,500 years later.

People did not give up hunting and gathering as soon as they had learned how to domesticate plants and animals. Hunter-gatherers in Syria and China cultivated crops thousands of years before their successors became full-time farmers. There was a

▲ Rock paintings from the Tassili plateau in the heart of the Sahara show that the land was fertile enough to support the raising of cattle around 6,000 years ago, when the paintings were created.

transition to agriculture

■	before 8000 B.C.
■	before 6000 B.C.
■	before 3000 B.C.
■	before 500 B.C.
■	hunters and gatherers
□	uninhabited

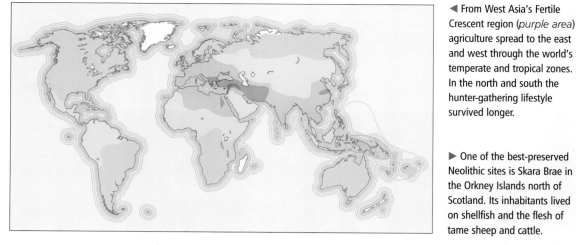

◄ From West Asia's Fertile Crescent region (*purple area*) agriculture spread to the east and west through the world's temperate and tropical zones. In the north and south the hunter-gathering lifestyle survived longer.

► One of the best-preserved Neolithic sites is Skara Brae in the Orkney Islands north of Scotland. Its inhabitants lived on shellfish and the flesh of tame sheep and cattle.

⊛ **c.11,000 B.C.** Rye cultivated east of Aleppo, Syria.

⊛ **c.8500** Sheep domesticated in Iraq.

⊛ **c.8000** Wheat cultivated in Syria and Turkey; barley cultivated in Jordan, Iran, and Israel; squash cultivated in Ecuador.

⊛ **c.8000** Pigs domesticated in China.

⊛ **c.7500** Goats domesticated in Iran.

⊛ **c.7000** Pigs domesticated in Turkey.

⊛ **c.6000** Cattle, probably bred from the wild aurochs, domesticated in Greece and Turkey; guinea pigs domesticated in Peru.

⊛ **c.6000** Wild rice cultivated along the Chang (Yangtze) River, China.

⊛ **c.5700** The first irrigation works are built in Mesopotamia.

⊛ **c.5600** Beans cultivated in Peru.

⊛ **c.4500** Horses domesticated in Ukraine.

⊛ **c.3500** Llamas domesticated in Peru.

⊛ **c.3000** Asses domesticated in Egypt; bottle gourds cultivated in Missouri.

⊛ **c.2000** Sorghum cultivated in Niger; cereals first cultivated in North America.

simple reason for this slow transition to settled agriculture: While the human population remained small and wild food was abundant, it was easier to make a living by hunting and gathering than by planting, tending, and harvesting crops.

It is harder to explain why sizable towns grew up in this changeover period. Scholars used to think that the first towns were established by farming communities, but recent excavations at 9,000-year-old sites in Turkey show that the inhabitants were at best part-time farmers and may have supported themselves mainly by hunting and gathering.

Towns did grow more numerous and populous when people made the shift to full-time farming—a development probably speeded up by rising populations and overhunting. Faced with such conditions, farmers had one great advantage over foragers: While hunter-gatherers could eat only what nature provided, farmers could increase their output by extending the area of land under cultivation.

Farming seems to have become the main livelihood in parts of West Asia about 10,000 years ago, in China 1,000 years later, and in the Americas and Africa by about 7,000 years ago. By the 4th millennium B.C. some farming communities were producing a food surplus that they could trade or barter for other goods, such as tools or pottery. Once they had reached that stage, people were poised to take the next leap forward—the urban revolution and the establishment of what we call civilization.

The Domestication of the Horse

Of all the animals domesticated by people, none has had a greater effect on history than the horse. When horses were first domesticated in the Ukraine about 6,500 years ago, they were kept mainly for their meat, milk, and hides. The early Babylonians used them to pull wagons, but considered it undignified to ride them—probably because the horses of the period were still small and wild. Although the Egyptians harnessed horses to two-man war chariots, it was not until about 1000 B.C. that individual mounted soldiers appeared. From that time on the horse brought a new and rapid tempo to the way people lived. Horses speeded up overland trade and communication and, as cavalry mounts, dramatically changed warfare, becoming the swiftest form of battlefield transportation until the invention of the tank almost 3,000 years later.

AMERICAS

⊛ **c.3000** Potatoes are cultivated in the Andes mountains of Peru.

⊛ **c.3000** The earliest known pottery in the Americas is produced in Ecuador and Colombia.

⊛ **c.3000** An early form of corn is cultivated in the Valley of Tehuacán, Mexico.

EUROPE

⊛ **c.3000** The ox-drawn plow, invented in the Near East, changes the landscape as farmers clear forests to make bigger fields.

⊛ **c.3000** Wealth from olive and vine culture encourages the growth of the first towns in the Aegean Sea region.

📖 **c.3000** A marble industry producing fine sculptures flourishes in the Cyclades, a group of Greek islands in the Aegean Sea.

⊛ **c.3000** Communities in Scandinavia build passage tombs and dolmens—stone monuments made with blocks weighing up to 40 tons.

⊛ **c.2800** The Beaker People, a culture that buries their dead with characteristic earthenware beaker vessels, spread out from Spain to northern Europe.

AFRICA

⊛ **c.3000** Yam and palm-oil cultivation develops in West Africa.

👑 **c.2950** Egypt's 1st Dynasty comes to power under the Pharaoh Menes, with its capital at Memphis in Lower Egypt.

Tomb stele of King Wadj from Abydos, Egypt, c.2850 B.C.

⊛ **c.2900** Egyptian astronomer-priests devise the first 365-day calendar.

📖 **c.2800** Egyptian scribes begin to write on papyrus made from the crushed stems of a fibrous plant growing along the banks of the Nile River.

WESTERN ASIA

👑 **c.3000** Independent Sumerian city-states flourish in southern Mesopotamia (Iraq).

👑 **c.3000** Non-Sumerian Semitic tribes move into the northern parts of Mesopotamia, settling the plains of Shinar and Akkad.

👑 **c.2900** The Early Dynastic Period gets under way in Sumer as different city-states battle for supremacy, appointing *lugals* (military leaders) to steer their destiny.

📖 **c.2900** The most likely date for the Great Flood, commemorated in Sumerian myth. Archaeological evidence in fact suggests that there may have been more than one such deluge.

👑 **c.2900** The Phoenicians, a seafaring people of the Mediterranean's eastern shore, settle on the Lebanese coast, establishing settlements at Tyre and Sidon.

☀ **c.2900** The first ziggurats—stepped temple-towers—are built in Sumer.

👑 **c.2750** Troy is founded on the eastern coast of the Aegean Sea in what is now Turkey. At this time it is a small walled settlement ruled by a local chieftain.

👑 **c.2750** Gilgamesh rules the city-state of Uruk. He will later enter legend as the hero of the *Epic of Gilgamesh*, the world's first literary classic.

EAST ASIA & OCEANIA

⊛ **c.3000** At Banpo in northern China, communities build large meeting houses over 60 feet (18 m) long.

⊛ **c.3000** Walga Rock in Western Australia is used as a shelter by Aboriginal hunter-gatherers and remains in use for the next 5,000 years.

☀ **c.2900** According to tradition, the first, mythical emperors of China—divine beings who were half-human and half-animal—ruled from about this time.

✳ **c.3000** Natives of western Nevada inhabit rock shelters furnished with skin blankets, baskets, and featherwork.

✳ **c.2600** Natives of fishing villages in the Chinchorro region on the Chile–Peru border develop a simplified method of mummifying their dead.

AMERICAS

Waisted drinking cups with flared lips and incised decorations were the distinctive feature of the Beaker People, who spread from Spain across much of central and western Europe in the course of the 3rd millennium B.C. They were farmers and herders who brought with them knowledge of metalworking, being skilled in the production of copper and bronze artifacts. Their weapon of choice was the bow and arrow, but they also used copper-bladed daggers and spears.

✳ **c.2800** Neolithic (New Stone Age) settlers at Skara Brae in the Orkney Islands north of Scotland build stone houses sunk beneath ground level and covered with turf.

✳ **c.2800** Grand Pressigny in western France becomes the export center for a high-quality flint suitable for making knives and daggers.

☀ **c.2800** In England Stonehenge first becomes a ceremonial center. At this date it has none of the giant standing stones for which it will later become famous: only circular earthworks and, perhaps, wooden posts, now long since rotted away.

📖 **c.2700** Early Minoan civilization develops on Crete, reaching its zenith after 2000 with the building of sumptuous palaces.

EUROPE

☀ **c.2650** The world's first massive stone monument, the Step Pyramid, is built for the Pharaoh Djoser.

👑 **c.2575** Egypt's Old Kingdom Period gets under way with the foundation of the nation's 4th Dynasty.

Egyptian scribe writing on papyrus. Old Kingdom Period.

☀ **c.2550** The Great Pyramid at Giza is built as a 480-foot-high (146-m) tomb for the Egyptian Pharaoh Khufu.

AFRICA

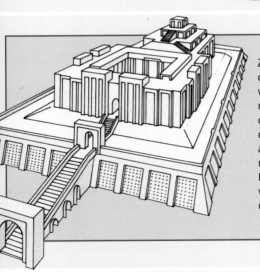

Ziggurats developed out of the Sumerian custom of building temples on platforms; when the mud-brick walls collapsed, the ruins provided a base for a new structure, creating a staggered effect. Over the centuries architects across Mesopotamia adopted this stepped plan, creating temple-mountains that reached toward the heavens. Later examples like this one from Qatara were part of elaborate temple complexes that dominated the cities in which they stood.

📖 **c.2600** Magnificent golden artworks, along with dozens of human sacrifices, are buried in the Royal Tombs of Ur, to be rediscovered by the British archaeologist Leonard Woolley in the 1920s.

WESTERN ASIA

✳ **c.2700** The production of silk from silkworms starts in China.

👑 **2698** Traditional date for the accession of Huang Di, the Yellow Emperor, a mythical early ruler of China.

✳ **2637** According to later tradition, Year 1 of the Chinese calendar falls in this year.

EAST ASIA & OCEANIA

THE SUMERIANS

WHILE MOST OF THE WORLD *lived in caves or huts, the Sumerians created the first urban civilization in southern Mesopotamia—the land between the Tigris and Euphrates rivers in today's Iraq. Their origins are uncertain, but they may have migrated from the Caspian Sea area, reaching Mesopotamia by about 5500 B.C. Over the next 3,000 years they built the first cities, established hereditary kingship, and devised a writing system that made them the first people in history to record history itself.*

▲ Wealthy Sumerians placed small pottery figures of themselves, with their hands clasped in prayer, in shrines dedicated to the gods.

▶ Sumer's heartland lay close to the ancient coastline of what is now southern Iraq. In time Sumerian influence spread northward through all of Mesopotamia.

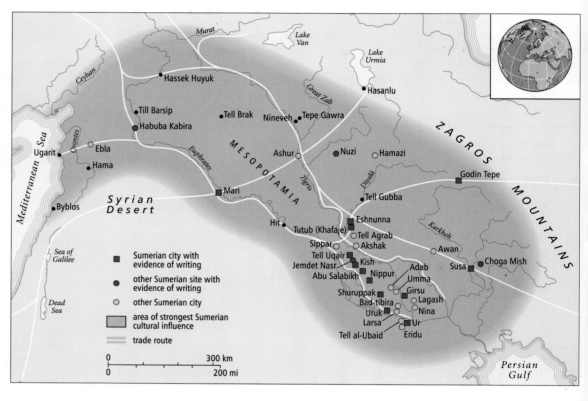

Sumerian city with evidence of writing
other Sumerian site with evidence of writing
other Sumerian city
area of strongest Sumerian cultural influence
trade route

| 0 | 300 km |
| 0 | 200 mi |

❋ **c.5500 B.C.** The first archaeological evidence of Sumerians in Mesopotamia.

❋ **c.5400** Advanced farming methods, including irrigation projects, first appear in Mesopotamia.

❋ **c.3500** The first Sumerian towns appear. Primitive writing is developed.

❋ **c.3400** Uruk becomes the first large Sumerian city, with an area of at least 500 acres (200 ha) and a population of around 50,000.

❋ **c.3300** The Sumerians invent the potter's wheel and the plow.

❋ **c.3000** Early cuneiform writing begins to replace pictographs.

❋ **c.2900** Parts of Mesopotamia are devastated by a severe flood, an event that may have influenced stories of the worldwide flood described in the Old Testament.

📖 **c.2750** Gilgamesh becomes ruler of Uruk. He will later be immortalized as a semidivine king in the world's first literary epic, the *Epic of Gilgamesh*.

Sumerian Writing

Sumerian writing originated in primitive accounting; merchants and tax collectors inscribed numbers and pictures (pictographs) in wet clay to represent quantities and objects. As time passed, a more stylized system developed in which reeds were used to make wedge-shaped impressions known as cuneiform (from the Latin *cuneus*, "wedge"). Early cuneiform had no grammatical elements; it was only after 2500 B.C. that signs were used to show the order in which words should be read. Finally, symbols that stood for sounds were invented, which meant that scribes could express abstract ideas like "love" or "justice."

The key to the Sumerians' achievements was irrigation. Because Mesopotamia's rivers are unreliable, its people built reservoirs and canals on a grand scale, turning large areas of barren soil into fertile farmland. Crop production was also boosted by technological innovations: The plow, the wheeled cart, and the sailboat are all Sumerian inventions.

Plentiful food supplies led to population increase, the growth of cities, and the opportunity for some people to quit farming for urban occupations. Some Sumerians became merchants and traders, exchanging the region's surplus harvests for the metals, timber, and other resources that Sumer lacked. Others were skilled craftsmen. Many must have been officials working for Sumer's political and religious leaders.

At first, Sumerian cities may have been governed by a council of elders. During times of conflict the council appointed a military commander called a *lugal*—literally, "great man." The position was supposed to be temporary; but as competition for land and water intensified, the *lugals* assumed power permanently and made their position hereditary. Eventually the title came to mean "king."

The Sumerian kings ruled about a dozen independent city-states, each consisting of one or more urban centers surrounded by villages and farmland. At the heart of each city stood the temple of its patron god or goddess. Over time these temples evolved into massive stepped structures, called ziggurats, that rose up to 165 feet (50 m) high.

The Sumerians were also capable mathematicians. As well as counting in tens, they used 60 as an arithmetical unit; from them come our 360-degree circle, 60-minute hour, and 60-second minute. But their greatest contribution was their writing system, used to record everything from business transactions to treaties and laws. Setting words down in writing was a key step because it gave them a status independent of the people who promulgated them.

Despite their accomplishments, the warring city-states were vulnerable to invasion. From about 2350 B.C. on, they were overrun by Semitic tribes from the north. By about 1950 B.C. their political power had been destroyed, but their writing, laws, religion, and much else lived on in the civilizations of such later Mesopotamian powers as Babylon and Assyria.

▼ The Standard of Ur, a mosaic designed to be carried in royal processions, illustrates scenes from a military campaign waged by the powerful city-state of Ur in about 2500 B.C. In this detail cattle, goats, and other tribute provided by the defeated enemy are paraded before a council made up of the city's ruling elders.

👑 **c.2600** Rulers of the southern city-state of Ur are buried in tombs together with their attendants.

⊛ **c.2500** Sumerian writing spreads abroad as trade routes are opened.

👑 **c.2350** The Sumerian city-states are overrun by Sargon of Akkad, a ruler of Semitic stock whose power base lies farther north within Mesopotamia. Sargon subsequently establishes the first empire known to history.

⊛ **c.2100** From Ur, King Ur-Nammu reasserts Sumerian power, founds schools for scribes, establishes the first legal code, introduces calendar reforms, and promotes international trade.

⚔ **c.1950** Ur is sacked by the Elamites from western Iran, bringing the era of Sumerian political power to an end.

EGYPT'S OLD KINGDOM

▲ The Palette of Narmer shows Narmer, king of Egypt in about 3000 B.C., smiting an enemy with his war club; other defeated foes lie under his feet. The falcon symbolizes the god Horus, usually shown with a falcon's head; the papyrus reeds on which he perches are the symbols of marshy Lower Egypt.

SEEN FROM SPACE, *the Nile Valley cuts a ragged green slash across an otherwise uninterrupted expanse of desert. It is water that makes the difference: Even in the dry season the Nile never ceases to flow, and it is dramatically swollen by summer rains in the Ethiopian Highlands. Today the river is controlled by hydroelectric dams that provide modern Egypt with much-needed energy; but the dams have also brought to an end a natural cycle that had continued unbroken for countless generations. The annual flood not only watered the Nile Valley but also replenished its fields with rich, river-borne soils. In so doing, it allowed overworked lands to renew themselves, creating the necessary conditions for the development of one of the world's longest-lasting civilizations.*

By 4000 B.C. agriculture in the Nile Valley was so productive that it could support a significant nonfarming population. It was concentrated in small urban clusters like the one excavated at Naqada, just downriver from modern Luxor (formerly Thebes). Prosperous though these communites were, however, their neighbors had as yet no need to envy them: Climate change was only just starting to set the lush Nile Valley apart in an increasingly arid region. The trend was irreversible, though, and an emergent Egypt gathered impetus from this wider crisis.

⊛ **c.6000 B.C.** Hunter-gatherers start turning to settled agriculture along the Nile Valley.

⊛ **c.4000** At Naqada, near modern Luxor, a simple village culture flourishes.

⊛ **c.3500** Rectangular brick houses replace circular huts at Naqada and other sites. Walled towns appear.

⊛ **c.3500** Desertification of the Sahara intensifies.

⊛ **c.3300** By this date Egyptians are using both river- and ocean-going sailing boats.

⊛ **c.3200** The first known examples of hieroglyphic writing date from about this time.

👑 **c.3100** Upper (upstream, or southern) and Lower (northern) Egypt are united under the kings of the Predynastic Period.

👑 **c.3000** Narmer, the best-known of the Predynastic kings, rules a united Egypt from the city of Abydos.

👑 **c.2950** Egypt's Early Dynastic Period begins when the First Dynasty is established under the Pharaoh Menes.

⊛ **c.2650** Djoser's Step Pyramid is built.

👑 **c.2575** The Fourth Dynasty gets under way as Sneferu succeeds Huni as pharaoh.

⊛ **c.2550** Work begins on the Great Pyramid, built at Giza (on the outskirts of modern Cairo) for the Pharaoh Khufu.

👑 **c.2450** Userkaf comes to power, inaugurating the Fifth Dynasty.

👑 **c.2325** The reign of Teti introduces Egypt's Sixth Dynasty.

👑 **c.2250** Reign of Pepi II begins.

👑 **c.2200** Drought throughout northeast Africa leads to famine along the Nile and prompts persistent raiding by increasingly desperate desert nomads.

👑 **c.2170** Pepi II's increasingly troubled reign ends with his death; his successors fail to maintain pharaonic authority over a disintegrating state.

👑 **c.2125** The Old Kingdom gives way to a time of troubles called by modern scholars the "First Intermediate Period."

Around 3100 B.C. Egypt's various centers came together as a single state whose rulers, the pharaohs, controlled the whole valley from the First Cataract (rapids) of Upper Egypt down to the delta. They did so by means of a powerful mystique: The pharaoh was seen as a god, the provider of the flood and its fertility, and the protector of his people in this life and the next. Hence the importance of the "mortuary cult"— the construction of lavish tombs was not just the religious focus but the economic engine of Egyptian life.

The ordinary Egyptian owed everything to his pharaoh and paid not only in produce but in labor on public works, from palaces and temples to irrigation projects. A vast civil service of scribes administered the whole complicated system, recording everything in their hieroglyphic (picture-based) script. The pharaoh's bureaucracy loomed large in the lives of ordinary Egyptians, but it was this organizational spirit that made possible the development of city life and great works like the pyramids.

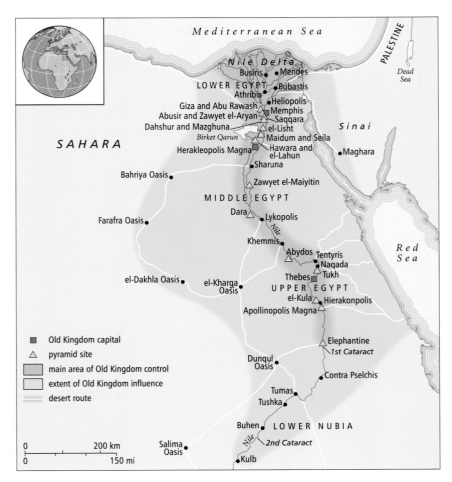

◀ The wealth of ancient Egypt was built on agriculture, which flourished in the rich soil of the Nile Valley. The river was also the nation's main highway; most heavy goods, including the stones for the pyramids, were transported by boat.

▶ Ancient Egypt grew up around the Nile, which formed a ribbon of life in the surrounding desert. The nation was born when the two separate kingdoms of Upper and Lower Egypt united under a single ruler from about 3100 B.C. on.

The Pyramids

At the beginning of the Old Kingdom Period, leading Egyptians were buried in flat-roofed mud-brick tombs known as mastabas. When the first pyramid, that of the Pharaoh Djoser, was built in about 2650 B.C., it took the form of a number of mastabas piled one on top of another, each slightly smaller than the one below. The stepped result offered the departed pharaoh a convenient staircase toward the sun, seen as the source of life.

Shortly afterward pyramids began to be built with the familiar straight edges, intended to represent the rays of Ra, the sun god. The first such was also the most impressive: Khufu's Great Pyramid at Giza is still a spectacular sight, towering above the high-rise apartment blocks of the nearby Cairo suburbs. No taller building would be built until the Eiffel Tower in 1889; the pyramid contains a staggering 6 million tons of stone.

THE INDUS VALLEY CIVILIZATION

IN THE EARLY 1920S *British archaeologists investigated two ancient mounds in the Indus Valley region of what is now Pakistan, one close to the village of Mohenjo-Daro and the other at a place called Harappa. To their amazement, at both sites they found the buried remains of large cities lying close to the dried-up courses of old rivers. Excavations subsequently turned up impressive mud-brick city walls, large public buildings, and streets laid out on a regular grid pattern.*

▲ This soapstone bust, just 7 inches (18 cm) high, was found in a small house in the ruins of Mohenjo-Daro. No one knows for sure who it represents, but the figure's ceremonial garb and air of authority have led the sculpture to be commonly known as the "Priest King."

The discovery of these cities was the first indication that a major civilization—known today as the Indus Valley or Harappan civilization—had arisen in the Indian subcontinent more than 4,000 years ago. Archaeologists now believe that the culture first emerged in about 2600 B.C. and lasted until about 1750 B.C. They estimate that Mohenjo-Daro and Harappa had populations of between 30,000 and 40,000—as large as, if not larger than, the cities of Mesopotamia at the same period.

Archaeologists have now uncovered hundreds of towns and villages belonging to the Indus Valley civilization spread over an area of around 260,000 square miles (680,000 sq. km). Buildings were almost invariably constructed of baked brick made to a standard size throughout the region. At Lothal, on the coast, archaeologists have discovered a deepwater dock built entirely of brick.

Brick was also used to build embankments that protected the citadels—the areas where the main public buildings lay—from flooding. As a further precaution they were constructed on flattened earth mounds, raising them safely above the floodplain.

The people in the towns were skilled craftworkers. They made jewelry of polished shell and semiprecious stones, pottery, and copper tools and ornaments, and traded these goods as far as the Persian Gulf and Mesopotamia. Pottery toys found at many sites show that they had wheeled carts and sailed flat-bottomed boats much like those in use on the Indus River today. Their stone seals (probably used as identification tags) were carved with animals such as elephants, rhinos, and oxen. Many seals have writing on them, but scholars are unable to read the pictographic script.

Archaeologists once thought that outside invaders brought the Indus civilization to a violent end. But it now seems rather to have declined gradually, probably during a period of climate warming when the rivers dried up. People abandoned the cities, and writing and craft production fell gradually into disuse, although life in the countryside continued largely unchanged for several centuries more.

Cities of Equals

A striking feature of the Indus Valley cities is that they contained neither palaces nor large monuments similar to the pyramids of ancient Egypt and no rich burial sites like the Royal Cemetery at Ur. From this fact archaeologists conclude that the civilization lacked a ruling elite (privileged class). The cities were usually divided into separate public and residential sectors. The public buildings were located in the upper part of the city (sometimes called the citadel). At Mohenjo-Daro (*right*) the main public building was the Great Bath, probably used for ritual washing. The houses in the residential area, or lower city, were often several stories high and were laid out around courtyards. Most had a well, a brick-paved bathroom, underground drains, and a lavatory.

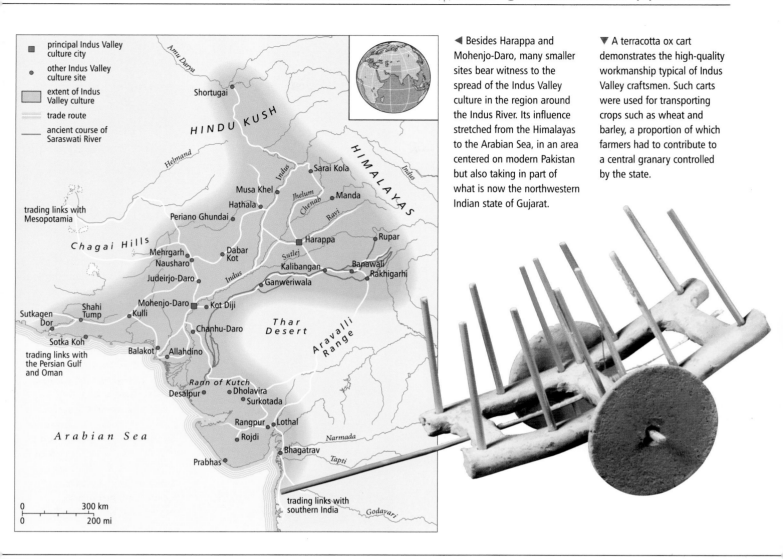

principal Indus Valley culture city

other Indus Valley culture site

extent of Indus Valley culture

trade route

ancient course of Saraswati River

HINDU KUSH

Amu Darya

Shortugai

HIMALAYAS

Helmand

Indus

Sarai Kola

Musa Khel   Jhelum   Manda

Hathala   Chenab   Ravi

Peniano Ghundai

Sutlej

trading links with Mesopotamia

Chagai Hills

Mehrgarh   Dabar Kot   Harappa   Rupar

Naushano   Kalibangan   Banawali

Judeirjo-Daro   Indus   Rakhigarhi

Ganweriwala

Shahi   Mohenjo-Daro   Kot Diji

Sutkagen Dor   Tump   Kulli

Sotka Koh   Thar Desert   Aravalli Range

trading links with the Persian Gulf and Oman   Balakot   Allahdino   Chanhu-Daro

Rann of Kutch

Desalpur   Dholavira

Surkotada

Arabian Sea

Rangpur   Lothal

Rojdi   Narmada

Bhagatrav   Tapti

Prabhas

trading links with southern India   Godavari

0   300 km
0   200 mi

◀ Besides Harappa and Mohenjo-Daro, many smaller sites bear witness to the spread of the Indus Valley culture in the region around the Indus River. Its influence stretched from the Himalayas to the Arabian Sea, in an area centered on modern Pakistan but also taking in part of what is now the northwestern Indian state of Gujarat.

▼ A terracotta ox cart demonstrates the high-quality workmanship typical of Indus Valley craftsmen. Such carts were used for transporting crops such as wheat and barley, a proportion of which farmers had to contribute to a central granary controlled by the state.

⊕ **c.6500 B.C.**   Sheep and goats are farmed at Mehrgarh in the mountains on the northern edge of the Indus Valley.

⊕ **c.4000**   Humped cattle (zebu) are by now the most common domesticated animal; wheat and barley are being cultivated.

⊕ **c.4000**   Farmers begin to settle on the Indus floodplain and to construct dams and canals for irrigation.

⊕ **c.4000**   Copper is in use in the Indus region.

⊕ **c.3500**   The potter's wheel is introduced to the Indus region.

⊕ **c.2600**   Cities emerge in the Indus Valley.

📖 **c.2350**   A reference in a Sumerian text to trade with a distant land called "Meluhha" may refer to the Indus Valley civilization.

👑 **c.2300**   Indus Valley civilization is at its height and continues to flourish for the next four centuries.

⊕ **c.2000**   First evidence of bronze in the Indus region.

👑 **c.1900**   The Indus cities begin to decline.

👑 **c.1750**   The cities are finally abandoned at about this time.

NEW KINGDOM EGYPT

ANCIENT EGYPT REACHED THE HEIGHT *of its power and its magnificence in the New Kingdom period, from about 1550 to 1075 B.C. At its peak in the 13th century B.C. the pharaoh's power spread northward up the Mediterranean coast as far as Syria and southward deep into Nubia. The wealth that came from trade and conquest went to build great temples and palaces, as well as the magnificent royal tombs uncovered by archaeologists in the Valley of the Kings outside the capital, Thebes.*

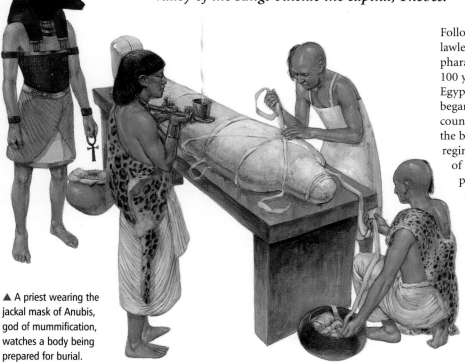

▲ A priest wearing the jackal mask of Anubis, god of mummification, watches a body being prepared for burial.

Following the collapse of the Old Kingdom and the lawlessness of the First Intermediate Period, the pharaohs' authority was restored after a gap of almost 100 years by a fresh royal dynasty, the eleventh since Egypt's history had begun. The Middle Kingdom began when Mentuhotep II managed to reunite the country under his sole rule. Succeeding reigns saw the bureaucracy growing ever more important, regimenting and rationalizing just about every aspect of Egyptian life. The greatest monuments of this period were not imposing royal tombs (although there were some of those) but rather ambitious irrigation projects, which brought extensive areas under cultivation for the first time. Fortresses were also built, notably at Buhen in the south to protected the frontier with Nubia, in what is now the Sudan.

In time the Middle Kingdom's wealth attracted the envy of outsiders. In about 1640 B.C. warriors known as the Hyksos swept into the Nile Delta. They came from the eastern shores of the Mediterranean, and they were equipped with a revolutionary new weapon, the

---

☟ **c.2040 B.C.** Mentuhotep II reunites Egypt, and the Middle Kingdom begins.

☟ **c.1991** Amenemhet I and his 12th Dynasty expand Egyptian territories southward into Nubia.

✳ **c.1897** Senusret II's reign begins, a time of great achievement for Egypt, with major irrigation projects and other public works.

☟ **c.1640** The Second Intermediate Period begins as a dynasty of Hyksos kings supplants the pharaohs of the 13th Dynasty in the Nile Delta region.

☟ **c.1550** Ahmose comes to power, driving out the Hyksos and inaugurating the 18th Dynasty and the New Kingdom. He goes on to bring much of Palestine and Syria under Egyptian rule.

☟ **c.1473** Queen Hatshepsut comes to power.

☟ **c.1350** Amenhotep IV takes the name Akhenaten and starts a religious revolution focused on worship of the aten, or sun's disk.

☟ **c.1333** The boy-king Tutankhamen succeeds to the throne. Worship of the old gods is restored.

☟ **c.1307** Ramses I ascends the throne, to be followed by the Ramessid rulers of the 19th and 20th dynasties.

☟ **c.1290** Accession of Ramses II, the Great, whose 66-year reign marks the peak of Egyptian power.

✕ **c.1285** Ramses II's invasion of Syria is fought to a standstill by the Hittites at the Battle of Kadesh.

☟ **c.1163** The death of Ramses III marks the beginning of the end for New Kingdom Egypt: his successors rule over an empire in decline.

◀ This gold funerary mask was one of the amazing finds from the tomb of Tutankhamen, a boy-pharaoh who ruled Egypt briefly at its New Kingdom peak in the 14th century B.C.

▼ Under a succession of warrior pharaohs New Kingdom Egypt extended its rule far up the Mediterranean's east coast and southward deep into Nubia (today's northern Sudan).

horse-drawn war chariot. The pharaohs were driven out of the delta, but managed to hold on to power in the south, ruling Upper Egypt (the southern half of the country) from Thebes, about 600 miles (1,000 km) upriver.

There, after almost a century had passed, a strong leader, Ahmose, arose to drive out the Hyksos. The interlopers were expelled around the year 1550, bringing Egypt's Second Intermediate Period to an end and ushering in the New Kingdom. Over the next three centuries a succession of warlike pharaohs went on the offensive, striking north up the Mediterranean coast and south into Nubia. For the first time in its history Egypt built up a sizable foreign empire. With military power came economic might. The next few centuries saw Egyptian civilization at its height, with stupendous achievements in art and architecture, medicine, science, and engineering.

The golden age continued until about 1150, at which point events beyond the nation's borders forced it into slow decline. In a time of general economic disarray a wave of uprooted refugees called the Sea Peoples swept across the Mediterranean. Egypt fought off their attacks but lost its empire, and the trade routes that had assured its wealth were disrupted. As its prosperity declined, its military power weakened. The New Kingdom itself came to an end in about 1070 B.C. with the death of its last ruler, Ramses XI.

Over the ensuing centuries Libyans, Nubians, Persians, and Greeks would all at different times hold power in Egypt, putting dynasties of their own on the pharaoh's throne. The final one was that of the Greek Ptolemies, who ruled for almost 300 years. The last of the Ptolemies was the famous Queen Cleopatra; when she committed suicide in 30 B.C., pharaonic rule came to an end, and Egypt became a province of the Roman Empire.

Map

HITTITE EMPIRE

Carchemish

ASSYRIA

Orontes
Euphrates
Tigris

Ugarit

Cyprus

Qadesh

Byblos

Damascus

Mediterranean Sea

Megiddo

Syrian Desert

Jerusalem • Amman
Dead Sea

Tanis
Kom el-Hisn Qantir
LOWER EGYPT Memphis

Sinai

Timna

Sidmant el-Gebel Serabit el-Khadim

Bahriya Oasis

Hermopolis Magna Akhetaten
Lykopolis

Farafra Oasis

MIDDLE EGYPT

Abydos

el-Dakhla Oasis

el-Kharga Oasis Thebes

UPPER EGYPT Apollinopolis Magna
Elephantine

SAHARA

Aniba Contra Pselchis
Abu Simbel
Buhen LOWER NUBIA
Semna
Kumma

Red Sea

Soleb

UPPER NUBIA

Kerkis

Napata
Sanam

■ New Kingdom capital

Thebes site with royal tomb of New Kingdom

○ site of temple or chapel

maximum extent of New Kingdom c.1500 B.C.

0 — 400 km
0 — 300 mi

👑 **c.945** A Libyan dynasty takes power under Shoshenq I.

👑 **c.750** Piye extends Nubian control over Lower Egypt.

👑 **c.671** Assyrian forces invade Egypt. They struggle with local rulers for control of the country for the next 24 years.

👑 **525** Cambyses of Persia invades Egypt, bringing the nation temporarily into the Persian Empire.

The Heretic Pharaoh

The most revolutionary pharaoh in Egypt's history was Amenhotep IV (c.1353–1336), who changed his name to Akhenaten (*right*). Coming to the throne when the New Kingdom was at its height, he made the momentous decision to abandon the worship of the country's many gods and to replace them with a single deity: Aten, the sun's disk. To distance his court from the high priests of the old faith, he moved the capital from Thebes to a new city built in the desert, Akhetaten. There he patronized a fresh style of art, more realistic than the stylized sculpture of earlier times. After his death all his reforms came to nothing. The old gods were restored, the capital was moved back to Thebes, and his successors did all in their power to erase his memory from the historical record.

THE KINGDOM OF ISRAEL

IN COMPARISON TO OTHER ANCIENT EMPIRES *the Israelite kingdom was small and short-lived, but its foundation would resonate through history. The homeland of Israel became a powerful spiritual and political symbol for Jewish people, sustaining them through the centuries of exile and dispersion that followed the kingdom's collapse.*

The Bible describes how Moses led the Israelites out of captivity in pharaonic Egypt to the "promised land" of Canaan, between the Jordan River and the Mediterranean Sea. There they lived in tribes, which were united under their first king, Saul, who reigned from about 1020 to 1006 B.C. David (1006–965) was Israel's next "beloved" king. He conquered the city of Jebus (Jerusalem) and made it the Israelites' center of political power and worship, installing the precious Ark of the Covenant there.

In Jerusalem David's son Solomon (965–928) built a magnificent temple, cedar paneled and richly decorated with bronze and gold. To pay for this and other projects, the king taxed his people heavily, and his son Rehoboam continued the practice. Resenting the burden, the northern tribes split away from the southern kingdom of Judah, forming a separate Jewish kingdom called Israel.

Meanwhile the Assyrians, a Mesopotamian people from the Tigris Valley, began to threaten the other powers in the region. Aided by technological developments such as siege engines and mail armor, the Assyrians were formidable fighters. Internal

- 🜲 **c.1220 B.C.** Hebrew people (Israelites) begin settling in Canaan.

- 🜲 **c.1150** Israelites live in tribes led by elders referred to as "judges."

- 🜲 **c.1020** Saul becomes the first Israelite king.

- 🜲 **c.1006** David rules first over the southern kingdom of Judah and later over all Israel, establishing his capital at Jerusalem.

- 🜲 **c.965** Solomon comes to the throne, presiding over a splendid court; to pay for its expense, he exacts high taxes from the Israelites.

- ☀ **c.950** King Solomon builds the Temple in Jerusalem.

- 🜲 **c.930** The Assyrian Empire becomes dominant in the Tigris Valley region.

- 🜲 **c.928** Solomon's son Rehoboam becomes king, but antagonizes the northern tribes: "My father chastised you with whips," he tells them, "but I will chastise you with scorpions."

- ✗ **c.925** The northern tribes rebel, splitting away from the southern kingdom of Judah to set up a separate, northern kingdom of Israel.

- ✗ **c.924** Shoshenq I of Egypt invades Judah and Israel.

- ✗ **c.854** Israel joins forces with other states to check Assyrian progress at the Battle of Karkar.

- 🜲 **c.841** Israel is forced to pay tribute (a payment acknowledging submission) to Assyria.

- ✗ **c.732** Tiglath-Pileser III of Assyria conquers Damascus. Over the next 17 years the Assyrians also overcome Babylon and make Israel and Judah vassal (subject) states.

- ✗ **c.724** Hoshea, king of Israel, rebels against Assyrian rule.

- ✗ **c.721** Samaria, the capital of Israel, is captured by the Assyrians after a three-year siege; its inhabitants are deported to Assyria.

- 🜲 **612** The Assyrian Empire breaks down.

discord had weakened Israel, which was conquered by the Assyrians in 721.

The southern Jewish kingdom of Judah survived the defeat as a vassal (subject) state of the great empire of Babylon, another Mesopotamian power. When the people of Judah revolted against Babylonian rule in 598, the Babylonian king, Nebuchadrezzar II (604–562), known in the Bible as Nebuchadnezzar, crushed the uprising. Ten years later, after another rebellion, he besieged Jerusalem, destroying the city and temple and deporting thousands of Jews to Babylon.

Babylon was a magnificent city, famed for its Hanging Gardens, but the Babylonian Captivity was harsh for the exiles. Accordingly, they welcomed Babylon's overthrow in 539 by the Persians, who had risen to greatness under Cyrus the Great (died 530). As the new ruler of Babylon, Cyrus encouraged the exiled Jews to return to their own land, which now also formed part of his empire. Many went home, but thousands remained in Babylon or in Egypt, beginning the dispersion, or "diaspora," of the Jewish people that continued into modern times.

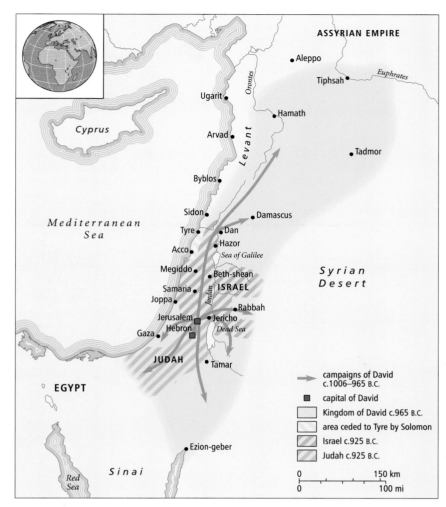

◀ As described in the biblical Book of Kings, the temple that Solomon built in Jerusalem to house the Ark of the Covenant consisted of three rooms: an outer porch or vestibule, an inner place of worship, and the Holy of Holies, where the Ark rested.

▶ Israel reached its greatest extent in the reign of David, but shrank back after his death. In about 925 B.C. the remaining lands split into two separate states: Israel in the north, with its capital at Samaria, and Judah in the south, ruled from Jerusalem.

Map legend:
- → campaigns of David c.1006–965 B.C.
- ■ capital of David
- Kingdom of David c.965 B.C.
- area ceded to Tyre by Solomon
- Israel c.925 B.C.
- Judah c.925 B.C.

0 — 150 km
0 — 100 mi

The Ark of the Covenant

The Ark of the Covenant was a box of acacia wood and gold, topped with two sculpted cherubs and carried on two long poles; the Bible relates that God instructed Moses to have it made to store the tablets listing the Ten Commandments. When the Israelites went to war, the ark was always carried with their soldiers; it served as a focal point for worship and was also believed to have the power to kill people. King David brought the ark to Jerusalem, where it was eventually housed in the temple built by his son, Solomon. But when the Babylonians captured Jerusalem and destroyed the temple in 586 B.C., the ark disappeared. Although the fictional Indiana Jones was able to track it down in the 1981 film *Raiders of the Lost Ark*, its real-life whereabouts remain a mystery.

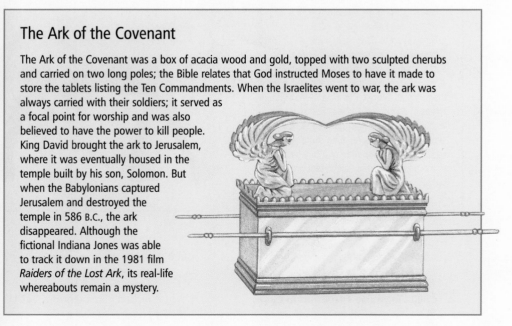

👑 **609–605** Judah comes under Egyptian control.

👑 **c.600** The Neo-Babylonian Empire is established.

⚔ **586** Jerusalem, capital of Judah, is destroyed after a long siege by the Babylonian ruler Nebuchadrezzar II; its inhabitants are deported to Babylon.

👑 **539** Cyrus the Great takes over from the Chaldeans as ruler of Babylon and allows exiled Jews to return to their homeland.

☀ **c.515** A new temple is completed in the rebuilt Jerusalem.

AMERICAS

c.900 The Chorreran Culture flourishes in Ecuador; among its fine pottery products are distinctive "whistle bottles," which produce a whistling sound when liquid is poured into them.

c.900 The Olmec ceremonial center at San Lorenzo in Mexico is destroyed, and the monumental stone heads that adorned it are ritually defaced and buried in piled-earth ridges.

c.900 A phase of intense cultural activity in the Valley of Mexico, marked by the extraordinary pottery produced at Tlatilco near modern Mexico City, comes to an end, leaving the central Mexican region as something of a cultural backwater for several centuries to come.

c.900 The great ceremonial center at Chavín de Huantar in Peru is built from about this time on.

EUROPE

c.900 Sparta is founded in the southern Peloponnese region of Greece; its citizens become renowned for their military discipline and austere lifestyle.

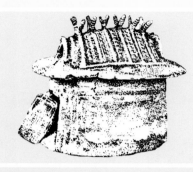

Villanovan hut-shaped burial urn.

c.900 The Villanova Culture emerges in the Bologna region of Italy; Villanovan society is notable for its bronzeworking and early use of iron.

AFRICA

c.900 The state of Kush emerges in Nubia, south of Egypt, with its capital at Napata.

c.817 Under the 23rd Dynasty Egypt breaks up into rival power centers.

c.814 The Phoenician colony of Carthage is founded in North Africa.

WESTERN ASIA

c.900 The people of the kingdom of Urartu, based around Lake Van in what is now eastern Turkey, adopt the Assyrian cuneiform script.

c.900 Phoenician colonists continue their westward expansion, founding settlements near metal deposits.

c.883 Assurnarsipal II ascends the throne of Assyria, further expanding the empire into Syria as far as the Mediterranean Sea.

The homeland of the Phoenicians was a narrow strip of the eastern Mediterranean shoreline in what is now Lebanon. Their only outlet for expansion was by sea, and from about 1000 B.C. on, they became famous as traders and voyagers, traveling even beyond the Straits of Gibraltar to explore the western coasts of Africa and Europe. Trade brought in wealth, which in turn supported skilled craftworkers producing dyed cloth, jewelry, and metalwork. This statuette of a bull, reminiscent of the biblical Golden Calf, is thought to symbolize the Phoenician fertitlity god Baal.

SOUTH & CENTRAL ASIA

c.900 The later Vedas are composed in India, completing the *Rig Veda*, a collection of 1,028 Hindu hymns that is the world's oldest sacred book.

c.900 The first states emerge on the Ganges plain in India.

c.800 Towns are established in India's Ganges Valley.

c.800 In India the Brahmanas are composed as instructions to priests, designed to provide direction in matters of ritual.

AMERICAS

While the Olmec heartland lay near Mexico's Gulf Coast, the Zapotecs came to dominate the Oaxaca Valley region inland from the Pacific Ocean. In its early stages the Zapotec Culture was influenced by the Olmecs, and Zapotec society reflected Olmec models in being ruled by an elite warrior class dedicated to the worship of gods and ancestors. In time, however, the Zapotecs developed a cultural identity of their own; they were the first Americans to devise a written script. Their capital of Monte Albán, shown here, was built from 500 B.C. on.

📖 **c.850** Olmec cave paintings in southern Mexico depict figures combining human and animal features.

✷ **c.800** Numerous villages are established by this date in the tropical lowland regions of Guatemala.

📖 **c.800** Zapotecs—Central American Indians inhabiting southern Mexico—develop a hieroglyphic script that is the earliest in the Americas.

EUROPE

👑 **c.850** Greece begins to emerge from the dark ages that began around 1200 B.C., establishing city-states in Ionia and Aeolia.

👑 **c.850** The first settlements appear on the site of Rome's Palatine Hill.

👑 **c.800** Corinth is founded in the northeastern corner of Greece's Peloponnese Peninsula; it will become the largest and richest Greek city-state after Athens.

👑 **c.800** Athens and Sparta grow in power and grandeur.

✷ **c.800** The Celtic Hallstatt Culture spreads out across Europe. Adherents have distinctive burial practices and use bronze and iron tools.

AFRICA

✷ **c.800** Ironworking begins to spread across sub-Saharan Africa.

WESTERN ASIA

👑 **c.880** Nimrud, near the present-day city of Mosul in Iraq, becomes the capital of the Assyrian Empire.

👑 **c.876** Phoenicia agrees to pay tribute to the Assyrians.

👑 **c.873** Ahab comes to the throne of Israel.

👑 **c.858** Shalmaneser III ascends the throne of Assyria; the empire expands further during his reign.

⚔ **c.856** Shalmaneser III of Assyria defeats Aramu, the first known king of Urartu.

⚔ **c.854** The Assyrians defeat a coalition of Levantine forces, including Israel, at the Battle of Karkar; despite the victory, their advance is checked.

👑 **c.853** The Babylonian kings become reliant on the military assistance of the Assyrians.

☀ **c.850** In Israel the prophets Elijah and Elisha attack the cult of the Phoenician god Baal.

👑 **c.850** The Medes migrate from Central Asia to the area southwest of the Caspian Sea.

⚔ **c.842** In Israel Jehu seizes power; King Ahab's widow Jezebel is thrown from a window and crushed to death under the wheels of Jehu's chariot.

👑 **c.841** A weakened Israel is forced to pay tribute to Assyria.

👑 **c.840** The kingdom of Urartu emerges as a significant power in the Middle East.

SOUTH & CENTRAL ASIA

☀ **c.800** The early Upanishads also date from about this time; a departure from the old Vedic beliefs, these texts represent an attempt to get close to the inner meaning of life.

HOMER'S GREECE

Greece has a unique place *in Western tradition as the central source of our civilization, yet around the year 2000 B.C. its prospects hardly looked promising. In the Middle East and Egypt great cities had already come and gone; in the valley of the Indus the Harappan civilization was at its height. Greece, however, had only recently shaken off a Stone Age lifestyle as Bronze Age culture had been brought across the Aegean Sea by "island-hopping" immigrants from Anatolia, in what is now Turkey.*

▲ Very little is known of the life of Homer, Greece's great epic poet, but legend claims that he was Ionian—born across the Aegean Sea from mainland Greece—and that he was blind.

▶ From the 11th century B.C. on, when northern Dorians swept into mainland Greece, colonists chose to sail east in search of new homes. They settled on Aegean islands and on the shores of Asia Minor, in what is now Turkey.

| | Greek settlement, 10th century B.C. |
| | Greek influence, 10th century B.C. |

⊛	**c.2300 B.C.**	Immigrants from Anatolia bring Bronze Age culture to Greece.
⊛	**c.2000**	The first Minoan palaces are built in Crete.
☀	**c.1600**	The Mycenaean civilization emerges in mainland Greece.
☀	**c.1450**	Mt. Thera erupts, causing devastation across the eastern Mediterranean and destroying some cities of Minoan Crete.
☀	**c.1250**	Mycenaean civilization collapses.

☀	**1184**	Traditional date of the Fall of Troy.
⊛	**c.1050**	Dorian nomads invade Greece from the north, bringing with them the secrets of ironworking.
☀	**c.1000**	Greek settlers start to establish colonies on the Aegean's eastern coast in regions that will become known as Aeolia and Ionia.
📖	**776**	The first Olympic Games.
☀	**c.750**	Greece's Archaic Period begins; the first city-states date from this time.

📖	**c.750**	The first evidence of a Greek alphabet comes from this period.
📖	**c.750**	The great epics of Homer are composed (although not yet written down).
☀	**c.734**	The first Greek colonies are founded in Sicily.
📖	**c.700**	The poet Hesiod's *Theogony* records traditional stories of the Greek gods.

The first significant civilization of mainland Greece emerged in about 1600 B.C. Its capital lay at Mycenae on the Pelopennese, the peninsula forming the southern part of the Greek mainland. The awe-inspiring ruins excavated there suggest a militaristic culture, yet Mycenae was also a merchant civilization. Soldiers and traders worked together to spread its influence across the eastern Mediterranean region.

The civilization's success was glorious but fleeting: By 1250 B.C. it had collapsed. The reasons for its fall remain unclear. A time of troubles was affecting the eastern Mediterranean, and a mysterious coalition of displaced migrants, known in Egyptian records as the "Sea Peoples," was on the move. Even if they did not destroy Mycenae itself, their activities would certainly have disrupted its seaborne trading network.

Mycenae fell leaving no successor civilization; instead, local warlords fought over a land of scattered settlements. Later scholars talked of the years from 1250 to 850 B.C. as Greece's "Dark Age," although we have no way of knowing how bleak it really was for those who lived through it.

By the 8th century B.C., however, the outlook was certainly brightening. The growing wealth of successful local rulers stimulated craft industries and trade, creating perfect conditions for the evolution of the *polis*, or self-governing city-state, often consisting of little more than one large community and its surrounding countryside. Young adventurers from these cities founded trading posts abroad, enriching their home states even further. While individual cities grew independently, their sense of a common Greek identity was growing too, fostered by a shared set of stories of gods and heroes. Almost nothing is known of the poet Homer (some even suggest "he" was actually more than one anonymous bard), but his great epics, the *Iliad* and the *Odyssey*, became an inspiration to the Greeks of future generations.

Crete's Minoan Civilization

Graceful athleticism triumphed over brute strength in Minoan culture, which flourished from around 2000 B.C. on the Mediterranean island of Crete. This spectacular civilization took its name from the legendary King Minos, whose name also lived on in Greek myths of the Minotaur. This monster lived in a mazelike structure called the Labyrinth, perhaps inspired by tales of the genuinely labyrinthine palace in the Minoan capital, Knossos (*above*). Under royal supervision a trading economy prospered, making commercial connections from pharaonic Egypt to Asia Minor. However, the island's sea-trade empire suffered a fatal blow in about 1450, when Mount Thera, a volcano on the nearby island of Santorini, erupted, devastating much of the eastern Mediterranean region. Political oblivion soon followed; the island was conquered by Mycenaean Greeks by about 1400 B.C.

◄ The palace at Knossos in northern Crete was the focal point of the Minoan civilization that flourished on the island from c.2000 to 1400 B.C. Sprawling across 5 acres (2 hectares) of hilly ground, the many-storied building served not just as a royal residence but also as a statehouse, a religious shrine, a center of craft production, and a warehouse for many different kinds of goods.

▼ Greek legends of youths sacrificed to the monstrous Minotaur—half-man, half-bull—may have been inspired by the real-life Cretan sport of bull leaping. Contestants caught a charging bull by the horns and tried to somersault over its back, as shown in this fresco from the palace at Knossos, dated c.1500 B.C.

AMERICAS

⚜ **c.800** The Dorset Culture begins to emerge around Cape Dorset on Canada's Baffin Island; its people display a new grace and precision in the crafting of flint blades and ivory figures.

⚜ **c.800** The Chavín Culture becomes established through much of the Andean region. Chavín craftsmen produce intricate artworks of hammered gold.

☀ **c.800** By this date La Venta, near Mexico's Gulf Coast, has taken the place formerly occupied by San Lorenzo as the main focus of Olmec religious and cultural activity.

EUROPE

⚜ **c.800** Etruscans establish the first towns in Italy, building on hillside terraces and surrounding their settlements with huge timbered walls.

👑 **c.800** The success of Euboea's trading post at Al Mina, on the coast of Syria, starts a trend among other Greek cities for colonization.

👑 **776** The first Olympic Games are held at Olympia in southern Greece.

👑 **753** The traditional date of the foundation of Rome.

📖 **c.750** First use of the Greek alphabet dates from this period: The Greeks use the existing Phoenician letters, but introduce vowels to allow the accurate reproduction of spoken language.

Painted Greek vase of the Archaic Period from Corinth.

AFRICA

⚔ **c.780** King Kashta's Kush (in what is now Sudan) starts encroaching on the southern territories of a weakened Egypt.

⚔ **c.770** Kashta takes control of Upper Egypt.

⚔ **c.750** Kashta's son Piye invades Lower Egypt, making it too subject to Nubia.

WESTERN ASIA

Hebrew captives of the Assyrian King Sennacherib.

👑 **c.800** By this date the Phoenician trading empire extends through much of the coastal Mediterranean.

⚔ **c.760** A weakened Assyria can find no economic or military answer to the rise of Urartu to the north: There are insurrections in several nominally subject cities.

👑 **c.744** Tiglath-Pileser III comes to the throne of a much reduced and enfeebled Assyria. He sets about building, by both military and diplomatic means, what will later be known as the "Neo-Assyrian" Empire.

👑 **c.738** Midas becomes king of Phrygia in central Anatolia: The legend of his "golden touch" gives some sense of the stupendous wealth of his newly powerful realm.

⚔ **c.732** Tiglath-Pileser incorporates Damascus into his empire.

⚔ **c.727** Sargon II seizes the Assyrian throne. In a 16-year reign he defeats both Elam and Urartu, and reimposes Assyrian power over much of the Middle East.

⚔ **c.721** Assyrian forces take the Israelite capital of Samaria after a three-year siege.

EAST ASIA & OCEANIA

⚜ **c.800** Wet rice cultivation and bronze technology are exported from China to Korea.

👑 **c.800** Rapid urban expansion takes place in China despite increasing lawlessness as the king's power is weakened.

⚔ **771** King Yu is dethroned and killed by an alliance of rebellious noblemen and steppe nomads.

✴ **c.750** In the Mayan region of Central America work begins on the ceremonial site at Los Mangales, which will eventually feature temple platforms, tomb complexes, and residential areas.

📖 **c.750** Greek craftsmen increasingly use animal figures rather than geometric patterns in ceramic decoration, showing that they are importing cultural ideas, as well as raw materials, from their Asiatic colonies.

🏛 **750** The conventional starting point for the Archaic Period in preclassical Greece.

🏛 **c.734** Greeks from Corinth establish the colony of Syracuse in Sicily.

✕ **c.716** The Nubian ruler Shabako formally annexes Lower Egypt, thereby officially reuniting the country.

✕ **c.707** Sargon II conquers Babylon.

🏛 **c.705** Sennacherib suceeds to the throne of an Assyrian Empire that is bigger and stronger than it has ever been.

✕ **c.701** Poised to seize Jerusalem, the all-conquering army of Sennacherib is forced to withdraw for reasons that remain obscure—perhaps an outbreak of plague; the Jews believe they have been saved by their god Yahweh.

Archaic Greek marble bust of a lady holding a pomegranate.

⊕ **c.700** Earliest date for construction work at Kaminaljuyú, on the outskirts of modern Guatemala City, which in time will become an important Mayan site.

✕ **c.730** The Greek city-state of Sparta attacks neighboring Messenia: after a bitter, 20-year war the Messenians' territory is taken and they themselves enslaved.

📖 **c.700** Drawing on preexisting oral traditions, Hesiod's *Theogony* relates the origins and histories of the Greek gods.

For more than seven centuries the Assyrians were among the most feared military powers in the Middle East. From a homeland around the city of Assur on the Tigris River in what is now northern Iraq they spread their influence by conquest, subduing neighboring peoples and demanding tribute from them. At its peak in the 8th century B.C. their empire stretched all the way from the Zagros Mountains of Persia to the Mediterranean coast and into Israel. This bronze image of a charioteer comes from the Balawat Gates, commissioned by Shalmaneser III to celebrate his victories.

🏛 **770** Yu's son moves his capital eastward from Hao to Luoyang to distance it further from the steppe nomads. The Eastern Zhou Period gets under way.

🏛 **722** The start of the Spring and Autumn Period of Chinese history.

AMERICAS

EUROPE

AFRICA

WESTERN ASIA

EAST ASIA & OCEANIA

800–700 B.C.

39

THE OLMECS

THE FIRST GREAT CULTURE *of Central America arose in a seemingly unlikely spot—the steamy rainforests of southern Mexico. There, sometime about 1250 B.C., a previously unknown people suddenly started raising spectacular ceremonial centers where previously there had only been scattered villages. Even more surprisingly, they decorated them with huge stone sculptures that still stand comparison with the finest produced anywhere in the world.*

▲ A tiny bust of a woman carved in rare blue jade demonstrates the Olmecs' skill in stone carving. Their sculptors only had stone tools with which to grind and chip the figures into shape.

▶ From a heartland in the steamy rainforest lands around the Gulf of Mexico, Olmec cultural influence spread out over the course of several centuries through much of Mexico and on into Guatemala, Honduras, and El Salvador.

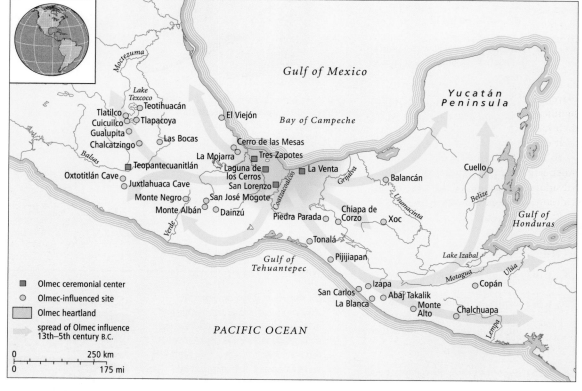

■ Olmec ceremonial center
○ Olmec-influenced site
▧ Olmec heartland
⬈ spread of Olmec influence 13th–5th century B.C.

0   250 km
0   175 mi

✴ **c.6500 B.C.** Chili peppers, cotton, and a variety of squash are cultivated in southern Mexico.

✴ **c.4000** Indian corn (maize) first cultivated in Central America.

✴ **c.3500** Beans first cultivated in Central America. Semipermanent villages appear, with pit huts replacing the rock shelters used by hunter-gatherers.

✴ **c.2300** First pottery made in southern Mexico.

✴ **c.2000** By this date agriculture has replaced nomadic (wandering) hunting and gathering as the typical lifestyle in the region.

✴ **c.1400** First evidence of a raised earthen mound in the Olmec region, from a site on Guatemala's Pacific coast.

✴ **c.1250** The first great Olmec ceremonial center built at San Lorenzo in the Gulf region of southern Mexico.

✴ **c.1200** The earliest stone sculptures are erected at San Lorenzo.

✖ **c.900** San Lorenzo is destroyed, and the great stone statues are defaced and buried.

♛ **c.800** La Venta, near the Gulf Coast, becomes the main center of Olmec Culture.

✖ **c.400** La Venta is demolished and its monuments buried.

♛ **c.200** The ceremonial center of Tres Zapotes falls into disuse, marking the end of the Olmec civilization.

San Lorenzo, the first such center, was built on an earth platform 150 feet (45 m) high—the height of a 10-story building. On this base its builders raised additional earthen mounds arranged in clusters around rectangular courtyards. They decorated the courts with huge sculpted heads, the biggest of them up to 11 feet (3.4 m) tall and weighing as much as 20 tons. The stone from which they were shaped was brought laboriously by raft—the Olmecs had no wheeled vehicles—from mountains 50 miles (80 km) away and carved with stone tools, since their craftsmen had no metals.

Scholars think that the heads probably represented dead rulers. Some are shown wearing helmets rather like those now worn by football players. The connection may not be entirely far-fetched, since the Olmecs are known to have devised a ritual ballgame, played on special courts, that was later passed on to almost all subsequent Central American civilizations. Players of the game, which probably had some ritual significance, were not allowed to touch the ball with their hands or feet; instead, they controlled it with their elbows, hips, and thighs.

To judge from small sculptures, ornaments, and other artifacts found from northern Mexico to El Salvador and Costa Rica, the Olmecs controlled widespread trade networks across Central America.

Apart from small numbers of craftsmen and traders, their society seems to have divided between a wealthy ruling class and the peasant farmers who provided the labor to build the ceremonial centers. Maybe the peasants resented the demands made on them; certainly San Lorenzo was deliberately destroyed around the year 900 B.C., when the monumental heads lining its courts were defaced and buried.

Subsequently, other centers rose to prominence to replace it, first at La Venta on an island in the Tonalá River, and then, when that in turn was overthrown, at Tres Zapotes. That site too seems to have fallen into disuse by about 200 B.C., bringing Olmec civilization to an end.

Yet its influence lived on in later Central American cultures—peoples such as the Maya, the Toltecs, and the Aztecs all borrowed heavily from the Olmecs. The innovations that they passed on to their successors went well beyond the ballgame to also include astronomic calendars, a taste for massive stone architecture, and even a form of pictographic writing.

▼ This colossal stone head is one of 17 found at the ceremonial site of La Venta. All were sculpted from volcanic basalt rock between about 1200 and 900 B.C. The heads range in height from 5 to 11 feet (1.5–3.4 m) and weigh as much as 20 tons. This figure is wearing the headdress that may be associated with the Olmecs' ritual ballgame.

The Jaguar Cult

Olmec sculptures and carvings often depict people whose faces have the slit eyes and snarling mouths of jaguars. Frequently the figure shown is a baby or infant, its forehead imprinted with the stylized image of a big cat's pawmarks. Scholars call these creatures "were-jaguars," after the manner of werewolves, and think that they indicate the existence of a cult devoted to the big cats—the top predators of the Central American jungles. It may be that Olmec nobles traced their origins back to a mythical founder who was himself half-man, half-jaguar, thereby claiming for themselves some of the jaguar's attributes of fierceness and cunning. In one chief's grave the bones of a child have been found buried alongside those of two jaguars, strengthening the idea of a direct link between the animals and nobly born young.

AMERICAS

⚙ **c.700** The Adena Culture is by now firmly established in the Ohio River valley region. Over 200 Adena sites, built over several centuries, have been identified in Ohio and neighboring areas of West Virginia, Pennsylvania, Kentucky, and Indiana.

For more than 1,000 years the building of burial mounds was a central feature of America's eastern woodlands cultures. Ohio's famous Serpent Mound is thought by some experts to be an Adena site (there are others nearby), although others link it to the later Hopewell Culture.

EUROPE

⚙ **c.700** Scandinavian craftsmen exhibit their bronzeworking skills by making lurs—trumpetlike musical instruments probably used in ritual ceremonies.

⚙ **c.700** The peoples of Central Europe build wooden trackways to carry carts over marshy areas.

📖 **c.700** The first known inscriptions in the Etruscan language date from this time.

👑 **683** In Athens, Greece, hereditary kingship comes to an end, to be replaced with elected officials.

👑 **654** The Phoenicians found trading colonies on the Balearic Islands in the western Mediterranean.

👑 **c.650** Tyrants seize power in several Greek city-states in opposition to aristocratic rule (–600).

AFRICA

⚔ **c.671** The Assyrian King Esarhaddon raids Egypt, conquering Memphis and demanding tribute.

⚔ **c.667** Esarhaddon's successor Ashurbanipal defeats Taharqa, the last of the Kushite (Nubian) pharaohs of Egypt.

👑 **c.665** Driven out of Egypt, the Kushites continue to rule most of Nubia from their capital at Napata.

WESTERN ASIA

👑 **c.700** Achaemenes founds the Persian Achaemenid Dynasty.

⚙ **c.700** Babylonian astrologers identify the signs of the zodiac.

📖 **c.690** The Assyrian King Sennacherib rebuilds the ancient capital of Nineveh and decorates the walls of his palace with reliefs of his military victories.

⚔ **689** The Assyrians sack Babylon after the Babylonians rebel against Assyrian rule.

⚙ **673** Babylonian astrologers correctly predict a solar eclipse.

👑 **640** Persia becomes a vassal state of the kingdom of the Medes.

☀ **c.630** The Persian prophet Zoroaster is born.

The Ishtar Gate at Babylon, made of blue-glazed bricks.

👑 **626** Nabopolassar, appointed governor of Babylon by the Assyrians, rebels and sets up his own Chaldean dynasty.

👑 **614** Cyaxares, ruler of the Medes, allies himself with Nabopolassar, king of Babylon, against the Assyrians.

⚔ **612** The Assyrian Empire falls to the Medes and Babylonians.

EAST ASIA & OCEANIA

👑 **c.670** Qi, in the northeast, becomes the dominant state in China during the early Spring and Autumn Period.

👑 **660** According to early Japanese legend, Jimmu becomes the first emperor of Japan.

⚙ **c.600** Iron casting spreads across China from this date.

📖 **c.700** In Central America red-orange pottery of the Mamón style is in use among the Mayan people of the Petèn Lowlands of northern Guatemala.

☀ **c.600** The Middle Formative Period of Mesoamerican culture is now fully under way. In the Mayan lands construction has begun at ceremonial sites including Nakbe, Chalchuapa, Komchen, Rio Azul, and Seibal.

☀ **c.600** The Olmec ceremonial center at Teopantecuanitlán, near Copalillo in the mountains of southwestern Mexico, is abandoned for unknown reasons.

AMERICAS

👑 **c.650** At about this time Perdiccas I is traditionally supposed to have founded the kingdom of Macedon in northern Greece.

👑 **621** The Athenian politician Draco draws up a code of laws that become notorious for their "draconian" severity.

👑 **c.616** A line of Etruscan kings is established in Rome.

📖 **c.600** The poetess Sappho flourishes on the Greek island of Lesbos.

⊕ **c.600** Coinage comes into use on the Greek mainland.

👑 **c.600** Greek colonies are founded at Massilia (modern Marseille) in southern France and at Emporia in southern Spain.

👑 **c.600** Celtic peoples cross the Pyrenees and settle on the Iberian Peninsula.

EUROPE

✕ **c.651** An Egyptian uprising, led by Psammetichus I, forces the Assyrians to leave Egypt.

⊕ **c.600** Ironworking is known in Kush.

⊕ **c.600** The Egyptian Pharaoh Necho II builds a canal linking the Nile River with the Red Sea.

⊕ **c.600** According to the 5th-century Greek historian Herodotus, Necho also sends a Phoenician fleet to sail around Africa, a voyage that takes three years.

AFRICA

👑 **604** Nebuchadrezzar II becomes king of Babylon and revives its fortunes; his empire is known to historians as the Neo-Babylonian Empire.

📖 **c.600** The Scythians, nomadic herders of Central Asia, begin making gold objects in the "animal style," depicting leaping animals such as deer, horses, and eagles in intertwining patterns.

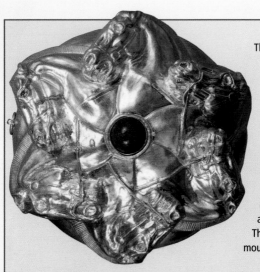

The Scythians owe their name to classical Greek historians, who used the term to describe horse-riding nomads living north of the Black Sea. Unbeknown to the Greeks, similar nomadic peoples could be found all the way across the steppes of Central Asia as far as eastern Siberia. As this relief molded on the base of a gold cup suggests, horses were central to their way of life: The Scythians traded them, rode them to move their herds of cattle between winter and summer pastures, and fought on them as mounted warriors. They buried dead leaders under massive earth mounds that have yielded many treasures.

WESTERN ASIA

👑 **c.600** In the South Pacific Polynesian voyagers from Fiji and Tonga sail east to settle the Cook and Society Islands.

EAST ASIA & OCEANIA

700–600 B.C.

THE ETRUSCANS IN ITALY

ANCIENT INHABITANTS OF A REGION *of central Italy known as Etruria, the Etruscans are one of history's mystery peoples. Although they were able to write, scholars today can decipher little of their script. Their literature, which was extensive, is lost except for a few fragments, and what we know of Etruscan history has come down to us through the unflattering comments of Greek and Roman writers.*

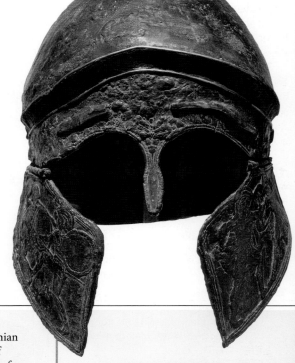

▲ The Etruscans grew rich by exploiting the mineral wealth of their land, which contained the only major sources of copper and iron in the central Mediterranean region. Their craftsmen used the metals to create magnificent artworks like this bronze statue of the Chimera—a monster with a lion's head and a snake tail.

Etruria, an area roughly equivalent to the modern Italian region of Tuscany, was rich in iron and copper ores. Its coastline possessed many natural harbors. Thus the Etruscans were skilled metalworkers and sailors. They grew rich by trading iron ingots, bronze, and other goods in their ships up and down the coast of Italy and across to southern France. By about 800 B.C., when Rome was still a hilltop cluster of huts, they had already begun to live in cities.

Etruscan traders faced competition from Phoenician and Greek traders in the western Mediterranean. In about 600 B.C. the Greeks founded a trading colony at Massilia (modern Marseille) in southern France. From this base they were able to seize control of the valuable trade route along the Rhône River into central Europe. To offset this loss, the Etruscans formed an alliance with the trading city of Carthage in North Africa.

⊛ **c.900 B.C.** The iron-using Villanova Culture emerges in northern Italy.

⊛ **c.800** Etruscan ships begin to voyage along the west coast of Italy.

⊛ **c.700** First use of Etruscan alphabetic script.

♔ **c.616** An Etruscan, Tarquin I, becomes king of Rome.

♔ **c.600** Twelve Etruscan cities come together to form the Etruscan League.

♔ **c.550** The Etruscans gain control of the Po Valley to the north of Etruria and begin to build cities there.

⚔ **539** A joint Etruscan–Carthaginian force defeats the Greeks off Corsica, halting the spread of Greek colonies in the western Mediterranean. The Etruscans take control of Corsica.

♔ **c.525** The Etruscans establish a number of settlements in Campania (southern Italy).

⚔ **525** The Etruscans unsuccessfully attack the Greek city of Cumae in southern Italy.

♔ **510** The Romans expel Tarquin II, the last Etruscan king of Rome.

⚔ **504** The Etruscans suffer a major defeat in southern Italy at the Battle of Aricia.

♔ **423** The Samnites take control of Capua in Campania, previously under Etruscan rule.

⚔ **405–396** The Romans capture the city of Veii in southern Etruria after a 10-year war.

♔ **c.400** The Gauls (Celts) cross the Alps to invade northern Italy and settle in the Po Valley. Etruscan power in the region begins to decline.

⚔ **296–295** After a series of defeats by the Romans most of the Etruscan cities sign a truce with Rome.

⚔ **285-280** Rome puts down a series of rebellions in the Etruscan cities.

The Etruscans were technologically advanced and built roads, bridges, and canals. They adopted the alphabet, vase painting, and temple building from the Greeks. During the 6th century B.C. the Etruscans expanded north and south out of their homeland of Etruria. According to Roman writers, 12 of the major Etruscan cities formed a loose political alliance, or "league" of states, at this time.

For a time Etruscan kings ruled the city of Rome. A group of Roman aristocrats overthrew the last Etruscan king of Rome in 510 B.C., an event that traditionally marked the foundation of the Roman Republic, and from that time on the Romans gradually replaced the Etruscans as the dominant power in Italy. The Etruscans finally disappeared from history early in the 3rd century B.C., swallowed up in the expanding political sphere of Rome.

The Romans took many cultural ideas from the Etruscans, such as augury—the belief that people can foretell the future by observing natural phenomena such as the flight of birds. They also inherited the Etruscans' knowledge of engineering and metalwork, and even some military tactics.

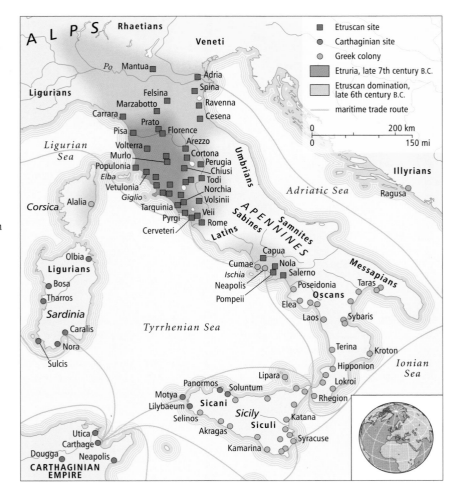

◀ There were Etruscan warriors, as this fearsome war helmet suggests. Yet the Etruscans are better known today for their artistic abilities, and in the long run they proved no match for the Romans as soldiers.

▶ The Etruscans' heartland lay in the region of Italy now known as Tuscany. They grew rich on sea trade, exporting metal ores from their mines, and used their wealth to spread their influence across much of northern Italy.

Cities of the Dead

The Etruscans buried their dead in extensive cemeteries that were laid out almost like cities. In southern Etruria they carved the tombs out of the soft tufa rock of the region and furnished them like houses. Such a tomb often contained a sculpted effigy of a deceased husband and wife reclining together on a couch, as if taking part in a banquet. Painted scenes of banquets attended by musicians and dancers decorated other tombs. Grave robbers have looted large numbers of the tombs, but archaeologists have excavated many that have survived the centuries intact. Their contents typically include enormous numbers of Greek vases, together with chariots and goods of gold, ivory, and amber, testifying to the wealth of the Etruscan aristocrats buried within them.

AMERICAS

c.600 The Paracas Culture flourishes on the Peruvian coast, producing spectacular colored textiles featuring a big-eyed figure known as the Oculate Being.

On a windswept peninsula on the coast of south-central Peru, a series of excavated burial sites have revealed the existence of an extraordinary early culture. Mummified by the dry desert heat, the Paracas corpses were laid to rest in richly decorated capes and blankets thought to have been specially woven by a local cottage industry.

EUROPE

c.594 Solon becomes sole archon (governor) of Athens. His laws lay the foundations of Athenian democracy.

585 The Greek philosopher Thales successfully predicts an eclipse of the sun.

578 Death of Tarquin I (Tarquinius Priscus), the first Etruscan ruler of Rome.

561 Peisistratus makes himself tyrant of Athens, dominating the city-state's politics for the next 34 years.

c.540 The Peloponnesian League unites most of the city-states of the Peloponnese, Greece's southern peninsula, under the leadership of Sparta.

539 The first known Greek tragedy is performed at Athens.

AFRICA

c.600 Carthaginians establish a colony at Marseille on the coast of southern France.

c.600 Iron- and bronzeworking develop in West Africa.

c.600 Phoenicians complete their circumnavigation of Africa.

591 Meroë becomes the capital of Nubia after Psammetichus II of Egypt sacks the former capital, Napata.

525 A Persian invasion force under Cambyses defeats Psammetichus III of Egypt at the Battle of Pelusium. For the next 121 years Egypt falls under Persian rule.

WESTERN ASIA

598 Judah rebels against Babylonian overlordship.

597 Nebuchadrezzar II conquers Jerusalem, but withdraws to quell a revolt at home.

597 Zedekiah is put on the throne of Judah by Nebuchadrezzar. He conspires with Egypt against the Babylonians.

c.590 The Zoroastrian religion spreads across Persia.

586 After a lengthy siege, Jerusalem falls to Nebuchadrezzar, who lays the city waste and takes many captives to Babylon.

585 Astyages succeeds his father Cyaxares as ruler of the short-lived empire of the Medes.

573 The Phoenician port of Tyre falls to Nebuchadrezzar's forces after a 13-year siege.

562 The death of Nebuchadrezzar marks the end of the great days of the Neo-Babylonian Empire.

560 Croesus becomes king of Lydia, a legendarily rich kingdom in Asia Minor (today's Turkey).

SOUTH & CENTRAL ASIA

599 Possible date of the birth of Mahavira ("Great Hero"), the founder of the Jain religion, which renounces the destruction of any living thing.

563 Possible date for the birth of Siddhartha Gautama, the Buddha, in India.

EAST ASIA & OCEANIA

c.600 The *Book of Songs*, the first anthology of Chinese poetry, is compiled.

551 Birth of Kongfuzi, known in the West as Confucius.

Confucius (Kongfuzi).

☀ **c.600** The Middle Formative ceremonial centers of the Mayan region expand as populations in Central America continue to grow. New centers emerge at Cobá and Copán.

☀ **c.550** The Olmecs build a ceremonial center at Tres Zapotes in the Gulf Coast region.

☀ **c.500** Zapotecs establish a ceremonial center at Monte Albán in southern Mexico that flourishes for more than a thousand years.

⊛ **c.500** Corn-growing farmers settle the valleys around San Agustín in southern Colombia, which in time will become that country's most spectacular archaeological region.

AMERICAS

👑 **510** Tarquin II is expelled from Rome, bringing to an end the Etruscan line of kings.

👑 **510** Cleisthenes overthrows Peisistratus's heirs, replacing tyranny with democracy in Athens.

👑 **509** Traditional date for the foundation of the Roman Republic.

✕ **508** Lars Porsena of Clusium attacks Rome in an unsuccesful attempt to restore Etruscan rule.

Bronze cast of the type of mask worn by Greek tragic actors, c.500 B.C.

EUROPE

From humble beginnings, the Persian Cyrus built one of the ancient world's great empires. First conquering his overlords the Medes, he went on to defeat the Babylonians and Lydians. Under his successors Persia ruled a realm stretching from Egypt to the borders of India. Rich tribute like this Lydian bracelet flowed in to fill the imperial coffers.

⊛ **c.525** Camels are introduced into North Africa from Persia.

👑 **c.500** The Bantu-speaking peoples begin to expand from their West African homeland.

AFRICA

👑 **558** Cyrus becomes ruler of Persia.

✕ **550** Cyrus defeats his overlord, the Mede Astyages, launching Persia on the road to empire.

✕ **547** Cyrus defeats Croesus, sacking his capital of Sardis and bringing all of Asia Minor under Persian control.

✕ **539** Babylon falls to Cyrus, bringing Mesopotamia under Persian rule. Jewish exiles are permitted to return to Judah.

👑 **530** Death of Cyrus the Great. He is succeeded by his son Cambyses, who conquers Egypt.

✕ **521** On Cambyses' death Darius comes to the Persian throne, putting down a number of revolts led by rival candidates.

☀ **c.515** The Temple in Jerusalem is rebuilt at the urging of the prophet Haggai.

📖 **c.500** The palace of Persepolis is built in Persia.

WESTERN ASIA

👑 **540** King Bimbisara rises to power in the Ganges kingdom of Magadha.

☀ **524** Gautama has the vision on which the Buddhist religion will be founded.

👑 **521 on** Darius extends the borders of the Persian Empire beyond the Indus into northern India, defeating disunited Aryan forces.

SOUTH & CENTRAL ASIA

📖 **530** Confucius marries and enters the service of the duke of Lu.

👑 **501** Confucius is made governor of the city of Chungtu.

EAST ASIA & OCEANIA

600–500 B.C.

CONFUCIUS'S CHINA

CHINA PRODUCED THE FIRST *great East Asian civilization, boasting major philosophers and poets at a time when much of the rest of the world was still illiterate. In the works of later historians myth and reality blended in tales of legendary early dynasties peopled by hero-kings who were often credited with superhuman powers. Recent archaeological finds have shown that powerful, wealthy kings did indeed rule sizable kingdoms from ancient times.*

According to legend, China's civilization dates back to Huang Di, the Yellow Emperor, who ruled in about 2700 B.C. and invented boats, bows and arrows, and writing. In fact, the first dynasty (line of kings) that can be confirmed is the Shang, said to have come to power in 1766 B.C. The Shang were Bronze Age kings, sweeping into battle in metal chariots and practicing human sacrifice on a large scale. More positively, their era saw the birth of writing in China and the development of an accurate calendar.

In about 1027 B.C. the last Shang king was overthrown by Wu, king of Zhou in central China. The Zhou Dynasty that Wu founded was the longest lasting in Chinese history, surviving for 800 years. The Zhou claimed they had been granted a "Mandate of Heaven," giving the king absolute authority to rule as long as he took care of the welfare of his subjects.

Under the Zhou kings Chinese society developed on feudal lines into a pyramid with the king and

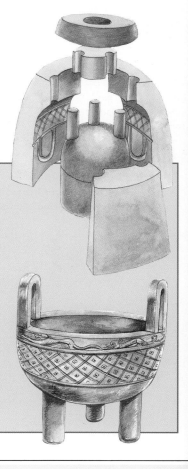

Bronze making in China

China's Bronze Age began sometime in the 3rd millennium B.C., when craftsmen learned to combine copper with tin or other metals to create bronze. By Shang Dynasty times bronze-working was well established. Early bronze vessels featured birds, dragons, and monster masks, but by the late 10th century B.C. the elements of the traditional *taotie* (an imaginary creature with horns, staring eyes, and a fearsome jaw) were incorporated into more abstract designs. Artifacts produced under the Zhou included weapons and spade-shaped coins, as well as sacrificial food vessels (*right*) to honor dead ancestors. The light vessels favored in the Shang period became more highly decorated and heavy bottomed.

🜲 **c.1766 B.C.** The Shang Dynasty is founded by King Tang.

🜲 **c.1027** King Wu of Zhou overthrows the last Shang king and founds the Zhou Dynasty.

✳ **c.1000** Skilled bronze casting proliferates, with the *taotie* animal mask a favorite motif.

🜲 **c.950** Death of King Mu, remembered in later legends as a world traveler.

✳ **c.800** Rapid urban expansion begins.

✳ **c.800** Wet rice cultivation and bronze technology are exported to Korea from China.

✗ **771** Barbarians and alienated Chinese nobility attack the Zhou capital and kill King Yu.

🜲 **770** The Zhou capital moves from Hao to Luoyang, marking the start of the Eastern Zhou Dynasty; thereafter the power of the Zhou rulers declines as rival states battle for supremacy.

📖 **722–481** The *Spring and Autumn Annals* chronicle the history of the state of Lu, retrospectively giving their name to the period.

🜲 **685** Huan of Qi assumes the role of hegemon, building up the economic power of the Qi state with the help of his minister Guan Zhong.

✳ **c.600** Ironworking begins to develop.

📖 **c.600** *Shi-jing* (The Book of Songs), a collection of 305 poems, reaches its final form.

📖 **c.600** The philosopher Lao-Tzu inspires Taoism, which urges disciples to connect to the *tao*, or "way," of nature.

📖 **551** The philosopher Confucius is born in the state of Lu.

🜲 **c.550** After a period of prolonged interstate warfare the dual hegemony of the states of Jin and Chu ensures an uneasy peace for some years.

✳ **c.550** Cast iron is manufactured.

📖 **c.500** The *Analects*—a collection of Confucius's sayings as recorded by his disciples—is assembled.

✳ **c.500** Bronze coins are introduced.

◄ The Chinese were the only people to use the "piece-mold" system of casting for creating large vessels. In this method clay was pressed against a roughly patterned model to produce a mold. When dry, the mold was cut away in several pieces from the model, and more intricate designs were then carved into the clay. The pieces were reassembled upside down in a frame, and molten bronze was poured in. Finally, the mold was removed to reveal the finished bronze object.

► This elaborate jug with a stylized tiger's head for a lid shows just how skilled China's bronzeworkers had become by the late Shang period, in about 1200 B.C.

nobles at the top and millions of peasants at the bottom. Later historians saw its early years as a golden age of peace and stability. Things changed for the worse after a nobles' revolt in 771, when the ruling king was killed; the capital was then moved from Hao to Luoyang, 200 miles (350 km) to the east. The so-called Eastern Zhou kings who ruled thereafter reigned less securely than their Western predecessors. Having tasted power, the nobility proved unwilling to give it up, and central authority was weakened. China increasingly split into a number of states, each controlled by a dominant ruler, or "hegemon," owing only nominal loyalty to the Zhou king.

The first centuries of the Eastern Zhou era are known as the "Spring and Autumn" Period (722–481 B.C.), from the *Spring and Autumn Annals*, a chronicle detailing events in Lu, one of the empire's states. This was a time when the power of the states, each one controlled by a different noble family, was on the rise at the expense of the central power. Even so, the period saw much artistic and technological innovation and creativity. Bronze making reached new heights, ironworking developed, and the earliest Chinese poetry was composed. In addition, religious and philosophical thinkers came to the fore as people sought to find order in troubled times. The most influential of them, Confucius (551–479 B.C.), spent

his life traveling from court to court, teaching and advising. The *Analects*, compiled by his disciples, record his ideas: He emphasized humanity, respect for authority, and responsibility to others.

After Confucius's death the emperor's power was further eclipsed as the nation moved into a time of civil strife known as the Warring States Period (481–221). Through this dark era Confucianism—the ethical system based on the philosopher's thoughts—served as a beacon, and it remained a blueprint for social behavior in China until modern times.

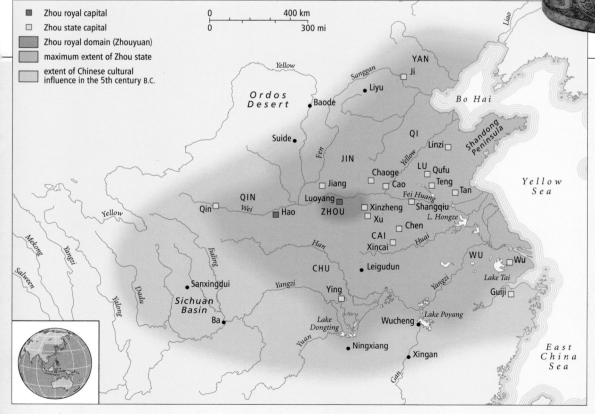

◄ The first Chinese civilizations grew up in the north of today's China, where the long-lasting Zhou Dynasty had its power base on the middle and lower reaches of the Huang (Yellow) River. Its first capital lay at Hao, on a western tributary of the river. But in time it proved too remote, and the capital was moved east to Luoyang in 770 B.C. Even so, the kings who ruled there could not prevent provincial nobles from developing power bases of their own in the various state capitals.

Map legend:
■ Zhou royal capital
□ Zhou state capital
▨ Zhou royal domain (Zhouyuan)
▨ maximum extent of Zhou state
▨ extent of Chinese cultural influence in the 5th century B.C.

0   400 km
0   300 mi

Chavín carving from a temple wall in Peru.

AMERICAS

⬤ **c.500** The Zapotec people of the Oaxaca Valley of central Mexico establish a political and ceremonial center at the hilltop site of Monte Albán.

✳ **c.500** In Peru the Chavín temple culture, developed from 1200 B.C. on, is still dominant from the edge of the Amazon Basin to the Pacific Coast.

EUROPE

✳ **c.500** Ironworking is introduced into Scandinavia.

⬤ **c.500** Powerful chiefdoms develop in the area between the Rhône, Rhine, and Danube rivers in central Europe; two-wheeled chariots are now in use.

⬤ **494** The Roman people (plebeians) form an assembly to represent their interests against the aristocrats.

✖ **474** The Etruscans are defeated in a naval battle against the city of Cumae in southern Italy.

✳ **c.460** The Greek physician Hippocrates, traditionally regarded as the founder of the scientific study of medicine, is born.

✖ **457** In Greece war breaks out between the city-states of Athens and Sparta (–445).

⬤ **451** In Rome the Laws of the Twelve Tables, which extend legal privileges to all Roman citizens, are laid down.

📖 **c.450** The Celtic peoples of central Europe begin to develop a style of art known as La Tène (after the site in Switzerland where it was first rediscovered in the 19th century).

AFRICA

⬤ **c.500** Traders from Saba in Arabia (the biblical land of Sheba, in modern Yemen) found trading settlements on the Red Sea coast of East Africa.

The Nok Culture is named for the village in Nigeria where its artifacts were first discovered in the 1940s. In all, some 150 stylized terracotta heads and figurines have been found. Although the Nok tradition itself died out by about 200 A.D., a sculptural tradition survived in the area: The worldfamous Ife bronzes were produced in the same region more than a millennium later.

WESTERN ASIA

✖ **499** The Greek cities of Ionia on the Aegean coast of Asia Minor (modern Turkey) rebel against Persian rule.

✖ **490** King Darius of Persia launches an attack against mainland Greece to punish the city-states there for their support of the Ionian cities. His forces are defeated at the Battle of Marathon.

✖ **480** Darius's successor, Xerxes I, resumes the attempt to conquer Greece. The Persian invasion force is first temporarily checked at Thermopylae and then suffers a naval defeat at the Battle of Salamis.

✖ **479** The Persian invasion force is compelled to withdraw after further defeats at Plataea and Mykale

⬤ **448** The Peace of Kallias secures the independence of the Ionian cities from Persia.

✖ **424** The assassination of King Xerxes II leads to a period of political weakness and disintegration in Persia.

SOUTH & CENTRAL ASIA

⬤ **c.500** The Sinhalese begin to settle Ceylon (modern Sri Lanka) from India.

✴ **c.500** The *Upanishads*, collections of sacred Hindu texts, are written down.

⬤ **c.500** Magadha, ruled by King Bimbisara, is the most powerful of the Hindu states of northern India.

✴ **c.483** Death of Siddhartha Gautama, the Buddha or Enlightened One.

⬤ **c.480** King Vijaya is reputed to have founded the first state on Ceylon.

EAST ASIA & OCEANIA

✳ **c.500** Ironworking begins in Southeast Asia (Vietnam, Cambodia, and Thailand).

⬤ **c.500** Jin is the most powerful state in Zhou China.

📖 **c.500** Sun Tzu writes the *Art of War*, the earliest military handbook.

👑 **c.400** The Olmec civilization of the Gulf Coast is by now in steep decline. Its main ceremonial center at La Venta is demolished at about this time.

⊛ **c.400** At El Mirador, an early Mayan site in the Petén lowlands of southern Mexico, construction begins on the central acropolis (raised earthen mound).

☀ **448** The Athenian statesman Pericles starts construction of the Parthenon, a temple to the goddess Athena completed over the following 10 years under the supervision of the sculptor Phidias.

👑 **c.400** As the Gauls (Celts) begin to cross the Alps and settle in northern and central Italy, Etruscan power goes into decline.

⊛ **c.400** The La Tène culture reaches Britain.

📖 **c.430** The Greek writer Herodotus, regarded as the first historian of the western world, completes his nine-book history of the conflict between Greece and Persia.

The plain of Thermopylae in northern Greece, where Greek forces delayed a Persian army.

⊛ **c.500** The Nok Culture, noted for its striking terracotta sculptures, emerges in northern Nigeria.

⊛ **c.500** Meroë, capital of Nubia, flourishes as an important center of ironmaking.

✕ **480** Carthaginian forces invade Sicily in support of the island's Phoenician colonists, but are defeated by Greek troops.

⊛ **c.470** Carthaginians under Hanno explore the West African coast.

✕ **404** The Egyptians rebel against their Persian rulers, who have governed the country since 525; Egypt becomes more or less independent once again.

👑 **c.420** The Nabateans establish a kingdom in western Arabia, with its capital at Petra in what is now Jordan.

⊛ **410** The earliest surviving horoscope, made by a Babylonian astrologer, dates from this time.

Head of baked clay from the Persian capital, Persepolis, c.450 B.C.

✕ **401** Cyrus, the Persian governor of Anatolia, recruits a Greek army to support a rebellion against his brother, the Emperor Artaxerxes II. After Cyrus's death in battle the Greeks find themselves stranded in the middle of Persia, but fight their way through to the Black Sea and so to safety. The Greeks' fighting retreat is described by their leader, Xenophon, in his classic *Anabasis*.

⊛ **c.450** Reindeer are domesticated by nomadic herders in the Sayan Mountains of Central Asia.

👑 **437** Anuradhapura is founded as the capital of a kingdom in northern Ceylon.

✕ **481** The Warring States Period begins in China, lasting until 221 B.C.; the Zhou realm breaks up amid constant warfare between rival kingdoms.

📖 **479** Death of Confucius (Kongfuzi), the Chinese sage whose name is given to the body of Chinese beliefs known as Confucianism.

AMERICAS

EUROPE

AFRICA

WESTERN ASIA

SOUTH & CENTRAL ASIA

EAST ASIA & OCEANIA

500–400 B.C.

THE GREEK CITY-STATES

AT THE BEGINNING OF THE 5TH CENTURY B.C. *the Greek world was divided among a number of powerful city-states—independent cities that controlled a surrounding territory of land and had their own system of government. A Greek's first loyalty was to his city, and wars between the city-states were frequent. Nevertheless the Greeks (who called themselves Hellenes) shared many cultural ties, including a common language, system of writing, and religion.*

▲ Of all the Greek city-states Athens, with its democratic tradition, won the greatest fame. The foremost Athenian statesman was Pericles (c.495–429 B.C.), who oversaw the building of the Parthenon temple and steered the city in the time of its greatest prosperity.

By 500 B.C. the two leading city-states in Greece were Sparta and Athens. Sparta was a militaristic state—at age seven boys were taken away from their families and raised as future soldiers. Sparta had used its great military strength to acquire mastery over a large part of the Peloponnese Peninsula of southern Greece.

Athens, situated on the coast near the neck of land leading to the Peloponnese, had grown rich on seaborne trade. It was a democracy, allowing its citizens to vote on important issues such as whether to declare war. However, there were limitations to its democratic franchise: Citizenship was restricted to free men aged at least 20 who were born in Athens and whose parents were Athenians. Women, slaves, and foreigners were excluded.

Some centuries earlier, migrants from Greece had founded a number of city-states along the Aegean coast of Asia Minor (present-day Turkey), an area that the Greeks called Ionia. The Ionian cities had been ruled by Persia since the mid-6th century B.C. When they rebelled in 499 B.C., Athens and other mainland city-states came to their aid. As soon as the Persian King Darius had quelled the uprising, he assembled a huge army and navy to punish the rebels' supporters across the Aegean Sea. In all, the Persians sent three invasion forces to Greece between 492 and 480 B.C., but each time they were driven back by the sheer courage of the much smaller Greek armies pitted against them.

The fear of invasion united Sparta and Athens as never before; but once the Persian threat had

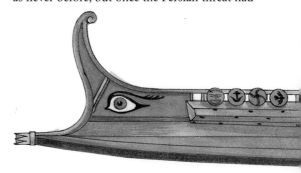

The Classical Age of Greece

Scholars give the name "the Classical Age" to the culture of 5th-century-B.C. Greece, when Greek architecture, literature, art, and science were unsurpassed throughout the Mediterranean world. In the time of Pericles, the politician who dominated Athenian life from 461 to 430 B.C., artists and sculptors adorned the city with magnificent monuments, including the Parthenon (*right*), a temple dedicated to Athene, whose interior was dominated by a huge statue of the goddess. Each year during the festival of Dionysus citizens flocked to the theater to see performances of plays by dramatists such as Aeschylus and Sophocles, while thinkers like Socrates and (in the following century) Plato and Aristotle raised the study of philosophy to new heights.

▶ By the 5th century B.C. the influence of the city-states stretched well beyond the Greek mainland. Greeks had long before settled the west coast of Asia Minor, where they came under the sway of the Persian Empire. Now they also controlled much of southern Italy and Sicily.

▼ When Athenians consulted the Delphic oracle to learn how to face up to the power of Persia, they were told to seek safety in wooden walls. The walls in question turned out to be those of ships like this trireme, so called because it held three banks of rowers. Athens used its fleet first to defeat the Persians at the Battle of Salamis, then to build a maritime empire.

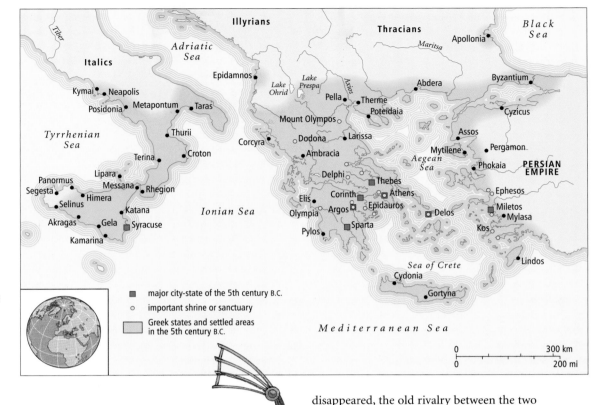

■ major city-state of the 5th century B.C.

○ important shrine or sanctuary

▢ Greek states and settled areas in the 5th century B.C.

disappeared, the old rivalry between the two reemerged stronger than ever. Both Sparta and Athens wanted to dominate Greece, and for the next 75 years their bitter quarrels plunged them and the other Greek city-states into a series of costly conflicts, known as the Peloponnesian Wars. Although Greek culture continued to flourish, the constant strife weakened Greece politically and sapped its economy.

⚔ **490 B.C.** King Darius of Persia invades Greece, but is defeated by an Athenian army at Marathon. A soldier, Pheidippides, runs 24 miles (39 km) to bring news of the victory to Athens; the modern marathon race is named for this feat.

⚔ **480** Spartans fight to the last man in an attempt to halt a fresh Persian invasion at Thermopylae, but fail. The Persians, under Xerxes, overrun Athens, but are turned back after defeat in the naval Battle of Salamis.

⚔ **479** A combined Spartan and Athenian army decisively defeats Xerxes' army at the Battle of Plataea. The Greeks destroy the remnants of the Persian fleet at Mykale, ending further Persian attempts to invade Greece.

👑 **478** Athens makes itself head of an anti-Persian league of Greek cities: Sparta withdraws from the alliance against Persia.

👑 **461** The politician Pericles comes to power in Athens and undertakes a series of reforms.

⚔ **457–445** The First Peloponnesian War breaks out between Athens and Sparta.

📖 **448** The Parthenon—a marble temple dedicated to the goddess Athene—is built as a thanks offering for the Athenian victory over the Persians; Phidias, the greatest sculptor of ancient Greece, carves the great gold and ivory statue of Athena that dominates the temple.

⚔ **431** Hostilities are renewed between Athens and Sparta (the Second Peloponnesian War).

📖 **430** Socrates begins his career as a teacher and philosopher in Athens.

⚔ **416** The Athenians lead an expedition against the island of Sicily, but are forced to withdraw in 413.

⚔ **405** The Spartans defeat the Athenian fleet at Aegospotami, spelling the end of Athens as a major power.

📖 **c. 404–396** The Athenian historian Thucydides writes his masterwork, *The History of the Peloponnesian War*.

400–300 B.C.

AMERICAS

c.370 In southern coastal Peru a new art style—the Nazca—emerges; it features highly colored textiles, mostly tapestries.

Nazca vase decoration featuring stylized hunters and parrots.

c.350 Cities and states develop among the Maya people of Central America.

EUROPE

399 The philosopher Socrates, convicted of corrupting the youth of Athens by his teachings, is forced to drink hemlock, a deadly poison.

396 Rome begins to expand territorially by capturing its northern neighbor, the Etruscan city of Veii.

390 A band of Gauls led by Brennus attacks and occupies the city of Rome for seven months.

c.385 Plato founds the Academy in Athens as a school for teaching philosophy.

371 The city of Thebes defeats Sparta to become the leading city-state in Greece.

348 Rome concludes a nonaggression treaty with the North African city of Carthage, the strongest power in the western Mediterranean.

AFRICA

c.400 Ironworking spreads to the Ethiopian Highlands of East Africa.

380 Nectanebo I seizes the throne of Egypt, starting the nation's 30th and last native dynasty.

343 Persian forces under Artaxerxes III reconquer Egypt.

332 Alexander the Great takes Egypt from Persian control.

331 Alexander founds the city of Alexandria on Egypt's Mediterranean coast.

305 In the power vacuum following Alexander's death Ptolemy, Egypt's Macedonian governor, proclaims himself pharaoh; the Ptolemaic Dynasty that he founds will rule Egypt until 30 B.C.

WESTERN ASIA

358 After a period of unrest Artaxerxes III succeeds to the throne of Persia and reasserts royal authority over the rebellious satraps (governors).

c.350 The widow of King Mausolus of Caria in Asia Minor commissions leading Greek sculptors to build his tomb, the Mausoleum, at Halicarnassus; it becomes one of the Seven Wonders of the Ancient World.

335 Darius III becomes Persia's ruler.

334 Alexander the Great of Macedon invades the Persian Empire.

331 Alexander defeats a Persian army at the Battle of Gaugamela, winning control of Mesopotamia.

SOUTH & CENTRAL ASIA

364 Under the Nanda Dynasty (– 321), the Kingdom of Magadha dominates the Ganges Plain.

c.350 Scythian tribes in the Black Sea area of southern Russia are abandoning nomadism to establish permanent trading settlements on the Dnieper and Don rivers.

329 Alexander the Great conquers Bactria and Sogdiana (modern Afghanistan and Uzbekistan) and invades the Indus Valley (– 326).

EAST ASIA & OCEANIA

c.371 Birth of Mengzi (known in the West as Mencius), Chinese philosopher and moralist in the tradition of Confucius, whose teachings are preserved in the *Book of Mengzi*.

361 Xiao becomes ruler of Qin in western China; his chief minister, Shang Yang, introduces sweeping reforms to end the power of the aristocracy and strengthen the army.

c.350 The crossbow is invented in China.

Chinese warrior with crossbow.

⊛ **c.300** Pottery, introduced to North America from Mexico, is thought to be in use in the Southwest by this time.

☀ **c.300** In Peru the influence of the Chavín Culture has now reached a peak; its style of art and architecture dominates the entire region.

✕ **343** Rome begins a series of wars against its neighbors, the Samnites; by 290 it will emerge as the major power in central Italy.

✕ **338** Philip II of Macedon defeats a Greek army at the Battle of Charonea and wins control of the Greek city-states.

👑 **336** After the murder of Philip II his son Alexander becomes king of Macedon and adopts Philip's plan to invade Persia; he will be known to history as Alexander the Great.

📖 **335** The philosopher Aristotle sets up a school at Athens, the Lyceum.

⊛ **c.330** The Greek navigator and geographer Pytheas makes a voyage of exploration in the Atlantic, sailing past Spain, France, and the east coast of Britain to reach a country he calls "Thule," probably northern Norway.

📖 **c.300** Ptolemy founds the Museum at Alexandria.

Alexandria on Egypt's Mediterranean coast was one of the chief centers of the Hellenistic (Greek-inspired) culture that spread across the Near and Middle East in the wake of Alexander the Great's conquests. Shown here in a 19th-century print, its library—housed in Ptolemy's Museum—was the finest in the world in its day, and such famous scholars as the mathematician Euclid and the scientist Archimedes studied there.

✕ **330** Alexander burns down the Persian royal palace at Persepolis. Darius III is subsequently murdered by one of his own satraps (governors), leaving Alexander in undisputed control of all the Persian Empire's lands.

👑 **323** The death of Alexander the Great unleashes a lengthy power struggle between his successors for control of the lands he conquered.

👑 **305** Seleucus, one of Alexander's former generals, establishes the Seleucid Kingdom in Mesopotamia and Persia.

✕ **301** Seleucus employs war elephants to defeat his rival Antigonos at the Battle of Ipsos in Anatolia.

👑 **c.321** Chandragupta Maurya, founder of India's Mauryan Empire, seizes power in Magadha; he reigns until about 297.

✕ **c.311** Chandragupta extends his kingdom as far as the Indus Valley, where he encounters resistance from Alexander's successors.

✕ **c.350** Earthen frontier walls are built in northern China as a defense against invading nomads; they will eventually be linked together to form the Great Wall of China (− 214).

✕ **312** Qin is now the strongest state in China after a series of military campaigns against its neighbors and border nomads.

AMERICAS

EUROPE

AFRICA

WESTERN ASIA

SOUTH & CENTRAL ASIA

EAST ASIA & OCEANIA

400–300 B.C.

ALEXANDER THE GREAT

GREEK POWER, PREVIOUSLY LIMITED *to the Mediterranean region, was carried deep into Asia by Alexander the Great, a military genius who ranks among the greatest generals of all time. From the small mountain kingdom of Macedon in northern Greece he set out on a seemingly foolhardy campaign to conquer the vast Persian Empire, a task he in fact accomplished with supreme success. He went on to extend Greek control as far as the borders of India.*

▲ Before setting out to conquer the mighty Persian Empire, Alexander had first to put down a rebellion in mainland Greece, which his father had brought under Macedon's sway. In a ruthless campaign he stormed the city of Thebes, killing 6,000 of its citizens. Thereafter no Greek city dared to openly defy him.

▶ Alexander set out to conquer the Persian Empire, which at the time included both Asia Minor (Turkey) and Egypt, with an army only 35,000 strong. He succeeded in extending his realm as far as the Indus River, founding more than a dozen cities (several of them called Alexandria) along the way.

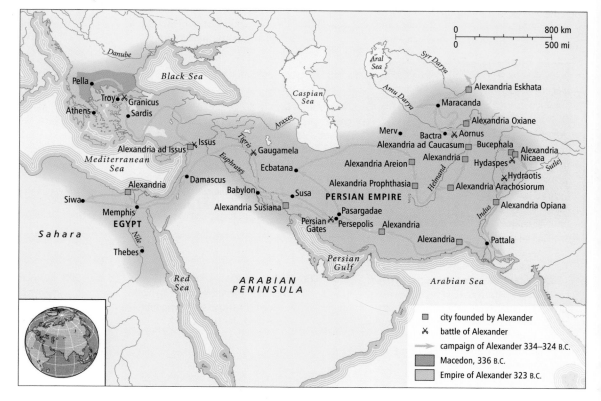

- ☐ city founded by Alexander
- ✕ battle of Alexander
- → campaign of Alexander 334–324 B.C.
- ▨ Macedon, 336 B.C.
- ▨ Empire of Alexander 323 B.C.

👑 **359 B.C.** Philip II comes to power in Macedon and sets about transforming his small kingdom into a major power.

👑 **343** Philip employs the philosopher Aristotle as tutor to his son Alexander.

👑 **336** Philip is murdered at a wedding, and Alexander succeeds to the throne.

✕ **334** Alexander invades Anatolia and routs a Persian army at the Battle of Granicus.

✕ **333** Alexander defeats the Persian ruler Darius III at the Battle of the Issus River in Syria.

👑 **332** Alexander takes control of Egypt, previously under Persian control.

✕ **331** Alexander defeats Darius once more at the Battle of Gaugamela, finally winning control of the Persian Empire.

✕ **330** Alexander burns the palace of Persepolis.

✕ **329–328** Alexander campaigns in Bactria and Sogdiana (Afghanistan and Uzbekistan) to complete his conquest of the Persian Empire.

✕ **327** Alexander crosses the Indus River and wins a battle against an Indian king.

✕ **326** Alexander reaches the Hyphasis River, a tributary of the Indus and the easternmost point of his expedition; an army revolt forces him to give up his plans to conquer India.

Alexander was only 20 years old when he succeeded to the throne of Macedon in 336 B.C., following the brutal murder of his father, Philip II. Philip had made his kingdom the most powerful state in Greece and was on the point of invading the Persian Empire when he was killed.

Alexander wasted little time in putting his father's daring plan into action. In 334 B.C. he invaded and conquered Anatolia (present-day Turkey), which at the time was a Persian province. He met and defeated two of the empire's armies, one of them led by the Persian King Darius III in person, before turning south along the Mediterranean coast to Egypt—also a Persian possession—which he conquered in 332 B.C.

Now Alexander headed into the heart of Darius's empire. He defeated his rival for a second time before entering Persepolis, the capital of the Persian kings, which he burned to the ground. Darius fled and was murdered soon afterward by one of his own satraps (governors), disillusioned by the ruler's military failures. For more than three years the Macedonian army campaigned ceaselessly through Central Asia. They reached the Indus River in present-day Pakistan, and Alexander decided to invade northern India. But his army had had enough, and Alexander was forced to agree to their demands to return home.

Alexander died suddenly in 323 while in Babylon planning his next campaign. His empire immediately collapsed into chaos. His heirs, a mad brother and an infant son, were murdered, and his Macedonian generals, whom he had appointed provincial governors, fought to carve out independent kingdoms for themselves in the lands Alexander had conquered.

While on his campaigns, Alexander founded Greek cities across the lands he conquered, all the way from Alexandria in Egypt to Bactria (in present-day Afghanistan). In his wake the Greek language, together with Greek architecture, sculpture, learning, and cultural pursuits, dominated much of the ancient world for several centuries. Historians call this period the Hellenistic Age (from "Hellene," the word the Greeks used to describe themselves).

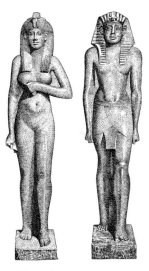

▲ The Ptolemaic Dynasty set up in Egypt after Alexander's death combined Greek and Egyptian traditions in its art.

Alexandria: A Greek City in Egypt

Alexander founded his first city at the mouth of the Nile, naming it Alexandria after himself. Under the Ptolemies, a line of pharaohs descended from Alexander's Macedonian general Ptolemy, Alexandria became the greatest city in the Greek-speaking world. Among the men who made it the foremost center of learning of the Hellenistic Age were Euclid, the father of geometry, the engineer Hero, inventor of a stationary steam engine, and the mathematician Eratosthenes. Best known of Alexandria's monuments was the Pharos, or lighthouse (*right*), one of the Seven Wonders of the Ancient World, which stood 400 feet (120 m) tall at the entrance to the harbor. Today the ruins of the city's ancient center lie offshore under the sea; marine archaeologists are currently investigating them.

⚔ **325–324** After sailing down the Indus River to the coast, Alexander returns to Persia on an overland route across the Baluchistan Desert; his army suffers great losses.

⚔ **323** Alexander dies suddenly in Babylon.

👑 **322** Perdiccas becomes regent on behalf of Alexander's infant son. Ptolemy, one of Alexander's finest generals, seizes control of Egypt.

👑 **321** Perdiccas is murdered by rivals on an expedition to Egypt.

⚔ **320–301** Alexander's empire breaks up as his generals seize territory for themselves in the course of the Wars of the Diadochi ("Wars of the Successors").

👑 **317** Philip III, Alexander's half-brother, is murdered.

👑 **310** Murder of Alexander IV, son of Alexander the Great and last member of the dynasty.

👑 **305** Ptolemy has himself proclaimed pharaoh of Egypt, founding a dynasty (the Ptolemaic) that will rule for 275 years until 30 B.C.

⚔ **301** At the Battle of Ipsos Seleucus establishes his hold over the eastern portion of Alexander's empire, extending the Seleucid Kingdom, which will survive until 63 B.C.

AMERICAS

⚙ **c.300** Earliest date proposed for the emergence of the Hohokam Culture in Arizona, with a lifestyle based on the cultivation of corn, beans, cotton, and tobacco.

⚙ **c.300** The city of Izapa flourishes in southwestern Mexico: its culture represents an intermediate phase between those of the Olmecs and the Maya.

EUROPE

⚔ **298** The Third Samnite War begins; the Romans' final victory over the Samnites and their Celtic allies eight years later will ensure their dominance over the whole of central Italy (–290).

👑 **287** Rome's plebeians (common people) are accorded equal rights with patricians (nobles).

⚙ **287** Archimedes is born in the Greek colony of Syracuse, Sicily: He will be remembered for calculating the value of pi and for breakthroughs in science and mechanics.

⚔ **280** Pyrrhos, king of Epiros, crosses the Adriatic Sea to defend his allies in the Greek cities of southern Italy against the Roman threat.

Roman plate showing a war elephant.

AFRICA

⚙ **c.300** Euclid, a Greek mathematician working at the court of Ptolemy I in Alexandria, outlines the main principles of geometry.

⚙ **297** Construction begins on Alexandria's Pharos lighthouse, which will become one of the Seven Wonders of the Ancient World.

👑 **285** Ptolemy I gives up his throne as Egypt's pharaoh to his son, Ptolemy II Philadelphus.

WESTERN ASIA

👑 **280** Antiochos I, the son of Alexander the Great's companion Seleucus, inherits the Seleucid Kingdom, made up of Alexander's conquests in Syria, Mesopotamia, and Persia.

👑 **278** Tens of thousands of Celts cross the Dardanelles Strait into Asia Minor. They come as mercenaries, but stay to establish their own state of Galatia in central Anatolia.

⚔ **247** After decades of raiding, Parthian nomads from Central Asia settle down more permanently as rulers of an empire in northern Iran.

⚔ **219** The Seleucid ruler Antiochos III invades the Bible lands, previously a possession of Ptolemaic Egypt. After a bitter struggle he is driven back by the forces of Ptolemy IV.

SOUTH & CENTRAL ASIA

📖 **c.300** Valmiki begins the compilation of the great Indian epic poem, the Ramayana.

Hanuman, the monkey general—a popular character from the Ramayana.

👑 **c.297** Chandragupta Maurya dies, having exploited the chaos following the invasion of Alexander the Great to found an empire extending across the whole of northern India.

EAST ASIA & OCEANIA

⚙ **c.300** The Yayoi Culture spreads north and east from western Japan, sustained by systematic rice cultivation and bringing skills in metalworking (both bronze and iron), spinning and weaving, and ceramics.

⚙ **c.300** The appearance of a Sanskrit-based alphabet in Cambodia implies the presence of Indian traders in this part of Southeast Asia.

📖 **c.300** The late Ban Chiang Period in Thailand is marked by fine pottery with extravagant swirling and spiraling designs.

Bronze panels from the Yayoi Culture, Japan.

👑 **c.300** With a massive circular pyramid at its heart, Cuicuilco reaches its height as an urban center, dominating the Valley of Mexico, where Mexico City now lies.

⊗ **c.300** Deep shaft tombs are dug in western Mexico at Jalisco, Nayarit, and Colima. Sophisticated ceramic pots and figures are buried with the dead.

☀ **c.300** The city of El Mirador begins to eclipse its Mayan neighbor, Nak'be. Its temple, decorated with giant limestone masks, sets a pattern for later Mayan sites.

✕ **279** Celts invade Macedonia and northern Greece.

✕ **275** Pyrrhos is forced to abandon his campaign against Rome despite considerable military success.

✕ **264** The First Punic War breaks out between Rome and the North African city of Carthage.

✕ **241** The First Punic War ends in victory for Rome; Carthage loses its trading colonies in Sicily.

✕ **218** The Second Punic War begins. The Carthaginian general Hannibal crosses the Alps with a force of 46,000 men and 37 war elephants to invade Italy from the north.

✕ **216** Hannibal defeats the Romans at the Battle of Cannae.

✕ **201** At the Battle of Zama Romans led by Scipio Africanus succeed in reversing Hannibal's victory. The Second Punic War ends with Rome in undisputed control of the Mediterranean.

⊗ **c.250** Ironworking reaches sub-Saharan Africa, probably brought across the desert from southern Mauritania to the Niger Valley.

⊗ **240** Eratosthenes, a Greek scholar working in the North African colony of Cyrene, calculates the circumference of the Earth.

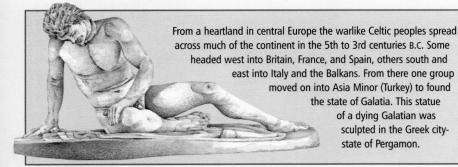

From a heartland in central Europe the warlike Celtic peoples spread across much of the continent in the 5th to 3rd centuries B.C. Some headed west into Britain, France, and Spain, others south and east into Italy and the Balkans. From there one group moved on into Asia Minor (Turkey) to found the state of Galatia. This statue of a dying Galatian was sculpted in the Greek city-state of Pergamon.

✕ **203** Antiochos III's second attempt to take the Bible lands from the Ptolemies is again fiercely resisted (although supported by the local population). By the end of the century he is finally master in Jerusalem.

👑 **c.269** The Mauryan Empire reaches its height with the accession of Ashoka: In his 37-year reign he will extend his power over all but the far south of the Indian subcontinent.

✕ **c.261** Ashoka conquers Kalinga, the last outpost of resistance to Mauryan rule.

📖 **c.250** The Sanskrit language, once confined to the northern Indian territories settled by the Aryans, starts to penetrate to southern areas around this time.

📖 **c.289** Death of Mengzi, the Chinese philosopher who did more than anyone else to popularize the creed of Confucius.

📖 **c.278** Qu Yuan, widely revered as the father of Chinese poetry, dies. He is believed to have been born around 340 B.C.

✕ **221** The Warring States Period ends with final victory for the Kingdom of Qin and the unification of China under the First Emperor, Shihuangdi.

👑 **210** Shihuangdi dies and is buried with a "Terracotta Army" of more than 7,000 pottery soldiers.

👑 **206** Traditional date for the foundation of the Kingdom of Nam Viet, located in southern China and what is now northern Vietnam.

👑 **c.200** The first settlers occupy the Marquesas Islands in Polynesia, bringing with them the skills of the Lapita Culture.

AMERICAS

EUROPE

AFRICA

WESTERN ASIA

SOUTH & CENTRAL ASIA

EAST ASIA & OCEANIA

300–200 B.C.

CHINA'S FIRST EMPEROR

AS THE 5TH CENTURY B.C. BEGAN, *the vast country we think of as China barely existed: Instead, a score of separate states sparred and jostled for advantage across its lands. In theory all of these states acknowledged the overlordship of the Zhou Dynasty, which had ruled the country since the 11th century B.C.; in practice, however, the Zhou emperors' powers had been in decline for centuries. In the course of the early 3rd century B.C., however, one kingdom succeeded in forcing its dogged way to military and political supremacy. The triumph of Qin represented the historic birth of imperial China.*

▲ The Great Wall of China had its origins in a series of earthworks built from the 4th century B.C. on to defend the nation's northern borders against nomadic tribesmen. The First Emperor linked these fortifications together into a single earth-and-masonry defensive line. Much of the wall was subsequently rebuilt in later times.

The Terracotta Army

Shihuangdi's burial mound rises high above the fields near the city of Xian in central China; it has yet to be excavated, but ancient sources suggest that a fabulous complex of passages and chambers lies within it. Legend has it that 700,000 prisoners labored for years to throw up this extraordinary earthwork. Equally astonishing, however, are the treasures uncovered in three pits found about a mile (1.6 km) away. Here, concealed in wood-roofed vaults, stands an army of lifesize terracotta figures 7,000 strong, lined up in defense of their dead commander-in-chief to serve as his bodyguards in the afterlife. The force includes officers and generals as well as ordinary soldiers armed with spears; there are mounted cavalrymen and charioteers as well as crossbowmen. Each is an individual: No two faces are the same, and a wide range of ages, physiques, and characters is represented.

👑 **481 B.C.** The "Warring States" Period begins: A weakened China is divided among about 20 different kingdoms vying for supremacy. In theory the emperors of the Eastern Zhou Dynasty still have overall control, but in practice their authority counts for little.

👑 **361** The philosopher Shang Yang becomes chief minister of the Kingdom of Qin, at the time a small realm in western China. Over the next 21 years he turns it into a strong, centralized state.

⚔ **314** The Kingdom of Qin wins a victory over nomads from the north, marking its emergence as a new military power in western China.

👑 **312** The Ba and Shu kingdoms of northern Sichuan, as well as parts of the Han Kingdom to the east, fall under Qin dominance.

👑 **c.280** By this date the conflicts of the Warring States are slowly drawing toward a resolution: Only six main kingdoms—Qin, Zhao, Wei, Han, Chu, and Zhou—now survive as independent states.

👑 **259** The Kingdom of Qin defeats its main rival, Zhao. The remaining states are subjugated in the decades that follow.

👑 **258** Ying Sheng, the future First Emperor, is born.

⚔ **256** The Qin army defeats forces loyal to the last Zhou emperor, forcing him to abdicate (give up power).

👑 **246** At the age of 12 Ying Sheng succeeds his father, Zhuang Xiang, as ruler of the Kingdom of Qin.

Qin used to be transliterated as "Ch'in," from which comes our word "China": It is fitting that this state should have given the modern country its name. Less just is the way Westerners have let the name of Qin's mightiest ruler be forgotten, for few historic figures have towered so imposingly as Ying Sheng, who united China under Qin rule. Born in 258 B.C., the son of Xiao Wen, the ruler of Qin, Ying Sheng was raised at a time when the conflicts of China's Warring States Period were heading toward resolution. Of the crowd of petty kingdoms that had once vied for supremacy, only a handful remained, among which Qin's ascendancy was becoming clear.

The way had been well prepared for the reunification of China, which took place early in Ying Sheng's reign. He then set about shaping his conquests into a coherent whole. In 221 he formalized the unification of all the former kingdoms into a single gigantic state, a feat that subsequently earned him the title of Shihuangdi, or First Emperor.

With the determination of a visionary and the brutality of a despot, he then launched an extraordinary program of nationbuilding. First, he took possession of his empire, disarming local warlords and subjecting them to his rule; for administrative purposes he divided his realm into 36 provinces, each overseen by officials answering to him. A network of new roads and canals improved communications. To encourage trade, weights and measures were standardized across China, as was the width of wagon axles, so all carts could trundle along the same road ruts. All the emperor's dominions had to accept a single, harsh legal code; he also took steps to reform the Chinese written language so as to make it understandable to all his subjects.

More sinister, to modern eyes, was Shihuangdi's concern to police his people's minds. Fearing the disruptive effect of philosophical arguments on his newly united realm, he had books burned in their

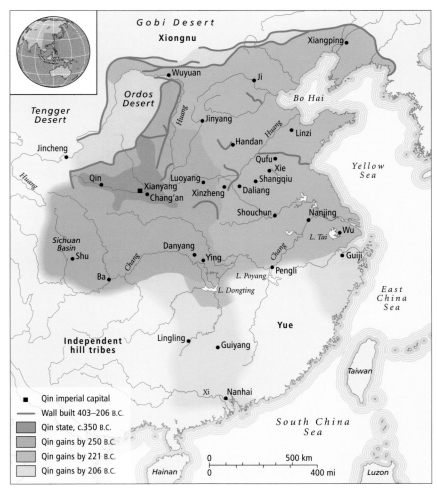

thousands at public ceremonies and also reportedly had some 400 dissident scholars killed. Opponents of his rule were treated mercilessly. Yet, tyrant that he was, Shihuangdi forced a great nation into being; without him imperial China would never have survived, as it did, for over 2,000 years.

▲ Between 350 and 206 the Qin state expanded from its heartland near the upper reaches of the Huang (Yellow) River to take over much of the area of modern-day China.

⚱ **221** Ying Sheng confers on himself the title of Huangdi, or emperor, of a newly unified China; historians after his death will call him Shihuangdi, or "First Emperor."

⚱ **219** Shihuangdi tours his empire, underlining his determination to rule China as a whole.

⚱ **214** The Great Wall of China is completed.

✕ **213** Shihuangdi sends out a military force against the nomads of Xiongnu to the northwest.

⚱ **213** When several scholars criticize the emperor's centralizing policies, an increasingly despotic Shihuangdi responds by ordering a series of public book burnings aimed at destroying "useless books."

⚱ **212** On the emperor's orders 460 scholars are buried alive for "throwing the common people into confusion."

⚱ **210** Shihuangdi dies. On his death civil war breaks out among his heirs.

⚱ **206** The entire Qin royal family is massacred by rebels led by a peasant warrior, Liu Bang.

⚱ **202** Liu Bang establishes a new dynasty, the Han, becoming its first emperor under the name of Gaozu.

⚱ **220 A.D.** The last Han emperor is deposed, and China splits into three kingdoms.

AMERICAS

☀ **c.200** By this date the influence of Peru's Chavín Culture is in marked decline.

⚙ **c.200** Defensive ramparts are built at Monte Albán in southern Mexico; massive carvings are inscribed with an early Zapotec text.

☀ **c.200** A sacred complex is built at El Mirador, with three temples clustered together on a single platform mound.

A stele from Monte Albán displays glyphs (characters) of an early Zapotec text.

EUROPE

👑 **197** Hispania (Spain) becomes a province of the Roman Empire.

⚙ **c.150** The Romans revolutionize engineering and construction with the discovery of how to make and work with concrete.

⚔ **149** The Third Punic War begins.

⚔ **146** Corinth, leader of the Achaean League, is sacked, effectively bringing Greek resistance to Roman rule to an end.

⚔ **146** The Third Punic War comes to an end with the final destruction of Carthage, leaving Rome as the unchallenged master of the Mediterranean Sea.

AFRICA

⚙ **c.200** The Nok Culture reaches its height in central Nigeria.

⚙ **196** Texts celebrating Pharaoh Ptolemy V are carved on the Rosetta Stone in Greek and Egyptian scripts; 2,000 years later they will be the key to deciphering hieroglyphics.

👑 **168** Rome intervenes in a dispute between the Seleucid Kingdom and Ptolemaic Egypt, signaling growing Roman influence in the land of the pharaohs.

WESTERN ASIA

⚔ **191** The Seleucid army of Antiochos III the Great is defeated by the Romans at Thermopylae in northern Greece.

⚔ **190** A Roman navy defeats the Seleucid fleet off Crete, leaving the way clear for the conquest of Asia Minor; Roman power is confirmed by a crushing land victory over Antiochos's army at Magnesia.

👑 **171** Mithradates I becomes king of the Parthians: By his death in 138 he will have built an empire extending from Afghanistan to the Euphrates River.

☀ **167** Antiochos IV Epiphanes ("God Manifest") outlaws the practice of Judaism even in Judah itself, rededicating the Temple of Jerusalem to the Greek god Zeus. His actions spark off the Revolt of the Maccabeans (followers of Judas Maccabeus).

SOUTH & CENTRAL ASIA

⚔ **c.185** Pushyamitra assassinates the last Mauryan emperor in front of his troops to seize power for himself and his successors of the Shunga Dynasty, restoring Hindu rule in India.

2nd-century-B.C. coin from Bactria (in modern Afghanistan) bears Greek inscriptions.

⚔ **c.183** Nomadic raiders from Central Asia attack India's northern frontier. So too do the forces of Demetrius, Greek king of Bactria, who establish a foothold in the valleys of northwestern India.

EAST ASIA & OCEANIA

⚙ **c.200** The Sohano Period begins in the Solomon Islands: Its craftspeople make fine pottery decorated with geometric forms.

⚙ **c.200** The water buffalo is used as a draft animal in Southeast Asia from around this time.

👑 **141** Wudi becomes emperor of China: He undertakes a series of military campaigns against nomadic Xiongnu raiders and extends the Great Wall west to the Tarim Basin.

⊕ c.200 Development starts on the North Acropolis at Tikal, Guatemala, with the construction of a massive stone platform that will subsequently provide a foundation for several Mayan pyramid temples.

⊕ c.200 Excavated villages suggest an agrarian lifestyle is being adopted in the region known as Greater Chiriquí, incorporating southern Costa Rica and northern Panama.

☀ c.100 Fine necklaces and other jewelry, made from green, semiprecious stone such as jadeite, are buried with the dead in tombs in parts of Costa Rica.

👑 c.150 The eruption of Mt. Xitle devastates Cuicuilco, forcing surviving residents to abandon the city in Mexico.

✕ 133 In Rome, Tiberius Gracchus, Tribune of the People, is assassinated—a dangerous escalation in the longstanding power struggle between the popular Assembly and the aristocratic Senate.

✕ 133 Celtiberian rebels against Roman rule are starved into submission by Scipio Aemilianus after a 15-month siege: The victory marks a shift toward a more aggressive imperial policy.

⊕ 125 Death of Hipparchos (born c.180), the first man to fix location by calculating latitude and longitude.

✕ 102 Uprisings by the Germanic Cimbri and Teutones tribes are ruthlessly put down by the Romans (– 101).

✕ 146 Carthage is laid waste by the forces of Rome.

✕ 104 Jugurtha, ruler of Numidia (in modern Algeria), dies in prison after an unsuccessful rebellion against Roman rule.

✕ 164 The Maccabeans prevail in Jerusalem; Antiochos is forced to rescind his law, and Judas is left in charge of what will in time emerge as an independent Jewish state (–142).

A 19th-century engraving shows Judas Maccabeus inciting the Jews to revolt.

✕ 141 Mithridates I defeats and captures the Seleucid ruler Demetrius Nicator, ending Seleucid rule in Persia and Mesopotamia.

👑 133 King Attalos III of Pergamon (in modern Turkey) bequeaths his kingdom to the Romans upon his death; it is soon absorbed into the Roman province of Asia.

✕ c.150 Menander, the most celebrated of the Indo-Greek kings, assassinates his predecessor Eucratides to take control of Bactria; he leads an army of conquest across northern India.

👑 c.141 The Chinese Emperor Wudi's actions against Xiongnu nomads have repercussions well to the west, pushing Kushan and Saka steppe nomads southward into northern India.

👑 138 Wudi sends embassies westward in the hope of establishing alliances against the Xiongnu, thereby helping to open up the Silk Road linking China to western Asia and Europe.

👑 117 In China iron and salt are made state monopolies, increasing the Han Dynasty's control over the nation's economic life.

👑 111 Wudi's armies conquer the Kingdom of Nam Viet, completing the conquest of southern China and bringing part of today's Vietnam under Chinese control.

⊕ 105 Traditional date for the invention of paper, made from scraps of cloth and wood chips, in China. For the next two centuries paper will only be used for wrapping and packing, not for writing.

⊕ 112 The minting of coins is made a state monopoly in Han China.

✕ 108 Wudi annexes northern Korea.

AMERICAS

EUROPE

AFRICA

WESTERN ASIA

SOUTH & CENTRAL ASIA

EAST ASIA & OCEANIA

200–100 B.C.

THE GROWTH OF BUDDHISM

DESTINED FOR GREATNESS, *according to the soothsayers, the young prince was kept in isolation from the ills of the world, the pampered prisoner of the palace where he lived with his beautiful wife, the Princess Yasodhara, and their small child. Yet, his curiosity growing, he stole out alone into the city and was shocked by some of the sights that met his eyes. He saw signs of suffering and sickness, old age and mortality— and, most moving of all, a holy man who had chosen a life of simplicity.*

▲ For the first four centuries of the Buddhist era representations of the Buddha were discouraged; it was only in the 2nd century A.D. that the earliest images began to appear. This statue comes from medieval Japan.

The young man's name was Siddhartha Gautama, and he had been born in the Himalayan foothills of northern India. Leaving his home and family to wander as a beggar, he spent six years in poverty and hunger, yet his sacrifices brought no spiritual return. Realizing that to find enlightenment he would have to start looking inside himself, he sat down beneath a tree, resolved not to move until he had attained a state of spiritual ecstasy. The forces of evil thundered and hurled down lightning bolts, but, transformed by his peaceful presence, they fell as blossoms. Three nights later, his struggles over, Siddhartha stood up and resumed his journey: The bodhisattva (holy man) had become the Buddha.

For over 40 years he wandered through northern India spreading the injunction "Cease to do evil; learn to do good, and purify your heart." Like other Indian thinkers of his time, he believed the dead were reincarnated innumerable times in different human— or even animal—forms, rising or falling in status according to how well they had lived their previous lives. Only when the sacred state of *bodhi* (enlightenment) had been reached could an

individual hope to transcend the swirling cycles of death and rebirth known as *samsara,* and find the final peace he himself had attained as the Buddha.

Simple as the Buddha's message sounded, it was open to endless differences of interpretation; and no sooner had he died, than his followers fell out among themselves. The gravest of many splits would come in the 3rd century B.C., when the Theravada ("Doctrine of the Elders") and Mahayana ("Greater Vehicle") schools separated. Theravada Buddhism emphasized the search for individual enlightenment as outlined by the Buddha in his doctrine of the Eightfold Path: right thinking, right aspiration, right speech, right conduct, right lifestyle, right effort, right mindfulness, and right meditation. Mahayana Buddhism was an altogether more popular faith, encouraging the worship of bodhisattvas—Buddhist saints who had delayed their own attainment of *nirvana,* or release from suffering, to help others do so.

Despite the Buddha's best efforts, his religion remained a minority creed until about 259 B.C., when it was taken up by Ashoka, India's Mauryan ruler, thus becoming the official religion throughout most of

* **483 B.C.** Siddhartha Gautama, the Buddha, dies. The First Great Council of his followers is held to agree on the main tenets of his teaching.

* **c.383** Said to have been held about a century after the Buddha's death, the Second Great Council concerns itself with details of ritual observance and monastic practice.

* **c.259** Buddhism finds its most influential convert when the Indian Emperor Ashoka becomes an adherent. His emissaries carry the creed not only across India but beyond, to Sri Lanka and into Southeast Asia.

* **c.250** Ashoka presides over the Third Great Council at Pataliputra, where doctrinal divisions arise, and the basic tenets of the Theravada tradition are established.

* **c.185** Buddhism in India suffers a major setback when Pushyamitra seizes power from Ashoka's Mauryan successors: Under the new Shunga Dynasty the Brahmin elite of Hinduism returns to power.

* **c.1 A.D.** The *Tripitaka* ("Three Baskets"), or Pali Canon—the nearest thing Theravada Buddhism has to a scripture—is thought to have been completed by about now.

* **c.50** Brought by Indian merchants and missionaries, Buddhism establishes a presence in China, but makes headway only slowly against the country's own strong spiritual traditions.

* **c.100** The main elements of Mahayana Buddhism are upheld at a council called by the Kushan ruler Kanishka in Kashmir.

* **c.200** The *Jatakamala*—a set of stories describing the different former lives of the Buddha—is said to have been written around now by the (perhaps legendary) Aryasura.

The Mountain of Life

The universe, according to Buddhist tradition, rises like a mountain from an endless plain, its sides curving gently upward toward a distant summit. Beneath the ground at its base lie 136 distinct hells where different sins are punished; on the slopes above, the souls of mortals find varying degrees of happiness. The purer the spirit, the higher the place, until, at the mountain's peak, lies the zone of *nirvana* in which the most blessed transcend selfhood and all time. This scheme finds symbolic representation in the lovingly sculpted form of the stupa— a domelike monument of a sort found throughout the Buddhist world. This example (*far right*) is enclosed in a rock-cut temple at Karli in western India.

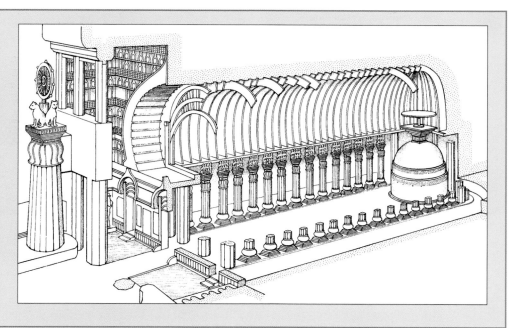

mainland India. Ashoka also sent out missionaries to the island of Sri Lanka and overland to Southeast Asia. In time, missionaries would set out from these places in their turn to preach Buddhism in China, Korea, Japan, and Indonesia. The message would prove more enduring in these far-flung lands than in its Indian birthplace, where, in the years after Ashoka's death, the Hindu Shunga Dynasty worked hard to suppress the upstart faith.

▶ Buddhism's original heartland lay in the prosperous Indian state of Magadha, in the Ganges Valley. Its spread owed much to the Emperor Ashoka, who became a convert around 259 B.C.

☀ **c.367** The first Buddhist missions are established in Tibet.

☀ **372** Missionaries bring Buddhism to Korea, where it will become the state religion for over a millennium.

☀ **c.470** Birth of Bodhidharma, who as a young missionary travels from his native India to China; there he is credited with founding the Chan sect of Buddhism, better known in its later Japanese form as Zen.

☀ **552** Buddhism is introduced from Korea to the Japanese court.

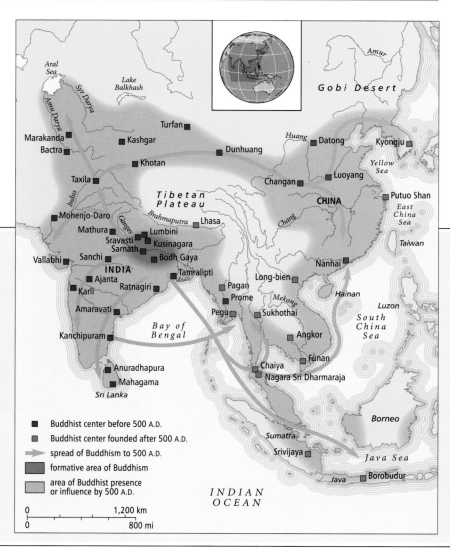

■ Buddhist center before 500 A.D.
■ Buddhist center founded after 500 A.D.
→ spread of Buddhism to 500 A.D.
▬ formative area of Buddhism
▬ area of Buddhist presence or influence by 500 A.D.

0 — 1,200 km
0 — 800 mi

AMERICAS

☀ **c.100** The Hopewell Culture emerges in the Ohio Valley, extending gradually along the Illinois and Mississippi rivers. A development of the Adena Culture, its ritual life centers on burial mounds.

☀ **c.100** Maya nobles at Kaminaljuyú (within modern Guatemala City) are buried with sacrificial attendants and grave goods of jade, obsidian, and mica.

EUROPE

⚔ **85** Athens is stripped of all political privileges after revolting against Roman rule.

⚙ **c.80** The Greeks invent a calculator for astronomical or calendrical purposes that uses an elaborate system of intermeshing gears.

Julius Caesar was the greatest general that republican Rome produced, and he was also a talented writer and politician. He used his conquest of Gaul (France) to build up a military power base. When summoned back to Rome by a Senate nervous about his growing ambitions, he came at the head of an army, triggering a civil war that he finally won. However, his rise aroused deep hostility, and he was eventually assassinated by republican conspirators in 44 B.C.

AFRICA

📖 **c.100** Alexandria, on the Mediterranean coast of Egypt, produces Greek-style mosaics and frescoes that are eagerly copied in wealthy Roman homes.

👑 **51** Cleopatra becomes ruler of Egypt as coregent with her brother. The two become involved in a power struggle that Cleopatra wins with the help of the visiting Julius Caesar (–48).

👑 **45** Carthage, destroyed by the Romans a century earlier, is refounded as a Roman city.

WESTERN ASIA

⚔ **64** The Roman general Pompey conquers Syria.

⚔ **63** Pompey wins control of the Bible lands for Rome, making Judea part of the province of Syria.

⚔ **53** The Parthians inflict a humiliating defeat on a Roman army at Carrhae (Haran, in what is now southeast Turkey). Their victory gives them control of the Silk Road, the main trade route between China and the West.

⚙ **c.50** The invention of glassblowing in Syria revolutionizes the glassmaking industry.

👑 **40** Herod the Great is appointed king of Judea by the Roman Senate. He builds a new temple in Jerusalem.

⚙ **c.10** Using concrete blocks, Herod constructs the first large harbor in the open sea, at Caesarea.

SOUTH & CENTRAL ASIA

👑 **c.100** The Silk Road trade route between China and the West across Central Asia is in full swing by this time.

The Silk Road winds through what is now Xinjiang Province, China.

EAST ASIA & OCEANIA

📖 **c.90** Sima Qian (c.145–80 B.C.) produces an official Chinese history that becomes a model for government-sponsored histories until modern times.

⚙ **c.85** The earliest known Chinese lacquerware dates from this time.

⚙ **52** Chinese astronomer Ken Shou-Ch'ang builds an armillary ring, a metal circle that represents the equator and is used in observing stars.

AMERICAS

👑 **c.50** El Mirador in Guatemala develops into the largest lowland Mayan center, covering more than 6 square miles (10 sq. km).

⚙ **36** The earliest Mayan date yet identified is carved on a stele at Chiapa de Corzo in southern Mexico. It corresponds to December 8, 36 B.C.

EUROPE

⚙ **63** A freed slave employed by the Roman orator Cicero invents a Latin shorthand system.

👑 **60** Rome founds colonies in Switzerland.

✕ **58** Julius Caesar begins a 10-year campaign to conquer Gaul (France).

✕ **55** Julius Caesar briefly invades Britain on what amounts to a military reconnaissance trip.

✕ **54** Julius Caesar returns to Britain and defeats a British army, but then returns to Gaul.

⚙ **46** Julius Caesar introduces the Julian calendar of three 365-day years followed by one of 366 days.

✕ **44** Julius Caesar is assassinated on his way to a meeting of the Roman Senate.

✕ **31** Caesar's heir Octavian triumphs over his rival Mark Antony in the civil war following Caesar's death.

👑 **27** Octavian takes the title Augustus, inaugurating the imperial period of Roman history.

AFRICA

📖 **40** Mark Antony gives Cleopatra 200,000 volumes from the library at Pergamon to add to Ptolemy I's collection in Alexandria, making the latter the greatest in the world.

✕ **31** Octavian's navy, under the command of Agrippa, defeats Antony and Cleopatra's forces at the Battle of Actium.

👑 **30** Antony and Cleopatra commit suicide. Rome annexes Egypt.

WESTERN ASIA

The Bible lands had been a Roman province for 23 years when Herod the Great was chosen to rule them in 40 B.C. Although a client of Rome, he was an ambitious monarch, noted for his building work. The site of the Herodium, a fortified palace atop an artificial mound, can still be seen near Jerusalem today (*left*).

☀ **4** Probable year of birth of Jesus Christ in Bethlehem, Judea.

SOUTH & CENTRAL ASIA

☀ **c.100** The Great Stupa, a Buddhist monument at Sanchi, India, is doubled in size and clad in lavishly carved stone.

☀ **c.100** A new form of Buddhism, called Mahayana ("Great Vehicle"), starts to take shape. It offers salvation through the help of bodhisattvas—humans who delay the attainment of enlightenment in order to help others.

⚙ **c.50** The *Ayurveda*, a Hindu medical treatise, establishes a holistic medical system that is still practiced today.

EAST ASIA & OCEANIA

⚙ **28** Chinese imperial histories begin recording sunspots—dark patches that appear periodically on the sun's surface.

⚙ **c.10** The Chinese invent methods for drilling wells over 3,250 feet (1,000 m) deep to obtain water and natural gas.

THE RISE OF ROME

IN 500 B.C. ROME WAS A TINY *republic hemmed in by other Latin tribes and more advanced Etruscan and Greek city-states. Over the next 250 years it succeeded in dominating Italy by conquest, colonization, or alliance. Victories over Carthage then made it the chief Mediterranean power. But as Rome's overseas territories grew, unrest at home led to dictatorship, civil war, and the replacement of the republican political system by imperial rule.*

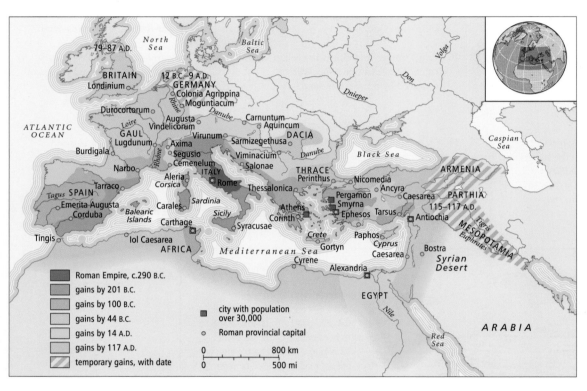

▲ According to legend, Rome was founded by Romulus, who as a child was abandoned with his twin, Remus; the two only survived because a she-wolf suckled them. This bronze statue illustrating the story dates from c.500 B.C., although the twins were added later.

◀ Roman power expanded steadily from the area around Rome itself to take in first Italy and eastern Spain, and then the Mediterranean empire of its defeated rival Carthage. Julius Caesar added Gaul (France) and Germany up to the Rhine frontier. Other territories in Europe, Africa, and Asia followed under the early emperors.

Map legend:
- Roman Empire, c.290 B.C.
- gains by 201 B.C.
- gains by 100 B.C.
- gains by 44 B.C.
- gains by 14 A.D.
- gains by 117 A.D.
- temporary gains, with date
- ■ city with population over 30,000
- ○ Roman provincial capital
- 0   800 km
- 0   500 mi

494 B.C. After going on military strike, Roman plebeians (commoners) win the right to appoint tribunes to protect their interests.

451 A code of laws known as the Twelve Tables is drawn up; it defines the rights and obligations of Roman citizens.

312 The first major Roman road, the Appian Way, is begun. Running south from Rome to Capua, it is the first link in a network that will eventually stretch over 50,000 miles (85,000 km).

287 A law (the *Lex Hortensia*) makes resolutions passed in the plebeian assembly binding on all Romans.

275 Victory against an invading army led by King Pyrrhos of Epiros (a Greek kingdom) confirms Rome's mastery over all of Italy.

241 Victory in the First Punic War (264–241) between Rome and Carthage gives Rome control of Sicily, its first overseas province.

218 Hannibal of Carthage starts the Second Punic War (218–201) by invading Italy across the Alps.

203 Despite having inflicted crushing defeats on Roman armies, Hannibal, having failed to take Rome itself, is eventually recalled to Africa.

146 The Third Punic War (149–146) ends with the destruction of Carthage. The province of Africa is founded.

88 After a conflict known as the Social War Rome is forced to grant citizenship to all Italians.

82 Lucius Sulla is appointed dictator of Rome. He butchers his opponents.

In the myths Aeneas, founder of the Roman race, was a prince of Troy, a city famed in Greek legend. In fact, the ancestors of the Romans were immigrants from north of the Alps who spoke the language that was later to develop into Latin. They moved into central Italy in about 1000 B.C. and built villages on hills overlooking the Tiber River. By the 8th century the settlements had merged into the town of Rome.

Early Rome was ruled by kings, including three Etruscan monarchs. Having expelled its last Etruscan ruler, Rome declared itself a republic in 509 B.C. From that time on the state was governed by two elected officials, called consuls, and by the Senate, which drew its membership from the ranks of aristocrats known as patricians. The commoners, or plebeians, in time set up their own assembly and elected officials called tribunes to protect their interests.

The new republic gradually imposed its power over the other Italian states by a combination of military force and diplomacy. Conquered rivals were offered alliances and given privileges, which in some cases included Roman citizenship. In return, the allies had to pay taxes and provide soldiers to serve in the Roman army. The Romans also consolidated their hold on Italy by founding colonies linked by a well-maintained network of roads.

Alliances with Greek cities in southern Italy brought Rome into conflict with Carthage, a trading city on the North African coast. In three campaigns known as the Punic Wars (from the Latin *Punicus*, or "Phoenician," the nationality of Carthage's founders), Rome first achieved naval supremacy, then survived an invasion by the Carthaginian general Hannibal, and finally (in 146 B.C.) destroyed Carthage itself.

The defeat of Carthage opened the way for more Roman conquests. Greece, Asia Minor, Syria, Palestine, and Gaul (modern-day France) all fell to its generals. At home, though, the republican political system was breaking down. The patricians used their wealth to create large country estates worked by slaves. Landless peasants flocked to the cities or joined the army, where they provided the power base for a series of military dictators: Lucius Sulla, Pompey the Great, and Julius Caesar.

After Caesar was murdered by patricians jealous of his power in 44 B.C., civil war broke out between his adopted son, Octavian, and Mark Antony, who planned to create a separate empire with Cleopatra, queen of Egypt. The defeat of Mark Antony's navy at Actium left Octavian as sole ruler of the Roman world. His new title "Augustus," meaning "revered one," would be used by Roman emperors for the next five centuries.

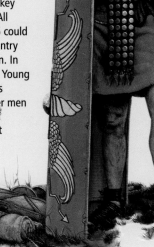

The Roman Army

Rome's well-disciplined citizens' army was a key factor in the early successes of the republic. All property-owning citizens between 17 and 46 could be called up. Soldiers were grouped into infantry units called legions, each of about 4,200 men. In battle a legion was organized in three ranks. Young men armed with thrusting spears and swords formed the first rank. Behind them were older men with better weapons and armor. A reserve of veterans made up the third rank. The poorest soldiers, who could not afford decent weapons, fought as skirmishers. In time the conscript army came to seem unwieldy, and from 104 B.C. on it was replaced by a professional standing force.

👑 **71** A slave revolt led by a Thracian gladiator named Spartacus is crushed.

👑 **59** The Roman general and politician Pompey the Great forms an illegal alliance with Marcus Crassus and Julius Caesar, intended to further the trio's political ambitions.

✕ **58–50** In a series of brilliant campaigns Caesar conquers Gaul and raids Britain and the German lands.

✕ **53** Crassus is defeated and killed by Parthians at the Battle of Carrhae.

✕ **49** Julius Caesar takes his troops without permission across the Rubicon, a stream separating Italy from Gaul. He fights a civil war with the armies of Pompey.

👑 **45** Following the defeat and death of Pompey, Caesar becomes sole ruler.

👑 **44** Declared dictator for life, Julius Caesar is assassinated by colleagues unwilling to accept one-man rule.

👑 **43** Caesar's adopted son and heir Octavian joins forces with Mark Antony and Marcus Lepidus to reconstitute the government.

👑 **37** Mark Antony, who is married to Octavian's sister, provokes anger in Rome by flaunting his relationship with Cleopatra, queen of Egypt.

✕ **31** The defeat of Antony and Cleopatra's forces at the naval Battle of Actium leaves Octavian master of the Roman world.

👑 **30** Antony and Cleopatra commit suicide.

👑 **27** Octavian assumes the name Augustus and is given overriding authority over all Rome's territories.

0–100 A.D.

AMERICAS

c.0 The first "Basketmaker" phase of the Anasazi Culture gets under way in the American Southwest; its economy is based on settled agriculture and on hunting large animals with spearthrowers.

The Pueblo peoples of the American Southwest have one of the continent's oldest cultural traditions. Its deepest roots lie in the Basketmaker Culture, named for the neatly woven baskets that were its most distinctive products. Around 500 A.D. the Basketmaker people started making pottery and living in sunken pithouses—distinctive features of the ensuing Anasazi Culture.

EUROPE

c.0 The Greek geographer Strabo publishes a detailed description of the known world.

9 Three Roman legions are wiped out by German tribes in the Teutoburg Forest, north of the Rhine River, which becomes the imperial frontier in Germany.

43 A Roman army under Claudius conquers Britain and establishes the city of London on the Thames River.

50 Cologne on the Rhine in Germany becomes a Roman colony.

AFRICA

c.0 Egyptian-style temples dedicated to the lion god Apedemek are built at Naga in Nubia.

42 Mauretania (made up of coastal regions of modern Morocco and Algeria) is annexed by Rome.

c.50 The Greek-influenced Kingdom of Axum is established in Ethiopia and dominates the Red Sea trade in incense.

WESTERN ASIA

6 Rome annexes Judea as a province of the empire; one of its governors, Pontius Pilate, will later convict Jesus of sedition.

c.30 Jesus of Nazareth, founder of Christianity, is crucified in Jerusalem.

Roman coin showing Judea in bondage.

53 Tiridates I founds a line of Armenian kings that lasts for several centuries.

c.68 A Jewish sect hides more than 600 religious manuscripts in caves at Qumran, Jordan. Discovered in 1947 and known as the Dead Sea Scrolls, the documents include the earliest known copies of the Old Testament.

SOUTH & CENTRAL ASIA

c.0 Romans establish trading links with southern India, using the monsoon wind system for rapid sea travel.

c.50 The Kushans, a people from Central Asia, gain control of northwest India, establishing a cosmopolitan empire that lasts for over 300 years.

c.60 Indian exports of spices, jewels, and textiles become such a drain on the Roman economy that the Emperor Nero bans the import of pepper.

EAST ASIA & OCEANIA

2 A census gives the population of China's Han Empire as 57 million.

9 Wang Mang seizes the Chinese throne and introduces radical reforms, including reallocation of land to peasants and restrictions on slave ownership.

c.10 The Chinese build cast-iron suspension bridges strong enough to carry vehicles.

25 Wang Mang is assassinated by Han princes who found the Later Han Dynasty.

c.39 Chinese control of northern Vietnam is challenged by a rebellion led by two sisters, who rule as queens of an independent state before their defeat in c.42.

👑 **c.0** Teotihuacán starts to emerge in the Valley of Mexico, replacing Cuicuilco as the region's main urban center.

☀ **c.0** The Moche people, inhabiting river valleys on the coast of northern Peru, emerge as a significant presence in a region previously dominated by the Chavín Culture.

☀ **c.50** In the desert 300 miles (500 km) south of the Moche lands Peru's Nazca people create vast line drawings that only take on recognizable form when seen from a great height.

👑 **c.50** El Mirador, the largest lowland Mayan city, goes into decline.

☀ **c.57** The Christian apostle and missionary Paul, a Roman citizen, is sent for trial to Rome and eventually executed under Emperor Nero.

✕ **61** The Iceni tribe in Britain revolt under their leader Boudicca (Boadicea).

⊕ **79** The volcano Vesuvius erupts, burying the Roman towns of Pompeii and Herculaneum on Italy's west coast.

⊕ **c.60** The inventor Hero of Alexandria designs a steam engine.

⊕ **c.80–95** Wheat, olive, and grape production is boosted across Roman Africa, making the region the granary of Rome.

✕ **70** Jerusalem is captured by imperial troops following a Jewish revolt against Roman rule. The last rebels commit suicide rather than surrender at Masada (–73).

👑 **97** A Chinese diplomatic mission sets out for Roman Syria but gets only as far as Characene, a state at the head of the Persian Gulf.

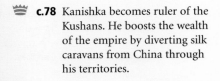

Jewish rebels make a last stand against Roman troops at the hilltop fortress of Masada in 73 A.D.

👑 **c.78** Kanishka becomes ruler of the Kushans. He boosts the wealth of the empire by diverting silk caravans from China through his territories.

📖 **c.90** Greek-influenced art, including statues of the Buddha, is created at Gandhara, a region in what is now northwestern Pakistan.

👑 **57** Chinese chronicles record a visit to the imperial court by Japanese emissaries.

⊕ **c.70** Work begins on China's Grand Canal, which eventually reaches a length of more than 1,100 miles (1,800 km).

⊕ **c.80** The Chinese make primitive compasses from lodestone, a magnetic iron ore. They were probably used in divination rather than for navigation.

⊕ **c.100** The Chinese make an insecticide from dried chrysanthemum flowers; its active ingredient, pyrethrum, is still widely used as an insecticide that is virtually harmless to birds and mammals.

AMERICAS

EUROPE

AFRICA

WESTERN ASIA

SOUTH & CENTRAL ASIA

EAST ASIA & OCEANIA

0–100 A.D.

THE ROMAN EMPIRE

UNDER THE RULE OF THE EMPERORS *Rome set about expanding its power. By the beginning of the 2nd century A.D. its empire stretched from the north of England to southern Egypt and from Spain to Syria; never before had so many different peoples lived together under one government. In their heyday Rome's emperors presided over an era of relative peace and prosperity in which national differences gradually weakened as Roman citizenship was progressively extended to all the empire's provinces.*

▲ A grandnephew of Julius Caesar, Octavian rose to power in the civil war that followed Caesar's assassination in 44 B.C. By 31 B.C. he had defeated all his rivals and was ruling Rome in effect as a dictator. Taking the title Augustus ("revered one"), he was to be the first Roman emperor, bringing to an end almost 500 years of republican rule.

When Augustus became Rome's first emperor, he made a pretence of restoring republican government while continuing to hold all real power himself. He was supreme commander of the army, which included a new personal bodyguard, the Praetorian Guard.

Augustus stamped out corruption, established a civil service, and rebuilt Rome. But his death exposed the weakness of a system that depended on the emperor's personal qualities for its success. Over the next 50 years Rome's rulers included Caligula, who made his favorite horse a consul, and Nero, who murdered his mother and two of his wives.

Despite the flaws of some of its rulers, the empire continued to grow. One reason lay in the efficiency of the administrative machine Augustus had created. The empire's main prop, however, was the Roman army, which was by far the most efficient fighting machine of its day; its disciplined legions, staffed by highly trained career soldiers, rarely failed to defeat their less organized opponents. Britain was conquered by legionaries in 43 A.D., Dacia (Romania) in 106,

▶ The emperors sought to keep urban populations happy with bloodthirsty spectacles such as gladiatorial combats.

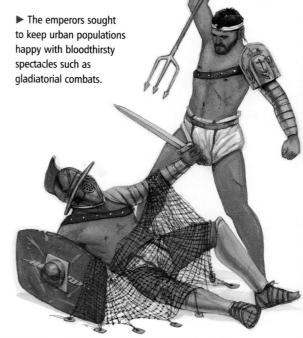

Roman Roads

"They have built paved roads throughout the country," the Greek geographer Strabo reported in the 1st century A.D., "leveling ridges and filling up hollows so as to make possible the movement of heavily loaded wagons." Road building was indeed one of the Romans' supreme achievements, providing highways that allowed their legions to cover over 30 miles (50 km) on foot a day. Roadbeds were layered (*inset, right*), with the paving stones resting on beds of sand and gravel; the surface was cambered to allow rainwater to run off into gutters.

Armenia and Parthia (northwest Persia) by 117. In the wake of military victory taxes and tributes poured into Rome. The emperors spent some of this wealth on massive building projects. They also used their wealth to buy public support, handing out free grain and paying for lavish gladiatorial games.

If Rome grew rich from its conquests, many of its provinces also prospered under early imperial rule. In return for paying taxes, their citizens received the protection of the world's mightiest military power. In regions where city living had long been established, merchants found a huge new export market for their goods. In more remote areas the Romans introduced the benefits of urban living. Most large provincial towns had Roman-style public buildings, including amphitheaters, law courts, and public baths.

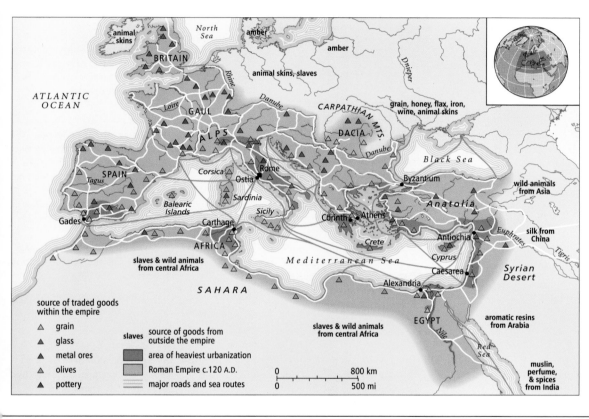

◀ In an age of horse and sail power the Roman Empire was a triumph of good communications as much as of military might. Covering more than 3 million square miles (5 million sq. km) at its peak, its network of paved roads and well-used sea routes provided not just highways for the legions but also vital arteries for trade.

🏛 **14**   Augustus dies and is succeeded as emperor by the 55-year-old Tiberius.

🏛 **37**   Tiberius is succeeded by the crazed Caligula, who, two years later, proclaims himself a god.

🏛 **41**   Caligula is murdered by soldiers of the Praetorian Guard (his own bodyguard), who replace him with his uncle, Claudius.

✕ **43**   A Roman army under the emperor Claudius conquers Britain.

🏛 **54**   Claudius dies, reputedly poisoned by his own wife, to be replaced by Nero, her 17-year-old son by a previous husband.

☀ **64**   Much of Rome is destroyed by a fire. The emperor Nero blames the disaster on Christians.

🏛 **68**   Nero is deposed by an army revolt. The Year of the Four Emperors follows, a time of anarchy ended when Vespasian seizes power.

⊕ **80**   The Colosseum, an amphitheater holding over 50,000 spectators, is completed in Rome.

✕ **106**   The Emperor Trajan conquers Dacia (Romania).

✕ **117**   The conquests of Armenia and Parthia (northwest Persia) mark the high point of imperial expansion.

🏛 **117**   On the death of Trajan the new emperor, Hadrian, abandons the policy of further expanding the empire.

🏛 **122**   In Britain work begins on Hadrian's Wall, built to protect Roman England from unconquered tribes to the north.

🏛 **138**   Antoninus comes to the imperial throne. His 23-year reign is a time of peace and prosperity.

🏛 **161**   The philosopher-emperor Marcus Aurelius succeeds Antoninus and continues his humanitarian policies.

🏛 **212**   All free adult males in the empire are granted Roman citizenship.

AMERICAS

c.120 The Moche people of northern Peru now control vast areas of lowland; they produce gold and silver artifacts, pottery, and textiles.

c.150 At Teotihuacán in Mexico, work gets under way on the Pyramid of the Sun; it will become the largest building in pre-Columbian America.

EUROPE

c.100 The Roman historian Tacitus begins his *Histories*, chronicling the history of the empire from 68 to 96 A.D.

c.101 The Roman Emperor Trajan begins his campaign against the Kingdom of Dacia, north of the Danube River, which becomes a Roman province in 106.

113 In Rome Trajan's Column is built; the spiraling reliefs carved around it depict the story of Trajan's wars against Dacia.

Under a succession of talented rulers— Trajan, Hadrian, Antoninus, and Marcus Aurelius—the Roman Empire enjoyed its heyday in the 2nd century. Its greatness was founded on trade as much as on military success. This marble carving of a merchant ship comes from Trajan's Column in Rome.

115 The Jews of Cyprus, Egypt, Cyrene (Libya), and Mesopotamia revolt against the rule of Trajan and the Romans (– 117).

117 Hadrian becomes Roman emperor, ruling to 138; he builds stone and turf walls to protect his borders in Germany and Britain.

c.120 Plutarch, the Greek historian, biographer, and philosopher, dies; his famed *Parallel Lives* describes and compares 46 great figures from Greek and Roman history.

AFRICA

c.100 By this date Greco-Roman merchants are sailing to East Africa for ivory.

168 Claudius Ptolemy, Egyptian astronomer and geographer, dies. His legacy is the Earth-centered view of the universe that becomes known as the Ptolemaic System.

173 In Egypt shepherd brigands stage revolts against the Roman Empire; they are crushed by governor Avidius Cassius.

WESTERN ASIA

106 The Kingdom of Nabataea, whose capital is Petra, is annexed by the Romans to become the province of Arabia.

Reliquary dating from Kanishka's reign, c.100 A.D.

115 In this year and the next the Roman Emperor Trajan wages a dramatically successful military campaign against the Parthians, capturing their capital of Ctesiphon and putting a puppet ruler on the throne.

134 In Cappadocia (eastern Turkey) Roman troops repel an attack by Alans from southeast Russia.

193 The governor of Syria, Pescennius Niger, is declared emperor by part of the Roman army, but is defeated and executed soon afterward.

SOUTH & CENTRAL ASIA

c. 100 Under Kanishka the Kushan Empire reaches its greatest extent, stretching from the Aral Sea to the Ganges River. The king promotes the spread of Mahayana Buddhism through Central Asia.

107 The Roman Emperor Trajan sends envoys to India (presumably to Kanishka).

EAST ASIA & OCEANIA

c.100 Buddhism begins to spread in China.

109 The earliest extant example of Chinese hemp paper with writing on it dates from this year.

120 China is by this time the largest and most densely populated state in the world.

c.148 An Qing (Anshigao), a Parthian missionary and translator, actively seeks converts to Buddhism at the Chinese court and in the area around the capital, Luoyang.

AMERICAS

♨ **c.150** The city of El Mirador is abandoned; Tikal replaces it as the chief Mayan center in Central America's Petén lowlands.

♨ **c.200** The eruption of Mt. Ilopango precipitates the decline of the southern Maya of modern-day Guatemala.

EUROPE

The Roman Emperor Hadrian, shown in profile on a coin.

⊕ **133** Hadrian's Wall across northern Britain is completed.

📖 **c.140** Death of Juvenal, the Roman lawyer and satirical writer; his *Satires* rail against Roman vices and society's evils.

📖 **c.190** One of the earliest examples of Christian figurative art, a fresco on the arch in the Catacomb of Santa Priscilla in Rome, is completed. Four men and three women are seated around a table; the central figure is breaking bread.

✕ **192** The despotic Emperor Commodus is strangled by the Roman athlete Narcissus, bring the Antonine Dynasty to an end.

♨ **197** The governor of Britain, Clodius Albinus, declared emperor by his troops, vies for power with Septimius Severus. By defeating him, Severus reunites the Roman Empire.

AFRICA

⊕ **c.190** Ironworking in Africa spreads as far south as the Limpopo Valley in southern Africa.

♨ **c.200** The Kingdom of Axum in Ethiopia is now a major power in the area, trading with the Roman Empire, Arabia, and India through its Red Sea port, Adulis.

WESTERN ASIA

✕ **197** The Parthian capital Ctesiphon (in modern-day Iraq) is sacked by Septimius Severus, who was proclaimed Roman emperor in 193.

Septimius Severus, conqueror of the Parthians.

♨ **198** Northern Mesopotamia becomes a Roman province.

SOUTH & CENTRAL ASIA

✕ **c.130** The Saka state in western India wins control of Ujain in central India.

📖 **c.150** Date of the earliest known Sanskrit inscription, carved on the orders of the Saka King Rudraman at Junagadh in western India.

⊕ **c.200** On the Deccan Plateau in India cities appear for the first time.

EAST ASIA & OCEANIA

✕ **184** Peasant farmers known as the Yellow Turbans rebel, challenging the corruption and ineffectual leadership of the Han court. The revolt is suppressed, but the Han Dynasty is greatly weakened.

✕ **189** General Dong Zhuo seizes power in the Han capital, Luoyang, presiding over a vicious dictatorship fronted by a puppet ruler, 15-year-old Emperor Xian.

♨ **c.200** The Kingdom of Champa is founded in what is now central Vietnam. It will becomes the most enduring Hinduized state in Southeast Asia.

100–200 A.D.

THE JEWISH DIASPORA

S OME HISTORIANS DATE THE START *of the Diaspora, or "dispersal," of the Jewish people as far back as 586 B.C., when many Jews were forced into exile in Babylon in the "Babylonian captivity." The next millennium witnessed several other forcible dispersals, particularly after unsuccessful uprisings against Roman rule in Judea in 66–73 A.D. and 132–135 A.D. In addition, many Jews chose to leave their homeland voluntarily in order to live and work in wealthier countries. By 500 A.D. Jewish communities were established in lands from southern Spain to the borders of India.*

▲ One of the treasures seized by Jerusalem's Roman conquerors in 70 A.D. was the seven-branched golden lampstand, or menorah, that had graced the city's Temple. In future centuries the menorah would become an enduring symbol of Jewish cultural identity.

▶ The Diaspora saw Jews moving out from Israel to locations around the Mediterranean world and also deep into Asia. The area around Babylon in the ancient Mesopotamian lands became an important Jewish center; so did Alexandria in Egypt.

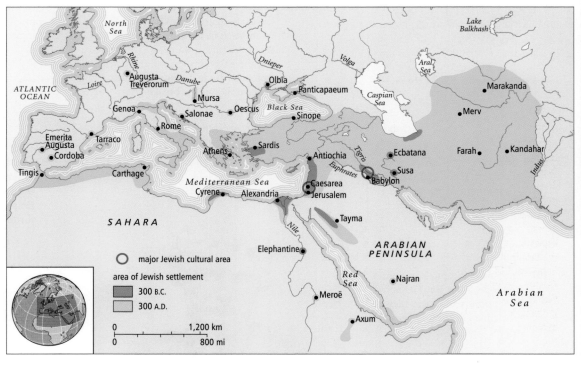

major Jewish cultural area

area of Jewish settlement
300 B.C.
300 A.D.

0   1,200 km
0   800 mi

🜲 **332 B.C.** Alexander the Great conquers the Bible lands in the course of defeating the Persian Empire. In the ensuing Hellenistic (Greek) Period, Jewish people are encouraged to embrace Greek culture.

🜲 **323** On Alexander's death the Bible lands fall under the control of the Ptolemies—Greek rulers of Egypt.

🜲 **198** The Seleucids—Greek rulers of western Asia—wrest control of the Bible lands from the Ptolemies.

🜲 **175** Antiochos IV becomes Seleucid emperor; in the course of his 12-year reign he proscribes the Jewish religion, attempting to force worship of the Greek gods on the Jews.

⚔ **167** Judas Maccabeus leads a Jewish uprising (the Maccabean Revolt) against Antiochos's measures.

⚔ **164** The Maccabean rebels win back and rededicate the Temple in Jerusalem, which had temporarily been given over to the Greek god Zeus.

🜲 **142** Judas Maccabeus's brother Simon establishes an independent Jewish state under the rule of the Hasmonean Dynasty.

⚔ **63** The Roman general Pompey forces the Hasmoneans to accept Rome's authority over the lands the Romans call Judea.

🜲 **40** The Roman Senate appoints Herod as king of Judea, replacing the last king of the Hasmonean line.

🜲 **4** Herod dies, and his kingdom is divided among three of his sons.

In the centuries following the Babylonian Captivity Judah and Israel fell under the control of a series of foreign powers. First they formed part of the Persian Empire; when that succumbed to Alexander the Great, they came under Greek control. In the 2nd century B.C. Maccabean rebels, taking their name from their leader Judas Maccabeus, were able to establish a semi-independent state; but in 63 B.C. the Hasmonean Dynasty that ruled it was forced to accept the overlordship of a fresh imperial master, and the Bible lands became the Roman province of Judea.

Since their own homeland was too small to hold a large population, many Jews were drawn to cities such as Egypt's Alexandria, founded by Alexander the Great in 331 B.C., in search of a better life. The communities of the Diaspora centered on the synagogue (meeting house) and courts of law; Jewish people often lived in a separate quarter of their adopted city. In general they were free to follow their laws and religious practices, although in the Hellenistic Period (323–30 B.C.) Jews were encouraged to adopt a Greek lifestyle.

The Roman era in Jewish history began with Jerusalem's fall to the Roman general Pompey in 63 B.C. In 66 A.D. its inhabitants launched a revolt against Roman rule that was savagely suppressed; Vespasian and his son Titus, both future Roman emperors, led the Roman forces, which captured Jerusalem after a 139-day siege and largely destroyed it, deporting Jews to Syria and Italy.

A further uprising in 132 A.D., this one led by Simeon bar Kokba, was also put down bloodily. In its wake Judea was renamed Palestine, and Jerusalem became a Roman city that Jews were forbidden to enter. Thereafter more than 1,800 years would pass before an independent Jewish state would be reestablished in the region.

The Dead Sea Scrolls

In 1947 a shepherd made a remarkable discovery near Qumran, 10 miles (16 km) south of Jericho in the Dead Sea region. In caves on a cliff face he found clay jars containing ancient parchment scrolls; over the next 10 years others would be discovered in caverns nearby. The texts—mainly written on parchment, some on papyrus—were dated by experts mostly to about 100 B.C. They included copies of the Hebrew Bible and writings describing the beliefs of a Jewish sect that had lived at Qumran from about 130 B.C. to 70 A.D. This sect—the Essenes—believed that they had been chosen by God to survive the "end of days." The scrolls probably formed their library, stored for safekeeping at a time when war with Rome was raging nearby.

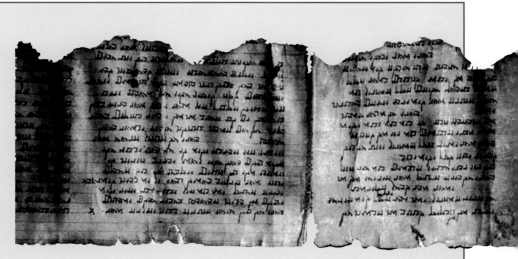

👑 **44 A.D.** Rome assumes direct rule over all of Judea.

✕ **66** The First Jewish Revolt breaks out against Roman rule.

✕ **70** Jerusalem falls to Roman forces under the future Emperor Titus after a 139-day siege. The Temple is destroyed, and many Jews are forced into exile.

✕ **73** The last of the Jewish rebels commit mass suicide at the clifftop fortress of Masada in southern Judea to avoid having to surrender to Roman troops.

✕ **115–117** Diaspora Jews in North Africa, Cyprus, and Mesopotamia rise up unsuccessfully against the rule of the Emperor Trajan.

✕ **132** In Judea the Second Jewish Revolt breaks out under the leadership of Simeon bar Kokba, seen as a messiah or Jewish national savior.

✕ **135** The bar Kokba revolt is crushed by Roman forces. In its wake Judea is renamed Palestine, and its former Jewish population is scattered; Jews are forbidden to enter Jerusalem.

☀ **c.200** The Mishnah, a collection of Jewish oral law that makes up part of the Talmud, is compiled.

☀ **219** Babylonia becomes the focus of Jewish life with the establishment of the first Jewish academy at Sura.

☀ **388** The Romans pass legislation forbidding intermarriage between Christians and Jews.

☀ **476** As the Roman Empire collapses, the definitive edition of the Talmud—the most authoritative compilation of Jewish oral law—is compiled in Babylon.

AMERICAS

Noted for its lively artworks, including this vase scene of a religious ritual, the Moche Culture takes its name from a Peruvian river valley. At its peak in the 3rd century its influence stretched over much of northern Peru.

c.200 The Moche state in northern Peru moves into its most influential era; the culture is notable for its gigantic mud-brick (adobe) ceremonial platforms.

EUROPE

205 Plotinus, the Neoplatonist philosopher, is born. He will study in Alexandria before settling in Rome in 244, becoming a popular teacher and producing a collection of philosophical essays, the *Enneads*.

212 Roman citizenship is extended to everyone living within the empire's boundaries in an attempt to raise more taxes.

260 The Roman Emperor Valerian, marching against the Persians, is defeated at Edessa (eastern Turkey).

267 The Goths, a Germanic tribe occupying the Black Sea region (the Ukraine and modern Bulgaria), make one of several incursions into Roman territory, pillaging Thrace, Macedonia, and Greece.

AFRICA

203 During a persecution of Christians ordered by the Emperor Septimius Severus, Perpetua and her pregnant slave Felicitas are martyred at Carthage.

248 Anti-Christian rioting breaks out in Alexandria.

250 The Emperor Decius issues an edict against Christians, forcing Cyprian, bishop of Carthage, into hiding. In the course of a further persecution in 258 Cyprian is executed.

WESTERN ASIA

c.200 The Mishnah, a collection of Jewish oral law that forms part of the Talmud, takes its final form.

219 The first Jewish academy is established at Sura; Babylonia becomes the focus of Jewish spiritual life.

224 The Parthian realm is overthrown by Ardashir I, from Fars in Persia, who founds the Sassanian Empire.

226 Ctesiphon, previously the winter capital of the Parthian emperors, becomes the Sassanian capital until 637.

240 Shapur I, son of Ardashir I, becomes Sassanian emperor.

c.250 A series of wall paintings illustrating biblical narratives is created to decorate the interior of the synagogue at Dura-Europos.

c.260 The capture of Emperor Valerian by the Sassanians at Edessa is commemorated in a cliff-face carving at the Persian site now known as Naqsh-i Rustam.

269 Zenobia, queen of Palmyra, conquers Egypt; the following year she conquers many of Rome's eastern provinces in Asia Minor, enthroning her son as eastern emperor.

SOUTH & CENTRAL ASIA

c.200 Over the next century Hindu laws are systematized.

c.213 Vasudeva, last of the great Kushan emperors, dies; the Kushan Empire is divided into western and eastern parts.

c.224 Kushan territories in Bactria and northern India are seized by the Sassanian Shapur I (to 240).

EAST ASIA & OCEANIA

220 The last Han emperor is deposed and the empire divided into three separate kingdoms.

239 Himiko, queen of a Japanese state known from Chinese sources as "Yamatai," sends a friendly mission to China.

259 Buddhists from China begin to make pilgrimages to India.

Earthenware model of an ox cart, Jin Dynasty, China.

👑 **c.250** By this time Teotihuacán has developed into a major urban center laid out on a grid pattern, with residential blocks surrounding a central avenue of palaces and temples.

✳ **c.300** Commemorative steles—stone pillars—are erected in the central lowland forest area by the Maya; the earliest found is at Tikal.

✳ **c.300** For the first time Mayan builders incorporate corbeled arches and vaults in their constructions.

👑 **286** Troubled by barbarian attacks, the Emperor Diocletian divides the Roman Empire into western and eastern parts, appointing Maximian to rule the west.

👑 **287** Marcus Aurelius Carausius, commander of the Roman fleet in the English Channel, stages an unsuccessful rebellion, finally put down by Diocletian in 296.

The Roman Empire's corulers, Diocletian and Maximian.

👑 **c.250** Aphilas becomes king of Axum and conquers surrounding territories. The kingdom begins to mint its own coins in gold and silver.

✕ **260** Pirate raids are launched on North Africa by Franks who have seized ships at Tarraco (Tarragona in modern Spain).

☀ **c.270** St. Anthony becomes a hermit in the Egyptian desert; in the years to come, many others will follow him into the wilderness.

✕ **272** Zenobia, having been defeated in several battles and besieged at Palmyra, is captured by the Roman Emperor Aurelian. A lively and beautiful woman, she is feted by the Romans and lives out her days in comfort in Italy.

For over 400 years, from its foundation in 224 A.D., Persia's Sassanian Empire rivaled Rome for influence in western Asia. Taking their name from Sassan, the dynasty's founder, its rulers—one of whom is shown (*right*) hunting rams—embraced the Zoroastrian religion and sought to revive the glories of the Persian Empire created by Cyrus the Great seven centuries earlier. To the east the empire confronted the threat of the Central Asian nomads; one such people, the Ephthalite Huns, briefly forced its rulers into subjection in the late 5th century.

✕ **c.225** The empire of the Satakani or Andhra Dynasty, which has ruled substantial territories in the Deccan and southern India for almost 300 years, breaks up.

👑 **c.270** The Kushans lose control of the plains around the Ganges River.

✕ **263** Wei, straddling the Yellow River Valley, is the strongest of China's three kingdoms, conquering the weaker Shu Kingdom to the south.

👑 **265** In China the Wei general Sima Yan is enthroned as Wudi, the first emperor of the Jin Dynasty.

✕ **280** Wu, the third of the Chinese kingdoms created in 220, is conquered by the Jin, thus reunifying China under the victorious general Sima Yan.

✕ **291** After Sima Yan's death his sons battle for control, enlisting support from the steppe peoples beyond China's boundaries; the northern kingdom breaks up into Chinese and nomad states.

👑 **c.300** Easter Island is settled.

AMERICAS

EUROPE

AFRICA

WESTERN ASIA

SOUTH & CENTRAL ASIA

EAST ASIA & OCEANIA

200–300 A.D.

THE INDIAN EMPIRES

▲ This capital once topped a 50-foot (15-m) high pillar set up by the emperor Ashoka at Sarnath in the Ganges Valley, where the Buddha first preached. Ashoka had several dozen such pillars erected around his realm.

I N 500 B.C. THE INDIAN SUBCONTINENT *was a land of petty kingdoms, the wealthiest of which were concentrated in the Ganges and Indus river valleys. In the course of the next millennium two great empires—those of the Mauryas and of the Guptas—would for a time impose some unity on the divided states. The Mauryan rulers helped spread the Buddhist faith, but the later Guptas encouraged a revival of Hinduism.*

Hinduism had originated in the 2nd millennium B.C. with the Aryans, a pastoral people who produced the first Hindu scriptures. These works—the Vedas—laid down a "caste" system of hereditary social ranks, with the priestly class of Brahmins at the top and a fixed hierarchy of warriors, merchants, and servants beneath them. By 500 B.C. people irked by the rigidities of the caste system had begun to resent the power wielded by those at the top; they turned to less hierarchical new sects, such as Buddhism and Jainism.

At this time some 16 states dominated northern India, of which Magadha, straddling the Ganges Valley, was the most strategically and economically important. In about 321 B.C. Chandragupta Maurya seized the throne there. His efficiently run empire was administered by a civil service; it had a huge army that in time came to include up to 600,000 infantrymen and 9,000 elephants. Chandragupta ruled from a vast royal city surrounded by a moat and a timber palisade. By the time he passed on the throne to his son in about 300, his empire stretched over much of the continent, including some of the lands on India's northwestern frontier that had been captured by Alexander the Great just 35 years before.

Chandragupta's grandson Ashoka, who reigned from about 269 to 232 B.C., was another great Mauryan ruler. His kingdom extended over most of the subcontinent. He conquered Kalinga in eastern India, but was so shocked by the suffering caused by the fighting that he decided to convert to Buddhism, which preached nonviolence. Ashoka set up stone pillars along pilgrimage routes; they carried carved messages urging compassion, respect for all animal life, considerate behavior, and courtesy to all.

By 185 B.C. the Mauryan Empire had collapsed, and the region dissolved into small kingdoms under a series of weaker dynasties. It was not until the 4th century A.D. that the next great empire arose, when a marriage alliance brought another ruler named Chandragupta—no relation to the Mauryan emperor of that name—control of Magadha. By the time of Chandragupta II, who reigned from 380 to 414

👑 **c.321 B.C.** From a power base in northwestern India Chandragupta Maurya seizes control of the kingdom of Magadha and founds the Mauryan Empire.

👑 **c.305** Chandragupta signs a peace treaty with Alexander the Great's successor Seleucus; by its terms the Mauryans receive much of today's Afghanistan and Pakistan in return for their alliance and a corps of 500 war elephants.

👑 **c.300** Chandragupta hands the throne to his son Bindusara, who further extends Mauryan rule into India's deep south.

👑 **c.269** Bindusara's son Ashoka ascends the throne.

⚔ **c.261** Ashoka conquers Kalinga, a previously independent kingdom on India's east coast, in a battle said to have cost the lives of 100,000 men.

☀ **c.259** Sickened by the violence of his victory, Ashoka converts to Buddhism.

☀ **c.250** Ashoka sends Buddhist missionaries to Ceylon (Sri Lanka).

👑 **c.232** Ashoka's death marks the start of the Mauryan Empire's decline.

👑 **c.185** The decline of the Mauryan Empire culminates in the overthrow of the last Mauryan ruler; the region dissolves into smaller kingdoms.

👑 **c.183** The Greek rulers of Bactria, a breakaway province of the Seleucid Kingdom, briefly reconquer the lands ceded to the Mauryans by Seleucus a century before.

👑 **c.135** The Sakas, a nomadic people from Central Asia, conquer Bactria from the Greeks.

👑 **c.100** By this time the Sakas have established a powerful kingdom in northern India.

⚔ **50 A.D.** At about this date the Kushans, nomads originally from China, invade northwestern India, defeating the northernmost Sakas and establishing an empire of their own.

A Buddhist Holy Site

In 1818 the first of a large group of Buddhist monuments was uncovered at Sanchi in central India. The remarkably well preserved buildings offered a fascinating record of the development of Buddhist art and architecture over some 1,300 years. The Mauryan Emperor Ashoka was probably the first to build on the site. He erected an inscribed pillar and a stupa—a solid dome of masonry built to encase relics of the Buddha or other Buddhist holy men. In the 2nd century B.C. a stone railing was built around the stupa, along with four elaborately carved gateways depicting scenes from the Buddha's life; a second stupa was also built at this time. Pilgrims walked clockwise around the stupas as an act of veneration.

A.D., the Gupta realm rivaled the Mauryan Empire in its extent. The Guptas were strong patrons of the arts and sciences, and they were also devout Hindus. The period became known as a golden age in India for literature, architecture, astronomy, and mathematics, heralding what has been called a "Hindu renaissance."

▶ Gupta rule expanded from the Ganges Valley across much of northern and eastern India in the 4th century A.D.

☀ **c.100** The Kushan Empire reaches its peak under the Buddhist Kanishka, who promotes the spread of Buddhism throughout Central Asia.

🏛 **320** Chandragupta I, the founder of the Gupta Empire, expands his kingdom from a small heartland on the southern banks of the Ganges River (–335).

🏛 **335** In the course of a 45-year reign Chandragupta's son Samudragupta conquers much of northern and eastern India, bringing the Kushan Empire to an end (–380).

🏛 **380** The Gupta Empire reaches a peak under Chandragupta II, almost rivaling the Mauryan Empire in size (–414).

⚔ **510** The Ephthalite Huns invade the Gupta lands, bringing the empire to an end.

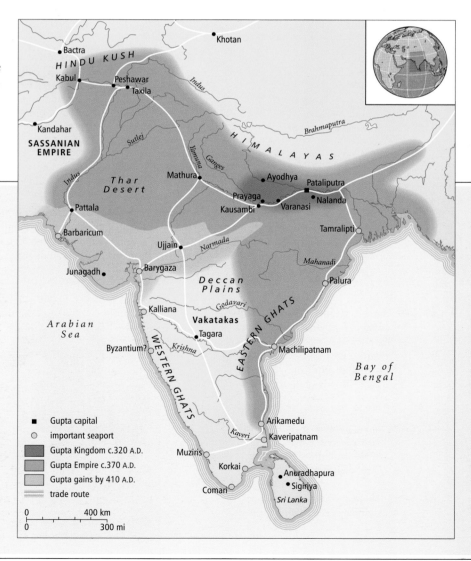

Gupta capital
important seaport
Gupta Kingdom c.320 A.D.
Gupta Empire c.370 A.D.
Gupta gains by 410 A.D.
trade route

0 400 km
0 300 mi

AMERICAS

 c.300 Latest date proposed for the Hohokam Culture's emergence in the American Southwest. Its ball courts and temple mounds show a Mexican influence.

c.300 The city of Teotihuacán is by now the most powerful state in central Mexico.

c.300 In the highlands of South America around what is now the Peru–Bolivia border a new urban center is emerging at Tiahuanaco, on the southern shores of Lake Titicaca.

EUROPE

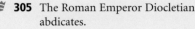

The Emperor Constantine celebrated victory over Maxentius, his rival for imperial power, at the Milvian Bridge in 312 A.D. by ordering the construction of this monumental arch in Rome. The battle also greatly helped the cause of Christianity, since Constantine had reportedly seen a vision of the cross before the fighting started. In the following year he issued the Edict of Milan, confirming religious toleration throughout the Western Roman Empire.

305 The Roman Emperor Diocletian abdicates.

306 The army in Britain proclaims Constantine as Augustus (co-emperor) in the west following the death of his father Constantius.

313 Constantine issues the Edict of Milan granting toleration to Christians in the Western Empire.

324 Constantine becomes sole emperor following the defeat and execution of Licinius, emperor in the east.

AFRICA

305 Donatus, bishop of Casa Negra, teaches that only those without sin belong in the church; his Donatist doctrines will split Africa's Christian community for much of the century.

c.350 The Kingdom of Meroë in Nubia (present-day Sudan) collapses after being conquered by Axum; Nubia splits into three states: Nobatia, Makkura, and Alwa.

c.350 King Ezana of Axum is baptized a Christian; converted by missionary monks from Syria, he is the earliest known Christian in sub-Saharan Africa.

WESTERN ASIA

c.303 The Kingdom of Armenia becomes the first country to adopt Christianity as an official religion.

348 Shapur II, Sassanian ruler of Persia, defeats the Emperor Constantius at Singara, but fails to drive the Romans from Mesopotamia.

c.350 White (Ephthalite) Huns begin raiding across the eastern Persian border.

SOUTH & CENTRAL ASIA

320 In the vacuum left by the collapse of Kushan power Chandragupta I, founder of India's Gupta Dynasty, creates a powerful Hindu kingdom on the Ganges Plain (– 335).

335 The Gupta King Samudragupta, reigning to 380, fights major campaigns in northern and eastern India.

EAST ASIA & OCEANIA

c.300 In Japan the Yamato kings extend their power throughout the island of Honshu; they build large "keyhole" tombs.

 c.300 The stirrup is introduced to China by horse-riding nomads.

Bronze statue of a horseman from Gansu, western China.

c.300 Over the following century northern China fragments into a mosaic of warring states.

313 In Korea the former Han colony of Luolong falls to the powerful northern Korean state of Koguryo.

👑 **c.400** In the eastern woodlands of North America the Hopewell mound-building culture passes its prime as the trade network sustaining it starts to break down.

👑 **330** Constantine founds the city of Constantinople on the Bosporus strait between Europe and Asia.

☀ **361** The Emperor Julian attempts to revive paganism in the Roman Empire (– 363).

✕ **c.372** The Huns, nomadic horsemen from Central Asia, conquer the Ostrogoths of the Black Sea area.

☀ **391** The Emperor Theodosius I officially ends paganism within the Roman Empire.

👑 **395** On the death of Theodosius the empire is permanently divided into eastern and western halves.

👑 **395** Stilicho, a successful Roman general of barbarian origin, becomes virtual ruler of the Western Empire as guardian to Honorius, Theodosius's son, emperor in the west.

✕ **396** The Visigoths, led by Alaric, rampage through the Balkans and Greece (– 398).

Half Vandal by birth, Stilicho was the Western Empire's true ruler in the late 4th century.

Axum was a major African power in the 4th and 5th centuries, dominating the Red Sea trade routes. After its ruler Ezana converted to Christianity, the kingdom became a bastion of the faith famed for its rock-cut churches (*right*). As such, it held out against the Islamic conquests of the 7th century, eventually forming the basis of the Christian Kingdom of Ethiopia.

☀ **391** Christianity is proclaimed the official religion of Egypt. Many temples of the old gods are destroyed.

⊕ **c.400** Iron is produced at Castle Cavern, a site in present-day South Africa.

✕ **363** Constantius's successor, Julian, invades Persia; he is killed in battle, and Shapur II regains control of eastern Mesopotamia.

✕ **c.370** The Huns move westward from the borders of China, encroaching on the Ostrogoths inhabiting the Russian steppes.

☀ **c.350** Dunhuang, an oasis town at the edge of the Gobi Desert on the Silk Road from China to the Mediterranean, becomes a flourishing Buddhist center.

✕ **380** Chandragupta II succeeds Samudragupta. During his 34-year reign he will conquer the Sakas of western India, bringing the Gupta Empire to its peak.

☀ **c.400** Hinduism revives in India under Gupta patronage; there is a flowering of classical Sanskrit literature.

👑 **c.350** Funan (in present-day Cambodia and southern Vietnam) is the most powerful state in Southeast Asia.

✕ **369** According to a later Japanese source, a Yamato army invades southern Korea.

☀ **372** Buddhism reaches the Korean Peninsula.

✕ **386** Toba nomads invade northern China (– 397) and establish a state in Wei on the northern frontier.

☀ **399** A Chinese Buddhist monk, Fa-hsien, travels by foot along the Silk Road from China to India and back (– 413).

AMERICAS

EUROPE

AFRICA

WESTERN ASIA

SOUTH & CENTRAL ASIA

EAST ASIA & OCEANIA

300–400 A.D.

THE SPREAD OF CHRISTIANITY

▲ In this 2nd-century carving the familiar Christian sign of the cross is combined with the *chi-rho* symbol (displayed within the ring), which combines the Greek letters making up the initial characters of Christ's name.

CHRISTIANITY IS THE RELIGION *based on the teachings of Jesus Christ, a charismatic figure who preached and healed the sick in the towns and villages of Palestine, then part of the Roman Empire, in the first third of the 1st century* A.D. *His religious and political views were unacceptable to many of his fellow Jews, as well as to the Romans, and in about 30* A.D. *he was condemned to death and crucified.*

Jesus's followers, the Christians, believed that he was the Messiah, or son of God, who had risen from the dead. They began meeting in small groups to spread his teachings and the news of his resurrection. In the first decades after his death the new religion began to spread outside Palestine. Its first great missionary was Paul of Tarsus, a Roman citizen from a well-to-do Jewish family. Paul traveled throughout the eastern Mediterranean as far as Rome itself to preach the Christian gospel to Jews and non-Jews alike.

The Roman authorities distrusted the early Christians because they refused to submit to the official state religion and to make sacrifices to the Roman gods. In 64 A.D. the Emperor Nero blamed them for starting a fire that destroyed much of the city of Rome, and many Christians were rounded up and executed. It was the first of a series of mass persecutions of Christians carried out by the Roman authorities over the next 250 years. As a result, the early Christians lived and worshiped in secret, adopting clandestine emblems such as the sign of a fish to identify their places of worship to each other. These signs can still be seen carved on the walls of the catacombs, their underground cemeteries, in Rome.

The last great persecution of Christians took place under the Emperor Diocletian in 303. Shortly afterward the Emperor Constantine adopted a policy of toleration throughout the empire. From then on Christianity could be practiced openly, and the faith witnessed a period of rapid growth.

early monastic community up to the 6th century A.D.
capital of Diocletianic diocese
spread of Christianity
Christian communities around 100 A.D.
largely Christian by the 6th century

0   800 km
0   500 mi

* **c.30 A.D.** Jesus is crucified in Jerusalem; Peter, his disciple, brings his followers together in the days after his death.

* **c.46–62** Paul makes four missionary journeys, founding churches in Syria, Asia Minor, Macedonia, and Greece, and visiting Rome.

* **c.49** Jesus's followers hold a council in Jerusalem in which it is decided not to impose Jewish law on non-Jewish Christians.

* **c.60–100** The four Gospels, telling the story of Jesus's life and death, are written down at this time.

* **64** Nero executes Christians after a great fire in Rome; Peter, the first bishop of Rome, is believed to have died in this persecution.

◄ Christiantity spread from its original base on the Mediterranean's eastern shores across the Roman Empire and also into Armenia and Axum (Ethiopia).

Constantine the Great

In 312 Constantine, who had been proclaimed joint emperor in the west in 306, won a crushing victory over his fellow emperor, Maxentius. The battle took place at the Milvian Bridge just outside Rome. In the course of the battle Constantine is reported to have seen a vision of the cross of Jesus in the sky and to have heard the words "In this sign, conquer." The following year Constantine formally recognized Christianity as one of the religions legally permitted within the Western Empire. Thereafter Constantine gave considerable support to Christian communities throughout the empire and ordered churches to be built in many cities. The greatest of them was St. Peter's at Rome (*right*), built on the spot where the apostle of that name was believed to be buried. Constantine was baptized a Christian on his deathbed in 337.

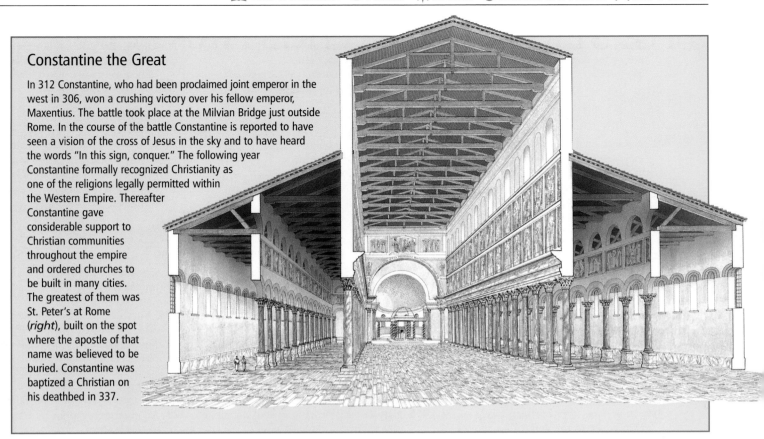

☀ **c.67** Paul is executed in Rome.

☀ **c.95** The Emperor Domitian resumes the persecution of Christians.

☀ **197** Tertullian, a Roman soldier's son converted to Christianity, writes his *Apology*, arguing that Christians can be trusted as good citizens.

☀ **222** All persecution of Christians temporarily ceases under the rule of the Emperor Alexander Severus.

☀ **250** The Emperor Decius renews the persecution of Christians. Fabian, the 20th pope (bishop of Rome), is martyred.

☀ **252** Cyprian, bishop of Carthage in North Africa, holds a council of bishops that reaffirms the pope's position at the head of the Christian Church.

▶ Diocletian, seen here with his three imperial coregents, was a fierce persecutor of the early Christian Church.

☀ **303** The Emperor Diocletian unleashes a violent persecution of Christians across the Roman Empire.

☀ **c.305** St. Anthony founds colonies of hermits in the Egyptian desert.

☀ **312** Constantine adopts the symbol of the cross at the Battle of the Milvian Bridge.

☀ **c.319** The theologian Arius propounds his theory of the Trinity, which argues that God the Son is not equal with God the Father.

☀ **325** Constantine presides over the first General Council of the Church, held at Nicaea, which condemns Arius's views as a heresy.

☀ **405** St. Jerome completes the first Latin translation of the Bible.

☀ **c.430–460** St. Patrick preaches Christianity in Ireland.

☀ **451** The Eastern Emperor Marcian calls the Council of Chalcedon; more than 500 bishops attend.

☀ **c.480** St. Benedict is born at Nursia, near Spoleto in Italy. The Benedictine rule he will devise for his monastery at Monte Cassino, dividing the monk's day into set periods for work and prayer, will become the model for monastic life in western Europe.

400–500 A.D.

AMERICAS

411 According to Mayan inscriptions, Tikal is the dominant Mayan city during the reign of King Stormy Sky (–457).

c.450 With an estimated population of 200,000 people and covering an area of 8 square miles (20 sq. km), Teotihuacán is at the peak of its influence in central Mexico.

c.500 The ceremonial site of Moche, in the Moche Valley of northern Peru, is abandoned after heavy flooding; the associated Moche Culture begins to decline.

EUROPE

402 Ravenna, on the Adriatic coast of Italy, replaces Rome as the capital of the Western Empire.

407 Britain ceases to be part of the Western Empire after the Roman garrison is withdrawn.

408 Stilicho is executed on the orders of the Western Emperor Honorius on trumped-up charges of treason.

410 Alaric leads a Visigoth army to sack Rome.

413 Theodosius II builds a strong defensive wall to protect Constantinople.

c.450 Groups of Anglo-Saxons, originally from northern Germany and Denmark, begin to settle in eastern and southern England.

455 Pope Leo the Great negotiates a peace with the Vandals after they attack Rome.

475 Julius Nepos, the last legitimate western emperor, is driven out of Italy by a palace coup; Romulus Augustulus, a young boy, is made emperor in his place.

476 Romulus Augustulus is deposed by Odoacer, a barbarian general who declares himself king of Italy, thus marking the end of the Roman Empire in the west.

c.480 Boethius, statesman and author of the *Consolations of Philosophy*, one of the most widely read books of the Middle Ages, is born.

AFRICA

c.400 Jenné-Jeno, in present-day Mali, has grown by this date into a city with defensive walls; at the southern end of the caravan routes across the Sahara, it is a flourishing center of trade.

415 Hypatia, a mathematician and philosopher of Alexandria, is murdered by a Christian mob, perhaps on the instructions of Cyril, archbishop of Alexandria, who resented her influence.

429 A Vandal army crosses from Spain to North Africa.

WESTERN ASIA

409 The Sassanian Emperor Yazdigird issues an edict allowing Christians in Persia to worship openly; he later rejects it and authorizes the persecution of Christians once again.

455 The Persians suppress Christianity in Armenia, now a Persian province, and forcibly convert the population to Zoroastrianism, the Persian state religion (–456).

484 The Sassanian ruler Peroz is killed while campaigning in the east against the White (Ephthalite) Huns.

SOUTH & CENTRAL ASIA

c.400 A new group of nomads, the Juan-Juan, now control the oasis towns at the eastern end of the Silk Road.

5th-century Hindu sculpture of the god Vishnu in the form of a boar.

414 The death of Chandragupta II ends further expansion of the Gupta Empire in India.

c.415 From this time on the Guptas' northwest border is increasingly threatened by the Huns.

EAST ASIA & OCEANIA

c.400 Indian traders introduce Hinduism to parts of Southeast Asia.

c.400 Polynesian seafarers settle the Hawaiian Islands.

407 The Juan-Juan repeatedly invade China's northern frontier (to 449), but are repulsed by the Wei state.

427 King Changsu moves the capital of Koguryo (Korea) to Pyongyang.

439 The state of Wei now controls all of northern China.

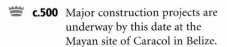
AMERICAS

🌊 **c.500** In the Andes a new state, Huari, emerges to the north of Tiahuanaco, with which it will compete for control of lowland trade.

🌊 **c.500** Major construction projects are underway by this date at the Mayan site of Caracol in Belize.

EUROPE

Founded in 330 A.D. by the Emperor Constantine, Constantinople was built on the site of the existing settlement of Byzantium to serve as the capital of the eastern half of the Roman Empire (which in later years would become the Byzantine Empire). The city grew in size and importance as the Western Empire fell apart, and in 413 Theodosius II ordered the building of new land defenses that almost doubled its size. Recently restored, the Theodosian walls are shown at left.

✕ **486** Clovis, king of the Franks, defeats a Roman general at Soissons and begins the southern expansion of his kingdom.

✕ **489** Theodoric, king of the Ostrogoths, defeats Odoacer and takes control of Italy (–493).

☀ **491** Possible date of Clovis's conversion; he is baptized as a Catholic.

AFRICA

✕ **431** The Vandals capture the Roman town of Hippo after a siege during which St. Augustine, bishop of Hippo and one of the greatest leaders of the early Christian Church, dies.

✕ **439** The Vandals capture Carthage and make it their capital.

✕ **468** A Byzantine fleet, sent to reconquer Africa from the Vandals, is destroyed off Cape Bon, Tunisia.

WESTERN ASIA

🌊 **484** Persia's new ruler, Balas, agrees to pay tribute to the White (Ephthalite) Huns.

☀ **498** Balas's successor Kobad is forced to abdicate the throne because of his support for Mazdak, a Zoroastrian high priest who preaches an extreme form of the religion.

SOUTH & CENTRAL ASIA

✕ **c.460** The Gupta King Skandagupta defeats an invasion of White (Ephthalite) Huns from Central Asia.

☀ **c.500** Rock-cut temples at Ajanta, central India, are painted with religious frescoes at this time.

Buddhist wall painting from Ajanta, India.

EAST ASIA & OCEANIA

☀ **c.450** By this time 90 percent of the population of northern China is Buddhist.

✕ **c.500** The Kingdom of Champa in central Vietnam takes advantage of Chinese weakness to launch crossborder raids.

400–500 CE

THE FALL OF THE ROMAN EMPIRE

IN 476 A.D. A GERMAN GENERAL *named Odoacer overthrew the last Roman emperor in the west, thereby ending nearly 500 years of imperial rule. The collapse of the empire was not sudden or unexpected. The threat to Rome had been building up for years as the weakened Roman army faced increasing pressure from beyond its borders.*

▲ In the late 3rd century A.D. the Emperor Diocletian made a valiant but short-lived attempt to restore the fortunes of the declining empire. This bust of Diocletian comes from Nicomedia in Asia Minor (Turkey), where he established his headquarters.

▶ In the 5th century the Roman Empire's western half fell apart, divided up between invading peoples. Its eastern lands remained mostly intact as the core of the Byzantine Empire, which survived for another 1,000 years.

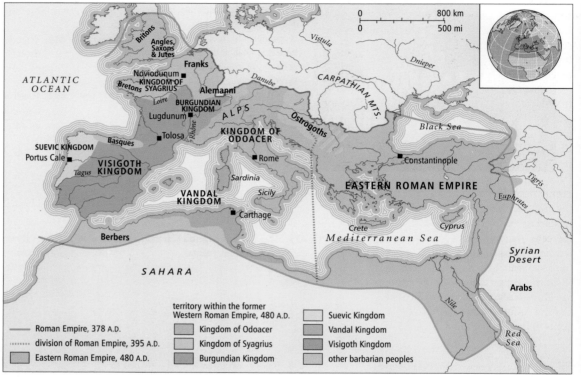

territory within the former Western Roman Empire, 480 A.D.

— Roman Empire, 378 A.D.
⋯⋯ division of Roman Empire, 395 A.D.
▢ Eastern Roman Empire, 480 A.D.

▢ Kingdom of Odoacer
▢ Kingdom of Syagrius
▢ Burgundian Kingdom

▢ Suevic Kingdom
▢ Vandal Kingdom
▢ Visigoth Kingdom
▢ other barbarian peoples

👑 **224 A.D.** Rome loses one foreign rival when the Parthian kingdom comes to an end, only to be confronted by a new one: the Parthians' conquerors, the Sassanian rulers of Persia.

⚔ **231** Emperor Alexander Severus launches a first campaign against the Sassanians.

👑 **235** A chaotic period begins in which power rests with the army; in all, 37 different men are declared emperor over the next 35 years, although many fail to win the supreme office.

⚔ **240** For the first time the empire finds itself attacked on several fronts: in Africa, in Europe, and in Persia.

⚔ **256** The Franks take advantage of the withdrawal of a Roman garrison from Gaul to cross the Rhine frontier into the empire.

👑 **260** The Emperor Valerian is seized by the Sassanian Emperor Shapur while attempting to negotiate a truce. He ends his life in Persian captivity.

⚔ **269** Claudius II wins a great victory over the Goths at the Battle of Naissus, taking the title of Gothicus.

⚔ **c.280** The Romans build a series of strongholds known as the Saxon Shore forts to protect the coasts of Britain and Gaul from pirate raids.

👑 **284** Diocletian comes to power and sets about restoring the authority of the emperors.

👑 **286** Diocletian splits control of the empire with his friend Maximian. He takes control of the eastern half, giving Maximian authority over the west.

👑 **293** Diocletian further subdivides control over the empire, establishing the Tetrarchy (rule of four), under which two separate *augusti* (rulers) share control in each half of the empire.

👑 **324** Constantine reunites the empire under one-man rule.

For centuries past the Romans had traded with the Germanic tribes settled beyond the empire's northern frontier. In the 3rd century, however, relations worsened. German raiders, attracted by the empire's wealth, made frequent attacks across its borders. On the eastern frontier, too, the Romans were under military threat from the Sassanian rulers of Persia.

After a century and a half of stability the Roman emperors now found themselves almost constantly at war. No individual could hope to rule without the support of the army, which was frequently withdrawn. In all, 26 emperors ruled between 235 and 284, reigning on average for less than two years each; all but one died violently. The cost of raising armies and defending the frontiers brought financial ruin.

In 284 Diocletian became emperor. He decided that the empire was too large to be ruled by one man and divided it into eastern and western halves, placing each half in the charge of two *augusti*, or co-emperors. He also doubled the size of the army. As a result of these measures, taxes rose, forcing farmers to leave the land. Famines were frequent, and the population declined, especially in the western half of the empire. A shortage of manpower led the Romans to start recruiting German mercenaries (soldiers fighting for pay) into their armies.

In the late 4th century the Huns burst out of Central Asia to ravage the lands to the west of the Black Sea, establishing a kingdom in Hungary. Their devastating raids

The Huns

The Huns who exploded out of Central Asia into Europe in the 4th and 5th centuries have earned one of the most fearsome reputations in history—their name is still used to invoke extreme savagery. Their war leader Attila was known as "the scourge of God." Under his leadership the Huns swept through the Balkans, defeating the Emperor Theodosius II in three battles and threatening the walls of Constantinople. In 451 the Huns invaded Gaul, but a combined army of Romans and Visigoths defeated them at the Battle of Châlons, and Attila retreated to Hungary. He led one further invasion into Italy, but died in 453. Deprived of his leadership, his empire quickly collapsed.

caused widespread panic among the German tribes, who fled for safety across the Roman frontier. The Romans had no resources to hold back the waves of invaders, and in the course of the next century the Germans carved out kingdoms for themselves in Gaul, Spain, North Africa, and Italy. The eastern half of the Roman Empire clung on to survive for another millennium as the Byzantine Empire, but by 500 A.D. all traces of Roman authority had vanished from western Europe.

▶ Romans gave the name "barbarians" to the tribal peoples who lived beyond their borders and did not share their culture. This mounted Germanic warrior clutching a lance and shield was carved on a tombstone in the 7th century A.D.

👑 **376** The Visigoths seek refuge from the Huns within the Roman Empire; the Emperor Valens allows them to settle on land in the Balkans.

⚔ **378** The Visigoths rebel and kill Valens at the Battle of Adrianople.

⚔ **406** A barbarian army of Vandals, Suevi, and Alans crosses the Rhine and invades deep into Gaul.

⚔ **c.435** The Roman general Aetius uses Hun mercenaries against the Burgundians and other Germanic tribes settled in Gaul.

⚔ **441–451** The Huns invade the empire.

⚔ **451** Aetius defeats Attila's army in Gaul.

⚔ **455** A Vandal army crosses from North Africa to sack Rome.

👑 **476** Odoacer declares himself king of Italy and is recognized by the Eastern Emperor Zeno.

👑 **480** Julius Nepos, the last legitimate western emperor, dies.

👑 **488** Zeno encourages the Ostrogoth leader Theodoric to invade Italy.

👑 **493** Odoacer is murdered, and Italy becomes part of the Kingdom of the Ostrogoths.

THE BYZANTINE EMPIRE

▲ The Emperor Justinian holds a golden bowl in this mosaic from the Church of San Vitale in Ravenna, Italy. Justinian presided over the Byzantine Empire at the time of its greatest expansion. He also codified Roman law and rebuilt Constantinople's great cathedral, St. Sophia.

THE BYZANTINE EMPIRE DEVELOPED *out of the eastern half of the Roman Empire. In the process it became something quite distinct. Although its rulers called themselves "kings of the Romans," oriental influences gradually eroded Roman traditions. Greek ousted Latin as the official language, and Orthodox Christianity replaced Roman Catholicism as the state religion. The emperors also introduced a type of feudal system, granting lands to warriors in return for military service; in so doing, they created a landowning aristocracy (upper class) that came to challenge their own power.*

Byzantium's first great emperor was also the last truly Roman ruler. Justinian I, who came to the throne in 527, spoke Latin, assembled the heritage of Roman law into one body, and attempted to restore imperial rule in the west. Belisarius, his leading general, recovered North Africa from the Vandals and then embarked on a 20-year struggle to drive the Ostrogoths from Italy.

Justinian's gains were short-lived. Soon after his death the Lombards—another "barbarian" people—conquered northern Italy, while Avars, Bulgars, and Slavs depopulated much of the Balkans. Persian armies reached the walls of Constantinople in 609 and again in 625. Locked in a struggle for survival, the empire grew less and less concerned with the west. Greek replaced Latin as the official language of a Chinese-style bureaucracy famed for its secretiveness.

In 627 the Emperor Heraclius inflicted a crushing defeat on the Persians, only to be confronted shortly after by an even more formidable enemy. Arabs inspired by the new religion of Islam seized Palestine, Syria, and Egypt from Byzantine hands. They might have taken Constantinople itself but for the supremacy of the Byzantine navy and its secret weapon, "Greek fire"—an inflammable substance that was pumped over enemy ships.

Wars with the Arabs were partly responsible for a serious rift between the Orthodox ("right-believing") and Roman Catholic churches. In 726 the Emperor Leo III, who attributed the military successes of the Muslims to their strict ban on religious images, ordered the destruction of Byzantine icons—religious pictures and statues. When the news reached the pope in Rome, he denounced the emperor as a heretic. The Iconoclastic ("image-breaking") Controversy raged in Byzantium itself until icons were restored in 843. But by then the gulf between Byzantium and Rome was too wide to be bridged.

♛ **529** Justinian I codifies Roman law. In the same year he closes the Athens Academy founded by Plato.

⚔ **534** In the opening move of a campaign to regain the Western Empire Justinian's leading general, Belisarius, takes North Africa from the Vandals.

♛ **542** Bubonic plague kills up to half the population of Constantinople (−543).

⚔ **568** Lombards invade Italy and occupy most of the country north of the Po River.

⚔ **572** Renewed warfare breaks out between Byzantium and Persia (−591).

Constantinople

Constantinople's position at the confluence of major sea and land trading routes helped make it the largest and most splendid city in Christian Europe. Built on a bluff controlling the seaway between the Black Sea and the Aegean, it included a deepwater harbor in an inlet called the Golden Horn. On the landward side a massive wall built in the 5th century resisted all enemies until 1204. The social hub of the city was the Hippodrome, where the public gathered to watch horse and chariot racing and theatrical performances. Below the Hippodrome palace buildings and classical monuments jostled with magnificent churches, including the 6th-century Hagia (Saint) Sophia (*right*), which remained the largest church in the world until 1547, when Michelangelo raised the dome of St. Peter's in Rome.

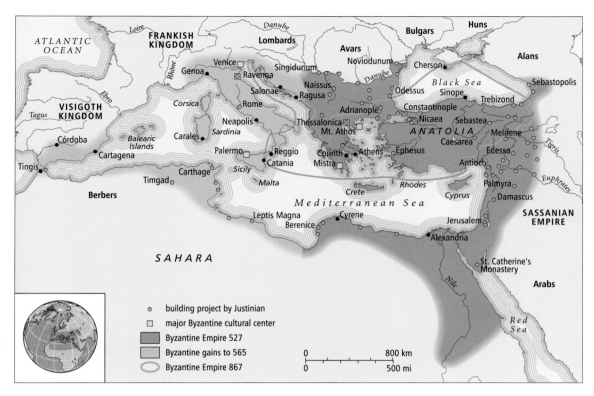

◀ The Byzantine Empire started out as the eastern half of the Roman Empire, which survived the fall of the Western Empire in the 5th century. Under Emperor Justinian and his brilliant general Belisarius the Byzantines managed to temporarily reconquer many of the lost western lands in the course of the 6th century. But the gains were short-lived. Under pressure from the Arabs the empire retrenched, and by the 9th century it was mostly restricted to the area of modern Turkey, Bulgaria, Greece, and the eastern Adriatic seaboard.

Map legend:
- ◎ building project by Justinian
- ☐ major Byzantine cultural center
- Byzantine Empire 527
- Byzantine gains to 565
- Byzantine Empire 867

0　800 km
0　500 mi

In response to the Arab threat the Byzantine rulers organized their territories into military districts called themes, governed by professional soldiers. The new system worked well, and Byzantium enjoyed a golden age under the Macedonian Dynasty founded by Basil I in 867. But the creation of military provinces also laid the foundation for the emergence of great landed families. These newly empowered nobles would jockey for imperial power during the 11th century, at a time when Byzantium faced new threats from Normans in the west and Turks in the east. Even so, the empire survived, although in a shrunken form, until 1453, when its capital Constantinople finally fell to the Ottoman Turks.

⚔ **626** Emperor Heraclius survives a siege of Constantinople by an alliance of Persians, Slavs, and Avars, then (in 627) defeats the Persians decisively at Nineveh, in present-day Iraq.

⚔ **637** Byzantium is seriously weakened by the Arab conquest of Mesopotamia, Syria, and (in 639) Egypt.

⚔ **649** Arab pirates from Spain seize Cyprus from the Byzantines.

🏛 **663** Constans II makes the last visit to Rome by a Byzantine emperor.

⚔ **673** An Arab fleet blockades Constantinople (–678).

⚔ **717** Leo III repulses an Arab army besieging Constantinople and destroys its fleet (–718).

☀ **726** Leo III issues the first decrees banning the worship of icons and other religious images. His iconoclast policies open a rift with Rome and spark a bitter controversy at home that lasts until 843, when holy images are finally restored.

⚔ **860** From their base in Russia Swedish Vikings known as Varangians mount their first attack on Constantinople.

🏛 **867** Basil I, an ex-horsebreaker who murdered his way to the Byzantine throne, establishes the Macedonian Dynasty.

⚔ **880** Basil I reconquers Calabria (in southern Italy) from the Arabs.

📖 **945** After ruling for 30 years in the shadow of his father-in-law, Constantine VII seizes sole power. A guiding spirit of the Byzantine cultural revival, he encourages the compilation of historical writings.

⚔ **961** Byzantines recapture Crete from the Arabs.

🏛 **976** Basil II, known as Bulgaroktonos ("Slayer of the Bulgars"), becomes Byzantine emperor.

🏛 **988** Basil II cements an alliance with Vladimir, prince of Kiev, who marries Basil's sister and converts to Orthodox Christianity.

🏛 **1453** The Byzantine Empire comes to an end when Constantinople falls to the Ottoman Turks.

AMERICAS

⊛ **c.500** By this date North American hunters on the Great Plains are using the bow and arrow.

⊛ **c.500** Ceramics in vivid colors are produced in many parts of Costa Rica and Panama.

♛ **c.500** Growing rich on the breeding of llamas and alpacas, the city of Tiahuanaco, to the south of Lake Titicaca in the Bolivian Andes, has by now spread its influence widely across the central Andes.

EUROPE

St. Benedict, shown in this 13th-century painting with his disciple St. Maur, has been called the father of Christian monasticism. His Rule, dividing the day into separate periods for work, study, and prayer, was hugely influential not just for his own Benedictine Order but also for all subsequent orders of monks. The son of a nobleman, Benedict put his precepts into practice at the monastery he founded at Monte Cassino, Italy.

⚔ **507** Alaric II, king of the Visigoths in Gaul, is killed in battle near Poitiers by the Frankish King Clovis.

♛ **511** Clovis, king of the Franks since 481, dies, and his realm is divided among his four sons, with courts at Paris, Metz, Soissons, and Orléans.

☀ **515** St. Benedict (c.480–547), the Italian founder of Western monasticism, composes his *Regula Monachorum* ("Monks' Rule"), which becomes the rule for monastic life in the west.

AFRICA

⊛ **c.500** In South Africa's Transvaal seven fired earthenware heads are carefully buried—the most impressive works of Iron Age art yet discovered in southern Africa.

⚔ **c.523** Caleb, ruler of the Kingdom of Axum (Ethiopia), conquers the Yemen.

⊛ **c.525** Cosmas Indicopleustes (meaning "Indian traveler"), a merchant of Alexandria, travels up the Nile to Ethiopia.

WESTERN ASIA

☀ **c.500** The Nestorians, a Christian sect that separated from the Orthodox Church in 431, settle in eastern Mesopotamia (Iraq).

⚔ **502** War breaks out between the Sassanian rulers of Persia and the Byzantine Empire. Neither side gains a clear advantage (–505).

⚔ **524** The Sassanians renew the war against the Byzantines, again with indecisive results (–531).

SOUTH & CENTRAL ASIA

⚔ **c.500** Toromana, a Hun leader, seizes the Punjab from India's Guptas.

♛ **c.500** The Buddhist trading state of Srivijaya emerges in Sumatra, modern Indonesia.

☀ **510** Suttee, a Hindu rite in which a widow dies on her husband's funeral pyre, is first recorded.

Carved wooden figures of musicians dating from the Gupta period in India.

EAST ASIA & OCEANIA

♛ **502** Xiao Yan founds China's Liang Dynasty after forcing Qi rulers to submit to his authority.

☀ **517** The Emperor Wu Ti becomes a Buddhist and introduces the new religion to central China.

☀ **523** The oldest known pagoda is built in China. Constructed in brick, it is a towerlike structure derived from the Buddhist stupa of India.

☀ **528** The Korean state of Silla adopts Buddhism; it is the last of the three kingdoms into which the Korean peninsula is divided to do so.

AMERICAS

🏛 **c.504** Waterlily Jaguar, ruler of the southeastern Maya city of Copán, begins a major expansion of the city's ceremonial center, the Acropolis..

🏛 **534** A mysterious lull sets in at Tikal, one of the main lowland Maya centers in Guatemala. Until 593 few monuments are erected.

🏛 **537** A dated Maya inscription records that Double Bird is the 21st ruler of Tikal.

EUROPE

📖 **523** The Roman philosopher Boethius (c.480–524) writes his *De Consolatione Philosophiae* (The Consolations of Philosophy), which for the next millennium is one of the most widely read books after the Bible.

☀ **529** St. Benedict founds the monastery of Monte Cassino near Naples in Italy and establishes the Benedictine monastic order.

🏛 **529** Justinian I (c.482–565), emperor of the Eastern Roman Empire, publishes his *Code of Civil Laws*, a work that will influence the law of most European countries down to modern times.

⚔ **535** The Byzantine general Belisarius invades Italy.

⚔ **c.537** Arthur, semilegendary king of the Britons, is killed in battle fighting Saxon invaders of Britain.

☀ **538** The church of St. Sophia in Constantinople, the first building with a large domed roof, is consecrated. It will remain the largest church in the Christian world until the 16th century.

⊕ **542** Bubonic plague, imported from Constantinople, ravages Europe for two years. Three further epidemics follow before the century's end.

☀ **c.550** St. David starts the conversion of Wales to Christianity.

AFRICA

⚔ **534** The Byzantine general Belisarius overthrows the Vandal kingdom in North Africa and makes it a Byzantine province.

☀ **536** Justinian orders the closure of the temple of Philae on the Nile River, marking the official end of the cult of the ancient Egyptian gods.

WESTERN ASIA

🏛 **531** Khusrow I (died 579) becomes ruler of the Sassanian Empire. Under his rule the empire reaches its greatest height.

🏛 **533** Khusrow concludes the Endless Peace with the Byzantines. In fact, war breaks out again between the two powers just seven years later.

⚔ **540** Khusrow's Sassanian army sacks the Byzantine city of Antioch on the Syrian coast.

SOUTH & CENTRAL ASIA

⊕ **c.520** Aryabhata, Hindu astronomer and mathematician (476–c.550), compiles a manual of astronomy. Aryabhata correctly states that the Earth rotates on its axis.

⚔ **c.530** Yasodharman, a legendary hero from central India, is credited with repelling the invading Huns.

⊕ **c.550** The game of chess originates in the Indus Valley in India.

EAST ASIA & OCEANIA

⊕ **534** The Koreans introduce Chinese mathematics into Japan.

⚔ **547** The Chinese crush a Vietnamese revolt led by Li-bon.

The tapering, multistoried buildings known as pagodas, usually associated with a temple complex, became East Asia's most distinctive form of religious architecture. Their shape derived from India's stupas—dome-shaped sanctuaries built to house Buddhist relics. The brick-built Pagoda of Songshan (*right*) is the oldest in China; it stands over 130 feet (40 m) high.

500–550 A.D.

THE FRANKISH KINGDOM

AS THE WESTERN ROMAN EMPIRE COLLAPSED, *barbarian warlords fought each other for land and power in the territories it had once ruled. The most enduringly successful was Clovis, king of the Franks from 481 to 511, who created a realm that extended from modern Belgium to the Mediterranean Sea. By the mid-6th century his successors ruled a kingdom roughly equivalent to modern France, Switzerland, and part of western Germany.*

The early Frankish kings belonged to the Merovingian Dynasty, named for an ancestor called Meroweg. The Frankish churchman Gregory of Tours (c.538–594), who wrote the first history of the Merovingian kings, reported that they were known as "the long-haired kings" because they grew their hair over their shoulders. At the time long hair and beards were considered the mark of a barbarian; the Romanized citizens of Gaul were clean-shaven and wore their hair cropped. While the Merovingians clung to this link with their barbarian past, they were also ready to accommodate the customs of their Gallic subjects. Thus in 491 Clovis was baptized as a Catholic. His was probably a political rather than a religious conversion—to rule his new lands effectively, he needed to have the church on his side, since bishops played an important role in local administration.

▲ As this silver filigree earring suggests, a modest trade in luxury items survived in Frankish times, even though the great trade networks of the Roman era had been disrupted.

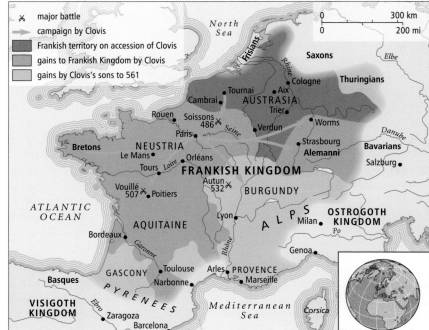

Map legend:
- ✕ major battle
- → campaign by Clovis
- Frankish territory on accession of Clovis
- gains to Frankish Kingdom by Clovis
- gains by Clovis's sons to 561

Map labels: North Sea, Frisians, Saxons, Elbe, Cologne, Thuringians, Rhine, Tournai, Aix, AUSTRASIA, Cambrai, Trier, Rouen, Soissons 486 ✕, Seine, Verdun, Worms, Danube, Paris, Strasbourg, Bavarians, Bretons, NEUSTRIA, Alemanni, Le Mans, Orléans, Salzburg, Tours, Loire, FRANKISH KINGDOM, Autun 532 ✕, Vouillé 507 ✕, Poitiers, BURGUNDY, ATLANTIC OCEAN, AQUITAINE, Lyon, ALPS, Milan, OSTROGOTH KINGDOM, Po, Bordeaux, Garonne, Rhône, Genoa, GASCONY, Toulouse, Arles, PROVENCE, Basques, Narbonne, Marseille, PYRENEES, Mediterranean Sea, Corsica, VISIGOTH KINGDOM, Ebro, Zaragoza, Barcelona

0 — 300 km / 0 — 200 mi

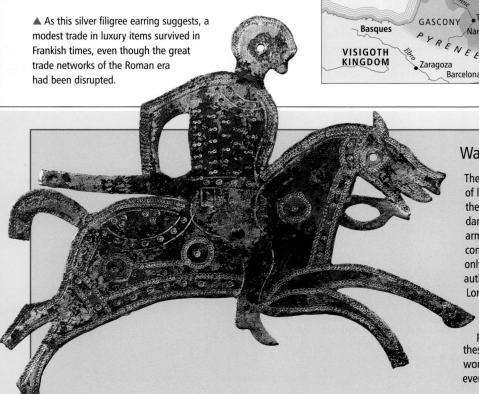

Warrior Kings

The collapse of the Roman Empire saw an end to the rule of law in Europe. Local kings tried to keep order as best they could, but for the majority of people life was more dangerous and uncertain than it had been when Roman armies guaranteed their security. Barbarian kings struggled constantly with rival monarchs and remained in power only for as long as they could win battles. To bolster their authority, they maintained groups of fighting men (like the Lombard cavalryman shown at left) in their households at their own expense. The soldiers had to be ready to do battle at any time and were given a share of any plunder that was looted while on campaign. It was from these household soldiers—known in the Anglo-Saxon world as housecarls—that the knights of medieval Europe eventually developed.

When Clovis died in his new capital of Paris in 511, his kingdom was divided between his four sons in accordance with Frankish tribal law. For most of the next 200 years the Frankish lands were separated into distinct kingdoms and were only rarely united under a single king. Rival heirs were constantly at war with one another, and assassinations were frequent. Real power passed from these *rois faineants* ("do-nothing kings") to the stewards of the royal household, known as "mayors of the palace."

By the mid-7th century the mayors of the palace were drawn exclusively from the Carolingian family (their name derives from Carolus, the Latin form of Charles). Outstanding among the Carolingian mayors was Charles Martel ("the Hammer"), who earned his nickname after defeating an Arab army near Tours in 732—a crucial victory that stemmed the advance of the forces of Islam into Christian Europe. Charles Martel actively promoted the mission of St. Boniface to convert the Germans to Christianity and was a great supporter of the church. He was succeeded by his son Pepin the Short. In 751 Pepin obtained permission from the Pope to depose the reigning Merovingian king, Childeric III, and contrived that an assembly of Frankish nobles should elect him king instead as the first ruler of a new Carolingian line.

◀ The Frankish Kingdom was largely the creation of Clovis, greatest of the Merovingian kings. Striking south from a homeland near the Rhine River, he conquered much of central and eastern France. Clovis made Paris his capital shortly before his death in 511.

▶ A medieval manuscript illustration shows Charles Martel confronting an Arab army at the Battle of Tours, just 100 miles (160 km) southwest of Paris. Charles's victory after six days of fighting stemmed the Arab advance into northern Europe.

🏛 **481** Clovis becomes king of the Franks, whose territory consists at the time of an area in present-day Belgium.

✕ **486** Clovis defeats Syragius, the last Roman general in Gaul, at Soissons in northern France.

✕ **507** Clovis drives the Visigoths from Aquitaine (southwest France).

🏛 **511** Clovis dies in his new capital of Paris; his kingdom is divided among his four sons.

🏛 **536** Burgundy (eastern France and Switzerland) becomes part of the Frankish Kingdom.

🏛 **537** The Franks win control of Provence (southeastern France).

🏛 **613** Lothair II reunites the Frankish Kingdom.

🏛 **638** Dagobert I, last of the great Merovingian kings, dies. He is succeeded by a series of short-lived kings in whose reigns power passes to the "mayors of the palace."

✕ **687** Pepin of Héristal, the Carolingian mayor of the palace, unites all the Frankish territories at the Battle of Tertry.

✕ **689** Pepin begins the conquest of the Frisians (present-day Netherlands).

🏛 **714** Charles Martel succeeds his father Pepin as mayor of the palace and effective ruler of the Franks.

✕ **732** Charles Martel wins a decisive victory over an Arab army at Tours in central France.

🏛 **741** Charles Martel dies and is succeeded by his son Pepin.

🏛 **754** Pepin is crowned by the pope in a ceremony at Reims, northern France, that formally affirms the Carolingian Dynasty as kings of the Franks.

550–600 A.D.

AMERICAS

556 The Mayan states of Caracol and Tikal go to war; Caracol finally wins the conflict in 562.

c.585 Some Early Classic Maya sites in the Petén lowlands of Guatemala are destroyed, perhaps as the result of drought.

c.600 The Huari Empire begins to expand north in the Andean highlands of southern Peru and west across the coastal plain.

EUROPE

c.550 The Slavs, farming peoples probably from present-day Belarus and Ukraine, migrate south across the Danube River.

552 A Byzantine army led by Narses expels the Ostrogoths from all of Italy south of the Po River (–554).

554 The armies of the Byzantine Emperor Justinian reconquer southern Spain from the Visigoths.

Crown of the Lombard King Agiluf

AFRICA

c.550 The Byzantine Empress Theodora sends missionaries to seek converts in North Africa.

c.550 The African Kingdom of Axum struggles with Sassanian Persia for control of Arabia (–574).

570 A Christian army from Axum attacks Mecca but is driven back.

WESTERN ASIA

554 The Sassanian rulers of Persia defeat the Ephthalite Huns, driving them beyond the Oxus (Amu Darya) River.

562 The Treaty of Edessa establishes temporary peace between the Byzantines and Sassanians. The Sassanians abandon claims to the Black Sea region in return for an annual payment of 30,000 gold pieces.

c.570 The Prophet Muhammad, founder of Islam, is born in Mecca into a merchant family.

572 The Byzantine Emperor Justin renews the war against the Sassanians.

SOUTH & CENTRAL ASIA

c.550 The Gurjaras establish a dynasty in northwest India.

553 The Juan-Juan—the confederation of Mongol tribes controlling the Silk Road—are overthrown by their Turkish subjects. One group, the Avars, migrates to eastern Europe.

572 The Turks establish a khanate (state) in Central Asia, which almost immediately splits into eastern and western divisions.

EAST ASIA & OCEANIA

c.550 The Kingdom of Chenla overthrows Funan in modern Cambodia and Thailand.

552 Buddhism is introduced to Japan.

557 The Northern Zhou Dynasty extends its power into the western and eastern parts of Wei, reuniting northern China (–577).

Silla was the easternmost of the three kingdoms set up in Korea in the mid-1st millennium A.D., when Chinese power in the peninsula came to an end. Thriving through its position on the China–Japan trade routes, it survived to the 10th century. The burial mounds of its kings can still be seen in their former capital of Kyongju (*left*).

High in the Peruvian Andes, the city of Huari housed perhaps 70,000 people, among them the potter who shaped this ceramic drinking vessel. From about the year 600 on, its people embarked on a series of successful military campaigns, building an empire that survived until the 9th century.

AMERICAS

EUROPE

✗ **559** The Byzantine general Belisarius defeats an army of Slavs and Huns at the gates of Constantinople.

✗ **c.560** A new wave of nomads, the Avars, enter eastern Europe from Central Asia; the Byzantines hire them to wipe out the last of the Huns.

☀ **563** St. Columba, an Irish monk, founds a monastery on the island of Iona off the Scottish west coast.

✗ **568** The Lombards, a Germanic people formerly allied to the Romans, invade northern Italy (–582) but fail to take control of Rome and Ravenna; they make their capital at Pavia.

✗ **571** The Visigoths recapture Córdoba in southern Spain.

✗ **c.580** The Avars overrun the Balkans and threaten the Byzantine Empire.

☀ **590** Gregory I (the Great) is elected pope.

📖 **591** Gregory of Tours completes *The History of the Franks*.

✗ **592** The Byzantine Emperor Maurice campaigns against the Avars in the Balkans (–602).

☀ **597** Pope Gregory I sends St. Augustine at the head of a mission to Britain to convert the Anglo-Saxons.

AFRICA

☀ **c.570** The Nubian Kingdom of Makurra (in today's Sudan) is converted to Christianity.

☀ **c.580** The missionary Longinus similarly converts Makurra's neighbor, the Kingdom of Alwa.

WESTERN ASIA

✗ **574** Having ravaged Syria, Khusrow I of Persia drives the Axumites out of Yemen in southern Arabia and joins it to the Sassanian Empire.

👑 **579** Death of Khusrow I; he is succeeded by Hormazd I.

✗ **589** The Sassanian general Bahram invades Colchis on the Black Sea but is defeated by a Byzantine army near the Araxes River.

✗ **589** Hormazd is murdered. His son Khusrow II succeeds him.

👑 **590–591** Bahram overthrows Khusrow II of Persia, who is later restored with the help of the Byzantine Emperor Maurice. Bahram takes refuge with the Turks but is murdered by them.

SOUTH & CENTRAL ASIA

👑 **c.575** In India the Pallava warrior dynasty extends its control of the southern Deccan as far as the Kaveri River.

✗ **c.590** The western Turks threaten the frontiers of the Persian Empire.

⊛ **c.600** Indian mathematicians have developed the decimal point and the concept of zero by this date.

EAST ASIA & OCEANIA

✗ **562** The state of Silla expels the Japanese from Korea.

✗ **581** Yang Jian overthrows the Northern Zhou Dynasty and founds the Sui Dynasty; he rules as Sui Wendi.

👑 **589** Sui Wendi reunifies China.

👑 **593** In Japan Prince Shotoku adopts Chinese models of government; he introduces Chinese craftsmen to the Japanese court (–622).

👑 **c.600** A Thai kingdom is established in Yunnan (southern China).

Chinese sculptures of two Sui Dynasty officials.

550–600 A.D.

TEOTIHUACÁN

IN THE MID-1ST MILLENNIUM A.D. *a city the size of early imperial Rome flourished in the highlands of central Mexico. Its population of perhaps 200,000 people made it one of the world's largest metropolises at the time. Yet its inhabitants knew neither iron- nor bronzeworking and had no writing. As a result, even the city's name has not been recorded. Today it is known by the title given to it by later peoples, who marveled at its ruins more than 500 years after its final destruction by fire. They called it Teotihuacán, "place of the gods."*

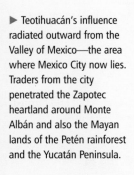

▲ Lying about 30 miles (50 km) north of modern Mexico City, Teotihuacán was the biggest city in the Americas in its day. This stone head decorated the Pyramid of the Feathered Serpent, a shrine built over the graves of at least 137 individuals, many of whom are thought to have been offered as sacrificial victims at its dedication.

The Valley of Mexico is a 3,000-square-mile (8,000-sq.-km) basin 5,000 feet (1,500 m) up in the mountains of central Mexico. Despite its temperate highland climate, well suited for the growing of maize (corn), the valley had been a cultural backwater until the final centuries B.C. Then, suddenly, its population started to grow.

One reason may have been improved agricultural techniques: The local peasants began terracing their fields and digging irrigation canals. Another was the discovery of one of Central America's best deposits of obsidian nearby. This volcanic glass can be flaked to produce a razor-sharp edge, making it invaluable for the manufacture of tools and weapons among people who, like the Teotihuacans, had no iron.

In time a town grew up that by the year 100 A.D. already housed perhaps 60,000 people. Unusually for the time, it was laid out on a grid pattern, with a dead-straight central thoroughfare that was lined with plazas, palaces, and monuments. The greatest of them were two towering pyramids, known to later peoples as the Pyramid of the Sun (see box) and the Pyramid of the Moon.

Beyond the main axis residential quarters spread out across the plain. Archaeological excavations have shown that the city's ruling class lived in spacious villas with painted walls built around central courtyards. Most citizens, however, inhabited single-story apartment complexes, each the size of a city block, divided into warrens of rooms often no bigger

▶ Teotihuacán's influence radiated outward from the Valley of Mexico—the area where Mexico City now lies. Traders from the city penetrated the Zapotec heartland around Monte Albán and also the Mayan lands of the Petén rainforest and the Yucatán Peninsula.

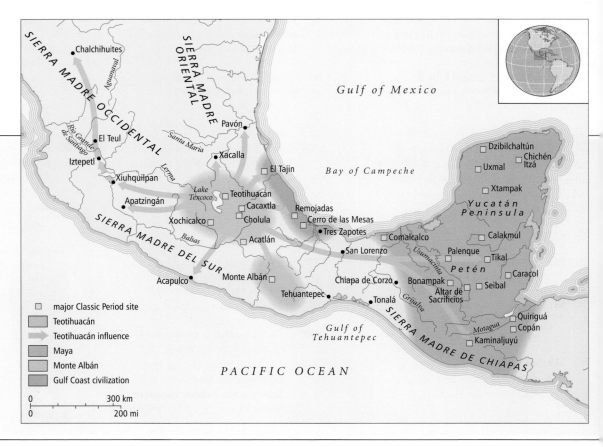

major Classic Period site
Teotihuacán
Teotihuacán influence
Maya
Monte Albán
Gulf Coast civilization

0   300 km
0   200 mi

The Pyramid of the Sun

The Pyramid of the Sun was the largest of Teotihuacán's monuments; at 738 feet (225 m) square, its base was almost as big as that of Egypt's Great Pyramid, although it stood less than half as high. In its final form it rose in four steps to a flat summit, where a shrine once stood. The tradition that the pyramid was dedicated to the sun dates from Aztec times; in reality, no one knows for sure what was worshiped there. A clue to its original purpose, however, turned up in 1971, when archaeologists discovered a tunnel leading into its depths. At its end was a cave artificially enlarged into the shape of a clover leaf. Scholars have speculated that it represented a "Place of Emergence"—a cave of a type familiar in Central American mythology, from which tribal ancestors were believed to have emerged in the distant past.

than closets. The residents supported themselves by agriculture, cultivating crops on small parcels in the surrounding countryside, and by industry that capitalized on local materials: There were more than 400 obsidian workshops in the city as well as over 200 potteries. Trade was also important, for merchants carried the goods produced in Teotihuacán's workshops all over Mexico.

By 450 A.D. Teotihuacán was at its peak. Then, around 650, disaster struck. For unknown reasons the temples and monuments at its heart were put to the torch, and in the ensuing decades the city's population collapsed, leaving nothing but ruins. Historians speculate that the metropolis may have foundered as a result of its own success; the burgeoning population may have exhausted the wood and other resources of the surrounding area. But whether the final destruction was accomplished by outside invaders or by Teotihuacán's own restive citizens remains a mystery.

Teotihuacán's builders did not date their monuments as the Maya of southern Mexico and Guatemala did, so all dates for its history can only be approximate.

👑 **c.0 A.D.** Teotihuacán starts to emerge as an important urban center in the Valley of Mexico.

👑 **c.100** By this date the city already covers more than 2 square miles (5 sq. km).

☀ **c.150** Work gets under way on the Pyramid of the Sun, the city's largest building and one of the biggest in the Americas.

👑 **c.250** By this time Teotihuacán has developed into a major metropolis, laid out on a grid pattern with residential blocks surrounding an avenue of palaces and temples.

👑 **c.300** The city of Teotihuacán is by now the hub of the most powerful state in central Mexico.

👑 **c.400** A Zapotec quarter develops in the city, inhabited by traders and craftsmen who produce pottery and utensils in the Zapotec style, use Zapotec characters for writing, and bury their dead in the manner favored at the Zapotec capital of Monte Albán.

👑 **c.450** Teotihuacán is at the peak of its influence and power; it has an estimated population of 200,000 people and covers an area of 8 square miles (20 sq. km).

⚔ **c.650** Teotihuacán is sacked and burned by unknown assailants.

👑 **c.700** Cholula takes Teotihuacán's place as the major urban center in the Valley of Mexico. Its central pyramid will in time rival the Pyramid of the Sun in size.

AMERICAS

c.600 Perhaps on account of an El Niño-influenced drought, the Moche people forsake their settlements on Peru's coastal plain, founding a new capital farther to the north.

c.600 The Tiahuanaco civilization, based around Lake Titicaca in the Andean altiplano (high plateau), is at its peak. Its prosperity is built on irrigated agriculture, copperworking, and trade.

c.600 In the American Southwest the Anasazi—successors of the earlier Basketmaker Culture—begin the transition from small, sunken pithouses to aboveground, multiroomed pueblos.

EUROPE

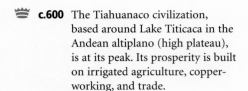

After the collapse of city life following the withdrawal of Roman troops in 407, England gradually returned to some kind of order in the 7th century. The land was no longer united, as it had been under the Romans; now it was divided into half a dozen separate kingdoms ruled by Anglo-Saxon kings (one such is shown with his council at left). The native people mostly integrated with the settlers, although Celtic groups held out in the southwest and in Wales.

602 The Byzantine army commander Phokas becomes emperor in what amounts to a military coup.

610 With Byzantium weakened by war with Sassanian Persia, Heraclius, governor of Carthage, displaces Phokas as emperor.

AFRICA

c.600 In West Africa the Kingdom of Ghana emerges to the north of modern-day Ghana.

c.600 As climate change increases aridity, the Sahara spreads slowly south.

WESTERN ASIA

614 Jerusalem falls into Sassanian hands. The "True Cross" of Jesus is seized and carried off to Persia.

620 Khusrow II is captured and executed by the Byzantine Emperor Heraclius, heralding the decline of Persia's Sassanian Dynasty.

c.620 The Turkic Khazars establish an empire in the northern Caucasus.

622 The year of the *hijra*, or Hejira—the flight of Muhammad and his followers from Mecca to Medina.

627 Byzantine armies defeat the Sassanians at Nineveh, Iraq.

629 Heraclius retakes Egypt, Syria, and Palestine for Byzantium but almost immediately faces a new threat from the forces of Islam.

632 The Prophet Muhammad dies. His succession by Abu Bakr stores up trouble for the future.

633 Arab forces invade Sassanian territories.

635 The Arabs take Damascus from the Byzantines.

636 Byzantine forces are decisively defeated by the Arabs at the Battle of Yarmuk in Jordan.

637 Arab forces smash Sassanian power for good at the Battle of Qadisiya, following which the dynasty's capital at Ctesiphon (Iraq) quickly falls.

638 The Arabs take Jerusalem.

SOUTH & CENTRAL ASIA

606 The "Age of Small Kingdoms" comes to an end with the accession of Harshavardhana; over the next four decades he will build an impressive Buddhist empire in north and east India.

608 Pulakesin II, greatest ruler of the Chalukya Dynasty, comes to the throne (−642). Much of south India will eventually be united under Chalukya rule.

7th-century Tibetan Buddhist decoration.

EAST ASIA & OCEANIA

c.600 The Champa civilization comes of age in central Vietnam, its kings promoting Hindu religion and a highly Indianized culture.

605 A four-year program begins in China to build the 1,200-mile (2,000-km) Grand Canal.

612 The first inscription in the Khmer language at Angkor in Cambodia dates from this year.

✳ **c.600** Long past its prime, the Hopewell Culture of the American Midwest fades further as communities are drawn south by the attractions of a corn-based agricultural lifestyle.

👑 **c.615** Classic Mayan civilization reaches a peak in Palenque with the accession of 12-year-old King Pacal ("Shield"). His 68-year reign will see the city become one of Mesoamerica's finest.

👑 **c.640** The Mayan city-states of Dos Pilas and Aguateca are founded by Ruler 1, a member of Tikal's ruling family.

⚔ **c.615** By now the Anglo-Saxon conquest of England is largely complete.

👑 **623** The Frankish merchant Samo brings Slavic Czechs and Slovaks together to fight the Avars. The union breaks up after his death in 659.

⚔ **626** Constantinople resists a siege by the Avars, Slavs, and Persians.

👑 **c.630** East Anglia emerges as foremost in the heptarchy (literally "rule of seven") of Anglo-Saxon kingdoms of England. The others are Kent, Wessex, Essex, Sussex, Mercia, and Northumbria.

☀ **635** St. Aidan founds a monastery on Lindisfarne, off the coast of Northumbria.

👑 **641** Heraclius dies, leaving the Byzantine Empire beset by barbarian tribes from the north and west, Arabs from the south, and Persians from the east.

👑 **c.600** The Zhagawa people settle by Lake Chad; their descendants will found the Kanem Kingdom there.

👑 **c.600** Axum goes into steady decline, Persian conquests having disrupted its trade routes.

⚔ **639** Arab armies conquer Egypt (–642).

⚔ **643** Arab victory at Nehavend, in the Zagros Mountains, effectively ends Sassanian resistance in Iran.

👑 **645** The Umayyad caliphs establish their capital in Damascus.

⚔ **649** The Arabs take the Sassanian city of Istakhr, massacring its inhabitants, and desecrate the ruins of the ancient Achaemenid capital of Persepolis nearby.

The Sassanian Dynasty, one of whose kings is shown hunting boar at left, ruled Persia for more than 400 years after overthrowing the Parthian Empire in 224 A.D. In that time its rulers revived much of the glory of the Old Persian Empire of Cyrus the Great. However, ongoing warfare with their Byzantine neighbors sapped their resources, and they quickly fell victim to the forces of the new faith of Islam in the decade after 633.

👑 **c.609** King Songtsen Gampo comes to power in Tibet. His reign will see the introduction of Buddhism to the country and its establishment as the official state religion.

⚔ **620** Pulakesin II's forces stem the southward expansion of Harshavardhana's empire.

⚔ **632** Pulakesin is defeated by the Pallava King Narasimha Varman.

📖 **646** Chinese monk Xuanzang publishes his *Records of the Western World*, an account of a trip to India.

👑 **647** Harshavardhana dies heirless, and his empire dies with him.

👑 **618** Usurping his Sui cousin, Li Yuan seizes power in China, founding the Tang Dynasty and ruling under the name of Gaozu.

👑 **626** Li Yuan's son takes power as the Emperor Taizong. The key achievement of his 23-year rule will be the quelling of nomadic tribes to the north and the opening up of trade routes to western Asia.

👑 **646** A series of measures taken by the Japanese Emperor Kotoku, the Taika or "Great Change" represents a concerted attempt to remodel Japanese society along Chinese lines.

AMERICAS

EUROPE

AFRICA

WESTERN ASIA

SOUTH & CENTRAL ASIA

EAST ASIA & OCEANIA

600–650 A.D.

MUHAMMAD AND ISLAM

▲ Shown here in a 19th-century woodcut, Muhammad was both a visionary prophet and a charismatic leader. In 627 he confirmed his authority by defending his adopted home city of Medina against rivals from Mecca in a two-week struggle known as the Battle of the Ditch.

FOR CENTURIES THE ARABIAN PENINSULA *seemed to be a backwater, its inhabitants all but forgotten by the rest of humanity. Wild horsemen and camel drivers, the Arabs emerged from the depths of the desert only on occasional raids against outlying settlements before returning to the desert from which they came. One man, Muhammad, would change all that, giving his people first a spiritual and then a military mission. By the end of the 7th century the Arabs had made themselves the masters of vast territories and carried the Muslim message through much of the world.*

"The distant Arabs dwelling in the desert … know neither overseers nor officials." This was the disdainful view of Sargon II of Assyria around 700 B.C. No anthropologist, the emperor overlooked the perfection with which the Arabs' lifestyle as nomadic camel herders was adapted to one of the world's most hostile environments. Yet it was true that they lived a marginal existence, far beyond the reach of what was generally recognized as civilization. A thousand years later it was still the same. To the east the Iran-based empire of the Sassanians flourished, to the north were the Greco-Roman realms of Byzantium, but the Arabs stood apart, as though history had passed them by.

All this would change, however, when in 610 a middle-aged businessman in the city of Mecca started seeing visions. In the years that followed, the Angel Gabriel appeared to Muhammad again and again,

dictating to him the word of Allah—God. The name for the new religion, Islam, meant "surrender" to the divine will: It resembled Judaism and Christianity in many respects, notably its monotheism—worship of a single deity.

Inspired by religious zeal and a message of charity for the poor, Muhammad and his followers could not help but find themselves at odds with the Quraysh, Mecca's wealthy elite. In 622 they left for the neighboring city of Medina. Relations with Medina's three tribes of Jews were good at first, although as hostilities with Mecca escalated, they deteriorated, the Muslims fearing that the Jews might make alliance with their Arab enemies.

In time the Muslims gained control of Mecca, and their victory marked the start of one of the most amazing campaigns of conquest the world has ever

The Kaaba

Mecca had been a holy place for Arabs long before Muhammad was born. For centuries they had flocked to the city to venerate the Kaaba, a shrine enclosing a sacred black stone fallen from heaven—in scientific terms a meteorite. Muhammad's falling out with the city's rulers owed much to his indignation at the way in which they exploited the pilgrims who came to worship there. Yet, radical as he was in rejecting paganism, Muhammad was also a traditionalist, and he made the Kaaba the object of a specifically Islamic pilgrimage. To this day all Muslims are expected at some stage in their lifetime to make the *hajj*—the journey to Mecca to walk around the Kaaba—and each summer crowds fill the vast shrine that now surrounds it (*right*).

☀ **c.570** Birth of the Prophet Muhammad in Mecca, Arabia.

☀ **c.610** Muhammad's divine mission begins with the first appearance to him of the Archangel Gabriel.

☀ **622** The *hijra*, or "emigration": Muhammad and his followers leave Mecca for the city of Yathrib, since known as Medina, "city of the Prophet," in his honor. The *hijra* marks the start of the Muslim calendar; all dates are calculated from this year.

✕ **624** Muslims defeat the Meccans at the Battle of Badr.

✕ **625** Muhammad's forces suffer a setback when they are defeated at Uhud.

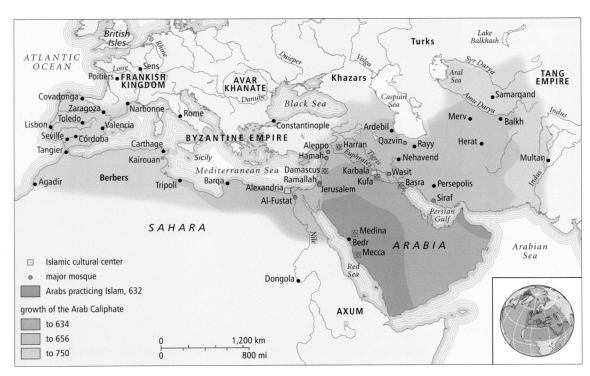

◀ From a heartland near the Red Sea Islam first spread over the Arabian Peninsula, then the Near East and Persia. By 750 Muslims ruled lands stretching from the Indus River to Spain. However, the Byzantine Empire succeeded in checking Islam's progress along the Mediterranean's northern shores.

Map labels: ATLANTIC OCEAN · British Isles · FRANKISH KINGDOM · Loire · Sens · Poitiers · Rhine · AVAR KHANATE · Danube · Dnieper · Volga · Turks · Lake Balkhash · Khazars · Aral Sea · Syr Darya · TANG EMPIRE · Covadonga · Zaragoza · Narbonne · Rome · Black Sea · Caspian Sea · Amu Darya · Samarqand · Indus · Toledo · Valencia · Constantinople · Ardebil · Merv · Balkh · Lisbon · Seville · Córdoba · BYZANTINE EMPIRE · Aleppo · Harran · Qazvin · Rayy · Herat · Tangier · Carthage · Hamah · Euphrates · Tigris · Nehavend · Multan · Kairouan · Sicily · Damascus · Karbala · Wasit · Mediterranean Sea · Ramallah · Kufa · Basra · Persepolis · Agadir · Berbers · Barqa · Alexandria · Jerusalem · Siraf · Tripoli · Al-Fustat · Persian Gulf · SAHARA · Nile · Medina · ARABIA · Arabian Sea · Bedr · Mecca · Red Sea · Dongola · AXUM

Legend:
□ Islamic cultural center
◉ major mosque
▨ Arabs practicing Islam, 632
growth of the Arab Caliphate
▨ to 634
▨ to 656
▨ to 750

0 — 1,200 km
0 — 800 mi

seen. By the time the Prophet died in 632, to be controversially succeeded by his father-in-law, the Arabs had already carried the word by force of arms—and inspiration—through much of West Asia. Although their warlike nature had always been recognized, the Arabs had hitherto been dismissed as little more than raiders, a mere nuisance: Now, however, their aggression was channeled by a passionate faith. Within a few decades these forgotten desert nomads made much of the known world their own, building an Islamic empire that stretched all the way from the edges of India to southern Spain.

▼ The chief vehicle for Islam's message is the Koran, which Muslims hold to be the word of God as revealed to Muhammad over a 20-year period. This manuscript fragment dates back to the time of the Abbasid Dynasty in the 8th or 9th century.

✕ **627** A Meccan army is turned back from Medina at the Battle of the Ditch. After the victory Muhammad attacks the city's chief Jewish tribe, suspected of conspiring with the Meccans; the men are massacred, the women and children enslaved.

✕ **630** Meccans surrender their city, and the Kaaba, to the Muslims. Muhammad launches a raid through northern Arabia to the borders of Byzantine Syria.

♛ **632** Death of Muhammad. A meeting of elders elects his father-in-law, Abu Bakr, to inherit his authority as *khalifah*, or caliph ("successor"), rather than his cousin and son-in-law Ali ibn Abi Talib. The decision will have enormous implications for subsequent Islamic history.

✕ **634** Battle of Ajnadyn brings victory over Byzantine forces in Syria.

♛ **634** Umar ibn al-Khattab (Omar I) becomes second caliph.

✕ **636** Victory over Byzantines at the Yarmuk River brings all Syria under Muslim control.

✕ **637** The Persians are defeated at the Battle of Qadisiya, opening the way into Iraq and the Sassanian heartland of Iran.

✕ **641** The Arabs take Cairo, Egypt; the Mediterranean port of Alexandria falls in the following year.

♛ **644** Umar is assassinated. His successor as caliph, Uthman, is most famous for having gathered Muhammad's various visionary pronouncements into a single book, the Koran.

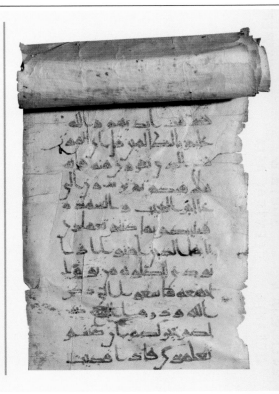

AMERICAS

⚔ **c.650** The monumental center of Teotihuacán in central Mexico is sacked and burned by unknown assailants. The city is abandoned sometime afterward.

Detail from a painted ceramic vase found at the Mayan city of Tikal.

EUROPE

⚔ **c.650** Visigoth rule in Spain is increasingly riven by internal faction fighting.

☀ **664** The Synod of Whitby, a church council held in northern England, establishes papal control over the English church, rejecting practices favored in the Celtic churches of Wales, Ireland, and Scotland.

⚔ **c.670** Bulgar raiders of Turkic origin move into the Balkan Peninsula.

⚙ **678** Byzantine forces use "Greek fire" — a flammable mixture of sulfur, naphtha, and quicklime fired from bronze tubes—to end a five-year blockade of Constantinople, marking a first significant setback for Islam's forces.

AFRICA

♛ **c.650** The centuries-long Bantu migration from West Africa ends, with Bantu speakers now found through east and southern Africa.

☀ **c.650** Islamic influences start to spread down the East African coast through what is already longstanding maritime trade.

⚔ **651** The Arab rulers of Egypt launch their first expedition against the Christian Nubian kingdoms of Alwa and Makurra.

WESTERN ASIA

☀ **651** Caliph Uthman brings Muhammad's teachings together to form a single sacred volume, the Koran.

⚔ **654** Having taken Armenia from Byzantium, Arab forces turn westward into the empire's heartland in Anatolia (Turkey).

♛ **656** Uthman's assassination precipitates the outbreak of Islam's first civil war.

♛ **661** The civil war comes to an end with the murder of Ali, the Prophet's cousin and son-in-law. The victorious Umayyads establish their capital in Damascus.

⚔ **680** The sons of Ali (Hasan and Husayn) and their supporters are massacred at Karbala, Iraq.

⚔ **683** The death of Umayyad Caliph Yazid I triggers a second Islamic Civil War.

♛ **692** Abd al-Malik succeeds in holding on to the caliphate for the Umayyads, although his ruthlessness will be resented by Shiites for generations.

SOUTH & CENTRAL ASIA

♛ **c.650** The disintegration of Harshavardhana's empire brings a return to regionalism and local cultures in India.

☀ **651** The Arab capture of Merv, in modern Turkmenistan, brings Islam to Central Asia.

♛ **659** Tang Dynasty victories against the Turks extend Chinese control of the Silk Road westward.

Earthenware figurine of a dancer from Tang Dynasty China.

EAST ASIA & OCEANIA

☀ **c.651** Islam is brought to China for the first time by Arab traders.

♛ **653** The first known Tang Dynasty law code dates from this year; its influence will linger for centuries.

♛ **657** Jayavarman I founds the dynasty that (in a century or so) will rule the powerful and prosperous Khmer Empire in Cambodia.

AMERICAS

👑 **682** "Ruler A" comes to power in the Mayan city of Tikal, Guatemala: nothing is known of him except that he seems to have transformed the flagging fortunes of his state.

✗ **695** Tikal finally defeats its northerly neighbor and longstanding enemy Calakmul. The city enjoys a boom in commerce and a renaissance in art and sculpture, its population rising to about 50,000 people.

👑 **695** The Mayan city of Copán, Honduras, begins its golden age with the accession of Waxaklajuun Ub'aah K'awiil.

EUROPE

👑 **681** The Bulgars sign a treaty agreeing to help protect Constantinople against Slavic raiders. In return the Byzantines recognize the new Kingdom of Bulgaria.

👑 **685** The Byzantine Emperor Constantine IV negotiates a treaty with the Arabs establishing a firm frontier between the Byzantine and Arab spheres.

👑 **687** The people of Venice, Italy, organize their city as a republic, with an elected "doge," or leader.

☀ **c.690** English missionaries are at work spreading Christianity in Scandinavia and the Netherlands.

✗ **700** The Balkans are overrun by Avar and Slavic tribes.

AFRICA

✗ **670** Uqba ibn Nafi leads Arab armies into what is now Tunisia, launching a new campaign in the Maghreb—western North Africa.

👑 **675** Kairouan, in modern Tunisia, is founded as a base for the conquest of the Maghreb.

✗ **698** After several years' intermittent assault Arab forces take the ancient city of Carthage.

WESTERN ASIA

☀ **692** The Dome of the Rock is completed in Jerusalem.

👑 **692** Abd al-Malik introduces new coinage with Koranic verses for use throughout the Islamic world. To the disapproval of many purists the caliph's vision of Islam transcends the religious sphere to comprise a whole new social and economic order.

The Dome of the Rock in Jerusalem is one of Islam's holiest shrines. Commissioned by the Umayyad Caliph Abd al-Malik in 687, it was completed five years later. Inside its octagonal walls lies the rock on which Abraham was said to have offered his son Isaac to God; according to Muslim tradition, the Prophet Muhammad, founder of Islam, ascended to heaven from the spot.

SOUTH & CENTRAL ASIA

✗ **664** The Arab advance reaches Kabul in what is now Afghanistan.

✗ **670** Sustained Tibetan attacks expel Tang forces from the Tarim Basin in present-day western China. The victory cuts off China from westward trade.

✗ **674** The Arabs reach the Indus River in modern Pakistan.

✗ **692** Tang forces, with their Turkic allies, seize back the Tarim Basin from the Tibetans.

EAST ASIA & OCEANIA

✗ **660** The southern Korean Kingdom of Silla invades neighboring Paekche.

✗ **668** Silla attacks its other Korean rival, Koguryo, then imposes peace on the peninsula.

✗ **676** Having established its dominance throughout Korea, Silla drives Chinese forces out of the peninsula.

👑 **690** Wu Zetian takes power as China's first and only empress.

📖 **699** Birth of Wang Wei, Buddhist scholar and one of China's greatest painters and poets.

650–700 A.D.

SUNNIS AND SHIITES

EXPLOSIVE IN ITS IMPACT, *Islam seemed to carry all before it in the 7th century when the power of faith was backed up by force of arms. The speed and stamina of its warriors' horses, their skill in the saddle, their military prowess, and their sense of destiny—all conspired to make the Arab advance irresistible. Yet as time went on, there would increasingly be wars within Islam itself, creating tensions that would ultimately split the entire Muslim community.*

▲ Islam may have begun life as a religion of the Arabian desert, but in a very short time its adherents brought most of the great cities of the Middle East under its sway. This mosaic townscape comes from the Great Mosque in Damascus, capital of Syria.

Najaf

Some 80 miles (130 km) south of Baghdad, Iraq, stands the sacred shrine of Mashad Gharwah, reputed to be the burial place of Ali, Muhammad's son-in-law and would-be successor. The story goes that having been mortally wounded by his murderers, he asked his followers to tie him to the back of a camel and turn the beast loose: Wherever it stopped to rest, there they should build his tomb. Today the site is one of the holiest shrines of Shia Islam: Many thousands make the pilgrimage to it each year. An idea of its importance to Shiites can be had from the fact that a visit in turn to Najaf and to Karbala (where Ali's sons Hasan and the martyred Husayn lie buried) is held by many to be spiritually equivalent to the *hajj*, or pilgrimage to Mecca.

632 Muhammad dies, and Abu Bakr, his father-in-law, is elected to succeed him as first of the *ar-Rashidun*, or "rightly guided" caliphs. In choosing him over the Prophet's son-in-law, Ali ibn Abi Talib, the Islamic elders are sowing the seeds of future strife.

656 Ali eventually becomes caliph, but his succession is disputed. Outbreak of first civil war between Ali and dissident Muslims led by Muawiya, governor of Syria.

661 The war ends with Ali's murder and Muawiya's recognition as caliph. His Umayyad descendants will hold sway over the Islamic world for the next 90 years.

680 The conflict passes down a generation as Husayn, son of Ali, attempts to seize power from Muawiya's heir, Yazid. He and his supporters are massacred at Karbala, Iraq.

683 Yazid dies, and a second civil war breaks out. Power passes eventually to Abd al-Malik, who reasserts Umayyad power at the cost of permanently alienating his Shiite opponents.

692 The Dome of the Rock, Jerusalem, is completed on the spot from which the Prophet is reputed to have ascended to heaven.

706 Construction of the Umayyad Mosque, Damascus, begins: It still stands as one of the architectural wonders of the world.

711 The first Muslim raids across the Straits of Gibraltar into southern Spain take place.

715 The Arab conquest of the Iberian Peninsula (Spain and Portugal) is completed.

732 The Arab advance into Europe is finally checked outside Tours in central France.

Although it was a moment of great sadness, the Prophet's death in the June of 632 was a time too of considerable hope and expectation. The visions Muhammad had experienced had already formed the basis of a significant religion, with adherents and territories through much of Arabia and beyond. The Prophet himself had already mounted expeditions in Byzantine Syria—perhaps sensing that a common military project was the best way of uniting his people's traditionally quarrelsome tribal factions.

But first of all it had to be decided who was to succeed the Prophet as leader of the Muslims: Muhammad had left no son. The seeds of future division were sown when a meeting of elders chose Abu Bakr, the Prophet's father-in-law, as *khalifah*, or caliph—a title that implied both spiritual authority and political rule. In making this choice, they passed over Muhammad's cousin and son-in-law, Ali, whose moral rigidity and religious fervor seem to have caused the elders some nervousness.

In a series of civil wars fought over the next 53 years, first Ali himself and then his sons attempted to wrest back the succession that they saw as rightly theirs. Over time doctrinal differences would also develop to further separate the rival groups. Those who followed Abu Bakr and the succession of "rightly guided" caliphs who came after him called themselves Sunni Muslims, because they followed the *sunnah*, or "customs," established by the Prophet. Shiites argued that this succession had been corrupted from the start, and that Islamic tradition should have flowed directly through the person of Ali to the line of imams, or "teachers," who came after him.

In 680 Ali's son Husayn and a small band of partisans were killed near Karbala in what is now Iraq as they traveled to join rebels in Iran pressing his

claim to the caliphate. The deaths gave Shiism its first martyrs and, although a defeat, lent the movement a new impetus. By 750 the Sunnis of the Umayyad Dynasty had been swept away by the Abbasid caliphs, based in Baghdad. Although their advent was not, strictly speaking, a Shiite revolution—Shiism recognized no rule higher than that of its own imams—the Abbasids could hardly have prevailed without the backing of the Shiite scholars. Divisions between Sunni and Shia Islam have persisted to this day, a source of distrust and at times of open warfare.

▲ In a 19th-century painting pilgrims commemorating the martyrdom of Muhammad's grandson Husayn approach the town of Karbala. Husayn, a claimant to the caliphate, was killed nearby by troops sent by the Caliph Yazid in 680. The town remains one of Shiite Islam's holiest sites.

⏝ **747** The province of Khorasan, Persia, rebels against Umayyad rule, the first open display of resistance to a dynasty whose legitimacy is increasingly coming into question.

⏝ **750** Muhammad ibn Ali ibn al-Abbas, a descendant of Ali, mounts a successful revolt against the Umayyads. He establishes his own Abbasid Dynasty, which reigns throughout the Middle East and North Africa (the Maghreb). The last Umayyads hold out in al-Andalus, southern Spain—the region now known as Andalusia—which they make their kingdom.

⏝ **762** Foundation of Baghdad by al-Mansur. The new Abbasid capital becomes the center of a thriving commercial empire, with trade (through the port of Basra) to China and East Africa.

📖 **786** The accession of Harun al-Rashid ushers in a golden age, with astonishing achievements in art, literature, music, mathematics, medicine, and science.

⏝ **913** Abbasid power sustains a major blow when Persia is overrun by the Buyids, an alliance of nomadic peoples from the southern shores of the Caspian Sea.

⏝ **930** Rebels sack Mecca, confirming a weakening of Abbasid power that has been becoming more evident for decades. The dynasty's difficulties are compounded by the westward advance of the Seljuk Turks from Central Asia.

⏝ **945** The Buyids conquer Iraq, the heartland of Abbasid rule.

✳ **969** A North African tribe, the Fatimids, seizes power in Egypt on its way to a wider dominance in the Islamic world. A Shiite group, they see their descent from Ali as being doubly sacred, through his relationship both with the Prophet himself and with his daughter, Fatima.

700–750 A.D.

AMERICAS

c.700 Monte Albán, the major Zapotec center in the Oaxaca Valley, is in decline by this time.

c.700 The Huari Empire conquers the Moche state of northern Peru.

735 The Mayan city of Seibal is conquered by Dos Pilas.

738 King Canac Sky of the Mayan city of Quiriguá rebels against King 18 Rabbit of Copán, whom he captures and beheads.

EUROPE

Icons like this image of the Virgin and Child from the Church of the Nativity in Bethlehem were at the center of a controversy that split the Byzantine Empire for more than a century from 726 on. In that year Emperor Leo III condemned the veneration of the much-loved images as a form of idolatry. Orthodox Christians remained deeply divided on the issue until 843, when the worship of holy images was officially restored.

c.710 Willibrord, an Anglo-Saxon monk, leads a mission to the pagan Danes.

711 An Arab army invades and conquers Spain as far as the Pyrenees (–715).

718 An Arab force fails to capture Constantinople.

718 The Danes build an earthen frontier in the south to defend their kingdom from the Saxons.

AFRICA

702 Berber resistance to Arab rule ends when the rebels' leader, Kahina "the Prophetess," is defeated and commits suicide.

706 Arabic becomes the official language of Egypt.

709 Arabs conquer Tangier.

725 Egypt's Christian Copts revolt unsuccessfully against Islamic rule.

WESTERN ASIA

c.715 The Islamic caliphate, ruled from Damascus, now extends from the Indus region to North Africa and Spain—the largest empire the world has yet seen.

720–724 Quarrels between Yemenites and Modharites—also known as southern and northern Arabs—spread through the Islamic world.

747 A major rebellion in the province of Khorasan is sparked by discontent among new converts to Islam who do not enjoy the same tax privileges as Arabs.

749 The rebels proclaim as caliph Abu-al Abbas, a member of the Abbasid family descended from Abbas, Muhammad's uncle.

SOUTH & CENTRAL ASIA

c.700 The Pallava rulers of south India build a temple complex at Mahabalipuram, with many fine rock-cut monuments.

The Shore Temple, Mahabalipuram, India.

c.700 Persian Zoroastrians take refuge from the advance of Islam by fleeing to western India, where they settle and become known as Parsis.

EAST ASIA & OCEANIA

c.700 China enjoys a period of great artistic creativity under the Tang emperors; poetry, figure painting, and pottery all reach high levels of attainment.

708 Official coinage is issued in Japan for the first time.

710 The Yamato emperors of Japan make a permanent capital at Nara.

712 Japan's oldest extant book, the *Kojiki*, which records the succession of Japan's ruling dynasty from mythical times, is written, employing Chinese characters.

⚙ **c.750** The Great Pyramid at Cholula in the Valley of Mexico is enlarged.

A stele from Quiriguá in what is now Guatemala depicts a Mayan king.

AMERICAS

✕ **718** A Christian army defeats an Arab army at Covadonga in the mountains of Asturias in northern Spain.

☀ **719** Pope Gregory II commissions St. Boniface, an Anglo-Saxon originally named Wynfrith, to convert the Germans.

☀ **726** The Iconoclast Controversy (over the worship of images) causes a deep breach between the Orthodox and Roman churches.

✕ **732** An Arab army from Spain advances far into France but is turned back at Tours by a Frankish army led by Charles Martel.

📖 **735** Bede, chronicler of the English church, dies in his monastery at Jarrow in northern England.

🏛 **741** Charles Martel dies.

☀ **744** St. Boniface founds an abbey at Fulda in Germany that will become a great center of learning.

🏛 **750** The Lombards capture Ravenna, ending Byzantine power in central Italy.

EUROPE

⚙ **734** Ali Ubaida leads an expedition across the Sahara in search of gold.

✕ **739** Maisara leads an uprising of Berbers and followers of the Kharijite sect of Islam against Arab rule in Morocco.

✕ **742** The Kharijite and Berber revolt is suppressed.

AFRICA

The caliphs of the Abbasid Dynasty, which replaced the Umayyads from 750, ruled much of the Islamic world from their capital Baghdad until its sack by the Mongols in 1258. They were great builders, responsible for such monuments as the Tarik Khana Mosque in Damghan (*left*), the oldest in Iran. Abbasid rule reached a peak in the 8th century under Harun al-Rashid, the caliph of *The Arabian Nights*.

✕ **750** The Abbasids win a decisive victory at the Battle of the Zab (near Mosul in present-day Iraq). They overthrow the last Umayyad caliph, Marwan II, and massacre almost the entire Umayyad family.

WESTERN ASIA

✕ **705** Arab armies extend Islamic rule into Central Asia (Bukhara, Samarkand, and Ferghana), the Indus Valley, and part of the Punjab in northwest India (–715).

🏛 **c.740** Nagabhak I, a ruler of the Gurjara–Pratihara Dynasty, unites much of north India and stems the Arab advance into northwest India.

SOUTH & CENTRAL ASIA

⚙ **c.725** Chinese potters produce the first true porcelain ware at about this time.

⚙ **738** Schools are established in every prefecture and district of China by imperial edict.

⚙ **c.750** The Chinese develop woodblock printing on paper; at first it is used mainly to print devotional Buddhist pictures and literature.

EAST ASIA & OCEANIA

700–750 A.D.

THE RISE OF JAPAN

*C*LAIMING DESCENT FROM THE SUN GODDESS *Amaterasu herself, the emperors of Japan traced their political origins back to the Yamato rulers who, from a base on the Yamato Plain near the present-day city of Osaka, had brought southern Japan under their rule by about 600 A.D. Chinese culture was at first an important influence, but Japan rapidly developed a rich court culture of its own in which belief in Japan's traditional gods, or* kami, *lived side by side with Buddhism.*

▲ The arrival of Buddhism in Japan in the 6th century stimulated new forms of architecture. Pagodas like this 7th-century example from the Horyuji Monastery in the imperial capital of Nara were built to house relics of the Buddha.

▶ The largest of Japan's keyhole tombs is preserved in a park in the modern city of Sakai. It was built to house the body of the Emperor Nintoku, a 5th-century ruler. This colossal monument is 1,600 feet (500 m) long and is surrounded by three moats.

The earliest history of Japan, the *Nihon Shoki* ("Chronicles of Japan"), was written in the 8th century. It describes the mythological origins of the country and throws little historical light on the origins of the first Yamato kings. Archaeology tells us more. Before 300 A.D. people living around the Inland Sea of southern Japan began to build massive, keyhole-shaped tombs, called *kofun* in Japanese, containing quantities of pottery, weapons, jewelry, and ritual objects such as bronze bells. The tombs probably belonged to high-status warrior chiefs who were rivals for regional power.

By the 4th century the strongest of these local chiefs appear to have been the rulers of the Yamato Plain on Honshu, the largest of the islands that make up Japan. The biggest of the *kofun* tombs, traditionally said to belong to Nintoku, one of the early emperors mentioned in the *Nihon Shoki*, probably dates from the early 5th century. By the end of the 6th century the Yamato kings had extended their rule over southern Japan and for a time may even have controlled an area of southern Korea.

By now a new cultural force—Buddhism—had spread to Japan from Korea and China. With it came other aspects of Chinese culture, including Chinese script and the Chinese calendar. In 710 a permanent imperial court was established at Heijo (modern Nara). It was laid out in a grid-shaped pattern similar

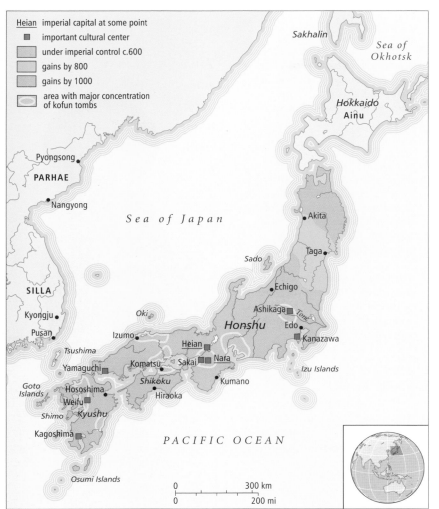

Map legend:

Heian — imperial capital at some point
■ important cultural center
▨ under imperial control c.600
▨ gains by 800
▨ gains by 1000
⬭ area with major concentration of kofun tombs

Sakhalin
Sea of Okhotsk
Hokkaido
Ainu

Pyongsong
PARHAE
Nangyong

Sea of Japan

Akita
Taga
Sado
Echigo
Ashikaga
Tone
Oki
Honshu
Edo
SILLA
Kyongju
Izumo
Heian
Kanazawa
Pusan
Komatsu
Sakai
Nara
Tsushima
Yamaguchi
Izu Islands
Goto Islands
Hososhima
Shikoku
Kumano
Weifu
Hiraoka
Shimo
Kyushu
Kagoshima

PACIFIC OCEAN

Osumi Islands

0   300 km
0   200 mi

Prince Shotoku

One of the first Yamato rulers to emerge from the shadows of prehistory is Prince Shotoku (572–622), seen at right as an infant. Shotoku is supposed to have introduced the "Seventeen Article Constitution," or plan of government, which stressed Chinese principles of loyalty, harmony, and dedication as ideals to be followed in political life. He introduced new ranks of nobility (the twelve "cap ranks"), also based on Chinese practice, which had the effect of weakening the power of the old clan chieftains and promoting men of talent to government office. The constitution gave special protection to Buddhism, and Shotoku is credited with founding many Buddhist temples, including the Horyuji Temple at Nara, which is the oldest surviving monastery compound in Japan. He was so revered as a statesman, sage, and patron of Buddhism that a cult in his honor sprang up shortly after his death.

▲ Imperial power in Japan spread northward up the main island of Honshu from a heartland in the south where the country's successive capitals, Nara and Heian, both lay.

▼ Todaiji Monastery was built in the imperial capital of Nara in 743. Its Great Buddha Hall, shown here, contains the largest statue of the Buddha in Japan, a massive 50 feet (15 m) tall.

to that of Chinese cities. Several important Buddhist monasteries were built nearby.

In time the monks gained so much influence that they began to undermine imperial authority, and in 794 the Emperor Kammu moved the capital to Heian in order to lessen their interference. Heian (today's Kyoto) became the center of a leisured aristocratic culture in which court life itself became a kind of art. Fine handwriting and the composition of poetry were valued above the skills of the warrior, and elaborate rituals of dress and etiquette set the court elite apart from the common people.

750–800 A.D.

AMERICAS

⚔ **c.760** Warfare appears to be on the increase among the Mayan cities of the Petén lowlands; some begin to build defensive walls.

📖 **c.790** Murals painted at Bonampak are left unfinished.

👑 **c.800** The lowland Maya suffer a sudden decrease in population, which declines from a peak of around 8–10 million people; many cities are abandoned.

👑 **c.800** The Toltecs begin to migrate into the Valley of Mexico from the north.

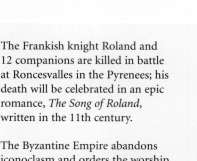

Mosaic portrait of the Byzantine Empress Irene.

EUROPE

👑 **751** Pepin the Short, mayor of the palace, deposes the Merovingian king of the Franks, Childeric III, and becomes king himself.

⚔ **755** The Byzantine Empire fights a series of campaigns against the Bulgars in the Balkans, forcing them to sue for peace (–764).

👑 **756** Abd ar-Rahman, a member of the Umayyad family, founds an independent emirate (Muslim state) at Córdoba in Spain.

⚔ **778** The Frankish knight Roland and 12 companions are killed in battle at Roncesvalles in the Pyrenees; his death will be celebrated in an epic romance, *The Song of Roland*, written in the 11th century.

☀ **787** The Byzantine Empire abandons iconoclasm and orders the worship of images at the Council of Nicaea, a notable victory for the church party over the court.

AFRICA

⊛ **c.750** Arab merchants from North Africa trade across the Sahara, exchanging salt, glass, and horses for African gold, ivory, and slaves.

👑 **750** The caliphs of the Abbasid Dynasty take control of Egypt in the wake of their victory over their Umayyad rivals.

👑 **c.770** The Soninke Dynasty is established in the Kingdom of Ghana by the ruler of that name, replacing an earlier Berber line.

WESTERN ASIA

⊛ **c.750** The first paper mill is established in the Islamic empire.

⊛ **c.760** The Arabs adopt Indian numerals; they are the "Arabic" numerals in general use today.

👑 **762** The Abbasid Caliph Al-Mansur establishes a new capital at Baghdad in Iraq.

SOUTH & CENTRAL ASIA

⚔ **751** The ruler of Tashkent (present-day Uzbekistan) asks the Arabs for protection from the Chinese; an Arab army scores a notable victory over Chinese forces at the Battle of the Talas River.

Rock-cut architecture in India was originally associated with Buddhism and Jainism, but in the 7th and 8th centuries Hindu rulers also commissioned finely carved sanctuaries. The complex at Ellora in central India has monuments from all three traditions, most notably the Hindu Kailasa Temple (*left*).

EAST ASIA & OCEANIA

⚔ **755** In China the general An Lushan leads a damaging rebellion against the Tang emperors (–763).

⚔ **763** Tibetan forces sack Chang'an, the western capital of the Tang Dynasty.

👑 **780** A power struggle between the monarchy and the nobles weakens the Kingdom of Silla in Korea.

The extraordinary Mayan murals at Bonampak—
"Painted Walls"—only came to the world's attention in
1946, when local people in the Mexican state of
Chiapas directed an American photographer to a
previously unrecorded three-room building. Its walls
were lined with brilliantly colored paintings of war,
sacrifice, and feasting, providing a vivid glimpse of
Mayan life as the Classic Period neared its end.

AMERICAS

☀ **c.790** Irish monks sail to the Faeroe
Islands and Iceland in the North
Atlantic.

⚛ **792** The Byzantine Emperor
Constantine VI makes his mother
Irene coruler.

✕ **793** Vikings sack the monastery on
Holy Island in northeast England,
their first major raid in Europe.

✕ **795** Viking raiders attack the coast of
Ireland.

⚛ **797** Irene becomes the first Byzantine
empress after having Constantine
VI imprisoned and blinded.

✕ **799** First Viking raids along the coast of
France.

⚛ **800** Charlemagne, king of the Franks, is
crowned Holy Roman emperor by
the pope in Rome on Christmas
Day.

EUROPE

⚛ **789** The Idrisid Dynasty, adhering to
the Shiite branch of Islam, founds
an independent caliphate in
Morocco.

⚛ **800** The Aghlabid Dynasty rules in
Ifriqiya (present-day Algeria and
Tunisia), recognizing the authority
of the Abbasid rulers of Baghdad.

⚛ **c.800** Arab merchants found trading
towns on the East African coast,
including Kilwa Kisiwani (in
present-day Tanzania).

AFRICA

⊕ **c.776** Jabir ibn Hayyan writes a
scientific treatise describing such
techniques as the refining of
metals and glassmaking.

⚛ **786** Harun al-Rashid becomes caliph
(until 809); a patron of the arts,
he is known to history as the ruler
of *The Arabian Nights*.

✕ **791** War breaks out anew between the
caliph's forces and the Byzantine
Empire in Asia Minor (–809).

WESTERN ASIA

⚛ **756** Dantidurga of the Rashtrakuta
Dynasty overthrows the Chalukya
Dynasty, which had dominated
central India since the 5th century.

☀ **758** Ruling as Krishnaraja I,
Dantidurga commissions the
Kailasa rock-cut temple at Ellora,
one of the great monuments of
Indian medieval art.

☀ **788** Birth of Sankaracharya, the great
Hindu philosopher and guru; he
will reinterpret the Vedas and
found four mathas (monastic
centers of learning) in India that
still survive today (died c.850).

✕ **791** The Tibetans defeat the Chinese at
the Battle of Tingzhou, forcing the
Tang emperors to abandon their
gains in Central Asia.

SOUTH & CENTRAL ASIA

📖 **780** The Chinese writer Lu Yu writes
The Classic of Tea, describing the
use of tea.

✕ **781** Japan's Emperor Kammu launches
a campaign against the Ainu
people of northern Honshu that
finally brings these early settlers
under imperial sway (–812).

⚛ **794** Emperor Kammu of Japan moves
his court to Heian, modern Kyoto.

EAST ASIA & OCEANIA

750–800 A.D.

THE EMPEROR CHARLEMAGNE

THE MOST FAMOUS OF THE CAROLINGIAN RULERS *of the Franks is known to history as Charlemagne, literally "Charles the Great." Charlemagne was the son of the first Carolingian king, Pepin the Short, and the great-grandson of Charles Martel, the leader who halted the Arab advance into Europe. In the course of his reign (768–814) he more than doubled the territory of the Franks.*

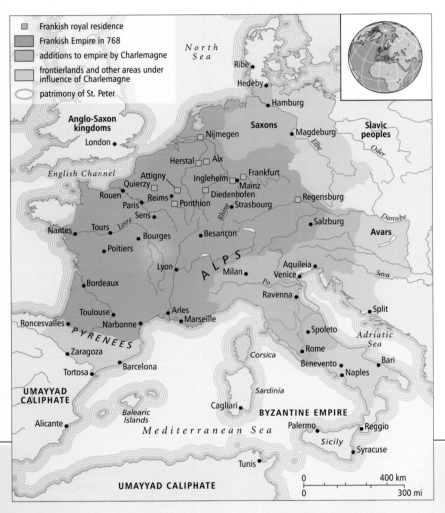

Map legend:
- Frankish royal residence
- Frankish Empire in 768
- additions to empire by Charlemagne
- frontierlands and other areas under influence of Charlemagne
- patrimony of St. Peter

▶ Charlemagne consciously set out to revive the glory of the Roman Empire. This small statue of the emperor is based on a Roman model.

According to Einhard, his biographer, Charlemagne was an outstanding figure who always dressed in the Frankish costume of tunic and leggings. Nearly 6 feet (1.8 m) tall, he had boundless energy and was rarely out of the saddle for long. In the course of more than 50 campaigns he extended the Frankish kingdom in all directions: south of the Alps into Italy; east to Saxony in Germany; westward into Brittany, France; and south across the Pyrenees into northeast Spain.

Charlemagne was a devout Christian. He encouraged missionaries, built numerous monasteries and churches, and gave generous grants of land to the papacy. On Christmas Day in the year 800, when on a visit to Rome (the fifth such journey he had made), Charlemagne attended mass in the Church of St. Peter. As he was kneeling in prayer, Pope Leo III placed a crown on his head, and the congregation acclaimed him as "Caesar" and "Augustus." By this act—which in all probability was carefully staged with Charlemagne's full cooperation—the pope established a Catholic emperor in the west independent of the

◀ By tireless campaigning Charlemagne extended the reach of the Frankish realm in several different directions, particularly to the east and south.

👑 **768** Charlemagne succeeds his father Pepin the Short as king of the Franks, ruling with his brother Carloman.

👑 **771** On the death of Carloman Charlemagne becomes sole ruler.

👑 **774** Charlemagne visits Rome for the first time.

👑 **781** The pope crowns Charlemagne's son Pepin as king of Italy.

📖 **782** The Anglo-Saxon scholar Alcuin, born in York, takes up residence at the court of Charlemagne.

✕ **785** Charlemagne subdues Saxony after a long campaign; he begins the conversion of the Saxons to Christianity.

👑 **788** The duke of Bavaria (southern Germany) becomes a vassal of Charlemagne.

✕ **799** Rioters force the pope out of Rome; he seeks refuge with Charlemagne until restored by Frankish troops.

☀ **800** The pope crowns Charlemagne Holy Roman emperor.

A New Style of Building

One of the strongest surviving links with Charlemagne today is the palace chapel at Aachen, in northwest Germany, where he is buried. It is built in the Romanesque style with round arches, vaulted ceilings, and high, small windows. The interior is decorated with mosaics, including the scene of angels around an altar shown at right. As its name suggests, this style of architecture was based on Roman models and particularly on the buildings of the empire in its late, Byzantine-influenced phase; Charlemagne was one of the first patrons to introduce the style north of the Alps. To ordinary men and women the Romanesque buildings spelled out the message that Charlemagne was the successor of the Caesars and could rightfully claim to have restored the glories of the Roman age. Romanesque remained the principal style of building in Europe until replaced by the soaring pointed arches of Gothic architecture in the 12th century.

Byzantine ruler in Constantinople. Charlemagne's coronation came to be viewed as the inauguration of the Holy Roman Empire, an institution that flourished under his successors. It survived for another 1,000 years until abolished by the French ruler Napoleon in 1806.

When not at war, Charlemagne traveled around his vast territories, setting up court wherever he happened to be. He sent roving emissaries to check on the conduct of local administrators, usually bishops and counts. Although he was probably barely literate himself, Charlemagne employed the leading scholars of the day, such as Alcuin of York, at his court, and was a great collector of manuscripts. For this reason his reign is sometimes described as "the Carolingian renaissance," or revival of learning.

✕ **801** Frankish troops capture Barcelona from the Arabs, marking a significant step in the southward drive into Muslim Spain.

👑 **812** The Byzantine Emperor Michael I recognizes Charlemagne's title in the west.

👑 **814** Charlemagne dies and is succeeded by his sole surviving son, Louis the Pious.

👑 **843** Breakup of the Carolingian Empire; Charlemagne's heirs divide it among themselves into three parts at the Treaty of Verdun.

AMERICAS

⊛ **c.800** People in the Eastern Woodlands region of North America begin to farm new varieties of corn and beans, improving food supplies and sparking population growth.

👑 **c.800** In the Peruvian Andes the city of Huari, which at one time had as many as 70,000 inhabitants, is abandoned for unknown reasons, marking the end of the Huari Empire.

⊛ **c.800** The Anasazi are by now establishing villages of adobe houses at cliff sites in the American Southwest.

EUROPE

📖 **810** Death of Nennius, Welsh historian whose *History of the Britons* contains the first reference to King Arthur, described as a Celtic leader.

⚔ **811** Krum, ruler of the Bulgars, defeats Byzantium's Emperor Nicephorus.

👑 **814** On Charlemagne's death his empire passes to his eldest surviving son, Louis the Pious.

👑 **817** Louis divides the empire between his sons, who agree to rule as coregents during his lifetime.

👑 **817** The Bulgars conclude a 30-year peace with the Byzantines.

⚔ **825** Arabs expelled from Spain conquer Crete.

☀ **c.831** A Christian bishopric is established in Hamburg as a center for missionary work in the Viking lands.

👑 **833** Mojmir founds the Kingdom of Moravia.

👑 **835** Viking raiders (mostly Norwegians) start to settle in Ireland.

AFRICA

👑 **c.800** The Kingdom of Kanem is established by the Zaghawa people on the northeastern shore of Lake Chad.

👑 **c.800** The state of Takrur is founded in what is now Senegal, on the western edges of the Kingdom of Ghana.

👑 **809** The city of Fez is founded by the Idrisid caliphs of the Maghreb (Morocco) as their capital city.

WESTERN ASIA

👑 **809** Caliph Harun al-Rashid dies while suppressing a rebellion in Samarkand.

👑 **813** Al-Mamun ascends the throne in Baghdad. His 20-year reign will be called the most glorious in the history of the caliphate.

📖 **c.820** Al-Mamun establishes the House of Wisdom, an academy that sponsors the translation of important Greek and Indian scientific and philosophical works.

⊛ **827** The *Megale Syntaxis* of the Greek astronomer Claudius Ptolemy is translated into Arabic as the *al-Majisti*, or *Almagest*.

⊛ **c.830** The Arab mathematician Al-Khwarizmi introduces the concept of algebra.

SOUTH & CENTRAL ASIA

☀ **c.800** Construction starts at Borobudur, a major Buddhist site on the island of Java that will eventually comprise more than 70 stupas.

👑 **c.800** The state of Srivijaya reaches the height of its power, dominating the sealanes of eastern Indonesia from its base on Sumatra.

👑 **831** The Dravidian Chandella Dynasty comes to power in north-central India; its principal monument will be the spectacular Hindu temples at Khajuraho.

EAST ASIA & OCEANIA

The people who in later times would be known as the Maoris are thought to have arrived in New Zealand in the 9th century. Previously its two main islands were uninhabited, making the new land the last sizable territory to be populated on Earth. Shown at left is a decorative greenstone Maori fish hook.

👑 **c.800** The first Polynesian seafarers, perhaps from the Society Islands, arrive on Aotearoa ("the Land of the Long White Cloud"), later to be known as New Zealand.

☀ **c.800** The populist Amida sect of Buddhism becomes established in the Korean Kingdom of Silla.

⊛ **c.800** First appearance of the Mississippian tradition in eastern America's moundbuilding cultures, typified by large, flat-topped earthworks often referred to as temple mounds.

👑 **820** The Classic Period dynasty at the Mayan city of Copán comes to an end as population levels in the Petén lowlands continue to fall.

✕ **837** Christians and Jews revolt unsuccessfully against Muslim rule in Córdoba, Spain.

👑 **840** Viking settlers in Ireland found Dublin as a trading center.

✕ **840** Louis the Pious dies, and civil war breaks out among his heirs.

✕ **841** Viking raiders invade Normandy.

👑 **843** By the Treaty of Verdun the heirs of Louis the Pious formally break up Charlemagne's empire. Lothair, the eldest, keeps the central territories, Louis the German takes the eastern, and Charles the Bald gets the western Frankish lands.

Britain's semilegendary King Arthur, shown in a medieval tapestry.

✕ **827** The Aghlabid rulers of North Africa conquer Sicily (–878).

☀ **831** The last Coptic Christian armed rising against Egypt's Islamic rulers is put down, leading to a period of rapid conversion to Islam.

✕ **846** An Aghlabid fleet raids Rome.

👑 **836** Caliph Al-Mutasim transfers the caliphate from Baghdad to Samarra.

✕ **838** Al-Mutasim defeats the Byzantine Emperor Theophilus at the Iris River, but abandons an attempt to take the Byzantine capital Constantinople when a storm destroys his fleet.

⊛ **c.840** The Arab astronomer Abu al Fadl Jafar records sunspots.

👑 **846** The capital of Sri Lanka is moved south to Polonnaruva to lessen the threat from seaborne Tamil invaders.

👑 **849** The city-state of Pagan is founded in Burma (modern Myanmar).

A temple complex at Khajuraho, India, built by rulers of the Chandella Dynasty.

📖 **801** In China Tu Yu completes the compilation of the *Tung T'ien*—the world's first historical encyclopedia.

👑 **802** Jayavarman II reunites the Khmer people from his base in the Angkor region of Cambodia.

☀ **804** The Tendai and Shingon sects of Buddhism are founded by two Japanese monks, both sent by their emperor on an embassy to China. Both sects will achieve lasting popularity in Japan.

⊛ **811** The Tang emperors of China issue "flying cash"—money drafts exchanged by merchants that are an early form of paper currency.

☀ **845** Nonnative religions, including Buddhism and Christianity, are banned in China; Confucianism is restored as the state ideology.

AMERICAS

EUROPE

AFRICA

WESTERN ASIA

SOUTH & CENTRAL ASIA

EAST ASIA & OCEANIA

800–850 A.D.

THE MAYA

THE MAYA ORIGINATED IN THE HIGHLANDS OF GUATEMALA. *From about the year 1000 B.C. they began to spread into the lowlands of the Yucatán Peninsula, where they dug canals to drain the swamps to grow food. By the 8th century B.C. they were building monumental temple pyramids, and city-states began to form. Writing, the use of the astronomical calendar, and the sacred ball game were probably adopted from the Olmecs and Zapotecs as long-distance trade developed.*

▲ This life-size stone head was found under the tomb of Pacal, ruler of the city-state of Palenque. It is thought to show him at age 12, when he first came to the throne.

▼ Palenque in the Petén lowlands (see map, p.14) was one of the most powerful Mayan states, reaching a peak during Pacal's 68-year reign in the 7th century.

Around 300 A.D. the Maya living in the Petén lowlands on what is now the Guatemala–Mexico border began to erect stone monuments. These stelae record the deeds of royal ancestors and commemorate important events. Many have survived, hidden in the forest vegetation, and archaeologists have learned how to decipher their inscriptions, which were written in an advanced glyph (picture) script. They paint a scene of more or less continuous conflict between such Mayan city-states as Tikal and Palenque.

Warfare was necessary to supply captives to serve as human sacrifices, who were offered to the gods on fixed dates in the astronomical calendar or to mark important events, such as royal funerals. Victims had their hearts cut out and put on display. Special temple complexes and pyramids were built to provide a setting for these rituals. A corps of priests oversaw and controlled the ceremonies.

Mayan kings were themselves expected to participate in painful rituals involving bloodletting. Typically, their tongues were pierced with cords barbed with thorns. They offered their blood to sustain the gods, who were thought in turn to have undergone ritual sacrifices to sustain the human race.

The Maya used a complex and highly accurate calendar based on precise astronomical observations. In later times they produced sacred books written on bark, which they illustrated with intricate paintings. These works, like their stone carvings, tell us something of their violent cosmos and powerful gods.

Wars and famine brought about by overcultivation of the land may have caused the rapid collapse that led the lowland Mayan cities to be deserted in the years after 800 A.D. The highland settlements survived longer, only to be eventually conquered by Spanish invaders in the 16th century.

0 ♔ **c.750 B.C.** Mayan forms of kingship develop, and the first monuments are built from about this time.

♔ **c.350** The Late Preclassic Period begins with the emergence of the first city-states.

✳ **c.200** The earliest known form of Mayan writing is thought to date from about this time.

The Ballgame

The Maya played a ballgame that was also popular in other cultures across Mesoamerica. In it two opposing teams struck a solid rubber ball around a specially made court. The game seems to have resembled basketball in that the object was to knock the ball through stone rings set high on the court walls. Players were not allowed to touch the ball with their hands, however, only with their hips and knees. They wore protective clothing, including a heavy belt made of wood and leather, and leather hip-pads, kneepads, and gloves. Spectators flocked to the ballcourt to place bets and cheer on their favorite team. The game was not simply a test of strength and skill. For the players it could be, quite literally, a contest to the death. Carvings around the walls of the Great Ballcourt at Chichén Itzá show members of the winning team sacrificing a defeated opponent by cutting off his head, while elsewhere in Mesoamerica the losing captain's heart was sometimes cut out.

▶ The Maya used three basic number symbols: a stylized shell for zero, a dot for one, and a bar for five. Time was recorded in units of 1, 20, 360, 7,200, and 144,000 days. Each interval was represented by a different symbol. The 260-day calender (*right*) had an inner cog with 13 numbers on it rotating around a wheel with 20 named days. As the wheel turned, each number fitted with a day symbol. After 13 days the cycle started anew.

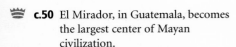

〰 **c.50** El Mirador, in Guatemala, becomes the largest center of Mayan civilization.

⊕ **36** The earliest known Mayan calendrical inscriptions, found at Chiapa de Corzo, date from this year.

〰 **200 A.D.** The eruption of Mt. Ilopango devastates the southern Maya lands. Lake Ilopango now fills the crater left by the eruption.

⊕ **292** Earliest known lowland inscription, found at Tikal in Guatemala.

⊕ **c.300** Elaborate monuments are built in the central lowland rainforests, marking the beginning of the Classic Period of Mayan civilization.

⊕ **c.300** Corbeled arches and vaults first appear in Mayan architecture.

☀ **300** Teotihuacán becomes a major influence on the Maya through its trading networks.

⊕ **c.325** The Maya begin to use stone instead of wood in their buildings.

〰 **411** Tikal is the dominant Maya center during the reign of King Stormy Sky.

✕ **562** Tikal goes into decline after it is defeated by its eastern neighbor, Caracol.

〰 **695** King Jaguar Paw of Calakmul is captured and sacrificed by Ah Cacau of Tikal.

〰 **738** Quiriguá becomes the major center of power during the Classic Period.

✕ **c.790** Murals painted at Bonampak provide evidence of the warlike character of Mayan civilization.

☀ **799** The last monuments are erected at the eastern city of Palenque.

⊕ **c.800** The "long count" Mayan calendar, with its five separate time cycles, falls into disuse.

〰 **c.800** Many central Mayan states fall into decline, marking a shift in power to the highland areas.

〰 **c.850** Mayan power and population move north, and Chichén Itzá on the Yucatán Peninsula becomes the dominant Mayan center.

☀ **889** The last monuments are erected at Tikal.

AMERICAS

📖 **c.850** In the Lambayeque Valley of northern Peru the Sicán art style comes into its own, notably at Batán Grande; distinctive features include black ceramics and shaft tombs.

The Toltecs established an empire in the Valley of Mexico that lasted from the 9th to 12th centuries. Their civilization was a somber one, dominated by concerns with war and sacrifice. This reclining stone figure in Chichén Itzá was shaped to receive the hearts of human victims.

EUROPE

👑 **c.850** Magyars from the lands north of the Black Sea settle in Hungary, displacing the Avars.

👑 **c.855** Eastern Vikings, known to the Byzantines as Varangians and to the local Slavs as Rus (from which the word "Russia" will derive), establish the state of Kiev in Ukraine.

⚔ **859** Vikings raid the Mediterranean (–862).

⚔ **860** Varangians unsuccessfully besiege Constantinople.

☀ **862** Saints Cyril and Methodius are sent to convert the Slavs to Christianity.

👑 **c.862** Viking Rus under Rurik found the state of Novgorod.

☀ **865** Boris I, king of the Bulgars, is baptized into the Orthodox Christian Church.

⚔ **866** Danish Vikings invade England.

👑 **867** Basil I seizes the Byzantine throne from Michael the Drunkard, founding the Macedonian Dynasty, which will oversee a revival in the empire's fortunes.

👑 **874** Vikings start to settle Iceland.

👑 **878** Oleg becomes ruler of Novgorod; he will unite it and Kiev to form the first Russian state.

AFRICA

👑 **c.850** Trade is on the increase in southern Africa, as shown by substantial finds of imported goods at Schroda, a site on the Limpopo River.

☀ **862** The Karaouine Mosque is built at Fez.

👑 **868** The independent Tulunid Dynasty is established in Egypt (–905).

📖 **c.871** Ibn Abd al-Hakam writes the first known history of the Arab conquest of Egypt.

WESTERN ASIA

👑 **861** Caliph al-Muttawahil is assassinated by his Turkish bodyguards, now the real power in the Abbasid realm.

⚔ **869** The Zenj rebellion devastates Mesopotamia (–883).

👑 **870** Caliph al-Mutamid temporarily checks the power of the Turkish guards.

☀ **873** Muhammad al-Muntazar, twelfth imam of the Shiite Imami sect, disappears; his followers still await his return today.

SOUTH & CENTRAL ASIA

👑 **c.850** The Chola State is founded among the Tamil people of southeastern India.

👑 **c.850** Uighurs driven westward by Kirghiz and Karluk tribesmen establish a new base in the Tarim Basin region of Central Asia, north of Tibet.

EAST ASIA & OCEANIA

⚙ **c.850** In China gunpowder is mentioned for the first time.

👑 **858** Yoshifusa establishes the Fujiwara family as the power behind Japan's throne, assuming the title of regent.

Low-relief carving from Bakong, Cambodia, dating from Indravarman I's reign.

☸ **868** The Diamond Sutra, the earliest known printed book (actually a scroll), is produced in China.

✕ **c.850** The Toltec people establish military supremacy in the Valley of Mexico.

👑 **c.850** Chichén Itzá is founded on the northern Yucatán Peninusla, marking a population shift to the north in the Mayan lands.

👑 **862** The long drought afflicting the Mayan lowlands peaks at about this time, contributing to massive population loss in the region.

👑 **889** The last dated inscriptions found in the Mayan lowlands date from this year.

AMERICAS

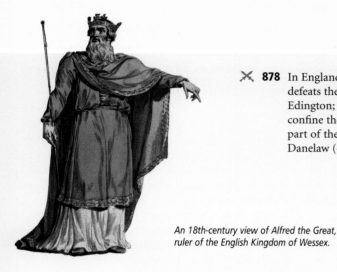

✕ **878** In England Alfred the Great defeats the Danes at the Battle of Edington; he will eventually confine the invaders to the eastern part of the country known as the Danelaw (–886).

👑 **884** Charles the Fat, ruler of Germany, takes control of the Frankish lands, temporarily reuniting the empire of Charlemagne.

👑 **888** Charlemagne's empire finally breaks up on the death of Charles the Fat.

An 18th-century view of Alfred the Great, ruler of the English Kingdom of Wessex.

EUROPE

📖 **872** The historian and geographer Al-Yaqubi writes a description of eastern Africa.

⊕ **876** Egypt's Tulunid rulers construct a hospital, racecourse, and the Ibn Tulun Mosque in Cairo (–879).

⊕ **c.890** The Arab astronomer al-Battani calculates the exact length of the year and the precession of the equinoxes.

The Ibn Tulun Mosque in Cairo, made of brick and plaster.

AFRICA

WESTERN ASIA

👑 **871** Arabs inhabiting what is now southeast Iran and Pakistan establish their independence from the Abbasid caliphs of Baghdad under the Saffarid Dynasty, which goes on to conquer all Iran.

👑 **c.880** The Palas, a dynasty of Buddhist kings ruling Bengal and Magadha, reach the peak of their power.

👑 **888** Under Aditya I the Cholas extend their rule up India's southeast coast at the expense of the Pallava rulers to their north.

SOUTH & CENTRAL ASIA

 874 A series of peasant rebellions fatally weakens China's Tang Dynasty, damaging the emperor's authority and strengthening the hand of local warlords (–884).

👑 **877** Indravarman I ascends the Khmer throne in Cambodia. In his 12-year reign he will extend Khmer rule over the Mon and Thai people to the north and west.

 c.880 Major uprisings weaken the authority of the Korean Kingdom of Silla.

EAST ASIA & OCEANIA

850–900 A.D.

121

THE VIKINGS

*F*OR THOSE WHOM THEY ATTACKED, THE VIKINGS WERE PIRATES—*robbers who came by sea. Worse still for the Christian monks who chronicled their raids, they were heathens; themselves venerating old Norse gods such as Odin and Thor, they respected neither the church nor churchmen. Viking warriors were indeed fearsome foes, yet there was also a hugely positive side to the Viking achievement. While Norse craftsmen constructed artworks of great beauty, boatborne adventurers settled Iceland and Greenland, made the earliest known European landfall in North America, and helped found the first Russian state.*

▲ Although the Vikings are now best remembered for their fighting skills, they were also fine craftsmen, as this elaborately decorated bronze brooch from Denmark suggests. Viking taste ran to intricate, semiabstract designs in which human and animal heads emerged from a mass of ornamentation.

The Vikings were drawn from a number of different peoples living in the lands we now know as Norway, Sweden, and Denmark. All, however, were linked by a common language, religion, and way of life. Originally farmers for the most part, they were propelled from their Scandinavian homeland apparently by a shortage of available land. Some found previously uninhabited regions to settle, for example, in Iceland and Greenland. Other voyages were carried out for plunder first and only secondarily for settlement.

Different Viking communities tended to concentrate their activities in different areas. Norwegian Vikings began to settle in the islands off the north coast of Scotland at the beginning of the 8th century and then moved down the west coast of Britain and across to Ireland, as well as north to Iceland. Danes attacked the coasts of the western European mainland and, in the mid 9th century, invaded England in force, eventually occupying the eastern half of the country, which they ruled as "the Danelaw." Vikings from Sweden moved across the Baltic Sea into eastern Europe. Traveling by river, they eventually reached Constantinople, besieging it unsuccessfully in 860. Many of these eastern Vikings settled in the burgeoning river ports as merchants; known to the local Slavs as Rus, they were instrumental in setting up the first Russian state.

By the 9th century the Viking merchant-warriors had built up a large trading network across the Baltic Sea and Europe. The Vikings supplied timber, furs, and honey in exchange for gold, silver, and luxury goods. Slaves were also an important commodity—the very word stems from the Slav peoples whom Viking slavers plundered mercilessly. Another important source of wealth came in the form of protection money, for many western European rulers chose to buy off Viking raiders, offering them huge sums of money in return for guarantees of peace.

⚔ **c.790** Viking raids on western Europe begin.

⚔ **793** Vikings raid Lindisfarne Monastery on Holy Island, off the coast of northern England.

⚔ **c.830** Viking raids on the English and French coast increase, with many towns being sacked.

👑 **c.835** Vikings set up the first winter camps in Ireland.

👑 **845** The Franks buy off Viking raiders by paying the tribute known as Danegeld.

The Viking Longship

The Viking longships represented the most important advance in shipbuilding since the fall of the Roman Empire. First recorded in the late 700s, the slim, beautifully constructed vessels carried warriors on raids across western Europe and into the Mediterranean, and also took settlers in stages across the Atlantic Ocean as far as the North American coast. Like all Viking craft, the longship sailed well; it was narrow and sat shallow in the water, which meant that it could be rowed up rivers. The Vikings sometimes chose to bury their dead leaders in longships, and several of the resulting boat graves have been excavated, providing vital information on the vessels. One famous example was found at Gokstad in Norway in 1880. The Gokstad ship was 75 feet (23 m) long and had 16 oarsmen on each side.

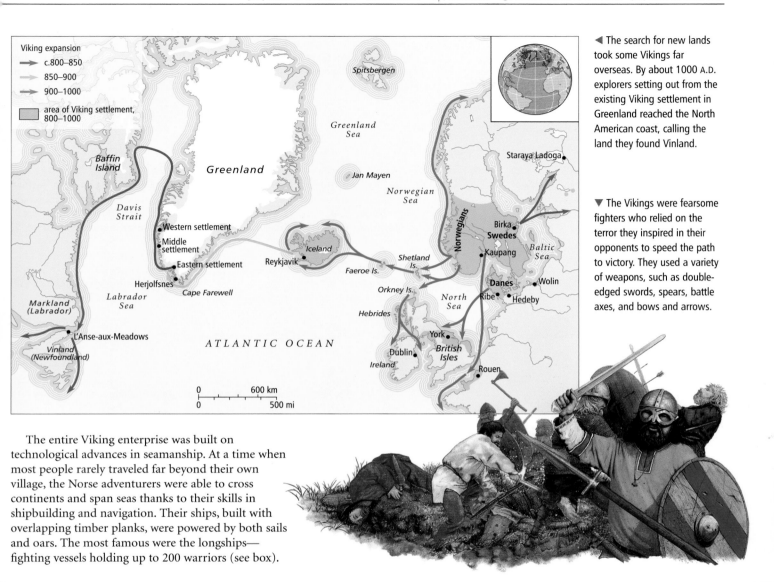

Viking expansion
→ c.800–850
→ 850–900
→ 900–1000
▨ area of Viking settlement, 800–1000

Spitsbergen

Baffin Island

Greenland

Greenland Sea

Jan Mayen

Norwegian Sea

Staraya Ladoga

Davis Strait

Western settlement
Middle settlement
Eastern settlement

Reykjavik

Iceland

Norwegians

Birka

Swedes

Kaupang

Baltic Sea

Herjolfsnes

Labrador Sea

Cape Farewell

Faeroe Is.

Shetland Is.

Danes   Wolin

Markland (Labrador)

Orkney Is.

North Sea

Ribe   Hedeby

L'Anse-aux-Meadows

Hebrides

ATLANTIC OCEAN

York

Vinland (Newfoundland)

Dublin   **British Isles**

Ireland   Rouen

0 ____ 600 km
0 ____ 500 mi

◄ The search for new lands took some Vikings far overseas. By about 1000 A.D. explorers setting out from the existing Viking settlement in Greenland reached the North American coast, calling the land they found Vinland.

▼ The Vikings were fearsome fighters who relied on the terror they inspired in their opponents to speed the path to victory. They used a variety of weapons, such as double-edged swords, spears, battle axes, and bows and arrows.

The entire Viking enterprise was built on technological advances in seamanship. At a time when most people rarely traveled far beyond their own village, the Norse adventurers were able to cross continents and span seas thanks to their skills in shipbuilding and navigation. Their ships, built with overlapping timber planks, were powered by both sails and oars. The most famous were the longships—fighting vessels holding up to 200 warriors (see box).

⚔ **859** Vikings raid ports in Spain and in the western Mediterranean (–862).

👑 **c.860** The first Viking settlement is established in the Faeroe Islands.

⚔ **866** The Danish Great Army lands in East Anglia (England).

⚔ **867** Danish Vikings occupying England capture the town of York.

⚔ **878** Alfred, king of Wessex in southwest England, defeats the Danes at the Battle of Edington.

👑 **882** Oleg makes Kiev capital of the Rus state, which extends from the Gulf of Finland to the Black Sea.

👑 **911** Charles the Simple allows Vikings under Rollo to settle Normandy.

👑 **954** Erik Bloodaxe, the last Viking king of York, is killed at the Battle of Stainmore.

☀ **965** Harald Bluetooth of Denmark becomes the first Scandinavian monarch to be baptized as a Christian.

👑 **c.986** Erik the Red founds Viking settlements in Greenland.

👑 **c.1000** Viking Greenlanders found a shortlived settlement on the North American coast at L'Anse aux Meadows in Newfoundland.

⚔ **1013** Danes under Svein Forkbeard invade England.

⚔ **1016** Cnut (Canute), Svein's son, is recognized as king of England.

👑 **1028** Cnut unites England, Denmark, and Norway under his rule in a short-lived North Sea empire.

👑 **1035** Magnus the Good is crowned king of Norway.

⚔ **1085** A large-scale Danish invasion of England is prepared but is abandoned.

AMERICAS

c.900 A remarkable road network is begun in northwestern New Mexico. Radiating out from Chaco Canyon, the roads are up to 35 feet (10 m) wide—far wider than seems necessary for a small society that does not even have pack animals.

c.900 The Pueblo Culture of southwest North America begins to build multistory houses arranged around a kiva, a ceremonial center.

c.900 Mayan civilization finally collapses in the southern lowlands, and the surviving cities are abandoned. Overpopulation, disease, warfare, and social revolution as well as drought are among the theories put forward to explain the collapse.

EUROPE

900 A medical school is founded at Salerno on the west coast of southern Italy.

c.906 Magyars from Hungary destroy the Slav empire of Moravia and capture Slovakia, which remains a Hungarian possession for the next thousand years.

910 Duke William of Aquitaine founds the Benedictine Abbey of Cluny, the most magnificent monastery in Europe.

911 The French king buys off Norman (Northmen) settlers by granting their leader, Rollo, the duchy of Normandy in northern France.

911 The Byzantine Emperor Leo VI signs a treaty with Oleg, ruler of Kiev, granting Varangian traders from Rus special privileges.

AFRICA

The Fatimid Dynasty took its name from Fatima, daughter of Muhammad and wife of Ali, from whom Shiite Muslims trace the succession of the Prophet. In the course of the 10th century Fatimid rulers established a powerful Shiite state in North Africa that rivaled the Sunni Abbasids for domination of the Islamic world. This Fatimid-era manuscript illustration shows the sport of stick fighting.

WESTERN ASIA

c.900 The Persian scholar ar-Razi, known in the west as Rhazes, first classifies matter as animal, vegetable, or mineral. Rhazes also describes infectious diseases.

c.900 Resurgence of Byzantine power in Anatolia.

901 Beginning of Saminid rule in Persia.

935 The text of the Koran, the sacred book of Islam, is finalized.

SOUTH & CENTRAL ASIA

c.900 Tribes of Turkish nomads are driven into Afghanistan and Persia by China's westward expansion.

c.900 The Hindu Shahi family controls the Kabul Valley region in Afghanistan.

916 The Khitans, horse-riding nomads, found a kingdom in Mongolia.

EAST ASIA & OCEANIA

900 Woodblock printing is widely used in China, Japan, and Korea.

906 Annam, in central Vietnam, achieves independence from China.

907 The last Tang emperor of China is deposed, and China splits into ten separate states (the Ten Kingdoms).

Chinese woodblock printer at work.

👑 **c.900** The Toltecs establish a capital at Tula (northwest of Mexico City), with a population that grows to about 40,000.

Monumental stone sculptures of warriors from the Toltec capital of Tula.

👑 **929** Abdurrahman III (891–961), emir of Córdoba in Spain, proclaims himself caliph—chief civil and religious leader of the Islamic world.

👑 **930** Norse settlers in Iceland establish the Althing, the world's oldest parliament.

✕ **944** London, England, is beset by a combined force of Danish and Norwegian Vikings.

⊕ **c.945** Gerbert of Aurillac, a French philosopher and future pope, introduces Hindu–Arabic numbers to Europe, but the new system does not at first catch on.

Wood carving from the Igbo Culture, Nigeria.

👑 **909** The Fatimid Dynasty, leaders of the Ismaeli branch of Shia Islam, is established in Kairouan, Tunisia.

✕ **915** The Fatimids invade Egypt.

👑 **935** Algiers founded by Arabs.

⊕ **c.950** The Igbo people of the east Niger Delta (Nigeria) develop an advanced Iron Age culture. They also import copper for bronzemaking, exporting ivory and slaves in return.

📖 **939** Birth of Firdausi, Persian poet (d.1020), who in later life wrote the Persian national epic, the *Shahnama* (Book of Kings).

👑 **945** The Buyids, an Islamic military group, establish themselves in Baghdad, ruling in the name of the Abbasids.

☀ **c.930** A royal inscription recording the foundation of a temple to the god Siva is the first known specimen of the Telugu language of southern India.

✕ **947** The Khitans overrun northeast China and establish the Liao Dynasty, with its capital at Beijing. The Khitans adopt many Chinese administrative techniques.

👑 **935** Koryo, the northern state that gave Korea its name, becomes the dominant power and unifies the country.

👑 **939** Annam (northern Vietnam) wins independence, although nominally remaining a tributary of China.

✕ **939** Revolts against imperial rule set off a period of civil war in Japan.

⊕ **c.945** The Dunhuang star map is produced in China; it uses a type of projection not known in the West until reinvented in 1568 by the Flemish geographer and mapmaker Gerardus Mercator.

AMERICAS

EUROPE

AFRICA

WESTERN ASIA

SOUTH & CENTRAL ASIA

EAST ASIA & OCEANIA

900–950 A.D.

Settling Oceania

▲ A traditional Maori good-luck charm, this *tiki* is made of jade. New Zealand was the last major landfall of the Polynesians who settled the South Pacific islands in the 1st millennium A.D.

HUNDREDS OF YEARS BEFORE *western peoples crossed the Pacific, Polynesians voyaging in canoes built with stone and coral tools settled islands scattered over an ocean area of 10 million square miles (26 million sq. km). It is impossible to date or track these journeys accurately, but the main migrations took place during the 1st millennium A.D.—a period of climate warming, when reliable trade winds and stable seas allowed for long sea journeys. The available evidence suggests that colonization involved deliberate voyaging by seafarers who were able to navigate with remarkable precision.*

Similarities between the languages of Polynesia and Southeast Asia are the strongest evidence that settlers entered the Pacific from the northwest, perhaps as long as 3,500 years ago. Traveling in outrigger canoes, the migrants brought with them a distinctive pottery, staple crops including the banana, breadfruit, and coconut, and domesticated chickens, dogs, and pigs.

By 1000 B.C. the newcomers had settled Fiji, Tonga, and Samoa. In the course of time the skill of potterymaking was lost on the islands, probably for lack of suitable clay; the settlers used shells and gourds instead. A Polynesian farming and fishing culture evolved, with its own distinctive toolkit of

shell, coral, and stone implements. From the Tonga–Samoa region Polynesian culture reached the Marquesas Islands by 300 B.C. This island group is ideally placed for dispersal, since it is located at the center of the "Polynesian triangle," with its corners at Easter Island, Hawaii, and New Zealand.

Easter Island was the first of this trio to be settled, by about 300 A.D. On the then densely wooded island the colonists in time established an impressive and enigmatic culture, sculpting huge stone statues and developing the only written language to be found in Oceania. About a century later, seafarers completed the 2,400-mile (3,800-km) voyage to the Hawaiian

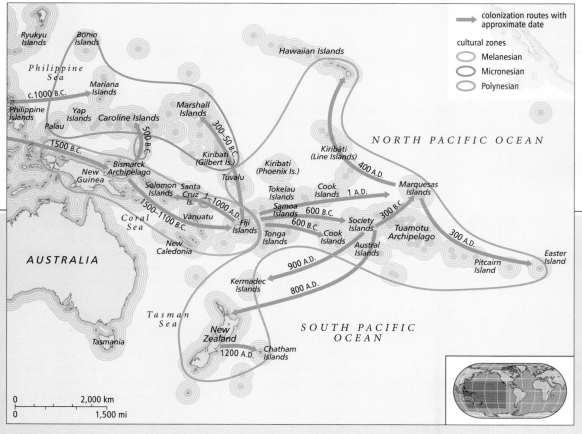

◄ It took many centuries to discover and settle the Pacific islands, but by 1000 A.D. the quest was almost over. The Marquesas Islands were important staging posts in the final round of exploration, serving as a base for voyagers traveling north to Hawaii, east to Easter Island, and south to New Zealand.

Islands, a chain of lush volcanic islands ringed by coral reefs teeming with fish.

When Polynesians reached New Zealand around 800 A.D., they found a very different world. There were no coral reefs, and the climate was too cool to grow the usual crops. Instead, the settlers' staple became the sweet potato, which they supplemented with native plants, including a giant rhizome (root) that needed several days' cooking to make it edible.

Pigs and chickens had not survived the sea voyage, but settlers found other sources of meat. New Zealand's long isolation and the scarcity of natural predators meant that some of its birds had lost the power of flight. The most remarkable were the islands' 19 species of moa, the largest of which stood 12 feet (3.5 m) high. At first the moa were so numerous that the settlers ate only their legs, discarding the rest of the carcass; in time so many were killed that the birds became extinct.

The colonists established tribes, each named for the giant canoe that brought them (they did not call themselves Maoris until after contact with Europeans). By the 13th century they still lived in small, scattered communities; but as the population increased, competition for diminishing food resources produced a militaristic society living in fortresses.

▲ The breadfruit was one of the staple foods that settlers helped spread across Polynesia. Its pulpy fruit is usually roasted or dried and ground into flour.

▼ Statues line a platform on Easter Island. Scholars still argue over the exact meaning of the sculptures, which are thought to represent the spirits of dead ancestors.

Way Finding

In the past it was often claimed that Polynesian seafarers made their discoveries by accident in the course of so-called "drift voyages." Now, however, computer modeling of ocean currents and experiments with replica canoes (*above*) have suggested this explanation is almost certainly wrong. Some scholars now think that the voyagers may have had a deliberate strategy to increase their chances of survival. They believe that they waited for a shift in the normal wind direction (from east to west), then sailed east hoping to find land. If they failed, the homeward journey was thereby made easier when the wind shifted back to its normal direction. The mariners navigated by interpreting natural signs, following birds that roosted on land and looking for the characteristic clouds that form over islands. They also noted telltale changes in wave patterns. At night they studied the heavens, steering toward a point on the horizon where known stars rose in succession.

〰 **c.0 A.D.** Polynesians begin to spread out from the Marquesas Islands.

〰 **c.300** Settlers reach Easter Island.

〰 **318** Earliest date given by carbon dating of a grave on Easter Island.

〰 **c.400** Settlers from the Marquesas Islands reach Hawaii.

📖 **c.700** The inhabitants of Easter Island begin carving stone statues (called *moai*) set on platforms (*ahu*).

〰 **800** Destruction of the forests on Easter Island is already under way—an ecological disaster confirmed by pollen records.

〰 **c.800** Polynesian settlers, possibly from Tahiti or the Society Islands, reach New Zealand's North Island, which they call Aotearoa, "the Land of the Long White Cloud."

〰 **c.1000** Migrants from Tahiti reach Hawaii and enslave the earlier settlers.

〰 **c.1250** The global climate begins to deteriorate, making lengthy sea journeys more hazardous. By the time European explorers reach the Pacific, the Polynesians no longer make voyages between the central islands and Easter Island, Hawaii, or New Zealand.

950–1000 A.D.

AMERICAS

 c.987 The Toltec ruler Topiltzin is driven into exile in "Tlapallan"—probably the Yucatán Peninsula.

 c.1000 Under Toltec influence the Mayan city of Chichén Itzá embarks on two centuries of prosperity.

 c.1000 The Chimú people of coastal Peru build a capital, Chan Chan, that at its height will house around 50,000 people.

EUROPE

The origin of the Holy Roman Empire, which came to dominate much of central Europe in medieval times, is usually traced back to the coronation of Charlemagne by Pope Leo III in Rome in 800 A.D. When Charlemagne's empire was divided after his death, the line of succession passed to the rulers of its central lands, incorporating much of modern Germany and northern Italy. The title implied a close relationship between the rulers of this huge realm and the popes, who saw the emperors as their secular champions. Something of the pomp associated with the emperors can be seen in this jeweled golden crown, created for the coronation of Otto I in Rome in 962.

954 Eric Bloodaxe, the last Viking king of York, is killed; England is united under the Anglo-Saxon King Edred.

955 Otto I (912–973), king of the Germans, defeats the Magyars at the Battle of Lechfeld, putting an end to 60 years of Magyar attacks.

962 After conquering Italy, Otto I is crowned Holy Roman emperor in Rome.

966 Six years after founding the Polish state, King Mieszko converts to Roman Catholic Christianity.

AFRICA

965 Birth of al-Hazen, Arab scientist (died 1038) who did pioneering work on vision. His *Book of Optics* remains the most authoritative treatment of optics for centuries.

969 The Fatimids conquer Egypt and found Cairo.

972 A university is founded at Cairo.

c.980 Arab settlers found towns along the eastern coast of Africa.

c.985 By now Islam is penetrating the Christian kingdoms of Nubia.

WESTERN ASIA

963 In Baghdad the Arab astronomer al-Sufi produces *The Book of Fixed Stars*, which mentions nebulae—clouds of interstellar gas and dust.

965 Sviatoslav, ruler of Kiev, crushes the Khazars, a Turkish people who converted to Judaism and built an empire north of the Black Sea.

973 Birth of al-Biruni, Arab mathematician and traveler whose *History of India* helps spread knowledge of Indian numerals.

SOUTH & CENTRAL ASIA

962 Alptigin, a Turkish warrior, founds a Turkic Islamic kingdom in Afghanistan, with its capital at Ghazni. The Ghaznavid Dynasty will control this region for two hundred years.

980 Avicenna (ibn Sina), the great Arab philosopher and physician, is born near Bukhara, in present-day Uzbekistan.

985 Rajaraja inherits the Chola throne in Southeast India. He restores Chola power and goes on to conquer south India.

998 Mahmud of Ghazni, grandson of Alptigin, inherits the Ghaznavid crown, vowing to carry Islamic power into Hindu India.

EAST ASIA & OCEANIA

960 Taizu becomes first emperor of the Song Dynasty.

965 Taizu begins a program of Chinese reunification by taking Szechwan.

976 Chang Ssu-Hsun invents the chain drive for use in a mechanical clock.

978 Chinese scholars begin compiling a 1,000-volume encyclopedia.

979 The Song Dynasty's second emperor takes Wuh-Teh, last of the Ten Kingdoms, completing Chinese reunification.

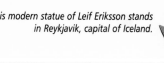

⊕ c.1000 Leif Eriksson, son of Erik the Red, establishes a settlement in Vinland on the coast of Newfoundland.

This modern statue of Leif Eriksson stands in Reykjavik, capital of Iceland.

AMERICAS

👑 c.982 Vikings, led by Eric the Red, set up a camp on Greenland, establishing a larger colony four years later.

✕ 982 The Slavs revolt against German rule and recover most of their territories to the east of the Elbe River (–983).

👑 987 Hugh Capet is crowned king of France, founding the Capetian Dynasty.

☀ 988 Vladimir, ruler of Kiev, marries Anna, sister of the Byzantine Emperor Basil II, and introduces the Eastern Orthodox form of Christianity to his Russian subjects.

☀ 999 Gerbert of Aurillac, inventor, mathematician, and philosopher, becomes the first French pope, taking the title of Sylvester II.

☀ 1000 The Magyars of Hungary convert to Roman Catholic Christianity.

☀ 1000 King Olaf introduces Christianity to Sweden.

EUROPE

The remains of the Viking settlement at Brattahild in southwestern Greenland.

⊕ c.1000 First Iron Age settlements in Zimbabwe.

👑 c.1000 The Kingdom of Ghana in today's Mauretania is at the height of its power. It controls the salt and gold trade to Egypt and coastal West Africa.

AFRICA

⊕ 977 A hospital is founded in Baghdad that employs 24 physicians and houses a surgery and a department for eye disorders.

⊕ 984 Ahmad and Mahmud, two brothers from Isfahan (Persia), make the earliest surviving dated astrolabe.

WESTERN ASIA

✕ 1000 Rajaraja invades Ceylon (Sri Lanka) and destroys its capital, Anuradhapura.

Ibn Sina, shown here in a manuscript illumination (seated in red), became the best known of all medieval Arab scholars in the west under the Anglicized version of his name, Avicenna. His *Canon of Medicine*, drawing on the classical writings of Aristotle and Galen, was the most influential medical textbook of the Middle Ages.

SOUTH & CENTRAL ASIA

⊕ 984 Chiao Wei-Yo invents the canal lock—an enclosure with gates at each end—for raising or lowering boats as they pass from one level to another.

👑 995 Fujiwara Michinaga (died 1027) becomes the true ruler of Japan. Through strategic marriages he becomes the father-in-law to three emperors, a retired emperor, and a crown prince.

⊕ c.1000 By this time the Chinese are burning coal for fuel.

EAST ASIA & OCEANIA

950–1000 A.D.

AMERICAS

⚙ **c.1000** The Hohokam of Arizona are the first known people to employ etching, using the fermented juice of cactus fruit to incise designs in shells.

⚙ **c.1000** The Mississippian Culture is by now well established in midwestern and southeastern North America.

Around 1000 A.D. artists of Arizona's long-lasting Hohokam Culture devised a revolutionary new way of producing pictures. The method involved partially covering stones or shells with resinous pitch, and then daubing the exposed portions with the acidic juice of a desert cactus. The resulting images, of which this bird is a typical example, were the world's first etchings.

EUROPE

⚔ **1000** Venice eliminates Dalmatian pirates to gain control of the Adriatic.

⚔ **1002** The Byzantine Emperor Basil II defeats the Bulgarians at Vidin in western Bulgaria.

⚔ **1004** Arab raiders sack Pisa.

⚔ **1014** At the Battle of Clontarf the Irish King Brian Boru breaks Viking domination of Ireland.

👑 **1015** The death of Vladimir, ruler of Kievan Russia, is followed by a violent succession struggle among his 11 sons.

⚔ **1016** Cnut, son of the Danish king, defeats an English army and becomes king of all England.

AFRICA

⚙ **1005** The House of Knowledge, a science library, is founded in Cairo, Egypt.

👑 **1007** The Hammadids, a Berber dynasty, found the city of Qalat Bani Hammad, with one of the largest mosques in North Africa, in the Algerian highlands.

⚙ **c.1010** Arab astronomer ibn-Yunis completes the *Large Astronomical Tables of al-Hakkim*, the most accurate yet compiled, named for the Fatimid caliph in Cairo.

WESTERN ASIA

⚙ **c.1005** The Arab scholar Avicenna (ibn Sina) writes his five-volume *Canon of Medicine*, which becomes the standard Islamic work on the subject.

📖 **1008** The Persian poet Firdausi completes the Persian national epic the *Shahnama* (Book of Kings) and dedicates it to the Ghaznavid ruler Mahmud.

SOUTH & CENTRAL ASIA

⚔ **1007** Rajendra, heir to southern India's Chola Empire, invades the Deccan in eastern India.

☀ **1007** In northeastern Iran the 166-ft (51-m) Gunbad-i Qabus is built as a funerary tower to house the body of an Islamic prince.

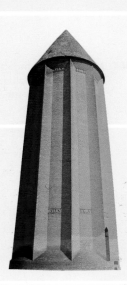

The Gunbad-i Qabus Tower in northeastern Iran

⚔ **1008** Mahmud of Ghazni, the Turkish ruler of an Islamic empire based in Afghanistan, defeats a coalition of northern Indian Hindu rulers at Peshawar.

EAST ASIA & OCEANIA

⚙ **c.1000** The seven-day week is introduced to China, probably from Persia; before this the week was commonly ten days.

☀ **c.1000** Date generally given for the arrival of Buddhism in Thailand (it may have arrived earlier).

📖 **c.1000** Sei Shonagon, a lady in the Japanese imperial court, completes *The Pillow Book*, a collection of anecdotes, lists, and personal thoughts.

AMERICAS

👑 **c.1000** Tula, the Toltec capital, is central Mexico's chief city, with a population of about 60,000.

✕ **c.1000** Following a catastrophic population decline, the southern lowlands of Mayan Central America are by now sparsely inhabited; most people no longer live in cities but in small waterside settlements.

👑 **c.1002** Following in the wake of his brother Lief, Thorvald Ericsson makes a journey of exploration to North America and is killed by Native Americans.

👑 **c.1010** Icelandic explorer Thorfinn Karlsefni attempts to found a settlement in North America. Hostilities with the native inhabitants and desertion by some of his companions force him to leave after three winters.

👑 **c.1020** The main period of Viking exploration of North America comes to an end.

EUROPE

✕ **1017** Norman soldiers first appear in southern Italy, fighting as mercenaries.

👑 **1018** The Byzantines annex Bulgaria.

👑 **1019** Cnut inherits the throne of Denmark in addition to his English possessions, creating a short-lived North Sea empire.

👑 **1019** Yaroslav the Wise, the greatest ruler of Kievan Russia, deposes his brother Sviatopolk and gains the throne, but faces continued opposition.

👑 **1020** Yaroslav the Wise embarks on an ambitious building program.

AFRICA

☀ **1013** The al-Hakim mosque is built in Cairo for the Fatimid caliph al-Hakim, whom the Druze religious sect will later revere as an incarnation of God.

WESTERN ASIA

☀ **1009** Caliph al-Hakim orders the destruction of the Church of the Holy Sepulcher in Jerusalem.

📖 **1020** Death of the Persian poet Firdausi.

Page from an illuminated manuscript of the Shahnama (Book of Kings).

SOUTH & CENTRAL ASIA

👑 **1014** On the death of his father Rajendra succeeds as ruler of India's Chola Empire.

✕ **1018** The forces of Mahmud of Ghazni pillage the sacred city of Mathura in northern India.

✕ **1021** Rajendra sends a Chola expeditionary force to Bengal.

✕ **1023** Mahmud of Ghazni destroys and loots the wealthy Hindu temple of Somnath on the Gujarat coast, returning to Afghanistan with about 6 tons of gold.

EAST ASIA & OCEANIA

👑 **1004** China's Song emperor agrees to pay an annual tribute to the Khitans, who control an area covering most of present-day Mongolia, Manchuria, and part of northeast China.

📖 **1010** Lady Murasaki, a Japanese noblewoman, completes *The Tale of Genji*, the world's earliest surviving novel.

⊕ **1012** After a devastating famine China's Song government imports a double-cropping, drought-resistant strain of rice from Champa (central Vietnam).

1000–1025 A.D.

SONG DYNASTY CHINA

AFTER 50 YEARS OF CHAOS *following the collapse of the Tang Dynasty the emperors of the Song Dynasty reunified China and imposed internal peace. A succession of enlightened rulers and a scholarly civil service presided over an intellectual and artistic renaissance. The Song fostered technical innovation that helped create economic prosperity and an urban middle class. Agricultural productivity increased thanks to the introduction of new strains of rice from Vietnam, and trade flourished. National defense, however, was the Song Empire's great weakness. Diplomacy and tributes kept enemies at bay until 1126, when invaders from the north captured the capital, Kaifeng. The Song retreated south to Hangzhou, where they enjoyed another 150 years of prosperity before the empire was finally engulfed by the Mongols.*

▲ The Song era was one of artistic creativity and religious freedom. This statuette of the period shows Laozu, founder of the ancient Daoist faith, seated on a water buffalo—a symbol of the Daoist belief in harmony between humans and the natural world.

When Taizu, the first Song emperor, came to power in 960, one of his first acts was to place the army under civilian control. Civil servants would come to dominate most aspects of Song government and society. In Taizu's reign about 30,000 candidates took the civil service examinations; by the dynasty's end the number had risen to nearly 400,000. Many high-ranking civil servants came from humble backgrounds and were educated at publicly funded schools.

Breaking from Buddhist traditions, the Song fostered a return to Confucian rationalism, promoting a philosophy that encouraged curiosity about the workings of the physical world. Advances in printing enabled the new ideas to circulate widely. Song inventive genius also produced gunpowder, the needle compass, and the mechanical clock.

New technology helped boost food production and industrial output. The population grew rapidly, and so did the cities, which changed from being mainly administrative units to commercial and residential centers. Landlords and gentry moved into towns to enjoy the urban pleasure grounds—theaters,

---

960 Seizing power in a military coup, Taizu becomes the first emperor of the Song Dynasty.

970 Taizong, the second Song emperor, completes the reunification of China, which had split into ten separate kingdoms after the Tang Dynasty collapsed.

1004 Zhenzong, the third Song emperor, is forced to pay the Khitans an annual tribute of 200,000 rolls of silk and 6,237 pounds (2,830 kg) of silver.

1034 At this time the Song imperial library contains 80,000 volumes.

c.1042 Bi Sheng, a commoner, invents a movable type using baked clay characters glued with wax in an iron frame.

1044 The Song agree to pay the Tanguts an annual tribute of 130,000 rolls of silk, 50,000 ounces (1,400 kg) of silver, and 20,000 pounds (9,000 kg) of tea.

1044 The Song administrator Fan Zhongyan introduces a program of bureaucratic, military, and land reforms. Measures include civil-service recruitment strictly on academic merit and the abolition of appointments by patronage.

1054 Chinese astronomers observe a supernova (exploding star). Their records of the event have enabled modern astronomers to establish that the explosion was the origin of the Crab Nebula.

1069 Wang Anshi begins a radical reform program aimed at boosting agricultural output.

1078 Iron production in China reaches 125,000 tons a year; a single ironworks employs nearly 3,000 workers.

1083 Sima Guang, Chinese scholar and statesman, completes a history of China from 403 B.C. to the beginning of the Song Dynasty.

1085 Death of Shenzong, sixth Song emperor. He is succeeded by his son Zhezong, but real power rests in the hands of a regent, the Dowager Empress Gao, who dismisses Wang Anshi and reinstates the conservatives.

1092 The engineer Su Song completes a remarkable 29-foot (9-m) astronomical clock driven by water power.

restaurants, and shops. Taking their lead from the emperors, who were themselves either artists or patrons of the arts, the middle class became avid collectors of paintings, ceramics, and calligraphy.

Not everyone benefited from the growing sophistication. Women's status declined in the cities, where their labor was less needed than in the countryside. The practice of foot-binding—deforming the feet of girls from the age of five to make them small and dainty—became widespread.

The Song preferred to buy off external enemies rather than fight them, but by the mid 11th century the annual tributes were a considerable financial drain. In 1069 the statesman Wang Anshi tried to tackle the problem. Realizing that government wealth was ultimately dependent on the prosperity of individual peasant taxpayers, Wang reduced land taxes, introduced credit plans, and provided food relief. The wealthy landowners blocked many of his reforms, but revenues rose.

In 1122 the Song allied with the Jin Dynasty of eastern Manchuria to defeat their old enemy, the Khitans. But then the Jin turned on the Song, capturing the emperor and taking Kaifeng. The Song retreated south and established a new capital at Hangzhou, where they enjoyed another golden age before Mongol hordes swept it away by 1279.

▶ The Song lost a substantial part of their empire in the 1120s, when the Jin rulers of Manchuria successfully invaded China, establishing their own rule in the northern part of the country.

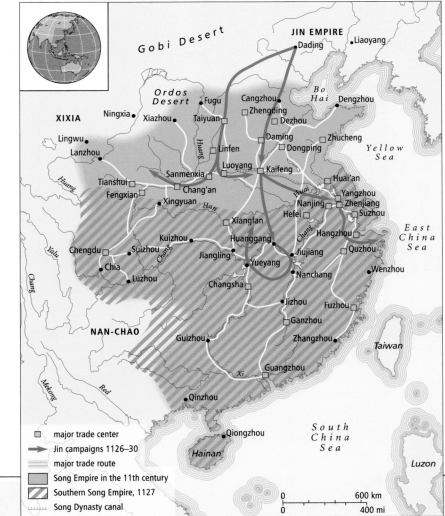

Legend:
□ major trade center
➤ Jin campaigns 1126–30
▬ major trade route
▨ Song Empire in the 11th century
▨ Southern Song Empire, 1127
▨ Song Dynasty canal

0   600 km
0   400 mi

☰ **1093** Following the death of the Dowager Empress Gao, the Emperor Zhezong puts the reformers back in power.

A Boom in Seaborne Trade

When hostile neighboring peoples cut off China's overland trade routes through Central Asia, the Song were forced to become a sea power. Chinese mariners had long taken to the seas in junks like the model shown here; now shipwrights produced improved versions, partly inspired by Arab designs. Innovations included four-deck vessels with watertight holds, navigational aids, and rigging that enabled them to sail close to the wind—that is, to keep the ship heading as close as possible into the wind while keeping the sails filled. The largest ships could carry 1,000 men and had 12 sails. Junks weighing 250 tons transported bulk cargos of silks, porcelain, and other manufactured goods as far west as the Red Sea. On the return voyage their holds were filled with raw materials and luxury items such as gems, ivory, and spices. Overseas trade became the mainstay of China's economy. Between 960 and the end of the 12th century export revenues multiplied 130 times.

☰ **1095** 80,000 candidates take civil service examinations.

☰ **1100** China's population reaches 97 million.

✕ **1126** The Jin of eastern Manchuria seize the Song capital of Kaifeng and imprison the emperor and his son.

☰ **1135** Emperor Gaozong establishes a new capital at Hangzhou, marking the start of the Southern Song period.

✕ **1268** The Mongol leader Kublai Khan embarks on the conquest of the Southern Song lands (–1279).

AMERICAS

⊛ **c.1025** Metalworkers in Costa Rica and Panama make gold pendants in the shape of frogs, turtles, and crocodile-headed figures.

📖 **c.1025** A new style of polychrome ceramics appears in Panama, abstract and geometric designs replacing figurative decorations.

EUROPE

King Cnut (or Canute) has been known to generations of schoolchildren for the story that he once tried unsuccessfully to order back the incoming tide. The tale, invented in the 12th century by a monk eager to contrast earthly rulers' powers unfavorably with those of God, does scant justice to a hard-headed and able king. By his own efforts Cnut created an empire that straddled the North Sea, bringing his native Denmark together with England and Norway for a time under his sway. Although he won the thrones of England and Norway by conquest, he proved a wise and competent monarch, restoring churches, patronizing the arts, and enforcing the rule of law.

📖 **1026** Guido D'Arrezzo, an Italian monk, introduces solmization in music (do, re, mi, fa, sol, la).

👑 **1027** Birth of William I, illegitimate son of Robert, duke of Normandy, and future king of England.

⚔ **1028** King Cnut of England and Denmark conquers Norway, expanding his North Sea empire.

⚔ **1028** King Sancho of Navarre takes Castile from the Arabs.

AFRICA

⊛ **c.1038** Al-Hazen, Arab physician and pioneer of the science of optics, describes a room-size camera obscura.

⊛ **1039** Al-Hazen dies in Cairo, Egypt.

☀ **1047** Christodoulos, pope (head) of Egypt's Coptic Church, transfers the patriarchate from Alexandria to Cairo.

WESTERN ASIA

⊛ **c.1030** The Persian philosopher-physician Avicenna (ibn Sina) writes *The Book of Healing*, a medical encyclopedia.

⊛ **1037** Avicenna dies at Hamadan, Iran.

⚔ **1043** Seljuk Turks capture the Persian city of Isfahan.

📖 **1048** Omar Khayyam, Persian poet, mathematician, and astronomer, is born in Nishapur, Iran.

SOUTH & CENTRAL ASIA

⚔ **c.1030** The Chola King Rajendra I sends a fleet to seize key points in the Srivijaya Empire of Sumatra and Malaya.

👑 **1030** Death of Mahmud of Ghazni.

⚔ **1037** Seljuk Turks seize the Ghaznavid-controlled cities of Nishapur and Merv, in the Persian region of Khurasan.

⚔ **1040** The Seljuks defeat the Ghaznavids at the Battle of Dandanqan.

👑 **1044** The Chola King Rajendra I dies.

EAST ASIA & OCEANIA

⊛ **1035** A painting shows a spinning wheel in use in China.

⊛ **1035** The Japanese make new paper from recycled paper.

👑 **1036** Birth of Su Shi, great Chinese poet and statesman.

⚔ **1038** Li Yuanhao, ruler of the Tibetan-speaking Tanguts, launches an attack on Song China.

⊛ **c.1042** A Chinese artisan named Bi Sheng invents movable-type printing.

📖 **c.1050** An offshoot of the Anasazi, Utah's Fremont Culture is at its peak now, producing distinctive figurines and pottery.

👑 **1031** The caliphate of Córdoba, Spain, splinters into a number of petty states.

☀ **1033** Birth in Italy of St. Anselm, philosopher and future archbishop of Canterbury.

👑 **1035** King Cnut dies, and his empire is divided among his three sons.

👑 **1035** Yaroslav the Wise emerges as undisputed ruler of Kievan Russia.

☀ **1037** The Church of St. Sophia is completed in Kiev.

⚔ **1048** The Almoravids, a Berber clan who will shortly come to rule much of North Africa, launch their first campaign.

👑 **1040** Macbeth, earl of Moray, kills Duncan I to become king of Scotland.

👑 **c.1043** Birth of Rodrigo Diaz, the Spanish warrior hero immortalized as El Cid (from the Arabic *sayyidi*, "my lord").

👑 **c.1050** Mapungubwe is established as a trade center in southern Africa's Limpopo Valley. Its elite live behind monumental walls.

Marble end-panel from the tomb of Yaroslav the Wise, St. Sophia Cathedral, Kiev, Ukraine.

📖 **1045** At the Abbey of Bec in Normandy a school is founded that will draw scholars from all over Europe.

👑 **1046** Henry III, king of the Germans, is crowned Holy Roman emperor in Rome.

👑 **c.1050** The city of Oslo is founded in Norway.

⊕ **1048** Death of al-Biruni, Arab mathematician, geographer, and physicist.

In the 11th century the Chola Dynasty reached its zenith. Its kings had long ruled one of the small kingdoms into which the Tamil-speaking lands were traditionally divided. Now they conquered an empire that covered not just most of southern India but also Sri Lanka. Their ships even raided Srivijaya, 1,250 miles (2,000 km) away on the Indonesian island of Sumatra. The wealth flowing into Chola coffers went to build splendid temples and graceful artworks like this stone carving of the Hindu god Shiva.

☀ **c.1050** Dedicated to the Hindu god Shiva, the magnificent Kandarya Mahadeva Temple is completed in north-central India. More than 900 carvings of gods, dancing girls, and demons decorate its exterior.

👑 **1044** King Anawrahta founds the first unified Burmese state at Pagan.

⊕ **1044** A Chinese text describes what is possibly the world's first needle compass.

👑 **1044** After six years of border warfare China agrees to pay annual tribute to the Tanguts.

⊕ **1044** In China Zeng Gongliang publishes the first formula for gunpowder, mixing charcoal, saltpeter, and sulfur.

AMERICAS

EUROPE

AFRICA

WESTERN ASIA

SOUTH & CENTRAL ASIA

EAST ASIA & OCEANIA

1025–1050 A.D.

135

THE NORMANS

THE NORMANS WERE THE DESCENDANTS *of Vikings who put down roots in northern France and swapped the Norse longboat for the warhorse. The finest European soldiers of the 11th century, they carved out a piecemeal empire stretching from the British Isles to the Mediterranean. In Arab Sicily they provided strong government while leaving many Muslim governors at their posts. In England they swept away the semi-independent Anglo-Saxon kingdoms and imposed a centralized feudal monarchy that became a model for medieval European government. For all their achievements, the Normans were not destined to survive as a separate culture. Like their Viking ancestors, they made their mark on history and then disappeared, swallowed up in the societies they had transformed.*

▲ Despite their Viking origins, the Normans were more used to fighting on land than to seaborne raiding by the time they invaded England in 1066. Even so, they relied on Viking-style longboats like the one shown here to make the 55-mile (90-km) crossing of the English Channel from the mouth of the Somme River to Pevensey on England's southeast coast.

Norman recorded history begins with Rolf, a Viking leader who in 911 swore homage to the Frankish king in return for land around the mouth of the Seine River in what would later be known as Normandy. Within two generations the Normans had adopted the Franks' language, religion, laws, and cavalry tactics. Mounted knights came to form an aristocracy who held lands granted to them by the duke of Normandy in return for providing military service.

Because estates usually passed to the firstborn son, many Norman younger sons sought to make their fortunes abroad. In Italy feuding between Lombard, Byzantine, and Arab rulers offered rich opportunities for mercenaries. The most remarkable Norman adventurers were three brothers of the de Hauteville family who between 1061 and 1091 conquered southern Italy and Sicily.

On the other side of Europe a succession struggle brought war between the Normans and the English. Edward the Confessor, king of England, died childless in 1066, having promised the throne to his cousin, William, duke of Normandy. On his deathbed, however, the king bowed to pressure from the nobility and chose Harold, earl of Wessex, to succeed him.

William assembled an invasion force to take by conquest what he believed was his by right. As Harold prepared to meet it, he received news that another rival, King Harald Hardrada of Norway, had landed in northeast England. Marching north, Harold surprised the Norwegians and achieved an overwhelming victory at the Battle of Stamford Bridge.

Less than three weeks later Harold was back on the south coast, confronting the Norman army at Hastings. The battle was in the balance before the

Norman Castles

William I conquered England with an army of fewer than 10,000 men. To secure his grip on the country, he built castles at strategic points. The first castles were earth and timber structures with a central tower, or "keep," built on an artificial mound, or "motte," adjoining a courtyard, or "bailey," that was enclosed by a fence of wooden stakes. The lord's family was housed in the keep, while his followers occupied buildings in the bailey, which usually contained a hall, a chapel, buildings for livestock, and workshops. Before the end of the 11th century the wooden motte-and-bailey castles began to be replaced by stone structures. The White Tower—the original Tower of London—is one of the earliest surviving examples; completed about 1078, it stood 87 ft (27 m) high with walls up to 10 ft (3 m) thick.

👑 **911** Rolf, a Viking leader, is granted lands in Normandy.

👑 **1013** When Danes invade England, Prince Edward—eldest son of King Ethelred of England and his wife Emma, sister of the duke of Normandy—goes for safety into exile in Normandy.

👑 **1027** Birth of William, illegitimate son of Robert, duke of Normandy.

👑 **1030** Rainulf, the first Norman to secure territory in Italy, is given the town and territory of Aversa.

👑 **1035** At the age of 8 William succeeds his father as duke of Normandy.

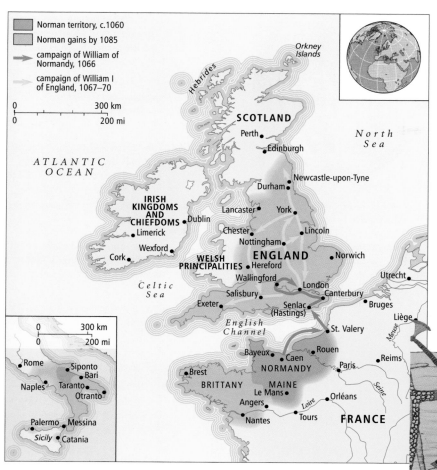

Norman territory, c.1060
Norman gains by 1085
campaign of William of Normandy, 1066
campaign of William I of England, 1067–70

0   300 km
0   200 mi

SCOTLAND
Perth
Edinburgh
Orkney Islands
North Sea
ATLANTIC OCEAN
Hebrides
Newcastle-upon-Tyne
Durham
Lancaster   York
IRISH KINGDOMS AND CHIEFDOMS
Dublin
Limerick
Chester   Lincoln
Nottingham
Wexford
ENGLAND
Cork
WELSH PRINCIPALITIES
Hereford   Norwich
Wallingford
Celtic Sea
Salisbury   London   Utrecht
Canterbury
Exeter   Senlac (Hastings)   Bruges
English Channel   Liège
St. Valery
Bayeux   Rouen   Reims
Caen   Paris
Brest   NORMANDY
BRITTANY   MAINE   Meuse
Le Mans   Orléans
Angers   Seine
Nantes   Tours   FRANCE
Loire

0   300 km
0   200 mi
Rome   Siponto Bari
Naples   Taranto
Otranto
Palermo   Messina
Sicily   Catania

▲ From Normandy Norman power spread through Brittany and southern Italy as well as England.

▶ A mounted Norman knight strikes an Anglo-Saxon footsoldier in a detail from the Bayeux Tapestry.

Normans, fighting on horseback, finally triumphed over the English, fighting on foot. Harold perished, and with him went the old Anglo-Saxon order; for the next 500 years England would be linked to France.

William confiscated most of the Anglo-Saxon estates. He kept about a fifth of the land for himself and distributed the rest to his barons, attaching military obligations to each grant. He also reorganized the church and installed Frenchmen as bishops. The English became an oppressed majority in their own land, but the Normans did not obliterate English identity. William and his heirs left many Anglo-Saxon institutions untouched and actually strengthened some of them—the shire courts and sheriffs, for example. And if the English were forced to become more Norman, the Normans also became more English. Only a century after the Battle of Hastings a court official reported that "the peoples have become so mingled that noone can tell...who is of English and who of Norman descent."

✕ **1042** A year after Edward returns from exile in Normandy, he succeeds to the English throne.

✕ **1047** Duke William defeats rebellious barons at the Battle of Val-ès-Dunes, confirming his hold on Normandy.

⬇ **1051** King Edward of England names Duke William of Normandy as his heir.

✕ **1053** The Normans defeat and capture Pope Leo IX at Civitate, Italy.

✕ **1060** Norman forces under Robert de Hauteville (also called Guiscard "the Cunning") complete their conquest of Calabria and Apulia.

✕ **1061** Robert de Hauteville invades Sicily.

✕ **1066** Following the death of King Edward, the English throne goes to Harold, earl of Wessex. William invades England, defeats Harold at the Battle of Hastings, and is crowned king.

✕ **1069** King William I smashes an English and Danish uprising in northeast England.

✕ **1071** The fall of Bari completes the conquest of Byzantine Italy.

✕ **1072** The Normans invade Scotland, many of whose lords offer their allegiance.

⊕ **c.1078** The Normans build the White Tower, a stone fortress that forms the core of the present-day Tower of London.

⬇ **1086** The Domesday Book, an economic survey of England, is commissioned (–1087).

⬇ **1087** King William I dies in France, leaving Normandy to his son Robert and England to his second surviving son, William II, known as Rufus.

✕ **1091** The Normans complete the conquest of Sicily.

AMERICAS

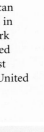

c.1050 The largest North American town emerges at Cahokia in Illinois. Construction work begins on the four-terraced Monks Mound, the largest earthen structure in the United States.

c.1050 Copper bells made by the lost-wax technique are worn as ornaments in Mexico and southwestern North America.

Mimbres pottery bowl deliberately holed to serve as a burial offering.

EUROPE

c.1050 Yaroslav the Wise compiles the first Russian legal code.

1052 The Italian city-state of Pisa captures Sardinia from the Arabs.

1052 Edward the Confessor, king of England, begins building Westminster Abbey.

1053 Danegeld (tribute paid to the Danes) is abolished in England, only to be transformed into an all-purpose tax, paid until 1162.

1054 The schism between the Eastern Orthodox and Roman Catholic churches becomes permanent.

1054 The death of Yaroslav the Wise leads to a division of Kievan Russia and renewed civil war.

1066 King Harold of England defeats and kills the Norwegian King Harald Hardrada at the Battle of Stamford Bridge in northern England.

1066 William, duke of Normandy, defeats and kills King Harold at the Battle of Hastings and is crowned king of England.

AFRICA

c.1050 Courtly life in Fatimid Egypt is depicted on beautiful lusterware—a type of pottery first developed in Iraq in the 9th century.

c.1050 In West Africa the Mossi peoples of what is now Burkina Faso resist the spread of Islam.

c.1050 The culture of the Yoruba people of Ife flourishes in Nigeria in West Africa.

WESTERN ASIA

c.1050 In Iran tall cylindrical minarets begin to replace the earlier style of square, stepped structures.

1055 The Seljuk Turks capture Baghdad from its Buyid rulers and restore the caliphate.

1058 Birth of the great Islamic theologian al-Ghazali at Tus in eastern Persia.

1064 Seljuk Turks invade Armenia and occupy the old capital of Ani.

1067 The Seljuk vizier Nizam al-Mulk founds the Nizamiya madrasa (religious college) in Baghdad.

1071 Seljuk Turks under Alp Arslan rout the Byzantines at the Battle of Manzikert in eastern Anatolia.

SOUTH & CENTRAL ASIA

c.1050 The influential Hindu philosopher Ramanuja writes of the importance of devotional worship.

c.1050 In India iron beams are used in the construction of buildings.

EAST ASIA & OCEANIA

c.1050 The sweet potato, native to South America, becomes a staple in New Zealand and Polynesia. It is unclear how it reached the islands, which are at no point less than 1,875 miles (3,000 km) from America.

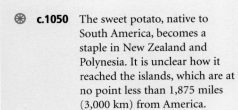

c.1050 The name of the Japanese city Heian-kyo is changed to Kyoto, meaning "capital."

The sweet potato, whose presence in Polynesia s[u] otherwise unrecorded links with South America.

AMERICAS

☀ **c.1050** Black-on-white pottery from New Mexico's Mimbres Valley is produced to serve as grave goods. The fact that most examples have holes in the bottom indicates that they were not intended for practical use.

👑 **c.1070** Through conquest and alliances Lord 8 Deer Jaguar Claw establishes a small Mixtec city-state in southern Mexico.

EUROPE

☀ **1073** Pope Gregory VII (Hildebrand) is elected and launches a reforming program, alienating rulers by denying them the right to make clerical appointments.

👑 **1075** Pope Gregory's ban on lay appointments to the church is challenged by Henry IV, Holy Roman emperor. The struggle between papacy and empire is known as the Investiture Contest.

Almost 500 years before the Reformation split Christians into Protestant and Roman Catholic camps, an earlier schism had separated the Catholic church from the Eastern Orthodox one. In the reign of the Byzantine Emperor Constantine IX (*right*), Cerularius, patriarch of Constantinople and so head of the Orthodox church, refused to meet envoys sent by Pope Leo IX, who then excommunicated him. The step marked the final breach between the two branches of Christianity, long divided by different forms of worship and administration.

AFRICA

👑 **1056** The Berber Almoravid Dynasty begins the conquest of Morocco and part of Algeria.

👑 **1062** The Almoravids establish their capital at the Moroccan city of Marrakesh.

📖 **1067** The Arab traveler al-Bakri publishes his *Description of North Africa*, an account of life in the region along the middle reaches of the Niger River.

WESTERN ASIA

👑 **1072** Alp Arslan dies and is succeeded by his son Malik Shah, whose title "shah," meaning "king" in both Arabic and Persian, indicates the Seljuk ruler's ambition to unite the Muslim world.

⊕ **1074** Omar Khayyam, commissioned by Seljuk patrons, begins work at an astronomical observatory in Iran on an accurate solar calendar.

SOUTH & CENTRAL ASIA

👑 **1070** Kulottunga I of Vengi ascends the Chola throne.

👑 **1072** The Seljuk Sultan Alp Arslan is stabbed to death in Central Asia.

EAST ASIA & OCEANIA

☀ **1053** The Byodo-in Buddhist temple, considered the finest surviving example of Fujiwara Period (894–1185) architecture, is built in Kyoto.

☀ **1066** Udayadityavarman II builds the Baphuon, a Buddhist temple-mountain, at Angkor, Cambodia.

👑 **1069** Wang Anshi launches a radical reform program in Song China.

📖 **1073** Death of the philosopher Zhou Dunyi, responsible for laying the groundwork of neo-Confucianism in China.

1050–1075 A.D.

THE SELJUK TURKS

I N 1071 A MUSLIM ARMY CAPTURED *the Byzantine emperor in a battle at Manzikert in eastern Anatolia. The victors were not Arabs but a Turkic dynasty called the Seljuks, who had risen to power with breathtaking speed. A minor clan of nomadic mercenaries at the start of the century, within two generations they won an empire covering most of present-day Iraq and Iran. Their rise had far-reaching consequences, provoking a reaction in Europe that led to the Crusades and establishing the permanent Turkic presence that turned classical Asia Minor into today's Turkey.*

▲ The Seljuks were famous warriors, reputed as much for their skills as mounted archers as for their infantrymen, shown in the relief above wearing chain-mail tunics and characteristic pointed helmets. The Seljuks began their rise as mercenary soldiers in the pay of the Ghaznavid rulers of Central Asia.

▶ The Seljuks first wrested eastern Persia from the Ghaznavids, then swung west to take control of Baghdad. In the 1060s they attacked the Christian Byzantine Empire, eventually conquering most of today's Turkey and the eastern Mediterranean lands.

major battle
Seljuk advance 1028–92
Seljuk Sultanate at maximum extent, around 1092

🜲 **c.1010** Approximate date of the death of Seljuk at the reputed age of 107. He is succeeded by his son Arslan ("Lion").

🜲 **c.1020** The Seljuks are border mercenaries in the region of Transoxiana, the land beyond the Oxus River (now Amu Darya).

⚔ **1029** Responding to Seljuk pillaging, Mahmud of Ghazni takes Arslan hostage and drives the Seljuks out of Khurasan (now northeastern Iran).

🜲 **1035** The Seljuks return to Khurasan under Chaghri-Beg and Tughril-Beg.

⚔ **1037** The Seljuks capture Nishapur, the capital of Khurasan, and Merv, an ancient trading city.

⚔ **1040** The Seljuks defeat a Ghaznavid army at Dandanqan, north of Merv.

🜲 **1055** Tughril-Beg restores the power of the Abbasid (Sunni) caliphs in Baghdad and is given the title of sultan.

⚔ **1063** Tughril-Beg dies childless. His nephew Alp Arslan ("Heroic Lion") becomes sultan after defeating rivals, including his cousin Kutulmush. He kills his father's vizier and replaces him with Nizam al-Mulk ("Order of the Realm").

⚔ **1064** Alp Arslan leads a campaign against Armenia.

☀ **1067** The Seljuk vizier Nizam al-Mulk founds the Nizamiya madrasa (college) at Baghdad.

The Assassins

Persecuted by the Seljuk upholders of Sunni Islam, the Shiites found a ruthless champion in Hasan-i Sabbah. In 1090 Hasan seized the mountain fortress of Alamut near the Caspian Sea—another Assassin fortress, at Masyaf, is shown below— and built up an army of fanatical disciples. Hasan's followers aimed to achieve maximum effect by murdering important personalities in public places—usually at a mosque during Friday prayers. Orthodox Muslims, who believed that the terrorists were drugged on hashish, called them *hashishin*, the origin of the English word "assassin." In 1092 the Assassins struck a lethal blow when they killed the Seljuk vizier Nizam al-Mulk. After his murder an Arab historian reported that the Seljuk state "disintegrated."

After Mahmud's death the Seljuks returned under two brothers called Chaghri-Beg and Tughril-Beg. This time they were after power, not just plunder. In 1037 they captured Nishapur, the capital of Khurasan, and the city of Merv. Three years later they smashed a Ghaznavid army.

Leaving Chaghri in Khurasan, Tughril-Beg moved west. After campaigning against Byzantine Armenia, he marched on Baghdad, whose Sunni caliphs had become puppets of the Shiite Buyid Dynasty. Declaring himself the champion of Sunni Islam, Tughril-Beg drove the Shiites out of Baghdad and was awarded the title of sultan—"holder of authority."

Under Alp Arslan ("Heroic Lion") the Seljuk realms became a unified empire based on a partnership between Turkish warriors and a mainly Persian bureaucracy. The chief minister was the Persian vizier Nizam al-Mulk, who filled bureaucratic posts with graduates of newly established colleges called madrasas.

In 1071 Alp Arslan led an army against the Shiite rulers of Egypt. As he was heading south, the Byzantine Emperor Romanus was marching to recover Armenia. When news of Romanus's advance reached Alp Arslan, he hurried back and caught up with the Byzantines near Manzikert, now the town of Malazgirt in eastern Turkey. The battle that followed ended with the Byzantine army in tatters and Romanus a prisoner.

Alp Arslan was succeeded by his 18-year-old son, Malik Shah. Taking advantage of the new sultan's youth, a member of the ruling dynasty carved out the Sultanate of Rum (so called in memory of ancient Rome) in Asia Minor. Malik Shah regained some of Rum in 1086 and also conquered much of Syria, marking the high point of Seljuk rule. After he and Nizam al-Mulk both died in 1092, the empire broke into a number of principalities. Rum, the front line of defense against the crusaders, survived their assaults and finally fell to the Mongols in the 13th century.

▼ The Seljuks left many monuments of their rule across western Asia, including this tomb, one of two at Kharragan in the desert of southern Iran. The domed sepulcher dates back to 1093.

Seljuk, the founder of the dynasty, was a member of a Turkish tribe that migrated from Mongolia in the 8th century. Early in the 11th century, having converted to the majority Sunni branch of Islam, the Seljuks moved into Khurasan, a Persian region controlled by the Afghan ruler Mahmud of Ghazni. Remarkable horsemen and archers, the Seljuks wreaked so much havoc that Mahmud eventually took up arms against them and drove them back across the Oxus River.

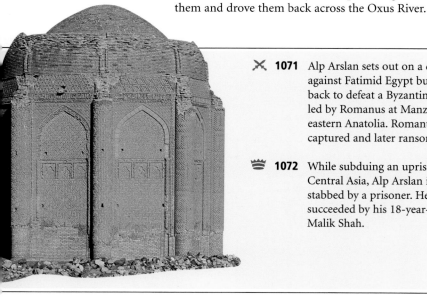

✕ **1071** Alp Arslan sets out on a campaign against Fatimid Egypt but turns back to defeat a Byzantine army led by Romanus at Manzikert in eastern Anatolia. Romanus is captured and later ransomed.

👑 **1072** While subduing an uprising in Central Asia, Alp Arslan is fatally stabbed by a prisoner. He is succeeded by his 18-year-old son, Malik Shah.

⊕ **1079** Omar Khayyam and a team of scientists under Seljuk patronage produce a reformed calendar that is the world's most accurate until the introduction of the Gregorian calendar in 1582.

✕ **1090** The Shiite sect of Assassins seizes the fortress of Alamut in the Elburz Mountains south of the Caspian Sea.

✕ **1092** Assassins murder Nizam al-Mulk. In the same year Malik Shah dies.

AMERICAS

c.1075 The Thule Inuit expand from eastern Alaska into Greenland, replacing most other arctic cultures, including the Dorset.

c.1100 The pyramid at Cholula, central Mexico, reaches its greatest extent.

c.1100 The proto-Iroquois people build longhouses in New York State.

EUROPE

Shown in battle in this illumination, Rodrigo Diaz de Bivar, known as El Cid, is the best-remembered figure of the long struggle between Christians and Muslim Moors for control of Spain. Although his fame spread widely through courtly romances only after his death, El Cid was a real warrior whose greatest exploit was the capture of Valencia in 1094. Unlike the Christian champion of the stories, however, the real El Cid was quite happy to make alliances with Moors when it suited his purpose in the complex politics of 11th-century Spain.

1076 Pope Gregory VII excommunicates the Holy Roman Emperor Henry IV for his refusal to give up the right of lay investiture and agree to other reforms; Henry's Saxon subjects rebel, and in 1077 Henry is forced to ask the pope's forgiveness at Canossa in Italy.

c.1080 The Bayeux Tapestry, telling the story of the Norman invasion of England, is made for Bishop Odo of Bayeux.

AFRICA

1076 According to Arab histories, Islam reaches the West African Empire of Ghana following military defeat by an Almoravid army.

1083 The Almoravids complete the conquest of all of North Africa west of Algiers from the Fatimids.

c.1100 The Empire of Ghana falls into decline in West Africa as new trade routes open up farther to the east.

WESTERN ASIA

1080 The Seljuk ruler Malik Shah captures Nicaea from the Byzantines, making it his capital.

1086 Malik Shah invades Palestine and expels the ruling Egyptian Fatimid Dynasty.

1090 The Assassins, a Shiite Muslim sect violently opposed to the Seljuks, make their stronghold at Alamut in the Elburz Mountains of Iran.

1092 The Assassins murder Nizam al-Mulk, vizier (chief minister) to Malik Shah, who has led two campaigns against them.

1092 On the death of Malik Shah the Seljuk sultanate begins to fragment.

EAST ASIA & OCEANIA

c.1075 The Japanese warrior class of samurai is growing as powerful landowners hire large private armies for protection.

c.1075 Magnetized needle compasses are in use as navigational devices on Chinese ships.

c.1075 Landscape painting on panels or long rolls of silk flourishes in China under the Song emperors.

1075 In China the reform program of Wang Anshi continues despite complaints of excessive taxation (–1085).

1083 In Japan Minamoto Yoshiie increases the influence of the Minamoto warrior clan during the Latter Three Years' War (–1087).

1083 Sima Guang (1018–1086), sometimes called the father of Chinese history, completes his monumental history of China, *Zizhi Tongjian* ("Comprehensive Mirror for Aid in Government").

1085 A conservative faction led by Sima Guang overturns the reforms of Wang Anshi during the regency of the Dowager Empress Gao (–1095).

👑 **c.1100** The Mayan city of Uaxactún, a neighbor of Tikal whose earliest constructions date back to about 500 B.C., is finally abandoned at about this time.

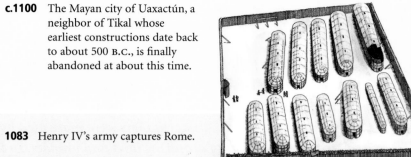

Iroquois longhouses as they looked at the time of the first European contact, c.1690.

⚔ **1083** Henry IV's army captures Rome.

⚔ **1084** Gregory VII appeals for aid to the Normans of southern Italy under Robert Guiscard; the Normans repel Henry's army but go on to sack Rome itself, forcing Gregory into exile.

⚔ **1085** King Alfonso VI of Castile captures the city of Toledo, in central Spain, from the Muslims.

👑 **1086** King William I of England orders a survey of all the property in England; the findings are recorded in a document known as the Domesday Book.

⚔ **1086** The Almovarids invade southern Spain from Morocco at the invitation of local Muslim rulers and defeat Alfonso VI near Badajoz; they establish their rule over much of Spain (–1091).

📖 **1088** The first European university is founded at Bologna in northern Italy.

⚔ **1091** The Norman adventurer Roger de Hauteville completes the conquest of Sicily with the capture of Syracuse.

☀ **1095** Pope Urban II proclaims the First Crusade at Clermont, central France.

☀ **1098** Robert of Molesme founds the Cistercian monastic order, which observes strict rules of manual labor and poverty.

⚔ **1099** The Spanish soldier Rodrigo Diaz de Bivar, nicknamed El Cid, dies defending Valencia from the Muslims.

☀ **c.1100** Islam has spread by this date to Kanem–Bornu, a trading kingdom on the southern edge of the Sahara Desert.

👑 **1095** The Byzantine Emperor Alexius I appeals to the West for military help against the Seljuk Turks.

⚔ **1097** A combined army of Greeks and crusaders from western Europe captures Nicaea, the Seljuk capital.

⚔ **1098** The Fatimids retake Palestine from the Seljuks.

⚔ **1098** The crusaders capture Antioch in Syria from the Seljuks.

⚔ **1099** The crusaders take Jerusalem.

👑 **1086** In order to escape the control of the Fujiwara clan, the Japanese Emperor Shirakawa abdicates but continues to control affairs behind the scenes as a "cloistered" emperor, introducing the system of government known as *insei*.

⊕ **c.1086** Shen Gua writes a scientific work, the *Dreampool Jottings*, considered to be a milestone in the history of Chinese science.

⊕ **1092** A water-driven mechanical clock is built for the Song court.

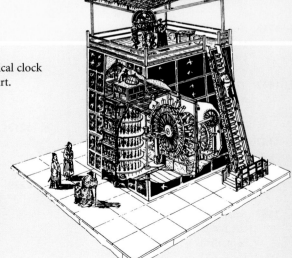

Su Song's astronomical clock featured a celestial globe and an armillary sphere showing the angle for sighting stars.

AMERICAS

EUROPE

AFRICA

WESTERN ASIA

EAST ASIA & OCEANIA

1075–1100 A.D.

143

THE CRUSADES

BETWEEN 1095 AND 1291 ARMIES *from Western Europe fought a series of wars known as crusades to recapture Palestine from Muslim control and to protect the holy places of Christianity. Crusaders wore a cross (the word "crusade" derives from* crux, *the Latin for "cross"). While many crusaders were motivated by religious zeal, others saw the crusades as a way of acquiring land and plunder. In the long run the campaigns failed, and Palestine was reclaimed by the forces of Islam.*

▲ In a scene from a 13th-century manuscript mounted crusaders confront Muslims. At the time Islamic armies had no real equivalent to the lance-wielding knights; their cavalry units were lightly armed with swords and bows, relying on mobility more than the momentum of the charge.

Pope Urban II launched the First Crusade in 1095 in response to an appeal from the Byzantine Emperor Alexius for help against the Seljuk Turks, who had recently overrun Anatolia and Syria. An army consisting mostly of French and Norman knights fought its way overland to Jerusalem, which it took in 1099. Fulcher of Chartres, a Frenchman who wrote an account of the crusade, left a vivid account of the bloody massacre of Muslims that followed the storming of the city.

One reason for the crusaders' success was that the Seljuk Turks, divided by internal feuding, had ceased for the time being to be a military threat. Taking advantage of their divisions, the crusaders set up a number of states in Palestine and Syria known collectively as Outremer ("Overseas"). Commerce flourished as fleets of ships from Venice and Genoa carried a steady stream of pilgrims and supplies to Outremer and brought exotic goods such as silks and spices back to Europe.

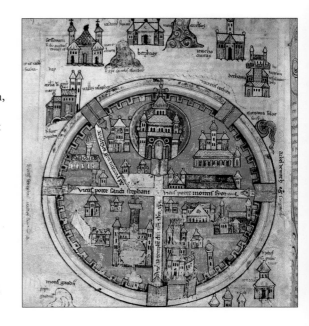

1095 Pope Urban II appeals for the launch of the First Crusade.

1096 The First Crusade ends with the capture of Jerusalem (−1099).

1113 The Order of the Hospital of St. John in Jerusalem (the Hospitalers) is founded.

1147 The Second Crusade, led by Louis VII of France and the Emperor Conrad III, ends in failure (−1149).

1147 Crusaders from England and the Low Countries on their way to the Holy Land capture Lisbon, Portugal, from the Muslims.

1187 Saladin defeats a crusader army at the Battle of Hattin and recaptures Jerusalem.

1190 The Third Crusade, led by King Richard I of England and King Philip Augustus of France, fails to retake Jerusalem but captures Acre.

1204 The Fourth Crusade sacks Constantinople, capital of the Christian Byzantine Empire.

1208 Pope Innocent III calls for a crusade against the Albigensian heretics in southern France.

1217 The Fifth Crusade attacks Muslim power in Egypt but makes no real gains (−1221).

1229 The Sixth Crusade, led by the Holy Roman Emperor Frederick II, secures Jerusalem by treaty with the sultan of Egypt; it is lost again in 1244.

1230 The Teutonic Knights begin crusading against the pagan Prussians in the Baltic region of northern Europe.

1248 King Louis IX of France leads the Seventh Crusade to Egypt (−1254).

1261 The Byzantine Empire regains Constantinople.

1270 King Louis IX dies besieging Tunis on the Eighth Crusade; he is later canonized as St. Louis.

1291 The Mamelukes of Egypt capture Acre, the last Christian stronghold in Palestine.

The Muslim reconquest of Outremer began with the fall of Edessa in 1144. The Second and Third Crusades failed to halt the Muslim advance, and by 1191 the crusader enclaves had been reduced to just the port of Acre on the Syrian coast.

By that time the Byzantines had come to resent the crusaders bitterly. The final insult came in 1204, when the Fourth Crusade sacked Constantinople, massacred its inhabitants, and established a Latin Empire in place of the Greek-speaking Byzantine one (it lasted until 1261). Although four more expeditions were sent to the Middle East during the 13th century, the crusades had lost their purpose and impetus.

The ventures to the Holy Land were only part of a wider crusading movement in Europe. Christian armies gradually reconquered Spain and Portugal from the Muslims. The Teutonic Knights, a German and Danish crusading order, were active in converting the pagan Slavs and Balts of the eastern Baltic to Christianity. And in 1208 Pope Innocent III declared a crusade against the Albigensians, followers of a heretic sect based in southern France that was wiped out amid much bloodshed over the next two decades.

◀ Christians in the Middle Ages regarded Jerusalem as the center of the world—a view made explicit in this map of the city, showing the Church of the Holy Sepulcher, where Jesus Christ's body was said to have been laid, as the main feature of the city.

▶ The First Crusade was one of history's epic treks. After crossing most of Europe on foot, the crusaders had to fight their way through the Seljuk lands in Anatolia before capturing Antioch after a seven-month siege to win a vital base in the Holy Land.

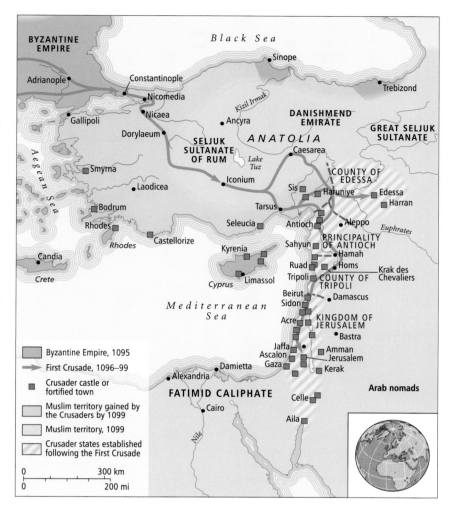

Legend:
- Byzantine Empire, 1095
- → First Crusade, 1096–99
- ■ Crusader castle or fortified town
- Muslim territory gained by the Crusaders by 1099
- Muslim territory, 1099
- Crusader states established following the First Crusade

0 — 300 km
0 — 200 mi

Crusader Castles

Relatively few in number, the crusaders relied on castles to provide strong defensive positions. Although castle building was already well advanced in Europe by the late 11th century, the defenders of the Holy Land took military architecture to new heights, building massive stone structures defended with projecting towers, concentric lines of fortification, and angled entrances. The greatest of these fortresses was Krak des Chevaliers in Syria (right). Built on the site of an earlier Islamic castle by the Knights Hospitalers, a military order of monks founded to defend the Holy Land, Krak originally housed a garrison of more than 2,000 troops. Access to the inner citadel was by a ramp that wound past four gates, making the castle virtually impossible to take by siege.

AMERICAS

c.1100 The Tarascan Kingdom emerges in Michoacán, northwest Mexico; the warlike Tarascans are highly skilled metalworkers.

c.1100 At Mesa Verde in southern Colorado and Canyon de Chelly in Arizona Anasazi farmers build villages of stone apartment dwellings beneath the overhangs of cliffs.

c.1100 The Mogollon Culture of Arizona and New Mexico is passing its peak by this time.

EUROPE

c.1100 Padded horse collars are introduced into Europe; they make it possible for horses to pull heavy plows, so improving agricultural productivity.

1100 King William II (Rufus) of England is killed by an arrow while out hunting; the throne passes to his younger brother, Henry.

1103 Malcolm Barelegs, king of Norway, is killed on a raiding expedition against Ireland.

1106 King Henry I of England gains the duchy of Normandy from his eldest brother, Robert, after winning the Battle of Tinchebray.

1108 Louis VI (the Fat) becomes king of France; he reigns until 1137 and strengthens the power of the French monarchy.

1115 St. Bernard founds a famous Cistercian abbey at Clairvaux, in the Champagne district of France.

AFRICA

1106 The Almoravid Empire in North Africa begins to break up following the death of its ruler, Yusuf ibn Tashfin.

1107 The Friday Mosque is completed at Kizimkazi on the island of Zanzibar.

1120 Ibn Tumert, a religious reformer, establishes a Berber state in Morocco's Atlas Mountains; his followers are the Almohads.

WESTERN ASIA

c.1100 Caravansaries (hostels providing free shelter for travelers) are built along important trade routes in Asia Minor.

1103 Tughtigin, a former Seljuk official who will go on to found the Burid Dynasty, becomes the independent atabeg (governor) of Damascus, Syria.

1109 By this date the crusaders have established a number of states— the so-called Latin kingdoms— in Palestine and Syria.

SOUTH & CENTRAL ASIA

c.1100 The Ghurid Dynasty takes control of northwestern Afghanistan from the Ghaznavids.

c.1100 Temple building is at its height in India; the Jagannath Temple at Puri in Orissa is begun about this time.

c.1125 The rulers of central India's Sena Dynasty begin to extend their influence northward from Orissa into Bengal.

EAST ASIA & OCEANIA

c.1100 The Pure Land Sect (a Buddhist cult) spreads among the aristocrats of the Heian court of Japan.

1101 The power of the reactionary faction at China's Song Dynasty court is reduced, and some of Wang Anshi's reforms are restored (–1104).

1106 An embassy from Pagan (Burma) is received at the Song court.

To the sophisticated Chinese of Song Dynasty times the Jürchen people of Manchuria were uncivilized nomads. But they were also fine warriors, and in 1127 they seized the Song capital of Kaifeng, together with about a third of China's land. In fact, the Jin Dynasty that the invaders set up in the conquered territories soon developed Chinese tastes, as this elegant porcelain headrest suggests. The regime survived for just over a century, finally falling to Genghis Khan's Mongols in 1234.

👑 **c.1125** Cahokia, Illinois, is by now the most important urban center of the mound-building peoples living in the Mississippi Valley.

The complex known as Cliff Palace at the heart of Colorado's Mesa Verde National Park.

AMERICAS

⚔ **1118** King Alfonso I of Aragon captures Saragossa from the Muslims and extends his kingdom to the Mediterranean.

⊕ **c.1120** Windmills first come into use in Europe.

☀ **1121** A church council condemns the teachings of French theologian Peter Abelard as heretical.

👑 **1122** An agreement between the pope and the German Emperor Henry V, the Concordat of Worms, ends the contest over lay investiture.

👑 **1125** Henry V dies and is succeeded by Lothair II of the Welf family.

☀ **c.1125** A bishopric is founded at Gardar in the Norse settlement on Greenland.

⊕ **c.1125** Land is cleared for farming, towns are built, and local fairs are founded as economic prosperity and trade revive in western Europe.

EUROPE

👑 **c.1120** Traders from Kilwa oust rivals from Mogadishu at Sofala (Mozambique), establishing a monopoly on its gold trade.

AFRICA

📖 **1111** Death of al-Ghazali (born 1058), the most important Muslim jurist and theologian of his day, who taught at Baghdad and Nishapur (Persia).

📖 **1122** Death of the Persian astronomer, mathematician, and poet Omar Khayyam.

⚔ **1124** Tyre falls to the crusaders; most of the coast of Palestine is now in the hands of the Latin Kingdom of Jerusalem.

WESTERN ASIA

The Jagannath Temple in Orissa remains one of India's most visited Hindu pilgrimage sites.

SOUTH & CENTRAL ASIA

📖 **c.1110** The Song Emperor We Zong founds the Imperial School of Painting and catalogs his collections of paintings and ancient bronzes.

👑 **1114** The Jürchen people of Manchuria stop paying annual tribute to the Khitan state of Liao on China's northern border.

👑 **1115** The Jürchen establish the Jin Dynasty in former Khitan lands.

⚔ **1117** With Chinese help the Jürchen invade and destroy Liao (–1124).

📖 **c.1120** *Konjaku monogatari* ("Tales of Time Now Past") is compiled; a collection of more than 1,000 Buddhist and secular tales, it is notable for its rich descriptions of the lives of Japanese nobles and common people.

👑 **1123** The Jin force the Korean state of Koryo to recognize them as overlords.

👑 **1125** We Zong abdicates in favor of his son, Qin Zong.

☀ **c.1125** The Khmer ruler Suryavarman II builds the temple of Angkor Wat in present-day Cambodia.

EAST ASIA & OCEANIA

1100–1125 A.D.

SOUTHEAST ASIAN EMPIRES

IN THE 12TH CENTURY *most of mainland Southeast Asia was divided between two great empires: Pagan in Myanmar (Burma) and the Khmer Empire in Indochina. Both were influenced by Indian culture. The rulers of Pagan saw it as part of their duties to build and embellish Buddhist temples and monasteries. The Khmer Empire was ruled by a Hindu* devaraja *(god-king) who resided in the temple-city of Angkor.*

◄ Part dog, part lion, this mythical beast guards a Buddhist temple at Pagan.

Buddhism entered Southeast Asia from India in the 3rd century B.C. An early Buddhist state emerged among the Pyu people of the upper Irrawaddy Valley in Myanmar about 600 A.D. It was destroyed by the warlike Thai kingdom of Nan Chao about 835. Soon afterward a new wave of immigrants—the Burmans, originally from the highlands east of Tibet—settled in the region and founded the city of Pagan.

In 1044 Anawrahta became king of Pagan. He subdued the once mighty state of Mon to the south and set about uniting Burma into a single kingdom by making the walled city of Pagan a central shrine of Buddhism. He and his successors built monasteries, shrines, pagodas, and libraries, all paid for out of royal taxes. Pagan's resources were probably exhausted by the mid 1250s, when the Mongols attacked and destroyed Nanchao. Pagan itself suffered a similar fate when forces dispatched by Kublai Khan, the Mongol emperor of China, invaded it two decades later.

The Khmer Empire, which flourished from the 9th to the 13th century, was one of the largest in Southeast Asian history, covering much of the Indochina Peninsula. Angkor, its capital city in northern Cambodia, was founded in about 880. It was laid out as the residence of a god-king in accordance with religious concepts borrowed from Hindu cosmology. At its center was a temple symbolizing Mt. Meru, the home of the gods; around it were lesser temples recalling the mountains believed to ring the edge of the world. A vast system of reservoirs, canals, and moats represented the waters of the cosmos and also provided irrigation for rice cultivation.

Chou Ta-kuan, a Chinese envoy of the 13th century, left an account of a visit to Angkor, which he described as one of the most magnificent capitals in all Asia. But within 200 years the temples and palaces had been abandoned, and Angkor had become a lost city in the jungle.

Angkor Wat

The most famous of all the Khmer temples is Angkor Wat, on the outskirts of Angkor. An enormous structure 1,700 yards (1,550 m) long by 1,500 (1,400 m) wide, it contains five major shrines, all surrounded by a wall and a moat. The temple was built by King Suryavarman II, who reunited the Khmer people after more than 50 years of unrest and introduced the cult of the Hindu god Vishnu. The temple—designed to contain Suryavarman's remains after his death—is decorated with sculptures that show the king reviewing troops and carrying out other duties; some portray him in the guise of Vishnu. Sadly, looters have stripped it of many of its carvings. Since 1992 the temple and the city have been given protection as a UNESCO World Heritage Site.

◀ Covered in gold leaf, the pagoda of Schwezigon is one of the most splendid of the 3,000–4,000 temples built in the Pagan region in the 11th and 12th centuries.

▼ A narrow, mountainous strip of land occupied by stateless farming peoples cut the Kingdom of Pagan off from the Khmer Empire at the start of the 12th century.

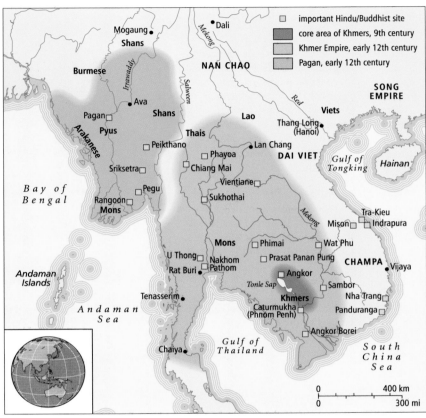

👑 **849**   Burmans establish Pagan as their capital city.

☀ **881**   The earliest surviving temple mountain, the Bakong, is built at Angkor.

👑 **c.1004**   Reign of King Suryavarman I of Khmer; he extends the Khmer Empire westward into Thailand (–c.1050).

👑 **1044**   Reign of King Anawrahta of Pagan (–1077).

⚔ **1057**   Anawrahta conquers the Mon city of Thaton in southern Myanmar; he transports the Mon royal family, and their scholars and craftsmen, to Pagan.

👑 **c.1112**   Reign of King Alaungsithu of Pagan (–c.1167).

👑 **c.1113**   Reign of King Suryavarman II of Khmer, who introduces the Vishnu cult to Angkor (–c.1150).

⊕ **c.1125**   Construction of Angkor Wat begins; it is uncompleted on Suryavarman's death.

⚔ **1177**   An army from the Vietnamese Kingdom of Champa seizes and sacks Angkor.

👑 **1181**   Reign of King Jayavarman VII of Khmer (–c.1220).

⚔ **1181**   Jayavarman invades Champa and makes it part of the Khmer Empire.

☀ **c.1190**   Jayavarman adopts Buddhism; he builds a Buddhist temple, the Bayon, at Angkor.

⚔ **1253**   Mongols invade the Thai Kingdom of Nan Chao bordering Pagan, using it as a base from which to attack southern China

⚔ **1277**   Forces dispatched by Kublai Khan attack Pagan, ending its days as a major regional power (–1287).

⚔ **1431**   The Thai state of Ayutthaya captures and sacks Angkor; the city is abandoned.

AMERICAS

c.1125 In Chaco Canyon, New Mexico, an extensive road system by now links several well-planned Anasazi ancestral Pueblo towns and around 100 smaller settlements in a trade network extending as far as coastal California and Mexico.

c.1150 The Hohokam people of Arizona begin to build platform mounds.

c.1150 The Chimú people of northern Peru are expanding territorially from their capital city at Chan Chan on the Pacific coast.

EUROPE

c.1125 Cistercian abbeys are founded across western Europe; the monks clear land and make agricultural improvements.

1126 Monks in Artois, France, make an artesian well by drilling a bore hole to draw up underground water at pressure.

1135 On the death of Henry I the English throne is contested between his daughter Matilda and his nephew Stephen of Blois, leading to civil war (– 1153).

The Gothic style of church architecture that spread across Europe from the 1130s was one of the great glories of the medieval age. The use of pointed arches and of high roofs supported by so-called "flying" buttresses (external wall supports) served to direct the eye upward toward God, while brilliantly colored stained-glass windows bathed the interiors in a reverent glow. The aim was to create theaters whose soaring spaces would inspire worshipers with a sense of the mystery and majesty of the divine presence.

AFRICA

1130 Al-Amir, Fatimid caliph of Egypt, is killed by the Assassins.

c.1130 On the death of Ibn Tumart Abd al-Mumin becomes leader of the Almohads.

c.1137 The Christian Zagwe Dynasty comes to power in the highlands of northern Ethiopia.

WESTERN ASIA

c.1125 Minarets are by now architectural features of mosques throughout the Muslim world.

1126 Zangi is appointed atabeg (governor) of Mosul and sets about creating an independent principality for himself in northern Syria.

1144 Zangi captures Edessa from the crusaders, prompting the Second Crusade.

SOUTH & CENTRAL ASIA

c.1140 The Chalukya rulers of Gujarat patronize Jainism under the influence of Hemchandra, a Jain monk.

1143 Kumarapala, a disciple of Hemchandra, becomes Chalukya ruler, prohibiting alcohol, dice, and animal sacrifice, and restoring the property rights of widows.

c.1150 The Chandella Dynasty of Khajuraho is now in decline.

EAST ASIA & OCEANIA

c.1125 Heian artists develop the art of *emaki*—the production of horizontal painted narrative handscrolls of great artistry.

1126 The Jin capture the Song capital of Kaifeng and take We Zong and Qin Zong prisoners. Other members of the dynasty flee south, where Gao Zong declares himself emperor, establishing the Southern Song Dynasty with a new capital at Hangzhou on the Yangtze (Chan) River (–1135).

1129 In Japan the Emperor Toba abdicates to rule as a "cloistered emperor," continuing the *insei* tradition.

c.1130 Ships powered by paddlewheels are in use on lakes and rivers in China.

Before the rise of the Inca Empire the Chimú Kingdom of Peru's north coast was the most developed state in the Andean lands. Developing out of the earlier Sicán Culture, it came to dominate a strip of land running from what is now southern Ecuador to the region around Peru's modern capital, Lima. Its craftsmen were famed for their gold and silver work, as well as for intricately decorated textiles like this image of a god.

⊛ **c.1150** The Inca people begin to farm intensively in the area north of Lake Titicaca.

AMERICAS

📖 **c.1136** Suger, abbot of St. Denis near Paris, rebuilds the abbey church in a new architectural style, with high pointed arches; it is now regarded as the first example of Gothic architecture.

🏛 **1137** Eleanor of Aquitaine, wealthy heiress of the duke of Aquitaine in southwest France, marries King Louis VII of France.

🏛 **1138** Conrad III, of the Hohenstaufen family, becomes German emperor on the death of the Welf Lothair II.

☀ **1139** Peter the Venerable, abbot of Cluny in France, commissions a Latin translation of the Koran.

🏛 **1143** Afonso Henriques is proclaimed first king of Portugal, having secured its independence from the neighboring Spanish Kingdom of León.

🏛 **1146** Bernard of Clairvaux launches the Second Crusade.

☀ **1150** Erik "the Saint" becomes king of Sweden; he leads a campaign to convert the Finns to Christianity.

📖 **c.1150** The University of Paris is founded.

📖 **c.1150** Averroës (Ibn Rushd), the most famous Islamic philosopher of his day, is active in Córdoba, Spain; his writings, translated into Latin, will be responsible for reintroducing knowledge of Aristotle's works to western Europe.

EUROPE

⚔ **1143** Roger II, the Norman ruler of Sicily, ravages the North African coast.

⚔ **1147** The Almohads become the chief power in North Africa, seizing the Almoravid capital of Marrakesh.

🏛 **c.1150** The Zagwe Dynasty establishes a capital at Roha (Lalibela) in the Ethiopian highlands.

AFRICA

⊛ **c.1145** Death of the astronomer and mathematician Jabir ibn Aflah, designer of a portable celestial sphere explaining the movement of celestial objects.

🏛 **1146** Death of Zangi; he is succeeded by his son Nur al-Din.

⚔ **1148** The Second Crusade fails to take the city of Damascus in Syria.

⚔ **1149** Nur al-Din defeats Raymond of Antioch and reestablishes Muslim power in Syria.

WESTERN ASIA

📖 **c.1150** The Tamil author Kampan composes the *Iramavataram*, a Tamil-language version of the Hindu epic the *Ramayana*.

SOUTH & CENTRAL ASIA

⚔ **1130s** The Southern Song, led by General Yui Fei, make war on the Jin and win a number of victories (–1141).

The emaki *handscrolls of Japan often show a cartoonlike sense of humor, as in this image of a monkey dressed up as a Buddhist monk.*

🏛 **1141** At the urging of Yui Fei's political enemies Gao Zong recalls his general to Hangzhou and has him executed before making peace with the Jin.

⊛ **c.1150** By this date the Chinese are using gunpowder in weapons.

EAST ASIA & OCEANIA

1125–1150 A.D.

FEUDALISM

HISTORIANS SOMETIMES CALL *the early Middle Ages in Europe—the period from roughly the 9th to the 13th century—"the age of feudalism." The term describes the contractual system by which a king or noble made a grant of land, known as a fief, in return for military service. The beneficiary then became the lord's vassal by swearing an oath of loyalty. In similar fashion the peasants who worked the land were considered to have an obligation to provide labor for their master in return for the protection he offered, plus a share of the crop.*

▲ In a scene from the Bayeux Tapestry Harold of England swears fealty to William, duke of Normandy, over a reliquary containing a saint's holy relics. The solemn oath of allegiance, by which one man promised to provide stipulated services to another, lay at the heart of the feudal contract between master and vassal.

Feudalism originally developed in the Carolingian lands—the territories in western Europe ruled by Charlemagne and his successors in the 8th and 9th centuries. The emperor granted land in return for "knight service," meaning that vassals had to be ready to send armies of knights (mounted soldiers) to serve in the imperial armies when required to do so, and to maintain them at their own expense. As feudalism developed, vassals were also expected to provide other duties and services, such as giving advice in the lord's council or paying a ransom if he was taken prisoner. In exchange they received both the income of the land and legal authority over all who lived on it.

Feudal lords lived in castles on their estates (manors). The land itself was farmed by peasants, who paid part of their annual harvest to the lord of the manor as rent; another part went to the church. In return the lord was expected to protect peasants in times of war and to act as a judge in their disputes. They paid him in kind for the right to fish in his ponds and rivers, to grind flour for bread in his mills, and to hunt and gather wood for fuel in his forests.

By the 11th and 12th centuries fiefs had become hereditary and were added to by marriage or inheritance. Some feudal lords reigned as semi-independent rulers of vast estates. In France, for example, the royal lands were confined to a small area around Paris, while the lands held by powerful nobles such as the counts of Anjou and Aquitaine were significantly larger than those of their feudal overlord.

This imbalance of power had some odd results. In 1152 Henry of Anjou married Eleanor of Aquitaine, the divorced wife of Louis VII of France and heiress to the vast wealth of Aquitaine, which at the time took in much of France south of the Loire River. Two years later Henry became King Henry II of England and duke of Normandy. Yet even though he was the most powerful ruler in Europe, he tried to avoid open warfare with the French king, his feudal lord, since to do so would set a bad example to his own vassals.

Chivalry

By the 12th century relations between lords and vassals were governed by the code of chivalry (from the French word *chevalier*, meaning "knight"). A knight was expected to show honesty, loyalty, courage, and strength. He was bound to obey his lord, protect the church, respect women, and go on crusade. Knights trained for warfare by jousting in tournaments—combats between horsemen armed with lances. *Chansons de geste* ("songs of deeds"), poems that celebrated the noble actions of such heroes as King Arthur, helped spread chivalric ideals, while *chansons d'amor* ("songs of love"), performed by musicians known as troubadours, celebrated themes of courtly love. The court of Eleanor of Aquitaine at Poitiers was especially famed for its troubadour music.

▲ A peasant plows his lord's land in an illumination from a medieval calendar illustrating the month of March.

▶ Feudal Europe was a patchwork of lands owned by the church, by ruling families, or by nobles holding royal fiefs.

England & France, c.1175
- French royal holdings
- Angevin Empire of Henry II of England
- other lands

Holy Roman Empire, c.1175
- Hohenstaufen holdings
- Welf holdings
- Church lands
- other lands

0 — 600 km
0 — 400 mi

≋ **843** The Treaty of Verdun states as a principle that "every man should have a lord."

≋ **911** The Viking leader Rolf does homage to King Charles III of France for lands in Normandy.

📖 **c.1095** The *Song of Roland*, a popular *chanson de geste* (epic poem) describing the heroic deeds of Charlemagne's knight Roland, spreads the ideals of chivalry.

≋ **1099** After capturing Jerusalem, the crusader leaders decide to rule the Holy Land as a feudal kingdom divided into four great baronies held by tenants-in-chief of the king of Jerusalem, their suzerain (overlord).

📖 **c.1135** Chrétien de Troyes, the greatest of the French poets of courtly love, is born (died 1183); his best-known romance will be *Yvain and Lancelot*.

📖 **c. 1140** Geoffrey of Monmouth's *History of the Kings of Britain* spreads the popular legends of King Arthur and the Round Table.

≋ **1152** Henry of Anjou marries Eleanor of Aquitaine, a dynastic marriage that unites two large fiefdoms.

≋ **1156** The Emperor Frederick Barbarossa creates the Duchy of Austria as a fief of the Holy Roman Empire to counter the influence of the rival Welf family in Bavaria.

≋ **1202** King Philip Augustus of France asserts his authority as the suzerain of King John of England, declaring him a "felonious vassal" for his failure to attend court.

⚔ **1209** Philip Augustus encourages Simon de Montfort, a northern baron, to lead a crusade against the Albigensian heretics of southern France, thereby reducing the power of the southern nobility, particularly the count of Toulouse (–1229).

≋ **1215** King John is forced to confirm the privileges of England's feudal lords by assenting to the declaration of baronial rights called Magna Carta ("the Great Charter").

AMERICAS

👑 **c.1150** A prolonged drought starts to affect the Chaco Canyon trade networks in New Mexico from this time on.

✳ **c.1150** The Salado Culture, blending Hohokam, Mogollon, and Anasazi influences, is taking shape in southeastern Arizona.

EUROPE

👑 **1152** Eleanor of Aquitaine, divorced wife of Louis VII, marries Henry of Anjou, making him master of much of western France.

✳ **1152** Byzantium and Hungary begin a two-year war.

👑 **1154** Henry of Anjou inherits the English crown, founding the Plantagenet Dynasty as Henry II.

Stained-glass image of England's martyred archbishop of Canterbury, Thomas Becket.

✳ **1157** Abd al-Mumin's armies invade Islamic Spain, taking Almería and Granada for Almohad rule.

👑 **1159** Frederick I Barbarossa sets up his own puppet "antipope" in opposition to the Vatican's power.

AFRICA

👑 **c.1150** Gao on the Niger River emerges as a center for trade with Algeria across the Sahara Desert.

👑 **c.1150** By this date Normans based in southern Italy and Sicily have established a series of fortified trading posts along the coast from Tripoli to Tunis, but without any attempt to establish a foothold farther inland.

👑 **1151** Abd al-Mumin extends the sway of his Almohad Dynasty, taking Algiers and Morocco from the Almoravids.

👑 **1160** Lalibela becomes king in Ethiopia. The most famous ruler of the Christian Zagwe Dynasty, his reign is remarkable for its richly decorated churches carved out of solid rock.

✳ **1167** Cairo is captured by Amalric, the Christian king of Jerusalem, only to be retaken by the Arabs the following year.

👑 **1169** Saladin emerges as vizier of Egypt on behalf of the Fatimid sultans.

👑 **1171** Saladin brings Fatimid rule to an end, establishing himself as Egypt's first Ayyubid sultan.

WESTERN ASIA

👑 **c.1150** The Seljuk Turks' Sultanate of Rum (named in honor of imperial Rome) now extends deep into Byzantine territory in what will come to be known as Turkey.

👑 **c.1150** Farther east, in northern Iran, the smaller Seljuk sultanates are under attack from yet another wave of Turkic invaders from Central Asia, the Khwarazmian Turks.

SOUTH & CENTRAL ASIA

✳ **c.1150** Vijayasena further extends the territories of the Sena Dynasty into Bengal, bringing to an end the 400-year reign of the Pala Dynasty.

✳ **1151** Turks from Ghur, Iran, raze Ghazni in Afghanistan, capital of the once mighty Ghaznavid Dynasty, earning their leader Ala al-Din the title of "the World-Burner."

Statue of Sri Lanka's King Parakramabahu I, from his capital of Polonnaruwa.

EAST ASIA & OCEANIA

👑 **1150** Suryavarman II dies, having brought Cambodia's Khmer civilization to as yet unprecedented heights. His passing leaves a power vacuum and leads to several decades of instability.

✳ **1156** Civil war breaks out in Japan as the Fujiwara clan begins to lose its hold. The ensuing conflict will continue for the next 29 years.

☀ **1163** A synagogue is built in Kaifeng, capital of Song China, reflecting the cosmopolitanism of a highly successful trading culture.

c.1150 The Tiahuanaco Culture of the Peruvian Andes is by now in rapid—and unexplained—decline.

✗ **c.1175** The Toltec capital of Tula in central Mexico is destroyed, possibly by Chichimec nomads from farther north.

☀ **1163** Construction begins of Notre Dame Cathedral, Paris.

🏛 **1164** Henry II of England attempts to boost the power of the crown at the expense of the church through the Constitutions of Clarendon: The resulting conflict ends with the exile of the archbishop of Canterbury Thomas Becket.

📖 **1165** French writer Chrétien de Troyes produces the first Arthurian romance, incorporating ideas of romantic love and chivalry.

🏛 **1170** Returned from exile, Thomas Becket is assassinated by knights of Henry II. The popular backlash compels the king to curtail his plans to reduce ecclesiastical power.

🏛 **1171** Henry II begins the conquest and colonization of Ireland.

🏛 **1173** Bela III succeeds to the throne of Hungary, by now one of the leading powers in southeastern Europe.

Saladin, shown in an imagined joust with his Christian rival Richard I "the Lionheart" of England, was a charismatic Muslim leader in the struggle with the crusaders for the Holy Land. A Kurd from Syria, he rose to prominence as vizier to Egypt's Fatimid sultan but seized power in his own right in 1171, restoring Egypt to the Sunni mainstream of Islam (the Fatimids had upheld the minority Shiite branch). Reuniting Egypt and Syria, he led their combined forces against the crusaders, whom he defeated decisively at the Battle of Hattin in 1187, recapturing Jerusalem itself three months later.

🏛 **1157** Sultan Sanjar dies. His death is now widely held to have spelled the start of the decline of the Seljuk Turks.

🏛 **1159** The Byzantine Emperor Manuel I asserts his authority over the crusader kingdoms, marching through Antioch in triumph, but his army is savaged by Turks as it makes its way home.

⊕ **1174** Saladin conquers Syria from the crusaders.

🏛 **1153** Parakramabahu I comes to power in Sri Lanka.

🏛 **1165** Accession of Paramardi, the last major ruler of the Chandella Dynasty that controls northern India's upper Ganges Valley.

☀ **1166** Death of Ahmad ibn Ibrahim al-Yasavi, a wandering Sufi (Muslim mystic) of key importance in spreading the Islamic word among the Turkic nomads of Central Asia.

🏛 **1173** Muhammad Ghuri is appointed Ghurid governor of Ghazni in Afghanistan.

🏛 **c.1163** Temujin is born about now, son of a chieftain of one of the nomadic Mongol tribes of the eastern steppe: He will later be known to the world as Genghis (or Chingis) Khan.

⊕ **1164** Burma (Myanmar) is attacked by a Sri Lankan expedition sent by Parakramabahu I in punishment for the mistreatment of one of his delegations.

🏛 **1170** Growing instability in Korea is compounded when the military elite effectively wrests power from the Koryo monarchy and its governing bureaucracy.

AMERICAS · EUROPE · AFRICA · WESTERN ASIA · SOUTH & CENTRAL ASIA · EAST ASIA & OCEANIA

1150–1175 A.D.

155

NORTH AMERICAN CULTURES

FAR TO THE NORTH OF THE MOUNTAINS *and valleys of Mesoamerica and the Andes, where spectacular civilizations had been rising and falling for centuries, the peoples of what are now the United States had for the most part been leading a simpler life based on small communities rather than large cities. But by the start of the 2nd millennium* A.D. *communities in the Mississippi Valley and the deserts of the Southwest were building impressive urban civilizations of their own.*

▲ The finest pottery in early North America was produced in the Mimbres Valley of southwestern New Mexico. Its makers formed a branch of the Mogollon Culture but put their own distinctive stamp on plates decorated with stylized images of people, gods, and animals such as the bat shown here.

▶ North America's early cultures formed two main clusters. The eastern woodlands tradition centered on the Mississippi River and its tributaries. The western Anasazi, Hohokam, and Mogollon cultures grew up in the dry lands of Arizona, New Mexico, Utah, and Colorado.

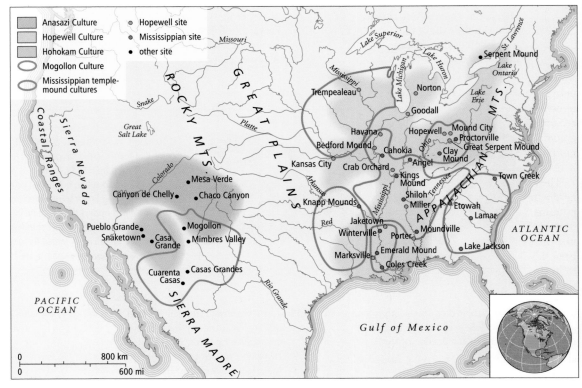

* **c.300 B.C.** First appearance of Hohokam Culture in Arizona.

* **c.100** The Hopewell Culture emerges in the Ohio River valley.

* **c.1 A.D.** Hohokam communities are practicing agriculture under irrigation.

* **c.300** The Mogollon Culture emerges in the mountains of southern Arizona and New Mexico; as yet, though, there is no sign of their practicing agriculture.

* **c.400** The Anasazi have developed their own system of irrigated agriculture.

* **c.500** The Mogollon people are incorporating agriculture into their traditional hunter-gatherer lifestyle.

* **700** The conventional cutoff date for the Hopewell tradition. From this time on it makes more sense to talk of a Mississippian Culture.

* **c.1000** The Mississippian Culture reaches its height.

* **c.1125** The Chaco Canyon urban complex reaches its fullest extent; its Anasazi inhabitants live in 70 separate villages linked by 500 miles (800 km) of roads.

* **c.1200** The Anasazi settlement at Mesa Verde attains its most sophisticated level; one complex, the so-called Cliff Palace, has well over 200 rooms and houses up to 350 people.

* **c.1300** Mesa Verde is abandoned.

* **c.1400** Cahokia is abandoned.

The culture that arose in the Mississippi Valley in the centuries leading up to the year 1000 A.D. did not, of course, come out of nothing; it can clearly be seen as a development of earlier Adena and Hopewell traditions. There was the same cultivation of crops—above all squash, beans, and corn—in fertile valley bottoms, the same supplementary pursuit of game and gathering of fruit, nuts, and other foods. There were also similarities in ceremonial life, with the construction of burial mounds for dead dignitaries.

Even so, the sheer scale and social complexity of the Mississippian communities were something new; with populations in their thousands, these were not villages but real cities. The mounds, too, dwarfed their predecessors; they were monuments not only to the departed but also to the spirit of collective endeavor that drove this society. Farming on a much expanded scale, with more productive strains of crops and in particular an improved strain of corn (maize) perhaps imported from Central America, the Mississippians accumulated surpluses for storage in huge communal granaries. Energies and resources were thus released not only for the manufacture of (and trade in) luxury items but for dancing, sports, and social activities.

The sun-seared deserts of the Southwest could hardly be more different from these lush valley bottoms, nor could less promising agricultural lands be easily imagined. For hundreds of years, however, first the Hohokam and then the Anasazi people had been slowly building an agrarian civilization by capturing the snowmelt that came cascading down the region's rivers every spring. Already by 1 A.D. Arizona's Hohokam had learned to divert precious water along irrigation channels; by 800 they had an extensive network, much of which is still in use today. In nearby uplands, meanwhile, the Mogollon were also cultivating corn and beans, although still for the most part living as hunter-gatherers.

The Anasazi emerged a little later and farther to the north, their territories extending into what are now Utah and Colorado. They were comparative latecomers to agriculture, very likely acquiring their skills by imitating their neighbors, but by 1000 they were the most sophisticated society the Southwest had seen. Their circular pit huts of sandstone and adobe, at first semisunken for insulation, were increasingly built above ground and clustered together with shared walls like the cells in a beehive—early apartment complexes, in other words. These pueblos (from the Spanish word for "village") were built in the most protected places possible, even up against cliff faces, as at Mesa Verde, Colorado. Such sites still rank among the humanmade wonders of the New World.

▲ A petroglyph (rock marking) decorates an outcrop in Arizona's Saguaro National Park. The design is a work of the Hohokam Culture, which flourished around the Gila and Salt rivers from 300 B.C. to 1450 A.D. The Hohokam used sophisticated irrigation techniques to increase the agricultural productivity of their lands.

Mississippian Metropolis

Just east of St. Louis a 100-foot (30-m) hill rises abruptly from a plain—all that remains of the Mississippian city of Cahokia. In its day almost 1,000 years ago this artificial knoll was the largest structure in North America; more than a mound, it was really a rounded earthen pyramid. Topped, presumably, by temples, it was once the centerpiece of a ceremonial complex 5 miles (8 km) square, its open esplanades punctuated by no fewer than 100 smaller earthworks. A wooden stockade enclosed this central area: Beyond sprawled the city itself, where up to 30,000 people may once have lived. The signs of their habitation extend for 12 miles (20 km) along both banks of the river; the inhabitants seem to have lived in communal, wood-framed, thatch-walled lodges. This apparently flourishing settlement was abandoned around 1400; the reason why remains unknown, one of the great mysteries of America's pre-Columbian past.

1175–1200 A.D.

AMERICAS

1200 The Mayan city of Chichén Itzá on the Yucatán Peninsula is in terminal decline; its last dated inscription comes from this year.

c.1200 Although it has centuries to run elsewhere and has still to extend its influence into some remoter areas, the Mississippian Culture is already passing its peak at its center in the Mississippi Valley.

c.1200 The Mogollon Culture of America's southwestern desert uplands is beginning slowly to merge with that of the Anasazi of adjacent lowland areas.

EUROPE

1176 At the Battle of Legnano the merchant cities of Lombardy maintain their independence against Frederick I Barbarossa and the Holy Roman Empire.

1180 In France Louis VII is succeeded by his son Philip II "Augustus."

1180 Stephen Nemanja establishes the monarchy in Serbia.

1182 Philip II expels Jews from France.

1185 Russia's Prince Igor Svyatoslavich leads a campaign against Kipchak invaders from the east.

1186 Bulgaria gains its independence from Byzantium.

AFRICA

c.1175 Gold is now being mined on a significant scale at the southern African site that will be known as Great Zimbabwe.

The Yaqub al Mansur Mosque, Rabat, Morocco.

1180 Under the kings of the Kante Dynasty, Soso starts making inroads on the territories of the Ghanaian Empire.

WESTERN ASIA

1176 Byzantine forces are defeated by the Turks at Myriokephalon.

1177 Saladin is defeated at the Battle of Montgisard by the forces of Baldwin IV of Jerusalem.

1179 Saladin lays siege to the port of Tyre.

1180 Baldwin IV and Saladin agree on a truce.

1180 Caliph al-Nasir attempts to restore the authority—both spiritual and temporal—of the Abbasid Dynasty, based in Baghdad.

1184 Queen Tamar ascends the throne of Georgia. Her 28-year reign is a golden age of literature and art in the Christian Caucasian kingdom.

1187 Saladin defeats the crusaders at the Battle of Hattin; his way is then clear to sweep on and take Jerusalem.

SOUTH & CENTRAL ASIA

1175 Using Ghazni as his base, Muhammad Ghuri begins attacking northern India, taking the city of Multan on the Indus River the following year.

1182 Forces of the Chandella Dynasty sack the Chauhan capital.

1186 Muhammad Ghuri occupies the Punjab, establishing a Muslim power base in northern India.

1189 Chalukya rule on southwestern India's Deccan Plateau finally collapses under pressure from the forces of the rival Hoyasala and Yadava Dynasties.

EAST ASIA & OCEANIA

1177 Zhu Xi writes the *Lun Yu*, commentaries on Confucius's thought that reestablish the early master at the center of Chinese tradition.

1177 Champa invaders from coastal Vietnam take advantage of continuing instability in the Khmer lands, sailing up the Mekong River to sack Angkor.

1180 The longstanding civil conflict in Japan moves up a gear as the Taira and Minamoto clans battle for power in what becomes known as the Gempei War.

1181 Jayavarman II ascends the Khmer throne, restoring order to the empire, for which he will build a completely new capital at Angkor Thom.

1185 Minamoto Yoritomo emerges victorious from Japan's exhausting civil war, initiating the Kamakura Period, so called after the capital from which he and his successors hold sway.

AMERICAS

👑 **c.1200** The Hohokam Culture enters its classic phase, strongly influenced by the Salado Culture that has emerged immediately to the south.

⚙ **c.1200** Cliff-dwelling towns similar to those at Mesa Verde are being built about now by Anasazi farmers in other sites in the San Juan Basin region of the American Southwest.

EUROPE

👑 **1189** Richard I, "the Lionheart," succeeds Henry II in England.

👑 **1189** Richard I, Philip II, and Frederick I join forces in a Third Crusade.

👑 **1190** Frederick I Barbarossa drowns on his way to the Holy Land.

👑 **1192** Richard is taken hostage by Duke Leopold of Austria on his way home from the Third Crusade. A ransom paid, he returns to England two years later.

⚔ **1195** In Spain a Muslim army defeats Christian forces at Alarcos.

☀ **1198** Innocent III is elected pope, resolved to protect the power of the church.

👑 **1198** Otakar I becomes king of Bohemia (today's Czech Republic).

AFRICA

👑 **1184** Yaqub al Mansur succeeds his father Abu Yaqub Yusuf as caliph in North Africa: His reign arguably sees the zenith of Almohad power.

👑 **c.1190** Yemrahana Krestos is crowned king in Ethiopia.

👑 **c.1200** Hausa states emerge along the valley of the Niger River.

WESTERN ASIA

⚔ **1191** Despite capturing Cyprus and Acre, the overstretched crusader forces are unable to press their advantage: The Third Crusade ends in failure.

⚔ **1193** Saladin dies in Damascus, Syria

⚔ **1194** The Khwarazmian Turks begin their conquest of Khurasan, in eastern Iran; they go on to take Iraq, assassinating Tughril, the last Seljuk sultan.

SOUTH & CENTRAL ASIA

⚔ **1193** The armies of the Ghurid Dynasty take Delhi, extending Islamic rule into central India.

☀ **1197** Ghurid forces begin attacking monasteries—the start of a concerted effort to stamp out Indian Buddhism and replace it with Islam.

👑 **1199** Ala al-Din Muhammad assumes authority over the expanding Turkish kingdom of Khwarazm, based in the lands south of the Aral Sea; he looks to extend its power eastward into India.

EAST ASIA & OCEANIA

In the Kamakura Period (1185–1334) Japan knew almost 150 years of relative peace and prosperity under a joint system of government. While the emperor exercised nominal sovereignty from Heian (today's Kyoto), real power lay in the hands of the shoguns—military governors—ruling from Kamakura, 300 miles (480 km) to the northeast. Trade and the arts flourished under their watchful eye, as did Japan's uniquely tolerant approach to religion—this statue shows Hachiman, a god of the nation's traditional Shinto faith, in the guise of a Buddhist priest.

👑 **1192** Yoritomo takes the title of shogun, confirming his position as leader of Japan's warrior class and thus as the real ruler of the country.

👑 **1200** Polynesian immigrants arrive in the Chatham Islands east of New Zealand, completing the settlement of the South Pacific.

1175–1200 A.D.

ISLAM COMES TO INDIA

▲ Muslim incursions into India in the 10th to 13th centuries brought not just a new faith and fresh systems of government but a different style of art, exemplified by this geometrically patterned Islamic arch. The blending of Hindu and Muslim elements was to flower later in the magnificent artistic accomplishments of the Mughal Empire.

*F*ROM THE SACRED WATERS *of the Ganges River to the shrines of the deep south, India is a land sanctified by some of the world's great faiths. Hinduism and Buddhism were already ancient when the religion of Muhammad arrived as an outsider's creed brought by invaders from the north. Islam's enduring presence on the Indian subcontinent owed much to the rulers of the Delhi Sultanate, who provided firm government for all their subjects while tolerating the practice of other faiths.*

Islam arrived on the subcontinent as early as 711, when the first Arab armies spilled across the mountains of the Hindu Kush onto the plains of the Indus Valley. There, in the region of Sind (now part of Pakistan), they established their own ruling dynasties, even making converts among the native population.

No concerted attempt at more systematic Islamization was made until 998, however, when the Afghan Muslim ruler Mahmud of Ghazni came to power swearing *jihad*—Islamic holy war—for the conversion of India. By 1001 his forces were attacking in earnest, and the raids went on relentlessly for almost three decades, culminating in the sack of the famous Hindu temple-city of Somnath. By his death in 1030 Mahmud had brought the entire northern Indian province of Punjab under his own Islamic rule.

The empire Mahmud built did not long survive his death, although his successors kept his Ghaznavid Dynasty alive in its original heartland around the Afghan city of Ghazni. In 1173, however, they were swept away by the forces of the Ghurid Dynasty, which originated in the district of Ghur in eastern Iran. Originally installed as governor of Ghazni by his

Might of Islam

No monument proclaims the pride of the Delhi Sultanate more eloquently than the Quwwat al-Islam ("Might of Islam") mosque, 10 miles (15 km) south of the modern Indian capital. Construction began in the 1190s in the aftermath of the Ghurid victory and was clearly designed to broadcast word of the conquest to India at large. Islamic supremacy is built into the very fabric of the complex, which was constructed from the razed remains of 27 Hindu temples; the ebullient ornamentation and extravagant forms of the reused fragments contrast markedly with the quieter austerities of Islamic architectural convention. Beside the mosque a freestanding tower, the Qutb Minar, rises an awesome 240 ft (72.5 m) high. Built to serve as a minaret from which the muezzin (crier) chanted the summons to daily prayer, it too carried an unmistakably triumphalist message to non-Muslims.

✗ **711** First Arab invasion of the Indian subcontinent (Sind).

✗ **998** Mahmud of Ghazni declares *jihad* for the conversion of India.

✗ **1001** Ghaznavid forces first invade Sind.

♛ **1030** Mahmud of Ghazni dies; under his successors his dynasty limps on, though much reduced.

♛ **1173** Muhammad Ghuri takes power in Ghazni; within 2 years the Ghurid Dynasty begins attacks on India.

✗ **1193** Delhi is captured and made the center of a new sultanate.

♛ **1206** Muhammad Ghuri dies; his successor, Qutbuddin Aibak, inaugurates the "Slave Dynasty."

✗ **1222** Ghengis Khan's Mongols invade India but do not stay to occupy it, allowing the Delhi Sultanate to recover, although without ever regaining its former power.

♛ **1290** The Slave Dynasty is displaced by the Khalji Dynasty.

♛ **1296** Alauddin's 20-year reign brings the Delhi Sultanate to its imperial height.

✗ **1398** The Delhi Sultanate is destroyed during Timur's invasion of India.

elder brother Ghiyas-ud-Din, Muhammad Ghuri emerged from his shadow with a vengeance when, from 1175, he started using Ghazni as a base for a series of raids deep into India. By 1193 his forces had captured Delhi. He subsequently made the city the capital of a rich and powerful Muslim state that in time spanned the entire northern part of the subcontinent from the Indus River through the Himalayan foothills to the Bay of Bengal.

After Muhammad's death in 1206 the Delhi Sultanate was taken over by one of his generals, Qutbuddin Aibak. He and several of his successors

had been born slaves before achieving greatness as soldiers, thus becoming known to history as the "Slave Dynasty." They were overthrown in 1290 by the sultans of the Khalji Dynasty, whose most illustrious ruler, Alauddin (1296–1316), conquered much of southern India also. Yet, for all their military might, the sultans were living on borrowed time: A new and terrifying threat was looming in the north. The sultanate survived the first wave of Mongol assaults, although in diminished form, but could not resist the invasion of Timur the Lame in 1398, which smashed the power of the Delhi sultans once and for all.

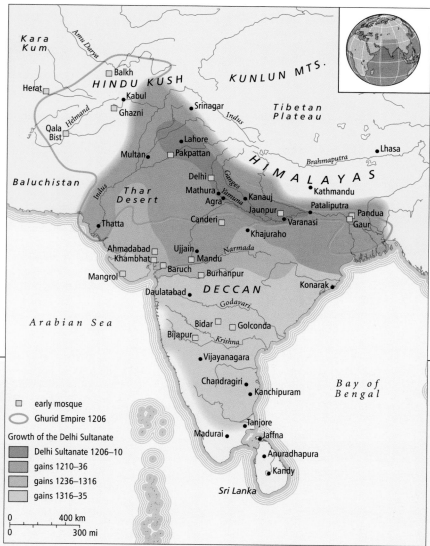

◀ Mahmud of Ghazni, whose mausoleum (monumental tomb) still stands in the Afghan city of that name (left), spearheaded the Islamic assault on India. The raids he staged from 1001 on paved the way for permanent occupation in the following century.

▲ Islamic rule entered India from the north, spreading from Afghanistan to present-day Pakistan and east to the Ganges Delta. In the 13th and 14th centuries the Muslim rulers of the Delhi Sultanate gradually expanded their power southward over much of the country.

AMERICAS

c.1200 Manco Capac establishes the Inca Dynasty with its capital at Cuzco, Peru.

c.1200 Mounds are constructed at Moundville, Alabama.

c.1200 The Chimú people conquer the coastal valleys of Peru.

EUROPE

1201 Riga, in present-day Latvia, is founded by Albert, bishop of Livonia, a German crusader who goes on to found the Sword Brethren, a military crusading order later absorbed into the Teutonic Knights.

1202 The Italian mathematician Leonardo Fibonacci of Pisa (c.1170–1240) completes his *Book of the Abacus*—the first European work to explain Indian numerals.

1203 Forces of the Fourth Crusade capture the Byzantine port of Zara (in present-day Croatia) for the Venetians.

One of the most influential Christian figures of the Middle Ages, St. Francis of Assisi founded the Franciscan order of mendicant (begging) friars, restoring a sense of idealism to a church grown wealthy and corrupt. The son of a cloth merchant, he renounced worldly goods and embraced poverty, choosing to live on charity like Christ's own disciples. This fresco from the Basilica of St. Francis in his hometown of Assisi shows the saint exhibiting the stigmata—the wounds suffered by Christ in the crucifixion.

1203 Muslim forces sent by the Almohad Dynasty in Spain capture the Balearic Islands.

1203 The German poet Wulfram von Eschenbach composes *Parzival*, a romance of the Holy Grail.

AFRICA

c.1200 Lalibela, king of Ethiopia, orders the carving of churches out of solid rock at a new capital city that will come to bear his own name.

c.1200 The Kingdom of Mwenemutapa is established in Zimbabwe.

c.1200 The Great Enclosure is built at Zimbabwe in southern Africa.

c.1200 The first coinage in East Africa is minted on the orders of the sultan of Kilwa.

1203 Sumanguru establishes himself as the ruler of the Kingdom of Soso on the Niger River, a surviving remnant of the Empire of Ghana; Muslims migrate north.

WESTERN ASIA

1204 The kingdoms of Nicaea and Trebizond are created from the ruins of the Byzantine Empire.

1221 En route to Russia, Mongol forces overrun nothwestern Persia and defeat Georgia and Armenia.

1222 John III Vatatzes becomes king of Nicaea; Byzantine fortunes will revive in his 32-year reign.

SOUTH & CENTRAL ASIA

1203 Muhammad Ghuri completes the Muslim subjection of northern India.

1206 Following the murder of Muhammad Ghuri, the Islamic Delhi Sultanate is established in northern India by his general Qutbuddin Aibak, a former slave.

1206 The Mongol warrior Temujin establishes his hold over all the Mongol tribes of Central Asia. He takes the title Genghis Khan ("Universal Ruler").

EAST ASIA & OCEANIA

c.1200 Birth of the Japanese Zen master Dogen (d.1253).

c.1200 The first chiefdoms develop in Polynesia.

c.1200 Water-powered textile machinery is in use by this date in China.

1211 Genghis Khan's Mongols invade the Jin Empire lands in northern China.

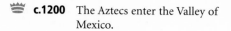

Black burnish pottery mug from Moundsville, Alabama.

👑 **c.1200** The Aztecs enter the Valley of Mexico.

✕ **1221** Hunac Ceel, founder of the Cocom Dynasty in Mayapán, conquers Chichén Itzá.

AMERICAS

✕ **1204** Constantinople falls to the forces of the Fourth Crusade; the Byzantine Emperor Alexius III is forced to take flight.

✕ **1204** Danes under King Waldemar conquer Norway.

✕ **1209** At the request of Pope Innocent III a crusader army invades southern France to suppress the Albigensian heretics (–1229).

☀ **1209** St. Francis of Assisi wins papal approval for the religious order known as the Franciscans—the first mendicant (begging) friars.

📖 **c.1210** The German poet Gottfried von Strassburg writes *Tristan and Isolde*.

✕ **1212** Muslim defeat at the battle of Las Navas de Tolosa marks a turning point in the Christian reconquest of Spain, leading to the collapse of the Almohad Dynasty.

✕ **1212** The Children's Crusade to free the Holy Land ends in disastrous failure.

✕ **1214** France's King Philip II decisively defeats the English at the Battle of Bouvines; his victory enables him to win back all English-held territory north of the Loire River.

👑 **1215** England's King John is forced by rebellious barons to sign the Magna Carta, limiting royal power.

☀ **1215** Pope Innocent III approves the establishment of the Dominican Order of preaching monks.

👑 **1220** Frederick II becomes Holy Roman emperor and ruler of southern Italy.

✕ **1222** A Mongol force sent by Genghis Khan invades Russia (–1223).

📖 **1222** The Icelandic poet Snorri Sturluson writes the *Prose Edda*—a vital sourcebook on Norse mythology.

EUROPE

☀ **1218** St. Peter Nolasco founds the Order of Our Lady of Mercy to ransom Christian captives held in North Africa.

✕ **1219** The forces of the Fifth Crusade capture the Egyptian port of Damietta, holding it until 1221, but fail to take Cairo.

👑 **1221** Dunama Dubalemi becomes emperor of Kanem; during his 38-year reign the empire will reach its peak.

The Great Enclosure at Zimbabwe is surrounded by a wall 270 yards (250 m) long and over 30 feet (10 m) high.

✕ **1224** Nicaean forces win back many of the lost Byzantine lands from the Latin ruler of Constantinople.

AFRICA

WESTERN ASIA

✕ **1218** Genghis Khan's Mongols sweep west, conquering Khwarazm and going on to overcome eastern Persia (–1225). The invasion will be remembered for centuries for the total devastation in its wake.

✕ **1222** Mongol forces conquer Afghanistan and invade northern India.

SOUTH & CENTRAL ASIA

✕ **1215** Mongols take the Jin Dynasty capital of Zhongdu (near modern Beijing) and press on to reach the Yellow River. The Jin set up a new capital further south at Kaifeng.

👑 **1219** The last Minamoto shogun is assassinated in Japan. The Hojo family takes control, ruling Japan as regents for the shoguns (military governors) until 1333.

☀ **1224** The True Pure Land Sect, a breakaway from the Pure Land Sect, is established in Japan; it will become the nation's most popular form of Buddhism.

EAST ASIA & OCEANIA

1200–1225 A.D.

THE MONGOL HORDES

IN THE EARLY 13TH CENTURY *Mongol horsemen erupted out of the steppes of eastern Asia to conquer the biggest empire the world had yet known. Under a series of brilliant military leaders, most notably the empire's founder Genghis (or Chingis) Khan, they made themselves masters of both China and Islamic Persia, the greatest civilizations of their day. Yet the Mongols' rule proved relatively shortlived, while the reputation for destruction they won in making their conquests has survived to this day.*

▲ The Mongols had long honed their riding skills as nomadic pastoralists driving flocks of cattle, sheep, and goats over the Central Asian steppelands. Under Genghis Khan they put their skills to good military use as mounted bowmen in the finest cavalry army the world had yet seen.

▶ From their Mongolian homeland the hordes first spread south and east into China and then west through the Islamic lands. After Genghis Khan's death they would extend their rule into Russia and to the shores of the Mediterranean Sea.

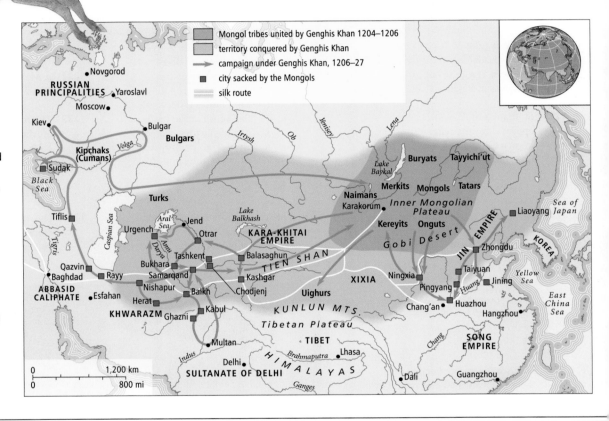

Mongol tribes united by Genghis Khan 1204–1206
territory conquered by Genghis Khan
campaign under Genghis Khan, 1206–27
city sacked by the Mongols
silk route

0   1,200 km
0   800 mi

👑 **c.1130** Kabul Khan creates a powerful, unified Mongol state. It breaks up into feuding clans following an unsuccessful war against the Jin Dynasty rulers of northern China (–1145).

👑 **c.1163** Temujin—the future Genghis Khan—is born in a direct line of descent from Kabul Khan (possibly his great-grandson).

👑 **1206** At a *kuriltai*, or gathering of clan chieftains, Temujin is proclaimed Genghis Khan ("Universal Ruler") of all the Mongol peoples.

⚔ **1207** Genghis Khan leads a combined Mongol force against the neighboring Tangut Kingdom of Xixia.

⚔ **1215** Genghis Khan's forces storm Zhongdu, the capital of the Jin Dynasty rulers of northern China.

⚔ **1217** Another Mongol horde under Jebe overwhelms the Kingdom of Kara-Khitai on Mongolia's southwestern border.

⚔ **1218** A Mongol horde led by Genghis Khan sweeps westward into the Turkish-ruled Kingdom of Khwarazm.

⚔ **1223** Another Mongol horde defeats a Russian army at the Battle of the Kalka River.

Before embarking on a career of conquest, the Mongols lived as nomadic livestock herders on the Central Asian grasslands. They worshiped nature spirits that dwelled in such elemental forces as fire, wind, and water, and that must not be offended; it was a mortal crime among them, for example, to bathe or wash clothes in a running stream.

The military genius who turned these hardy shepherds into worldbeaters was Temujin, born into a princely family. The first task he set himself was to unite the feuding Mongol clans. By 1206 he had achieved this goal, and at a general assembly of chiefs he was proclaimed Genghis Khan, "Universal Ruler."

He then set about living up to his new title. First he destroyed Xixia, the kingdom of the Tangut people that stood between the Mongol lands and China. At the time that great nation was split between two rival dynasties, the Jin in the north and the Song in the south. Genghis Khan's target was the Jin realm, and in 1215 his Mongols swept across the Great Wall that protected its western frontier. Before the year was out, they had devastated the Jin capital of Zhongdu.

Next the Mongols struck the Islamic world. They fell on the Turkish-ruled Kingdom of Khwarazm with a fury that became the stuff of legend. In a three-year campaign millions of men, women, and children died; pyramids of skulls marked the passage of the hordes from one razed city to the next.

Genghis Khan himself died in 1227, but the Mongol expansion continued under his successors. One group drove north into Christian Russia, establishing the Khanate of the Golden Horde. Another completed the conquest of western Asia, in the process capturing and destroying Baghdad. In the east the Mongols seized Korea and, under Genghis Khan's grandson Kublai Khan, eventually conquered the Song lands of southern China, finally reuniting all China under their rule.

By that time, however, Mongol expansion was reaching its limits. The hordes had suffered their first major military setback 11 years earlier at Ayn Jalut in Palestine, where a Mongol army was defeated by the Mameluke rulers of Egypt. Elsewhere Mongol rulers gradually succumbed to the attractions of the civilizations they had overcome: The Il-Khan rulers of Persia converted to Islam in 1295, while Kublai Khan ruled China amid an oriental splendor the rough-riding Genghis would have despised.

▲ Shown here in a Persian miniature painting, Genghis Khan used his political skills first to unite the Mongol clans and then to embark on a career of conquest that served to hold the union together.

The Yurt

The Mongols owed much of their military success to the mobility associated with their nomadic lifestyle. Their warriors had no fixed abode; instead, they lived in tents called yurts. These movable homes were made of willow poles and latticework held together with rawhide and covered with blankets of greased felt. Inside, skins or rugs covered the floor around a central hearth, creating warm, comfortable, but smoky dwellings. The yurts could be quickly disassembled and strapped onto pack horses, although the luxurious tents of chiefs required large ox carts to carry them.

☞ **1227** Genghis Khan dies of a fever while suppressing a Tangut revolt in Xixia.

☞ **1229** Ogodei, Genghis's favorite son, is confirmed as his successor at a fresh *kuriltai*.

✗ **1231** A Mongol horde invades Korea (−1259).

✗ **1236** Led by Subetei and Batu, a horde moves westward to attack first the steppe tribes and, later, Christian Russia (−1241).

✗ **1240** The Mongols capture and destroy the Russian capital Kiev.

✗ **1241** The same horde destroys a Polish army at the Battle of Liegnitz, then invades Hungary, only to abandon its conquests and return home on news of the death of the Great Khan Ogodei.

☞ **1251** Mongke, a grandson of Genghis Khan, is acclaimed as Great Khan.

✗ **1256** Hulagu leads a horde westward to crush the Assassins of Syria.

✗ **1258** Hulagu's horde sacks Baghdad; the caliph is captured and executed.

☞ **1259** Mongke dies while campaigning in China.

✗ **1260** The Mongols suffer their first major defeat, at the hands of Egypt's Mameluke rulers at the Battle of Ayn Jalut, fought in Palestine.

☞ **1264** Kublai Khan, Mongke's successor as Great Khan, opts to live in China rather than Mongolia.

1225–1250 A.D.

AMERICAS

☗ **c.1225** The small Mayan city of Tulum is established on the Yucatán Peninsula's Caribbean coast.

☗ **c.1250** Following the fall of Chichén Itzá, Mayapán rises to prominence as the most important Mayan city-state of the Yucatán.

☗ **c.1250** The Aztecs are scraping a living as mercenaries hired by some of the many city-states vying for power in the Valley of Mexico.

EUROPE

📖 **1225** Guillaume de Loris writes the *Roman de la Rose*, one of the great medieval chivalrous romances.

☗ **1226** Louis IX—later to be sanctified as St. Louis—ascends the throne of France at the age of 12.

☀ **1226** Death of Francis of Assisi, founder of the Franciscan order of monks; he is canonized (made a saint) two years later.

☀ **1226** The Knights of the Teutonic Order are commissioned to convert and subjugate the pagan Prussians.

☀ **1229** The Albigensian Crusade against Cathars in southwest France comes to an end.

☗ **1230** Fernando III of Castile inherits the Kingdom of León, uniting the two Spanish kingdoms.

☗ **1230** Wenceslas I ascends the Bohemian throne

✹ **1230** Returning crusaders bring leprosy back to Europe.

✹ **1231** Frederick II requires all medical practitioners in the Kingdom of Sicily to have a diploma from the medical school at Salerno.

While crusaders in the eastern Mediterranean were slowly losing the battle for the Holy Land, the Knights of the Teutonic Order were waging a long, bloody, and ultimately successful campaign to force Christianity on the pagan peoples of the Baltic Sea's southeastern shores. Prussians, Livonians, Letts, and Estonians were all converted at sword point by crusaders operating from strongholds like Malbork Castle (*left*). The knights created a self-governing military state in the conquered lands that effectively preserved its independence until the 16th century.

AFRICA

☗ **1228** Ifriqiya becomes independent under Abu Zakaria Yahya I, who makes his capital in Tunis.

✗ **1240** Sundiata Keita, Malinke ruler of Mali, razes Kumbe, capital of the Kingdom of Soso.

✗ **1249** On the Seventh Crusade Louis IX of France takes Damietta in Egypt but is taken prisoner in 1250.

WESTERN ASIA

☗ **1229** Frederick II gains Jerusalem by diplomacy in the Sixth Crusade.

✗ **1230** Mongol forces win western Persia from the Khwarazmian Turks; the last Khwaramian sultan is killed in flight.

✗ **1243** The Mongols defeat the Seljuks of Rum at the Battle of Kosedagh, turning Rum (western Turkey) into a vassal state.

SOUTH & CENTRAL ASIA

✗ **1227** Ghengis Khan dies on a campaign against the Tanguts of Xixia.

☗ **1229** Ghenghis Khan's son Ogodei is elected Mongol Great Khan.

☀ **1232** The Kutb Minar minaret is completed in Delhi.

☗ **1235** The Mongols establish their capital at Karakorum.

☗ **1236** On the death of her father Altamsh, Raziya succeeds to the Delhi Sultanate, becoming the only Muslim woman ever to rule in India (–1240).

EAST ASIA & OCEANIA

✗ **1226** Mongols destroy the Xixia Kingdom in northern China.

✹ **1227** Returning home after four years' study in China, the potter Toshiro starts porcelain manufacture in Japan.

✗ **1231** Mongols invade Korea (–1259).

☗ **1232** Japan's military rulers draw up the Joei Formulary (a legal code).

⚜ **c.1250** For unknown reasons the ceremonial center of Cahokia starts to decline in importance around this date.

☀ **1233** The Inquisition is established by the papacy to investigate and prosecute heretics.

⚔ **1236** Ferdinand III of Castile embarks on the conquest of the Moorish Kingdom of Andalusia in southern Spain (–1246).

⚔ **1237** Frederick II defeats the Lombard League—a coalition of north Italian cities—at Cortenuova.

⚔ **1238** Mongols led by Batu invade Russia; they take Kiev in 1240 and establish the Khanate of the Golden Horde.

⚔ **1240** Alexander Nevsky of Novgorod defeats the Swedes at the Battle of the Neva River.

⊕ **c.1240** Water-powered sawmills come into use in Europe.

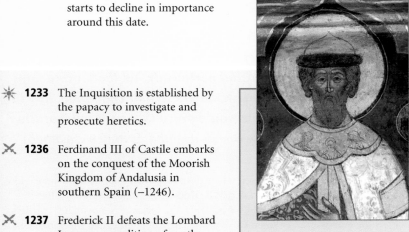

At a time when southern Russia had fallen under Mongol control, the northern Russian principality of Novgorod found a champion in its young prince, Alexander Nevsky. In 1240 he secured its northern borders by defeating a Swedish army on the Neva River, then drove back two attacks from the west, first by the Teutonic Knights and later by the Lithuanians. He maintained the independence of his lands to his death in 1263, winning a reputation as a hero and a saint—he was officially canonized in 1547.

⚔ **1241** The Mongols defeat a Christian army at Liegnitz in Poland; they proceed to invade Hungary but withdraw on the death of their Great Khan Ogodei.

⚜ **1241** The north German ports of Lübeck and Hamburg form an alliance from which the Hanseatic League will eventually develop.

⚔ **1250** Egypt's last Ayubbid sultan is overthrown, to be replaced by the Turkish Mameluke Dynasty.

⚔ **1244** Muslim forces under the Egyptian pasha Khwarazmi recapture Jerusalem from the crusaders.

⚔ **c.1236** Parakramabahu II of Ceylon repels an attack by Tambralinga, a kingdom on the Straits of Malacca, with the help of southern India's Pandya rulers.

⚔ **1234** The Mongols capture the new Jin capital of Kaifeng, extinguishing the Jin Empire in northern China.

⚜ **c.1250** The multistoried Anasazi villages at Chaco Canyon, New Mexico, are abandoned at about this time.

⚔ **1242** In dispute with the papacy Frederick II ravages papal lands.

⚔ **1242** Alexander Nevsky defeats the Teutonic Order in a battle on the frozen waters of Lake Peipus.

⚜ **1245** Pope Innocent IV formally deposes Frederick II as Holy Roman emperor.

⚜ **1250** Death of Frederick II.

⚜ **c.1250** Established by Manding peoples, Mali becomes the predominant state in West Africa.

A medieval manuscript illumination shows forces of the Seventh Crusade disembarking at Damietta in Egypt.

⚔ **1234** Following their success against the Jin, the Mongols launch their first attack on the lands of the southern Song Dynasty.

⊕ **1234** The earliest known use of cast metal movable type for printing books is recorded in Japan.

AMERICAS

EUROPE

AFRICA

WESTERN ASIA

SOUTH & CENTRAL ASIA

EAST ASIA & OCEANIA

1225–1250 A.D.

THE HOLY ROMAN EMPIRE

THE HOLY ROMAN EMPIRE AIMED TO *revive the grandeur of the old Roman Empire in Christian form. It became the chief European power of its day, with its emperors ruling as overlords over central Europe and north Italy. Yet there was a flaw in its makeup. For it to work, the emperor, as Christendom's secular champion, had to cooperate with the pope, its spiritual head. Events would prove that such collaboration was hard to come by; the two leaders were at loggerheads as often as they were allies.*

▲ The Holy Roman Emperor Frederick II appears in suitably Roman guise on this gold coin. A freethinker in a time of deep religious faith, he ruled over a brilliant court where Arab and Christian scholars freely exchanged ideas. His relations with the papacy were less happy, and his reign ended in prolonged warfare.

►A manuscript illumination shows a battle between Guelphs and Ghibellines—the names given in Italy to supporters of the Welf and Waiblinger (Hohenstaufen) claimants to the imperial throne. The Guelphs generally backed the papacy, the Ghibellines the emperors.

Unlike other rulers of the time, the emperor was elected by leading nobles of his realm. In practice, however, certain great families quickly came to dominate the post. From 1024 to 1125 the Salian family provided a succession of emperors. When the last Salian ruler died heirless, the electors chose as his successor Lothair II, a member of the powerful Welf clan, over the claims of a candidate from the equally mighty Hohenstaufen family. Thus started one of the great dynastic rivalries of the Middle Ages, as lesser lords sided with either Welfs or Waiblingers—an alternative name for the Hohenstaufens, drawn from their castle of Waiblingen in Germany. In Italy the names became corrupted into Guelphs and Ghibellines—the two factions that divided the northern cities at the dawn of the Renaissance.

However bitter the divisions separating rival claimants to the title, they paled in comparison with the gulf that opened between emperor and pope. The two first fell out in the 11th-century Investiture Contest (see box). Strife was renewed in the 12th century, when the Hohenstaufen family finally established itself on the imperial throne. One of the greatest Hohenstaufens, Frederick I, known as Barbarossa ("Red Beard"), sought to impose his authority on the papacy and the northern Italian cities by military means, only to be thwarted by their combined forces at the Battle of Legnano in 1176.

Even worse divisions emerged in the 38-year reign of Frederick II. Known as *Stupor Mundi* ("The World's Wonder"), Frederick was a brilliant, ruthless ruler. By dynastic chance he inherited the Kingdom of Sicily, made up not just of Sicily but also of southern Italy, as well as the imperial title, sandwiching the pope's central Italian possessions. When Frederick, like his earlier namesake, sought to impose his will, a bitter 12-year war broke out, in the course of which the emperor was repeatedly excommunicated (banned from the church). In return Frederick ravaged the papal lands and sought to depose the pope.

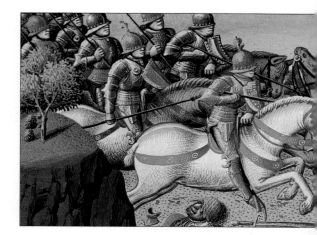

🕮 **800** Charlemagne, king of the Franks, is crowned in Rome as the first of the Holy Roman emperors.

🕮 **1024** Conrad II becomes the first member of the Salian family to hold the imperial title.

☀ **1075** Pope Gregory VII declares lay investiture (appointment) of bishops illegal, setting off the Investiture Contest.

👑 **1076** At the Synod of Worms bishops loyal to Henry IV declare Pope Gregory deposed. In return Gregory declares Henry deposed and excommunicates him and the bishops supporting him.

☀ **1077** Threatened by rebellion in Germany, Henry goes as a penitent to Canossa in Italy. After Henry has waited for three days, Gregory agrees to absolve (forgive) him and to reinstate him as emperor.

✕ **1084** Under threat from Henry Gregory calls on the Normans of southern Italy for aid. Norman troops drive back Henry but go on to sack Rome.

🕮 **1085** Gregory dies in exile in southern Italy.

🕮 **1122** The Concordat of Worms brings the Investiture Contest to an end.

🕮 **1138** Conrad III becomes the first Hohenstaufen emperor.

The Investiture Contest

In 1075 a reform-minded pope, Gregory VII, decided to insist on his right to invest (appoint) bishops. At a time when the church controlled great wealth, the ability to choose its leaders had huge political importance, and the

emperors had sought to claim it for themselves. The result was a bitter struggle in the course of which Gregory declared Emperor Henry IV excommunicated (banned from the church), forcing Henry to wait for three days in the snow outside the papal residence of Canossa to seek a lifting of the ban. While politically necessary, Henry's show of humility did not deter him from later declaring all-out war on the pope. The issue continued to trouble succeeding popes and emperors until a compromise solution was finally worked out in 1122. By the Concordat of Worms (a German city) the pope established the right to appoint bishops but conceded that nominees must have imperial approval.

main Hohenstaufen palace or castle

seat of archbishop within the Holy Roman Empire

Holy Roman Empire under the Hohenstaufen, c.1254

territory in Italy claimed by the pope

0 — 400 km
0 — 300 mi

Frederick died in 1250 with the struggle unresolved. The empire itself outlived the conflict for many centuries, being finally abolished by the French Emperor Napoleon as late as 1806; yet its position as a bulwark of the Christian faith was fatally weakened. The real loser in the conflict was Christendom itself, which saw the expansive energies unleashed in the Crusades dissipated in internal strife.

▲ From 1194 on the empire's lands in northern Europe were supplemented by the territories of the Kingdom of Sicily, comprising southern Italy as well as the island of Sicily itself.

👑 **1152** Frederick I Barbarossa succeeds to the throne.

✕ **1176** Frederick's forces are defeated by rebellious Italian cities, grouped together in the Lombard League, at the Battle of Legnano.

👑 **1183** By the Peace of Constance Frederick acknowledges the Italian cities' right to govern themselves, while they acknowledge his position as their overlord.

👑 **1197** The sudden death of Barbarossa's successor Henry VI unleashes 14 years of civil war in Germany.

👑 **1212** Frederick II is elected king of Germany at the age of 18. He will be crowned Holy Roman emperor eight years later.

👑 **1231** Frederick issues the Constitutions of Melfi, the most comprehensive legal code of the day, in a reorganization of his lands.

✕ **1237** Frederick defeats the forces of a revived Lombard League at the Battle of Cortenuova.

✕ **1238** Frederick is excommunicated by the pope, launching 12 years of all-out war between the emperor and the papacy in alliance with the northern Italian cities.

👑 **1250** Frederick dies with the struggle unresolved.

AMERICAS

c.1250 Casas Grandes, in what is now northern Mexico, emerges as an important outpost of the Mogollon Culture.

c.1250 The warlike Otomí establish a city at Xaltocan in central Mexico.

c.1250 Hohokam settlements are expanding in southern Arizona.

1260 The Acolhua, Nahuatl-speaking kinsfolk of the Aztecs, found the city of Coatlinchan in Mexico's Central Highlands.

EUROPE

1252 Pope Innocent IV authorizes the use of torture against heretics.

1254 The death of Conrad IV leaves the position of Holy Roman emperor vacant: The Great Interregnum (gap between reigns) begins.

Portrait of Louis IX of France (Saint Louis) in a 15th-century manuscript.

1258 James I of Aragon renounces all claims to Languedoc and Provence in southern France.

1258 By the Treaty of Paris, Henry III of England pledges fealty (loyalty and service) to Louis IX.

1259 The Nicaean ruler Michael VIII Palaeologus defeats the Latins (descendants of western Crusaders) at Pelagonia.

1260 At Montaperti the Ghibellines (supporters of the emperor) defeat their rivals the Guelphs (partisans of the papacy).

AFRICA

1250 The Seventh Crusade, led by Louis IX of France (Saint Louis), is interrupted when the French king is captured in Egypt. A ransom is paid and he continues on his way to Palestine.

1250 Egypt's Ayyubid Dynasty is overthrown by the Mamelukes.

1269 Almohad rule in Morocco comes to an end with the overthrow of Abbu Dabbas by Abu Yaqub, first ruler of the Berber Marinid Dynasty.

WESTERN ASIA

1251 Batu's Golden Horde brings much of western Asia and southern Russia under Mongol rule.

1254 The Seventh Crusade comes to an end, having successfully reinforced Crusader strongholds in Palestine but failed to retake the Christian holy places.

1256 A Mongol army led by Hulagu occupies Iran, establishing the Ilkhan Dynasty there.

SOUTH & CENTRAL ASIA

1251 Jatavarman Sundara begins the 17-year reign that will see the Pandya Dynasty at its imperial height in southern India.

1252 Mongols invade Tibet.

1254 Kublai Khan gives Phagspa Lodro Gyaltsen supreme power in Tibet, establishing the leading role of the lamas—but also their subservience to Chinese rulers.

EAST ASIA & OCEANIA

1253 The Mongol leader Kublai Khan embraces the Buddhist religion.

1253 Kublai Khan's Mongol forces invade the kingdom of Nan Chao in what is now southern China. Many refugees find sanctuary at Sukhothai, a Buddhist holy city in modern Thailand.

1259 The Mongols complete the conquest of Korea after 28 years of fighting.

1259 Kublai Khan becomes Great Khan of the Mongols.

The Mayan city of Mayapán was the main political and religious center of Yucatán for 250 years after the decline of Chichén Itzá in around 1200. Its 3,600 stone buildings include many ceremonial structures, such as the large pyramid or Castillo shown here. The city was abandoned after its leaders were overthrown in about 1450.

🌊 **1263** The Late Postclassic Mayan city-state of Mayapán is founded in Yucatán, southeastern Mexico.

AMERICAS

🌊 **1261** Michael VIII Palaeologus becomes Byzantine emperor.

✕ **1262** Michael VIII Palaeologus takes Constantinople back into Byzantine hands from the Latins after 58 years.

🌊 **1264** Simon de Montfort, earl of Leicester, leads a revolt of English barons against his brother-in-law, Henry III. Initially successful, they take control of Parliament.

✕ **1265** De Montfort's rebels are defeated at the Battle of Evesham.

🌊 **1266** Pope Clement IV crowns Charles of Anjou king of Sicily.

🌊 **1267** Henry III acknowledges Llywelyn ap Gruffudd's right to the title of prince of Wales and Wales's right to independent rule.

🌊 **1273** The Great Interregnum ends with Rudolf of Hapsburg's election as emperor.

☀ **1274** Death of Thomas Aquinas, western Christendom's leading theological scholar.

EUROPE

🌊 **1270** Louis IX dies at Tunis in the course of a new crusade.

Emperor Yekuno Amlak of Ethiopia, with slaves and Muslim ambassadors.

✕ **c.1270** Yekuno Amlak deposes Ethiopia's last Zagwe ruler. Claiming descent from the biblical Solomon, he establishes the Solomonid Dynasty, with its capital at Amhara.

AFRICA

✕ **1258** Hulagu's Mongols sack Baghdad.

📖 **1258** The Persian poet Sadi writes his *Gulistan* ("The Rose Garden").

✕ **1260** At the Battle of Ayn Jalut in Palestine the Mongol advance is halted by a Mameluke army.

✕ **1260** Baybars murders Quzut, seizing the Mameluke sultanate.

✕ **1268** The Mamelukes take the Christian-ruled cities of Jaffa, Beirut, and Antioch.

📖 **1273** The great Persian poet and mystic Jalaluddin Rumi dies.

WESTERN ASIA

🌊 **1266** Ghiasuddin Balban, last of the great "slave sultans," inherits the throne of the Delhi Sultanate.

🌊 **1269** Accession of Maravarman Kulasekhara, the last great Pandya king.

✕ **1271** Tughril Khan, Balban's assistant governor in Bengal, extends Muslim rule deep into eastern Bengal.

SOUTH & CENTRAL ASIA

🌊 **1262** Nan Chao's former ruler, Prince Megrai, founds a new kingdom, Lannatai, which allies with Burma (Myanmar) against Ayutthaya (Thailand).

🌊 **1267** The Islamic state of Samudra Pasai is established on the coast of northern Sumatra, Indonesia.

✕ **1268** Kublai Khan begins preparations for the invasion of Japan.

✕ **1274** The Mongols invade Japan, landing 30,000 troops on the island of Kyushu, but are forced to withdraw after meeting resolute resistance.

EAST ASIA & OCEANIA

1250–1275 A.D.

EGYPT'S SLAVE SULTANS

THE MAMELUKES STARTED OUT AS SLAVES *but ended up masters of western Asia, their dynasty holding sway in the region for over 200 years. Soldiers of skill and ferocity, they proved a match even for the Mongols, whose westward advance had seemed irresistible until a Mameluke army halted it at the Battle of Ayn Jalut. But the Mamelukes, great wagers of jihad, or holy war, were also happy to enjoy the benefits of peace and prosperity, ruling an empire of splendid cities from a glittering court.*

▲ Expansion brought prosperity to the Mameluke Empire and trade in valuable commodities such as woods, resins, and spices for use as incense. This brass incense burner was created for a Mameluke dignitary in Syria around the 1270s.

Slavery was taken for granted throughout the medieval Muslim world, with slaves performing many vital functions. While many slaves worked as laborers or household servants, others reached positions of great influence as scribes and public officials. Slave soldiers had a particularly important role. From the 9th century onward the rulers of many Muslim dynasties—among them the Ayyubid sultans of Egypt—bought boys, mainly from among the warring Turkic tribes of the western steppes, for military service. The young men, or Mamelukes (the word means "slave" in Arabic), were preferably old enough to have acquired some of their peoples' celebrated skills in mounted combat. It was important, however, that their minds should not yet be fully formed, for the other advantage of the slave soldier was his unquestioning loyalty to the only lord and master he had ever really known.

Egypt's rulers were to find out, however, that loyalty had its limits. When the last effective Ayyubid sultan, al-Salih Ayyub, died defending Egypt against King Louis IX's crusade in 1249, his Mameluke officers fought on until the French invaders had been defeated. A few months later, however, they murdered al-Salih's heir Turanshah and took over Egypt in their own name. Their reign did not go unchallenged: Not only the legitimate heirs of the Ayyubid dynasty but rival generals fought to carve out empires of their own in areas claimed by the Mameluke leaders.

A decade went by in a chaos of vicious but inconclusive factional fighting before the advance of the Mongols from the east once more united the Egyptians. After sacking Baghdad, in modern-day Iraq, in 1258, the Mongols paused to consolidate their gains. In 1260 they began pushing into Syria in the east of the Mameluke Empire. The Mameluke Sultan

---

☫ **1249** The Ayyubid Sultan al-Salih dies of a fever at a critical time, shortly after the troops of the Seventh Crusade, led by King Louis IX of France, have invaded Egypt.

✖ **1250** Egyptian forces led by Mameluke slave soldiers defeat the crusader army at the Battle of Mansura; Louis IX is subsequently taken prisoner.

☫ **1250** When the new Ayyubid sultan, Turanshah, appoints slaves from his own household over the Turkic Mamelukes, the Mamelukes stage a coup, killing the sultan.

✖ **1260** When Mongol forces strike Syria, a Mameluke army led by Sultan Qutuz stops their advance at the Battle of Ayn Jalut in Palestine. The battle marks the limit of Mongol expansion in West Asia.

☫ **1260** Six weeks after his victory, Qutuz is assassinated by rival Mamelukes led by Baybars, who had earlier engineered Turanshah's death. Baybars himself becomes sultan, ruling ruthlessly but effectively for 17 years (–1277).

✖ **1268** Baybars sacks the crusader enclave of Antioch.

☫ **1280** Following a fresh coup, Qalawun replaces Baybars's son as sultan (–1290).

✖ **1281** Qalawun defeats a Mongol army dispatched by the Ilkhan rulers of Persia at the Battle of Homs.

✖ **1289** Qalawun conquers the crusader state of Tripoli.

☫ **1290** Khalil becomes sultan on the death of Qalawun.

✖ **1291** Acre—the last Christian enclave in Palestine—falls to the Mamelukes after a six-week siege, bringing to an end nearly 200 years of crusader rule in the Holy Land.

☫ **1293** In a time of political instability, al-Nasir Muhammad briefly takes the Mameluke throne.

☫ **1310** Muhammad is restored to the throne. His 30-year reign marks the high point of Mameluke rule.

☫ **1340** The death of al-Nasir Muhammad unleashes a new period of instability and coups.

☫ **1382** The Turkic Bahri Mamelukes are overthrown by usurpers of the Circassian Burji line.

Qutuz was equal to the challenge. At Ayn Jalut, in Palestine, the Mongols were halted by a Mameluke army skilled at the same sort of warfare at which they themselves excelled— "defeated," in the words of one Arab scholar, "by pests of their own kind."

Before he could long enjoy the new authority he had won, however, Qutuz was assassinated by a Mameluke general, al-Zahir Baybars (1260–1277). Ruthless but effective, Babyars reigned successfully for 17 years, building an empire that stretched from southern Egypt to Armenia. Under his successors, al-Mansur Qalawun (1280–1290) and al-Ashraf Khalil (1290–1293), the "Latins," as the Christian crusaders were known, were driven out of the last crusader states, Tripoli falling in 1289 and Acre in 1291.

Suspicious of Christian ambitions in the region, the Mamelukes tended to treat the Christian subjects of their empire harshly. In other respects, however, they proved relatively enlightened and cultivated rulers. This first Turkish Bahri Dynasty declined through the 14th century. In 1382 it suffered a Mameluke coup of its own: The slave-soldiers who formed the new Burji Dynasty were not Turkic in origin like their predecessors but Circassians from the Caucasus Mountain region between the Black and Caspian seas.

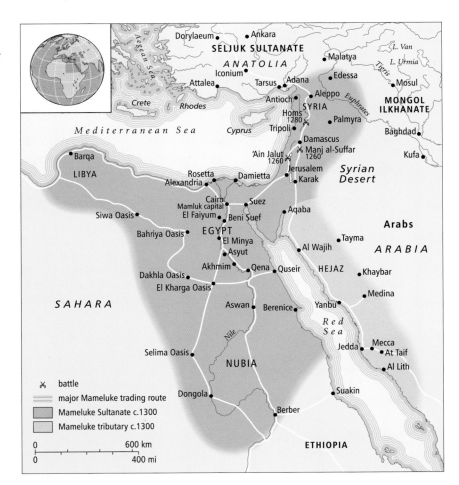

▲ The Mamelukes' military superiority brought them effective control of Mecca and allowed them first to defend their empire against Mongol attack from the east and later to conquer the last of the crusader states of the Holy Land.

The Mosque of al-Nasir Muhammad

The capital of Egypt since the 10th century, Cairo was strengthened in the late 12th century when Salah al-Din (Saladin), the founder of the Ayyubid Dynasty and the crusaders' most celebrated opponent, built a mighty citadel to garrison his troops. The city reached a peak of prosperity and magnificence under the Mameluke Sultan al-Nasir Muhammad, who ruled, with two short interruptions, between 1293 and 1340, a reign that saw the Mameluke Empire at its height. Cairo more than doubled in size in the course of his reign, which was a time of conspicuous prosperity. In typical Mameluke style Muhammad sought to proclaim the might of his dynasty and of Islam through impressive programs of public works. The centerpiece of his plans was the al-Nasir Muhammad Mosque (built from 1318 to 1335), which was designed as the monumental center of a revamped citadel, conceived by his architects as an Islamic version of the Athenian Acropolis. Today the mosque is considered Cairo's best-preserved Mameluke building.

1275–1300 A.D.

AMERICAS

1276 From this year on droughts (and perhaps also Athabascan raids) send the Anasazi Culture of the American Southwest into decline.

1283 The Kokom Dynasty seizes power in Mayapán and begins building an empire in Mexico's northern Yucatán Peninsula.

EUROPE

1276 Edward I of England begins the eight-year campaign that will complete the subjection of Wales.

1282 In a rebellion known as the Sicilian Vespers, the people of Sicily rise against the rule of Charles of Anjou, of the French Angevin Dynasty. King Peter III of Aragon takes power at the invitation of the people.

1282 The Serbs take the city of Skopje in Macedonia.

1285 Philip IV, "the Fair," begins his 19-year reign in France.

1287 Alfonso III of Aragón surrenders important powers to his barons.

1290 Edward I expels the Jews from England.

1292 Asked to judge who should occupy Scotland's vacant throne, Edward I appoints John Balliol, who offends some Scots by doing homage to the English king.

AFRICA

1280 Al-Mansur Qalawun comes to power as Egypt's Mameluke sultan.

1284 Qalawun orders the building of Cairo's Mansuri Maristan, the best medical facility of its time.

1290 Khalil succeeds Qalawun as sultan; he continues plans to capture the Latin enclave of Acre.

WESTERN ASIA

1280 Teguder Ahmed, Mongol Ilkhan ruler of Persia, converts from Buddhism to Islam about now. It will be a decade or two before his followers do the same.

1281 The Mameluke Sultan Qalawun defeats the Mongol Ilkhans, who had taken up the cause of his rival Sunqur, at the Battle of Homs.

1281 Osman (Uthman) makes himself master of the area around Bursa in eastern Asia Minor, founding what will eventually become known as the Ottoman Dynasty.

SOUTH & CENTRAL ASIA

1278 Tughril Khan, assistant governor in Bengal, sets himself up as an independent ruler and thwarts attempts by the Delhi Sultan Balban to dislodge him.

1279 Its realms already much reduced, southern India's Chola Dynasty comes to an end with the death of Rajendra III. The kingdom is absorbed into the territories of the Pandya kings.

1282 Balban's renegade official in Bengal, Tughril Khan, is defeated, captured, and executed.

1284 Pandya forces invade Sri Lanka, pushing its Sinhalese rulers southward and establishing the Tamil Kingdom of Jaffna in the north; a lasting linguistic division is thus created on the island.

1287 The death of Balban ushers in a period of instability for the Delhi Sultanate.

EAST ASIA & OCEANIA

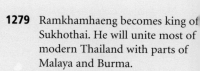

Kublai Khan, founder of the Yuan Dynasty in China.

1279 Kublai Khan becomes emperor in China, founding the Yuan Dynasty.

1279 Ramkhamhaeng becomes king of Sukhothai. He will unite most of modern Thailand with parts of Malaya and Burma.

1281 A second Mongol invasion of Japan fails when a storm sinks their fleet. The Japanese name the storm *kamikaze*, "divine wind."

👑 **1299** Formerly nomadic, the Aztecs settle at Chapultepec, near the Tepanec capital of Azcapotzalco in what is now part of Mexico City.

AMERICAS

The Scottish hero William Wallace, known as Braveheart, led resistance to Edward I's seizure of the Scots crown from John Balliol in 1296. In 1297 Wallace and an army of commoners defeated the English near Stirling, and Wallace was declared guardian of the kingdom. The next year, however, Edward defeated Wallace heavily at Falkirk. Wallace resigned as guardian and lost prominence. In 1305 he was arrested by the English and executed as a traitor. The next year Robert Bruce launched the rebellion that eventually won Scottish independence.

👑 **1293** The Ordinances of Justice transfer power in Florence, Italy, from the city's nobles to its craft guilds: The resulting surge in civic pride is one inspiration for the Italian Renaissance.

⚔ **1294** War breaks out between England and France over Gascony.

☀ **1294** The hermit Pietro di Morone is elected pope as Celestine V but refuses to take office. Boniface VIII becomes pope in his place.

📖 **c.1295** *The Harrowing of Hell*, the first surviving English miracle play, dates from about this time.

⚔ **1297** William Wallace ("Braveheart") leads a Scots revolt against English rule. The rebels win a crucial victory at Stirling Bridge.

⚔ **1298** An English victory at Falkirk marks the beginning of the end for Wallace's revolt.

EUROPE

⚔ **1299** Marinid forces launch a nine-year siege of the Zianid capital of Tlemcen (modern Algeria).

AFRICA

⚔ **1289** The Mamelukes capture Tripoli in Lebanon from the Latins.

⚔ **1291** Acre, the last Latin stronghold in West Asia, falls to the Mamelukes, bringing to an end the era of the crusader states.

👑 **1295** Mahmud Ghazan becomes Ilkhanid ruler. Under his rule Islam will spread widely among his Mongol subjects.

WESTERN ASIA

⚔ **1290** Jalaluddin Firuz Khalji, an Afghan Turk, overthrows the last slave sultan to establish his own Khalji Dynasty in Delhi.

📖 **1292** Marco Polo travels up western India's Malabar coast. His description of India will prove almost as revelatory for European readers as his account of China.

👑 **1296** Alauddin Khalji's 20-year reign begins, inaugurating a golden age for the Delhi Sultanate.

⚔ **1297** Alauddin's forces repulse an attempted Mongol invasion.

Alauddin's madrasa, or theological school, in the Quwwat al-Islam Mosque outside Delhi, India.

SOUTH & CENTRAL ASIA

⚔ **1283** Kublai Khan's Mongols attack the Angkor Empire of present-day Cambodia. Emperor Jayavarman VIII agrees to pay tribute rather than lose his throne.

⚔ **1293** Kublai Khan's forces attempt unsuccessfully to occupy Java. After resisting them, their conqueror Kertarajasa establishes the powerful Hindu Majapahit Dynasty.

⚔ **1295** Jayavarman VIII is overthrown by his son-in-law Srindravarman, who replaces Cambodia's Hindu regime with a Buddhist one.

👑 **1297** The Kamakura Shogunate shores up its position in Japan with the Tokusei Decree, canceling debts owed by the shogun's allies.

EAST ASIA & OCEANIA

THE MONGOLS CONQUER CHINA

WHEN THEY FIRST IRRUPTED INTO CHINA *in the early 13th century, the Mongols were dreaded as savage raiders, bent only on murder and plunder. Yet under the Yuan Dynasty, established by the grandson of Genghis Khan some 70 years later, a reunited China would grow in prosperity and power. Even so, the Chinese never took their foreign rulers to their hearts and in 1368 rose up to sweep them from power, replacing them with the native Ming Dynasty.*

▲ The Yuan Dynasty brought prosperity, cultural achievement, and religious tolerance to China. Kublai Khan himself was a Buddhist who worshiped bodhisattvas, or spiritual guides, such as Guanyin, shown here in a ceramic figurine.

▶ With Kublai Khan's conquest of China the Mongol Empire stretched from the South China Sea to the Black Sea. Beyond China, however, the empire was largely limited to the extent of grasslands that supported the horses of the Mongol cavalry.

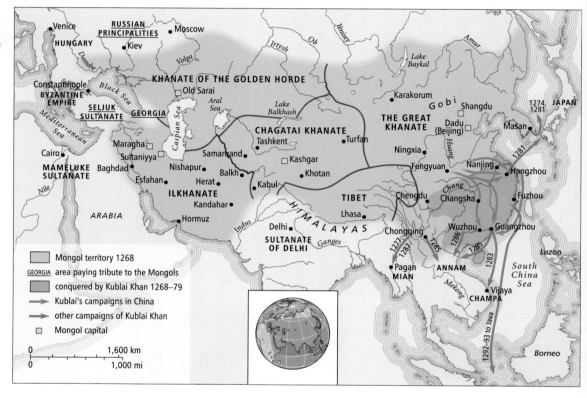

Mongol territory 1268
GEORGIA area paying tribute to the Mongols
conquered by Kublai Khan 1268–79
→ Kublai's campaigns in China
→ other campaigns of Kublai Khan
□ Mongol capital

0 ____ 1,600 km
0 ____ 1,000 mi

👑 **1211** Kublai Khan is born.

⚔ **1211** The Mongols launch their first attacks on the Jin Kingdom of northern China.

⚔ **1215** Genghis Khan captures the Jin capital of Zhongdu.

⚔ **1234** Genghis Khan's successors renew the Mongol attack on northern China, bringing all of the Jin lands under their control.

⚔ **1236** A Mongol horde attacks Hanzhou in the Song Kingdom of southern China.

⚔ **1253** Kublai Khan conquers the Thai Kingdom of Nan Chao on Song China's western border.

☀ **1253** Kublai Khan embraces Buddhism.

⚔ **1258** Kublai Khan invades the Song Kingdom.

👑 **1259** Kublai Khan becomes Great Khan.

👑 **1271** Kublai Khan establishes the Yuan ("First") Dynasty, reuniting northern and southern China under his rule.

⚔ **1274** Kublai Khan's forces attempt unsuccessfully to invade Japan.

📖 **1275** European traveler Marco Polo arrives at the Chinese court.

⚔ **1279** Kublai Khan defeats the last Song claimant to the imperial throne, completing the Mongol conquest of China.

Genghis Khan himself had invaded China as early as 1211, and by 1234 his successors had wrested control of the vast north of the country from the rulers of the Jin Dynasty, set up by Jurchen nomads from Manchuria a century earlier. That still left southern China in the hands of rulers of the native Chinese Song Dynasty, who maintained their hold on power for another generation.

China was finally reunited under Mongol rule by Kublai Khan (1215–1294), a grandson of Genghis who became Great Khan in 1259. Kublai had been educated largely by Confucian scholars, and in later life his tastes and manners became increasingly Chinese. Taking the title of emperor in 1271, he ruled from Khanbalik (today's Beijing) as the founder of the Yuan ("First") Dynasty. Himself a Buddhist since 1253, he tolerated other religions and respected Chinese traditions in everything from literature and law to agriculture and administration.

Kublai's reign was a time of legendary splendor and opulence. In palaces whose walls glittered with gold and silver, he gave banquets for up to 6,000 people. The winter palace that he built for himself near the ruins of the old Jin capital of Zhongdu stirred the imagination of the English poet Samuel Taylor Coleridge. More than six centuries later Coleridge wrote, "In Xanadu did Kubla Khan/A stately pleasure-dome decree…."

For all the prosperity that it brought, Mongol rule was never popular with the Chinese themselves. Despite his respect for Chinese culture, Kublai introduced a class system that regularly gave precedence first to Mongols and then to other foreign advisers; in effect the Chinese became second-class citizens in their own country. Two attempts to invade Japan, launched in 1274 and 1281, were both expensive failures whose costs had to be borne by Chinese taxpayers.

The failings of Kublai's rule grew worse in the decades following his death in 1294. Rivalries between Kublai's heirs combined with the growing oppressiveness of Mongol rule and spiraling inflation that rendered paper money worthless to drive the native Chinese to revolt. In 1368 a peasant army captured Khanbalik, and its leader proclaimed himself the first emperor of a new dynasty, the Ming. Mongol rule had lasted for less than a century, and it left China's population with a distaste for foreign influences that led the nation to cut itself off increasingly from the rest of the world, with disastrous long-term consequences.

Marco Polo

Marco Polo was just a teenager when in 1271 he set off from Venice with his father and uncle, both merchants, on the long journey overland to China—a trip only made possible by the cross-border peace that the Mongol conquests had imposed throughout much of Asia. Starting out through Syria and Iran, the Polos traversed the steppes and mountains of Central Asia before crossing the Gobi Desert to Kublai Khan's court. They arrived there to a warm welcome in 1275. But their travels were just beginning, for the emperor took a liking to the enterprising foreigners and sent them out as emissaries to different parts of his empire; he even made Marco governor of the eastern city of Yangzhou for three years. In 1292 the Europeans left, sailing via southern India to the Persian Gulf, and finally returned home to Venice in 1295. Marco's memoirs astonished his age and have since become an enduring classic of travel literature.

✕ **1281** Kublai's second attempt to invade Japan fails when his fleet is destroyed by a typhoon, which is dubbed by the Japanese *kamikaze* ("divine wind").

✕ **1283** Kublai Khan's forces attack the Kingdom of Angkor (in modern Cambodia), exacting tribute.

📖 **1292** Marco Polo leaves China for home by sea.

✕ **1293** Kublai Khan's Mongols attack the island of Java but fail to hold it.

👑 **1294** Kublai Khan dies at the age of 79.

👑 **1368** The Mongols' Yuan Dynasty is overthrown after a native uprising; the Ming Dynasty replaces it.

1300–1325 A.D.

AMERICAS

c.1300 Its population swollen by immigrants streaming in from farther north, the old Toltec city of Texcoco is becoming an important regional power.

c.1300 The Mississippian city of Cahokia is in continued decline, with falling population levels and the construction of a defensive rampart.

c.1323 Attending the marriage of his daughter to the Aztecs' chief, King Achitometl of Colhuacan finds an Aztec priest wearing her skin in a sacrificial ritual.

EUROPE

1302 Pope Boniface VIII affronts Europe's rulers with his claim that "every living creature" should be under the authority of the pope.

1302 The first meeting of the Estates General in Paris represents France's three "estates"—clergy, nobility, and commoners.

1303 After quarreling with Pope Boniface, France's Philip the Fair is excommunicated (expelled from the church community).

The Divine Comedy, by Italian poet Dante Alighieri, is one of the masterpieces of medieval literature. Its three books—Inferno, Purgatorio, and Paradiso—follow Dante's journey from the darkness of Hell to a vision of God. Guided through Hell and Purgatory by the Roman poet Virgil, the embodiment of human wisdom, Dante is joined for his journey though Paradise by his lost love Beatrice, shown here guiding the poet in a contemporary illustration. Dante's decision to write his poem in his native Tuscan rather than the more scholarly Latin was highly influential in the development of European poetry.

AFRICA

c.1300 Traditionally dated to the 16th century, Queen Amina of Zazzau is now thought by scholars to have lived around this time. Under her rule the Emirate of Zaria came to dominate the Hausa states of what is now Nigeria.

c.1300 In southern Nigeria the state of Benin comes into being with the unification of a group of hitherto quarrelsome tribes.

1312 Mansa ("King") Abubakar II of Mali sails west with his fleet into the Atlantic and is never seen again.

1313 Amda Siyon succeeds as Solomonid king of Ethiopia: In the course of a 40-year reign he will establish a significant empire in the region.

WESTERN ASIA

1302 Byzantine forces are defeated by the Ottoman Turks at the Battle of Bapheus, outside Nicomedia in modern Turkey.

1303 The Mongols invade Syria again. They are turned back outside Damascus by al-Malik en-Nasir's Mameluke army.

SOUTH & CENTRAL ASIA

1302 In Sri Lanka, the Sinhalese King Parakramabahu III has to acknowledge the overlordship of the Pandya King Maravarman Kulasekhara.

1311 Malik Kafur takes the Pandyan capital Madurai on behalf of the Delhi Sultanate.

The tomb of Ghiyasuddin Tughluq, founder of the Tughluq Dynasty, Tughlakabad, India.

EAST ASIA & OCEANIA

c.1300 The east Javan Singhasari Dynasty, having eclipsed the Kingdom of Srivijaya, falls in its turn to the rulers of neighboring Majapahit.

1304 The Franciscan missionary John of Montecorvino baptizes 6,000 Christian converts in Beijing.

1309 The death of Srindravarman ushers in an age of decline for Cambodia's Angkor Empire.

AMERICAS

☀ **c.1325** Arizona's Sinagua Culture, fusing numerous traditions, starts to decline; its major monument is the cliff dwelling known as Montezuma's Castle.

EUROPE

☀ **1305** Facing discontent in Rome, the papacy moves to Avignon in southern France.

🏛 **1305** Scottish rebel William Wallace is executed in London.

📖 **c.1307** Italian poet Dante Alighieri begins work on his *Divine Comedy*—the first significant work of literature to be written in a vernacular language (the author's native Tuscan) rather than in Latin.

🏛 **1308** The Ottoman Turks cross the Bosporus and enter Europe.

📖 **1309** The French crusader Jean de Joinville writes his *Life of Saint Louis*.

⚙ **1310** The Doge's Palace is built in Venice.

☀ **1312** The Knights Templar, a military religious order founded in the crusading era, are abolished by Pope Clement V.

⚔ **1314** At the Battle of Bannockburn Scots led by Robert Bruce defeat the English to win independence.

🏛 **1315** Famine hits northern Europe when harvests fail this year and for the next two summers.

⚔ **1321** Civil war breaks out in Byzantium between factions led by the Emperor Andronicus II and by his grandson, the future Andronicus III.

⚔ **1323** The Flemish inhabitants of the Low Countries rise against their rulers, the king of France and the count of Flanders (–1328).

⚙ **1324** Europe's first known cannon is forged in Metz, northern France.

AFRICA

☀ **1316** Sent by Pope John XXII, a party of eight Dominican friars travels to Ethiopia in search of the legendary Christian ruler Prester John.

Mansa Musa, king of Mali, seated on a throne in a 1375 European map of Africa.

☀ **1324** Mali's Mansa Musa makes a celebrated pilgrimage to Mecca.

📖 **1325** The Moroccan Muslim Ibn Battuta embarks on the famous travels that will take him through Egypt to Arabia and much of West Asia.

WESTERN ASIA

🏛 **1304** The Ilkhan ruler Mahmud Ghazan dies. His successor, Mahmud Uljaytu, is most famous for his tomb in Sultaniyya, Iran.

📖 **1313** Abu Hayan writes the first known treatise on Turkish grammar.

🏛 **1316** Abu Said succeeds his father as ruler of the Ilkhans.

SOUTH & CENTRAL ASIA

🏛 **1320** Ghiyasuddin Tughluq takes power in Delhi, replacing the previous Khalji rulers with his own Tughluq Dynasty.

☀ **1322** The scholar Buston completes a history of Tibetan Buddhism, distinguishing between the Buddha's own words (Kangui) and the additions of his commentators (Tenjur).

🏛 **1325** Muhammad ibn Tughluq takes the Delhi Sultanate. His reign will take the sultanate's territories to their greatest extent.

EAST ASIA & OCEANIA

🏛 **1324** The Shochu Conspiracy—a bid by the Emperor Go-Daigo to overthrow Japan's Kamakura Shogunate—ends in failure.

Emperor Go-Daigo in a silk painting from the Shojokoji Temple in the city of Fujisawa.

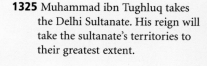

1300–1325 A.D.

THE EMPIRE OF MALI

THERE WERE NUMEROUS PRECEDENTS FOR THE EMPIRE OF MALI. *Down the centuries a series of West African states had grown prosperous on the proceeds of trans-Saharan trade. Yet despite the success of such earlier realms as Jenne-Jeno, Ghana, and Takrur, Mali was on a different scale: It awed contemporaries with its staggering wealth and wide extent. Even today, thanks to the many uncertainties that still surround its history, Mali retains an air of mystery.*

▲ The Empire of Mali was a center of scholarship, principally at Timbuktu, whose celebrated university drew some 25,000 students from all over the Islamic world to study Arabic manuscripts such as this one.

▶ Mali's rise to prominence was based on rich farmlands and goldfields, and above all on control of the lucrative trans-Saharan trade routes with the Islamic states of North Africa.

"It is said," an Egyptian historian reported of the time Mali's ruler Mansa Musa passed through Cairo on his way to Mecca in 1324, "that he brought with him 14,000 slave girls for his personal service. The members of his entourage proceeded to buy Turkish and Ethiopian slave girls, singing girls, and clothes, so that the rate of the gold dinar fell by six dirhams [a smaller unit of currency]."

Al-Maqrizi may have exaggerated, yet Mali must have been an astoundingly wealthy state, commanding as it did the great goldfields of Bambuk and Bure, in modern Guinea. Extending along the corridor formed by the Niger and Senegal rivers, it included some of Africa's richest agricultural land. There were towns, too, long famous for their metalwork and crafts. Upriver from the west and from the forests of the south came ivory and kola nuts (chewed as a stimulant), as well as a never-ending supply of slaves. Away to the north, meanwhile, camel columns up to 30 miles (50 km) long plied back and forth over ancient trails across the Sahara Desert. The Empire of Mali controlled the entire trans-Saharan trade, including the vital traffic in salt from the desert mines at Taghaza.

The empire had emerged from the confusion following the collapse of the Kingdom of Ghana in the 11th century. The successor kingdoms that emerged from Ghana's ruins included Takrur, which reached a peak early in the 12th century, and Soso,

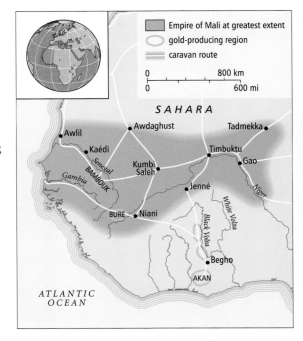

which was dominant in the later decades. By 1235 a new power had arisen: Mande, led by Chief Sundiata Keita of the Malinke people (also known as the Mandinka). In that year Sundiata prevailed over Sumanguru, the Soso king. Pronouncing himself mansa (emperor) of the region's tribes, he made his

✕ **c.1235** Sundiata Keita, founder of the Empire of Mali, overcomes Sumanguru, ruler of the Soso, at the Battle of Kirina.

♛ **c.1260** Sundiata dies after a 25-year reign.

♛ **c.1312** King Abubakar II sails off into the Atlantic at about this date. When he fails to return, Mansa Musa assumes power.

✕ **1320** Mansa Musa's forces seize Timbuktu from the Tuareg.

☀ **1324** Mansa Musa goes on pilgrimage to Mecca. The wealth and splendor of his entourage help draw Mali to the attention of the wider world (–1325).

✕ **1325** Malian forces conquer Gao, extending the empire eastward.

♛ **1337** Death of Mansa Musa.

♛ **c.1350** Mansa Suleiman reigns around now; little is known of his reign.

📖 **1352** The celebrated Arab traveler and writer Ibn Battuta visits the Empire of Mali, reporting that "their sultan does not permit anyone to practice oppression."

♛ **c.1370** Power passes to the tyrannical Mansa Djata at about this time.

Timbuktu

The Malian capital, Niani, was eventually eclipsed by Timbuktu, whose very name has become misted over with exotic legends. A lonely desert oasis before Sundiata captured it from the Tuareg nomads, Timbuktu became first a trading city then a center of culture and learning. Endowed by Mansa Musa with a mosque and a palace, the city in time became the commercial crossroads of the Sahara. It was the place where the great camel routes and the waterway of the Niger River converged. A trading center of great wealth, it was also the hub of a vigorous cultural traffic. At its height in the late 15th century students flocked to its renowned university to study the rare manuscripts in its libraries and to marvel at the grandeur of its mosques.

capital at Niani, near the Bure goldfield, laying the foundations of the Empire of Mali.

Mali's heyday came in the 14th century. At its peak its borders extended from the Atlantic shoreline eastward to the borders of modern Nigeria and from the Sahara south to the rainforests of Guinea. At the start of the century its ruler was Abubakar II, although little is known of him except that one day he sailed off into the Atlantic with a mighty fleet. Some enthusiasts claim that Abubakar and his fellows may have reached America. His successor, Mansa Musa, has a firmer place in the historical record: His pilgrimage aside, he built mosques in the conquered cities of Gao and Jenné. Influenced by their trading contacts with the Arab world, Mali's rulers had embraced Islam in the previous century, although they encouraged the people they governed to maintain their ancestral beliefs.

Mali declined from the early 15th century onward, assailed by raids by the Tuareg nomads of the Sahara and weakened by internal divisions. The eastern city of Gao on the Niger River grew in influence, soon eclipsing its former capital as the center of the new and powerful Songhai Empire.

▼ This 17th-century Italian engraving shows Timbuktu as a stately city amid the sands of the Sahara Desert. By that time, however, Mali's heyday had long passed.

🫔 **c.1382** The death of Mansa Musa II unleashes a power struggle for the succession.

⚔ **c.1400** Raids by Tuareg nomads weaken Mali.

⚔ **1433** Timbuktu falls to Tuareg raiders.

🫔 **c.1450** Mali is eclipsed by the growing Songhai Empire, of which it becomes a part.

1325–1350 A.D.

AMERICAS

⊛ **c.1325** The Aztecs begin building their capital of Tenochtitlán where Mexico City now stands.

Ancient mask found at Tenochtitlán.

✺ **c.1325** The Kachina Cult starts to develop in the American Southwest: It will be central to later cultures such as the Hopi.

EUROPE

⚔ **1326** Isabella, wife of Edward II, and her lover Roger Mortimer invade England and capture the king.

⚔ **1327** Edward is deposed by Parliament and murdered at Berkeley Castle. He is succeeded by his son, Edward III.

♛ **1328** King Charles IV, last of the Capetian kings of France, dies. He is succeeded by his nephew Philip VI, founder of the Valois line of kings.

♛ **1328** Muscovy (Moscow) first rises to prominence under Grand Duke Ivan I.

♛ **1331** Stephen Dushan comes to the Serbian throne and begins to create an empire in the Balkans.

📖 **1333** Under Caliph Yusuf I, Arabic civilization in Granada reaches its zenith.

⚔ **1337** Edward III's refusal to do homage to Philip VI for English lands in France precipitates the Hundred Years' War.

📖 **1337** Death of the Italian painter Giotto, whose work will influence the great Renaissance artists.

⚔ **1340** In the first major battle of the Hundred Years' War, an English fleet destroys the French navy off the port of Sluys in Flanders.

AFRICA

⚔ **1325** Mali captures Gao on the Niger River.

♛ **c.1325** The Arab trading town of Kilwa, built on an island off Tanzania, monopolizes the East African gold and ivory trade.

📖 **1331** The Arab traveler Ibn Battuta visits the wealthy city-states of Africa's east coast.

WESTERN ASIA

⚔ **1326** The Ottomans under Osman capture the Byzantine city of Bursa in western Anatolia and make it their capital.

♛ **1326** Death of the Ottoman ruler Osman. He is succeeded by his son Orhan.

⚔ **1331** The Ottomans seize the Byzantine town of Nicaea in western Anatolia and rename it Iznik.

SOUTH & CENTRAL ASIA

♛ **1327** Tughluq, sultan of Delhi, establishes a new, more central capital at Daulatabad in the Deccan but is unable to control the north and is forced to return to Delhi.

📖 **1333** Ibn Battuta, renowned Arab traveler, resides in India and later travels to China as an ambassador for Tughluq, sultan of Delhi.

♛ **1334** The governor of Madurai in southern India declares his independence from the Delhi Sultanate.

EAST ASIA & OCEANIA

⚔ **c.1325** Fortified sites known as *pas* begin to appear in New Zealand as conflict intensifies among the Maoris over limited food resources.

⊛ **1327** China's Grand Canal, started in 70 A.D., is completed. It is 1,100 miles (1,770 km) long.

The Grand Canal in eastern China.

182

AMERICAS

👑 **c.1350** In the Pueblo region of southwest North America, the population concentrates in fewer and larger settlements.

☀ **c.1350** The so-called Southern Cult, characterized by shared visual religious motifs, is now found across the American South.

EUROPE

📖 **c.1340** The madrigal, a form of vocal chamber music, originates in northern Italy.

📖 **1341** Francesco Petrarch is crowned poet laureate in Rome.

⚔ **1346** An English army defeats the French at the Battle of Crécy. The following year the port of Calais surrenders to Edward III.

👑 **1347** The Black Death reaches Europe from Asia.

The Hundred Years' War (1337–1453) between France and England occupied several generations of rulers on both sides disputing the right to rule parts of France. The English and French and their allies fought a series of battles, including Sluys (1340, right), Crécy (1346), and Poitiers (1356), while the conflict was complicated by civil war in France and changes of monarch in both countries. Eventual French victory in 1453 helped secure the rule of the Valois Dynasty within France.

AFRICA

📖 **1333** Ibn Khaldun, greatest of medieval Arab historians, is born in Tunisia.

👑 **1337** Mansa Musa dies; he is eventually succeeded by his brother, Mansa Suleiman.

⚔ **1347** The Moroccan Marinids capture Tunisia from its Hafsid rulers.

👑 **1348** The Black Death devastates Egypt.

WESTERN ASIA

⚔ **1333** Ottomans led by Orhan capture the town of Nicomedia (renamed Izmit), leaving the Byzantines only a toehold in Anatolia.

👑 **1335** The Mongol Ilkhan Dynasty of Persia, begun by Genghis Khan's grandson Hulagu, ends with the death of the last khan.

👑 **1346** In return for Ottoman military aid the Byzantine Emperor gives his daughter, Theodora, in marriage to Sultan Orhan.

SOUTH & CENTRAL ASIA

👑 **1345** Bhaman Shah, a Muslim noble, revolts against the Delhi Sultanate and founds the Bhamanid Dynasty, which rules the Deccan for nearly two centuries.

👑 **c.1346** Vijayanagar in southern India becomes the center of a Hindu empire. The city itself is one of the richest in the world at this time, noted for its palaces and enormous monumental gateways.

⚔ **1346** Muslim armies raid the Kathmandu Valley in Nepal, destroying Hindu images and temples.

EAST ASIA & OCEANIA

✱ **c.1330** The technique of decorating porcelain in underglaze cobalt blue is popular in China.

👑 **1336** Ashikaga Takauji seizes power in Japan and installs Prince Toyohito as Emperor Komyo.

👑 **1338** In Japan Emperor Komyo names Ashikaga Takauji as shogun.

👑 **c.1331** Plague devastates the population of northern China.

⚔ **1337** Popular rebellions against the Mongol Yuan Dynasty break out in central and southern China.

👑 **1344** China's Huang (Yellow) River floods, blocking the Grand Canal with silt.

👑 **1333** Japan's Emperor Go-Daigo and his supporters overthrow the Kamakura Shogunate in what becomes known as the Kemmu Restoration.

👑 **1337** Japanese emperor Go-Daigo escapes to Yoshino and sets up a Southern Court in competition with Takauji's Northern Court.

✱ **1349** A huge workforce reopens China's Grand Canal.

👑 **1349** First Chinese settlement at Singapore.

1325–1350 A.D.

THE BLACK DEATH

EUROPE IN THE 14TH CENTURY WAS RACKED *by wars, but the unstoppable Black Death—the name given to a pandemic of plague that swept the continent—was more deadly than any army. Between 1347 and 1352 the plague killed about one-third of the total population, making it the greatest demographic disaster in European history. The lower classes suffered worst; but after the scourge had passed, the survivors used their own scarcity to demand higher wages. Rulers responded with repressive laws, breeding resentment that was to erupt in popular revolts toward the end of the century.*

▲ In some places the Black Death left barely enough people alive to bury the dead.

The Black Death originated in Central Asia in the early 1340s and spread west along overland trade routes to the Black Sea, from where Genoese merchant ships transported it to Europe. In just four years it penetrated to almost every corner of the continent, claiming an estimated 20 million lives. The death toll was so great in some cities that, according to one contemporary chronicler, "the living did not suffice to bury the dead."

The disease struck in three different forms, all equally unpleasant and nearly as fatal. Bubonic plague, which was spread by contact with an infected person, affected the lymph glands. It caused painful black swellings—the buboes for which the disease was named—in the neck, armpits, and groin. The mortality rate was about 75 percent, and most victims died within a week of infection. Septicemic plague infected the blood, while pneumonic plague, a deadly airborne form, attacked the lungs; it killed more than 90 percent of its victims within three days of infection.

It would be another 500 years before scientists finally identified the cause of the Black Death as *Pasteurella pestis*, a bacterium that was transmitted to humans by fleas carried on rats. Fourteenth-century scholars attributed the disease to causes ranging from foul vapors released by earthquakes to a malign conjunction of the planets. The 14th-century church, meanwhile, argued that the contagion was clearly divine retribution on humans for their wicked and sinful ways.

The Flagellants

Self-scourging with whips as a form of penance was common to many religions, but in Europe during the Black Death the practice was taken to grotesque extremes. The flagellant movement flared up in Germany, where organized groups marching from city to city whipped themselves to reenact the scourging of Christ and thus atone for the wickedness they blamed for the onset of the plague. In 1349 the flagellants turned on the Jews, whom they accused of producing the plague by poisoning wells. By the end of the year they had wiped out most of the Jewish communities in Germany and the Low Countries.

✷ **c.1341** The plague that will become known as the Black Death starts in Central Asia.

✷ **1345** The plague reaches the Balkan region and Black Sea ports.

✷ **1347** Genoese merchant ships returning from the Black Sea carry the plague to Sicily, Venice, and Genoa.

✷ **1348** The Black Death penetrates western Europe, crossing the English Channel from France into southern England. Pope Clement VI speaks of "the pestilence with which God is afflicting the Christian people."

✷ **1349** The plague spreads into Scotland, the Low Countries, and Scandinavia. In England three archbishops of Canterbury die of plague within a year.

✕ **1349** Jewish communities are persecuted by flagellant groups in Germany and the Low Countries.

✷ **1350** By July the plague has gone from most of Europe.

♛ **1351** The plague reaches Russia. England's Parliament passes the Statute of Labourers, which fixes wages at preplague rates.

◀ The spread of the Black Death followed the main trade routes from Central Asia to Europe and then moved north and west throughout the continent. In the worst affected areas—Tuscany in Italy, East Anglia in England, and Norway—around half the population died.

▼ This skull and crossbones was carved in medieval Rouen, France, to mark an ossuary, a place where the bones of plague victims were deposited.

Map legend:
spread of Black Death
- 1347
- 1348
- 1349
- 1350
- 1351
- area lightly affected by the Plague
- maritime trade route
- ends of Silk route

0   800 km
0   600 mi

Medieval medicine had no cure for the plague. The only effective measure against its spread was quarantine, or trying to separate the sick from the healthy. The death toll in Milan was lower than in other Italian cities, for example, probably because its ruler ordered that any house struck by plague should be instantly walled up, entombing sick and healthy occupants alike.

Faced with the threat of imminent death, Europeans reacted in different and often extreme ways. Chroniclers left accounts of parents abandoning their dying children and of priests refusing to hear deathbed confessions. At one Paris hospital, however, nuns selflessly nursed strangers until they, too, were struck down. While many citizens turned to prayer and repentance, others resolved to enjoy themselves while they could and gave themselves up to a life of indulgent debauchery.

The scourge had lasting social and economic effects. So many priests died that the Catholic church was forced to ordain semiliterate replacements whose lack of piety caused widespread disillusion with established religion. Labor became so scarce that surviving workers could command wages three times higher than they had earned before the plague struck. In England the government reacted by passing laws that required laborers to work for the same pay as in 1347; these and other repressive measures stoked up widespread anger that would ignite in the Peasants' Revolt of 1381.

☀ **1352** In Cambridge, England, two guilds (medieval workers' unions) found Corpus Christi College, whose scholars are required to pray for guild members killed by the Black Death.

📖 **1358** In his introduction to the *Decameron*, a classic collection of stories, the Italian writer Giovanni Boccaccio estimates that the Black Death killed 100,000 people in his native Florence.

⊕ **1361** The Black Death reappears for a time in England.

⊕ **1377** Sailors and their cargoes arriving at the port of Ragusa (today's Dubrovnik, in Croatia) are held in isolation for 40 days—*quaranta giorni* in Italian, hence the English word "quarantine."

✕ **1381** Resentment in England over the Statute of Labourers and the Poll Tax (introduced in 1380) erupts in the Peasants' Revolt. After initial successes the rising fails, and its leaders are executed.

♨ **1400** Europe's population is thought to be 50 percent lower than it was 100 years earlier.

AMERICAS

⚙ **c.1350** Chocolatl, a drink made from cacao beans, becomes a favorite beverage of wealthy Aztecs.

👑 **c.1350** In Mexico's Oaxaca Valley Mixtecs marry into Zapotec royalty.

The Chimú, skilled potters and metal and textile workers who created this tabard from feathers around the 14th century, dominated the Peruvian Andes before the rise of the Incas after 1450. At their capital Chan Chan they left the remains of a city some 6 by 10 miles (10 by 16 km) square built from adobe bricks.

EUROPE

⚔ **1354** The Ottoman Turks gain their first territory in Europe when they take the Gallipoli Peninsula on the western side of the Dardanelles Strait.

⚔ **1356** In the Hundred Years' War an English army commanded by Edward the Black Prince defeats the French at Poitiers and captures France's King John II and his son Philip.

📖 **1358** Italian writer Giovanni Boccaccio completes the *Decameron*, earthy tales of love and intrigue.

👑 **1360** The Peace of Brétigny brings a nine-year truce between England and France.

⚔ **1361** Ottoman Turks capture Adrianople in Bulgaria. Renamed Edirne, it becomes the main Ottoman base in Europe.

📖 **c.1362** William Langland starts writing *Piers Plowman*, one of the first great English poems.

📖 **1364** The University of Kraków is founded in Poland.

AFRICA

📖 **1352** The Arab author and traveler Ibn Battuta explores the Sahara Desert and spends a year in Mali.

☀ **1352** Muslims persecute Christians in Egypt and imprison the Coptic Patriarch Marco.

⚔ **1352** The Marinids capture Algeria.

👑 **1360** Mansa Suleiman of Mali dies, and his empire begins to decline.

WESTERN ASIA

⚙ **c.1350** Glassmaking reaches a peak of refinement in Syria and other parts of the Mameluke Empire.

👑 **1360** Succeeding his father Orhan as Ottoman sultan, Murad puts down a revolt in Ankara (Turkey).

SOUTH & CENTRAL ASIA

👑 **1351** Firuz Shah succeeds Muhammad ibn Tughluq as sultan of Delhi. During his 37-year reign he consolidates the Delhi Sultanate.

👑 **c.1360** The Kingdom of Majapahit in Java enjoys a golden age under the rule of Rajasanagara (1350–1389).

👑 **1361** Timur establishes himself as leader of the Barlas tribe of Chagatai Mongols in Transoxiana.

A 14th-century Persian miniature shows the Mongol conqueror Timur the Lame on a hunting expedition.

EAST ASIA & OCEANIA

👑 **c.1350** A chief called Ruy Mata emerges in central Vanuatu.

☀ **c.1350** Cambodia adopts the Theravada form of Buddhism and changes the liturgical language from Sanskrit to Pali.

👑 **1351** King Ramathibodi I founds the Thai Kingdom of Ayutthaya, north of the mouth of the Chao Phraya River.

👑 **1353** Fa Ngum founds Lan Xang, the first unified state of the Lao people. The name, meaning "million elephants," is an allusion to Fa Ngum's formidable war machine.

⊛ **c.1350** The Iroquois of northeast North America build communal longhouses over 330 feet (100 m) long.

⚔️ **c.1370** The Chimú people complete the conquest of coastal northern Peru by overcoming the state of Sicán in the Lambayeque Valley.

Gold coin of Edward the Black Prince.

⊛ **c.1365** The French mathematician Nicole d'Oresme describes a precursor of calculus. He also gives a theory of the rotation of the earth, which he describes as "round like a ball."

⊛ **c.1367** The Kremlin in Moscow is rebuilt with white stone walls and towers.

⚔️ **1369** France renews the war against England.

⚔️ **1370** Edward the Black Prince sacks the French city of Limoges.

〰️ **1370** The Peace of Stralsund between Denmark and Germany's Hanseatic League sees the league at the height of its power, virtually controlling the Baltic Sea trade.

⚔️ **1372** French and Castilian fleets defeat the English navy off La Rochelle on France's Atlantic coast.

⚔️ **1365** Arabs ravage southern Egypt and kill the Christian king of Makurra (Nubia).

📖 **1375** In Algeria Ibn Khaldun prefaces his history of North Africa with the *Muqaddimah*, a philosophy of history and theory of society.

📖 **1368** Hafiz assembles his *Diwan* ("Collected Works"), one of the masterpieces of Persian poetry.

📖 **1372** Al-Damiri writes *The Lives of Animals*, the best-known Arabic zoological work.

The Majapahit Kingdom of Indonesia was founded in Java at the end of the 13th century by Vijaya, a prince of Singharsari. Vijaya's rule extended over the modern Indonesian regions of Bali, Madura, Malayu, and Tanjungpura. The Indianized Buddhist dynasty reached its height under the rule of King Hayam Wuruk in the middle of the 14th century and enjoyed a final golden age under the rule of Rajasanagara. The rule of the Majapahit was brought to an end by the spread of Islam through the area and the rise of Islamic states along the northern coast of Java.

〰️ **1369** Timur makes himself ruler of all the Chagatai Mongols.

⚔️ **c.1370** Vijayanagar conquers the Sultanate of Madurai to become the dominant state in southern India.

⚔️ **1355** Chinese rebel leader Zhu Yuanzhang seizes Nanjing from the Mongols.

⚔️ **1363** Zhu Yuanzhang defeats Chen Youliang, a rival Chinese leader, in a naval battle on Lake Poyang.

〰️ **1368** China's Mongol Yuan ruler flees to Mongolia, and Zhu Yuanzhang proclaims the new dynasty of the Ming Dynasty, assuming the imperial title Hongwu.

⚔️ **c.1370** Japanese pirates begin to pillage coastal areas of China and Korea.

📖 **c.1370** The dramatist Kanami establishes Japan's Noh theater in its classic form.

AMERICAS

EUROPE

AFRICA

WESTERN ASIA

SOUTH & CENTRAL ASIA

EAST ASIA & OCEANIA

1350–1375 A.D.

CHINA'S MING DYNASTY

I N THE 14TH CENTURY RESENTMENT AGAINST *China's Mongol rulers erupted in a wave of uprisings. One rebel group was led by a former monk, beggar, and bandit named Zhu Yuanzhang, who defeated all rivals and overthrew the Mongols to found the Ming Dynasty. The early Ming emperors rebuilt the Chinese economy, made their capital of Beijing the largest city on earth, and sent naval expeditions as far west as Africa. But after this dynamic start Ming China lost its spirit of adventure and turned in on itself, becoming increasingly conservative at a time when the mood of inquiry and exploration was rising in the west.*

▲ The Ming period was a golden age of Chinese cultural achievement. Among the luxury craft items produced was this intricately patterned lacquer tray from the 15th century, created using a traditional style of building up layers of varnish.

Zhu Yuanzhang, the peasant's son who would found the Ming Dynasty, was born at a low point in Chinese history. Under Kublai Khan's incompetent successors the Mongol Yuan Dynasty had become embroiled in murderous intrigues. Native-born Chinese, who for centuries had provided the nation with its bureaucrats, were barred from high office, leaving the administration in the hands of incapable foreigners. Huge tracts of land were taken out of cultivation, and floods, famines, and epidemics killed millions. Zhu Yuanzhang's own parents died of starvation when he was a teenager, and he himself survived only by entering a Buddhist monastery.

Widespread unrest broke out in the 1330s, culminating in the Red Turban rebellions, named for the characteristic headdress worn by the rebels. Zhu Yuanzhang joined the Red Turbans in 1352 and by 1356 had established a power base at Nanjing, where he campaigned against other nationalist groups in the Yangtze River valley. The decisive battle took place on Lake Poyang, where Zhu's forces used fireships to destroy his main rival's fleet of iron-sheathed galleys.

By 1367 Zhu was strong enough to launch an assault on the Mongol capital of Dadu. The Yuan court did not wait for the arrival of his army, instead fleeing to Mongolia. In January 1368 Zhu was

Ming Porcelain

It was during the Ming Dynasty period that characteristic Chinese blue-and-white porcelain first reached the west, creating a demand for fine china that was not satisfied until European potters discovered for themselves the secret of porcelain-making in the 18th century. The Chinese technique involved painting blue pigment—cobalt from Persia—on wares potted from a fine clay called kaolin, mixed with other minerals. The wares were then glazed and fired at about 1,300 °C (2,370 °F) so that the materials fused, producing ceramics that were thin and translucent but also hard and strong. Most of the best-quality Chinese porcelain was produced in state-sponsored kilns around the city of Jingdezhen, where there were plentiful deposits of the special china clay required for the process. Although much high-quality porcelain was exported to the west, the finest wares were reserved for the imperial court: In a single year alone, the Ming emperor placed orders for more than 400,000 pieces. Reign marks, usually comprising four or six characters to denote under which emperor a piece was produced, were first regularly used on porcelain in the Ming period.

proclaimed first emperor of the Ming ("Brilliant") Dynasty, taking the reign name of Hongwu ("Boundless Martial Valor").

Hongwu introduced an efficient tax system, increased the amount of land used for agriculture, and expanded trade. Chinese bureaucrats once again staffed the civil service, but Hongwu, unlike previous Chinese emperors, would not allow his senior administrators any independence. He grew paranoid and became convinced that his chancellor was plotting against him. The emperor had the minister and 30,000 of his associates executed. He then abolished the office of chancellor and for the rest of his reign ruled as a despot.

Hongwu was succeeded by his grandson, but in 1403 the throne was usurped by his fourth son, who, ruling as Yongle, presided over Ming China's most brilliant period. Yongle transferred the capital from Nanjing to Dadu, which he renamed Beijing. Between 1405 and 1424 he sponsored six major naval expeditions to Southeast Asia, India, the Persian Gulf, the Red Sea, and the east coast of Africa. China's conservative officials opposed these costly maritime adventures, however, and after Yongle's death only one more voyage was undertaken. Rather than extending its power and prestige abroad, Ming China retreated into semi-isolation at just the same time as explorers in the west were embarking on what is now called the "Age of Discovery."

▶ China's great maritime trade continued during the early Ming period, but a change was heralded by the transfer of the imperial capital in 1421 from the port of Nanjing north to Beijing. Henceforth China became far more inward looking.

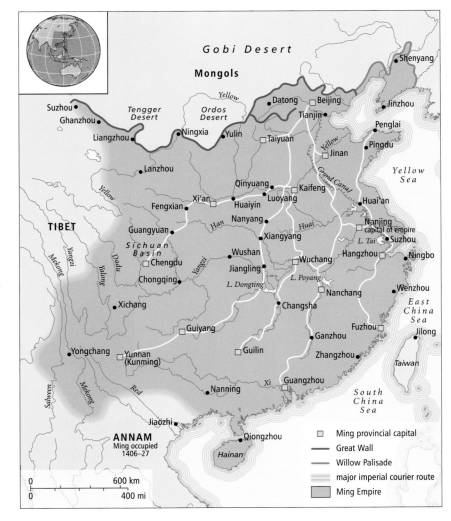

1328 Zhu Yuanzhang, future founder of China's Ming Dynasty, is born to a family of peasant farmers.

c.1331 Plague devastates northern China.

1335 Bayan, the Mongol grand chancellor of China, abolishes civil service examinations and reserves all high administrative positions for Mongols.

1344 China's Huang (Yellow) River bursts its banks, blocking the Grand Canal with silt.

1352 Zhu Yuanzhang joins the Red Turbans, a rebel movement.

1354 Toghto, the last efficient Mongol administrator of China, is dismissed by the imperial court.

1355 Zhu Yuanzhang seizes Nanjing from the Mongols.

1363 Zhu Yuanzhang defeats Chen Youliang, a rival Red Turban leader, in a battle on Lake Poyang.

1368 The last Yuan emperor flees to Mongolia, and Zhu Yuanzhang proclaims the new Ming Dynasty, taking the imperial title Hongwu.

1370 Hongwu institutes new civil service examinations.

1372 The Ming commander Xuda invades Mongolia but withdraws after suffering heavy casualties.

1380 Hongwu assumes direct rule.

1398 Hongwu dies, to be succeeded by his grandson, Jiangwen.

1402 Hongwu's fourth son usurps the throne. Ruling as Yongle, he begins to move the capital from Nanjing to Beijing (-1421).

1405 Yongle sends out the first of seven maritime expeditions; the first fleet comprises 317 ships and 27,870 men.

1424 Yongle dies; China soon surrenders its position as the leading naval power in the Indian Ocean and retreats into isolation.

AMERICAS

👑 **1376** Acamapichtli becomes the first Aztec ruler whose name has been preserved by history.

👑 **1396** Acamapichtli dies and is succeeded by his son Huitziláihuitl, who expands Aztec power in the Valley of Mexico.

👑 **c.1400** In southern Mexico the Tarascan Kingdom expands rapidly. Tzintzuntzan, its capital, has a population of approximately 35,000 people.

EUROPE

👑 **1376** Death of Edward the Black Prince.

☀ **1378** The Great Schism of the Catholic church begins when cardinals elect rival popes—one in Rome, the other in Avignon, France.

⚔ **1379** The Venetians defeat the Genoese at the naval Battle of Chioggia.

⚔ **1381** The Peasants' Revolt in England is suppressed, and its leader, Wat Tyler, is executed.

☀ **1384** English reformer John Wycliffe dies after overseeing translation of the Bible into English.

👑 **1386** Poland and Lithuania unite; a year later Lithuania converts to Christianity.

📖 **1386** The University of Heidelberg is founded in Germany.

📖 **c.1387** The English poet Geoffrey Chaucer starts writing *The Canterbury Tales*.

⚔ **1389** The Ottoman Sultan Murad I defeats the Serbs at Kosovo but is assassinated on the battlefield.

👑 **1396** Richard II of England marries Isabella of France at Calais. The Anglo-French truce is extended to 28 years.

AFRICA

👑 **1375** Gao secedes from Mali and eventually becomes the Songhai Empire.

✳ **1375** A map made for the French king shows Mali and a seated figure of its emperor.

The trading state of Songhai, a subject of which created this fetish in the 16th century, flourished in the 15th and 16th centuries along the Niger River in what is now Mali. From urban centers such as Gao and Timbuktu Songhai expanded to control a large Islamic empire that controlled trade with the north. The empire fell to Moroccan forces in the late 16th century.

WESTERN ASIA

⚔ **1375** A Mameluke army conquers the kingdom of Armenian Cilicia in present-day southern Turkey.

📖 **1377** Death of Ibn Battuta, Arab geographer and traveler.

👑 **1379** Bairam Khawaja founds the independent principality of the Kara Koyunlu ("Black Sheep") Turkmen, establishing his capital at Van in Armenia.

SOUTH & CENTRAL ASIA

☀ **c.1382** Jaya Sthiti of the Malla Dynasty in Nepal repairs the damage done by Muslim raids and introduces a legal and social code based on Hindu principles.

👑 **1388** Death of Firuz Shah, the last important sultan of Delhi. The sultanate begins to disintegrate.

👑 **1394** Jaunpur in northern India breaks free of the Delhi Sultanate under the control of an independent Muslim dynasty.

EAST ASIA & OCEANIA

👑 **1388** Yi Song-gye (1335–1408), the founder of Korea's Choson Dynasty, ousts the reigning Koryo king.

👑 **1392** Yi Song-gye establishes a new capital on the site of modern Seoul.

👑 **1392** Japan's Northern and Southern Courts are reconciled with the acceptance of Emperor Gokomatsu as sole sovereign.

✳ **1392** In Korea a foundry is built to produce bronze printing type.

⚔ **1394** Thais invade Cambodia, and the Khmer move their capital to Phnomh Penh.

A sukia figure from Costa Rica, around 1000–1550.

📖 **c.1400**   In central and eastern Costa Rica seated stone figures known as "sukias" (shamans), are produced, usually shown either smoking a large cigar or playing a flute.

AMERICAS

Geoffrey Chaucer's unfinished *The Canterbury Tales* (c.1387–1400) takes the form of a series of verse tales told by English pilgrims on the journey to venerate Saint Thomas Becket in Canterbury Cathedral. The structure of the work allowed Chaucer great freedom to experiment with contemporary forms. There are refined tales about courtly love and piety, such as the Knight's Tale, and more down-to-earth ribald tales such as the Miller's Tale.

✕ **1396**   The Ottomans under Bayezid I defeat an army of European crusaders at Nicopolis on the Danube River.

👑 **1399**   Richard II of England is deposed by Henry Bolingbroke, who succeeds as Henry IV. Richard is murdered the following year.

EUROPE

👑 **c.1380**   The Kongo Kingdom is founded near the mouth of the Congo River in Central Africa.

👑 **1382**   In Egypt Barquq becomes the first Mameluke ruler of the Burji (Circassian) line, seizing power from the previous Bahri (Turkic) one.

📖 **1382**   Ibn Khaldun, the great Arab historian, is appointed a professor and judge in Cairo.

👑 **1382**   David I becomes king of Ethiopia and makes contact with Christian nations outside Africa.

AFRICA

✕ **1381**   Timur leads an army into Persia for the first time.

👑 **1389**   Bayezid I succeeds his father Murad as the Ottoman sultan.

✕ **1390**   The Byzantines lose their last holdings in Asia Minor to the Ottomans.

✕ **1393**   Timur occupies Baghdad.

✕ **1395**   Timur defeats the rival Mongol Empire of the Golden Horde in south Russia and destroys its capital at Sarai on the Volga River.

WESTERN ASIA

✕ **1398**   Timur invades India and sacks Delhi, finally shattering the power of the Delhi Sultanate.

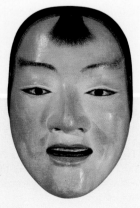

SOUTH & CENTRAL ASIA

👑 **1399**   Death of Hongwu, first emperor of the Ming Dynasty.

Noh mask showing a young monk, Japan, approximately 1370.

📖 **1400**   Zeami, one of the early writers of Noh plays, completes the first part of his *Fushi Kaden*, a treatise on Noh drama.

EAST ASIA & OCEANIA

1375–1400 A.D.

191

TIMUR THE LAME

THE MONGOL CONQUEROR TIMUR THE LAME *warned the citizens of Damascus in 1401, "You are wicked, but I am more wicked." When he entered the Syrian city, he matched deed to word by massacring thousands of its inhabitants—just as he had done in Delhi, Esfahan, and a dozen other cities during a 30-year campaign of conquest. Timur was a brilliant general who defeated the mighty Mamelukes and the Ottomans; he was also a committed Muslim and a lover of scholarship and the arts, who made his capital of Samarqand (Samarkand) an oasis of culture. His obsession, though, was with conquest; he failed to create an administrative machine that could hold his empire together after his death in 1405.*

▲ As Timur's capital, Samarqand in present-day Uzbekistan, was a flourishing center of Islamic culture. This star-shaped tile, typical of Islamic craftsmanship, was set into a wall in the mausoleum built for Timur in the city.

A shepherd's son who was born in about 1336 in Transoxiana—the region north of the Oxus (Amu Darya) River in what is now Uzbekistan—Timur was a Mongol of the Chagatai Khanate, a Central Asian realm that took its name from Genghis Khan's second son. As a young man he was injured during a rustling raid and sustained the wounds that gave him his nickname Timur-i-Lenk, "Timur the Lame" (often shortened to "Tamberlane" or "Tamerlane"). From such inauspicious beginnings, he rose by force and guile to make himself leader of the Chagatai by 1369.

Timur directed his first foreign campaign against Persia, where he established a lasting reputation for cruelty. In 1387 he punished a revolt in Esfahan by slaughtering tens of thousands of citizens and piling their skulls in pyramids around the city walls.

Although Timur committed similar atrocities wherever he went, he took pains to spare scholars and the craftsmen he needed to rebuild his capital, Samarqand. Campaigning, however, meant that Timur himself never spent more than two years in the city at a time. In one frantic seven-year period, which included a residence at Samarqand, he pillaged Georgia half a dozen times, occupied Baghdad, destroyed the Golden Horde, a Mongol state in Russia, then rode south to the decaying but still powerful Delhi Sultanate, where his troops indulged in a three-day orgy of murder and plunder.

Next Timur turned on two formidable opponents in the west: the Ottoman Turks and the Mamelukes of Egypt and Syria. Leading an army of 300,000 men, Timur invaded Syria in 1400 and defeated the local

---

👑 **c.1336** Timur is born at Kish, south of Samarqand.

👑 **1361** Timur is recognized as leader of the Barlas tribe of Chagatai Mongols, the group that rules the Central Asian steppelands.

👑 **1369** Timur makes himself master of the Chagatai Khanate of Transoxiana, a position he seeks to legitimize by taking two wives who are direct descendants of Genghis Khan.

⚔ **1381** Timur invades Persia, which has fragmented after the death of the last Ilkhan ruler in 1335.

👑 **1384** Timur makes Sultaniyya in northwest Persia the base for military campaigns to the north and west.

⚔ **1392** In a period known as the "Five Years' Campaign" Timur's army devastates Georgia, seizes Baghdad for a time, and wages war on the rival Mongol Empire of the Golden Horde in southern Russia (–1396).

⚔ **1395** Timur defeats the Golden Horde and destroys its capital of Sarai on the Volga River.

⚔ **1398** Timur invades India and sacks Delhi.

👑 **1399** In Egypt the Mameluke Sultan Barquq dies, leaving the throne to his 10-year-old son al-Nasir Faraj.

⚔ **1400** Timur defeats the Syrian army of the Mamelukes at Aleppo; the main Mameluke army turns back to Cairo.

⚔ **1401** Timur captures Damascus and Baghdad.

⚔ **1402** Timur defeats the Ottoman army of Sultan Bayezid near Ankara in present-day Turkey. Bayezid is taken prisoner and dies a few months later.

👑 **1405** Timur dies while leading a planned invasion of China. The Timurid Dynasty he founds effectively collapses within 15 years, but one of his descendants, Babur, will establish India's Mughal Empire in 1526.

Samarqand

The Arabs had originally made Samarqand a center of culture, but by the time Timur came to power, the oasis town lay in ruins, having been destroyed in 1220 by Genghis Khan. Determined to create a capital worthy of his greatness, Timur brought craftsmen from all over his empire and set them to work building mosques, bazaars, gardens, and workshops. The most spectacular surviving building is the Gur-i-Mir, "Tomb of the Prince," a mausoleum complex crowned with a turquoise-tiled dome lined inside with gilded and carved papier-mâché. Constructed for one of Timur's grandsons, it was completed shortly before Timur's death and became his own resting place. Another legacy of Timur's ruthless patronage was India's Mughal school of miniature painting, which was inspired by the exquisite work of artists deported to Samarqand from Baghdad.

Mameluke army outside Aleppo. On hearing news of the disaster, the main Mameluke force, led by the 11-year-old Sultan Faraj, turned back to Cairo in Egypt, leaving Timur to sack Damascus and then Baghdad, where each soldier was ordered to decapitate two male citizens.

That left the Ottomans, whose renowned Sultan Bayezid, known as Yildirim ("the Thunderbolt"), matched Timur for generalship and cruelty. When the two forces met near Ankara, however, some Turkish contingents deserted and joined the Mongols. Bayezid himself was captured, displayed in an iron cage, and reportedly was forced to watch while his favorite wife served naked at Timur's table.

Timur was now master of the whole of Asia from India to the Mediterranean. Although he was by now nearly 70 years old and his health was failing, his appetite for conquest remained undiminished. In 1405 he set out to attack China, only to fall sick and die on the borders of Transoxiana before he reached his destination.

The empire he had created soon broke into pieces. His chief concern had always been to plunder rather than administer his territories, so he had not created any kind of central government that could hold the empire together. Even by the standards of his time Timur was an anachronism, a warrior whose horseback, raiding style of warfare would soon be rendered obsolete by infantry armed with artillery.

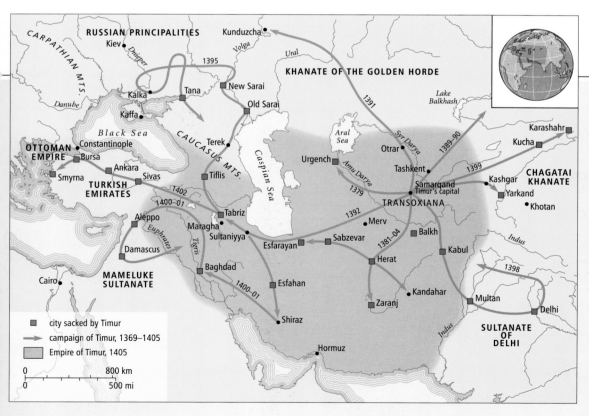

◀ Timur's campaigns of conquest led him west across Central Asia into Persia, the Caucasus, and the Mameluke Empire of Egypt and east to campaign against the Sultanate of Delhi in India. His conquests were accompanied by notorious barbarity: After he captured Baghdad in 1401, he massacred 20,000 of its citizens.

AMERICAS

👑 **c.1400** The Mayan site of Cobá in the Yucatán Peninsula, dating back as far as 600 B.C., is finally abandoned at about this time.

👑 **c.1400** The Quiché Maya build the fortress capital of K'umarcaaj (now known as Utatlán) in the Guatemalan highlands.

EUROPE

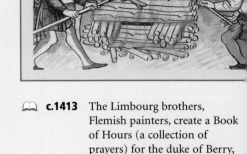

📖 **c.1400** The French historian Jean Froissart writes his *Chronicles*, describing events of the Hundred Years' War.

📖 **c.1403** Lorenzo Ghiberti designs the bronze doors of the baptistery at Florence, a masterpiece of early Renaissance art.

✕ **1410** A Polish–Lithuanian army defeats the Teutonic Knights at the Battle of Tannenberg (Grunwald), establishing the Jagiellon Dynasty of Polish kings.

Illustration from The Book of Hours by the Limbourg brothers.

📖 **c.1413** The Limbourg brothers, Flemish painters, create a Book of Hours (a collection of prayers) for the duke of Berry, one of the most beautiful books of medieval Europe.

AFRICA

📖 **c.1400** The lost-wax method of bronze casting is in use in West Africa.

✹ **c.1410** Most of the stone buildings at Great Zimbabwe in southern Africa have now been built; the city has a population of between 5,000 and 18,000.

✕ **1415** The Portuguese capture Ceuta, on the coast of Morocco, from the Muslims, giving them a foothold on mainland Africa.

WESTERN ASIA

✕ **1400** Timur invades Syria and sacks Damascus (–1401).

✕ **1401** Timur sacks Baghdad in Iraq.

✕ **1402** Timur invades Anatolia, defeating the Ottoman Sultan Bayezid, who dies in captivity.

SOUTH & CENTRAL ASIA

👑 **1404** Death of Harihara II, ruler of the Hindu Kingdom of Vijaynagar in southern India.

👑 **1405** Timur dies while setting off to campaign in China; his conquests are divided between two of his sons, Miranshah and Shah Rokh.

👑 **1407** Miranshah dies, and Shah Rokh becomes sole ruler of the Timurid Empire in Iran and Central Asia; he establishes a capital at Herat (Afghanistan).

👑 **1412** Death of Nasiruddin Muhammad, last of the Tughluq sultans of Delhi.

👑 **1414** Khizr Khan, founder of the Sayyid Dynasty, takes over the much-reduced Delhi Sultanate.

👑 **c.1415** The Kingdom of Bahmani in the northern Deccan is a center of Muslim culture under Sultan Firuz Shah Bahmani (ruled 1397–1422).

EAST ASIA & OCEANIA

✕ **1402** Zhu Di, prince of Yen in China, leads a rebellion against his nephew Jianwen and takes over the imperial throne, reigning as Emperor Yongle.

✹ **1405** Yongle sponsors the first of seven voyages of exploration by Admiral Zheng he to the Indian Ocean.

👑 **1407** Yongle imposes direct rule over the state of Nam Viet (Annam).

✕ **1410** Yongle personally leads five military expeditions against the Mongols (–1424).

AMERICAS

👑 **c.1400** The last remnants of the Dorset Culture Inuit, inhabiting northern Quebec and Labrador, die out about now.

👑 **c.1425** The Hohokam Culture finally disappears about this time as a result of crop failure and perhaps also of Apache raids.

EUROPE

Jan Hus's death in 1415 ended the Bohemian reformer's attempts to change the Catholic church a century before the Reformation began. Hus argued for church reform during the Great Schism, when the church was split between support for two popes. Guaranteed safe conduct, Hus attended the Council of Constance to argue his case but was executed for heresy.

🏛 **1414** The powerful Medici banking family of Florence become bankers to the papacy.

☀ **1414** A great church council is held at Constance in Germany (–1417).

☀ **1415** The Council of Constance condemns the Bohemian (Czech) reformer Jan Hus to death for heresy.

✗ **1415** King Henry V of England invades France and wins a major victory at the Battle of Agincourt.

☀ **1417** The Council of Constance ends the Great Schism of the papacy by electing Martin V as pope.

⊕ **1419** Prince Henry of Portugal (the Navigator) retires to study seamanship and navigation.

🏛 **1420** Henry V of England marries Catherine, daughter of the French king, who adopts Henry as his heir in the Treaty of Troyes.

⊕ **1420** The Italian architect Filippo Brunelleschi (1377–1446) starts to build the dome of Florence Cathedral; completed in 1461, it is a unique engineering feat.

✗ **1420** In Bohemia (the modern Czech Republic) a 13-year war begins as the followers of Jan Hus reject the authority of the emperor.

AFRICA

✗ **1415** An Ethiopian army attacks the Arab port of Seylac on the Red Sea and kills the Muslim ruler.

⊕ **1416** A Chinese fleet under Admiral Zheng-he sails for Africa, visiting the east coast ports of Mogadishu and Malindi, and bringing back a giraffe as a gift for the Chinese emperor (–1419).

WESTERN ASIA

✗ **1410** Black Sheep Turkmen capture Baghdad and establish a dynasty there.

🏛 **1413** Mehmed I wins back Ottoman control over Anatolia (Asiatic Turkey) from Timur's heirs.

SOUTH & CENTRAL ASIA

The Muslim Bahmani Sultanate dominated the Deccan in India from 1347 to 1518. It fought various Muslim and Hindu rulers for dominance of the Deccan Plateau through the 15th century before the sultanate divided into five separate powers, including Muslim Golconda (fortress, left).

✗ **1417** A war between Bahmani and Vijaynagar ends in a disastrous defeat for Bahmani; Firuz Shah is forced to abdicate two years later (–1420).

EAST ASIA & OCEANIA

⊕ **1415** In China the Grand Canal linking the Chang (Yangtze) and Huang (Yellow) Rivers, neglected for centuries, is repaired.

📖 **1420** In Korea a royal academy, the Chiphyonjon ("Hall of Worthies"), is established for young scholars to engage in study and research.

🏛 **1421** China's imperial capital moves permanently to Beijing with the completion of the Forbidden City as the emperor's residence.

1400–1425 A.D.

THE OTTOMANS

▲ Sultan Mehmed II was painted by the great Venetian artist Bellini. Despite the conflict between the Ottomans and Christendom, cultural links and, more importantly, trade bound the Islamic empire into the Mediterranean world.

IN THE MID-1300S TURKISH ARMIES *began making regular raids into the Balkan region of southeast Europe, which belonged at the time to the Byzantine Empire. They were led by the Ottomans, a Turkish dynasty from northwestern Anatolia named for its founder Osman I (1259–1326); the word is written as "Uthman" in Arabic. By 1500 the Ottomans had overthrown the Byzantine Empire, penetrated deep into eastern Europe as far as Hungary, and begun to expand into Iraq and Syria, laying the foundations for one of the greatest Muslim empires in history.*

The early Ottomans were *ghazis*, warriors dedicated to fighting for Islam and winning converts. From their small principality in the northwestern corner of Anatolia they made repeated attacks against the Christian Byzantine Empire, now in decline and weakened by internal disorder. The greatest of the early Ottoman sultans was Murad I (ruled 1360–1389). In 1361 he captured Adrianople, the second most important city of the Byzantine Empire, in present-day Bulgaria. Murad renamed the city Edirne and made it his capital. From there he sent his armies ever deeper into Europe. In 1389 he was killed at the Battle of Kosovo in Serbia, which despite his death was a great victory for the Turks. The memory of their defeat at Kosovo still haunts Serbs today.

Murad's namesake and grandson, Murad II (ruled 1421–51), oversaw the next great period of Ottoman expansion. Murad ruled with the support of the highly trained janissaries, a corps of soldiers made up of Christian slaves and converts to Islam who served as his personal guard. To ensure a constant flow of recruits, Murad devised the *devshirme* system by which drafts of Christian youths were sent from the Balkans to the sultan's capital each year. After undergoing conversion to Islam, they were given military training and joined the sultan's service for life. Although slaves, the janissaries were well treated and could rise to high positions of wealth and influence in the empire.

The *devshirme* system relied on conquest to produce fresh drafts of young men, and Murad renewed the Ottoman campaigns in Greece, Serbia, Walachia (now southern Romania), and Albania. By now the Byzantine Empire, reduced to little more than the city of Constantinople, was entirely encircled by the Ottomans. Its inevitable fall came in 1453, when the army of the 20-year-old Sultan Mehmed II (ruled 1451–1481) stormed the walls after a 53-day

The Fall of Constantinople

Constantinople was built on a peninsula on the Bosporus, the narrow strait that separates Asia from Europe. On its seaward side lay the harbor of the Golden Horn. The massive walls that guarded the city on its landward side, built by the Roman Emperor Theodosius II, had withstood countless sieges before the final siege of Constantinople began on April 2, 1453. The Greek Emperor Constantine IX Palaeologus had strengthened the city's defenses and stretched a great chain across the entrance to the Golden Horn, but the Ottomans hauled their ships overland into the harbor so that the city could not be supplied from the sea. On May 29 the Ottomans' huge cannons made a breach in the walls, and the janissaries flowed in. In the fighting that followed, the Greek emperor was killed. Days later the great domed cathedral of Saint Sophia was converted into a mosque.

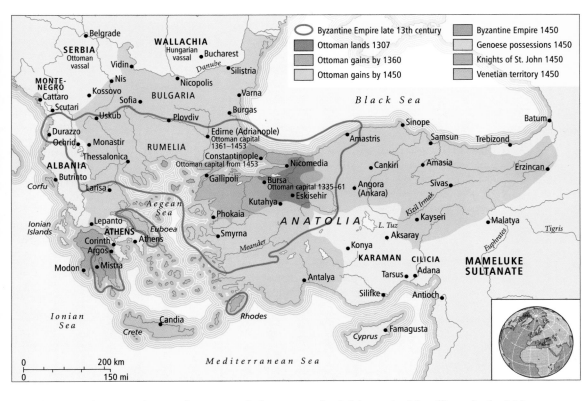

Key:
- Byzantine Empire late 13th century
- Ottoman lands 1307
- Ottoman gains by 1360
- Ottoman gains by 1450
- Byzantine Empire 1450
- Genoese possessions 1450
- Knights of St. John 1450
- Venetian territory 1450

◀ The Ottoman Empire expanded from its heartland to cover much of Anatolia and a sizable part of southeastern Europe. It took 150 years, however, before the Ottomans finally engulfed the rump of the Byzantine Empire with the fall of Constantinople.

▼ The famed Ottoman janissary corps was created from Christians from the Balkans who were converted to Islam and subjected to rigorous discipline, including not being allowed to marry.

siege, bringing the Byzantine Empire to an end after 1,000 years. From that time on Constantinople, now known as Istanbul, became the residence of the Ottoman sultans and the capital of their widespread and highly organized empire.

Like the Byzantine Empire before it, Ottoman rule proved long-lasting. It reached a peak of splendor under Suleiman the Magnificent in the 16th century but subsequently fell into a protracted decline; by the 19th century the Ottoman realm was widely known as "the sick man of Europe." Even so, the Ottomans saw out the century. The last emperor was not finally deposed until 1922, in the aftermath of Turkey's defeat in World War I.

👑 **1300** By this date Osman I has established himself as bey (prince) of a principality in northwestern Anatolia.

✕ **1354** The Ottomans capture the Gallipoli Peninsula on the European side of the Dardanelles (the strait leading into the Bosporus), giving them a permanent base in Europe.

✕ **1361** Murad II captures Adrianople, 350 miles (560 km) north of Constantinople, and renames it Edirne.

✕ **1389** The Ottomans inflict a crushing defeat on the Serbs at the Battle of Kosovo.

✕ **1402** Timur captures Sultan Bayezid at the Battle of Ankara; Bayezid dies later in captivity.

👑 **1402** The Ottoman Empire is thrown into disorder as Bayezid's four sons contest the succession (–1413).

✕ **1422** The Ottomans besiege Constantinople but end the siege in return for a payment of tribute from the Byzantine emperor.

✕ **1423** War with Venice for mastery of the Adriatic Sea ends with the Ottoman capture of Salonika, in northern Greece (–1430).

✕ **1448** Victory at the second Battle of Kosovo secures the Danube River as the Ottoman frontier in the Balkans.

👑 **1451** On the death of Murad II the janissaries bring about the succession of his son Mehmed II.

✕ **1453** Constantinople falls to the armies of Mehmed II.

📖 **1454** Construction of the Topkapi Palace, the Sultan's residence, begins in Istanbul, as Constantinople is now renamed.

✕ **1460** Mehmed II conquers Morea in southern Greece, eliminating the last claimants to the Byzantine throne.

👑 **1473** Ottoman rule now extends throughout Anatolia from the Euphrates River to the Black Sea coast.

AMERICAS

1427 Itzcóatl becomes Aztec ruler.

1428 In alliance with other city-states the Aztecs capture Azcapotzalco, which they replace as the main power in the Valley of Mexico.

1438 Pachacutec usurps the Inca throne; he expands the Inca Empire north to present-day Quito and south to Lake Titicaca.

EUROPE

Joan of Arc was a French peasant who became a national heroine and saint. Born around 1412, she was drawn by religious visions to lead the forces of the Dauphin, heir to the French throne, against the English. She fulfilled her promise to lift the English siege of Orléans and, after victory at Patay, went with the prince to Reims, where he was crowned Charles VII. Meanwhile Joan's bravery on the battlefield was matched by her impatience to recapture Paris from England's Burgundian allies. Taken prisoner by the Burgundians in 1430, she was passed to the English, tried as a heretic, and executed. She became a saint in 1920, the same year in which the French dedicated a national holiday to her memory.

1429 After Joan of Arc leads a French army to recapture Orléans, the Dauphin (heir to the throne) is crowned King Charles VII of France in Reims Cathedral—a turning point in the Hundred Years' War against the English.

1430 Joan of Arc is taken prisoner and handed over to the English. She is tried as a witch and burned at the stake the following year.

1434 Cosimo de Medici establishes the Medici family as effective rulers of Florence.

AFRICA

1433 In Mali Tuareg desert nomads take control of the trading city of Timbuktu.

1434 The Portuguese navigator Gil Eanes sails around Cape Bojador on the coast of Morocco, opening the way to European exploration of the west coast of Africa.

1441 Portuguese traders export the first slaves from Africa to Europe.

WESTERN ASIA

1426 The Mamelukes of Syria and Egypt raid Cyprus.

c.1430 Traders from East Africa introduce coffee into Arabia.

1439 Jahan Shah becomes leader of the Black Sheep Turkmen; he is known for his patronage of architecture and calligraphy.

1444 Ottoman Sultan Murad II voluntarily hands over power to his young son Mehmed II but resumes it two years later to suppress an insurrection.

SOUTH & CENTRAL ASIA

c.1425 Shihab-ud-Din Ahmad I moves the capital of Bahmani from Gulbarga to Bidar (Karnataka).

1432 In a series of campaigns Devaraya II of Vijayanagar expands the boundaries of his kingdom northeast to the Krishna River and south into Kerala (–1446).

1434 The Sayyid sultan of Delhi, Mubarak Shah, is assassinated.

1438 The Golden Horde of the Mongols breaks up into a number of smaller khanates, including Crimea, Astrakhan, and Kazan.

1440 Birth of the Indian mystic and poet Kabir (d. 1518), who will bridge Hindu and Muslim thought and be the future master of Nanak, the founder of Sikhism.

1443 A Persian visitor to the city of Vijayanagar describes it as having "no equal in the world."

EAST ASIA & OCEANIA

1428 The Chinese withdraw from Nam Viet after a series of military uprisings make it impossible for them to maintain control.

1428 There are widespread peasant uprisings in Japan (–1429).

1431 The Khmer abandon their capital of Angkor for Phnom Penh in Cambodia.

1441 The sixth Ashikaga shogun, Yoshinori, is assassinated.

👑 **1440** Montezuma I succeeds Itzcóatl; the Aztecs now rule a military empire in the Valley of Mexico.

✗ **c.1443** Mayapán, the leading Mayan city in Yucatán, is destroyed in the course of a feud with Uxmál.

☀ **1436** Through the Compacts of Prague, negotiated with the pope at the Council of Basel (1431–1436), the majority of Hussites are received back into the church.

✗ **1437** Prince Henry the Navigator leads a Portuguese expedition to capture Tangiers in North Africa from the Muslims, which fails disastrously.

👑 **1438** Albert of Hapsburg is elected Holy Roman emperor; from now on the title remains in the hereditary possession of the Hapsburg Dynasty until it is abolished in 1806.

👑 **1443** King Alfonso of Aragon and Sicily becomes king of Naples.

✗ **1443** Janos Hunyadi, a Hungarian soldier leading resistance to the Ottoman advance in Serbia and Transylvania, is defeated at the Battle of Zlatica.

✗ **1444** A papal crusade against the Ottomans is decisively defeated at Varna on the Black Sea (in present-day Bulgaria).

📖 **1445** The painter Fra Angelico, a Dominican friar, is active in Rome, where he paints a series of frescoes for the St. Nicholas Chapel in the Vatican (–1448).

✗ **1445** Zara Yakob of Ethiopia inflicts a crushing defeat on the neighboring Muslim state of Ifat.

Carving of an eagle from Great Zimbabwe.

👑 **c.1450** The Shona state of Mwenemutapa on the Zambezi River now dominates the gold trade in southeastern Africa; Great Zimbabwe is in decline.

👑 **c.1450** Damascus and Aleppo in Syria are centers for the textile trade between Asia and Europe.

Ruins in the Indian village of Hampi testify to the power of the empire of Vijayanagar, Sanskrit for "City of Victory," which arose in southern India after the city's foundation in 1336. The empire defended the region against Islam from the north and nurtured a flourishing of Hindu life and culture, unified by the use of the Sanskrit language. The empire fell in about 1614 thanks to internal struggles and pressure from neighboring sultanates.

📖 **1443** Hangul, the Korean phonetic alphabet consisting of 24 letters, becomes the official writing system of Korea by royal decree.

✗ **1449** The Ming Emperor Cheng Tung is captured by the Oyrat Mongols while on campaign; the Oyrat go on to besiege Beijing.

👑 **1450** Death of King Sejong, fourth king of the Yi Dynasty (since 1419), whose reign marked a period of high cultural achievement in Korea.

AMERICAS

EUROPE

AFRICA

WESTERN ASIA

SOUTH & CENTRAL ASIA

EAST ASIA & OCEANIA

1425–1450 A.D.

THE AZTECS AND THE INCA

TWO GREAT NEW WORLD EMPIRES ROSE TO POWER *in the course of the 15th century without having any direct contact with, or knowledge of, each other. The Aztecs in the Valley of Mexico and the Inca in the Andes Mountains of southern Peru both had complex, sophisticated societies, produced exquisite artworks, and built great cities. Yet neither employed draft animals, wheeled vehicles, or ironwork, and the only writing they knew was pictographic, employing visual signs rather than an alphabet. Both came to dominate their neighbors by military might, yet each would fall victim after less than a century of supremacy to Spanish conquistadors, whose technology of guns and armor they could not hope to match.*

▲ This ornate knife created by Inca craftsmen for use in religious rituals draws together two preoccupations common to both the Aztec and Inca cultures: blood sacrifice and gold.

The Aztecs originated as nomads who moved south from the northern deserts of Mexico in search of farmland. They arrived in the Valley of Mexico sometime around the year 1200. They initially served as mercenary soldiers, offering their services to rival city-states vying for supremacy in the power vacuum left in central Mexico by the collapse of the earlier Toltec civilization. In 1428 the Aztecs rose up against the people of Acapotzalco, their then employers, seizing their lands and massacring the citizens. At a stroke they made themselves masters of the region, a position they buttressed over the following decades by a widespread series of successful military campaigns.

The Aztecs owed their rise to their fighting skills, and their society was fiercely militaristic, geared to maximizing success in battle. All boys received army training from an early age and were taught to believe

that victory—and, if necessary, death—in battle was the highest honor. Aztec religion also turned on the shedding of blood, which the gods themselves were thought to have offered to set the Sun in motion; the Aztecs practiced human sacrifice on a larger scale than any other culture known to history.

Yet there was also a constructive side to the Aztec achievement. Built on islands in the shallow waters of Lake Texcoco, their capital city of Tenochtitlán grew into a well-ordered metropolis of some 200,000 people, a greater population than in any European city of the time. Aztec craftsmen produced beautiful objects of gold, jade, turquoise, and featherwork that were bartered across Central America by traveling merchants exploiting a sophisticated trading network.

The Inca too built their empire by force of arms, in their case largely under two exceptional leaders:

Machu Picchu

In 1911 the American explorer Hiram Bingham was directed by local people to a previously unrecorded Inca site on a Peruvian mountain ridge. There he found a ruined city, spectacularly located 6,750 feet (2,000 m) up against a backdrop of towering peaks. Machu Picchu had escaped detection by the Incas' Spanish conquerors even though it lay only 50 miles (80 km) from the Inca capital, Cuzco. Laid out on a series of terraces connected by more than 3,000 steps, it was probably built around 1500 and may have served as a summer retreat for the Inca royal family.

Pachacutec (reigned 1438–1471) and Tupac Yupanqui (1471–1493). Yet their culture was far less warlike than the Aztecs'. Under an emperor—himself known as the Inca—who claimed descent from the sun god, society was tightly organized under a hierarchy of functionaries ranging from governors of provinces down to local officials responsible for just 10 families. All able-bodied men and women were expected to serve the state by working on state-owned farmlands, as well as by taking part in public-work projects such as roadbuilding and the terracing of hillside land for agriculture.

In the long run both the warlike Aztecs and the communally minded Inca suffered a similar fate. The two empires crumbled before the onslaught of Spanish conquistadors ("conquerors")—soldiers who arrived in the wake of Christopher Columbus equipped with superior military technology, including horses, guns, and armor. By the 1540s the Aztec and Inca lands both formed part of Spain's burgeoning New World empire, and their people—demoralized by defeat and decimated by imported diseases such as smallpox—were in disarray and subjection.

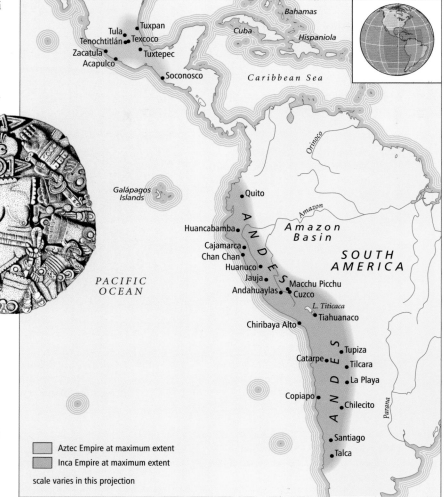

▲ The Aztec moon goddess Coyolxauhqui was shown on this vast stone circle, excavated at the foot of the Templo Mayor in Tenochtitlán.

▶ The Inca Empire dominated the Andes Mountains, while the Aztec heartland lay in the fertile lands of what is now central Mexico.

Aztec Empire at maximum extent
Inca Empire at maximum extent

scale varies in this projection

🍃 **c.1200** The nomadic Aztecs enter the Valley of Mexico seeking a secure homeland.

🍃 **c.1200** The Inca settle near Cuzco in the Peruvian Andes.

🍃 **c.1325** The Aztecs settle on an island in Lake Texcoco that will become their capital, Tenochtitlán.

⚔ **1428** After serving as mercenaries for the city-state of Acapotzalco, the Aztecs sack the city and make themselves the leading power in the Valley of Mexico.

🍃 **1438** Pachacutec ascends the Inca throne; a great military leader, he will lay the foundations of the Inca Empire.

🍃 **1471** Tupac Yupanqui succeeds Pachacutec as Inca ruler.

⚔ **1476** Inca forces led by Tupac Yupanqui conquer the Chimú Empire of the Peruvian north coast.

🍃 **1493** Huayna Capac becomes Inca on Tupac Yupanqui's death.

🍃 **1502** Montezuma (Moctezuma) II ascends the Aztec throne.

⚔ **1519** Spanish conquistadors under Hernán Cortés land on the Mexican coast and march on Tenochtitlán. Montezuma receives Cortés as a guest but is taken prisoner by the Spaniards.

⚔ **1520** Montezuma is killed by his own subjects in riots that temporarily drive out the Spanish occupiers.

⚔ **1521** Cortés takes Tenochtitlán after an eight-week siege, winning control of the Aztec Empire for Spain.

⚔ **1525** Civil war breaks out in the Inca lands as Huayna Capac's sons, Atahualpa and Huáscar, contend for his throne.

⚔ **1532** Atahualpa is victorious, but is taken captive by conquistadors led by Francisco Pizarro, who have marched inland from the coast.

⚔ **1533** Pizarro orders Atahualpa's execution; the Spaniards take control of Cuzco.

AMERICAS

c.1450 The population of the Aztec capital Tenochtitlán may have reached 300,000 by this time.

1461 The Mayan city of Mayapán is finally abandoned.

1469 Axayacatl becomes Aztec ruler. In his 12-year reign he will unite Tenochtitlán with its northern neighbor, Tlatelolco.

EUROPE

c.1450 Johannes Gutenberg sets up a printing press in Mainz, Germany.

1452 Italian architect Leon Battista Alberti publishes *On Architecture*, a major influence on the classical revival in the Renaissance.

1453 The French drive the English from France, ending the Hundred Years' War.

1453 The Byzantine Empire ends with the capture of Constantinople by the Ottoman Turks.

The Wars of the Roses (1455–1485)—named for the emblems of the respective sides—were fought by the noble houses of Lancaster and York for the English throne. Warfare brought the Yorkist Edward IV to the throne, then the Lancastrian Henry VI. Edward became king again after Henry's murder and was succeeded by Richard II. Richard was defeated in 1485 by the Lancastrian Henry Tudor, who became Henry VII. Henry's marriage to Elizabeth of York united the families and ended the conflict.

AFRICA

c.1450 The Muslim port of Mombasa (in present-day Kenya) has a population of 10,000.

1450 Emperor Zara Yakob of Ethiopia imposes church reforms and persecutes Falasha Jews.

1468 Sunni Ali seizes Timbuktu and establishes the Songhai of Gao as the leading power in West Africa.

WESTERN ASIA

1451 Death of the Ottoman Sultan Murad II; his son Mehmed II succeeds him.

1453 In a series of campaigns Jahan Shah extends the Kara Koyunlu (Black Sheep Turkmen) domains in Iraq and western Iran, and takes control of Baghdad (–1464).

1455 Construction of the Great Bazaar gets under way in the Ottoman capital of Istanbul (formerly Constantinople).

SOUTH & CENTRAL ASIA

1451 The last Sayyid sultan surrenders Delhi to an Afghan noble, Bahlul Lodi, founder of the Lodi Dynasty.

1463 Mahmud Gawan becomes chief minister of the Bahmani Kingdom on India's Deccan Plateau; he will campaign successfully against Vijayanagar in the south and Orissa in the east.

1469 Guru Nanak, founder of Sikhism, is born near Lahore in the Punjab region of northwest India.

EAST ASIA & OCEANIA

c.1450 The Ryoanji Zen temple is established at Kyoto; its drystone landscape garden is one of the finest in Japan.

1467 In Japan the Onin War undermines the authority of the Ashikaga Shogunate and leads to the rise of feudal warlords called *daimyo* (–1477).

c.1470 Doucai ("contrasting colors") porcelain, in which blue cobalt outlines are colored with enamels, reaches a peak of development in China.

1471 Dai Viet (northern Vietnam) conquers the kingdom of Champa in southern Vietnam.

Chinese doucai stem cup from the Ming era.

✕ **1470** The Incas capture Chan Chan, capital of the Chimú Empire of coastal Peru.

👑 **1471** Tupac Yupanqui becomes Inca (the title of the Inca ruler); he expands the empire southward into Chile.

AMERICAS

✕ **1455** Start of the Wars of the Roses in England, a struggle for power between the Yorkist and Lancastrian families (–1485).

👑 **1456** Vlad, known to history as "Vlad the Impaler," becomes prince of Wallachia (southern Romania). He is said to have impaled 20,000 prisoners during a raid against the Turks.

👑 **1458** Matthias I Corvinus, second son of the Hungarian hero Janos Hunyadi, is elected king of Hungary.

📖 **1461** François Villon writes his *Testament*, the greatest poem of medieval France.

👑 **1469** Lorenzo "the Magnificent" Medici comes to power in Florence; he gathers many of the great artists of the day to his court.

☀ **1471** Death of the German monk Thomas à Kempis, whose *Imitatio Christi* (Imitation of Christ) is one of the most influential works of medieval spirituality.

📖 **1472** Leonardo da Vinci leaves the workshop of the goldsmith and artist Andrea del Verrochio and sets up as an independent artist.

👑 **1472** On marrying Zoe, niece of the last Byzantine emperor, Grand Prince Ivan III of Moscow adopts the double-headed eagle of the Byzantine Empire as his symbol.

👑 **1474** Isabella, wife of King Ferdinand I of Aragon, becomes queen of Castile in her own right, thus uniting the two most powerful Spanish kingdoms.

EUROPE

👑 **c.1474** The Portuguese start to settle the island of São Tomé off the coast of Central Africa.

AFRICA

✕ **1467** The Kara Koyunlu are defeated by the Ak Koyunlu ("White Sheep") Turkmen of northern Iraq; Jahan Shah is killed, and the Ak Koyunlu take his territories.

👑 **1468** Qa'itbay begins a 28-year reign as Mameluke sultan (the longest of any of the Burji Dynasty rulers); he extensively restores the shrines of Mecca and Medina.

✕ **1473** In a campaign against the White Sheep Turkmen the Ottomans extend their hold over Anatolia eastward to the Euphrates River.

WESTERN ASIA

👑 **1470** Husain Baiqara becomes Timurid ruler of Herat, reigning until 1506; he is a patron of the arts and adorns Herat with many fine buildings.

SOUTH & CENTRAL ASIA

📖 **1472** Birth of Wang Yangming, Neo-Confucian philosopher whose ideas, advocating the unity of thought and action, influence Chinese thought for generations.

⊕ **1474** The Great Wall is repaired and extended to prevent further Mongol incursions.

The Great Wall of China.

EAST ASIA & OCEANIA

1450–1475 A.D.

THE SPREAD OF PRINTING

THE INVENTION OF THE PRINTING PRESS *has been likened to the birth of the Internet—it revolutionized information technology in 15th-century Europe. Until then books were copied laboriously by hand, making them costly items that only the very rich could afford. Now they could be produced cheaply and quickly in hundreds of identical copies, allowing a wider circulation and reducing the risk of errors.*

▲ Gutenberg drew largely on existing technology such as presses used to make illustrated books, but his introduction of movable type transformed the production of printed material and enabled the rapid spread of ideas that characterized the Reformation in Europe.

The person generally credited with setting up the first printing press in Europe was a German, Johannes Gutenberg. The first book he printed on his press, in about 1455, was the Bible. Gutenberg did not invent printing, however, which had been around for a very long time. The Chinese were printing books probably as long ago as the 8th century or even earlier. They carved a text onto a block of wood so that the characters stood out in relief, inked the block with a paintbrush, spread a sheet of paper on it, and transferred the inked text onto the paper by rubbing the back. Europeans were using similar methods to print religious pictures and short texts by the first decades of the 15th century.

Gutenberg's innovation was to develop a way of printing using reusable movable type. These rectangular pieces of cast metal, each bearing a raised letter, were arranged side by side on a strip of wood to form words and sentences. They could then be taken apart and reset to print something else. The Chinese had invented movable type long before, but because Chinese script has so many different characters—as many as 60,000—the invention did not catch on as a practical technology. Printing in European languages required only pieces of type for the letters of the alphabet (including capitals), numerals, and punctuation marks, a much easier undertaking.

❀ **c.750** By this time the Chinese are employing woodblocks to print single-sheet publications.	❀ **1421** Vespasiano da Bisticci establishes a bookshop in Florence that numbers Cosimo de Medici among its wealthy clients.	❀ **1438** Gutenberg begins experimenting with printing at Strasbourg.
❀ **c.900** Woodblock printing is widely employed by this date in China, Japan, and Korea.	❀ **c. 1430** Block printing using engraved metal plates develops in Holland and Germany.	❀ **c.1455** Gutenberg publishes the first commercially printed book, the Gutenberg Bible, at Mainz, Germany.
❀ **1399** Johannes Gutenberg is born in Mainz, Germany; he will later begin work as a silversmith.	❀ **c. 1435** A Dutchman, Laurens Janszoon Koster, is experimenting with movable type in Haarlem; some claim he invented it before Gutenberg.	❀ **1457** Color printing is first used in the Mainz Psalter, produced by Gutenberg's partners, Fust and Schöffer.
❀ **c.1420** Woodcuts (consisting of pictures of saints with short texts) are printed in Germany.		

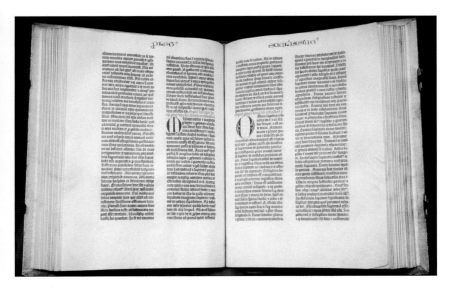

▲ The Gutenberg Bible, Europe's first complete book, was completed in around 1455. No one knows how many copies Gutenberg produced of the Latin, three-volume work: Around 40 are in existence today.

◀ Printers position paper and ink type in an open form in the foreground of this 16th-century engraving of a printer's shop. In the background men assemble type to make more pages.

The printer placed the lines of type within a frame known as a form. After use the type was removed from the form, broken up, and stored letter by letter in a case to be used again. To print a page, the inked form was covered with a sheet of paper and placed between two wooden boards in the press. The printer turned a screw to press the upper surface (the platen) down onto the sheet of paper. Such presses had been in use since Roman times for pressing grapes and were also used for binding manuscript books.

Gutenberg's printing press soon had many imitators, who found a ready market for their products among the growing numbers of literate people—lawyers, merchants, university teachers, and skilled artisans—in Europe's expanding cities. As presses were set up in one city after another, a stream of bibles, encyclopedias, religious works, classics, histories, and romances poured out to feed the demand for the printed word.

Incunabula

Books printed before 1501, like the examples below, are known as incunabula, a word that derives from the Latin for "cradle." Early printers competed with manuscript-copying workshops to feed the demand for books. These workshops produced beautiful books, illustrated in brilliant blues, reds, and golds, and with ornamented margins and initial letters. Early printers tried to give their books the same attraction by using decorative typefaces and sometimes leaving space around initial letters so that they could be decorated by hand. Printed books were large, like the manuscript books they emulated—people read books seated at tables and did not carry them around. Probably only about 200 or 300 copies of a book were printed at a time, but some 35,000 incunabula survive today.

⊛ **1468** Nicolaus Jensen establishes a printing shop in Venice; a metal punch-cutter by training, he experiments with casting different typefaces.

⊛ **1476** William Caxton sets up a printing press in London, England.

☀ **1485** A censorship office is set up in Frankfurt and Mainz to suppress dangerous publications sold at the Lenten Fair: its first edict bans translations of the Bible into European languages other than Latin.

📖 **1498** The first book of music is printed using movable type.

AMERICAS

⚔ **1476** Inca forces under Tupac Yupanqui conquer the Chimú state of northern Peru.

👑 **1486** The Aztec Emperor Tizoc dies, probably from poison, after leading an unsuccessful military campaign; he is replaced by Ahuitzotl, a successful commander.

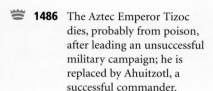

teçiquauhtitlā

Christopher Columbus, in a ruff collar at right of this 16th-century illustration, sailed the Atlantic in 1492 to find a westward route to the Indies. He died in 1506, still convinced that the "New World" he had encountered was part of Asia.

EUROPE

⚔ **1476** Vlad the Impaler, ruler of Wallachia (southern Romania), is killed in battle outside Bucharest.

⚔ **1476** Burgundy's Charles the Bold fails in his attempt to conquer the Swiss following defeats at the battles of Grandson and Morat.

👑 **1477** The Hapsburg rulers of the Holy Roman Empire acquire the Netherlands by marriage.

☀ **1478** The Spanish Inquisition is established.

⚔ **1478** In Florence, Italy, a bloody feud between the Medici and Pazzi families for control of the city ends in a massacre of the Pazzis.

👑 **1480** The Russians stop paying tribute to the Tartar (Mongol) rulers of the Khanate of the Golden Horde.

⚔ **1485** The Battle of Bosworth Field brings England's Wars of the Roses to an end and puts the Tudor Dynasty on the throne.

📖 **1486** Sandro Botticelli paints *The Birth of Venus*.

☀ **1486** Written by two Germans, *Malleus Maleficarum* ("The Hammer of Evildoers") will become the chief handbook for the witch-hunting mania sweeping Europe.

AFRICA

👑 **1476** Spaniards settle the Canary Islands off Africa and suppress the native culture (–1524).

⚙ **1488** Portuguese sailor Bartholomeu Dias becomes the first European to round the Cape of Good Hope.

☀ **1492** After the fall of Granada, the last Moorish state in Spain, many Muslims and Jews are forced into exile in North Africa. Among their number is the historian and traveler Leo Africanus.

👑 **1493** Askiya Muhammad founds the Songhai Empire's Askiya Dynasty. Under him Songhai will absorb much of the Manding Empire, and Timbuktu's Sankoré Mosque will become a center of learning.

WESTERN ASIA

👑 **1479** The Treaty of Constantinople ends a 15-year war between the Ottoman Empire and Venice.

⚔ **1480** The Ottoman Sultan Mehmet II dispatches a fleet that besieges the Greek island of Rhodes and takes Otranto in southern Italy.

👑 **1481** Bayezid II ascends the Ottoman throne on Mehmet II's death. His 31-year reign will see a further expansion of the Ottoman realm.

SOUTH & CENTRAL ASIA

👑 **1485** The Sangama Dynasty of Vijayanagar comes to an end; amid murderous factional fighting the throne passes to Narashima Saluva, a successful general.

⚔ **1486** African slaves in the Indian state of Gaur in Bengal rebel, setting their leader on the throne.

EAST ASIA & OCEANIA

⚔ **1477** Japan's 10-year-long Onin War ends, only to open the way for a century of strife between rival *daimyo* (warlords).

⚔ **1479** Annam (northern Vietnam) invades the neighboring kingdom of Lan Xang (Laos)

👑 **1492** Sailing from Spain, Christopher Columbus reaches the New World, making landfall in the Bahamas and sailing on to Cuba and Hispaniola.

👑 **1493** On his second voyage Columbus explores Dominica, Puerto Rico, and Jamaica, as well as sailing around Hispaniola.

👑 **1494** By the Treaty of Tordesillas Spain and Portugal agree a boundary line for New World discoveries; lands to the east go to Portugal, those to the west to Spain.

👑 **1497** Sailing from England, John Cabot reaches Newfoundland (Canada). Cabot and his fleet are lost on a return voyage the following year.

👑 **1498** On a third transatlantic voyage Columbus reaches Trinidad before making the first European landfall on the coast of South America near the mouth of the Orinoco River.

👑 **1499** Amerigo Vespucci and Alonso de Ojeda reach the mouth of the Amazon River.

Medal of Girolamo Savonarola.

✕ **1492** Ferdinand and Isabella conquer Muslim Granada, bringing all of Spain under Christian control.

👑 **1494** The puritanical reformer Savonarola comes to power in Florence; he will be burned at the stake for heresy four years later.

✕ **1494** Charles VIII of France invades Italy.

📖 **1497** Leonardo da Vinci paints *The Last Supper*.

👑 **1497** Vasco da Gama sets off from Lisbon on a pioneering sea voyage to India (–1499).

✕ **1499** A new French ruler, Louis XII, launches a more ambitious invasion of Italy.

⊕ **1498** En route for India, Vasco da Gama's fleet explores the coast of East Africa.

The Mosque of Sankoré was one of the leading schools of Arabic learning.

👑 **1497** In Persia Rustam Shah's death brings the end of the Turkmen White Sheep Dynasty and the rise of the Safavid Dynasty (–1502).

✕ **1499** Bayezid renews war with Venice, winning fresh lands in the Balkans.

✕ **1492** Sikandar II Lodi, sultan of Delhi, annexes Bihar, extending Muslim rule westward toward Bengal.

👑 **1498** Vasco da Gama's Portuguese fleet arrives at the port of Calicut in southern India, establishing a sea route around the Cape of Good Hope from Europe.

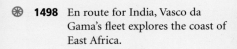

A Japanese woodblock print shows a lady boiling water to make tea.

📖 **1484** The tea ceremony is first recorded in Japan, introduced by the shogun Yoshimasa.

☀ **1488** Members of Japan's True Pure Land sect kill a feudal warlord in the first of many confrontations with the ruling *daimyo*.

AMERICAS

EUROPE

AFRICA

WESTERN ASIA

SOUTH & CENTRAL ASIA

EAST ASIA & OCEANIA

1475–1500 A.D.   207

THE AGE OF DISCOVERY

EUROPEAN SAILORS TRADITIONALLY AVOIDED *the open Atlantic Ocean. Although the Vikings had reached Newfoundland around the year 1000, their feat had long been forgotten. For much of the Middle Ages trading boats rarely ventured far from the sight of land. By the end of the 15th century, however, Portuguese ships had voyaged far into the Atlantic and sailed around Africa into the Indian Ocean, while Christopher Columbus had reached the Americas. The Age of Discovery had begun.*

▲ The great feats of European navigation depended on contemporary technological development. Instruments such as this astrolabe, used to calculate the position of the sun and other heavenly bodies, allowed sailors to track their position and record their discoveries.

Henry the Navigator

The guiding spirit behind the Portuguese voyages of exploration was a royal prince known to history as Henry the Navigator (1394–1460). Henry was a devout Christian who as a young man had taken part in the Portuguese capture of the Muslim stronghold of Ceuta in Morocco. The success inspired him with a desire to drive the Muslims out of North Africa, just as they had already been driven out of Portugal and most of Spain. Henry had heard stories of Prester John, a legendary Christian king rumored to rule a large empire somewhere in Africa. He thought that if an expedition sailed down the coast of Africa, beyond Muslim-held Morocco, it might meet up with the king's forces; the combined Christian armies could then launch a crusade against the Muslims. At his court at Sagres, on the southwest tip of Portugal, Henry brought together mapmakers and astronomers. His shipbuilders developed the caravel, a deep-bottomed boat that could turn quickly in the wind and was sturdy enough for long sea voyages. By the time of Henry's death Portuguese caravels had sailed as far as Sierra Leone in West Africa.

⊛ **1409** A Latin translation is made of Ptolemy's *Geography*. The ancient Greek showed how Earth's surface could be measured using latitude and longitude; rediscovery of his work greatly aided navigation.

⊛ **1420** After Portuguese navigators discover the uninhabited Madeira Islands, west of Morocco, Henry the Navigator sends an expedition to colonize them.

⊛ **1432** The Portuguese colonize the Azores Islands in the Atlantic.

⊛ **1434** The Portuguese navigator Gil Eanes passes Cape Bojador on the Moroccan coast.

⊛ **1445** The Portuguese reach the mouth of the Senegal River and round Cape Verde, the westernmost tip of Africa.

⊛ **1480** The astrolabe (an instrument for measuring latitude from the height of the sun at noon) is adapted for use at sea.

⊛ **1488** Bartholomeu Dias rounds the Cape of Good Hope—the southern tip of Africa—in a storm.

⊛ **1492** Christopher Columbus makes the first of four voyages to the Americas, visiting Hispaniola and Cuba.

⊛ **1497** Vasco da Gama sails from Lisbon to Calicut on the west coast of India and back again (–1498).

⊛ **1497** Italian navigator John Cabot sails across the North Atlantic from Bristol, England, to Labrador on the Canadian coast on behalf of the English King Henry VII.

⊛ **1498** On his third voyage to America Columbus discovers the mainland of South America, still believing it to be part of Asia.

⊛ **1500** The Portuguese navigator Pedro Cabral discovers the coast of Brazil while sailing from Lisbon to India.

The most pressing reason why European sailors began to venture into the Atlantic in the late medieval period was trade. Muslim states had won control of the western end of the overland routes from China and India, along which luxury goods such as silk, spices, gold, and rubies made their way to Europe. Some individuals therefore began to look for alternative routes to these riches and for alternative sources of wealth.

The Portuguese, on the western edge of Europe, knew that supplies of gold and slaves reached the Muslim cities of North Africa by overland routes across the Sahara from the south. In the early 1400s they began to venture south by sea down the African coast, and by the 1440s they had reached West Africa. The prevailing north winds in that part of the Atlantic made the return journey to Portugal hazardous, but the sea captains discovered that by sailing far out into the Atlantic, they could find southerly winds that would bring them safely home. Soon the Portuguese were sending regular shipments of gold and slaves back to Lisbon each year from the fortified trading stations they set up along the African coast.

In 1488 Bartholomeu Dias sailed around the southernmost tip of Africa and into the Indian Ocean, and a decade later Vasco da Gama became the first westerner to reach India by the sea route around the coast of Africa. He had opened up a direct passage to the wealth of Asia.

Meanwhile Christopher Columbus, in the service of King Ferdinand and Queen Isabella of Spain, had sailed west across the Atlantic in search of a sea route to China and discovered the Americas instead. Italian by birth, Columbus had spent many years as a sea captain in Lisbon. Sailing as far north as Iceland and south to Sierra Leone, he had come to know the winds and currents of the Atlantic very well. He studied the accounts of the Venetian traveler Marco Polo's journeys in Asia and pored over maps and works of astronomy, calculating that the island Polo called Cipangu (Japan) lay only about 2,000 miles (3,200 km) to the west of Europe. This was a serious underestimate, as Japan is actually about 12,000 miles (19,000 km) distant, separated from Europe by the vast width of the Americas and the Atlantic and Pacific Oceans. Nevertheless, Columbus's error does not detract from his skill as a navigator in guiding his three tiny vessels across the Atlantic Ocean. Facing the threat of mutiny from his despairing crew, Columbus continued westward on his voyage to make landfall in the Bahamas on October 12, 1492. He returned to the Americas three more times in the service of Spain.

▲ Vasco da Gama's sea voyage to India opened up a new trade route to the east that bypassed the Islamic middlemen who controlled Asia's overland trade.

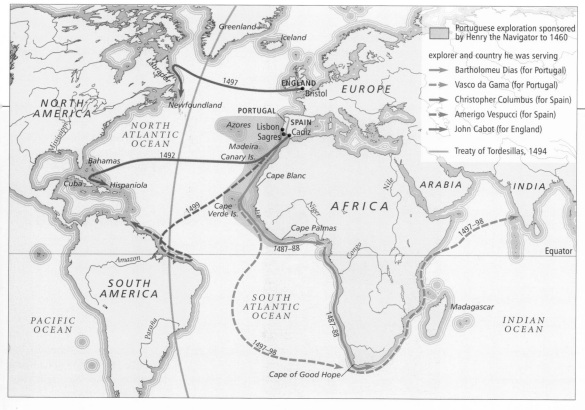

◄ The great age of exploration introduced by Henry the Navigator shifted Europe's economic focus away from the Mediterranean to the countries of the Atlantic seaboard: initially Spain, Portugal, and England, and later the Netherlands.

1500–1510 A.D.

AMERICAS

👑 **c.1500** The Inca Empire in Peru reaches its high point under Huayna Capac (r.1493–1525).

⚙ **1500** The Portuguese navigator Gaspar de Côrte-Real makes the first authenticated landfall on the North American mainland since Vikings explored Labrador five centuries previously.

👑 **1500** The Portuguese explorer Pedro Álvarez Cabral claims Brazil for Portugal under the terms of the Treaty of Tordesillas.

⚙ **1501** The colonial plantation system is initiated when Spain transfers sugarcane cultivation from Madeira to Hispaniola.

EUROPE

⚙ **c.1500** In Siegershausen, Switzerland, Jakob Nufer performs the first recorded caesarean birth operation on a living woman.

⚔ **1500** French forces under Louis XII overrun and annex the Duchy of Milan. The Treaty of Granada partitions Italy between France and Spain

⚔ **1501** Russia begins its expansion as Czar Ivan III invades Poland–Lithuania.

⚙ **1503** The Spanish office of American trade ("Casa de Contratación") is set up in Seville.

☀ **1503** Julius II becomes pope; a patron of the arts, he commissions the rebuilding of St. Peter's Cathedral by Bramante and the painting of the Sistine Chapel ceiling by Michelangelo (–1512)

👑 **1504** Death of Isabella I of Castile; Ferdinand II ("the Catholic") of Aragon rules Castile as regent in place of Isabella's mentally ill daughter Juana.

⚙ **c.1505** In Nuremberg, Germany, the clockmaker Peter Henlein introduces a timepiece driven by springs rather than weights, enabling the invention of portable watches

📖 **1506** Leonardo da Vinci paints the *Mona Lisa* and compiles his notebooks on mechanics, anatomy, and astronomy (–1509).

📖 **1507** German cartographer Martin Waldseemüller publishes *Cosmographiae Introductio*, a map on which the name "America" is first used.

AFRICA

⚔ **1504** In Sudan, the Muslim Funj defeat the Christian rulers of Sennar between the Blue and White Niles.

⚔ **1505** Kilwa on the East African coast is sacked by Francisco de Almeida's Portuguese troops.

👑 **1508** Lebna Denegel becomes emperor of Ethiopia and struggles against growing Islamic influence.

WESTERN ASIA

👑 **1501** Shah Esmail overthrows the "White Sheep" Turkmen rulers of Persia and founds the Safavid Dynasty.

⚔ **1502** Tatars destroy the last remnants of the Mongol Golden Horde, opening the way for Russian expansion into the Caucasus.

SOUTH & CENTRAL ASIA

👑 **c.1500** Muslim khanates emerge centered on the oasis cities of the Silk Road to the West.

Babur, founder of India's Mughal Dynasty, watches a wrestling match.

⚙ **1500** Pedro Álvarez Cabral lands at Cochin and Cannonore, establishing trade links between Portugal and India.

EAST ASIA & OCEANIA

👑 **c.1500** The Hindu–Buddhist kingdom of Majapahit is weakened by the spread of Islam to Borneo and Java.

⚙ **c.1500** The Chinese inventor Wan Hu is killed trying to pilot a flying machine made of a chair, two kites, and 47 rockets.

📖 ARTS & LITERATURE   👑 POLITICS   ☀ RELIGION   ⊕ TECHNOLOGY & SCIENCE   ⚔ WAR & CONFLICT

AMERICAS

⊕ **1502**   Amerigo Vespucci ventures down the east coast of South America.

👑 **1502**   Montezuma II becomes the last Aztec Emperor of Mexico; during his reign (to 1520) the empire reaches its zenith.

⊕ **1505**   The first African slaves arrive in the Americas, at Santo Domingo, starting the transatlantic slave trade.

👑 **1508**   The Spanish expand their territory in the Caribbean and Central America with the conquest of Puerto Rico (–1511).

A fanciful 16th-century engraving by Theodor de Bry shows the Italian explorer Amerigo Vespucci arriving in Bermuda.

EUROPE

👑 **1508**   The League of Cambrai is formed by Aragon, France, Spain, and the Holy Roman Empire against Venice.

👑 **1509**   Henry VIII ascends the throne in England and marries his first wife, Catharine of Aragon.

One of the greatest showplaces of the art of the Italian Renaissance, the Sistine Chapel in Rome's Vatican Palace was first commissioned by Pope Sixtus IV in the 1470s. Over the following years its walls were decorated with frescoes by some of the finest artists of the day, including Perugino and Botticelli. Its greatest masterpieces, however, were added from 1508 on by Michelangelo. Despite bitter quarrels with Pope Julius II, his patron, he spent four years working in uncomfortable conditions covering the building's ceiling in paintings. Twenty-five years later he was summoned back by a new pope to decorate the west wall behind the altar and produced another great work, *The Last Judgment*.

AFRICA

👑 **1508**   The Portuguese establish Mozambique as their first colony in Africa.

⚔ **1509**   Spain captures Oran in Algeria, beginning a campaign to take key bases on the North African coast.

WESTERN ASIA

⚔ **1503**   The war setting Venice and Hungary against the Ottoman Empire comes to an end.

⊕ **1504**   Venice sends an envoy to the Ottoman Sultan Bayezid II proposing the construction of a Suez Canal.

⊕ **1509**   The Ottoman capital Istanbul is rocked by a devastating earthquake that kills 10,000 people.

SOUTH & CENTRAL ASIA

⚔ **1504**   In Afghanistan Mughal forces under Babur begin a series of conquests that will eventually establish their rule over the whole Indian subcontinent.

⚔ **1509**   Krishnadevaraya, newly appointed king of the Hindu state of Vijayanagar, repels an attack by Sultan Mahmud of Bidar.

⚔ **1509**   A Portuguese fleet under Francisco de Almeida defeats an Egyptian–Gujarati fleet at Diu, securing control over the spice trade.

EAST ASIA & OCEANIA

👑 **1506**   In Korea the tyrant Yonsangun is deposed by a rebellion that brings Chungjong to the throne (–1507).

1500–1510 A.D.   211

IN THE WAKE OF COLUMBUS

▲ A Portuguese merchant gathers outsize sticks of cinnamon, collected in Sri Lanka, for transport back to Europe. Used as a flavoring, cinnamon was one of the most prized of the spices that spurred the European voyages of exploration; at one time it was said to be more valuable than gold.

DRIVEN BY THE URGE TO CHART *new territories and to explore new commercial opportunities, many intrepid seafarers followed the example of Christopher Columbus and set sail from Europe for distant regions to the west and east with only crude navigational instruments to guide them. The voyages of Magellan, Vespucci, and others opened up lands and oceans previously unknown to Europeans and established new trade routes. By 1600 the ground was laid for the system of international commerce on which all modern economies are based.*

Portuguese mariners were at the forefront of exploration in the 16th century. In 1511 Afonso de Albuquerque seized the port of Malacca on the Malaysian peninsula, securing a key center of the East Indian spice trade for Portugal. Venturing out from Goa—a base on India's west coast seized by Albuquerque the previous year—the Portuguese discovered the "Spice Islands" (the Moluccas, now part of Indonesia). Trade with China began in 1520, and by 1557 Portugal had founded a permanent base at Macao, on China's south coast. Farther east Japan's isolation ended with the landing of Portuguese merchants on the small island of Tanegashima in 1542. The supremacy of Portugal's seaborne trading empire in the East went unchallenged until the rise of the Dutch and British East India Companies in the following century.

Portugal's most famous 16th-century explorer, Ferdinand Magellan, was sailing in the service of the Spanish king in 1519 when he traveled to the tip of South America and through the strait that now bears his name. Crossing the Pacific, he pioneered a new westward route from Europe to the East Indies. Although he himself was killed on the Philippine island of Cebu, one of his ships under the command of Sebastian del Cano went on to complete the first circumnavigation of the world in 1522.

Like Columbus, Amerigo Vespucci was an Italian navigator–merchant working for Spain. On his second trip to America, from 1499 to 1500, he sighted the mouth of the mighty Amazon River. On further voyages, this time on Portugal's behalf, he explored the coast of what is now Brazil as far south as the River Plate. Vespucci was one of the first explorers to promote the idea that the New World was not part of the Indies, as Columbus had believed, but a seperate continent, and contemporary mapmakers duly named it "America" in his honor.

⊛ **1500** Portuguese explorers led by Pedro Álvarez Cabral discover Brazil.

⊛ **1507** The German cartographer Martin Waldseemüller names the continent of America in honor of the Florentine navigator Amerigo Vespucci.

✕ **1509** The Portuguese under Francisco de Almeida defeat a combined Indian and Mameluke Egyptian fleet off Diu, Gujarat, so gaining control of the Indian Ocean.

⊛ **1513** A Spanish expedition led by Vasco Nuñez de Balboa crosses the Isthmus of Panama and claims the "South Sea" (Pacific Ocean) for Spain.

⊛ **1519** Fernão de Magalhães (Ferdinand Magellan) sails through the Magellan Strait and discovers the western passage to the East Indies (–1522).

♛ **1522** The Ming Emperor Jia Qing expels the Portuguese from China for piracy.

⊛ **1531** The first international stock exchange opens in Antwerp, becoming the center of European trade and finance until 1576.

♛ **1557** Portugal establishes a permanent trading and missionary settlement at Macao in the Pearl River Delta of southern China.

⊛ **1570** Nagasaki in southern Japan is opened up to foreign trade by the local daimyo (lord) Omura.

✕ **1576** During the Dutch revolt against Spanish rule Antwerp is sacked by unpaid and starving Spanish troops (again in 1585). Its importance as a trading center begins to wane in favor of Amsterdam.

⊛ **1595** The first Dutch maritime expedition to the East Indies mark the beginning of the Dutch overseas trading empire (–1597).

⊛ **1600** Foundation of the English East India Company in India.

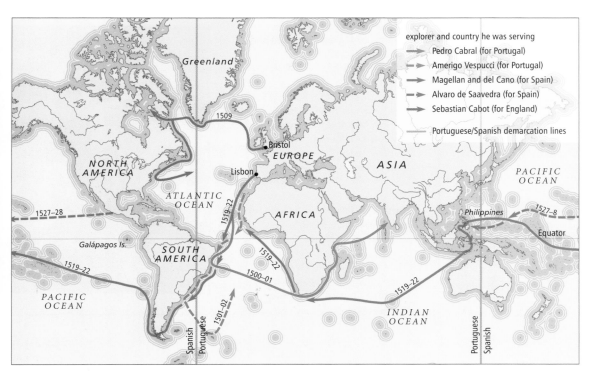

explorer and country he was serving
→ Pedro Cabral (for Portugal)
⇢ Amerigo Vespucci (for Portugal)
→ Magellan and del Cano (for Spain)
⇢ Alvaro de Saavedra (for Spain)
→ Sebastian Cabot (for England)
— Portuguese/Spanish demarcation lines

◄ The great voyages of exploration of the late 15th and early 16th centuries linked parts of the world that had previously been barely if at all aware of each other's existence. Sailing from Spain, Portugal, and England, brave mariners traveled west to the New World of America and east to India. In 1522 Sebastian del Cano—second in command to Ferdinand Magellan, who had been killed en route—completed the first circumnavigation of the world.

The Spanish were eager to set up colonies to exploit the New World's riches. Alonso de Ojeda, who had sailed with Columbus and Vespucci, claimed large parts of northeastern South America for Spain in 1509. He named Venezuela after seeing native houses built over the water—like those in Venice. Two years later Vasco Nuñez de Balboa founded the settlement of Darien (present-day Panama). Balboa's search for gold took him across the narrow Central American isthmus, and on September 29, 1513, he became the first European to see the Pacific Ocean, finally disproving Columbus's claim to have reached India.

Thus far Spain's American settlements were on a small scale. Soon, however, Hernán Cortés and Francisco Pizarro were to seize control of Mexico and Peru, ushering in the age of the conquistadors.

A Taste for Spices

Spices had been prized in Europe since Roman times as flavorings for food and ingredients in medicines. Grown in tropical regions, they were brought by land to ports in West Asia; from there Venice came to control their import into Europe. The urge to gain direct access to spices drove much of the eastward exploration in the 16th century. Portugal began to ship pepper from India (right), cinnamon from Sri Lanka, nutmeg and cloves from the Moluccas, and ginger from China. Spices were easy to carry in bulk and highly profitable. To cut transport costs to northern Europe, the Portuguese moved their main distribution center from Lisbon to Amsterdam and Antwerp. By 1530 Antwerp was Europe's richest city, and its wealth increased further when it became the hub for Spanish silver imports from Peru.

1510–1520 A.D.

AMERICAS

✗ **1511** Diego Velazquez leads the Spanish conquest of Cuba, a springboard for further invasions of Central America (–1515).

⚙ **1513** A Spanish force under Vasco Nuñez de Balboa crosses the Isthmus of Darien (Panama) and sights the Pacific Ocean.

EUROPE

✗ **1511** The pope forms an alliance (the Holy League) with Venice, Spain, and the Holy Roman emperor to drive the French from Italy; its forces are defeated at the Battle of Ravenna (1512).

👑 **1513** The Union of Kalmar, which has linked Denmark, Norway, and Sweden since 1397, comes under strain as Sweden (then including Finland) breaks away.

👑 **1513** The Italian political theorist Niccolò Macchiavelli writes *The Prince*, a key work on statecraft that instructs rulers on how to hold power.

⚙ **1515** The wheel-lock arquebus (early musket) is developed in Germany as a replacement for the unreliable matchlock.

📖 **1516** The English scholar Thomas More publishes *Utopia*, which describes an ideal social and political system.

AFRICA

👑 **1512** The Songhai Empire, ruled by Askia Mohammed, vies for supremacy with the Hausa Confederation in West Africa (–1517).

⚙ **1517** Archduke Charles of Austria (later Emperor Charles V) grants a monopoly on the trade in African slaves to merchants from Florence.

✗ **1517** Tuman Bey, the last Mameluke sultan of Egypt, is hanged after an Ottoman army sacks Cairo.

WESTERN ASIA

👑 **1510** Shah Esmail I of Persia drives the Uzbeks out of the disputed region of Khurasan; he has the skull of their leader Mohammed Shaibani made into a drinking cup. In the same year he makes the Shiite branch of Islam the state religion of Persia.

👑 **1511** Selim I ("the Grim") deposes his father Bayezid II to become Ottoman sultan and orders the death of 40,000 Shiite Muslims (–1512); in his nine-year reign the empire will double in size.

✗ **1514** At the Battle of Chaldiran Selim's Ottoman forces defeat Shah Esmail's Persians; the Ottoman Empire expands south and east.

SOUTH & CENTRAL ASIA

⚙ **1510** Afonso de Albuquerque establishes Goa as a Portuguese colony on the west coast of India.

☀ **1514** Under Khan Sayid of Kashgar the Taklamakan Desert region falls under the sway of Islam.

👑 **1518** Portugal signs a peace treaty with Kotte, a kingdom on Sri Lanka.

✗ **1519** Led by Babur, the Mughals undertake the first of many invasions of India.

EAST ASIA & OCEANIA

✗ **1510** Japanese pirates repeatedly pillage the coastal settlements of southern China.

⚙ **1511** Portuguese forces seize Malacca on the Malay Peninsula, center of the East Indies spice trade.

A Portuguese merchant trades in nutmegs, along with mace and cloves one of the main exports of the Moluccas or Spice Islands (now part of Indonesia). The Portuguese monopoly on trade with the islands was first challenged by the Dutch at the start of the 17th century.

AMERICAS

⊕ **1513** The conquistador Juan Ponce de León discovers and names Florida, claiming the territory for Spain.

⊕ **1517** The Spanish explorer Francisco de Córdoba discovers the Mayan civilization on the Yucatán Peninsula in Central America.

✕ **1519** An expeditionary force led by the conquistador Hernán Cortés sets out from Cuba to conquer the Aztec Empire of Mexico.

EUROPE

Charles V was the mightiest European ruler of his day. He owed his powers to the marriage alliances of his Hapsburg forebears, which led him to inherit the Netherlands in 1506 and the throne of Spain in 1516. In 1519 he was crowned Holy Roman emperor. He spent his long reign enmeshed in struggles with France, his main rival on the continent, and fighting to defend the Catholic church against the rise of Protestantism. Exhausted by the task, he abdicated all his powers in 1556 and spent the last two years of his life in a monastery.

👑 **1516** In Venice Jews are forced to live in a separate, walled area of the city—the world's first ghetto.

☀ **1517** Martin Luther publishes his *95 Theses* in Wittenberg, Germany, detailing abuses by the Catholic church and starting the Reformation.

☀ **1518** Ulrich Zwingli promotes the Reformation in Switzerland, persuading Zurich city council to ban the sale of indulgences by Catholic monks.

👑 **1519** Spain's Hapsburg King Charles I is chosen as Holy Roman Emperor Charles V, linking Spain and its colonies with Burgundy and the German lands in a single empire.

⊕ **1519** The Portuguese navigator Ferdinand Magellan leaves Spain with five ships to find a western route to the Spice Islands; one of his ships will eventually circumnavigate the world (–1522).

AFRICA

👑 **1518** The Barbary states of Tunis and Algiers are established on the North African coast; they will become notorious bases for raids on Mediterranean shipping.

⊕ **1518** The transatlantic slave trade gears up as the Spanish authorities grant a license permitting 4,000 African slaves to be imported into the New World.

WESTERN ASIA

⊕ **1515** The Portuguese viceroy Afonso de Albuquerque takes Hormuz at the mouth of the Persian Gulf.

👑 **1517** Mecca comes under Ottoman rule when the city's ruler surrenders to Selim.

This Ottoman pulpit tile bears a plan of the Muslim holy city of Mecca. The Kaaba, a square shrine, can be seen in the center.

SOUTH & CENTRAL ASIA

☀ **1519** Guru Nanak founds the Sikh religion at Kartarpur in the Punjab region of India.

EAST ASIA & OCEANIA

⊕ **1513** The first Portuguese ships reach the Moluccas, the fabled "Spice Islands"; Portugal enjoys a monopoly on the nutmeg and mace trade for almost a century.

👑 **1514** Ali Mughayat Syah becomes the first sultan of Aceh in western Sumatra, a rising power in Southeast Asia.

⊕ **1517** Portuguese sailors discover Taiwan off the Chinese coast, naming it Ilha Formosa ("beautiful island").

1510–1520 A.D.

GREAT ZIMBABWE

▲ An ivory carving shows one of the Portuguese merchants who eventually took over Africa's east coast trade.

FROM AROUND 1000 A.D. *several small chiefdoms rose and fell between the Zambezi and Limpopo rivers in southern Africa. By 1300 the royal center of Great Zimbabwe on the Zambezian plateau (covering the eastern part of the modern state of Zimbabwe) had come to dominate the whole region. Yet by the end of the 16th century even this great city-state had been eclipsed and was in decline.*

The Karanaga, a Shona-speaking people, built the palace-city of Great Zimbabwe between the 12th and 15th centuries. Apart from its sheer size—the site covered a huge area of 1,800 acres (7 sq. km)—its most striking feature was its stone architecture (the word *zimbabwe* comes from a term meaning "sacred houses of rock"). The city was by far the largest complex of stone buildings in sub-Saharan Africa, and many of its massive walls have survived into modern times. Like builders in the Inca Empire in South America, the masons who made Great Zimbabwe hewed blocks of granite and fit them together perfectly, using no mortar. The walls were then carved with intricate herringbone and zigzag patterns.

Because its builders had no written language and so left behind no records of their history, many mysteries surround the rise, zenith, and fall of the complex. At its peak in around 1400 it was probably home to some 20,000 people, most of whom lived in mud huts that have long since disappeared. The wide, grassy plains that surrounded the site were ideal for grazing the cattle that were a vital element of the kingdom's economy. But herding alone could not sustain the population, and the soil was too thin to support intensive agriculture.

Instead, many inhabitants are thought to have lived from trade. Their commerce was based on the rich gold deposits on the Zambezian Plateau, for Great Zimbabwe was strategically placed to control the supply of the mineral to Arab and Swahili traders. Its merchants transported the gold and ivory—another key trade commodity—to the port of Sofala, 280 miles (450 km) away on Africa's east coast. There the goods were exchanged for cotton cloth and other imports. The discovery of Chinese Ming pottery in Zimbabwe bears witness to such transactions.

The Great Enclosure

Of all the puzzles posed by Great Zimbabwe, the Great Enclosure is the most enigmatic. The most striking of the city's stone remains, this compound (also known as the Elliptical Building) has walls 32 feet (10 m) high and up to 17 feet (over 5 m) thick. Parts of the structure may have been plastered with a substance called *daga*, a mixture of decomposed granite and gravel. The fortifications clearly were built for defense, but archeologists disagree about what they were intended to protect. Some think that the enclosure, whose remains include a solid conical tower 30 feet (9 m) high (left), was designed as a place for the city's rulers to smelt gold. Others see it as a home for either the ruler himself or his principal wife, or as a sacred precinct reserved for religious worship.

Whatever its purpose, the Great Enclosure still dominates the site of Great Zimbabwe. Its remains so impressed the first European visitors to the site that they were convinced the city was the capital of the biblical Queen of Sheba.

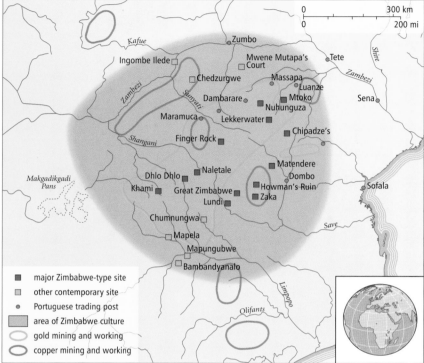

◀ For centuries Great Zimbabwe was unknown territory to Europeans until it was rediscovered in 1867. This Italian map of the Congo lands to the northwest dates to 1575.

▼ The lands ruled from Great Zimbabwe covered a wide area of what is now the eastern part of the state of Zimbabwe. Graves from the 14th century have been found at Ingombe Ilede, 300 miles (500 km) to the north.

Map legend:
- ■ major Zimbabwe-type site
- ▢ other contemporary site
- ● Portuguese trading post
- area of Zimbabwe culture
- ◯ gold mining and working
- ◯ copper mining and working

From around 1450 on, however, a new force emerged to challenge Great Zimbabwe's preeminence in the region. The gold-producing provinces rose up, taking control of most of the plateau region in their own name. They were led by Chief Mutota, who came to be known as Mwene Mutapa ("Lord of the Plundered Lands"), a name that came to be applied not just to his successors but also to the kingdom itself, which, weakened by rebellion, fell into decline in the early 17th century.

👑 **c.1200** The Shona-speaking Karanga people first rise to prominence in the Great Zimbabwe area.

👑 **c.1400** Great Zimbabwe is at its peak, grown rich by trading gold to the coast.

⊕ **c.1400** Swahili settlements thrive on the East African coast, trading in gold, ivory, iron, and slaves with Arabs from Zanzibar and elsewhere.

👑 **c.1400** The Zulu and Xhosa peoples establish kingdoms in southern Africa.

👑 **c.1450** Great Zimbabwe goes into decline as Mwene Mutapa rises.

☀ **1490** The Portuguese convert Nzinga Nkuwu, ruler of the Kingdom of Kongo, to Christianity. Mbanza Kongo, its capital, has 30,000 inhabitants when the Europeans arrive.

⊕ **1505** The Portuguese establish a trading post at Sofala on Africa's eastern seaboard (in present-day Mozambique).

👑 **c.1550** Mwene Mutapa is at the height of its power; lying between the Zambezi and Limpopo rivers, its sphere of influence extends from the Kalahari Desert in the west to the Indian Ocean in the east.

⊕ **1570** Portugal establishes a colony in Angola, southwest Africa, as a major center of the transatlantic slave trade.

👑 **c.1600** By this date the Rozwi Empire is dominant in the region once controlled by Great Zimbabwe.

⚔ **c.1610** Gatsi Rusere, ruler of Mwene Mutapa, cedes the mineral wealth of his kingdom in return for Portuguese help in putting down a rebellion.

👑 **1652** The Dutch establish a first colony at the Cape of Good Hope. Farmers ("Boers") forcibly take land from the native San and Khoikhoi peoples.

1520–1530 A.D.

AMERICAS

1520 A popular uprising forces the Spanish conquistadors led by Hernán Cortés to flee the Aztec capital of Tenochtitlán.

1520 The Portuguese navigator Ferdinand Magellan passes through the straits at America's southermost tip, later named after him.

1521 Cortés returns to capture Tenochtitlán, making the Spanish masters of the Aztec Empire.

EUROPE

1520 Christian II of Denmark and Norway defeats the Swedes at Lake Asunden and massacres their leaders in the Stockholm Bloodbath.

1520 Martin Luther is excommunicated and declared a heretic.

1520 Charles V is crowned Holy Roman emperor at Aachen.

1521 The Diet of Worms declares Martin Luther to be a heretic.

1521 Belgrade falls to the Ottoman Turks.

1521 War breaks out in Italy between the French occupying Milan and the forces of Charles V and the papacy.

Stirred into action by the ferment of the Reformation, farm workers across southern Germany took up arms against their landlords in the Peasants' War of 1524 to 1526. Although their grievances were mainly economic, many of the rebels also took up the Protestant cause, much to the horror of Martin Luther, who wrote a pamphlet *Against the Murdering, Thieving Hordes of Peasants*. The revolt was put down with much brutality; in all, 100,000 peasants were killed.

AFRICA

1520 The Portuguese priest Francisco Alvarez arrives in Ethiopia at the start of a six-year mission.

1524 The Ottomans put down an attempt by Egypt's governor Ahmad Pasha al-Khair to set himself up as an independent ruler.

1526 The ruler of the West African Kingdom of Kongo tries unsuccessfully to expel the Portuguese.

WESTERN ASIA

1520 Suleiman I, "the Magnificent," succeeds his father Selim as Ottoman sultan.

1521 Suleiman launches a major invasion of the Kingdom of Hungary.

1523 Ibrahim Pasha, born Greek and sold into slavery by pirates, becomes Suleiman's grand vizier.

SOUTH & CENTRAL ASIA

1524 The Mughal leader Babur seizes Lahore.

1525 Babur invades the Punjab.

1526 Babur defeats the sultan of Delhi at the Battle of Panipat and occupies Delhi and Agra.

EAST ASIA & OCEANIA

1521 Ferdinand Magellan is killed by natives in the Phillippines. His around-the-world voyage continues under his second in command, Sebastiano del Cano.

1521 The Portuguese establish a trading post at Amboina in the Moluccas, the famed Spice Islands of Indonesia.

Chinese Ming vase from the reign of the Emperor Shizung.

✕ **1522** Spanish forces conquer Guatemala.

⊕ **1522** Pascual de Andagoya leads a land expedition from Panama to Peru.

⊕ **1522** Francisco Montano ascends Mt. Popocatapetl in Mexico.

☀️ **1529** The Franciscan friar Bernardino de Sahagún starts his mission in Mexico.

AMERICAS

⊕ **1522** Magellan's flagship the *Victoria*, now under the command of Sebastiano del Cano, returns to Spain, completing the first circumnavigation of the world.

👑 **1523** Gustavus Vasa, leader of Swedish resistance to Danish rule, comes to power as Gustavus I.

✕ **1525** French forces in Italy are routed at the Battle of Pavia. King Francis I is taken prisoner.

☀️ **1525** In Germany the Catholic League is founded to combat Lutheranism.

👑 **1525** Sigismund I of Poland ends the rule of the Teutonic Knights in Prussia.

👑 **1526** The Peasants' War in Germany ends in brutal suppression.

✕ **1526** Ottoman forces defeat the Hungarian army at the Battle of Mohacs.

☀️ **1527** Sweden opts for Lutheranism, cutting its ties to the papacy.

✕ **1527** Mutinous imperial forces sack Rome, imprisoning Pope Clement VII and killing 4,000 inhabitants.

☀️ **1528** Finland adopts the Lutheran faith.

✕ **1529** Ottoman forces under Suleiman the Magnificent fail to take Vienna after a 17-day siege.

EUROPE

✕ **1529** The buccaneer Khayr ad-Din, known in the West as Barbarossa, seizes Algiers with Ottoman aid.

Barbarossa rose to fame attacking Christian shipping in the Mediterranean. Capturing Algiers from Spain, he ceded it to the Ottoman sultan, who responded by making him admiral of his fleet.

AFRICA

👑 **1524** Shah Esmail, founder of Persia's Safavid Dynasty, dies. He is succeeded by his 10-year-old son.

WESTERN ASIA

✕ **1527** Babur defeats the Hindu Rajputs at Khanua, successfully defending his conquests of the previous year.

✕ **1529** Babur completes the conquest of the Delhi Sultanate as far east as the frontier with Bengal.

SOUTH & CENTRAL ASIA

👑 **1521** Takakuni Masamoto drives the Japanese Shogun Yoshitane out of his capital, Kyoto, further reducing the prestige of the Ashikaga Shogunate.

👑 **1521** A Portuguese envoy, Thomé Pires, arrives at the Chinese court.

👑 **1522** The Portuguese are expelled from China following the piratical activities of Simao d'Andrade and other buccaneers.

👑 **1522** In China the Ming Emperor Shizung begins a long reign (−1567).

⊕ **1526** Portuguese vessels reach New Guinea.

👑 **1529** By the Treaty of Saragossa the Holy Roman Emperor Charles V and the Portuguese divide spheres of interest in East Asia. Portugal retains the Moluccas.

EAST ASIA & OCEANIA

1520–1530 A.D.

THE CONQUISTADORS

FOLLOWING THE EUROPEAN DISCOVERY *of the New World, sizable numbers of Spanish soldiers and adventurers crossed the Atlantic Ocean in search of gold and glory. Many went only to their deaths, but other conquistadors—so called from the Spanish word for "conquerors"—helped change the course of history. One group under Hernán Cortés conquered the Aztec Empire of Mexico, while another under Francisco Pizarro made themselves masters of the Inca Empire of Peru. The Hispanic Empire they created in Central and South America lasted for 400 years and made Spain itself for a century or more the wealthiest country in Europe.*

▲ Steel helmets provided protection from enemy slingshots and arrows.

▼ Emissaries of the Aztec emperor greet Hernán Cortés.

Cortés and Pizarro were both younger sons of minor Spanish noblemen who had come to the New World to seek their fortunes. In earlier centuries such men had found employment fighting the Moors who occupied parts of Spain itself, but with the collapse of the last Moorish kingdom in 1492 they were forced to look abroad instead.

Cortés landed in Mexico in 1519 with a force of just 508 soldiers. Crucially, he also had seven small cannons and 16 horses; both were unknown on the American continent at the time. His men had little idea of what they would find on the mainland and were startled to discover a well-organized empire with a capital city, Tenochtitlán, that was bigger than Madrid or London at the time. The Aztecs had built their empire by force, however, and the newcomers were able to find allies among local peoples eager to throw off their yoke. The Spaniards also benefited from the uncertain response of the Aztec ruler Montezuma II, who initially welcomed them, uncertain whether the strangers with unfamiliar weapons might not be emissaries sent by the gods, as foretold in certain Aztec myths.

Pizarro was equally fortunate to arrive in the Inca lands at a time when they had just been riven by civil war. When the victor, Atahualpa, agreed to meet him and his men, Pizarro's troops took him prisoner, slaughtering his vast retinue of unarmed bodyguards. With the emperor in their hands, the tiny force of 180 Spaniards were able to impose their will on the leaderless millions who had been his subjects.

1428 The Aztec people become the dominant power in the Valley of Mexico. By the end of the century most of Mexico also accepts their overlordship.

1438 Under a new ruler, Pachacutec, the Inca people of Peru embark on a course of military expansion, eventually building an empire stretching from Ecuador into northern Chile.

1492 Christopher Columbus crosses the Atlantic Ocean from Spain to discover the New World on its western shores.

1494 By the Treaty of Tordesillas Spain and Portugal agree to divide control of the New World along a line of longitude 370 leagues (about 1,150 miles/1,850 km) west of the Cape Verde Islands.

1500 Under the terms of the treaty the navigator Pedro Alvares Cabral claims Brazil, which lies east of the line, for Portugal.

1504 Hernán Cortés arrives on the island of Hispaniola from Spain as a 19-year-old fortune-seeker.

1511 A Spanish force under Diego de Velazquez occupies Cuba.

1519 Spanish conquistadors led by Hernán Cortés land on the Mexican coast and march on the Aztec capital, Tenochtitlán. The Aztec Emperor Montezuma receives the Spaniards as guests, only for them to take him prisoner.

A Mountain of Silver

More than anything else, the lure of gold and silver drew the conquistadors into Central and South America. They were not disappointed with what they found. Cortés sent beautifully crafted examples of Aztec gold- and silverwork back to Spain that became the wonder of Europe. In Peru Atahualpa's subjects filled a hall of his palace with gold to a depth of almost 7 feet (2 m) in a vain attempt to ransom their emperor from his captors. After the conquest the Spaniards found even greater riches in Mt. Potosí (right), a hill in Bolivia that eventually yielded more than 18,000 tons of silver ore. Annual silver fleets carried the treasure back to Spain, which became the wealthiest country in Europe for more than a century until the mines were finally exhausted.

Many conquistadors died in battle or of disease, but a lucky few made vast fortunes. More significantly, they won a vast and wealthy American empire for Spain; rarely have so few people left such a large mark on history.

For the native peoples, though, the Spaniards' triumphs were an almost complete disaster. Thousands died in the fighting, and millions more succumbed to diseases such as smallpox that entered the country with the Spaniards and to which they had no immunity. It has been estimated that the population of Mexico fell from 25 million to 2.7 million in the years after the conquest, while that of Peru plummeted from 9 million to 1.3 million.

Havana

Tenochtitlán   Cuba

PACIFIC OCEAN

route of Cortés

Aztec Empire

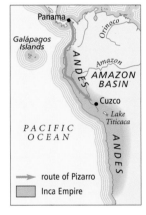

Panama

Galápagos Islands

ANDES

Amazon

AMAZON BASIN

Cuzco

Lake Titicaca

PACIFIC OCEAN

ANDES

→ route of Pizarro

▨ Inca Empire

◀ The Aztec Empire that Cortés conquered occupied much of modern Mexico (far left); his troops set out from Cuba. Pizarro's forces sailed south from Panama, landing in northern Peru (near left). Summoned to meet the Inca ruler Atahualpa, Pizarro accepted, only to stage a surprise attack. By taking Atahualpa prisoner, he made himself master of the Inca Empire and its captial, Cuzco.

⚔ **1520** The citizens of Tenochtitlán revolt, killing Montezuma and temporarily driving out the Spanish.

⚔ **1521** Cortés returns with reinforcements to take Tenochtitlán after an eight-week siege, winning control of the Aztec Empire for Spain.

⚔ **1525** In the Inca lands civil war breaks out between rival contenders for the throne.

⊛ **1530** Portuguese colonists found the first permanent settlements in Brazil.

⚔ **1532** Atahualpa emerges victorious from the Inca civil war only to be taken captive by Spanish conquistadors under Francisco Pizarro, who have staged a landing on the Peruvian coast.

⚔ **1533** Atahualpa is executed on Pizarro's orders. The conquistadors take control of the Inca capital Cuzco.

👑 **1535** Pizarro founds a new capital, Lima, on the Peruvian coast.

👑 **1535** The Holy Roman Emperor Charles V sends a viceroy to rule Mexico, now called New Spain, in his name.

👑 **1541** Pizarro is assassinated by rival conquistadors.

👑 **1542** A Spanish viceroy arrives in Lima to take control of Peru, bringing the era of the conquistadors to an end.

1530–1540 A.D.

AMERICAS

1530 The Portuguese found towns at São Vicente and São Paulo, their first colonies in Brazil.

1532 The Spanish conquistador Francisco Pizarro conquers Peru and captures the last Inca ruler, Atahualpa, who is executed a year later.

1534 The Portuguese ship the first African slaves to Brazil.

1534 French explorer Jacques Cartier is the first European to enter the St. Lawrence River; returning a year later, he reaches the future sites of Montreal and Quebec (–1535).

EUROPE

1530 Ten years after assuming the title, Charles V is crowned Holy Roman emperor at Bologna, Italy; he will be the last one to have a papal coronation.

1531 A Catholic Swiss army defeats the Protestants of Zurich at the Battle of Kappel. The Swiss reformer Ulrich Zwingli is one of the dead.

1531 German Protestant princes form the Schmalkaldic League to resist the attempts of Charles V to reintroduce Catholicism.

1532 François Rabelais, French monk and physician, publishes his two great satirical masterpieces, *Pantagruel* and *Gargantua* (–1534).

1533 King Henry VIII of England divorces his first wife Catherine of Aragon, leaving him free to marry Anne Boleyn. As a result, he is excommunicated by the pope.

AFRICA

1531 Muslim leader Ahmad Gran goes to war against the Christian rulers of Ethiopia, winning much land.

An Italian medal depicts the flagship of the Genoese admiral Andrea Doria.

WESTERN ASIA

1534 Suleiman I invades the Safavid Empire and takes Baghdad, which becomes part of the Ottoman Empire.

1536 Suleiman I forms an alliance with King Francis I of France against the Hapsburg Empire.

1538 The Ottoman navy defeats a Christian fleet at Prevesa, off the west coast of Greece.

SOUTH & CENTRAL ASIA

The Mughal Emperor Humayun, shown in this painting on a hunting expedition, inherited the Mughal Empire from his father Babur, lost it to the Afghans, then 15 years later won it back. He spent the intervening years first in the wilderness of Sind then in Persia, whose Shah Tahmasp provided him with the forces to regain his kingdom. He had little time to enjoy his restoration, dying six months later.

c.1530 The Nakaya Dynasty frees itself from the Vijayanagar Empire of southern India and becomes a great patron of Hindu temple construction.

1530 Humayun becomes Mughal emperor of India on the death of his father Babur, but has to share his lands with his brothers.

EAST ASIA & OCEANIA

c.1530 Shizung, Ming emperor of China, largely withdraws from government to concentrate on alchemy.

1533 The Dai Viet Kingdom of Indochina fragments into a number of small states.

⊕ **1535** Pizarro founds the city of Lima as the Spanish capital in Peru.

☀ **1538** The Spanish establish an archbishopric at Bogota, Colombia, the first in South America.

Cartier explores the St. Lawrence River, as shown in a 19th-century painting.

⊕ **1539** Conquistador Hernando de Soto embarks on a journey of exploration that will take him through Florida and Georgia in search of gold.

AMERICAS

☀ **1535** The Anabaptists, a strict Protestant sect, seize control of Münster, Germany, and prophesy the end of the world.

☀ **1536** William Tyndale, translator of the Bible into English, is burned at the stake for heresy.

〰 **1537** Cosimo I de Medici, a great patron of the arts, becomes duke of Florence.

📖 **1539** Agnolo Bronzino, a leading exponent of the Mannerist style, becomes court painter to Cosimo de Medici.

☀ **1535** Henry VIII assumes the title of supreme governor of the Church of England.

EUROPE

✕ **1534** Khayr ad-Din Barbarossa captures the North African stronghold of Tunis for the Ottomans.

✕ **1535** Andrea Doria, a Genoese admiral in the service of Charles V, drives the Ottomans out of Tunis.

✕ **1535** By this time Ahmad Gran controls most of Ethiopia; Christian resistance continues in the mountain areas.

AFRICA

✕ **1538** An Ottoman naval expedition to the Indian Ocean conquers Aden and brings the whole of the Red Sea coast of Arabia under Ottoman rule.

☀ **1539** Sinan, the most famous of all Islamic architects, becomes chief of the Corps of Royal Architects under Suleiman I.

Sinan's masterpiece, the Suleimaniye Mosque in Istanbul.

WESTERN ASIA

〰 **1535** The Portuguese fortify Diu on the coast of India.

✕ **1538** An Ottoman navy on service in the Indian Ocean combines with a Gujarati army to attack Diu and expel the Portuguese.

✕ **1539** Sher Shah Sur, an Afghan chieftain, rebels against Humayun and conquers Bengal.

📖 **1539** Guru Nanak, the founder of the Sikh religion, dies.

SOUTH & CENTRAL ASIA

〰 **1539** Tabinshweti of the Toungou Dynasty captures Pegu, capital of the Mon Dynasty, and begins to unify Burma (modern Myanmar).

EAST ASIA & OCEANIA

1530–1540 A.D.

THE RENAISSANCE

▲ Probably the world's most famous painting, the *Mona Lisa* owes its alternative name, the *Gioconda*, to its subject, the wife of the Marquis del Giocondo. Painted by Leonardo da Vinci, the work is a masterpiece of Italian Renaissance art.

THE WORD "RENAISSANCE" MEANS REBIRTH. *It refers to an artistic and cultural movement that arose in northern Italy in the 14th century and had spread throughout Europe by the mid-16th century. Historians today recognize in the Renaissance a period of transformation that brought an end to the medieval era, opening the way to new achievements in learning and science that led eventually to the 18th-century Enlightenment. In its origins, however, the Renaissance was backward-looking, seeking inspiration in the art and literature of the classical worlds of Greece and Rome.*

There had been revivals of interest in the classical past before—at the court of the Emperor Charlemagne in the 8th century, for example, and in the 12th century with the rediscovery of the works of Aristotle. One new factor in the 14th and 15th centuries was the decline and collapse of the Byzantine Empire. Well before the fall of Constantinople to the Turks in 1453, Greek scholars had taken large numbers of classical Greek manuscripts for safety to Italy. Previously unknown in the West, these works led to the development of new branches of study, such as mathematics, geography, medicine, and philosophy.

By the early 15th century Italian cities such as Florence, Ferrara, Urbino, Venice, and Milan had become wealthy through international trade and banking. They were hotspots of creativity, where artists and craftsmen such as the architects Alberti and Brunelleschi and the painters Donatello and Masaccio were developing new styles of painting, decoration, and architecture based on the ideals of the past. As interest in the classical world revived, members of the powerful families that ruled these cities, such as the Medici of Florence and the Sforza of Milan, became great patrons of the arts. They built libraries and churches in the classical style, with an ordered use of columns and symmetry. They also endowed universities that stimulated scholarship, and commissioned portraits and medals of themselves that often showed them as Roman emperors. Partly through the new medium of printing and partly as a result of the wars that brought rulers such as the Emperor Charles V and Francis I of France to Italy, the influence of the Renaissance traveled rapidly outside Italy to all the courts of Europe.

---

c.1420 The architect Brunelleschi, the sculptor Donatello, and the painter Masaccio—all important figures in the art of the early Renaissance—are at work in Florence.

1434 Cosimo de Medici begins a 30-year domination of Florence.

1440 The Platonic Academy is founded in Florence.

1450 Francesco Sforza becomes ruler of Milan.

1485 Sandro Botticelli paints *The Birth of Venus*.

1505 Albrecht Dürer, German artist and engraver, is present in Venice (–1506).

1506 Leonardo da Vinci completes his most famous painting, the *Mona Lisa*.

1508 Michelangelo paints the ceiling of the Sistine Chapel (–1512).

1508 The painter Raphael moves to Rome and is employed by Pope Julian II to decorate the papal chambers in the Vatican (–1509).

1509 Erasmus publishes *In Praise of Folly*.

1513 Niccolo Machiavelli publishes *The Prince*, a handbook for Renaissance monarchs.

1516 Sir Thomas More writes *Utopia*, in which he describes an imaginary land with an ideal form of government.

1519 Leonardo da Vinci dies in France while working for Francis I.

1519 Construction begins on the Château of Chambord, the first building in France in the new Renaissance style.

1532 Francis I invites Italian painters to his palace at Fontainebleau.

1543 Nicolaus Copernicus's *On the Revolutions of the Heavenly Bodies* is published, setting the sun at the center of the universe.

1547 Michelangelo is appointed architect of St. Peter's in Rome.

c.1550 Giorgio Vasari publishes the *Lives of the Artists*—biographies of the great Renaissance painters.

The scholars of the New Learning, as it was called, challenged the rigid authority of the medieval church. They found inspiration in the works of Plato and other classical writers, and were known as humanists, reflecting their people-centered view of the universe. In art the influence of humanist ideas called for a return to a more realistic depiction of nature, as seen in the works of Leonardo da Vinci (1452–1519). As well as a painter and sculptor, he was an architect and engineer, and his notebooks reveal an immensely inventive mind, way ahead of his time in investigating biology, anatomy, mechanics, and aerodynamics.

Erasmus of Rotterdam

If Leonardo da Vinci was the outstanding all-round genius of the Renaissance, Desiderius Erasmus (1466–1536) was its most famous scholar. Born in Rotterdam in the Netherlands, Erasmus became a monk and later went to study in Paris. There he turned against the rigid scholasticism of his youth, embracing instead the new doctrine of humanism, which stressed the power of human reason. He traveled widely, spending time at England's Oxford and Cambridge among other universities, and corresponded with Europe's foremost scholars. He was one of the first popular writers of the age of printing—his most famous work, *In Praise of Folly*, went into 43 editions in his lifetime. He also published a best-selling book of *Adagia* (literally "adages") as well as scholarly editions of classical texts. Erasmus was strongly critical of the abuses of the Catholic church, but he took no part in the Reformation and later attacked Luther for his extreme views.

▲ In the 16th century Renaissance styles of art and architecture moved north of the Alps, as shown by the Château of Chambord, built for France's King Francis I from 1519 on.

▼ Made rich by trade, Renaissance Italy was a fragmented land of rival city-states that competed with one another for the services of the finest artists and architects.

AMERICAS

1540 Pedro de Valdivia establishes a Spanish colony at Santiago de Chile.

1540 Francisco Vázquez de Coronado leads an expedition into what is now the American Southwest

1541 Hernando de Soto and his party, pushing westward across Georgia, discover the Mississippi River.

1541 Francisco Pizarro is hacked to death by rival conquistadors in Peru.

1541 Marooned in the Upper Amazon after exploring eastward over the Andes Mountains, Francisco de Orellanas and his men float on rafts downriver to the Atlantic.

1542 By the Laws of the Indies the Spanish crown abolishes *encomienda*—the right of colonists to exact tribute and labor from Native Americans.

1542 An *audiencia*—a Spanish court with governing powers—is established in Lima, Peru

EUROPE

1540 The Society of Jesus (the Jesuit order) is given official recognition by Pope Paul III.

1541 John Calvin begins preaching as chief pastor in Geneva, Switzerland.

1542 War breaks out between England and France (–1546).

1543 Hungary is conquered by the Ottoman Turks.

As shown here in a contemporary illustration, the Polish astronomer Nicolaus Copernicus pioneered the view that the planets moved around the sun; earlier authorities had followed the classical writer Ptolemy of Alexandria in viewing the Earth as the center of the universe. A lifelong churchman, Copernicus only agreed to publish his controversial views shortly before his death in 1543.

AFRICA

1540 Under the command of Barbarossa the Ottoman navy defeats Charles V's fleet off Crete.

1541 Barbarossa inflicts a second defeat on the Christians off Algiers.

1542 With Portuguese aid, Ethiopia's King Lebna Denegel takes the offensive against Ahmad Gran.

WESTERN ASIA

1540 The death of Ubayd Allah Kahn puts an end to Uzbek raids on the eastern provinces of Safavid Persia.

1547 The Ottoman Sultan Suleiman the Magnificent and Ferdinand of Austria sign a peace treaty.

1547 The Ottomans take control of the port of Basra in what is now Iraq. Former pirate Piri Reis takes command of the Ottoman Indian Ocean fleet.

SOUTH & CENTRAL ASIA

1540 The Afghan Sher Shah Sur defeats the Mughal Emperor Humayun and seizes power in Delhi.

1542 St. Francis Xavier begins his mission to Goa in western India.

1543 Sher Shah Sur extends his realm to the Indian Ocean.

1543 In Sri Lanka Portuguese colonists join the native Kingdom of Kotte in a disastrous attempted invasion of the northern Kingdom of Kandy.

EAST ASIA & OCEANIA

1541 King Tabinshweti of Toungou completes his conquest of the Mon Dynasty to make himself ruler of a reunited Burma (Myanmar).

1542 Sunan Gunung Jati founds Banten on the Sunda Strait. The new Islamic state will soon come to dominate the neighboring Hindu kingdoms of western Java.

1542 A group of Portuguese sailors making an accidental landfall become the first Europeans to set foot on Japanese soil.

Bartolomé de las Casas campaigned for the humane treatment of indigenous peoples.

⚙ **1545** A typhus epidemic in New Spain claims an estimated 100,000 native lives, along with those of a few European settlers.

⚙ **1545** The richest silver mine in the Americas opens at Potosí in what is now Bolivia.

⚙ **1545** Bartolomé de las Casas founds a utopian community based on partnership between Europeans and Indians at Verapaz in Honduras.

👑 **1549** Tomé de Sousa is sent from Portugal to govern Brazil.

AMERICAS

⚙ **1543** Nicolaus Copernicus publishes *De Revolutionibus Orbium Coelestium* ("On the Revolutions of the Heavenly Bodies"), suggesting that the planets orbit the sun.

⚙ **1543** Andreas Vesalius's *De Humani Corporis Fabrica* ("On the Structure of the Human Body"), widely regarded as the founding work of modern anatomical science, is published.

☀ **1545** The Council of Trent begins in Italy, launching the Counter-Reformation.

⚔ **1546** The Anglo-French War ends with England taking the French port of Boulogne.

👑 **1547** Ivan IV, "the Terrible," becomes the first czar of Russia.

👑 **1547** Francis I of France dies, to be succeeded by his son, Henry II.

⚔ **1547** Charles V's general in the Netherlands, the duke of Alba, gains a decisive victory over the Schmalkaldic League at the Battle of Mühlberg.

⚔ **1549** War breaks out again between England and France.

EUROPE

⚔ **1543** Ahmad Gran is killed in battle, bringing to an end the Muslim attempt to take over Ethiopia.

👑 **1543** Afonso I of Kongo dies, leaving his kingdom open to the slave trade's destabilizing influence.

AFRICA

⚔ **1548** Despite the help of a huge Ottoman army, Alqas Mirza, governor of Khurasan, fails to overthrow his brother, Persia's Shah Tahmasp.

⚔ **1548** The Ottoman admiral Piri Reis takes Aden back from the Portuguese.

Persia's Shah Tahmasp receives an ambassador in his palace.

WESTERN ASIA

👑 **1545** Sher Shah Sur takes Chitor, stronghold of the Rajputs, effectively completing his conquest of Rajasthan. He dies soon after, to be succeeded by his son Islam Shah.

⚔ **1546** The Ottoman Turks besiege the Gujarati port of Diu.

SOUTH & CENTRAL ASIA

⚔ **1545** King Prajai of Ayutthaya (Thailand) invades Chiengmai in northwestern Thailand. He is eventually sent packing by the Laotian army.

⚔ **1548** Portuguese mercenaries repulse an attack by Tabinshweti of Burma on Ayutthaya. The ruler is assassinated soon after.

☀ **1549** Jesuit missionaries led by St. Francis Xavier reach Japan.

EAST ASIA & OCEANIA

1540–1550 A.D.

THE REFORMATION

PROTESTANTISM WAS BORN OF *Martin Luther's attempt to reform the Catholic church, which in his eyes was riddled with greed and corruption. The religious upheavals that followed his call split the unity of Western Christendom and unleashed a century and a half of bitter warfare and vicious persecution. At a time when religion was an essential part of everyday life, the turmoil in the church affected all of Europe.*

▲ In 1520 Pope Leo X issued a papal bull (decree), shown above, condemning the views of Martin Luther as heretical. When Luther responded by burning the document, he was excommunicated (barred) from the Catholic church. The Reformation was under way.

▶ As the map shows, Protestantism in its Lutheran, Calvinist, and Anglican forms was at first mostly confined to northern Europe; the south remained loyal to the pope.

majority faith 1550
- Anglican
- Catholic
- Calvinist
- Lutheran
- Muslim
- Orthodox
- mixed

1517 Martin Luther posts his 95 Theses criticizing church abuses on the door of Wittenberg Cathedral in Germany.

1525 William Tyndale produces an English translation of the Greek New Testament.

1529 Henry VIII begins a dispute with Pope Clement VII over his wish to divorce Catherine of Aragon.

1533 Henry VIII marries Anne Boleyn in defiance of Pope Clement VII. He is promptly excommunicated (expelled from the Catholic church).

1534 Henry VIII breaks with Rome, establishing the Church of England.

1534 Luther completes his German translation of the Bible. Ignatius of Loyola founds the Society of Jesus (the Jesuits).

1536 John Calvin publishes the *Institutes of the Christian Religion*.

1540 The Society of Jesus receives official recognition from Pope Paul III. It will become a spearhead of the Counter-Reformation.

1541 Calvin is appointed chief pastor in Geneva.

1542 The Jesuit missionary St. Francis Xavier reaches Goa, western India.

1545 Catholic prelates meet to discuss church reform at the Council of Trent in northern Italy (–1563).

1549 St. Francis Xavier's missionaries reach Japan.

1549 The Protestant *Book of Common Prayer* is published for use in all English churches.

1553 Mary I becomes queen of England, which reverts to the Catholic faith. Many Protestants are tortured and killed in the persecution that follows.

Some historians maintain that the Catholic church has been in a state of rolling reformation since its earliest times: There was no shortage of reformers in the medieval period. But the crisis that began when the German monk Martin Luther nailed his 95 Theses criticizing church abuses to the door of Wittenberg Cathedral in 1517 represented a change of attitude on an altogether different scale. Outraged at the sale of indulgences—documents sold for cash to purchase the forgiveness of sins—Luther had boiled over in his anger at a church that seemed more concerned with earthly wealth and power than heavenly salvation.

Luther is generally considered to have been the first "Protestant," the catchall name given to all the various groups and individuals who followed his lead and eventually broke with the Catholic church. His belief that the structures of the church only interfered between individual men and women and their God quickly struck a chord throughout Germany and much of northern Europe. The spirit of revolt spread like wildfire, and the attack that Luther had launched on the pope's authority quickly broadened into a split.

Many of the protestors who took up the cause of reform were sincere believers like Luther himself, shocked by clerical misconduct. Others were more opportunistic. Henry VIII of England first denounced Luther's views, then underwent a change of heart when the pope refused to grant him a divorce from his marriage. The Church of England that he established was at first Catholic in everything but obedience to Rome, which Henry renounced.

Luther's own objections were to the institutions of the church and the conduct of its clergy; his faith in its central tenets remained unchanged. In Geneva, however, the French preacher John Calvin rethought Christian theology altogether, promoting a theological system that was severe and strongly Bible based. In his view the faithful, or "elect," would be saved, but sinners would be cast into hell forever: He even argued that God knew in advance which group was which, and that some people were thus predestined to be damned. In English-speaking countries his followers became known as Puritans, famed for their strict personal morality and their often intolerant attitude to those who did not share their beliefs.

The political effect of the Reformation was to split first Europe and later other parts of the world into opposing Protestant and Catholic camps. Protestants were persecuted in Catholic lands, Catholics in the growing number of Protestant ones, but many braved torture and death rather than surrender their beliefs.

Meanwhile, thoughtful Catholics quickly came to realize that there was some justice in Luther's complaints. Firm in their loyalty to the pope, they sought to combat the Protestants by cleansing the church of abuses from within. Leading churchmen met at the Council of Trent (1545–1563) to draft the necessary reforms, and a group of dedicated Catholic writers, artists, and priests mobilized to reinvigorate the faith in the intellectual and spiritual movement called the Counter-Reformation.

▲ The French reformer John Calvin preached a strict version of Protestantism that became a model for the Puritans. He got the opportunity to put his ideas into practice in Geneva in Switzerland, serving as its chief pastor for 28 years.

The Good Book

Today Christians take it for granted that reading the Bible is a pious duty: Prior to the Reformation it was regarded as an activity best left to priests. The Catholic church argued that there was less likelihood of error if the general public had the word of God interpreted for them by its own trained ministers. Biblical study was anyway difficult for nonscholars, for the only generally available copies of the sacred texts were in Latin, Greek, or Hebrew, languages that few ordinary citizens could understand. Reformers like Martin Luther felt that the Church's policy was obstructing the spreading of the Christian message. They sought to encourage access to the Bible by producing texts in the "vernacular"—the commonly spoken languages of their countries. Luther's own German translation (right) appeared in 1534. The church authorities fiercely resisted such efforts. William Tyndale, the English translator, was first forced into exile and eventually burned at the stake.

AMERICAS

📖 **1551** The first universities in the Americas are established in Mexico City and in Lima, Peru.

☀ **1551** Brazil gets its first bishop, based in Bahia and answerable to the archbishop of Lisbon.

📖 **1552** Bartolomé de las Casas's indictment of New World colonialism, *A Brief Account of the Destruction of the Indies*, is published in book form.

EUROPE

⚔ **1550** The Anglo–French War ends with France taking Boulogne back from the English.

⚔ **1552** The Russians conquer the former Mongol Khanate of Khazan, opening the way for later ventures across the Urals into Siberia.

☀ **1553** Mary I restores Catholicism as the state religion of England. Many Protestants are martyred for their faith, earning the queen the nickname "Bloody Mary."

The wealth flooding into Spain from its American colonies launched a golden age and made the Spanish ruler, Philip II, the most powerful king in Europe. Coming to power in 1556, Philip also inherited the Spanish Netherlands and lands in Italy; in 1580 he acceded to the Portuguese throne. A champion of Catholicism, Philip took on Protestant rebels in the Netherlands as well as England's Queen Elizabeth I, sending the Spanish Armada against her in 1588; ultimately, neither campaign was successful. In Spain Philip put down a revolt of the Moriscos (Christianized Muslims) between 1568 and 1570, but his incessant wars and the taxes needed to pay for them left the country bankrupt on his death in 1598.

AFRICA

⚔ **1550** The Marrakech warlord al-Shaykh takes Fez to make his Saadi Dynasty masters of Morocco.

⚔ **1551** The Ottoman Turks take Tripoli from the Knights Hospitallers.

👑 **1555** Diogo I, Christian king of Kongo, quarrels with his Portuguese backers, expelling all Portuguese nationals from his kingdom.

WESTERN ASIA

👑 **1551** Ottoman admiral Piri Reis expels the Portuguese from Muscat.

⚔ **1553** Suleiman I mounts a second invasion of Persia, ended by the Treaty of Amasya (–1555).

👑 **1553** Suspecting conspiracy, Suleiman orders the execution of his son Mustafa.

⚔ **1555** A rebellion by supporters of Mustafa is put down in Anatolia.

👑 **1556** Shah Tahmasp's son Esmail is appointed governor of Khorasan but promptly falls under suspicion of plotting a coup. The future shah will spend the next 19 years of his life in prison.

SOUTH & CENTRAL ASIA

⚔ **1551** Portuguese colonists renew their alliance with the Kingdom of Kotte in southwestern Sri Lanka, this time to attack neighboring Sitavaka.

👑 **1555** India's second Mughal emperor, Humayun, occupies Lahore and goes on to reestablish Mughal power in Delhi.

👑 **1555** Humayun dies and is succeeded by his 13-year-old son Akbar, who rules under the supervision of a regent, Bairam Khan.

EAST ASIA & OCEANIA

👑 **c.1550** Cambodia's King Anga Chan rediscovers the ruined Khmer capital of Angkor Wat in the jungle. His attempt to restore it to its former splendor is doomed to failure.

👑 **1551** In the confusion following the assassination of Tabinshweti, Bayinnaung becomes king of Burma.

☀ **1552** The missionary St. Francis Xavier dies on a small island off Macao after repeated, unsuccessful attempts to reach the Chinese mainland.

⚔ **1554** Bayinnaung invades the Laotian territory of Chiangmai, annexing it after a four-year war (–1558).

Bayinnaung's palace at Bago in Burma (Myanmar).

☀ **1554** Jesuit priests at odds with the bishop of Bahia leave for the São Vicente region: The settlement they found will eventually grow into the city of São Paulo.

👑 **1559** The *audiencia* of Charcas is established, centered on what is now Bolivia but extending south to include Paraguay, Uruguay, and Argentina.

👑 **1559** A Spanish expedition under Tristán de Luna seeks unsuccessfully to colonize the Carolinas (–1561).

👑 **1555** The Peace of Augsburg is signed. In his capacity as Holy Roman emperor Charles V acknowledges the right of local German rulers within the empire to decide the official religion in their territories.

☀ **1556** In England the archbishop of Canterbury, Thomas Cranmer, is burned at the stake for his Protestant beliefs despite a series of recantations that he retracts in his last moments.

👑 **1556** Charles V abdicates. His son Philip II inherits Spain with the Netherlands, Naples, and Milan, while the Hapsburg lands in Central Europe together with the title of Holy Roman emperor go to Charles's brother Ferdinand.

👑 **1558** Mary I dies, and Elizabeth I is crowned queen of England.

☀ **1559** The first national synod (council) of French Protestants ("Huguenots") is held.

✕ **1559** The Treaty of Cateau-Cambrésis brings an end to almost 70 years of on–off war between France and the Hapsburgs; France abandons all its Italian claims. The treaty also concludes hostilities between France and England, confirming England's loss of Calais, its last foothold in France.

👑 **1557** The Ottoman Turks have al-Shaykh assassinated but cannot check Morocco's revival under his Saadi successors.

👑 **1559** The Portuguese initiate contacts with Ndambi, king of Ndongo in what is now Angola.

☀ **1556** Istanbul's Suleimaniye Mosque is inaugurated after being under construction for six years.

✕ **1557** The Ottoman navy recaptures the Red Sea ports previously taken by Portugal.

👑 **1559** Though their father is still alive, Suleiman's sons Bayezid and Selim take up arms to contest the succession. Bayezid flees to Iran, seeking protection from Shah Tahmasp

✕ **1556** Akbar's authority as emperor is confirmed by a Mughal victory over a Hindu army at Panipat in northern India.

⚙ **1557** A Portuguese trading settlement is established on the coast of mainland China at Macao.

👑 **1558** Lan Na in Ayutthaya (modern Thailand) becomes a subject state of Bayinnaung's Burmese Empire.

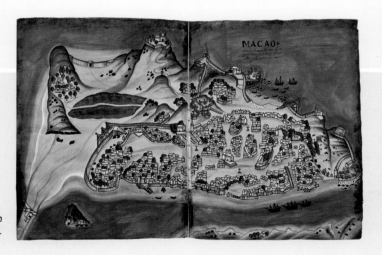

Taipa Island, Macao, as shown in a print dated to 1646.

AMERICAS

EUROPE

AFRICA

WESTERN ASIA

SOUTH & CENTRAL ASIA

EAST ASIA & OCEANIA

1550–1560 A.D.

SULEIMAN THE MAGNIFICENT

▲ A gold coin from the time of Suleiman the Magnificent describes the Ottoman sultan as "Lord of might and victory by land and sea." Under his rule Ottoman power stretched from the Arabian Sea almost to the Straits of Gibraltar.

▶ An Ottoman gouache (watercolor) painting shows Suleiman's forces arrayed outside Belgrade in 1521. The city fell to his troops after weeks of bombardment and 20 massed attacks.

IN THE TURKISH OTTOMAN EMPIRE *his own subjects called him "Suleiman the Lawgiver" in honor of his efforts to protect the individual from the excesses of arbitrary rule. To the West, though, he has always been "Suleiman the Magnificent." The title was awarded grudgingly—he was a bitter foe of Christendom—but his greatness could not be ignored. The tragedy for the Ottoman Empire was that his reign represented a culmination: Thereafter there would be only a long decline.*

The future Suleiman I was still a teenager when his father became sultan. Selim was to prove a highly effective ruler, defeating the Ottomans' chief eastern rival, the Safavid ruler of Persia, at Chaldiran in 1514 and conquering the Mamelukes to win Egypt and Syria two years later. Yet his means of winning and holding onto power justified the name that history was to give him: "Selim the Grim." He probably had his own father poisoned in his eagerness to inherit the throne; he certainly had his two elder brothers garroted and their five sons strangled to remove rival claimants. He also ordered the massacre of 40,000 Muslim heretics in eastern Anatolia to underline his role as the protector of Islamic orthodoxy.

When Suleiman came to the throne in 1520, he therefore inherited a tradition of despotic absolutism as well as a mighty empire. He was the tenth ruler of the Ottoman Dynasty, which had first risen to power in northern Anatolia (modern Asiatic Turkey) in the late 13th century. His predecessors had put paid to the Christian Byzantine Empire and forged a realm that incorporated Turkey and the Balkan lands as well as the eastern Mediterranean seaboard and Egypt.

Suleiman's first act on becoming sultan was to introduce sweeping reforms to the legal system,

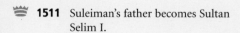

👑 **c.1494** Birth of Suleiman.	👑 **1536** The Grand Vizier Ibrahim is summarily executed.	👑 **1553** Suleiman orders the murder of his son, Mustafa, suspected of conspiring against him.
👑 **1511** Suleiman's father becomes Sultan Selim I.	⚔ **1543** In alliance with France the Ottoman fleet sacks Nice, held at the time by an ally of the Holy Roman emperor.	⚔ **1559** Suleiman's sons Selim and Bayezid begin fighting over the succession.
👑 **1520** Suleiman becomes Ottoman sultan after his father's death from cancer.	⚔ **1544** Barbarossa's fleet raids towns along the Italian coast.	👑 **1561** Bayezid is executed on his father's orders.
⚔ **1521** Suleiman captures Belgrade from the Hungarians.	👑 **1547** Suleiman agrees to a five-year truce with Emperor Ferdinand of Austria, allowing him to campaign in the east against Persia.	⚔ **1565** The island of Malta successfully resists an Ottoman siege.
⚔ **1522** The island of Rhodes is taken.		👑 **1566** Death of Suleiman. He is succeeded by his son, Selim II.
⚔ **1534** The Ottoman navy is placed under the command of Barbarossa.		

The Suleimaniye Mosque

"Whoever builds a mosque, desiring thereby God's pleasure, God builds the like for him in paradise." The Prophet Muhammad's words no doubt ran through the minds of the builders of Istanbul's Suleimaniye Mosque. Designed by Suleiman's chief architect Sinan and built between 1548 and 1557, it was intended not just to reflect God's glory but also to proclaim the wealth and power of the Ottoman Dynasty and to confirm the sultan's status as "God's shadow on earth." The Suleimaniye was always more than simply a place of worship: It was also a house of Islamic culture, with colleges and libraries attached, and a place of charity, with its own hospital and school and a soup kitchen to feed the poor. Distributions of food from the mosques played a vital political role, helping ease the empire through times of economic hardship.

introducing new laws to protect his subjects from arbitrarily imposed taxes, trade restrictions, and land confiscations. He extended the protection of the law not just to Muslims but also to other religious groups. Western visitors were staggered by the tolerance they found in Ottoman society under Suleiman. "He constrains no one," enthused a French traveler, "but permits everyone to live as his conscience dictates."

Abroad, Suleiman's policy was aggressive. In 1521 he captured Belgrade; the next year he seized the strategic island of Rhodes in the Aegean. In 1529 he terrified Europe by besieging Vienna; although that attempt was unsuccessful, he completed the conquest of Hungary in 1543. Earlier Ottoman sultans had been hampered by a lack of sea power, a weakness Suleiman addressed. Under the command of Khayr ad-Din Barbarossa ("Redbeard"), a North African corsair, his fleet harried Western shipping in the Mediterranean. Allying with France's Francis I against the Emperor Charles V, Barbarossa's fleet destroyed Nice, and Turkish Muslims wintered in Toulon.

At home Suleiman could be ruthless as well as just. In 1536 he had his Grand Vizier Ibrahim, long his most trusted adviser, executed—Suleiman's beloved Russian wife Roxelana is said to have had resented the vizier's power. In 1553 he ordered the murder of his own son Mustafa, whom he thought was conspiring against his rule.

Suleiman was to be last of the great Ottomans; his successor on his death in 1566 went down in history as "Selim the Sot" for his drunken ways, and some later rulers proved similarly deficient. Even so, the empire Suleiman had helped build was to survive for another 350 years. For that alone he merited the title history bestowed on him of "the Magnificent."

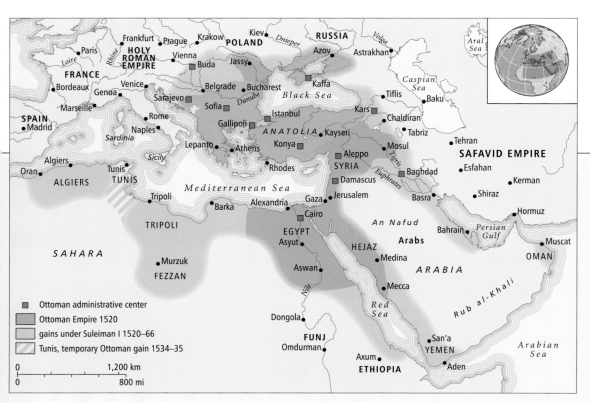

◀ Suleiman extended the Ottoman Empire in all directions. In the west he conquered Hungary; in the east he won Mesopotamia (modern Iraq) from the Persian Safavids. To the south he extended Ottoman rule from Egypt along the North African coast and down the Red Sea to Aden.

■ Ottoman administrative center
Ottoman Empire 1520
gains under Suleiman I 1520–66
Tunis, temporary Ottoman gain 1534–35

0   1,200 km
0   800 mi

AMERICAS

1564 A group of French Calvinists led by Jean Ribault establishes a settlement (Fort Caroline) at the mouth of the St. John's River in northern Florida.

1565 A Spanish expeditionary force wipes out the French outpost at Fort Caroline, Florida, and establishes a new colony along the coast at St. Augustine.

1565 The Portuguese drive the French from their settlement on the Brazilian coast and establish a new one of their own that is the origin of Rio de Janeiro (–1567).

EUROPE

Perhaps the most powerful woman in French history, Catherine de Medici became Queen of France in 1547 as the wife of Henry II. On his death in 1559 she served as regent first for their son Francis II and then, when he in turn died the next year, for the 10-year-old Charles IX. As the nation's true ruler, she became embroiled in the religious wars setting Catholics against the Protestant Huguenots and was considered responsible for the massacre of Huguenot leaders in Paris on St. Bartholmew's Day 1572. Her power waned when a third son, Henry III, came to the throne as an adult in 1574.

1562 The first Huguenot revolt breaks out in western France.

1562 St. Teresa of Avila receives the church's blessing to found the Convent of St. Joseph and a new order of rigorously disciplined Discalced Carmelite nuns.

1563 Work begins on the construction of the Escorial, Philip II's great palace–mausoleum in the mountains outside Madrid.

1561 Sweden conquers Estonia, embarking on what will be a steady campaign of expansionism over the coming decades.

1561 Charles IX inherits the French throne at the age of 13. Real power rests in the hands of his mother, Catherine de Medici.

1565 Malta successfully resists a four-month siege by the Ottoman Turks.

AFRICA

1562 Captain John Hawkins gets the English slave trade under way with a raid up West Africa's Sierra Leone River.

1567 Alvare succeeds Diogo I as king of Kongo, inheriting a kingdom badly weakened by the depredations of the slave trade.

1568 Kongo is devastated by nomadic Jaga raiders, themselves dislodged from home territories farther east by the activities of slavers.

WESTERN ASIA

1561 Shah Tahmasp of Persia surrenders Suleiman's rebellious son Bayezid to the Ottoman ruler in return for a substantial ransom and in order to prevent the possibility of a further war.

1566 Death of Suleiman I, "the Magnificent." He is succeeded by his son Selim II, who will become known as "Selim the Sot." The Ottoman decline is generally held to have started with his accession.

SOUTH & CENTRAL ASIA

1561 Akbar dispenses with the services of his regent and takes the reins as India's third Mughal emperor. Under his rule the empire will enjoy its golden age.

1564 Akbar subdues the Gakkhar rulers of Punjab and the Gonds of eastern India.

The ruins of Chittor Fort, Rajasthan, India.

EAST ASIA & OCEANIA

1560 After a series of floods, droughts, and earthquakes have exacerbated an already deep economic crisis, cuts in army rations spark off a violent mutiny in Nanking, China.

1564 King Bayinnaung of Burma strikes southeast into Ayutthaya (Thailand) and takes the city of that name, which is promptly lost again after a local uprising.

1565 Although claimed for Spain by Magellan in 1521, the Philippines only now receive their first European colonists—and their modern name, in honor of King Philip II.

👑 **1566** Angered by restrictions on their rights over indigenous peoples, colonists in Mexico City conspire to break away from Spanish rule, but their plans are discovered.

☀ **1569** The Spanish introduce the Inquisition to America, setting up tribunals in Mexico City and Lima (–1571).

⚔ **1567** Philip II sends the Duke of Alba to Brussells to quell unrest in the Spanish Netherlands, but he succeeds only in sparking an all-out rebellion.

👑 **1567** In Scotland the Catholic Mary Queen of Scots is ousted by a confederacy of Protestant lords.

👑 **1569** The Union of Lublin unites Lithuania and Poland under the rule of the Polish King Sigismund II, bringing the enlarged nation into conflict with Russia.

⚔ **1569** Moriscos—Muslim Spaniards only nominally converted to Christianity—rise in revolt against Philip II's attempts to force them to abandon their language and culture.

The Escorial was built by Philip II of Spain as a palace–monastery and a burial place for Spanish kings.

⚔ **1569** The Ottoman Turks take Tunis on the North African coast.

⚔ **1567** The Zeydis, Shiite heretics in Yemen, take advantage of Selim's weakness to stage an uprising. They are put down but retain a presence in the mountains (–1568).

👑 **1568** Czar Ivan IV invites the shah of Persia to join Russia in an alliance against the Ottoman Turks; Pope Gregory XIII proposes that both countries participate in a "crusade."

⚔ **1565** In India the Hindu Vijayanagar Empire is overthrown by the Deccani Sultanates, a Muslim alliance that wins a crushing victory at the Battle of Talikota.

⚔ **1568** The Mughal Emperor Akbar destroys the Rajput stronghold of Chittor in Rajasthan after a siege; about 30,000 Rajputs are massacred.

⚔ **1569** The last great Rajput fortress, Rathambor, falls to Akbar.

⚔ **1565** Relentless raids by Sultan Hairun of Ternate, one of the Molucca Islands (eastern Indonesia), finally drive Christian missionaries out of the islands.

👑 **1568** The *daimyo* (warlord) Oda Nobunaga seizes control of the area around Kyoto in Japan, installing Ashikaga Yoshiaki as a puppet shogun in a first step toward the reunification of the country.

👑 **1569** Bayinnaung takes Ayutthaya for a second time, placing it under the rule of a loyal puppet prince, Maha Thammarcha, but in its weakened state Ayutthaya is vulnerable to a series of invasions by Cambodia.

IVAN THE TERRIBLE

▲ Shown here in a contemporary woodcut, Ivan was an energetic but unbalanced ruler who became infamous for his impulsive cruelty. Even as a child he had a reputation for torturing small animas and birds.

I**VAN IV VASILYEVICH WAS THE FIRST RUSSIAN** *ruler ever to give himself the title "czar," but history has always known him as "Ivan the Terrible." The name is no exaggeration: In the later years of his reign he was truly terrifying in the unpredictability of his murderous moods and the savage cruelty with which he acted toward his subjects. And yet, for better or for worse, he helped shape the destiny of modern Russia and did much to create the character of his country.*

The people of Novgorod could hardly believe what was happening. They were herded like frightened livestock into city squares. Buildings burned all around as men, women, and children in their thousands were impaled, eviscerated, flayed, or boiled alive. The nature of the "Novgorod Treason" of 1570 for which they were so savagely punished was never entirely clear: The czar may have feared that the northern city meant to secede to neighboring Lithuania, itself recently joined to Poland by the Union of Lublin. Some people, however, suspected that the affluence and sophistication of the prosperous trading center had simply affronted the dour and suspicious czar, who was known to explode into anger at the least provocation.

Born in 1533, Ivan Vasilyevich had begun his apprenticeship in violent intrigue early: He became grand duke of Muscovy at the age of three. Only five years later his mother, the regent, died—probably poisoned—leaving him an orphan to be manipulated by the different factions of boyars (nobles) at the Moscow court. But Ivan had his own ideas and at 13 ordered his first assassination. In 1547 he took power personally, becoming the first Russian ruler to adopt the title "czar" (from the Roman "Caesar"). His marriage to Anastasia Zakharina soon after seems to have stabilized his life to some extent, and he gave up the dissolute pleasures that had marked his youth.

Ivan's reign began promisingly. The young ruler showed a capacity for effective action when in 1552 he conquered the Mongol Khanate of Kazan. The next year, in the aftermath of English navigator Richard Chancellor's discovery of the White Sea route to Russia's north coast, he reopened trade with the West. He extended his kingdom again in 1556, taking the Khanate of Astrakhan and so opening the way to the Volga River, the Caspian Sea, the Caucasus Mountains, and ultimately Siberia. In 1558 he attacked the Germanic Livonian Knights, who restricted Russian access to the Baltic Sea, but this campaign would turn into a protracted war involving Sweden, northern Europe's leading power at the time.

After Anastasia's death in 1560 Ivan's suspicions spiraled out of control. Paranoia became the determining characteristic of his rule. He divided his kingdom into two, the *oprichnina* or area around Moscow, which was under his own control, and the *zemshchina*, which was supposedly run by a boyars' council. In practice Ivan's own 6,000-strong secret police force, the black-hooded *oprichniki*, roamed the *zemshchina* at will, terrorizing the population and

---

👑 **1533** Birth of Ivan Vasilyevich.

👑 **1536** Ivan's father, Vasily III, dies: Ivan becomes grand duke of Muscovy (Moscow) with his mother as regent.

👑 **1538** Ivan's mother is murdered.

👑 **1547** Ivan takes personal power, becoming the first Russian ruler to bear the title "czar."

⚔ **1552** Ivan's forces conquer the Mongol Khanate of Kazan.

✳ **1553** The English explorer Richard Chancellor opens up the trade route around the North Cape of Norway to Russia's White Sea.

👑 **1553** Ivan's infant son Dmitri drowns in a tragic accident.

St. Basil's Cathedral

Standing on the south side of Moscow's Red Square, St. Basil's Cathedral is one of the world's most famous buildings, instantly recognizable around the globe as a symbol of Russia. With its gaudy onion spires, its ornate facades, and its dark interior honeycombed with small chapels, it proclaims Russia's pride in its unique culture and spirituality. The building was planned as a monument to the conquests of Ivan the Terrible, whose relations with the Orthodox church were often strained; the czar resented the church's hold over Russia's peasantry even as he needed its help in shoring up his authority with the people. He needed church support, too, as a spiritual bulwark against the threat of Protestantism and all the political consequences it was having for the kingdoms to the west. Work on St. Basil's began in 1555, but the building was only finally completed in 1679.

▲ A contemporary book illustration shows Ivan's marriage to Anastasia Romanovna in 1547.

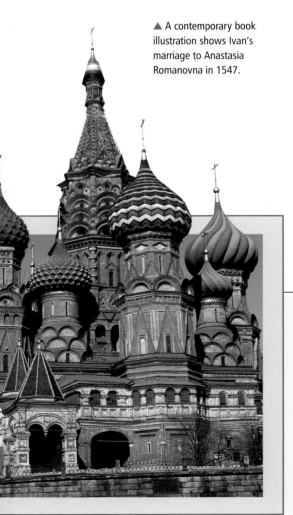

pulling in suspects for torture sessions in which Ivan himself sometimes took an eager part. No one was safe: The head of the Russian Orthodox Church was one victim of the terror; another was Ivan's cousin, Prince Vladimir Staritsky. In 1581, in a rage, the czar even murdered his own son, Ivan. He himself died in 1584, leaving behind a Russia that, although comparatively strong and coherent as a nation, was mired in economic backwardness and ruled by fear.

▼ For all the horrors of his reign, Ivan considerably expanded Russian power eastward, opening up new lands for settlement in the last decades of the 16th century.

☀ **1555** Construction of St. Basil's Cathedral, Moscow, begins.

✗ **1556** Ivan's forces conquer Astrakhan.

✗ **1558** Eager to gain access to the Baltic Sea, Ivan launches the first of a series of wars against Livonia that will stretch on for 25 years.

🜛 **1560** Ivan's wife Anastasia dies.

🜛 **1569** The Union of Lublin unites Lithuania with Poland.

✗ **1570** Ivan punishes the "Novgorod Treason" by launching a reign of terror in the city.

🜛 **1581** The czar murders his second son, Ivan.

🜛 **1584** Death of Ivan the Terrible. He is succeeded by his third son, Fyodor.

1570–1580 A.D.

AMERICAS

The *Popol Vuh*, some of whose characters are shown on this vase, is the main surviving Mayan literary work. It preserves the creation myths of the Quiché Maya, recounting the struggle of a monstrous bird deity known as Seven Macaw against two heroes, the twins Hunahpu and Xbalanque (seen here hunting waterfowl), in the time before the emergence of the first humans.

📖 **c.1570** The *Popol Vuh*, a compilation of Mayan myths, is written down in the Mayan language by scribes using the Roman alphabet.

EUROPE

⚔ **1571** An army of Crimean Tatars sacks Moscow.

⚔ **1571** A Christian fleet led by Don John of Austria defeats a large Ottoman fleet at the Battle of Lepanto, just off the coast of Greece.

⚔ **1572** The Dutch War of Independence gathers pace with a revolt against the Duke of Alba, the Spanish governor of the Netherlands (–1609).

☀ **1572** Over 2,500 leading Huguenots are slaughtered in Paris during the Massacre of St. Bartholomew's Day.

⊛ **1572** The Danish astronomer Tycho Brahe observes a supernova marking the birth of a new star (now known as Tycho's Star), disproving Aristotle's notion that the heavens are unchanging.

📖 **1572** The Portuguese poet Luis de Camoes publishes *The Lusiads*, Portugal's national epic.

AFRICA

👑 **1570** Under Idris III Aloma, the Saharan Kingdom of Kanem Bornu begins to expand its power.

⚔ **c.1572** The king of Kongo drives out the Jaga invaders who had laid waste to his country.

⊛ **1572** An epidemic in Algiers kills one third of the population.

WESTERN ASIA

⚔ **1570** The Ottoman Empire declares war on Venice and invades Cyprus.

👑 **1574** Murad III becomes Ottoman sultan.

👑 **1576** Shah Tahmasp I of Persia dies; his son succeeds him as Esmail II but reigns for less than a year.

SOUTH & CENTRAL ASIA

⚔ **1574** The Mughals conquer Gujarat, giving them access to the Indian Ocean.

☀ **1576** The first annual pilgrimage caravan sets out from India to the Muslim holy cities of Mecca and Medina, paid for and organized by the Mughal Emperor Akbar.

⚔ **1576** The Mughals conquer Bengal from the Afghans, extending their rule across the whole of northern India.

EAST ASIA & OCEANIA

⊛ **1570** The port of Nagasaki in Japan is opened to foreign trade.

⊛ **1571** The Spanish found Manila on the island of Luzon (Philippines).

👑 **1573** Oda Nobunaga drives the Ashikaga shogun out of Kyoto, ending the Ashikaga Shogunate.

👑 **1573** Accession of Wan-li as emperor of China; his reign is a time of great unrest.

This gilded copper statue represents Sonam Gyatso, the third Dalai Lama of Tibet.

AMERICAS

⊕ **c.1575** The Dominican friar Bernardino de Sahagún compiles an illustrated account of Aztec myths, history, and customs, based on firsthand accounts from native informants.

⊕ **1576** The English mariner Martin Frobisher explores the Labrador coast and Baffin Island, discovering and naming Frobisher Bay (–1578).

⊕ **1578** English seaman Francis Drake raids Spanish bullion ships off the Pacific coast of South and Central America.

⊕ **1579** Drake claims land near modern San Francisco and names it New Albion.

EUROPE

👑 **1574** Henry III becomes king of France on the death of his brother, Charles IX.

📖 **1575** The Greek painter Domenikos Theotokopoulos settles in Toledo, Spain, where he achieves fame as El Greco ("the Greek").

✕ **1576** In response to the Dutch revolt Spanish troops sack the city of Antwerp in the Netherlands, killing 7,000 people.

The victory of a Christian fleet over the Ottoman navy at the Battle of Lepanto revived Western morale after a string of defeats.

👑 **1576** Rudolf II of Hungary becomes Holy Roman emperor; his court at Prague is a center for writers, artists, and humanist scholars.

📖 **1577** Death of the Venetian-born painter Titian, court painter to Charles V and Philip II of Spain and the greatest artist of the late Renaissance.

👑 **1579** The seven rebel provinces of the Netherlands form the Union of Utrecht under the leadership of William the Silent.

AFRICA

👑 **1574** The Ottomans fight off an attempt by Christian forces to retake Tunis.

⊕ **1575** The Portuguese found a base at Luanda in Angola that becomes a center of the slave trade.

✕ **1578** The Moroccans defeat and kill King Sebastian I of Portugal at the Battle of Kasr al-Kabir.

WESTERN ASIA

✕ **1578** Murad III launches a war against Safavid Persia.

SOUTH & CENTRAL ASIA

Amritsar in the Punjab region of northern India was founded as a holy city by Ram Das, fourth guru (spiritual leader) of the Sikh faith, around a sacred pool, the Amrita Saras. Its most famous building, the Golden Temple, stands on an island in the lake. It owes its name to a covering of gold leaf added in the early 19th century.

☀ **1577** Amritsar is founded as a holy city of the Sikhs in the Punjab.

👑 **1579** Akbar abolishes the *jiziya*, an annual property tax levied on non-Muslim subjects.

EAST ASIA & OCEANIA

⊕ **1575** A Spanish expedition from Manila visits Canton, South China, in an attempt to gain trading privileges.

⊕ **1576** Oda Nobunaga constructs a mighty fortress at Azuchi, initiating a period of castle building in Japan.

☀ **c.1577** Altan Khan, ruler of the Tumed Mongols, adopts Buddhism and recognizes the spiritual authority of the Tibetan monk Sonam Gyatso, giving him the name of Dalai Lama ("Ocean of Wisdom"). Sonam is taken as the third incarnation of the Dalai Lama.

✕ **1577** Hideyoshi, Oda Nobunaga's general, begins the conquest of western Japan.

⊕ **1578** Chinese scholar Li Shih-Shen completes the *Great Pharmacopoeia*, in which he describes more than 2,000 drugs.

1570–1580 A.D.

239

INDIA'S MUGHAL EMPIRE

▲ The splendor of the Mughal emperors was captured in the works of a brilliant school of miniature painters. Here Humayun is shown holding a falcon.

THE MUGHAL DYNASTY RULED *most of India and Pakistan for more than 200 years. Theirs was one of three great Muslim empires that dominated western and southern Asia at this time, the others being the Ottoman Empire in West Asia and the Safavid Empire in Persia. The Mughals are remembered today for their rich legacy of Islamic art and architecture as well as for their administrative efficiency and stable government, which united Muslims and Hindus in a single state.*

The founder of the Mughal Dynasty was Babur, who claimed descent fromTimur and Genghis Khan, the great Mongol leaders of the past—Mughal (sometimes spelled Mogul) is the Arabic form of Mongol. Babur was the hereditary prince of Ferghana in Central Asia but was driven out of his lands by the Uzbeks. Inspired as a boy by tales of the deeds of his ancestors, he sought adventure and conquest on the battlefield and by 1504 had made himself ruler of Kabul in Afghanistan. From there he turned his attention to India. In 1526 Babur swept down into the Ganges Plain at the head of an army of 12,000 men. His soldiers, equipped with cannons and firearms, defeated the last sultan of Delhi at the Battle of Panipat, and by the time of his death in 1530 Babur had conquered most of northern India.

Babur's empire was all but lost during the reign of his son Humayun. Afghan rebels took over most of the Mughal territory in northern India, and Humayun himself was forced into exile for a time. It was Babur's grandson Akbar (reigned 1555–1605) who established the true greatness of the Mughal Empire. He was almost constantly at war and not only won back Babur's empire but also extended Mughal rule across the whole of northern India and into the Deccan Plateau. Although he did not hesitate to punish his enemies with brutal force when necessary, Akbar gave the Mughal Empire stability and a strong system of government by pursuing tolerant policies toward his Hindu subjects. He married the daughter of the Hindu ruler of Amber and, although he never renounced Islam, encouraged debate with other religions and even celebrated some of the major Hindu festivals at his court.

There were three more outstanding Mughal emperors after Akbar. Under Jahangir's tolerant rule

Mughal Architecture

The Mughals were descended from the nomadic Mongol rulers of Central Asia, whose courts were movable tented cities, complete with palaces and bazaars. The Mughal court, which was also the administrative capital of the empire, rarely remained in one place for long, regularly shifting between Agra and Delhi. The Mughal emperors were prolific builders and endowed their capitals with edifices in brick, marble, and stone. In 1570 Akbar took the unusual step of constructing a new capital from scratch. He named it Fatehpur Sikri ("City of Victory") but occupied it for less than 15 years before moving the capital to Lahore to cope with unrest in neighboring Afghanistan. Never reoccupied, Fatehpur Sikri today contains some of the finest examples of Islamic architecture in India, especially the Jami Mosque and the Diwan-i Khass, or audience hall, which lay at the heart of Akbar's palace complex.

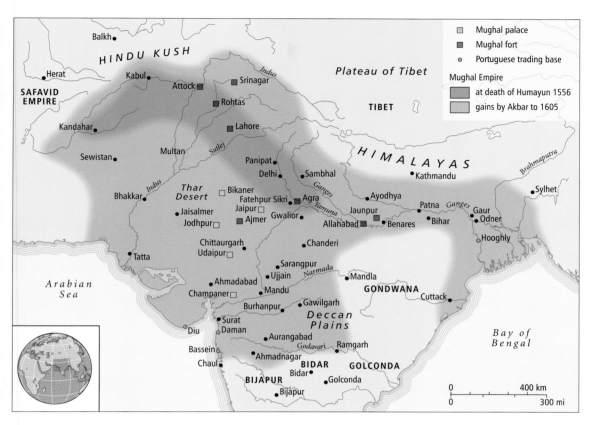

◀ The Mughal Empire in India was founded by Babur and partly lost by his heir Humayun. Its third ruler, Akbar, carried Mughal power across the subcontinent to the east coast and southward through land contolled by the various Rajput dynasties onto the central plateau known as the Deccan. In the 17th century Aurangzeb would extend its boundaries even farther into the deep south.

from 1605 to 1627 Mughal arts flourished, and miniature painting reached rare heights. In the reign of the next emperor, Shah Jahan (1628–58), the influence of Islam grew much stronger. The empire reached its greatest extent under Aurangzeb (1658–1707); but although it remained outwardly strong and prosperous, Aurangzeb's increasingly harsh treatment of Hindus caused rebellions in many parts of the country. Mughal power weakened rapidly after his death, and the empire began to break up. By 1748 the Mughals ruled only the area around Delhi, and in 1857 they passed out of history.

🌊 **1483** Birth of Babur in Ferghana, Central Asia.

🌊 **1504** Babur takes possession of Kabul, Afghanistan.

✕ **1526** Babur defeats Sultan Ibrahim Lodi at the Battle of Panipat, north of Delhi, and founds the Mughal Empire.

🌊 **1530** Death of Babur; he is succeeded by Humayun.

🌊 **1540** Humayun loses northern India to Afghan rebels and goes into exile in Persia.

🌊 **1555** Humayun recaptures Delhi; he dies soon after and is succeeded by his son Akbar, aged 13.

✕ **1556** Akbar's army defeats Hemu, a Hindu usurper, at the second Battle of Panipat.

✕ **1568** Akbar captures the Rajput fortress of Chittor, which is holding out against him, and massacres all its inhabitants.

🌊 **1570** Akbar builds and occupies a new capital at Fatehpur Sikri (–1584).

☀ **1580** Three Jesuit priests from Goa visit Fatehpur Sikri at Akbar's invitation to debate religion with him.

🌊 **1605** Akbar dies: Salim, Akbar's son, becomes emperor, taking the name of Jahangir.

📖 **1618** Abu'l Hasan, the greatest of the Mughal miniature painters, is given the title of *Nadiru-zaman* ("Wonder of the Age") by Jahangir.

🌊 **1627** On the death of Jahangir his son Khurram murders his brothers and nephews to ensure his succession as emperor (in 1628); he rules as Shah Jahan.

📖 **1638** Shah Jahan builds India's best-known building, the Taj Mahal, as a memorial to his wife, Mumtaz Mahal.

🌊 **1658** Aurangzeb, the last of the great Moghul emperors, comes to the throne; he will reign to 1707.

1580–1590 A.D.

AMERICAS

1583 Sir Humphrey Gilbert founds the first English colony in North America at what is now St. John's, Newfoundland.

1584 Walter Raleigh founds an English colony on Roanoke Island off the coast of Virginia, but it is quickly abandoned (–1585).

The scant remains of an earthen fort are all that survives of the colony on Roanoke Island.

1585 English navigator John Davis undertakes three Arctic voyages in search of the northwest passage; the Davis Strait between Greenland and Baffin Island is named for him (–1587).

EUROPE

1580 After defeating a Portuguese army at the Battle of Alcantara, Philip II of Spain claims the throne of Portugal.

1582 The Gregorian calendar, introduced by Pope Gregory XIII for whom it is named, replaces the Julian calendar. The new calendar is accepted at once by most Catholic countries but only gradually by Protestant ones.

1584 The port of Archangel is founded on the White Sea, giving Russia limited access to the ocean. (It is only open in the summer months since it lies within the Arctic Circle).

AFRICA

c.1580 Idris III Aloma buys firearms from the Ottoman Empire to strengthen his hold over the trade routes of the eastern Sahara.

1581 The Moroccans under Ahmed al-Mansur of the Sharifian Dynasty occupy Tuat in the northern Sahara.

c.1585 The Portuguese wage a series of military campaigns against local rulers in Angola and force them to accept their rule in return for a share in the slave trade.

WESTERN ASIA

c.1580 The Ottomans' *devshirme* system of recruiting Christian boys for the Janissaries, the sultan's crack troops, goes into decline under Murad III.

1582 Murad III, who is known for his love of display, gives a festival in Istanbul to celebrate his son's circumcision, with banquets and mock battles; it lasts for 55 days.

1583 The Ottomans take the city of Baku on the west coast of the Caspian Sea from the Safavid rulers of Persia.

SOUTH & CENTRAL ASIA

c. 1580 The Mughal Emperor Akbar brings together Hindu and Persian scholars to translate the Hindu religious epic, the *Mahabharata*, into Persian.

1582 Akbar sets out the Din-I Ilahi (Divine Faith); it incorporates ideas from other Asian religions, including Jainism and Hinduism, as well as Islam.

EAST ASIA & OCEANIA

1582 In Japan Oda Nobunaga is assassinated, and his general Hideyoshi seizes power.

1582 Ming Emperor Wan-li refuses to conduct court business, and power passes into the hands of the royal eunuchs.

Hideyoshi (1536–1598) was the only man of peasant birth to rule Japan. Rising through the ranks in the service of Oda Nobunaga, he staged a coup on Nobunaga's death, having himself made *kanpaku* (civil regent) by the emperor. He then forced the *daimyo* (feudal lords) into line and disarmed the peasants. In his later years he staged a futile attempt to conquer Korea that cost many lives and almost bankrupted the state.

Seen in a 17th-century map, Roanoke Island off the North Carolina coast was the site of the first English colony in the future United States, promoted by the explorer Walter Raleigh. The first attempt, in 1584, failed, with the survivors returning to England. The second three years later simply vanished; no trace of the colonists could be found when help finally came in 1591.

⊛ **1585** The first recorded commercial shipment of chocolate is sent from Veracruz, Mexico, to Spain.

⊛ **1587** Governor John White lands a party of 117 settlers on Roanoke Island in a second attempt to found a colony there.

AMERICAS

👑 **1584** Boris Godunov, a nobleman of nonroyal birth, becomes virtual ruler of Russia on the death of Ivan IV and the succession of his feeble son Fyodor.

👑 **1584** Death of William the Silent, leader of the Dutch revolt against Spain.

👑 **1589** Henry of Navarre, a Protestant, becomes the first of the Bourbon kings of France as King Henry IV.

⚔ **1589** Philip II of Spain declares war on France in support of the Catholics opposed to Henry IV.

EUROPE

⊛ **1588** The English Guinea Company is founded to trade with West Africa.

AFRICA

👑 **1588** Abbas I becomes shah of Persia; he will become the greatest of the Safavid rulers, famed for his patronage of the arts, especially miniature painting.

A miniature painting shows young noblemen serving food and drink to Persia's Shah Abbas.

WESTERN ASIA

👑 **1585** Akbar moves his capital to Lahore in Punjab.

📖 **1589** The *Memoirs* of the first Mughal emperor, Babur, are translated into Persian. Lavishly illustrated, they help promote the imperial image of the Mughal Dynasty.

SOUTH & CENTRAL ASIA

☀ **1583** The Jesuit priest Father Matteo Ricci arrives in Macao as the first Christian missionary to China.

👑 **1583** As a sign of his supremacy over central Japan, Hideyoshi begins to construct a great castle at Osaka.

👑 **1585** The Sultan of Aceh (Indonesia) sends a diplomatic letter to England's Queen Elizabeth.

👑 **1587** Hideyoshi orders the expulsion of Jesuit missionaries from Japan and takes control of the port of Nagasaki.

👑 **1587** Hideyoshi demonstrates his power over the Japanese court by hosting a lavish 10-day tea ceremony attended by Emperor Go-Yozei.

EAST ASIA & OCEANIA

1580–1590 A.D.

243

ELIZABETH'S ENGLAND

▲ Queen Elizabeth watched over her public image as carefully as any modern politician. This portrait of the ruler in all her finery was painted by Nicholas Hilliard in 1575, when she was 42 years of age.

*L*ATER GENERATIONS LOOKED BACK *on the reign of England's Queen Elizabeth I as a golden age, the time of "Merrie England." To her subjects she was "Good Queen Bess." During her long reign of nearly 50 years England was transformed from a divided country troubled by religious strife to one of comparative peace, stability, and prosperity, an outcome that owed much to Elizabeth's determination and strength of character.*

Born in 1533, Elizabeth was the daughter of King Henry VIII and his second wife, Anne Boleyn. Henry already had a daughter, Mary, by his first wife, Catherine of Aragon, but he desperately wanted a son. In order to divorce Catherine and marry Anne, Henry split with the Roman Catholic church and declared himself head of the newly created Church of England, displacing the pope. But Anne's failure to produce a son led to her downfall, and less than three years after Elizabeth's birth she was executed on the king's orders. Although the young princess rarely saw her father after that, she received the education usually reserved for the male heirs of Renaissance monarchs and was instructed in Greek, Latin, history, philosophy, and theology as well as French and Italian. She proved an intelligent and eager scholar.

Henry died in 1547 and was succeeded by his 10-year-old son Edward VI, the son of his third wife, Jane Seymour. Although young, Edward held strong

William Shakespeare

William Shakespeare, the greatest writer of the Elizabethan age, was born in 1564 in the small country town of Stratford-on-Avon. By the early 1590s he was living in London, where he became a member of the Lord Chamberlain's Men, a company of actors paid for by Queen Elizabeth. He soon found fame as the author of a stream of plays—comedies, histories, romances, and tragedies—that won him popular acclaim and favor at court. His use of language was unsurpassed, and his words, expressions, and characters have entered the English language and imagination. He died in Stratford in 1616.

◀ Elizabeth's onetime brother-in-law, Philip II of Spain, sent an armada (fleet) of 130 ships to invade her kingdom in 1588. The boats headed for the Spanish Netherlands, planning to take on extra troops, but their formation was wrecked by English fireships. Cutting anchor, the boats were swept north by a storm that completed the havoc the English warships had begun. Barely half the fleet eventually made its way back to Spain.

Protestant views, and the Reformation flourished in England. But when Edward died suddenly at the age of 16, his eldest half-sister, Mary, a devout Roman Catholic, became queen. Determined that England should become Catholic again, Mary had many Protestants burned at the stake. These were unhappy years for Elizabeth; and when she found herself queen on the death of Mary in 1558, she was already well skilled in the arts of political survival.

Her harsh early lessons in life served Elizabeth well. From the beginning she ruled wisely and strongly, kept her own counsel, chose her advisers carefully, and maintained good relations with Parliament. One of her first moves was to restore Protestantism in England, but she baulked at the extreme measures employed both by her brother Edward and by Mary to force religious change on her subjects, believing that England needed a period of stability and calm to recover from the religious and political upheavals of the recent past.

Many people thought it unnatural for a woman to rule over men, but Elizabeth did not consider herself inferior to any man, nor, as queen, would she submit to any man's authority. She never married but instead built up a strong personal cult, surrounding herself with courtiers, poets, and painters who celebrated her image as the Virgin Queen. Her reign was a time of expansion for England: Sir Francis Drake, Sir John Hawkins, and Sir Walter Raleigh, among other English adventurers, helped make the country rich through exploration, trade, and plunder. Their exploits overseas, especially against the power of Spain, added to the newfound sense of national pride that Elizabeth's long reign helped forge.

▲ The naval battles against the Armada in 1588 all took place along England's south coast. Thereafter storms swept the remnants of the Spanish fleet around Scotland and Ireland.

🎖 **1533** Elizabeth is born at Greenwich Palace, near London.

🎖 **1536** Elizabeth's mother, Anne Boleyn, is executed on charges of treason and adultery.

🎖 **1549** Thomas Seymour, lord high admiral of England and Elizabeth's guardian, is accused of plotting to marry Elizabeth and beheaded for treason.

🎖 **1554** Queen Mary suspects Elizabeth of treason and holds her prisoner.

🎖 **1558** On the death of Mary Elizabeth is crowned queen of England.

☀ **1559** Parliament declares Elizabeth supreme governor of the Church of England and restores the use of the English Prayer Book.

⊕ **1562** Elizabeth nearly dies of smallpox.

⚔ **1585** Elizabeth sends an army led by the earl of Leicester to the Netherlands to support the Protestant revolt against Spain.

🎖 **1587** Mary, queen of Scots, Elizabeth's cousin and an exile in England, is found guilty of plotting to murder Queen Elizabeth and is executed.

⚔ **1588** King Philip II of Spain sends the Armada, a fleet of 130 warships, to invade England.

📖 **1590** Edmund Spenser publishes the first three books of *The Faerie Queene*, a narrative poem written in celebration of Queen Elizabeth.

📖 **1598** The Globe Theater in London opens with a performance of William Shakespeare's *Henry V*.

🎖 **1601** Robert Devereux, earl of Essex, the queen's former favorite, leads a rebellion against her; he is executed for treason.

🎖 **1603** Elizabeth dies and is succeeded by James VI of Scotland, son of Mary, queen of Scots.

AMERICAS

1591 John White, governor of Roanoke Island, returns with supplies for the struggling colony but finds it abandoned.

1595 The English courtier and adventurer Walter Raleigh explores the coast of Trinidad and sails up the Orinoco River.

1595 The English buccaneer Francis Drake tries unsuccessfully to sack Panama, the commercial heart of Spain's overseas empire.

EUROPE

c.1590 John Harington, a courtier to Queen Elizabeth, invents the flush toilet and installs one in her palace at Richmond.

1592 Sigismund, king of Poland since 1587, succeeds his brother John III as king of Sweden; his attempts to restore Catholicism lead to a rebellion, and he is deposed (–1599).

1593 Henry IV brings the French wars of religion to an end by renouncing his Protestant faith and winning the acceptance of his Catholic subjects (–1598).

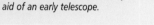

An astronomer searches the sky with the aid of an early telescope.

1594 Hugh O'Neill, earl of Tyrone, leads a rebellion in Ireland against English rule.

c.1595 The telescope is invented in the Netherlands.

1596 The Spanish crown is bankrupt, and the country's population falls as a result of several years of famine and plague.

1598 Henry IV signs the Edict of Nantes, guaranteeing religious toleration in France.

AFRICA

1590 The Moroccans mount a military expedition across the Sahara to overthrow the once-powerful Songhai Empire, now in decline (–1591).

1593 The Portuguese build Fort Jesus just outside Mombasa on Africa's east coast and sack the long-established Islamic trading port.

WESTERN ASIA

1590 The Ottoman and Safavid empires make peace, fixing their frontier at the Caspian Sea.

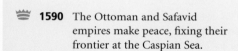

Shah Nematollah's Tomb, Mahan, Iran, built on the orders of Shah Abbas.

SOUTH & CENTRAL ASIA

1591 The sultan of Golconda, one of the principal Muslim rulers of India's Deccan Plateau, founds a new city at Hyderabad on the Musi River in what is now Andhra Pradesh.

1595 Emperor Akbar's forces capture Kandahar, bringing Afghanistan under Mughal control.

1598 With the northwest pacified, Akbar moves his capital to Agra.

EAST ASIA & OCEANIA

1591 Hideyoshi conquers the northern part of Honshu Island, effectively reuniting Japan.

1592 Hideyoshi invades Korea with the ultimate aim of attacking China, but the strength of the Korean navy forces him to retreat.

1592 The Ming court sends military aid to Korea.

1592 Wu Che'eng-en publishes *Monkey*, a classic Chinese novel.

1595 Matteo Ricci adopts the dress of a Confucian scholar and makes a first unsuccessful attempt to enter the Imperial City in Beijing; he then settles in Nanking.

1595 Cornelis Houtman leads the first Dutch trading expedition to the Spice Islands (Indonesia).

1596 The Japanese invade Korea for a second time, but an organized defense by combined Chinese and Korean forces halts their advance.

1597 Houtman's expedition visits Bali before returning home.

⊛ **1598** The Marquis de la Roche founds a short-lived French colony on Sable Island, off the coast of Nova Scotia (–1603).

⊛ **1598** Spanish settlers prospecting for precious metals occupy San Juan Pueblo in the Rio Grande Valley of what is now New Mexico.

AMERICAS

A favorite of Ivan the Terrible, Boris Godunov served on his death as regent for the czar's young heir Fyodor. As the true ruler of Russia at this time, he provided capable leadership, winning back land earlier lost to Sweden and encouraging the colonization of Siberia. When Fyodor died in 1598 without leaving an heir, Boris was chosen by a popular assembly to be czar. In contrast to the success of the regency, his short reign was beset by unrest, caused largely by a devastating three-year famine. Usurpers arose to challenge the legitimacy of his rule, and on his death in 1605 the nation was plunged into ten years of anarchy, the Time of Troubles.

👑 **1598** Boris Godunov is elected czar of Russia on the death of Fyodor.

✕ **1598** With the Treaty of Vervins Philip II of Spain ends the war with France.

👑 **1598** Death of Philip II; he is succeeded by his son Philip III.

EUROPE

👑 **1594** The Portuguese have by now established control over most of coastal Angola but are unable to penetrate far into the interior because of disease.

⊛ **1596** Dutch traders are present in Guinea on the West African coast.

⊛ **1596** The Dutch establish a trading base on the island of Mauritius in the Indian Ocean.

AFRICA

👑 **1595** On becoming Ottoman sultan, Mehmed III murders 20 of his younger brothers to prevent them setting up as rivals for his throne.

📖 **1597** Shah Abbas of Persia moves the Safavid capital to Esfahan, where he builds a new city adorned with many fine buildings.

✕ **1597** The Safavids win a major victory over the Uzbeks, halting their incursions into Khurasan in northeast Persia.

WESTERN ASIA

☀ **1599** The Portuguese archbishop of Goa calls a synod at Diamper at which the Syrian Church of Kerala (in southern India) is formally united with the Roman Catholic church.

SOUTH & CENTRAL ASIA

👑 **1598** Hideyoshi dies suddenly, and the invasion of Korea is abandoned; many Korean craftsmen are forcibly transported to Japan.

Cornelis Houtman's fleet returns to Amsterdam, as shown in a 17th-century Dutch painting.

EAST ASIA & OCEANIA

1590–1600 A.D.

THE GUNPOWDER REVOLUTION

▲ An Italian engraving shows a metalworker casting a section of a cannon in a forge. Heavy artillery was costly to produce, making it difficult for the private forces of individual nobles to compete against the armies of the state.

BY THE END OF THE 16TH CENTURY *the gunpowder revolution had finally come of age. By that time armies in Europe and Asia had been using gunpowder-fired weapons for nearly 300 years, and guns, which had at first been little more than military curiosities, had become the main battlefield weapon, transforming the way that war was waged. But the gunpowder revolution altered more than just the face of combat. It stimulated closer study of chemistry, mathematics, and mechanics, and brought about important advances in metal casting, so paving the way for the development of modern science. Unexpectedly, it also increased the power of the state.*

Gunpowder is a mixture of potassium nitrate (saltpeter), charcoal, and sulfur. When lit, it explodes with enough force to propel a missile along a barrel or tube. The Chinese knew about the explosive properties of gunpowder as early as the 1st century A.D. At first they seem to have used it only to set off firecrackers at religious ceremonies, but by the 10th century they were employing it on the battlefield to shoot fire-arrows down bamboo tubes. News of this startling technology reached Europe early in the 13th century, after Chinese troops used gunpowder-fired rockets in their wars against the Mongols.

It was in Europe that the first cannons were developed. Short tubes of bronze or iron firing stone balls, they proved useful in siege warfare. However, they often exploded while being fired, killing the

gunners, and it is doubtful how much damage they actually caused, although the noise and smoke of the explosion must have terrified the enemy.

Over the next two centuries weapon technology and design steadily improved. Metalworkers developed alloys of bronze and iron capable of withstanding the shock of the explosion. Trunnions (lugs) were fixed to the barrel so that the gunners could adjust the angle of fire. Cannons became steadily smaller and lighter, while the addition of

- ✲ **1232** First recorded use of gunpowder-fired rockets by the Chinese against a Mongol army.

- ✲ **1248** An Oxford scholar, Roger Bacon, makes the first-known reference to gunpowder in Europe.

- ✕ **1331** Cannons are used at the siege of Cividale, Italy.

- ✲ **1376** Reference is made to a cannon foundry at Venice.

- ✕ **1389** The Turks use cannons at the siege of Kosovo.

- ✲ **1411** First-known manuscript illustration of a matchlock trigger mechanism.

- ✕ **1420** Small artillery pieces and handguns are used during the Hussite Wars in the Czech lands (–1433).

- ✕ **1449** Mons Meg, a giant iron bombard (cannon), is made for Philip the Good, duke of Burgundy.

- ✕ **1450** The French use two culverins—long-barreled cannons—against English longbowmen at the Battle of Formigny.

- ✕ **1454** The French develop the two-wheeled gun carriage.

- ✕ **c.1525** By this time the shoulder stock is in use on small arms.

▶ A book illustration dated to 1512 shows various models of harquebus, the predecessor of the musket. At first it took two people to fire the gun—one to hold and aim it and another to light the fuse, as shown here. Later, the invention of the matchlock—a pivoting fuse that could be lowered with a flick of the thumb to ignite the charge of gunpowder—made it possible for a single person to aim and fire. In the early days supports were often used to steady the gun and bear the weight of the long barrel.

wheeled carriages gave them greater mobility. Finally, more efficient mixtures of gunpowder were found.

By the middle of the 15th century the first small arms were appearing on the battlefield. At first, one gunner held a small hand cannon fastened to a simple wooden stock braced against his arm, while a second person fired it. Then a pivoting firing mechanism called a matchlock was attached to the stock, making it possible for a single person to aim and fire the gun by squeezing a trigger. Arms of this sort were first developed in Germany and were called harquebuses. Their use spread rapidly throughout Europe and the Ottoman Empire. By the 16th century harquebuses had developed into muskets, comparatively accurate weapons that could kill a man at 300 paces. At the same time, powerful cannons had been place on board ships, transforming naval warfare.

One unexpected consequence of the revolution was to increase the power of rulers. Producing field artillery and arming infantry regiments with muskets were too expensive for even great lords to afford, so private armies fell into disuse. By the end of the 16th century guns and gunpowder were made under royal license, and armies and arsenals were maintained at the expense of the government. Large-scale warfare had become the monopoly of the state.

The End of the Castle Era

One of the main results of the spread of guns was the decline of the medieval castle. The fall of Constantinople to the bombardment of Ottoman siege artillery in 1453 showed that high stone walls and tall flanking towers were no defense against siege cannons. To counter the threat, military engineers were soon experimenting with new ways of constructing fortifications. As at England's Deal Castle (left), walls and towers were sunk behind a ditch and faced with a stone parapet. Beyond the ditch a sloping earthen bank, or glacis, exposed the attackers to cannon and harquebus fire from the parapet, while also serving to bounce incoming cannonballs harmlessly over the defenders on the walls. Rounded or pointed bastions projected out into the ditch to provide gun platforms to give flanking fire. The first bastioned fortresses of this kind were built in northern Italy to designs drawn up by artist–engineers such as Leonardo da Vinci and Francesco di Giorgio.

✗ **1527** Venetian galleys are equipped with lidded gunports.

⊕ **1537** Ligatures (stitches) are first used to treat gunshot wounds.

⊕ **1543** The English perfect an improved method for casting iron cannons.

✗ **c.1550** The musket replaces the crossbow as the main battlefield weapon (other than swords) in Europe.

✗ **1588** The Armada sees the first artillery battle between massed warships at sea.

AMERICAS

1602 Sebastian Vizcaino sails from Acapulco, Mexico, along the coast of California but fails to discover San Francisco Bay.

1606 The Plymouth Company is founded in London with the object of establishing colonies in North America; two unsuccessful expeditions are sent this year.

1607 Captain John Smith founds the Jamestown colony at the mouth of the James River in Virginia.

1608 French explorer Samuel de Champlain founds a colony at Quebec.

EUROPE

1600 Italian scientist and one-time friar Giordano Bruno is burned at the stake in Rome for his heretical views concerning the nature of the universe.

1603 On the death of Queen Elizabeth I, James VI of Scotland becomes King James I of England, uniting the two kingdoms.

In a time of religious tension in England the Gunpowder Plot was the most lethal threat to the nation's ruling class. In 1605 a small group of Catholics (right) conspired to blow up the Houses of Parliament while the Protestant King James I of England was there. Assigned to ignite the gunpowder, Guido, or Guy, Fawkes was arrested just before he did so. His effigy is still burned on Bonfire Night each November 5.

AFRICA

c. 1600 The empire of Mwene Mutapa—the successor state of Great Zimbabwe in southeastern Africa—is at its greatest extent.

c.1605 The Kingdom of Luba is by now beginning to emerge as an economic and political power in central Africa.

Wooden figurine by the Luba people of central Africa.

WESTERN ASIA

1602 Shah Abbas of Persia begins a campaign to win back the Safavid lands in Iraq from the Ottoman Empire.

1603 Ahmed I becomes Ottoman sultan.

1606 The Ottomans sign the treaty of Zsitvatörök with Austria, in which they are forced to recognize the Hapsburg emperor as an equal and grant trading concessions to Europeans.

SOUTH & CENTRAL ASIA

1601 Salim, son of the Mughal Emperor Akbar, rebels against his father but is later restored to favor (–1604).

1605 Akbar dies and is succeeded as emperor by Salim, who takes the title of Jahangir.

1605 Jahangir orders the execution of the fifth Sikh guru, Arjun, for his part in supporting a rebellion led by Prince Khusrau, Jahangir's son.

EAST ASIA & OCEANIA

1600 In Myanmar (Burma) the state of Pegu collapses, and the country fragments into a number of small states.

1600 After winning the Battle of Sekigahara, Ieyasu of the Tokugawa clan becomes the virtual ruler of Japan.

1602 An English trading station is established at Bantam in Java (Indonesia).

AMERICAS

⚙ **1609** Henry Hudson enters New York Bay and sails up the river that will later be named for him as far as the future site of Albany.

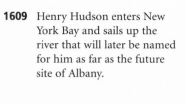

Shown in this fanciful illustration leading an attack on a fortified Iroquois village, Samuel de Champlain did more than anyone else to establish a French presence in North America. He led pioneering expeditions up the St. Lawrence River, founded Quebec, and ended his life as governor of New France, the colony set up in the lands he had explored.

EUROPE

⚔ **1604** The "Time of Troubles," a period of civil war in Russia, begins when a pretender, Dmitry, claims to be czar and wins widespread support from the Cossacks.

🏛 **1604** In Hungary an alliance between Protestants and an Ottoman army led by Istvan Bocskay forces the Hapsburgs to withdraw from Transylvania.

📖 **1605** In Spain Miguel de Cervantes publishes the first book of his masterpiece *Don Quixote*.

🏛 **1605** In England conspirators attempt to blow up the Houses of Parliament, but their Gunpowder Plot is discovered.

⚔ **1609** The United Provinces of the Netherlands agree on a 12-year truce with Spain.

🏛 **1609** Sweden gains Karelia (part of modern Finland) in return for supporting Boris, the new czar, in the civil war in Russia.

⚙ **1609** German astronomer Johannes Kepler publishes his first two laws of planetary motion, which show that the planets travel in elliptical paths around the sun.

☀ **1609** King Philip III orders the expulsion of the Moriscos (Christianized descendants of the Arabs) from Spain, an act of ethnic cleansing that sees more than 300,000 people forcibly deported in the next five years.

AFRICA

🏛 **c.1605** A dynasty of rulers, probably immigrants from East Africa, establishes a Merina state in the central highlands of Madagascar.

🏛 **1605** Rebels kill the Ottoman governor of Egypt.

WESTERN ASIA

📖 **1609** Construction begins on the Mosque of Ahmed I (more often known as the Blue Mosque) in Istanbul.

The Blue Mosque was the last of Istanbul's great imperial mosques to be built.

SOUTH & CENTRAL ASIA

🏛 **1606** Jahangir has Khusrau blinded and many of his followers killed.

⚙ **1608** English envoys land at Surat on India's east coast, seeking to negotiate trading rights.

EAST ASIA & OCEANIA

🏛 **1603** Ieyasu is formally appointed shogun (military ruler); his stronghold Edo (modern Tokyo) becomes the center of power in Japan.

⚔ **1605** The Dutch seize the Indonesian island of Amboina from the Portuguese; it will become the center of the spice trade to Europe.

1600–1610 A.D.

PERSIA'S GREAT SHAH

ABBAS I WAS THE MOST EFFECTIVE RULER OF PERSIA *since ancient times. He restored the fortunes of the Safavid Dynasty when they had fallen to a low ebb and secured the country's frontiers against the Ottomans and Uzbeks. He revived trade and encouraged merchants, craftsmen, and artists to settle in his new capital of Esfahan, which he transformed into one of the largest and most beautiful cities in the world.*

▲ Persia's Safavid Dynasty owed its hold on power to Turkmen warriors like this one.

▼ A fresco from a palace ceiling shows Shah Abbas receiving foreign envoys.

The Safavids were Sufis, members of an Islamic mystic order based at Ardabil, west of the Caspian Sea. The traditional leaders of the Turkmen tribes in this northwest corner of Persia, they embraced military conquest as a means of spreading the Shia branch of Islam to which they and their followers belonged. By 1502 Esmail I, the head of the order, was strong enough to declare himself shah (ruler) of Persia and to embark on a campaign of conquest. A great variety of peoples inhabited Persia at the time—Kurds, Armenians, and Arabs, as well as Turkmens and Persians—and Esmail I made Shiism the state religion as a means of imposing his authority on them.

The Ottoman rulers to the west of Persia and the Uzbeks to the northeast belonged to the Sunni branch of Islam, and Esmail's successors faced continual harassment from both of them. By the time that Abbas I came to the throne in 1588, the Safavids had lost considerable territory, and their authority was further weakened by intertribal factions and jealousy.

Abbas realized that he could not fight on two fronts at once. In 1590 he signed an unfavorable peace treaty with the Ottomans in order to leave himself free to deal with the Uzbeks. At the same time, he set about creating a strong, permanent army recruited mainly from non-Muslim Georgians, Armenians, and Circassians. Called *ghulums* ("slaves"), they converted to Islam and were then trained for the army or the royal administration like the janissaries, their equivalents in the Ottoman Empire. Abbas preferred the *ghulums* for high office over local tribal leaders whose loyalty was unreliable.

Esfahan, Abbas's capital

In 1597, soon after his defeat of the Uzbeks, Abbas decided to move his capital from Qazvin, which was dangerously close to the Ottoman war zone, to the small town of Esfahan in central Persia. Esfahan had briefly served as the nation's capital in the 11th and 12th centuries but had subsequently fallen into decline. Now the shah determined to rebuild it on a scale fitting his political ambitions. Over the next two decades he endowed it with stately, tree-lined avenues, ornamental fountains, palaces, bazaars, public buildings, and gardens. Visitors to the city marveled at its 162 mosques, 48 colleges, and 273 public baths. At its center was an immense open space, the Maidan, that was seven times larger than St. Mark's Square in Venice. The Royal Mosque, decorated with blue enameled tiles, stood on one side of this arena, while the Mosque of Sheikh Lutfallah, reserved for the shah's private devotions, occupied another. On a third stood the entrance to the central bazaar, painted with murals showing Abbas's victories over the Uzbeks. At the square's end a great gate led to a series of gardens and to a long boulevard, the Chahar Bagh, lined with parks, palaces, and pavilions for the royal family and nobles of the court.

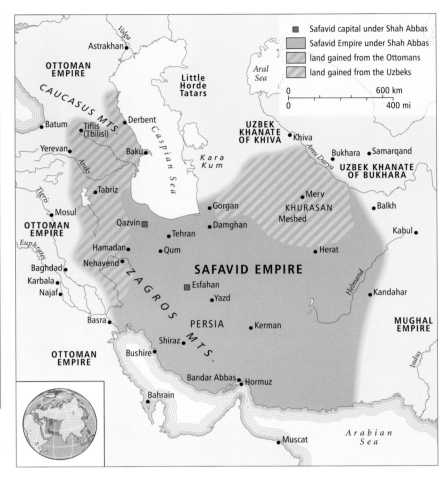

Abbas engaged an English adventurer, Sir Anthony Sherley, to train his new army in artillery tactics. Once he had expelled the Uzbeks from Khurasan he turned his attention to the Ottomans, winning back Baghdad, Mosul, and most of Iraq in a series of campaigns. Sir Robert Sherley, Anthony's brother, also became a close adviser, and in 1609 Abbas sent him on a mission to a number of European countries to try and win their support for a military alliance against the Ottomans.

During Abbas's reign Persia grew rich through its monopoly of the silk trade. A discerning patron of the arts, Abbas invited craftsmen and artists to settle in Persia, and he encouraged the production of textiles, carpets, and ceramics. Like his contemporaries the Mughal Emperor Akbar and Queen Elizabeth I of England, he presided over a great court at his capital of Esfahan, where he welcomed ambassadors and merchants from many European countries. He was open to new ideas and enjoyed discussing religious theories with foreign visitors. Unusually for an Islamic ruler, he allowed Christians to wear what they liked and to own property in Esfahan.

▲ Shah Abbas's foreign policy was dominated by wars against the Ottomans to the west and the Uzbeks to the east. He won large swaths of territory from each, building a Persian empire larger than any known since antiquity.

🏛 **1588** Abbas I, third son of Mohammed Shah, succeeds him on his death.

🏛 **1590** Abbas makes peace on unfavorable terms with the Ottoman Empire.

⚔ **1598** Abbas defeats the Uzbeks and recovers Khurasan and Herat; he moves his capital to Esfahan.

⚔ **1599** Sir Anthony Sherley arrives in Persia; he will be put in charge of training Abbas's army.

🏛 **1602** Abbas breaks his treaty with the Ottomans.

📖 **1603** The Mosque of Sheikh Lutfallah is built in Esfahan (−1619).

🏛 **1609** Abbas sends Sir Robert Sherley on an embassy to Europe.

📖 **1611** Work begins on the Royal Mosque.

⚔ **1622** Abbas ousts the Portuguese from the island of Hormuz at the entrance to the Persian Gulf.

⚔ **1623** In a major offensive against the Ottomans Abbas wins back Baghdad and establishes control over the Shia holy cities of Najaf and Karbala in Iraq (−1624).

🏛 **1629** Death of Abbas.

AMERICAS

1610 English explorer Henry Hudson discovers the bay in Canada that now bears his name; he disappears the following year after being set adrift by mutineers.

1610 The first Dutch settlers from New Jersey arrive on Manhattan Island, founding the colony of New Amsterdam (New York).

A later painting shows indigenous people greeting the explorer Henry Hudson in the course of one of his North American voyages.

EUROPE

1610 In the Plantation of Ulster, King James I of England encourages thousands of Scottish Protestants to settle in Catholic northern Ireland, creating a lasting religious divide.

1610 Henry IV of France is assassinated in Paris by a religious fanatic. He is succeeded by the nine-year-old Louis XIII, whose mother Marie de Medicis rules as regent under the guidance of Cardinal Richelieu.

1611 The King James Bible—the first authorized English translation—is published in London.

1611 Gustavus II Adolphus ascends the Swedish throne, starting Sweden's rise to become a major European power.

1613 Russia's Time of Troubles ends when Michael I is elected czar; a Romanov, his dynasty will last until the Russian Empire collapses in 1917.

1614 The Estates-General, France's administrative assembly since 1347, meets for the last time until 1789, marking the start of absolute monarchy in France.

1615 Spanish writer Miguel de Cervantes completes his epic novel *Don Quixote*.

1616 William Shakespeare, England's greatest playwright, dies in Stratford-upon-Avon aged 52.

AFRICA

1610 Ralambo takes power as the last ruler of the Merina people of highland Madagascar before French settlement begins.

1610 Queen Amina of the Hausa people dies after extending her West African empire south to the Niger Delta.

1612 Moroccan forces withdraw from western Sudan but retain control over the declining Songhai Empire east of the Sahara.

WESTERN ASIA

1614 Cossack pirates sack and burn Sinope on Turkey's northern coast; the Ottomans lose control of the Black Sea.

1616 Renewed warfare breaks out between the Ottomans and the armies of Persia's Shah Abbas.

SOUTH & CENTRAL ASIA

c.1610 With the defeat of the southern Toungou realm the Kingdom of Ava becomes the dominant force in Myanmar (Burma).

This gold commemorative coin issued by the Mughal Emperor Jahangir bears a portrait of his father Akbar.

EAST ASIA & OCEANIA

1612 Japanese Shogun Tokugawa Ieyasu outlaws Christianity, launching a persecution of converts and ordering all Christian missionaries to leave the country.

1614 Ieyasu lays siege to and captures Osaka Castle, ending a challenge to his rule from the warlord Hideyori (–1615).

1615 Nurhachi, leader of the Juchen (Manchu) people, unites the tribes on China's northeast frontier, laying the groundwork for his later conquest of China and the founding of the Manchu (Qing) Dynasty.

👑 **1611** Native American princess Pocahontas marries Jamestown settler John Rolfe, bringing a truce in the war between English settlers and the Algonquians.

⊕ **1615** Rubber and drinking chocolate are first exported from the Americas to Europe.

⊕ **1616** Willem Schouten, a Dutch East India Company captain, rounds the southern tip of South America, naming it Kap Hoorn (Cape Horn) after his hometown in the Netherlands.

👑 **1619** The first shipment of African "indentured laborers" to Jamestown, Virginia, heralds the start of the slave trade in North America.

👑 **1619** The first Thanksgiving Day is celebrated by settlers at Hampton, Virginia.

AMERICAS

⊕ **1616** Denounced as a heretic for confirming Copernicus's observation that the Earth moves round the sun, Galileo Galilei is barred from scientific study by the Catholic church.

✕ **1618** The Thirty Years' War begins with an uprising in Bohemia against Hapsburg rule after Protestant governors are thrown from a window at Hradcany Castle in the "Defenestration of Prague."

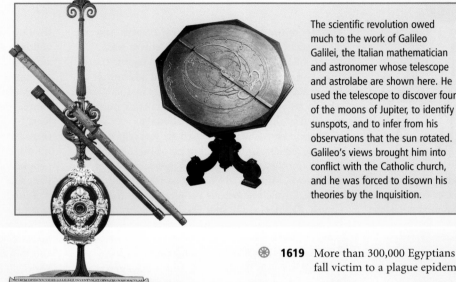

The scientific revolution owed much to the work of Galileo Galilei, the Italian mathematician and astronomer whose telescope and astrolabe are shown here. He used the telescope to discover four of the moons of Jupiter, to identify sunspots, and to infer from his observations that the sun rotated. Galileo's views brought him into conflict with the Catholic church, and he was forced to disown his theories by the Inquisition.

EUROPE

✕ **1614** A Portuguese fleet bombards the palace of the Sultan of Mombasa in what is now Kenya; the sultan visits Goa to protest.

⊕ **1619** More than 300,000 Egyptians fall victim to a plague epidemic.

AFRICA

👑 **1617** Ottoman Sultan Ahmed I dies and is succeeded by his brother Mustafa I, aged 26.

👑 **1618** Mustafa is declared unfit to govern and is replaced as Ottoman ruler by Osman II.

👑 **1618** Peace is restored with Persia when the Ottomans agree to abandon Azerbaijan and Georgia.

WESTERN ASIA

👑 **1611** The Mughal Emperor Jahangir marries Nur Jahan, who becomes a leading figure in the royal household and effectively rules India until the death of her husband.

✕ **1612** Forces of the English East India Company defeat a Portuguese fleet off Surat in Gujarat, western India, going on to establish the first permanent trading post ("factory") in India at the port.

👑 **1618** Birth of Aurangzeb, future ruler of India, under whose control the Mughal Empire will reach its greatest extent.

SOUTH & CENTRAL ASIA

⊕ **1616** Porcelain manufacture begins in Japan when imported Korean potters discover a kaolin deposit on the island of Kyushu.

👑 **1616** English involvement in the Southeast Asian spice trade gets under way when Nathaniel Courthope forms an alliance with the people of Banda Island in the Moluccas and withstands a four-year siege by Dutch forces.

👑 **1619** Batavia (modern Jakarta) on Java becomes the administrative center of the Dutch East India Company for its trade and plantation operations in Southeast Asia.

EAST ASIA & OCEANIA

1610–1620 A.D.

SETTLING NORTH AMERICA

▲ Relations between the European settlers and the indigenous peoples they met in the New World were usually hostile. This figure of a bow-wielding warrior decorated a Massachussets weather vane.

BEFORE THE 17TH CENTURY THE EUROPEAN POWERS *made few systematic attempts to settle North America. Early explorers went searching for riches or a northwest passage to East Asia. Spanish conquistadors looked in vain in the south for the fabled realm of gold, El Dorado, while far to the north the French sailor Jacques Cartier explored the St. Lawrence River from 1534 to 1541. By the late 1630s, however, several different European groups had gained a firm foothold along the eastern seaboard.*

The fate of the first English colony in North America is shrouded in mystery. A small settlement was established at Roanoke Island off the Virginia coast in 1584 and was reinforced by the famed adventurer Walter Raleigh, who sent more settlers in 1587. Yet when a relief party arrived three years later, no trace survived of the colony's 120 inhabitants.

No one knows whether Roanoke was wiped out by violence, illness, or famine, but all of these were real threats to other early colonists. English settlers at Jamestown, founded in Virginia in 1607, faced malaria, hostile indigenous people, and hunger, and almost abandoned the site. The planting of tobacco eventually assured the colony's prosperity; by 1619 some 50,000 pounds (22,500 kg) of the "sot-weed" hated by King James I were being exported to England. A more sinister trade began the same year when the first African slaves were landed from a Dutch ship. But life in Jamestown remained fragile; in 1622 a massive attack by a native alliance known as

the Powhatan Confederacy left 350 men, women, and children dead. In turn, imported diseases such as smallpox, typhoid, and malaria took a terrible toll on the native population.

At around the same time, French settlers under Samuel de Champlain came into conflict with the local Iroquois in the Great Lakes area. Yet Champlain forged amicable fur trading links with the Iroquois' traditional enemies, the Huron and Algonquian peoples. This alliance was to serve the French well in their war against the English in the following century.

European settlement began to focus on the Northeast from the 1620s on. In 1626 Peter Minuit, acting for the Dutch West India Company, bought Manhattan Island from the native Wappinger people and founded the town of New Amsterdam (later New York). The wider colony of New Netherland arose in the area between the Hudson and Connecticut rivers but never thrived, as Holland neglected it in favor of its East Asian interests.

⊛ **1540** Conquistador Francisco Coronado leads an expedition north from Mexico into southwestern North America (–1541).

👑 **1566** St. Augustine, the first European settlement on mainland North America, is founded as a military outpost in Florida by Spanish explorer Menéndez de Avilés.

👑 **1584** Walter Raleigh founds a colony on Roanoke Island, Virginia; the colony fails, and all trace of it has disappeared by the time a relief expedition arrives in 1590.

👑 **1607** The first continuous English settlement is founded by the London Company at Jamestown in Virginia; the colony supports itself through tobacco growing.

⊛ **1608** Exploring the St. Lawrence River, French explorer Samuel de Champlain establishes the colony of New France at Quebec, later becoming its commandant.

👑 **1619** The first elections are held in the colonies when 22 "burgesses" are elected to the Virginia Assembly by popular vote in Jamestown.

☀ **1620** The Pilgrims arrive at Cape Cod, Massachusetts, aboard the *Mayflower*; they choose New Plymouth as the site of the first Puritan colony.

⚔ **1622** The Powhatan Confederacy, a group of Algonquian-speaking peoples, attacks European settlements in Virginia, killing over 350 settlers.

⊛ **1624** Dutch merchants establish the colony of Fort Orange (Albany) up the Hudson River, predominantly to trade furs with the Iroquois Confederacy.

⊛ **1626** Fort Amsterdam (later New Amsterdam) is founded on the tip of Manhattan Island by Dutch traders.

👑 **1630** A large colonizing expedition sets sail from England, founding Boston, Massachusetts, and six other towns nearby.

⚔ **1637** Mystic, Connecticut, is destroyed by a mixed Narragansett, Pequot, and Mohican force, and over 600 inhabitants are massacred.

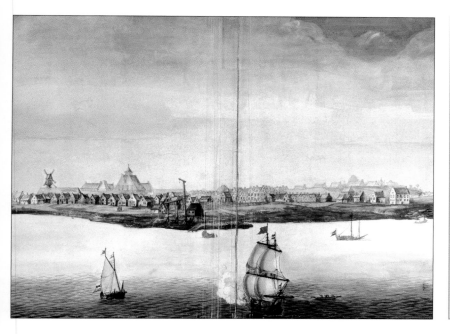

Pocahontas

As the Jamestown colonists began to starve, their leader, Captain John Smith, went upcountry from Chesapeake Bay in 1607 to barter for corn with the Algonquian people. Received with hostility and facing death, Smith was saved when Chief Powhatan's 12-year-old daughter Pocahontas pleaded for his life. Five years later she was herself taken as a captive to Jamestown, where she met the settler John Rolfe, marrying him in 1614. Rolfe took his wife, who had converted to Christianity and changed her name to Rebecca, back to England in 1616. There she was presented to the king and society, and was received with great curiosity and acclaim, but died of smallpox as she embarked on the return journey. Pocahontas is often seen as symbolizing harmony between different peoples; violence and exploitation, however, marked most settlers' response to Native Americans.

Commercial concerns were the driving force behind the earliest settlements, but a very different kind of settler soon arrived in growing numbers. Fleeing persecution in England, a group of Puritan religious dissenters set sail for the New World to create a community where they could practice their faith in peace. These Pilgrims founded the Plymouth Colony on Cape Cod in 1620. The Mayflower Compact, named for their ship, agreed to establish a "civil body politic" based on the will of the majority—an early expression of American democracy.

▲ A painting by the Dutch artist Johannes Vinckeboons shows how Manhattan Island looked in the early days when it was occupied by Dutch settlers and known as New Amsterdam rather than New York.

▼ The European settlement of North America began on the East Coast. Settlers from England, France, Sweden, and the Netherlands carved out terrritories, contesting the land with each other

👑 **1643** The New England Confederation, the first union of English colonies in America, is founded for mutual defense against Dutch and French settlers and hostile indigenous peoples.

⚔ **1664** English troops seize New Amsterdam from the Dutch and rename it New York.

⊕ **1671** English settlers are the first Europeans to cross the Appalachian Mountains.

⚔ **1675** Chief Metacomet, known to colonists as King Philip, leads the Narragansett and Wampanoag peoples in an uprising against New England settlements, killing some 600 colonists (–1676).

☀ **1681** William Penn begins to establish Quaker colonies in North America.

1620–1630 A.D.

AMERICAS

The Pilgrims who sailed from England on the *Mayflower* and settled at Cape Cod were the first permanent European settlers of New England. Some had been persecuted for their Puritan views and had first sought refuge in the Netherlands. Granted permission by the British government to settle in America, they were able to make the trip with the aid of financial backing from London merchants.

1620 The *Mayflower* arrives in Cape Cod, Massachusetts, carrying 102 settlers, including Puritans fleeing religious persecution in England.

1621 Potatoes, native to the Andes Mountains region of South America, reach Europe for the first time and are planted in Germany.

EUROPE

1620 At the Battle of the White Mountain near Prague a Catholic army defeats a Bohemian force led by Frederick V in the first major engagement of the Thirty Years' War.

1620 Sweden's Gustavus II Adolphus overruns Livonia (modern Latvia and Lithuania) and drives out Polish forces (–1629).

1620 Dutch engineer Cornelius Drebbel tests the first submarine, built of wood and leather.

1624 Cardinal Richelieu is appointed first minister by Louis XIII, becoming the most powerful political figure in France.

AFRICA

c.1620 The Akan Kingdom of Denkyera emerges as a growing power in the forested lands north of the Gold Coast.

1624 Queen Nzinga comes to power in Matamba (Angola); she will check Portuguese expansion inland from coastal slaving bases.

1626 French explorer Thomas Lambart makes landfall at the mouth of the Senegal River in West Africa.

WESTERN ASIA

1622 Persian forces in alliance with troops provided by the English East India Company capture the important trading base at Hormuz at the mouth of the Persian Gulf, under Portuguese control since 1507.

1622 Osman II tries to suppress the growing power of the janissaries (the elite palace guard of the Ottoman Empire) but is murdered by them.

1623 Murad IV, Osman's nephew, becomes Ottoman sultan and moves to crush the janissaries.

SOUTH & CENTRAL ASIA

1625 The Mughals under Emperor Jahangir lose control of the strategically important city of Kandahar in what is now Afghanistan to the Persian Safavid Empire.

A cameo brooch in gold, enamel, and sardonyx shows the Mughal Emperor Shah Jahan killing a lion.

EAST ASIA & OCEANIA

1621 The expansion of the Manchu people of Manchuria begins when Nurhachi, their leader, seizes land in northeastern China, including the city of Shenyang; renamed Mukden, it will become his capital (–1625).

1622 Dutch traders found a fortified settlement on the offshore Chinese island of Formosa (today's Taiwan).

1623 Dutch–English rivalry in Southeast Asia intensifies as 12 English traders are killed when Dutch troops sack Amboina on the island of Ceram (Moluccas).

258

✳ **1621** James I of England (author of *A Counterblast to Tobacco*) sends an emissary on a failed mission to persuade Virginia colonists not to grow tobacco.

✕ **1622** Native American warriors of the Powhatan Confederacy attack Virginia settlements, killing around 350 colonists.

✕ **1623** Dutch raiders seize the ports of Pernambuco (Recife) and Bahia, the capital of Brazil, from the Portuguese, who regain control shortly after (−1625).

✳ **1626** Fur traders in the service of the Dutch West India Company found New Amsterdam on Manhattan Island.

✕ **1626** Dutch admiral Piet Hein intercepts a Spanish bullion flotilla off Cuba, seizing a fortune in Peruvian silver.

AMERICAS

〰 **1625** James I of England dies and is succeeded by his son Charles I.

✕ **1625** Christian IV of Denmark intervenes on the Protestant side in the Thirty Years' War (−1629).

✕ **1628** Richelieu's troops capture the Huguenot (Protestant) stronghold of La Rochelle after a long siege.

✳ **1628** English physician William Harvey publishes *On the Motion of the Heart and Blood*, a pioneering study of the circulatory system.

〰 **1629** Charles I of England dissolves Parliament and rules as an absolute monarch (−1640).

✕ **1629** Denmark is forced to withdraw from the Thirty Years' War following defeats by Catholic forces under von Wallenstein.

EUROPE

✳ **1626** The first French colonists settle on the island of Madagascar.

✳ **1629** Portuguese settlers in Angola plant corn and cassava from America; the crops will become staples of the African diet.

AFRICA

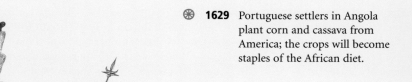

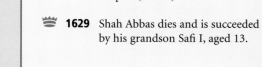

Shown here wearing ceremonial headgear, the janissaries were fearsome soldiers, the shock troops of the Ottoman Empire. Recruited largely from Balkan Christian families and forcibly converted to Islam, they owed their loyalty directly to the state. From the 17th century on they took an active part in politics, frequently making and unmaking sultans.

✕ **1623** Shah Abbas I of Persia completes his conquest of Iraq (begun in 1603) with the capture of Mosul and Baghdad from the Ottoman Empire (−1624).

〰 **1629** Shah Abbas dies and is succeeded by his grandson Safi I, aged 13.

WESTERN ASIA

☀ **1627** The first Westerners—two Jesuit missionaries—arrive in the Himalayan kingdom of Bhutan.

〰 **1627** Emperor Jahangir dies, to be succeeded by his son Shah Jahan.

〰 **1629** Uzbeks take over the city and region of Kandahar after the defection of the Persian governor.

SOUTH & CENTRAL ASIA

〰 **1623** Shogun Hidetada of Japan abdicates in favor of his son Iemitsu; the persecution of Christians continues.

✕ **1627** Manchu troops invade Korea and force it to become a vassal state.

✕ **1627** Peasant rebellions protesting harsh taxation by Ming rulers break out in central and northern China, and rapidly become widespread (−1644).

✕ **1628** From their enclave at Batavia the Dutch launch repeated attacks to spread their power across Java, now ruled by Sultan Agung of Mataram.

EAST ASIA & OCEANIA

1620–1630 A.D.

THE THIRTY YEARS' WAR

▲ Sweden's King Gustavus II Adolphus turned the tide of the war in the Protestants' favor when he intervened in 1630. When he was killed in battle two years later, imperial armies regained the initiative.

▶ The Treaty of Westphalia, which finally brought the war to an end, took four years to negotiate.

THE RELIGIOUS STRIFE THAT HAD PLAGUED EUROPE *since the Reformation climaxed in the horrors of the Thirty Years' War. Starting as a struggle between the Catholic Holy Roman emperor and his Protestant subjects, it quickly grew into a multinational struggle setting the Hapsburg emperor against foreign forces eager to tame his power. The chief losers were the people of the central European regions that served as battlegrounds; their populations were decimated and their lands laid waste.*

The first phase of the war began when the Hapsburg ruler Ferdinand II, an ardent Catholic who at the time was king of Bohemia and later became Holy Roman emperor, tried to impose anti-Protestant policies on his subjects. In protest, angry nobles threw two imperial counselors out of a high window in the Royal Palace in the "Defenestration of Prague." The rebels offered Elector Frederick V of the Rhenish Palatinate—a Calvinist—the crown, but his reign was brief; the so-called "Winter King" was defeated at the Battle of the White Mountain in 1620. Troops from Spain (also ruled by the Hapsburgs) occupied the Palatinate, and Bohemia was forcibly re-Catholicized.

Breaking a 12-year truce, Spain then moved to crush the enduring revolt against its rule in the Netherlands. To defend Dutch and north German Protestants, Denmark invaded Lower Saxony in 1625;

but its armies were repulsed, and it withdrew from the conflict four years later. By 1629 the forces of Catholicism were dominant, and in that year Ferdinand further tightened his grip with the Edict of Restitution, which deprived Protestants of hard-won freedoms held for over 70 years.

Yet at the very height of Catholic supremacy the tide started to turn. Splits arose within the imperial camp—even many Catholic princes suspected Ferdinand of

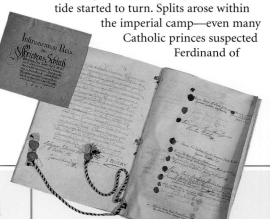

✕ **1618** Two imperial counselors are thrown from a window of Hradcany Castle in Prague; the Bohemian–Palatinate War begins.

👑 **1619** Ferdinand II, the repressive ruler of Bohemia whose actions sparked revolt, is elected Holy Roman emperor in Vienna; a Protestant siege of Vienna fails.

✕ **1620** Imperial forces under Johann Tilly triumph over Protestant champion Frederick V at the Battle of the White Mountain; Spain conquers the Rhenish Palatinate.

✕ **1621** Under its new ruler Philip IV Spain breaks its 1609 truce with the Netherlands and invades to restore Catholicism.

👑 **1624** Cardinal Richelieu is appointed first minister in France by Louis XIII.

✕ **1625** King Christian IV of Denmark joins the Protestant Union and invades northern Germany.

✕ **1626** Danish forces suffer a heavy defeat by armies of the Catholic League commanded by Tilly and Wallenstein at the Battle of Lutter, near Hamelin, Lower Saxony.

✕ **1628** Wallenstein unsuccessfully besieges the key Baltic port of Stralsund to disrupt trade between the chief Protestant allies, the Netherlands, Denmark, and Sweden.

☀ **1629** Ferdinand II's Edict of Restitution curtails Protestant freedom of worship and restores Catholic church estates in northern Germany.

👑 **1630** Following an electoral meeting (assembly of princes) at Ratisbon, Wallenstein is dismissed as commander of the imperial forces.

✕ **1630** Gustavus II Adolphus of Sweden becomes the new champion of the Protestant cause, landing in Pomerania and advancing south almost to Vienna.

✕ **1631** Besieged by Tilly, the city of Magdeburg capitulates, and its citizens are massacred. At the Battle of Breitenfeld in Saxony–Anhalt the Swedes and Saxons win a major victory over the forces of the Catholic League.

✕ **1632** Wallenstein is restored as imperial commander; Gustavus II Adolphus is killed at the inconclusive Battle of Lützen.

Legend:
- Austrian Hapsburg territory 1618
- Spanish Hapsburg territory 1618
- German Protestant states 1618
- United Provinces 1618
- borders 1648

0 — 300 km
0 — 200 mi

✕ major battle
→ French campaign
→ Hapsburg campaign
→ Protestant campaign
→ Swedish campaign

trying to extend his absolute power. The year 1630 marked a watershed when the emperor's ambitions were checked by his own allies at a meeting of German princes at Ratisbon. Meanwhile a new player's entry into the war tipped the military balance against the Hapsburg ruler. Under its dynamic king Gustavus Adolphus Sweden won a series of victories and advanced deep into southern Germany. Yet Swedish momentum faltered when Gustavus fell in the Battle of Lützen in 1632, followed by a defeat at Nördlingen (1634). Civilian casualties continued to mount; in the siege of Magdeburg an imperial army slaughtered almost all the city's 25,000 inhabitants.

An unlikely new ally of Protestantism now emerged in the form of Catholic France. To curb the power of the Holy Roman Empire, France's chief minister, Cardinal Richelieu, formed an alliance with anti-Hapsburg forces in 1635. Although French and Swedish armies made gains against the Spanish and imperial forces, neither side could win supremacy. When the moderate Ferdinand III succeeded to the imperial throne in 1637, the war entered a decade of bloody stalemate. Finally, in 1648, with the land exhausted by decades of bloodshed, an uneasy peace was concluded at the Treaty of Westphalia.

◀ The main theaters of conflict were in what are now southern and eastern Germany, Poland, and the Czech Republic, but fighting also spread into Italy, Austria, Denmark, and the Netherlands.

Wallenstein

The most charismatic military leader of the Thirty Years' War was Albrecht von Wallenstein. Brought up as a Protestant in Bohemia, he converted to Catholicism in 1606 and won distinction at the Battle of the White Mountain in 1620 (right). Amassing great wealth by confiscating Protestant noblemen's property, Wallenstein raised an army of 24,000 men for the imperial cause. Appointed supreme commander, he led his troops to victory over Danish forces in north Germany from 1624 to 1629. His success won him enemies, however, and the emperor was forced to dismiss him in 1630. Recalled two years later to counter the Swedish threat, he regained Bohemia but failed to achieve a decisive breakthrough. After a second dismissal in 1634 Wallenstein was accused of treason by Ferdinand II and murdered by British mercenaries.

〰 **1635** The Peace of Prague brings the conflict between the Holy Roman Empire and Saxony to an end; Cardinal Richelieu of France forms an alliance with Sweden.

✕ **1635** A long war of attrition breaks out between France and Spain; France seizes Martinique and Guadeloupe in the Caribbean from the Spanish (–1648).

✕ **1648** The Thirty Year's War is ended by the Peace of Westphalia. The power of the Hapsburgs is checked, and religious freedoms within Germany are reaffirmed.

1630–1640 A.D.

AMERICAS

1630 The city of Boston is founded.

1630 Dutch forces make their first attempt to conquer northeastern Brazil but are soon driven out by the Portuguese.

1632 French settlers found Acadia (modern Nova Scotia, Canada).

1634 Searching for a northwest passage to Asia, French explorer Jean Nicolet crosses Lake Michigan.

1635 The French occupy and colonize the Caribbean islands of Martinique and Guadeloupe.

EUROPE

1630 An outbreak of bubonic plague causes 500,000 deaths in Venice.

1630 At the Ratisbon electoral meeting (assembly of princes) Holy Roman Emperor Ferdinand II dismisses Albrecht von Wallenstein as supreme commander of the imperial armies.

1630 Swedish forces under King Gustavus II Adolphus intervene in the Thirty Years' War to aid the Protestant cause and invade northern Germany.

1631 Following the Siege of Magdeburg by imperial (Catholic) forces under Count Johann Tilly, the victorious army sacks the city and slaughters most of its 25,000 inhabitants.

1632 King Gustavus II Adolphus of Sweden is killed leading his troops at the Battle of Lützen (Saxony).

1633 Galileo Galilei is forced by the Inquisition to recant his view that the sun is at the center of the universe; he is subsequently put under house arrest and banned from studying the heavens.

1634 The Académie Française, an organization fostering France's cultural heritage and the French language, is founded by Cardinal Richelieu in Paris.

1634 Branded a traitor by the emperor, Wallenstein is murdered by English mercenaries in Eger, Hungary.

1637 "Tulipmania" reaches its height in the Netherlands, with one speculator swapping a house in Haarlem for just three bulbs; prices will eventually crash by 95 percent.

AFRICA

c. 1630 Ife is eclipsed as the dominant Yoruba state in what is now Nigeria by the rise of the Kingdom of Oyo.

1637 Elmina, a key Portuguese trading port on West Africa's Gold Coast, is captured by the Dutch.

WESTERN ASIA

1630 Ottoman Sultan Murad IV captures the Persian city of Hamadan.

Sultan Murad IV, ruler of the Ottoman Empire.

1638 After a month-long siege Ottoman forces recapture Baghdad from the Persian Safavids; Iraq becomes an Ottoman province until 1918.

SOUTH & CENTRAL ASIA

1632 Following the death of his wife Mumtaz Mahal, Mughal Emperor Shah Jahan orders the construction of her tomb, the Taj Mahal at Agra, which will take 22 years to complete.

1632 Shah Jahan embarks on the conquest of the Deccan (central India); at the same time, a famine in the region causes one million deaths, with cannibalism rife.

1634 Shah Jahan drives the Uzbeks from Kandahar in Afghanistan.

1639 The English East India Company founds a trading base at Fort St. George (modern Madras) on the southeastern coast of India.

EAST ASIA & OCEANIA

1634 Ligdan Khan, last ruler of the Great Khanate of Mongolia (originally established in 1206), dies, and the Manchus overrun the region.

1636 In Mukden, northeastern China, the Manchus proclaim the Qing Dynasty. The Ming Dynasty holds onto power in the rest of China, although in a weakened state.

1636 As part of a campaign to eradicate Western influence in Japan, all foreigners are forced to live on the artificial island of Dejima in Nagasaki harbor.

📖 **1636** Harvard University, the oldest university in the United States, is founded in New Towne (later Cambridge), near Boston, Massachusetts.

⚔ **1637** Conflict breaks out between New England settlers and the indigenous Pequots, resulting in hundreds of deaths on both sides.

⊛ **1638** The first printing press in North America is set up by Stephen Day in Cambridge, Massachusetts.

"I think, therefore I am," wrote the French thinker René Descartes, outlining the first step in a rationalist worldview that has led him to be called the father of modern philosophy. In his *Discourse on Method* and other works he laid out the basis of a system of thought that in future decades would come to underpin the scientific revolution. A practicing Catholic, Descartes nonetheless advocated the questioning of all established beliefs in an attempt to create a universal scheme of knowledge founded on mathematical standards of proof. The emphasis that he placed on the exercise of reason challenged the medieval notion of discovering truth through faith and prepared the way for a newly critical approach to intellectual activity.

👑 **1637** Emperor Ferdinand II dies in Vienna and is succeeded by his son Ferdinand III.

⊛ **1637** In his *Discourse on Method* French philosopher René Descartes proposes his principle of methodical doubt whereby science begins with observation, followed by analysis.

☀ **1638** Scottish Presbyterians sign the National Covenant, opposing the divine right of kings and English interference in Scottish Protestant affairs.

⊛ **1638** Firmly established at St. Louis on the Senegal River, French settlers begin to paticipate in the transatlantic slave trade.

👑 **1639** Shah Safi of Persia and Murad IV sign the Treaty of Qasr-i-Shirin, which establishes a permanent border between their empires.

📖 **1639** Shah Jahan orders construction of the walled city of Old Delhi. He will move the Mughal capital there nine years later (–1648).

The Taj Mahal, built as a mausoleum for the wife of Shah Jahan.

⚔ **1637** Japan's Shogun Iemitsu crushes a Christian peasant uprising in the Shimabara region. Iemitsu's forces capture Hara Castle and massacre its defenders (–1638).

⊛ **1639** Russian explorers reach the Pacific coast of Siberia.

👑 **1639** Portuguese traders are expelled from Japan.

👑 **1639** All Japanese ports except Nagasaki (used by Dutch merchants) are closed to trade with the outside world.

AMERICAS

EUROPE

AFRICA

WESTERN ASIA

SOUTH & CENTRAL ASIA

EAST ASIA & OCEANIA

1630–1640 A.D.

JAPAN CLOSES ITS DOORS

▲ A European trader as seen by a Japanese artist.

▼ Tokugawa power in Japan spread out from a base on the central island of Honshu.

JAPAN WAS FIRST EXPOSED TO WESTERN INFLUENCE *in the middle of the 16th century. Long accustomed to prosperous trade with China, the Japanese initially welcomed the growth in commerce stimulated by European merchants. Yet Japan was a country of strict social divisions and longstanding religious traditions, and its rulers soon reacted strongly against the activities of Christian missionaries. Fearing that European nations had colonial ambitions, Japan closed its doors on foreigners in 1641; over two centuries were to pass before they opened again.*

As a result of the conquests of Toyotomi Hideyoshi (1536–1598) Japan had become steadily more unified and stable before the Tokugawa Dynasty took control of the shogunate in 1603. Peace brought with it greater opportunities for trade, for the development of industry and agriculture, and for improved communications and transport.

Trade with China, which had been going on for a thousand years, grew considerably, with local feudal warlords adopting Chinese culture as a sign of their new respectability. As the 16th century went on,

however, another entirely unfamiliar influence—that of Europe—made its mark on Japanese society.

The first contact with Europeans happened by chance when a Chinese ship with two Portuguese travelers on board was shipwrecked off Tanegashima in 1542. Significantly, the foreigners sold their muskets to a local lord; soon replicated by the Japanese, these firearms transformed warfare there and played a vital role in the country's unification under strong military leaders.

The Portuguese seaborne empire, pushing ever farther east, began regular trade with Japan in 1570 with the opening of the port of Nagasaki to foreign commerce. The Japanese viewed the Europeans with cautious openness; after the English explorer Will Adams was shipwrecked on Kyushu in 1600, he served the ruling strongman Ieyasu, who became shogun three years later, as an adviser. Adams (who

1542 Portuguese travelers make a first, accidental landfall in Japan following a shipwreck off the southern tip of Kyushu.

1548 A missionary expedition led by the Jesuit Francis Xavier travels to the Japanese capital of Kyoto and to Kagoshima in western Japan to win converts to Christianity (–1551).

1570 The southern port of Nagasaki is opened to foreign trade.

1587 Japan's Shogun Hideyoshi bans Christianity and expels Jesuits from the country.

1598 The death of Hideyoshi leaves a power vacuum, plunging the country into civil war.

took the Japanese name of Miura Anjin) won permission for Dutch and English traders to operate in Japan and also developed Japan's own merchant fleet. The commodities the foreign merchants sought were gold, silver, and copper from new mines. They exchanged the metals for raw silk and finished textiles brought from China as well as new types of firearms.

Relations with the foreigners, however, soon worsened over the question of religion. Jesuit missionaries from Spain and Portugal arrived in the wake of the traders, converting many Japanese, particularly among the influential feudal daimyo (lords). Along with Christianity they brought new

technical knowledge, for example in mathematics, astronomy, engineering, and mining. But their influence came to be bitterly resented by enemies who suspected them of destabilizing the country in preparation for foreign invasion. A long series of persecutions followed. The final impetus for the expulsion of the Europeans and their religion came with the Shimabara Rebellion of 1637, after which Japan retreated into two centuries of isolation.

▼ A Japanese painting shows a Portuguese sea captain watching his men disembark on an early visit to the country. Europeans were at first welcomed as curiosities but were later expelled.

The Massacre at Hara Castle

A major uprising against Tokugawa rule broke out in December 1637 on the Shimabara Peninsula near Nagasaki. It was sparked by the levying of heavy taxes on the peasant population. The area had been Christianized in around 1612, and the repeated torture and murder of converts had fueled discontent. Under their young, charismatic leader Amakusa Shiro the rebels occupied Hara Castle and held out for three months against a large force sent to quell them. Yet starvation and overwhelming odds finally brought defeat. All 37,000 defenders were slaughtered; some 11,000 were beheaded, while others were burned alive. Archaeological excavation of the site, which began in 1992, has uncovered several small crucifixes, rosaries, and icons of Christ, the Virgin Mary, and the missionary leader Saint Francis Xavier.

✕ **1600** At the Battle of Sekigahara the warlord Tokugawa Ieyasu defeats three rivals to win undisputed control over Japan.

👑 **1603** After being awarded the hereditary title of shogun (military dictator) by the emperor, Tokugawa Ieyasu moves the seat of government to Edo (present-day Tokyo).

⊕ **1609** Breaking the Portuguese monopoly on trade with Japan, the Dutch East India Company establishes a base on Hirado Island near Nagoya at the invitation of the shogun.

☀ **1612** Ieyasu begins his persecution of Christians in Japan, particularly local converts to the faith.

⊕ **1613** The first English trading mission opens in Hirado; it will be abandoned in 1623.

✕ **1615** Ieyasu mounts a major operation against Osaka Castle, a stronghold of opposition to his rule under the control of Hideyori, Hideyoshi's only surviving son.

⊕ **1616** The shogun's English adviser Will Adams helps the Japanese build ocean-going vessels and sails to Siam to expand trade links.

👑 **1616** Ieyasu dies, to be succeeded by his son Tokugawa Hidetada.

👑 **1623** Hidetada abdicates in favor of his 19-year-old son Iemitsu.

👑 **1633** Decrees ban Japanese, on pain of death, from trading or living overseas (–1635).

✕ **1638** A Christian-led revolt on the Shimabara Peninsula near Nagasaki is put down brutally.

👑 **1639** Portuguese traders are expelled from Japan. Two years later the Dutch—the only remaining Europeans—are restricted to the artificial island of Dejima.

AMERICAS

1640 Violent conflict flares in Brazil as Jesuit priests attempt to prevent the enslavement of the indigenous peoples by Portuguese colonists.

1641 The General Court of Massachusetts Bay Colony sets out the Body of Liberties, a code of 100 laws that includes the legalization of slavery.

1642 French settlers found a colony at Ville de Marie in Canada, later to be called Montreal.

EUROPE

1640 Catalans revolt against the centralizing policies of Philip IV's chief minister, the Count–Duke of Olivares.

1640 Portuguese forces take advantage of the Catalan revolt to win freedom from Spanish rule. John of Braganza becomes king.

1642 In the Thirty Years' War Swedish forces defeat imperial troops in the Second Battle of Breitenfeld.

The Count–Duke of Olivares, Spain's chief minister, as painted by Diego Velázquez.

1643 A Baltic war breaks out between Sweden and Denmark.

1643 Philip IV's hated righthand man, the Count–Duke of Olivares, falls from power.

1644 Under pressure from Oliver Cromwell England's Parliament forms the New Model Army to fight the civil war against King Charles I; the army is commanded by Sir Thomas Fairfax, with Cromwell as his second-in-command.

AFRICA

1641 Dutch forces take Luanda, capital of Angola colony, from the Portuguese. They will hold it for the next seven years.

1641 Garcia II becomes king of Kongo (Zaire).

WESTERN ASIA

1640 Ottoman Sultan Murad IV dies and is succeeded—disastrously— by his son Ibrahim the Mad.

Ottoman Sultan Ibrahim the Mad, deposed and killed in 1648.

1642 With the help of Crimean Tatars Ottoman forces drive the Cossacks from Azov, a setback for Russian ambitions on the Black Sea coast.

SOUTH & CENTRAL ASIA

1641 The English East India Company establishes a trading base at the river port of Hooghly in Bengal, downstream from modern Calcutta.

1641 Russian forces begin an 11-year campaign to subdue the Buryat Mongols of the Baikal region, Siberia (–1652).

1642 Gushri Khan, ruler of the Qosot Mongols, conquers Tibet and installs the fifth Dalai Lama, Ngawang Lobsang Gyatso, in Lhasa as ruler of what will from now on be a theocratic state.

EAST ASIA & OCEANIA

1641 The Dutch capture of Malacca underlines their dominance throughout the East Indies.

1641 Safiyat ud Din Taj ul-Alam comes to the throne of Aceh, beginning half a century of female rule in the Indonesian sultanate.

1641 Japanese authorities move Dutch merchants from Hirado to the island of Dejima in Nagasaki harbor for closer supervision.

1642 In Cambodia King Chetta II's son Chan takes power after a bloody palace coup.

1642 Dutch navigator Abel Tasman becomes the first European to sight Van Diemen's Land (later Tasmania) and New Zealand.

1644 Russian forces reach the Amur Valley of eastern Siberia.

👑 **1643** Connecticut, Massachusetts Bay, Plymouth, and New Haven colonies come together in the New England Confederation, a defensive alliance.

⚔ **1644** A Native American uprising around Jamestown, Virginia, kills 400 colonists.

☀ **1648** A book by Miguel Sanchez hailing the apparition of the Virgin of Guadalupe, Mexico City, launches the greatest Catholic cult in the Americas.

AMERICAS

England's long list of kings and queens runs back for more than a thousand years with just one gap—the 11-year period known as the Interregnum between the execution of the deposed King Charles I in 1649 and the crowning of his son Charles II in 1660. The nation was ruled for most of this time by Oliver Cromwell, leader of the victorious parliamentary armies in the preceding civil war—his sword hilt is shown at left. Taking the title of lord protector, he proved a competent, dedicated leader who enforced order at home and raised the country's prestige abroad. But the harsh Puritanism of his regime roused hostility, and within two years of his death in 1658 leading figures in the kingdom had determined that England's future well-being would best be served by the restoration of the monarchy.

☀ **1647** George Fox founds the Society of Friends ("Quakers") in England.

⚔ **1648** The Treaty of Westphalia brings the Thirty Years' War to an end, guaranteeing independence for the Dutch Republic, the Swiss Confederation, and some 250 German states.

👑 **1649** A new law code restricts the rights of Russia's serfs (peasants) to such an extent that they can be bought and sold as slaves.

EUROPE

👑 **1643** The French establish the colony of Fort Dauphin in southwestern Madagascar.

⊕ **1645** The first slaves are exported from Mozambique to Brazil.

☀ **1648** Portuguese Jesuits and other western missionaries are expelled from Ethiopia for interference in the country's religious affairs.

AFRICA

👑 **1642** The Safavid Shah Safi of Persia dies; he is succeeded by his son Shah Abbas II, whose reign will be characterized by a new mood of religious intolerance.

⚔ **1648** Shah Abbas II takes Kandahar, Afghanistan, from the Mughals.

👑 **1648** Sultan Ibrahim is executed at the prompting of his own Janissaries.

WESTERN ASIA

⚔ **1646** Mughal forces embark on what will turn out to be an ill-advised campaign in Central Asia.

The Potala Palace rises majestically over the Tibetan capital of Lhasa.

SOUTH & CENTRAL ASIA

👑 **1646** Amangkurat I inherits the throne of Java. His tyrannical reign begins with mass executions of potential opponents and religious scholars; some 6,000 people are killed in the first year.

⊕ **1647** The first English colony in Myanmar (Burma) is founded at Syriam. Ten years later it will be abandoned, unable to contend in a region dominated by the Dutch, by that time at war with England.

⊕ **1648** Russian explorer Semyon Dezhnyov leads an expedition along the Arctic coast and around Asia's northeast cape (now Cape Dezhnyov) to the Pacific.

EAST ASIA & OCEANIA

1640–1650 A.D.

THE MANCHUS IN CHINA

THE NOMADS OF THE NORTHERN STEPPE *exerted an influence on Chinese history over many centuries, their lifestyle despised, their incursions deeply feared. These rootless raiders were an alien presence against whom the Chinese defined themselves as a settled, civilized, industrious, and peaceful people. Yet there were times when the nomads came to the rescue of the culture that so reviled them; the accession to power of the Manchu Qing Dynasty was one such occasion.*

▲ To Confucian intellectuals of the Ming Dynasty the Manchus were barbarians who could in no way match their own sophisticated culture, symbolized by the exquisite vase above. But the northerners took advantage of spreading disaffection to impose their rule.

The Juchen, or Manchus, a tribal grouping from the lands to the north of China, had already established a solid power base before they overthrew China's Ming Dynasty, having earlier united Manchuria under their rule and also won victories over the Mongols and Koreans. Their attention was inevitably drawn to the rich lands to the south, where growing economic disarray and political disaffection were causing a breakdown in order. In the early 1640s rebellion spread through much of the country, forcing the last Ming emperor to the dangerous expedient of inviting the disciplined and efficient northern forces to shore up his rule. The request came too late to save his throne; the rebels reached Beijing in 1644, and the ruler himself committed suicide. The Manchu army took advantage of the power vacuum that ensued to

▶ A contemporary painting shows Emperor Kangxi entering a Chinese town on a tour through his realm in 1699. By that time the ruler had already reigned for 37 years, but he still had more than two decades of power ahead of him.

1644 The Ming Dynasty collapses; the Manchu regent Dorgon declares that his protégé, the five-year-old Emperor Shunzi, has initiated a new imperial dynasty, the Qing.

1645 An imperial decree proclaims that all Chinese must shave their foreheads and wear their hair in a long plait in the Manchu style.

1650 Death of Dorgon.

1659 The last Ming holdouts on the Chinese mainland finally fall to Manchu forces.

1662 Emperor Kangxi comes to the throne at the age of seven, assisted by regents; he grants his Chinese subjects parity with the Manchus.

1667 The imperial regent Obei seizes power in a palace coup. Two years later the emperor reasserts his authority, and Obei is killed.

1673 The Revolt of the Three Feudatories breaks out (–1681) in southern China, led by rebellious generals.

1673 Emperor Kangxi embarks on a series of imperial tours to inspect his realms.

1683 The Qing Empire annexes Taiwan.

1722 Emperor Kangxi dies.

seize power in the Manchus' own name. Their leader Dorgon became the true ruler of China, although technically only as a regent for his five-year-old nephew, who took the regnal name of Shunzi, first emperor of China's new Qing, or "pure," Dynasty.

The man who did most to impose the authority of the Qing was Shunzi's successor Kangxi, who came to power at the age of seven on Shunzi's death in 1662. At first the empire was run by regents, but Kangxi disposed of the last of these in 1669, taking power in his own name at the age of just 15.

Kangxi proved in every way an exceptional ruler. A man of immense energy and intellectual curiosity, he set out to accomplish a delicate balancing act, winning the support of the native Chinese for the new dynasty without alienating the Manchu warriors who had put it in power. At first he had to cope with armed resistance, especially in the south, and in 1673 trouble broke out again when three generals who had been appointed provincial governors sought to break away in the Revolt of the Three Feudatories.

Kangxi overcame these challenges to his rule by adopting a carrot-and-stick approach, on the one hand inaugurating important programs of public works, restoring canals, and building flood defenses, while on the other clamping down hard on dissent and disorder. The emperor also succeeded in developing a power structure in which native Chinese subjects could rise to high office, and the traditional Confucian values of the empire's civil service were maintained. Kangxi lived on until 1722, bequeathing to his successors an empire basking in a golden age of peace and prosperity.

▶ The Manchus rose to power by expanding from a small homeland north of the Korean Peninsula to take control first of Manchuria and Inner Mongolia and then of China itself.

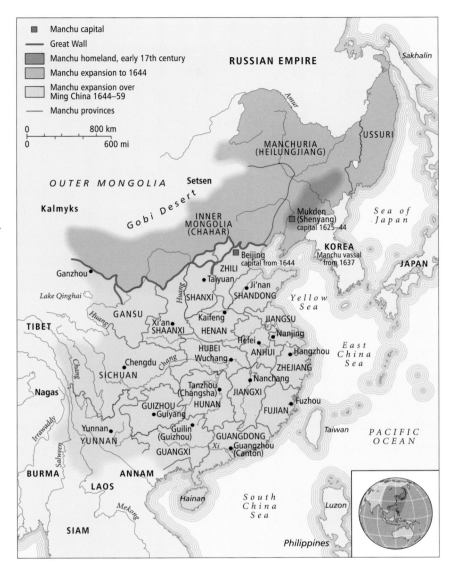

The Imperial Palace at Shenyang

The Imperial Palace at Shenyang (or Mukden, as the Manchus called it) was built by the Manchu emperors shortly before they conquered the rest of China and established the Qing Dynasty. The building lies in Liaoning, now a northeastern province of China but at that time an outlying territory that had recently been conquered by the nomads. Construction began under Nurhachi in 1625 and was completed by his successor Abahai 11 years later. The palace was built as a replica of the famous Forbidden City in Beijing, although only about one-tenth its size, and was intended from the start as a statement of the Manchus' ambitions to rival or supplant the declining Ming Dynasty. It remained in use as an imperial summer palace throughout the centuries of Qing rule, serving as a constant reminder to the emperors of their Manchurian roots.

1650–1660 A.D.

AMERICAS

✗ **1654** The Dutch West India Company gives up its attempt to suppress a Portuguese settlers' revolt in Brazil.

👑 **1655** Peter Stuyvesant, the Dutch governor of New Netherland (New York and New Jersey), expels the Swedish colonists of New Sweden (Delaware).

EUROPE

👑 **1651** England introduces the first of a series of protectionist Navigation Acts: All trade from its colonies must be carried in English vessels.

Dutch and English fleets confront one another in the course of the First Anglo-Dutch War.

✗ **1652** The Dutch Republic declares war on England in response to the Navigation Laws, starting the First Anglo-Dutch War (–1654).

AFRICA

✗ **1650** Dombo Changamire conquers the Torwa Kingdom in Zimbabwe, establishing the Rozwi Dynasty.

✗ **1650** Portuguese forces complete the recapture of Angola from the Dutch.

✱ **1651** English settlers establish Fort St. James at the mouth of the Gambia River as a base for trade inland.

A 17th-century book illustration depicts inhabitants of the island of Zanzibar, off the coast of East Africa.

WESTERN ASIA

✗ **1650** Muscat is taken from the Portuguese by Sultan bin Saif al-Yarubi of Oman.

👑 **1656** The appointment of Mehmed Kiuprili as Ottoman grand vizier brings stability after a period of near anarchy.

✗ **1658** Abaza Hashan Pasha leads a revolt in Anatolia. It will be put down by Mehmed Kiuprili the following year.

SOUTH & CENTRAL ASIA

✗ **1656** Dutch forces take the city of Colombo in Ceylon (Sri Lanka) from Portugal. Over the next two years they will seize the island's other Portuguese colonies.

✱ **1658** Fort St. George, the future Madras, becomes the overall headquarters of East India Company operations in India.

👑 **1658** The Mughal Emperor Shah Jahan is deposed and imprisoned by his son Aurangzeb. The new emperor will seek to enforce strict Sunni orthodoxy, repressing Sikhism and Hinduism along with minority Islamic groups.

✗ **1658** After 20 years of struggle the Dutch win the coastal region of Sri Lanka from the Portuguese, although the inland Kingdom of Kandy remains an independent state.

✗ **1659** Sivaji, a Marathan Hindu warlord from southwest India, takes the city of Bijapur from the Mughals.

EAST ASIA & OCEANIA

👑 **1651** Japan's Shogun Iemitsu dies, and Ietsuna succeeds to the Tokugawa shogunate. He puts down two coup attempts in his first two years and is then secure.

✗ **1652** The king of Tran Ninh's refusal to wed his daughter to his neighbor King Souligna Vongsa of Laos triggers an invasion, his forced compliance to the match, and the start of a 200-year feud.

👑 **1656** Narai becomes king of Ayutthaya (Siam). His 32-year reign will be marked by commercial and cultural openness to the outside world.

✕ **1655** England takes Jamaica from Spain.

⊛ **1658** French traders Médard Chouart des Grosseilliers and Pierre-Esprit Radisson explore territories to the west of Lake Superior.

☀ **1659** Fray García San Francisco y Zuniga establishes the mission that will form the nucleus of the city of El Paso.

AMERICAS

✕ **1652** Barcelona surrenders to Philip IV of Spain, bringing the Catalan Revolt to an end.

✕ **1654** Ukrainian Cossacks rise against Polish rule, offering their allegiance to Czar Alexis I and sparking a 13-year war that will end with Russia taking Ukraine.

✕ **1655** The First Northern War breaks out when Charles X of Sweden declares war on Poland.

✕ **1656** A Swedish victory at the Battle of Warsaw sparks declarations of war from Russia, Denmark, and the Holy Roman Empire.

✕ **1656** Britain joins France in a war against Spain.

✕ **1658** Anglo–French forces defeat the Spanish at the Battle of the Dunes. England gains Dunkirk.

👑 **1658** Leopold I is enthroned as Holy Roman emperor.

👑 **1659** The Treaty of the Pyrenees is signed by Spain and France, which makes territorial gains. The treaty marks the end of the Spanish ascendancy in Europe.

EUROPE

✕ **1652** Omani Arabs capture Zanzibar from Portugal; a 70-year struggle begins for control of East Africa's Swahili Coast.

👑 **1652** Dutch settlers found a colony at Cape Town, South Africa.

⊛ **1659** French merchants build a new, larger base at St. Louis on the Senegal River that will become the main French trading post in West Africa.

✕ **1659** Ottoman janissaries based in Algiers revolt, appointing their own *agha*, or commanding officer, as governor.

👑 **1659** The last Saadi sultan of Morocco is assassinated in Marrakech.

AFRICA

✕ **1658** The Ottomans begin a lengthy siege of Candia, the capital of Crete.

WESTERN ASIA

Known as the "World-holder," Aurangzeb was the last of the great Mughal emperors, noted as much for his religious zeal and building activities (at right, the Badshahi Mosque in Lahore) as for his military campaigns. In the course of a 48-year reign he pushed the boundaries of the empire to their greatest extent, but at a cost—his lengthy wars in the Deccan exhausted the imperial treasury. Meanwhile his intolerance of all faiths but the Sunni version of Islam alienated numbers of his subjects and built up future opposition to Mughal rule.

SOUTH & CENTRAL ASIA

👑 **1658** Cambodian princes depose Chan with the help of forces from Hué, which exacts pledges of loyalty and tribute in return.

👑 **1659** Yungli, the last serious Ming pretender to the throne of China, takes refuge in Burmese territory. His hosts are forced to return him four years later, and he is publicly executed.

✕ **1659** The Chinese rebel leader Zheng Chenggong, known in the West as Coxinga, fails in an attempt to sieze the city of Nanking from the country's new Manchu rulers.

EAST ASIA & OCEANIA

1650–1660 A.D.

ENGLAND'S REVOLUTION

▲ Charles I holds the royal scepter and a model church in a statue symbolizing his status as head of the Church of England, a role that antagonized his many Puritan opponents.

IN THE MID-17TH CENTURY *two concepts of sovereignty came into bloody conflict in England. On one side stood King Charles I of the Stuart Dynasty, a conscientious but blinkered ruler with an unshakeable belief in the "divine right of kings" to govern as they saw fit. On the other was the country's Parliament, representing the property-owning upper classes, who were equally convinced that they had a right to a say in the way the nation was run. The result was civil war.*

Charles I was unpopular with his Parliament from the outset: They suspected him of covert Catholic leanings, and he made no secret of his belief in his god-given right to rule as he pleased. They knew that he would do without them if he could, and from 1629 he did precisely that, for 11 years. Matters came to a head in 1640 when Charles was forced to recall parliament by shortage of money: He needed new taxes approved to wage the "Bishops' War," fought to force the Scots to accept the authority of the Anglican church. This policy was as unacceptable to English Puritans as it was to the Presbyterian Scots: Both were equally hostile to the established church hierarchy.

This first parliament proved uncooperative, so after 23 days Charles dissolved it and called another. This "Long Parliament"—with interruptions it sat for 20 years—exacted concessions in return for qualified support. The compromise proved inadequate to a deteriorating situation. Early in 1642 Charles invaded Parliament with 400 soldiers, hoping to arrest five radical members, only to find, in his words, that "the birds had flown." His heavy-handed action alienated moderate opinion, and both sides prepared for war.

The Royalist forces had the best of the opening exchanges, since the Parliamentarians had to build their own army from scratch. But Charles proved indecisive while his enemy was getting better organized all the time. The Parliamentarians found a military leader of genius in Oliver Cromwell, who fashioned an instrument to win the war in the "New

👑 **1625** Charles I becomes king of England on the death of his father James I.

👑 **1629** Charles dismisses Parliament, starting an 11-year period of personal rule.

👑 **1640** Charles summons, then promptly dissolves, the "Short Parliament."

👑 **1640** The "Long Parliament" gets under way.

⚔ **1642** Civil war breaks out between Royalists and Parliamentarians.

⚔ **1644** Cromwell's New Model Army defeats Royalist forces at the Battle of Marston Moor.

⚔ **1645** Parliamentary forces decisively defeat the Royalists at Naseby.

👑 **1646** Charles surrenders to the Scots.

Condemned to Death

Repeatedly defeated, Charles I gave himself up to the Scots army in England in 1646. The Scots handed Charles over to the English Parliamentarians but later fell out with them and with the leadership of the English army. In 1648 the Scots unsuccessfully invaded England on Charles's behalf, but were heavily defeated. The English army went on to purge Parliament and put Charles on trial for treason. The king defended himself stoutly, but the verdict was never in doubt. His death warrant (below), specifying that the king should be "put to death by the severing of his head from his body," had no fewer than 59 signatories (Cromwell's name comes third from the top in the lefthand column). Charles went to his death on January 30, 1649, wearing two shirts so that he should not be seen to shiver in the cold morning air. He won more support by his death than he had enjoyed in his life. Public opinion across the nation was shocked by the execution, and his persecutors had difficulty in establishing the legitimacy of their rule.

Model Army," a dedicated force that was strengthened in its resolve by the Puritan views of many of its soldiers. (Popularly they were known as "Roundheads," their hair being cropped far shorter than the flowing locks of the royalist Cavaliers.) They won at Marston Moor and then, decisively, at Naseby.

Defeated in battle, the king sought sanctuary with the Scots. Their loyalties were divided: Charles had been no friend to them, so they handed him over to the English. But when Charles escaped from captivity and the Scots fell out with the English Parliamentarians, they sent an army to invade England in his name. This force was defeated. The king, who had meanwhile been recaptured, was put on trial in London in 1649 and beheaded.

The Parliamentary victors then set about founding a republican "commonwealth," but it proved inherently unstable. Cromwell cut through the constitutional arguments to provide decisive rule; but when in 1653 he dissolved Parliament just as Charles had done, taking for himself the title of "lord protector," people came to the conclusion that they had merely exchanged one dictator for another. On his death in 1658 there was little appetite to replace him. Two years later Charles's son Charles II was invited back to England, and the monarchy was restored, although with additional safeguards against absolutism. England's revolution had come to an end.

▲ A crude woodblock illustration dating from 1649 shows Charles's execution, which took place in London before a huge crowd.

▼ Parliamentary forces held London throughout the war, gradually driving back the Royalists to the farthest parts of Britain.

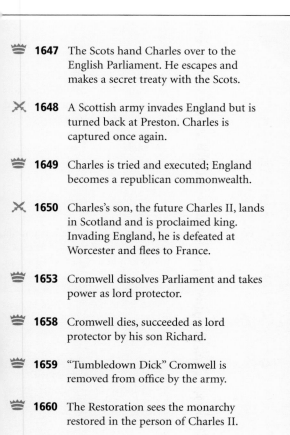

👑 **1647** The Scots hand Charles over to the English Parliament. He escapes and makes a secret treaty with the Scots.

✕ **1648** A Scottish army invades England but is turned back at Preston. Charles is captured once again.

👑 **1649** Charles is tried and executed; England becomes a republican commonwealth.

✕ **1650** Charles's son, the future Charles II, lands in Scotland and is proclaimed king. Invading England, he is defeated at Worcester and flees to France.

👑 **1653** Cromwell dissolves Parliament and takes power as lord protector.

👑 **1658** Cromwell dies, succeeded as lord protector by his son Richard.

👑 **1659** "Tumbledown Dick" Cromwell is removed from office by the army.

👑 **1660** The Restoration sees the monarchy restored in the person of Charles II.

✕ important battle 1640–51

⬭ Parliament control 1642

⬭ Royalist control 1642

▢ Parliament control at the end of 1645

▢ remaining Royalist areas at the end of 1645

➜ Cromwell's punitive campaigns 1649–50

Orkney Islands

Outer Hebrides

SCOTLAND under English control 1650–60

Inner Hebrides

ATLANTIC OCEAN

Tippermuir ✕ 1644   Scone •

Edinburgh • Dunbar ✕ 1650

Philiphaugh ✕ 1645

North Sea

Newburn ✕ 1640

Londonderry • • Ulster 1641 ✕

L. Neagh

Isle of Man

Marston ✕ Moor 1644

Drogheda ✕ 1649   *Irish Sea*   Preston ✕ 1648

IRELAND under English occupation 1649–60   • Dublin

Anglesey   Chester •   Nantwich ✕ 1644   • Newark

ENGLAND

• Limerick   **WALES**   Naseby ✕ 1645

Waterford • ✕ Wexford 1649   Worcester ✕ 1651   ✕ Edgehill 1642

Oxford • London

Newbury 1643/44 ✕   ✕ Basing House 1645

Lostwithiel ✕ 1644   Winchester •

• Plymouth   *English Channel*   **FRANCE**

Corfe Castle •

Celtic Sea

0 200 km
0 150 mi

Seine

273

1660–1670 A.D.

AMERICAS

1661 The Dutch West India Company formally renounces its interest in Brazil.

1662 Slavery is authorized in the English colony of Virginia.

1663 King Charles II of England grants a royal charter to the proprietors of the Carolina colony. Four years later he also grants them rights over the Bahama Islands.

1664 English forces take New Amsterdam from the Dutch. Fearing annexation by the newcomers, the colony of New Haven unites with Connecticut.

EUROPE

1663 An Ottoman army is turned back in the Alps at St. Gothard, an apparent triumph for European power, but the Ottoman Empire comes off best in the ensuing negotiations.

1665 The Second Anglo-Dutch War breaks out, with the Dutch supported by France and Denmark. The English win an initial victory over a Dutch fleet off Lowestoft.

1665 The Great Plague breaks out in London. Over the next 18 months it will claim 68,500 lives in England.

1665 Philip IV of Spain dies and is succeeded by the sickly Charles II.

1666 The Great Fire of London destroys over 13,000 houses and almost 90 churches.

1666 Reforms in the Russian Orthodox church lead to the defection of the conservative Old Believers.

1667 The Dutch defeat an English fleet at the Battle of the Medway River.

1667 The Treaty of Breda brings peace between the Dutch Republic, England, France, and Denmark.

1667 The Russo–Polish war ends with the Treaty of Andrussovo.

AFRICA

c.1660 In response to growing Western influence Islamic leader Nasir al-Din launches a *jihad* (holy war) in the kingdoms of northern Senegambia (between the Senegal and Gambia rivers).

Mulay Rashid, sultan of Morocco.

1661 Garcia II dies and is succeeded as king of Kongo by Antonio I. The kingdom is coming under increasing pressure from Portuguese forces based in the colony of Angola to the south.

WESTERN ASIA

1661 The Ottoman Grand Vizier Mehmed Kiuprili dies, to be succeeded by his son, starting a dynastic tradition in the post that will survive for more than a century.

1664 After their defeat at the Battle of St. Gothard the Ottomans salvage their authority in the Peace of Vasvar, concluded on favorable terms with the Austrians thanks to the Kiuprilis' diplomatic skills.

1665 Shabbetai Tzevi, the "False Messiah," proclaims his messianic mission. His claims are dismissed by rabbis but euphorically embraced by ordinary Jews throughout the Diaspora.

SOUTH & CENTRAL ASIA

1662 Mughal forces of the Emperor Aurangzeb conquer Assam, although they will be forced out again four years later.

1664 The Mughal armies continue their conquests in northeast India by taking Bengal.

1664 Sivaji sacks Surat: He is beginning to carve out a Marathan Hindu kingdom in the southern Deccan.

1666 The deposed Mughal Emperor Shah Jahan dies in prison in Agra.

EAST ASIA & OCEANIA

1662 Dutch forces drive the Spanish from the Moluccas.

1662 The Chinese rebel leader Zheng Chenggong (Coxinga) establishes a new base on Taiwan, taking control of the island from the Dutch.

1663 Spanish settlers abandon their fort at Zamboanga and with it their interest as a colonial power in the southern Philippines.

👑 **1665** French Jesuit Claude Jean Allouez founds the Chequamagon Bay Mission on Lake Superior's Wisconsin shore.

👑 **1669** Having been stung by French indifference into seeking English backing, Médard Chouart des Grosseilliers and Pierre-Esprit Radisson found Fort Charles by the shore of Hudson Bay.

⊕ **1669** René-Robert Cavelier, sieur de La Salle, sets out from Montreal to explore areas south of Lakes Ontario and Erie.

AMERICAS

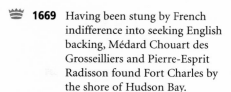

As the photograph suggests, the *starovery*, or Old Believers, remain a presence in Russia to this day. The movement had its origins in the 1660s, when the patriarch of the Russian Orthodox church announced sweeping liturgical reforms that conservatives within the church refused to accept. Breaking away, they formed their own schismatic movement, which subsequently split into a number of different sects. The Old Believers, who remain deeply traditional in their views, suffered persecution for the first two centuries of their existence but won official recognition from 1871 on.

EUROPE

⊕ **1663** An English trading post is established in Sierra Leone, West Africa.

👑 **1664** Mulay Rashid becomes ruler of the Alawid clan of southern Morocco.

✗ **1665** Antonio I is killed by the Portuguese at the Battle of Mbwila. Kongo begins to disintegrate.

👑 **1666** Mulay Rashid takes Fez from Morocco's ruling Saadi Dynasty, now in steep decline, and establishes his capital there.

👑 **1667** King Fasilides of Ethiopia dies, to be succeeded by his son John I.

AFRICA

👑 **1666** Safavid Shah Abbas II dies, but the persecution of non-Muslims in Persia continues under his son Shah Sulayman.

Memorial shrine in the house of the "False Messiah" Shabbetai Tzevi in Izmir, Turkey.

✗ **1668** Ottoman forces capture Basra on the southern coast of Iraq; the rule of the Afrasiyab Dynasty in the city is overthrown.

✗ **1669** Ottoman forces finally take Candia, and with it all Crete, from the Venetians.

WESTERN ASIA

⊕ **1668** The English East India Company is granted land for a colony at Bombay (Mumbai).

☀ **1669** Aurangzeb outlaws Hindu worship in India, a major step in enforcing an increasingly intolerant Sunni Islamic state.

SOUTH & CENTRAL ASIA

👑 **1664** Siam (modern Thailand) is forced into signing a treaty giving the Dutch a monopoly on its foreign trade.

✗ **1666** Mughal forces take the Burmese port of Chittagong.

☀ **1668** The Spanish Jesuit Diego Luis de San Vitores establishes a mission on Guam in the Mariana Islands.

EAST ASIA & OCEANIA

1660–1670 A.D.

FRANCE'S SUN KING

LOUIS XIV HIMSELF BEST SUMMED UP *his constitutional position in France when he proclaimed, "L'Etat, c'est moi" ("I am the State"). For much of his 73-year reign it seemed just so: France reached a zenith under the Sun King, emerging as Europe's preeminent power and eclipsing such earlier rivals as England and Spain. Yet there was a downside to Louis's rule: The cost of his endless wars overtaxed the treasury, and his absolutism eventually paved the way for the French Revolution.*

▲ The sun radiates in majesty above the Earth on a silver medallion coined in Louis XIV's time. France's all-powerful monarch delighted in solar imagery, seeing the splendor of his own rule as an earthly reflection of the sun's heavenly glory.

Few would have guessed when Louis XIV became king of France in 1643 that he was destined to be the dominant figure of his age. He was only five years old at the time and seemed an insignificant figure beside his capable regent Cardinal Mazarin, who quickly stamped his mark on an office he filled with energy and autocratic arrogance. Thanks to Mazarin's deft diplomatic footwork, the Treaty of Westphalia concluding the Thirty Years' War proved a triumph for France, now a leading actor on the European stage. At home, though, Mazarin came to be hated. Hunger and high taxes alienated the common people, while his high-handed treatment of the nobility provoked a bitter and protracted series of revolts, collectively known as the Fronde, against his rule.

Louis only emerged as a dominant figure in his own right on Mazarin's death in 1661. The expected announcement of a new chief minister never came; instead, Louis assembled a team of exceptional talents that were to serve him well over the ensuing decades.

These men included the Marquis de Louvois, who became minister of war; the engineer Vauban, famed for his defensive fortresses; and above all, Jean-Baptiste Colbert, controller of France's finances for over 20 years. The main goals the young king set himself were to tame the fractious aristocracy that had so troubled Mazarin and to replace the Hapsburg rulers of the Holy Roman Empire and Spain as Europe's most powerful monarch.

Louis's marriage to Maria Teresa, the heiress to the Spanish crown, gave him the perfect lever with which to chip away at Spanish power. Nominally his queen had given up all claim to the Spanish throne in exchange for the payment of a huge dowry, but Louis was able to use bankrupt Spain's inability to come up with the money as a pretext for war. France's early successes against the Spanish Netherlands alarmed not only the neighboring Dutch Republic but also the two main northern European powers, England and Sweden. Together they formed the Triple Alliance,

---

1643 Louis XIV becomes king of France at the age of five.

1648 The Treaty of Westphalia concludes the Thirty Years' War: The setbacks the settlement represents for Hapsburg Spain and the Holy Roman Empire are a boost for France.

1648 The Fronde (literally "catapult") breaks out—a five-year series of revolts against the crown (–1653).

1659 France's chief minister, Cardinal Mazarin, brokers the Treaty of the Pyrenees. Louis agrees to wed the Spanish Infanta (crown princess) Maria Teresa, who renounces her claims to the Spanish throne in exchange for the payment of a large dowry by Spain.

1661 Cardinal Mazarin dies; Louis XIV makes himself absolute monarch.

1667 The War of Devolution begins with a French invasion of the Spanish Netherlands, claimed by Louis on behalf of his queen.

1668 The Triple Alliance pits England, the Dutch Republic, and Sweden against France.

1668 The War of Devolution comes to an end with the Treaty of Aix-la-Chapelle. France keeps most of its conquests in the Spanish Netherlands.

1672 France goes to war with the Dutch, later joined by the Hapsburg emperor, from whom France makes sizable gains (–1678).

1685 Louis revokes the Edict of Nantes, which since 1598 has guaranteed the right of France's Protestant Huguenots to worship freely.

1688 Louis invades Protestant states of Germany, initiating the War of the League of Augsburg (–1697).

1701 The War of the Spanish Succession begins.

1713 The Treaty of Utrecht resolves the Spanish succession issue in favor of Louis's grandson Philip, but France loses territories in the Americas and along its own northeastern frontier.

1715 Louis XIV dies and is succeeded by his son Louis XV.

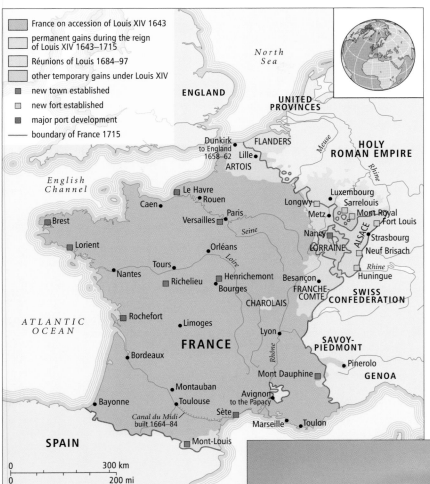

France on accession of Louis XIV 1643
permanent gains during the reign of Louis XIV 1643–1715
Réunions of Louis 1684–97
other temporary gains under Louis XIV
■ new town established
□ new fort established
■ major port development
— boundary of France 1715

which successfully checked further French expansion, although France was able to hold onto most of the conquests it had already made.

Subsequently Louis would fight three more wars against his European neighbors. The urge to defend Catholicism was a growing theme of his policy, and it also led him to launch a crackdown on France's own Protestant minority, the Huguenots. Although French armies for the most part held their own, the cost of taking on much of Europe exhausted the royal treasury and caused widespread economic hardship at home. By the later years of Louis's reign France's cultural preeminence was unchallenged, but its people were increasingly discontented, and the growing autocracy and religious intolerance of his rule had helped sow the seeds of the French Revolution.

◀ Louis XIV fought four major wars in his long reign, at first making substantial territorial gains, especially in the north and east. By the time of his death, however, his forces were overstretched and his people overtaxed, and some of the newly won lands were lost as rival powers allied to counter French might.

▼ The formality of Versailles's design was matched by the ordered ceremonial of the court life played out within its corridors and halls. Louis consciously set out to tame France's aristocracy by insisting that nobles spend most of their time at court, occupied in an unending theater of status and display.

Versailles

Louis XIV's self-promotion transcended mere vanity; he made no distinction between his own personal glory and that of the country he ruled. It seemed no more than fitting, then, that in 1668 he should give orders for a splendid palace to be built outside Paris at Versailles. Designed by Louis Le Vau and Jules Hardouin-Mansart, the edifice was conceived as a showcase for French wealth and power. The finished building was stunning in its magnificence and in its sheer scale, its western facade alone measuring 1,900 feet (580 m) long. Inside the palace hundreds of rooms were decorated with all the opulence appropriate to the royal residence of the greatest monarch of the age. Outside, in the ornamental gardens laid out by André le Nôtre, fountains played among spacious avenues and secluded walks.

AMERICAS

✕ **1670** The English pirate Henry Morgan captures Panama.

♛ **1670** English forces take possession of the Caribbean island of Jamaica.

✴ **1671** Two Englishmen, Batts and Fallam, are the first Europeans to cross the Appalachian Mountains.

☀ **1671** The Pope canonizes the first New World saint, Rose of Lima, the daughter of Spanish settlers in Peru who became a nun.

✴ **1673** French explorers Father Jacques Marquette and Louis Joliet reach the headwaters of the Mississippi River.

✴ **1674** Jacques Marquette founds a mission on the shores of Lake Michigan; it will become the city of Chicago.

♛ **1674** The Treaty of Westminster confirms the English possession of New Amsterdam; it is renamed New York.

✕ **1675** King Philip's War breaks out when native Americans under Metacomet (King Philip), chief of the Wampanoags, rise up against the colonists of New England. The rising is put down, but not before one in 16 of all adult male settlers in the region has been killed (–1676).

✴ **1679** The French begin to explore the upper Great Lakes and discover Niagara Falls.

EUROPE

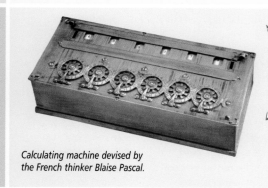

Calculating machine devised by the French thinker Blaise Pascal.

♛ **1670** By the Treaty of Dover, a secret agreement with Louis XIV, Charles II of England deserts the Triple Alliance and ends hostilities with France.

📖 **1670** The *Pensées* of Blaise Pascal, French mathematician and religious thinker, are published eight years after his death.

✕ **1672** The army of Louis XIV of France invades the Netherlands.

✕ **1674** William of Orange, leader of the Dutch Republic, floods low-lying coastal land in Holland to halt the French advance.

AFRICA

♛ **c. 1670** The Lunda Empire of central Africa extends its grip to the upper Zambezi River region.

♛ **c.1670** The Ashanti are by now beginning to emerge as a powerful state in West Africa.

♛ **1672** Mulay Ismail succeeds Mulay Rashid as sultan of Morocco.

WESTERN ASIA

✕ **1672** The Ottoman Empire goes to war with Poland, winning Podolia and parts of Polish Ukraine (–1676).

📖 **1673** French traveler Jean Chardin visits Esfahan on a great journey through Turkey and Persia.

✕ **1677** War breaks out between the Ottoman Empire and Russia following Cossack raids on Ottoman territory.

SOUTH & CENTRAL ASIA

♛ **1674** The French East India Company founds a base at Pondicherry, south of Madras in India.

♛ **1674** Sivaji, the leader of the Marathas of western India, has himself crowned as a Hindu king.

☀ **1675** Aurangzeb arrests and executes the Sikh guru Tegh Bahadur, who had refused to embrace Islam.

☀ **1675** Goband Singh becomes the last of the Ten Gurus of Sikhism and openly rebels against the Mughals.

📖 **1677** Jean Chardin reaches India on his travels, visiting the courts of the Mughals and the Deccani sultans before returning to Europe.

EAST ASIA & OCEANIA

✴ **1673** Mitsui Takatoshi of the Mitsui banking family opens a dry goods store in Edo, Japan; it is the predecessor of the celebrated Mitsukoshi department store.

♛ **1673** A French mission brings letters from the pope and King Louis XIV of France to the court of Siam (Thailand).

✕ **1673** The revolt of the Three Feudatories breaks out in China when Wu Sangui, governor of Yunnan and Guizhou provinces, refuses to accept an order to give up his office (–1681).

King Philip's War broke out in 1675 in response to settlers' encroachments on Native American lands in New England. Metacomet, known to the colonists as King Philip, led an alliance of the tribes living from Maine to Rhode Island in a ferocious campaign that took the insurgents within 20 miles (30 km) of Boston, attacking 52 of New England's 90 settlements and destroying 12 of them. Eventually the settlers' firepower told, and the war came to an end in 1676 with Metacomet's death. His wife and children were sold into slavery in the West Indies.

AMERICAS

👑 **1675** John Sobieski is elected king of Poland.

✗ **1675** Louis XIV's General Turenne defeats the armies of Prussia and Austria at the Battle of Turkheim.

✗ **1675** The Swedes invade Brandenburg–Prussia in support of the French but are decisively beaten at the Battle of Fehrbellin.

⊕ **1676** The Royal Observatory is founded in London, England.

👑 **1676** Fyodor III becomes czar of Russia.

📖 **1678** English Puritan writer John Bunyan publishes *The Pilgrim's Progress*.

👑 **1678** By the Treaties of Nijmegen concluding the Dutch War Louis XIV gains valuable territories in the north and east of France; he is now the most powerful ruler in Europe (–1679).

EUROPE

✗ **1677** The French capture Dutch trading posts on the coast of Senegal.

AFRICA

Kara Mustafa, Ottoman grand vizier from 1678 until 1683.

👑 **1678** Kara Mustafa, a brother-in-law of Ahmed Kiuprili, becomes grand vizier and effective ruler of the Ottoman Empire.

WESTERN ASIA

✗ **1679** Aurangzeb seizes the Rajput Kingdom of Marwar.

👑 **1679** Aurangzeb restores the *jiziya* tax levied by the Mughals on non-Muslims.

SOUTH & CENTRAL ASIA

✗ **1678** The Khanate of Kokand (modern Uzbekistan) overthrows the Khanate of Kashgar.

✗ **1679** Galdan, ruler of the Oirat and Zunghar Mongols, conquers much of present-day Xinjiang province with the help of the Dalai Lama.

Shanhaiguan Castle in northern China, held by Wu Sangui at the time of the Manchu takeover.

EAST ASIA & OCEANIA

1670–1680 A.D.

THE DUTCH REPUBLIC

THE STORY OF THE DUTCH REPUBLIC *is one of determination, enterprise, and good fortune. By the mid 17th century this small country on the coast of northern Europe, still less than 50 years old, had become the most powerful trading nation in the world. Dutch ships sailed far and wide, carrying grain and timber from the Baltic to France and Spain and bringing spices and luxury goods from Southeast Asia to Europe. As Dutch merchants and traders grew rich and prosperous, the country enjoyed a golden age of art and science.*

▲ A relief sculpture shows a Dutch warship of the type used to support the nation's far-flung mercantile interests. The prosperity of the Netherlands in the 17th century relied heavily on mastery of the sea.

▶ The Dutch trading empire had three main focuses. First and foremost came the Spice Islands of the Dutch East Indies, followed by trading posts on the Indian coast. The third area was the Caribbean, which supported a busy trade in sugar, tobacco, and slaves.

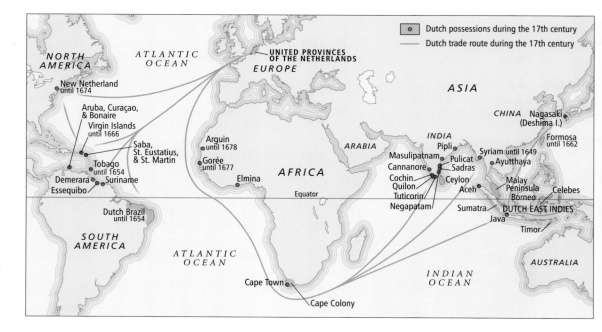

- ● Dutch possessions during the 17th century
- — Dutch trade route during the 17th century

1588 The United Provinces become a republic, having won their freedom from Spain.

1602 The Dutch East India Company is founded to trade with Southeast Asia.

1609 The Amsterdam stock exchange is founded.

1619 The Dutch East India Company founds a trading station at Batavia (now Jakarta) on Java, which becomes the center of its Asian trading empire.

1629 French philosopher René Descartes settles in the Dutch Republic, remaining there until 1649.

1642 Rembrandt paints *The Nightwatch*.

1642 Dutch navigator Abel Tasman discovers Tasmania (which he calls Van Diemen's Land) and New Zealand.

1648 Spain formally recognizes the independence of the Dutch Republic in the Treaty of Westphalia.

1656 Christiaan Huygens builds a pendulum clock.

c.1660 The painter Jan Vermeer is at his peak, painting domestic interiors such as *The Girl with a Pearl Earring*.

1667 A Dutch fleet sails up England's Thames and Medway rivers and destroys the naval shipyards at Chatham during the Second Anglo-Dutch War.

1672 Louis XIV of France sends an army to invade the Netherlands. To halt its advance, the Dutch open the dykes and flood lowlying lands. In this crisis William III of Orange comes to power (–1678).

1677 William marries Mary, eldest daughter of James, duke of York (later James II of England).

1689 William accepts the throne of England and rules jointly with his wife.

In the mid-16th century the Netherlands were part of the Catholic Kingdom of Spain. Most Dutch people were Protestant, however, and also disliked paying high taxes to Spain, so they rebelled. At first the Spanish put down the revolt with great ferocity. But in 1579 seven northern provinces formed an alliance to continue the struggle, and in 1588 these United Provinces declared themselves a republic. Although Dutch independence had in practice been gained, Spain refused to recognize the republic as an independent state until 1648.

The Netherlands lay at the crossroads of European trade. When the Spanish-held port of Antwerp went into decline as a result of the Dutch revolt, the port of Amsterdam was ready to take over. Soon enterprising Dutch merchants had seized control of the profitable spice trade from Portugal. Industries such as sugar refining and shipbuilding added to the wealth of the young state, while its policy of religious tolerance encouraged refugees from all over Europe to settle in its towns. The newcomers brought valuable skills with them such as clock- and telescope-making. Meanwhile Dutch engineers increased the amount of agricultural land by developing windmills to pump water and create polders (areas of land reclaimed from the sea).

The republic's prosperity encouraged an artistic blossoming. To show off their wealth, rich merchants had portraits painted of themselves and their families, and decorated the walls of their new townhouses with landscapes and scenes of everyday life by artists such as Vermeer, de Hooch, Cuyp, and Frans Hals. The outstanding Dutch painter of the day was Rembrandt, whose self-portraits and pictures such as *The Nightwatch* and *The Anatomy Lesson* are among the world's great masterpieces.

The republic was governed by the States-General, a parliament representing all the provinces, but the most powerful official was the stadtholder (chief magistrate) of Holland, the richest province. In practice this office was almost always held by the princes of Orange, whose forebear, William the Silent, had led the Dutch revolt. In effect, the office became hereditary, and in time the stadtholder was recognized as the head of government. When, in 1689, William of Orange became king of England following the expulsion of James II, he effectively became ruler of both countries. Previously the Dutch and English had fought three wars for mastery of the sea, but in future the English would take the leading role in colonial trade, bringing the republic's great days to an end.

Tulipmania

It is rare for a flower to bring about financial ruin, but that is what happened to hundreds of Dutch investors when the demand for tulip bulbs reached a peak in the 1630s. The vibrant colors of the blooms, recently introduced into Europe from Turkey, made them highly popular with gardeners. The sandy soils of the Netherlands proved well suited to growing the bulbs, which quickly became a fashionable status item. Soon people proved willing to pay high prices to get hold of them. In 1636 tulips began to be traded on the stock exchange of several Dutch towns, and the fashion turned into a speculative boom. People mortgaged their houses, land, and even businesses in order to make a killing in the tulip market, and bulbs were sold and resold while they were still in the ground. But the craze could not last. A panic set in in 1637, and the market collapsed overnight, sweeping away fortunes in its wake.

◀ Painted in 1642 when the great Dutch painter Rembrandt was 36 years old, *The Nightwatch* was commissioned as a group portrait of a civic guard

AMERICAS

⊛ **1681** French explorer the sieur de La Salle travels down the Mississippi River to reach the sea (–1682).

☀ **1681** English Quaker William Penn founds a colony on an area of land extending west from the Delaware River; it will later become Pennsylvania.

✕ **1683** Dutch and English pirates sack Veracruz, Mexico.

✕ **1687** La Salle is murdered by mutineers while leading an expedition to explore the Mississippi Delta.

✕ **1689** La Salle's colony on the coast of Texas is attacked and completely destroyed by Native Americans.

✕ **1689** War between England and France in Europe spreads to North America as King William's War, the first of the French and Indian Wars, which set settlers from the two nations against one another.

EUROPE

♔ **1682** Louis XIV moves his court to the new palace of Versailles outside Paris.

✕ **1683** The Polish King John Sobieski leads an army to the rescue of Vienna, which is under siege by an Ottoman army.

Shown here on an ivory vase decoration, John III Sobieski was a champion of the European struggle against the Ottoman Turks. Elected to the Polish throne in 1674, he made common cause with the Hapsburg ruler of Austria when Ottoman forces invaded his lands and, as commander of a combined Austrian and Polish army, raised the siege of Vienna. He subsequently joined the Holy League against the Turks, but his later attempts to detach Black Sea territories from the Ottoman Empire came to nothing.

AFRICA

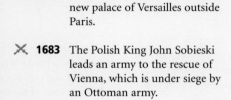

The dodo, made exinct by overhunting.

⊛ **1681** The last dodo, a large flightless bird, is killed by sailors on the island of Mauritius.

♔ **1682** Isayu I becomes king of Ethiopia and begins to open the country to trade with European and Arab states.

WESTERN ASIA

♔ **1681** Ottoman Grand Vizier Kara Mustafa assembles a large army to invade central Europe.

♔ **1683** After the defeat of the Ottoman army at the gates of Vienna Kara Mustafa is beheaded on the orders of the sultan.

♔ **1687** Mehmed IV, known for his love of hunting, is deposed as Ottoman sultan and replaced by his younger brother, Suleiman II.

SOUTH & CENTRAL ASIA

♔ **1680** The Maratha leader Sivaji dies. Known as the Grand Rebel, he had succeeded in thwarting the Mughal ruler Aurangzeb by establishing an independent Hindu kingdom in the Deccan.

♔ **1681** Prince Akbar leads an unsuccessful revolt against his father Aurangzeb, for which he is exiled.

♔ **1685** Aurangzeb expels the English East India Company from its base at Surat in western India.

EAST ASIA & OCEANIA

♔ **1680** The first Portuguese governor is appointed to Macao on the coast of China.

✕ **1683** The Chinese use their fleet to expel the warlords who have occupied Taiwan since 1662; for the first time the island comes under direct imperial administration.

♔ **1684** The Japanese chief minister Hotta Mastoshi is assassinated, leaving Shogun Sunayoshi without advisers; he imposes impractical reforms that create widespread hardship.

This painting by American artist Edward Hicks shows William Penn, the English Quaker leader and founder of Pennsylvania, signing a treaty with local Native Americans. Penn obtained the territory from King Charles II in repayment of a royal debt owed to his father. He established a constitution for the colony that guaranteed religious freedom, and he achieved lasting good relations with the neighboring Delaware tribes by insisting that the treaty obligations were rigorously observed.

AMERICAS

👑 **1684** Pope Innocent XI establishes the Holy League, an alliance of Poland, Venice, and Hapsburg Austria, to liberate Europe from Turkish rule.

☀ **1685** Louis XIV cancels the Edict of Nantes, ending toleration of French Huguenots; thousands flee to Protestant lands.

✗ **1687** The Venetians besiege Athens, Greece, during a war against the Turks. A stray shell ignites an ammunition dump inside the Parthenon, and the ancient Greek temple is badly damaged.

✗ **1688** The Holy League captures Belgrade (modern Serbia) from the Ottomans.

👑 **1688** James II of England is deposed for his Catholic views.

✗ **1689** England, the Netherlands, Spain, and other European nations ally against Louis XIV's France in the War of the League of Augsburg (–1697).

📖 **1689** English philosopher John Locke publishes *An Essay Concerning Human Understanding.*

EUROPE

👑 **1684** The English abandon Tangier, on the coast of North Africa, and it passes to Morocco.

✗ **1684** The French attack pirate bases on the North African coast.

✗ **1686** French settlers build a fort on the island of Madagascar, which they claim as a French possession.

☀ **1688** French Huguenot refugees arrive as settlers in the Dutch colony of South Africa.

AFRICA

👑 **1689** Suleiman II makes Mustafa Kiuprili his grand vizier; he begins to reform the Ottoman army and administration.

Ottoman Sultan Suleiman II, painted by an Italian artist.

WESTERN ASIA

✗ **1686** Aurangzeb conquers the Muslim Sultanate of Bijapur in the northwestern Deccan.

✗ **1687** Golconda, famous for its diamonds, falls to Aurangzeb.

✗ **1689** Sambhaji, Shivaji's son, is captured by a Mughal force; he is brought to Aurangzeb and executed.

SOUTH & CENTRAL ASIA

📖 **1684** The Japanese poet Saikuku composes 23,500 verses in 24 hours.

⊕ **1684** The Dutch East India Company occupies the Sultanate of Bantam on Java.

⊕ **1684** The English East India Company is granted permission to build a trading station at Canton (now Guangzhou) in southern China.

⊕ **1685** An English trading station is founded at Benkulen on the Indonesian island of Sumatra for the export of pepper.

EAST ASIA & OCEANIA

1680–1690 A.D.

RUSSIA'S DRIVE TO THE EAST

MOST PEOPLE HAVE HEARD OF *the great sailors such as Magellan, Tasman, and Cook who mapped the empty spaces of the Pacific Ocean, or of Lewis and Clark who made the first transcontinental crossing of North America. The story of the Russian pioneers who ventured overland across the vast expanses of Siberia to reach the Pacific Ocean is less well known, but it was filled with drama and excitement.*

Siberia stretches from the Ural Mountains in the west all the way across northern Asia to the Pacific Ocean in the east. The Arctic Ocean bounds it to the north and the mountains of Central Asia in the south. In between lie expanses of frozen tundra, vast forests, and swampy plains and lakelands, intersected at intervals by wide, northward-flowing rivers that empty into the Arctic Ocean.

Russians began to move beyond the Urals in the late 16th century. Encouraged by Czar Ivan the Terrible, a Cossack chief called Yermak Timofeyevich led an armed band of horsemen that in 1582 defeated Kuchum, the khan (ruler) of the local tribes, after a three-day battle. Yermak drowned soon after while crossing a river, dragged down, it was said, by his chainmail coat, a present from the czar.

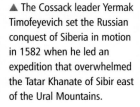

▲ The Cossack leader Yermak Timofeyevich set the Russian conquest of Siberia in motion in 1582 when he led an expedition that overwhelmed the Tatar Khanate of Sibir east of the Ural Mountains.

▶ Spectacular mountains like this peak near Petropavlovsk dot the Kamchatka Peninsula in the Russian far east, which has over a dozen active volcanoes. The first Russian to claim the peninsula was Vladimir Atlasov, who built two forts there in 1697.

🜲 **1574** Ivan IV "the Terrible" grants the Stroganov merchant family land along the Tura and Tubol rivers east of the Ural Mountains.

✕ **1582** Commissioned by the Stroganovs, the Cossack leader Yermak defeats Kuchum, khan of Sibir (a region of western Siberia), and captures his capital, Kashlyk.

✕ **1587** A Russian fort is built at Tobolsk, not far from Kashlyk.

✕ **1607** The Cossacks overcome resistance from the Tungus hunters of Siberia (–1610).

🜲 **1632** Yakutsk is founded on the Lena River.

✳ **1639** The first Russians reach the Pacific Ocean.

✳ **1644** Vassili Poyarkov crosses the watershed from the Aldan to the Zeya River and reaches the Amur Basin.

✕ **1648** A Russian fort is built on the upper Uda River beyond Lake Baikal.

✳ **1648** Semyon Dezhnyov sails through the Bering Strait.

✳ **1651** Yerofey Khabarov charts the Amur River (–1653).

🜲 **1689** The Russians give up the Amur Basin by the Treaty of Nerchinsk.

🜲 **1697** The Kamchatka Peninsula is claimed for Russia.

Semyon Dezhnyov, Arctic Explorer

Semyon Dezhnyov was a Cossack who made his way to northeast Siberia in search of furs and walrus tusks. In 1648 he led an expedition of about 100 men in seven small boats from the mouth of the Kolyma River on the Arctic coast eastward around the Chukotka Peninsula. Only three of the boats got as far as the entrance to the Bering Strait (later named Cape Dezhnyov), and only one made it all the way to the mouth of the Anadyr River. By making this perilous journey, Dezhnyov became the first person to show that the continents of Asia and North America were not joined. Some historians believe that the Dezhnyov expedition may have been the first to land in Alaska, but the theory remains unproven. It is known that Dezhnyov explored a number of islands in the Bering Strait and noted that the people inhabiting them decorated their lower lips with fragments of bone, stone, or walrus tusk.

Over the next century the Russians advanced rapidly. Most of the pioneers were Cossacks, warrior–adventurers from southern Russia. They traveled along the river systems in boats in the summer and in sleds when the steams were frozen in winter. As they advanced, they built fortified settlements where they could trade with local fur trappers, and each year a large consignment of the finest sables made its way back to the Russian court. They reached the Yenisey River by 1619 and the Lena River, where they founded the town of Yakutsk, by 1632. From there they made their way north to the Arctic Ocean. The first Russians reached the Sea of Okhotsk, an inlet of the Pacific, in about 1639. They founded the town of Anadyrsk on the Bering Sea and penetrated the mountainous Kamchatka Peninsula, Asia's northeasternmost point.

Meanwhile other explorers ventured south from Yakutsk. In 1643 Vassili Poyarkov led an expedition up the Aldan River to cross the mountains that divide Siberia from Outer Mongolia. His men reached the Amur River and journeyed down it to the Sea of Okhotsk, returning to Yakutsk in 1646. From 1651 to 1653 Yerofey Khabarov charted the length of the Amur River. A number of Russian forts were built along its banks, garrisoned by Cossacks who clashed with Chinese forces that were expanding into Mongolia from the south and considered the whole of the Amur Basin to be within their sphere of influence. At length the Russians agreed to abandon the forts. The Treaty of Nerchinsk (1689), which confirmed Chinese control over the Amur River, was the first treaty the Chinese ever made with a European power.

▶ An early print shows the city of Yakutsk, a Russian settlement in eastern Siberia built on the banks of the Lena River. The first fort was built there in 1632. Remote from other population centers and subject to extreme climate swings between winter and summer, the city served for centuries to harbor prisoners, political or otherwise, sentenced to internal exile.

▶ Russia's progress eastward across Siberia can be tracked by the new towns founded there in the 17th century. Most started out as forts or small fortified settlements.

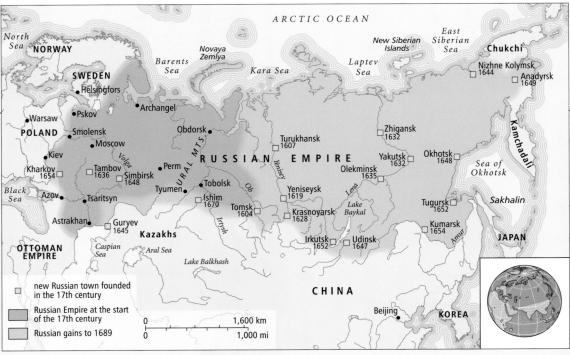

AMERICAS

The arrest of a witch in 17th-century New England as imagined by the illustrator Howard Pyle.

⚔ **1690** A Puritan force from Massachusetts lays unsuccessful siege to the city of Quebec during King William's War.

☀ **1692** In Salem, Massachusetts, 19 women and girls are executed for witchcraft.

👑 **1692** Food shortages in Mexico City lead to the "Corn Riots," in which public buildings are burned.

📖 **1693** William and Mary College is founded in Williamsburg, Virginia.

EUROPE

📖 **1690** The clarinet is invented in Nuremberg, Germany.

⚔ **1690** The Battle of the Boyne is fought in Ireland between England's deposed King James II, a Catholic, and his Protestant son-in-law and successor King William III. James's defeat ends his campaign to regain the English throne.

📖 **1694** François-Marie Arouet is born in France; he will become famous as the philosopher Voltaire.

⚔ **1696** Peter the Great, czar of Russia, captures the important seaport of Azov near the mouth of the Don River from the Ottomans (–1698).

👑 **1697** Peter the Great makes a grand tour of Europe; traveling incognito, he visits shipyards in England and the Netherlands.

👑 **1697** Charles XII becomes king of Sweden at the age of 15.

👑 **1697** The Treaty of Ryswick ends the War of the League of Augsburg; all the towns and forts seized by Louis XIV since the Treaty of Nijmegen (1679) are to be handed back to their original owners.

AFRICA

☀ **c.1695** Isayu I of Ethiopia builds many churches in his capital Gondar, located north of Lake Tana.

👑 **1697** A French expedition led by André de Brue lays claim to Senegal in West Africa.

Church decorations in Gondar, Ethiopia.

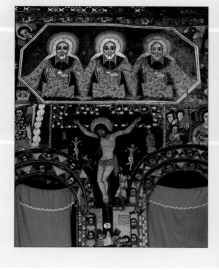

WESTERN ASIA

⚔ **1690** Mustafa Kiuprili organizes a large army that drives the Austrian army out of Serbia.

👑 **1691** Sultan Suleiman II is succeeded by his brother Ahmed II.

⚔ **1691** Mustafa Kiuprili is killed fighting the Austrians at the Battle of Slankamen.

👑 **1694** Shah Suleiman of Persia dies and is succeeded by Shah Hussein.

SOUTH & CENTRAL ASIA

⚔ **1690** Rajaram, Sambhaji's brother and successor as Maratha leader, is besieged in the great fortress of Senji by a Mughal army (–1698).

⚙ **1690** Job Charnock, chief agent for the English East India Company in Bengal, founds a trading station at Calcutta.

EAST ASIA & OCEANIA

⚔ **1690** The Manchu court sends an army to defend the Mongols of Khalka (Outer Mongolia) against their neighbors, the Zunghars (West Mongols).

Matsuo Basho (1644–94), Japan's master of the three-line haiku poem.

📖 **1694** Death of Matsuo Basho, considered the greatest of the Japanese *haiku* poets.

⊕ **c.1695** Gold deposits are discovered in Minas Gerais, Brazil, leading to a gold rush that attracts prospectors from Portugal.

✕ **1697** King William's War between England and France ends with the English in possession of Port Royal (now in Nova Scotia).

✕ **1697** The Spanish conquer Tayasal, capital of the last independent Maya state of Guatemala, which is located on an island in Lake Pétén Itzá.

⊕ **1698** The English Parliament passes the Woolens Act forbidding colonists in New England to ship wool or woolen products directly from one colony to another.

👑 **1699** The French colony of Louisiana is founded.

⊕ **1698** English engineer Thomas Savery develops the first practical high-pressure steam engine for pumping water out of mines.

👑 **1699** The Ottomans cede most of Hungary to the Hapsburg rulers of Austria by the Treaty of Karlowitz, which concludes the war between Turkey and the Holy League and brings the era of

Charles XII of Sweden made his reputation as a military leader at the start of the Great Northern War, winning important victories over Danish, Saxon, and Russian forces. But an attempt to invade Russia in 1707 led to disastrous defeat at Poltava in 1709. Charles escaped to Ottoman territory in the Crimea, where he remained as a virtual prisoner for five years. He eventually returned to the Baltic region in 1714, spending the last years of his life in inconclusive military maneuvers before he was shot dead at a siege in Norway in 1718.

✕ **1698** The Omani Arabs drive the Portuguese from their ports on the coast of East Africa and set up the Zanzibar Sultanate (–1700).

👑 **1699** Louis XIV of France sends an envoy to Ethiopia; he travels to Gondar overland from Egypt.

👑 **1695** Mustafa II succeeds Ahmed II as Ottoman sultan.

✕ **1697** A Hapsburg force defeats an Ottoman army at the Battle of Zenta; the Turks lose nearly 30,000 men, along with huge quantities of supplies and ten of the sultan's wives.

✕ **1693** The Dutch seize Pondicherry from the French and hold it until 1697.

☀ **1699** Goband Singh founds the Khalsa Brotherhood of the Sikhs. Khalsa means "pure."

A watercolor sketch by a Jesuit missionary shows the Dutch siege of Pondicherry in 1693.

✕ **1696** Chinese forces defeat a Zunghar army at Jao Modo in Outer Mongolia.

✕ **1697** The Chinese overrun and occupy Outer Mongolia.

⊕ **1699** William Dampier becomes the first Englishman to land on Australia's west coast; he goes on to discover the Dampier Archipelago, named for him.

AMERICAS

EUROPE

AFRICA

WESTERN ASIA

SOUTH & CENTRAL ASIA

EAST ASIA & OCEANIA

1690–1700 A.D.

287

THE SCIENTIFIC REVOLUTION

WE TAKE IT FOR GRANTED THAT THE HEART *pumps blood around the body, that the planets orbit the sun, and that there are tiny organisms smaller than the human eye can see. Yet few people before 1600 would have believed any of these things. The situation had changed markedly by the end of the century, for enormous advances in knowledge had transformed understanding of the physical world. These advances are what historians describe as the scientific revolution of the 17th century.*

▲ A 17th-century astrolabe, used to measure the altitude of stars and planets.

Seventeenth-century Europeans were not the first people to study the nature of things. The Greeks had a great understanding of mathematics, astronomy, and the natural world; the Arabs studied medicine and mechanics. In early modern Europe, however, the Catholic church held that the Earth was the center of the universe as created by God, and that the universe was perfect and unchanging. This Bible-based view also accorded with the teachings of the fourth-century-B.C. Greek philosopher Aristotle. Anyone who challenged Aristotle's ideas therefore challenged the authority of the church.

Polish astronomer Nicolaus Copernicus used his knowledge of mathematics to calculate that the planets move around the sun rather than the sun around the Earth. He did not publish his ideas until 1543, when he was on his deathbed. It would be more than 60 years before anyone dared agree with him. Then, in 1609, the German astronomer Johannes Kepler argued that the planets moved in elliptical, rather than circular, orbits (an ellipse is a flattened oval), and in Italy Galileo used a telescope—a recent invention—to observe the heavens more closely than anyone had ever done before. He was the first person to see the mountains on the moon, the moons of Jupiter, the phases of Venus, and the spots on the sun.

Galileo's observations led him to accept the Copernican system of a sun-centered universe.

Against the advice of friends he defended his ideas in a book published in 1632. The church immediately banned it and put Galileo on trial. Threatened with torture by the Inquisition, he recanted his views and was allowed to live under house arrest near Florence, where he carried on working until his death in 1642. Galileo's researches into mechanics and movement paved the way for the work of Isaac Newton, the

Large and Small

The discoveries of the scientific revolution would not have been possible without new instruments. A Dutch eyeglass-maker, Hans Lippershey, developed a telescope sometime before 1608; soon afterward Galileo Galilei used his own improved version to make revolutionary observations of the heavens. At the other end of the scale microscopes brought the world of the infinitesimally small into human view. Here again the pioneer was a Dutchman, Antoni van Leeuwenhoek, who used a lens he fashioned himself to study blood cells, fleas (right), and tiny bacteria. Another important invention was the airpump, which allowed Robert Boyle and others to investigate atmospheric gases.

⁕ **1543** Nicolaus Copernicus argues that the sun is the center of the solar system.

⁕ **1543** Andreas Vesalius publishes the first modern anatomical text.

⁕ **1600** William Gilbert, in his work on magnets, deduces that the Earth itself acts as a magnet.

⁕ **1609** Johannes Kepler publishes his first two laws of planetary motion.

⁕ **1610** Galileo describes his astronomical observations with a telescope in *The Starry Messenger*.

⁕ **1628** William Harvey proves that the heart pumps blood around the body.

⁕ **1632** Galileo publishes his defense of the Copernican system.

⁕ **1644** Evangelista Torricelli describes a mercury barometer.

⁕ **1652** To demonstrate atmospheric pressure, Otto von Guericke pumps the air from two large metal hemispheres to create a vacuum; two teams of horses cannot pull them apart.

⁕ **1662** Robert Boyle establishes that the pressure and volume of a gas are inversely proportional.

⁕ **1662** The Royal Society of London is founded under the patronage of King Charles II.

greatest genius of the scientific revolution. Newton's experiments into the nature of light and his discovery of the laws of motion and gravitation were outstanding achievements that laid the foundations of modern physics.

In the 17th century the words "science" and "scientist" did not exist, nor were the new discoveries taught in universities. Groups of people interested in "natural philosophy," as it was called, formed academies or societies where they could meet to exchange ideas, discuss their experiments, and publish their results. One of the earliest of these bodies was the Academy of the Lynx, formed in Florence, Italy, in 1603. The Royal Society, founded in England in 1662, included among its early members such men as the architect Sir Christopher Wren, the microscopist Robert Hooke, the astronomer Edmond Halley, and Isaac Newton himself. These societies had enormous influence in helping to spread the new ideas of the scientific revolution.

▼ Scientists and doctors had had a clear idea of the anatomy of the human body since the 16th-century studies of Andreas Vesalius (below). The 17th century added a new understanding of its inner workings, especially the circulation of the blood.

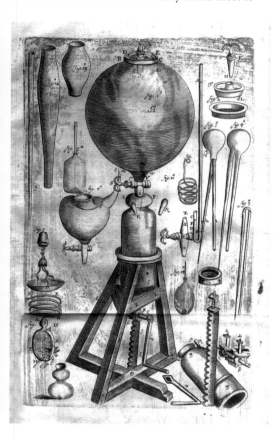

▲ An airpump devised by the English scientist Robert Boyle.

⊕ **1677** Antoni van Leeuwenhoek uses a microscope to examine male spermatozoa.

⊕ **1678** Christiaan Huygens proposes that light travels in waves.

⊕ **1687** Isaac Newton publishes *Principia Mathematica*, in which he sets out his three laws of motion.

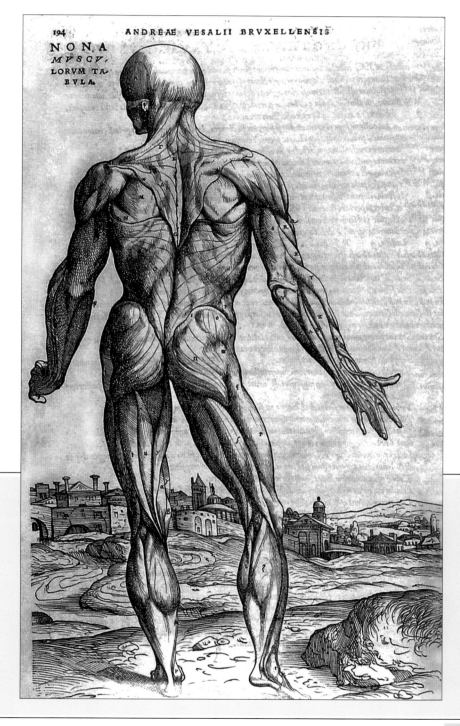

1700–1710 A.D.

AMERICAS

1701 Antoine de Cadillac founds Detroit as a trading post at a strategic site controlling trade routes between Illinois and the Atlantic coast.

1701 Yale College is established at New Haven, Connecticut.

Yale University as it looked at the turn of the 19th century.

EUROPE

1700 The Great Northern War breaks out, setting Sweden under Charles XII against Russia, Poland, and Denmark.

1700 The Academy of Sciences is founded in Berlin.

1701 England's Parliament passes the Act of Settlement, excluding Catholics from succession to the throne.

1701 Frederick III, elector of Brandenburg, has himself crowned King Frederick I of Prussia.

1701 England, the Netherlands, the Holy Roman Empire, and the German states form a Grand Alliance against France as the War of the Spanish Succession gets under way.

1702 The first English-language daily newspaper, *The Daily Courant*, starts publication in England.

1703 The Hungarians revolt against Austrian rule. Francis II Rakoczi leads the rising, which will last for eight years (–1711).

1704 England's Duke of Marlborough and Austria's Prince Eugene of Savoy lead the Grand Alliance to victory in the Battle of Blenheim.

1705 The Holy Roman Emperor Leopold I dies, to be succeeded by his son Joseph I.

AFRICA

18th-century gold head that once adorned an Ashanti royal stool.

1701 Osei Tutu embarks on a program of expansion that will unite the small principalities of the Gold Coast (modern Ghana) into a single Ashanti Kingdom.

1702 Murad III, last Muradid bey (Ottoman client ruler) of Tunis, is killed in a coup. In the ensuing confusion an army officer, Husain ibn Ali, seizes power.

WESTERN ASIA

1703 Ottoman Sultan Mustafa II abdicates in favor of his brother Ahmed III.

1704 Hasan Pasha is appointed Ottoman governor in Baghdad; his descendants will reign in the province for over 100 years.

1708 A treaty gives French merchants and missionaries special privileges in Iran, but the expected upsurge in trade does not materialize.

SOUTH & CENTRAL ASIA

1702 More than two million lives are lost to plague and famine in India's Deccan region.

1705 War breaks out in Tibet as Qosot Mongols, backed by China, attempt to oust the Zunghar Mongols. They assassinate the country's regent, Sangye Gyatso.

1707 Emperor Aurangzeb dies while on campaign against the Marathas in the Deccan. The already weakened Mughal Empire will now go into steep decline.

EAST ASIA & OCEANIA

1700 Dynastic struggles that began with the death of Souligna Vongsa without an heir in 1694 continue in Lan Xang (Laos); an exiled prince takes over the kingdom with Vietnamese backing.

1703 A major earthquake devastates Edo (modern Tokyo).

1704 The First Javanese War of Succession begins. The Dutch East India Company supports the claim of Pakubuwono I to the throne of Mataram, but exacts concessions in return (–1708).

✕ **1702** Queen Anne's War breaks out. Linked to Europe's War of the Spanish Succession, it is fought between the French and English colonies in North America (–1713).

✕ **1704** French colonists and their Native American allies raid Deerfield, Massachusetts, killing many inhabitants.

✕ **1704** The New England colonists try unsuccessfully to take Acadia from the French; they will try again—with the same result—three years later.

👑 **1706** Albuquerque, New Mexico, is founded. It is named after the then viceroy of New Spain.

AMERICAS

The Battle of Blenheim (left) was one of the chief Allied victories against the French in the War of the Spanish Succession. The conflict broke out in 1701 over rival claims to the vacant Spanish throne. Charles II of Spain had died childless, leaving two sisters, one married to Louis XIV of France, the other to the Holy Roman Emperor Leopold I. Both rulers pressed their claims, and the English and Dutch, fearful of French hegemony, came in on the emperor's side. The war dragged on for 12 years, ending in a compromise settlement at the Peace of Utrecht (1713).

✕ **1706** Alliance forces defeat the French at Ramillies and Turin.

👑 **1707** The Act of Union brings England and Scotland together in the United Kingdom of Great Britain.

✕ **1709** Alliance troops win a costly victory over the French at the Battle of Malplaquet.

✕ **1709** In the Great Northern War Peter the Great of Russia decisively defeats Charles XII of Sweden at the Battle of Poltava.

EUROPE

👑 **1705** The Husainid Dynasty is established in Tunis.

☀️ **1706** The Ethiopian Emperor Susenyos converts to Roman Catholicism.

☀️ **1706** Kimpa Vita is burned at the stake in Kongo for proclaiming her own, Africanized version of the Christian message.

✕ **1708** Algerian forces take Oran from Spain.

AFRICA

👑 **1709** Defeated by Peter the Great, Sweden's Charles XII and the Cossack leader Mazepa seek asylum in Ottoman territory.

Dancers entertain Ottoman Sultan Ahmed III in a gouache painting now in the Topkapi Museum, Istanbul.

WESTERN ASIA

✕ **1708** Banda Bahadur leads a Sikh uprising against Mughal rule in Punjab, northwestern India.

✕ **1709** Under the leadership of Mir Wais Hotaki, Ghilzai Afghans revolt against Iranian Safavid rule and occupy Kandahar.

SOUTH & CENTRAL ASIA

⊕ **1707** Mount Fuji erupts in Japan.

👑 **1707** Lan Xang is split as a group unhappy at the Vietnamese takeover forms its own breakaway kingdom, Luang Prabang.

👑 **1709** The Japanese Shogun Sunayoshi dies; his successor, Ienobu, will introduce a number of important economic reforms.

👑 **1709** The British establish a merchant colony in Myanmar (Burma).

EAST ASIA & OCEANIA

1700–1710 A.D.

PETER THE GREAT

PETER I OF RUSSIA IS SAID TO HAVE GIVEN HIMSELF *the title of "the Great," but history has not quibbled with his boast, given the legacy he left: The czar's impact on his homeland was vast. A visionary of resolution, even ruthlessness, he had the energy and determination necessary to bring the backward, feudal Russia he inherited into the modern world, turning it into a strong, confident, and forward-looking power.*

▲ To bring Russia into line with contemporary European fashions, Peter restricted the growing of beards among Russian nobles. Those who wished to sport facial hair had to pay a tax, receiving in return a copper token like the one shown here.

1672	Peter is born in Moscow, second son of Czar Alexis I.
1683	Fyodor III Alexeyevich dies childless; Peter is crowned "second czar" to his disabled half-brother Ivan V, but his half-sister Sophia Alexeyevna exerts real power as regent.
1692	Ivan's death leaves Peter sole ruler.
1696	A land and sea expedition captures the fort of Azov commanding the entry to the Black Sea.
1697	Peter undertakes a tour of western Europe (–1698).

1700	The Great Northern War breaks out, setting Russia against Charles XII of Sweden.
1709	Russian forces win a decisive victory over the Swedes at the Battle of Poltava.
1712	St. Petersburg becomes the new capital of Russia.
1712	Peter marries Catherine, a former servant.
1721	The Treaty of Nystad ends the Great Northern War, confirming Russian possession of Livonia, Estonia, and adjoining territories.

1721	Peter abolishes the patriarchate and appoints a synod in its place, putting authority over the Russian Orthodox church in lay hands.
1722	The Table of Ranks rationalizes Russia's armed forces and civil service.
1725	Death of Peter. Amid some controversy the crown passes to his widow, Catherine I.
1725	An Academy of Sciences, long projected by Peter, is founded shortly after his death.

▶ Russian ships escort captured Swedish vessels into the port of St. Petersburg following a naval victory at Hankoniemi in 1714. Peter built the Russian navy almost from nothing, ordering 52 battleships and nearly 600 oared galleys.

◀ The territories that Peter won in the Great Northern War were strategically vital in giving Russia access to the Baltic Sea. Previously, the nation's only major port had been Archangel, north of the Arctic Circle and only open to shipping for six months of the year. From Peter's day the newly won territories served as windows on the West, fostering trade and cultural relations with the European nations.

Born in 1672, Peter I became "second czar"—deputy ruler—at the age of 11 because his elder half-brother Ivan was mentally handicapped. Real power resided with his half-sister Sophia Alexeyevna until1689, when Peter wrested it from her to reign in his own right. Ivan's death in 1692 ratified Peter's position as Russia's sole ruler: His ambitions for his country were apparent from the start.

In 1696 he won his first military success, taking the Black Sea port of Azov from the Ottoman Turks. The victory served notice of Russia's emergence as an important power and also identified the nation firmly with the cause of the Christian West. The next year Peter set out on an extended tour of western Europe, observing everything from etiquette to the arts; he attended public lectures, visited factories and shipyards, and even underwent training in carpentry.

Back in Russia he did his best to inculcate the ideas and attitudes that he had encountered on his travels. He began with symbolic gestures, ordering the boyars (nobles) to shave off their beards and seeking to introduce French fashions (and the French language) in high society. Soon he was moving on to more substantive changes, bringing in foreign craftsmen and scientists in large numbers and promoting education on an unprecedented scale. He built a modern navy on the Western model and reformed many Russian institutions, including the army, the civil service, and the Orthodox church.

Peter's admiration for all things Western did not prevent him from picking quarrels with his European neighbors—notably with Sweden, then the main power in the Baltic region. The 21-year Great Northern War, which broke out in 1700, reflected Peter's resolve not only to expand Russia but also to reorient it geopolitically: Access to the Baltic Sea meant a "window on the West." By 1703 he was able to found a fort at the mouth of the Neva River, looking out across the Baltic; by 1712 Russia had a new capital on the site, St. Petersburg.

Peter was in many ways an unlikely modernizer: An intimidating, even thuggish figure, he stood almost 7 feet (2.1 m) tall and was loud and aggressive in his manner. He had little interest in the arts or scientific inquiry for their own sake, seeking rather to put the technological expertise of the Western world to use to advance Russian prosperity and power. In similar spirit most of his political reforms, which made the armed forces and bureaucracy more meritocratic, were inspired not by a sense of social justice but by the desire to strengthen the nation. So a law of 1721 helped galvanize Russian industry by allowing entrepreneurs to buy serfs like slaves from rural landowners: This advanced the economy but showed no concern at all for human rights.

St. Petersburg

Before Peter's day Russia had taken shape over the centuries around its historic capital, Moscow—a city far from coasts or borders and profoundly suspicious of the outside world. By building his new capital of St. Petersburg on the Baltic Sea, Peter tilted Russia on its traditional axis: From now on it would be a modern state looking outward to the West. An entirely new city, St. Petersburg was conceived along the most up-to-date Western lines, with wide boulevards and sweeping terraces of stone-built houses. Its setting on the Neva River was dramatic (*right*), with spacious vistas punctuated by palaces and churches. The new city was Peter's architectural manifesto, featuring state-of-the-art amenities such as street lighting, paved sidewalks, and public parks. It was also, crucially, a seaport; not only did it open a window to overseas trade and cultural commerce, but its construction announced Russia's arrival on the European stage as a naval power.

AMERICAS

⚔ **1710** New England colonists finally take French Acadia with British help.

☀ **1712** A Mayan girl's vision of the Virgin Mary sparks a revolt in Chiapas, Mexico. Her supporters renounce both the Spanish crown and traditional Christian beliefs for a cult dedicated to Mary.

👑 **1713** The Peace of Utrecht brings Queen Anne's War to an end. The French cede Newfoundland and Hudson Bay as well as Acadia to the British.

EUROPE

Louis XV, who came to the throne in 1715 at the age of five, was to rule France for almost 60 years. He proved a weak king, spending huge sums on court extravagances symbolized by the jeweled crown shown at left. Although France remained Europe's dominant power throughout his reign, its influence was gradually diminished by a series of unsuccesful wars. Internally Louis's repressive policies roused popular discontent, paving the way for the French Revolution.

👑 **1713** The War of the Spanish Succession ends with the Peace of Utrecht and the crowning of France's favored candidate, Philip V, as king of Spain.

👑 **1713** Holy Roman Emperor Charles VI announces the Pragmatic Sanction, ensuring the succession of his daughter Maria Theresa.

AFRICA

⚔ **1711** Civil war breaks out in Egypt between representatives of the Ottoman rulers of Turkey and the local governors, the Mameluke beys.

👑 **1711** Ahmed Qaramanli becomes Ottoman governor of Tripoli, establishing a dynasty that will increase the importance of the North African coastal city.

⚔ **1712** As leader of his *ton*, an initiate society turned private army, Mamari Kulibali begins extending the power of Segu across the inland delta of the Niger River.

WESTERN ASIA

⚔ **1711** Ottoman troops defeat the Russians at the Pruth River. Peter the Great returns all the Black Sea territories ceded to Russia by the Ottomans in the Treaty of Karlowitz (1699).

👑 **1711** Civil strife within the Druse community in Lebanon leads the defeated Yamani Druse to leave for Syria. Maronite Christians make up a majority of the remaining population.

⚔ **1714** The Ottoman Sultan Ahmed III declares war on the Holy Roman Empire and the Venetian Republic.

SOUTH & CENTRAL ASIA

⚔ **1710** The Sikh leader Banda Bahadur takes the Mughal fortress of Sirhind and sets up an autonomous Sikh nation in Punjab.

👑 **1712** On the death of Shah Alam (Bahadur Shah) the breakup of the Mughal Empire begins with the secession of Hyderabad as an independent state.

India's Mughal Emperor Bahadur Shah goes hunting.

⚔ **1715** Banda Bahadur is captured by the Mughal authorities and publicly executed; the Punjabi uprising is brutally put down.

⚔ **1716** The Abdali, former allies of the Safavids in western Afghanistan, take the city of Herat.

EAST ASIA & OCEANIA

👑 **1713** In Laos the breakup of Lan Xang is completed: There are now three kingdoms, centered on Vientiane and Luang Prabang in the north and Champasak in the south.

👑 **1716** Yoshimune becomes shogun of Japan. His reign will be a time of new economic and intellectual openness.

⊕ **1716** Kuzma Sokolov makes the first crossing of the Sea of Okhotsk, facilitating Russia's colonizing effort in East Asia.

👑 **1715** New immigrants and established settlers start to push into the Piedmont region of eastern Appalachia.

👑 **1717** The Viceroyalty of New Granada (Colombia, Ecuador, Venezuela, and Panama) is established, with its capital at Bogotá.

👑 **1717** The Compagnie d'Occident ("Company of the West") takes charge of French Louisiana. Two years later it will become part of the Compagnie des Indes ("Company of the Indies").

AMERICAS

👑 **1714** Queen Anne of England dies childless; she is succeeded by George I, founder of the Hanoverian Dynasty.

👑 **1715** Louis XV, aged five, succeeds to the French throne on the death of his great grandfather Louis XIV.

✗ **1715** The first Jacobite uprising breaks out in Scotland, aiming unsuccessfully to set James Edward Stuart, the "Old Pretender," on the British throne.

✗ **1717** Spain takes the Mediterranean island of Sardinia from Austria.

✗ **1718** Spain takes Sicily from Savoy.

📖 **1719** English author Daniel Defoe writes his classic novel *Robinson Crusoe*, inspired by the real-life experiences of marooned seaman Alexander Selkirk 15 years earlier.

EUROPE

☀ **1714** The Jesuits establish a mission in Sierra Leone.

👑 **1715** The Dutch buy forts on West Africa's Gold Coast established in the late 17th century by the German Duchy of Brandenburg.

👑 **1715** Oba Akenzua I takes power in Benin, West Africa, bringing to an end several decades of dynastic squabbling.

AFRICA

👑 **1718** The Peace of Passarowitz ends the war between the Ottomans and the Holy Roman Empire, which gains territory in the Balkans and Hungary.

📖 **1718** Damad Ibrahim Pasha is appointed Ottoman grand vizier, ushering in the Tulip Period, a time of cultural renewal in the empire.

WESTERN ASIA

👑 **1716** The Mughal Emperor Farrukhsiyar confers special trading privileges on the British East India Company.

✗ **1717** Manchu forces drive the Zunghar Mongols from Tibet. Within three years they will have established their own Dalai Lama and made the country a Chinese protectorate.

Mughal Emperor Muhammad Shah visits the countryside.

✗ **1717** Russia invades the Khiva khanate of Uzbekistan.

✗ **1719** Now led by Mir Wais Hotaki's son Mir Mahmud, the Ghilzai Afghans invade Iran, attacking Irfan and laying siege to Esfahan.

👑 **1719** Muhammad Shah becomes Mughal emperor following the assassination of Farrukhsiyar.

SOUTH & CENTRAL ASIA

👑 **1718** Spanish colonists reopen the fortress of Zamboanga on the island of Mindanao, renewing their presence in the southern Philippines after a break of almost 60 years.

✗ **1719** The Second Javanese War of Succession begins on the death of Pakubuwono I (–1723).

✗ **1719** Fernando Manuel de Bustamente, Spanish governor of the Philippines, is murdered by friars resentful of his financial reforms.

EAST ASIA & OCEANIA

1710–1720 A.D.

THE SLAVE TRADE

▲ This bill advertising the sale of a freshly arrived boatload of slaves was exhibited in Boston in about the year 1700. They came from "the Windward and Rice Coast"—the coastal area of West Africa stretching from modern Senegal to Liberia.

BETWEEN THE 15TH AND 19TH CENTURIES *some 12 million mostly African men, women, and children were crammed into the unlit, unventilated, and insanitary holds of cargo vessels and shipped to the Americas as slaves. Fully a sixth of them died in the dreadful conditions of the crossing, and many of those who survived may well have wished they had. Yet while the slaves themselves led lives of appalling suffering and their African homelands were devastated, the merchants who carried on the trade often made enormous fortunes.*

Slavery was an accepted feature of life in the Old World in the Middle Ages, sanctioned by Christian and Islamic tradition as well as by the pagan customs of earlier times. Conquered peoples—both soldiers and civilians—and those who had forfeited their rights by criminality or debt were bought and sold for employment in every conceivable field. From unskilled labor in agriculture and construction through domestic service of every kind to highly skilled work as artists, craftworkers, or scribes—slaves did it all. In the Islamic empires slaves made up the bulk of the armed forces and civil service, many rising to the topmost tiers.

Not until 1441 was a European ship—it came from Portugal—specifically chartered to sail down the coast of Africa and bring back slaves. It was to be the first of many, although the traffic would build only slowly, and the boom years would not get underway until the 17th century. Then the opening up of the Americas created a demand for labor that could not be met by an indigenous population decimated by Old World infections to which they had no immunity.

At first European unfortunates were enslaved—criminals or debtors brought out to work off their obligations. But with vast and fertile areas waiting to be worked in the American South, in Cuba and other

The Slave House

Just over 0.6 miles (1 km) off the coast of Senegal, West Africa, lies the island of Gorée, which was a major center of the slave trade for more than three centuries. The offshore base was as convenient for European shipowners as it was for native slavers, who could marshal their captives there in full confidence that they could not escape. The island was at different times a possession of the Portuguese, the French, and the British, but the procedure for transshipping slaves remained much the same whoever held it. In all, a human cargo of hundreds of thousands of people passed through the island, brought there in chains to await sale and shipment overseas. The "Slave House" to be seen today (*right*) was built in 1780, at the very height of the slave trade. Up to 200 inmates would be confined there at a time, crowded together in tiny cells.

► Coastal areas of central and southern Africa suffered worst from the depredations of the slave mechants, although local slavers also fed the trade by bringing in captives from the continent's interior. In addition to the passage to the Americas there were overland routes to the Islamic states of North Africa, which had a long slaving tradition of their own.

👑 **1662** Slaveowning becomes legal in Virginia Colony. All children born to slaves are to be slaves themselves.

👑 **1441** The first-known shipment of slaves from West Africa to Europe takes place.

👑 **1619** The first shipment of African workers arrives in Virginia. They are bought as slaves, although their legal status at the time remains ambiguous.

👑 **c.1700** By this time around 25,000 slaves a year are being shipped across the Atlantic Ocean to the American continent.

Caribbean islands, and in Brazil, the need for plantation labor quickly grew clamorous.

By 1700 a "triangular trade" had become well established in the Atlantic. On the first leg ships sailed south from the ports of Europe, laden with sought-after manufactured goods, guns, and trinkets. The vessels were met at markets on the African coast by local slavers who brought captives with them from their forays into the interior, having seized them themselves or bought them from local chiefs.

The second side of the triangle was the notorious "middle passage": Slaves were shackled and packed below decks in their hundreds in conditions of unimaginable squalor. After a journey that might take many weeks, those who survived were released from this horrific confinement to be examined like livestock and sold to their new owners. The third part of the triangle was the ship's passage home, carrying cotton, sugar, tobacco, and other plantation produce bought with the proceeds of the sale.

For the merchants who financed the trips, the trade could be highly profitable. A rapidly industrializing England benefited more generally from the supply of cheap raw materials the trade brought in and the demand for manufactured goods that it created in Africa and the American colonies. Ports like Bristol and Liverpool, which were sending out some 40 slave ships a year by 1750, thrived on the traffic. But the trade caused disruption and depopulation in regions of western Africa, while America inherited a problem that would eventually lead the nation to tear itself apart a century later in the Civil War.

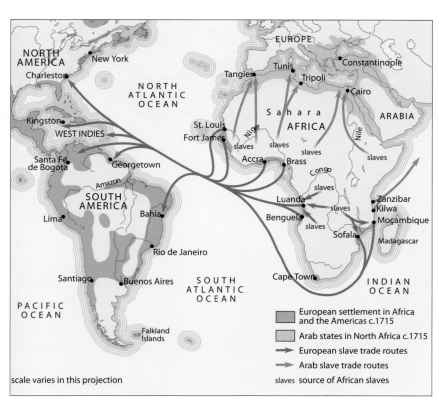

scale varies in this projection

European settlement in Africa and the Americas c.1715

Arab states in North Africa c.1715

→ European slave trade routes

→ Arab slave trade routes

slaves source of African slaves

▲ Under the watchful eye of overseers slaves in Brazil wash diamonds out of the mud of a river bed. Some 3.3 million Africans were taken to Brazil over the course of three centuries.

👑 **1705** The Slave Code passed by Virginia's General Assembly strips slaves of every human right, including the right to life.

✕ **1712** A slave revolt in New York City is put down by the local militia.

✕ **1739** A slave revolt breaks out at Stono River in South Carolina.

👑 **c.1780** By now the transatlantic slave trade is at its peak: Around 80,000 people are taken to the Americas every year.

✕ **1791** Toussaint L'Ouverture leads a slave uprising in the French colony of Saint-Domingue (Haiti).

👑 **1807** The tide begins to turn as Britain bans the slave trade; the United States will do the same the following year, but the owning of slaves already in the country is still allowed.

1720–1730 A.D.

AMERICAS

1720 A Spanish expeditionary force from Mexico occupies what is now Texas (–1722).

1721 A regular postal service is established between New England and London.

1721 Rifles are first introduced into North America by Swiss settlers.

1726 Spanish colonists found the city of Montevideo at the mouth of the Rio de la Plata.

1727 Quakers call for the abolition of the transatlantic slave trade.

1727 In Brazil coffee is planted for the first time; in time it will become the country's chief export.

EUROPE

1720 The collapse of Britain's South Sea Company ruins thousands of investors in the financial scandal known as the "South Sea Bubble."

1720 In France the Mississippi Company collapses, bankrupting the government.

1720 In Marseilles, southern France, the last major outbreak of the Black Death in western Europe claims 80,000 lives.

Portrayed here on an enamel snuff-box lid, Robert Walpole steered the government of Britain for 21 years from 1721, a tenure of power that established his claim to be the nation's first prime minister. Previously, executive duties had been shared collectively by a cabinet of advisers answering individually to Parliament and to the king. Walpole was an effective administrator who demanded strict loyalty from his colleagues and sought to avoid controversy at home. His liberal use of patronage to win political support opened his administration to charges of corruption, and he was eventually forced to step down in 1742.

AFRICA

18th-century Benin bronze mask from the Dahomey region of West Africa.

1720 Dutch settlers in South Africa venture inland from the Cape of Good Hope to the Orange River.

1721 French forces capture Mauritius from the Dutch.

1723 King Agaja of Dahomey in West Africa invades the neighboring territory of Allada to expand his catchment area for supplying slaves to European traders.

WESTERN ASIA

1722 Afghan ruler Mir Mahmoud invades Persia. Defeating the Safavids at the Battle of Gulnabad, he proclaims himself shah.

1722 Russia and the Ottoman Empire both invade Persia to counter the Afghan threat; Russian forces occupy Persia's Caspian Sea coast.

SOUTH & CENTRAL ASIA

1720 Tibet falls under Chinese control for the first time as the Manchus install a new Dalai Lama and garrison troops there.

1721 The Afghan Rohilla tribe establish the Kingdom of Rohilkhand in northern India.

1724 Asaf Jah, Mughal governor of the Deccan Plateau in central India, founds an independent kingdom in Hyderabad.

EAST ASIA & OCEANIA

1720 Japan's Shogun Yoshimune allows the import of Western books to promote scientific and technical learning; religious works are still banned.

1722 Dutch explorer Jakob Roggeveen discovers remote Easter Island in the Pacific Ocean.

1722 Chinese Manchu Emperor Kangxi dies after ruling for 60 years; he is succeeded by his son Shizu.

1727 The Treaty of Kyakhta fixes the border between China and Russia in the disputed Amur River region north of Manchuria.

👑 **1728** Diamonds from the Brazilian town of Tejuco reach Lisbon in Portugal, starting a diamond rush to the town, which is soon renamed Diamantina.

👑 **1729** North and South Carolina become colonies of the British crown.

👑 **1729** The city of Baltimore is founded as a center for shipbuilding.

✕ **1729** Natchez Indians massacre some 300 French settlers and soldiers in Fort Rosalie, Louisiana.

AMERICAS

👑 **1721** The Great Northern War between Sweden and Russia comes to an end. Russia gains substantial territories around the Baltic Sea, including Livonia and Estonia.

👑 **1721** Robert Walpole becomes the first British prime minister; his 21-year term of office brings the country great stability.

⊕ **1722** French physicist René de Réaumur discovers the crucial role played by carbon in making steel from iron.

👑 **1725** Czar Peter I dies and is succeeded by his wife Catherine I (–1727).

📖 **1726** Irish writer Jonathan Swift writes his famous satire *Gulliver's Travels*.

👑 **1727** Empress Catherine I of Russia expels Jews from the Ukraine.

✕ **1727** Spain begins hostilities with Britain and France, launching a siege of Gibraltar; the dispute is ended by the Treaty of Seville (–1729).

📖 **1729** German composer Johann Sebastian Bach writes the *St. Matthew Passion*.

A 19th-century illustration for Jonathan Swift's classic satire Gulliver's Travels.

EUROPE

👑 **1723** The British Africa Company is granted land in Gambia, West Africa.

✕ **1728** The Portuguese briefly recover the East African port of Mombasa (in modern Kenya) from the Sultanate of Oman, which has held it since 1698.

AFRICA

✕ **1723** An Ottoman army overruns the Persian stronghold of Tiflis (now Tbilisi, Georgia).

👑 **1724** Mir Mahmoud, who has grown increasingly insane, is replaced and executed by Shah Ashraf (–1725).

✕ **1726** The Safavids retake the key Persian city of Esfahan from the Afghans.

WESTERN ASIA

👑 **1724** The northern Indian Kingdom of Oudh also breaks free of Mughal rule.

SOUTH & CENTRAL ASIA

⊕ **1728** Danish navigator Vitus Bering sails through the strait that now bears his name, separating Siberia from Alaska.

👑 **1729** Emperor Shizu bans opium smoking in China.

Enameled glass bowl produced in China in the reign of Emperor Shizu.

👑 **1729** The Danish East India Company is chartered to conduct trade with the East Indies.

EAST ASIA & OCEANIA

1720–1730 A.D.

THE ENLIGHTENMENT

▲ Gotthold Ephraim Lessing was a leading figure of the Enlightenment in Germany, He won fame as a playwright and literary critic, arguing for a naturalistic style of drama and for freedom of speech. In his later years he took part in theological controversies, passionately advocating the cause of religious toleration.

THE ENLIGHTENMENT WAS A PHILOSOPHICAL MOVEMENT *that made its influence felt on many aspects of European society and culture in the 18th century, leading the era as a whole to be known as the Age of Reason. Basing their ideas on the principles of rational enquiry, its proponents believed that humankind could follow a path of steady material and spiritual progress that would gradually raise it toward perfection.*

Horrified by the widespread violence that religious strife had caused in the 16th and 17th centuries, many scholars sought alternative ways for people to bring meaning and order to their lives. In *An Essay Concerning Human Understanding*, published in 1690, the English philosopher John Locke stated a key principle of the new thinking by saying that people were not naturally evil and irrational but could be made so by their circumstances. Even when thinkers did not reject religion outright, they claimed for humankind a more personal, natural relationship with God than orthodox faiths, with their dogma and hierarchies, had traditionally allowed. In place of miracles and divine revelation this "deist" view proposed a benign but distant God who had given humans the capacity for reason and empowered them to control their own fate.

The rise of the natural sciences in the 17th century had discredited traditional explanations of the universe. Instead, thinkers of the time put their trust in close observation of natural phenomena and in experiment (a method known as empiricism) to reveal the workings of nature. The English scientist Isaac Newton epitomized the new approach, while personally retaining a deeply religious worldview.

Along with the challenge to established religion came a demand for social change. French philosophers such as Montesquieu, Voltaire, and Rousseau advocated civil liberties, including equality before the law, free speech, and government that obeyed the general will as the basis of a "social contract" between ruler and people. Modern notions of religious pluralism and racial tolerance also first found a voice at this time; in Germany the Jewish Enlightenment movement, or Haskalah, called for political emancipation and a strong Hebrew culture.

Many monarchs felt threatened by the new ideas; Voltaire himself was jailed and forced into exile. Yet some of Europe's absolute rulers, notably Catherine the Great of Russia, Joseph II of Austria, and Prussia's King Frederick II, adopted the new ideas and instituted social, educational, and legal reforms. Even

---

☀ **1730** *Christianity as Old as the Creation*, by the English deist Matthew Tyndale, attacks the supernatural element of organized religion.

📖 **1734** French writer François-Marie Arouet (Voltaire) publishes his *Lettres philosophiques* ("Philosophical Letters"), which call for political and religious toleration.

❀ **1735** In Sweden the botanist Karl Linné (still often known by the Latin version of his name as Carolus Linnaeus) sets out his system of plant classification, the *Systema Naturae* ("System of Nature").

❀ **1736** Medieval laws against witchcraft are repealed in England.

👑 **1740** Frederick II ("the Great") of Prussia ascends the throne; under his rule economic and social reforms are introduced, and the legal code liberalized.

📖 **1747** Diderot and d'Alembert begin their work on the *Encyclopedia*. The first volume is published four years later.

📖 **1750** Voltaire goes into in exile in Germany, where he enjoys the patronage of Frederick the Great at Sans Souci, the ruler's palace in Potsdam near Berlin (–1753).

❀ **1751** In Portugal the marquis of Pombal institutes administrative and educational reforms and encourages manufacturing. His work will culminate in the rebuilding of Lisbon as a modern, planned capital after an earthquake devastates the old city in 1755.

☀ **1755** Laws are passed in England permitting the naturalization of Jews.

📖 **1755** After nine years' work the English lexicographer Dr. Samuel Johnson produces his enormous *Dictionary of the English Language*.

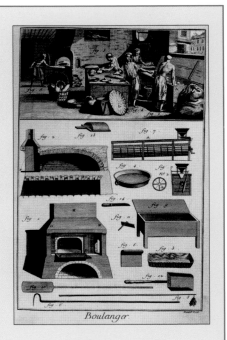

The *Encyclopedia*

One of the Enlightenment's key aims was to foster popular education: If people knew how the world around them worked, its promoters held, they could take greater control of their lives. In an attempt to build a compendium of knowledge the philosopher Denis Diderot and the mathematician Jean d'Alembert collaborated to produce the *Encyclopedia*. This monumental work, which ran to 33 volumes published over 26 years, contained articles by the leading French thinkers of the day. Practical subjects—for example, baking techniques (right)—were treated alongside radical topics such as progressive philosophical ideas and political liberalism. The first two volumes were suppressed because of the anticlerical tone of some entries.

Boulanger

▲ Frederick the Great of Prussia strolls around his palace of Sans Souci with his guest, the exiled French philosopher Voltaire.

▼ The ideas of the Enlightenment spread across much of western Europe, promoting scientific research alongside political reform.

so, these "enlightened despots" stopped short of introducing representative government.

Toward the end of the 18th century the American and French revolutions adopted many key Enlightenment tenets; yet in France the optimism of the Age of Reason gave way to the Reign of Terror, plunging the continent into a new cycle of bloodshed and turmoil.

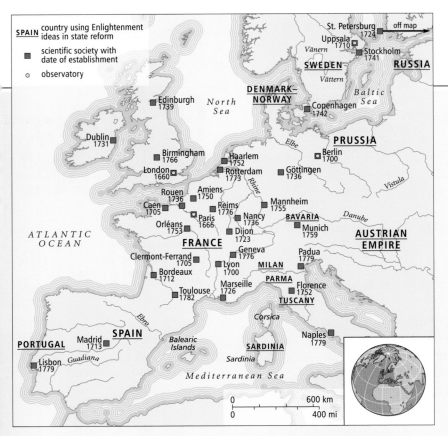

Map legend:
- SPAIN country using Enlightenment ideas in state reform
- ■ scientific society with date of establishment
- ○ observatory

St. Petersburg 1724 → off map
Uppsala 1710
Vänern
Stockholm 1741
SWEDEN RUSSIA
Vättern
Baltic Sea
DENMARK-NORWAY
Edinburgh 1739
North Sea
Copenhagen 1742
Dublin 1731
Elbe
PRUSSIA
Birmingham 1766
Haarlem 1752
Berlin 1700
London 1660
Rotterdam 1773
Göttingen 1736
Rhine
Rouen 1736
Amiens 1750
Vistula
Caen 1705
Reims 1776
Mannheim 1755
Paris 1666
Nancy 1736
BAVARIA
Orléans 1753
Dijon 1723
Munich 1759
Danube
ATLANTIC OCEAN
FRANCE
Geneva 1776
AUSTRIAN EMPIRE
Clermont-Ferrand 1705
Lyon 1700
MILAN
Padua 1779
Bordeaux 1712
Marseille 1726
PARMA
Toulouse 1782
Florence 1752
TUSCANY
Corsica
SPAIN
Naples 1779
PORTUGAL
Madrid 1713
Balearic Islands
SARDINIA
Ebro
Sardinia
Lisbon 1779
Guadiana
Mediterranean Sea

0 ___ 600 km
0 ___ 400 mi

⬡ **1764** The Italian legal theorist Cesare Beccaria publishes his *Tratto dei Delitti e delle Pene* ("Treatise on Crimes and Punishments"), advocating the abolition of torture and the reform of the penal code.

☀ **1766** Catherine II (the Great) of Russia grants freedom of worship to her subjects.

☀ **1776** Adam Weisshaupt, a Bavarian lawyer, founds the Order of Illuminati, a cult dedicated to spreading a new religion based on reason.

📖 **1779** *Nathan the Wise*, a blank verse drama by the German playwright Gotthold Ephraim Lessing, is a passionate plea for religious tolerance and common humanity.

1730–1740 A.D.

AMERICAS

📖 **1731** In Philadelphia Benjamin Franklin establishes the first subscription library in North America.

👑 **1733** The last of Britain's 13 American colonies is founded and named Georgia after King George II.

> Writer, statesman, and inventor, Benjamin Franklin was a man who embodied the entrepreneurial spirit of the infant United States. A proponent of civic improvement at home and an ambassador for the revolutionary government abroad, he also conducted pioneering scientific experiments and wrote a classic autobiography.

EUROPE

👑 **1733** The "Soldier King" Frederick William I lays the foundation for Prussia's later military expansion by introducing compulsory army service for all males aged over 18.

⚙ **1733** The flying shuttle loom, key to the industrialization of cotton milling, is patented by the English inventor John Kay.

👑 **1733** Augustus II ("the Strong") of Poland dies; his reign was characterized by repeated wars with Sweden to regain lost territory.

Iron-tipped shuttles designed for use on John Kay's loom.

⚔ **1733** The War of the Polish Succession begins when France and Spain reject the claimant to the Polish throne backed by Austria and Russia; most fighting takes place in the Hapsburg lands in Italy (–1735).

⚙ **1735** English clockmaker John Harrison builds the first marine chronometer; his invention makes position plotting and navigation at sea far more accurate and safe.

AFRICA

👑 **c.1730** In West Africa the Ashanti Kingdom expands to cover most of the area of modern Ghana.

WESTERN ASIA

⚔ **1730** The janissaries (elite soldiers) revolt in Istanbul, deposing Sultan Ahmed III and bringing Mahmud I to the throne.

⚔ **1730** Persia's Shah Ashraf is murdered by his followers after a defeat by Ottoman forces at Shiraz.

⚔ **1730** Nadir Kuli, a brilliant Persian general (and later shah), inflicts a heavy defeat on an Ottoman army at Nehavend in western Persia.

SOUTH & CENTRAL ASIA

👑 **c.1730** Bajirao I, ruler of Maharashtra in central India, greatly expands the area under the control of the Marathas; by 1740 they will govern more of India than the declining Mughals.

⚙ **1737** A major earthquake hits Calcutta (Kolkota) in Bengal, eastern India, killing 300,000 people and causing a tidal wave 40 feet (12 m) high.

⚔ **1738** Nadir Shah of Persia embarks on a campaign of eastward expansion, capturing the city of Kandahar in Afghanistan.

EAST ASIA & OCEANIA

👑 **c.1730** The world's first futures market opens in Japan, dealing in three-month forward contracts for rice.

👑 **1732** China's Emperor Shizu takes the first steps toward abolishing slavery in his realm.

👑 **1732** A widespread famine in Japan, caused by torrential rainfall and a plague of grasshoppers, claims some 12,000 lives.

👑 **1733** The Molasses Act, passed by the British Parliament, effectively prohibits direct trade between the American colonies and the French West Indies by imposing high tariffs.

👑 **1737** Richmond, Virginia, is founded by William Byrd.

👑 **1739** The Viceroyalty of New Granada (modern Ecuador, Colombia, Venezuela, and Panama) is permanently separated from the Viceroyalty of Peru.

✖ **1739** Conflict breaks out between Georgia and the Spanish territory of Florida (–1743).

⚙ **1739** French explorers Paul and Pierre Mallet reach Santa Fe after journeying west from the Mississippi River.

⚙ **1735** British iron manufacturer Abraham Darby first uses coke in his blast furnaces, enabling much greater efficiency and yield in the production of cast iron.

⚙ **1735** Swedish botanist Karl Linné (Carolus Linnaeus) publishes his first major work, *Systema Naturae*, which introduces a new system of plant classification.

⚙ **1738** Swiss mathematician Daniel Bernoulli publishes his *Hydrodynamica*, outlining a key discovery concerning the speed and pressure of fluid flow (the "Bernoulli principle").

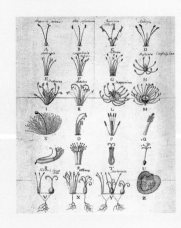

An illustration from Linnaeus's Systema Naturae *depicts plant reproduction.*

⚙ **1738** French inventor Charles de Labelye introduces the caisson, a watertight chamber that allows people to work below sea level.

👑 **1739** As an Ottoman army advances on Belgrade, Holy Roman Emperor Charles VI sues for peace; the settlement returns the city and all northern Serbia to the Turks, lost to them since 1718.

✖ **1739** Russian forces retake the city of Azov from the Ottomans.

✖ **1730** King Agaja of Dahomey is defeated in a four-year war with the neighboring Yoruba Kingdom of Oyo.

✖ **1732** A slave revolt forces the Dutch to abandon their slave trading post at Maputo in Mozambique.

> Nadir Shah was a ruthless conqueror who fought his way to the throne of Persia at a time of dynastic instability. Of Turkic origin, he first rose to prominence as a bandit leader. As shah of Persia he won victories against Mughal India, the Ottomans, and Russia, but tyrannized and impoverished his own subjects.

✖ **1730** Nadir Kuli unsuccessfully besieges Baghdad.

✖ **1731** After defeat at the Battle of Arijan Shah Tahmasp II of Persia signs a peace treaty with the Ottomans; Nadir Kuli denounces the treaty and deposes the shah.

✖ **1735** Nadir Kuli forms an alliance with the Russians and recaptures Tbilisi in Georgia from the Ottoman Turks.

👑 **1736** Shah Abbas III of Persia dies at the age of six and is succeeded by Nadir Kuli, now Nadir Shah.

✖ **1739** The collapse of the Mughal Empire in India accelerates as Persian forces under Nadir Shah defeat Muhammad Shah's army at Karnal and overrun his capital, Delhi.

👑 **1736** Emperor Qianlong ascends the Chinese throne, starting a 60-year reign that begins with a long period of peace and prosperity.

Chinese cloisonné enamel ram from Qianlong's reign.

⚙ **1739** Camellias first arrive in Europe from East Asia; they quickly become very fashionable and sell for high prices.

AMERICAS

EUROPE

AFRICA

WESTERN ASIA

SOUTH & CENTRAL ASIA

EAST ASIA & OCEANIA

1730–1740 A.D.

SPANISH RULE IN AMERICA

▲ Better known now as Mission Dolores, San Francisco de Asís is a surviving reminder of the Spanish colonial presence in modern downtown San Francisco. Built in 1791 to replace an earlier structure constructed 15 years before, the church is the oldest intact building in the city.

THROUGH MUCH OF THE 16TH AND 17TH CENTURIES *Spain was the dominant power in Europe. Its position on the contintent waned after 1700, when its ruler Charles II died childless, precipitating the War of the Spanish Succession, but its American empire continued to thrive. Tensions were growing within the caste-based society that had developed there, however, and as the 18th century came to an end, the pressure to gain independence from the mother country was becoming irresistible.*

Economically Spain's American empire went from strength to strength. Continuing huge revenues from the silver and gold mines of Mexico and Peru were supplemented by the growth of large-scale commercial agriculture. Under the hacienda system tracts of virgin territory and lands seized from native subsistence farmers were merged into large estates owned by wealthy families. The dispossessed Indians had little choice but to work as low-paid laborers (peons) on the estates. The great wealth generated by such enterprises stimulated further expansion; in 1776 the new Viceroyalty of Rio de la Plata (present-day Uruguay and Argentina) was created to exploit the prosperous cattle-ranching operations developing there and to increase the export of hides.

Challenges to Spanish dominance in the Americas from other imperial powers had little effect. From 1739 on, Spain and Britain fought the inconclusive War of Jenkins' Ear, named for an English sea captain

who claimed to have had his ear cut off by Spanish customs officials in the Caribbean; the conflict was in fact born principally of British merchants' frustration at their exclusion from trading with Spanish America. The empire's territory remained largely intact until the Seven Years' War (1756–1763), which Spain joined at a late stage to aid France; in the resulting fighting the British occupied Havana in Cuba, while the peace settlement of 1763 also forced Spain to cede Florida to Britain.

Although the Spanish gained the former French territory of Louisiana in return, they did little to exploit their new possession. Instead, internal tensions began to weaken the empire. In the 1780s, in an attempt to foster commerce, Spain's King Charles III liberalized the system of colonial trade, which had long been restricted to licensed guild merchants and particular ports in Spain; the administrative system was also reorganized, increasing the power of the

---

👑 **1702** Spanish and French colonists in the southern parts of North America ally against the British colony of South Carolina; the Peace of Utrecht forces the Spanish to grant Britain the right to trade with Spanish colonial territories (–1713).

👑 **1720** Texas is occupied by a Spanish force from Mexico. Nebraska marks the northern extent of Spanish penetration into North America when an expedition there is repelled by the Pawnee people (–1722).

⚔ **1739** The War of Jenkins' Ear breaks out between Britain and Spain after British merchants urge their government to force Spain to allow British ships to trade with their overseas empire (–1741).

⚔ **1739** Conflict breaks out between the British colony of Georgia and Spanish Florida (–1743).

👑 **1739** The Viceroyalty of New Granada is permanently separated from that of Peru, reflecting the growing prosperity of the new region.

⚔ **1741** An English naval expedition attacks the Spanish stronghold of Cartagena in what is now Colombia, but is forced to retreat to Jamaica after most of the attacking force succumb to yellow fever.

👑 **1750** The Treaty of Madrid updates the Treaty of Tordesillas of 1494, which divided the Americas between Spain and Portugal, definitively settling the borders of Brazil.

⚔ **1762** In the Seven Years' War British forces capture the city of Havana, Cuba, in response to Spain's alliance with France.

👑 **1763** The peace settlement following the Seven Years' War cedes Florida to Britain, while French areas west of the Mississippi River are granted to Spain.

☀ **1767** All Jesuits are expelled from the colonies by order of the Spanish king, and their missions are closed.

👑 **1776** Spanish settlers establish the garrison and mission of San Francisco on the coast of California.

The Revolt of Tupac Amarú II

A descendant of the last Inca ruler Tupac Amarú, executed by the Spanish invaders of Peru in 1572, José Gabriel Kunturkanki Tupac Amarú (*right*) was a respected figure. Growing frustrated with the injustices of Spanish rule, he staged an uprising in 1780 to restore Inca rule. He attracted many different groups to his cause, appealing to creoles and mestizos (mixed-race settlers) and also promising freedom to black slaves. He professed loyalty to the Spanish crown, claiming that it was local rulers who had corrupted the imperial ideal. After a siege of the capital Cuzco failed, however, and his supporters began indiscriminately killing whites, he was betrayed, captured, mutilated, and hanged in 1781, having first been forced to witness the execution of his wife and children. His revolt was the most serious challenge to Spanish rule in the Americas, costing over 200,000 lives.

1779   Spain joins the Revolutionary War against the British; at the Battle of Baton Rouge in Louisiana British forces are defeated by a mixed force led by Spanish commanders.

1780   Spanish forces retake western Florida from British control (–1783).

1780   Tupac Amarú II, an Inca of royal blood, leads indigenous peoples and other groups in Peru in an unsuccessful and bloody revolt against Spanish rule (–1781).

1810   The first wars of independence against Spanish rule break out in Colombia, Mexico, and Argentina.

crown at the expense of the local viceroys. Although these reforms boosted trade and improved local government, they also bred resentment in the colonies. Charles III also moved to suppress the church's influence, expelling the Jesuits from all parts of his empire in 1767. Among the chief losers by this move were the indigenous inhabitants of the Spanish lands, for the missions of this wealthy order had provided them with some degree of sanctuary from exploitation by white settlers.

The main impetus behind the growing urge for change came from the creoles. Although ranked above Indians, mestizos (people of Indian–white mixed race), mulattos (mixed black–white), and the numerous other divisions in the Spanish American racial hierarchy, these American-born whites were systematically disadvantaged by crown policy. All top positions were occupied by *peninsulares*—white immigrants born in mainland Spain. The rigid and discriminatory caste system was to prove the downfall of the empire after Napoleon invaded Spain in 1808, when disaffected creoles came to the forefront of the independence movements.

▼ Spanish power in the Americas was originally based in the Caribbean islands and the former Aztec and Inca lands of Central and South America. In the 16th and 17th centuries it expanded east into Argentina and north to what is now the southern United States, including Florida. Brazil owed allegiance to Portugal, while other European powers maintained smaller outposts in the Caribbean and on the South American coast.

1740–1750 A.D.

AMERICAS

✕ **1741** A major slave uprising in New York causes widespread damage.

✕ **1741** An English naval force under Admiral Vernon attacks the Spanish citadel at Cartagena, but disease forces it to withdraw.

⚙ **1742** Coal is first mined in the West Virginia region.

✕ **1742** British troops defending Georgia repel an attempted Spanish invasion.

✕ **1745** In King George's War New England settlers overrun Louisburg on Cape Breton Island, previously France's most secure stronghold in North America.

EUROPE

Maria Theresa was an able ruler who managed to hold together the Hapsburg lands she had inherited in the face of attempts by neighboring states to seize them from her. She continued in power for 40 years, introducing important reforms in taxation, local government, and education.

👑 **1740** Frederick William I of Prussia dies and is succeeded by his son Frederick II ("the Great").

✕ **1740** Maria Theresa inherits the Hapsburg realm on the death of her father, Emperor Charles VI.

✕ **1740** The War of the Austrian Succession begins when Frederick II seeks to annex Silesia from Maria Theresa. It widens when Bavaria, Saxony, and Spain also invade the Hapsburg lands.

👑 **1741** Elizabeth Petrovna, Peter the Great's daughter, deposes the infant Czar Ivan VI in a coup.

⚙ **1741** An outbreak of yellow fever in Cádiz, Spain, kills 10,000 people.

✕ **1742** The First Silesian War ends with the Treaty of Berlin; Austria concedes some territory in return for Prussian neutrality in the War of the Austrian Succession, withdrawn two years later.

⚙ **1742** Swedish astronomer Anders Celsius devises the centigrade scale, measuring temperature from 0° to 100°.

📖 **1742** German composer George Frederick Handel premieres his oratorio *The Messiah*.

AFRICA

✕ **1744** Portuguese forces invade the Kingdom of Matamba in Angola following the murder of a white trader, seizing some land.

✕ **1745** Firearms are used for the first time in an African tribal war when the Ashanti defeat the neighboring state of Dagomba.

WESTERN ASIA

✕ **1743** Hostilities resume between the Ottoman Empire and Safavid Persia.

Ahmad Shah Durrani, first emir of Afghanistan.

☀ **1744** Muhammad ibn Saud and Islamic scholar Muhammad al-Wahhab, founder of the Wahhabi sect, win control of much of Arabia.

SOUTH & CENTRAL ASIA

✕ **1740** The Marathas launch an invasion of the Carnatic region of southeastern India and defeat the nabob of Arcot at the Battle of Damalcherry.

👑 **1740** Alvardi Khan takes power as the independent ruler of Bengal, while maintaining the fiction that he governs in the name of the Mughal emperor.

✕ **1743** The nizam of Hyderabad in south-central India takes Arcot, the capital of the Carnatic, from the Marathas.

EAST ASIA & OCEANIA

✕ **1740** Wishing to restore their own ancient kingdom, the Mons of Pegu in what is now southern Myanmar begin a rebellion against Burmese rule.

⚙ **1741** The Danish explorer Vitus Bering, discoverer of the Bering Strait, returns to the area, again in the service of Russia. He explores the Alaskan coast and the Aleutian Islands, but dies on the voyage.

👑 **1742** In Japan Shogun Yoshimune orders a major codification of the criminal law that will provide the framework for the country's legal system for the rest of the Tokugawa period.

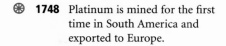

AMERICAS

⊛ **1746** The cities of Lima and Callao in Peru are destroyed by an earthquake that kills 18,000 people.

⊛ **1748** Platinum is mined for the first time in South America and exported to Europe.

👑 **1749** The British establish a naval base at Halifax, Nova Scotia.

✕ **1749** A French expeditionary force under Joseph Céloron, sieur de Blainville, is despatched from Canada to claim the Ohio Valley for France's King Louis XV.

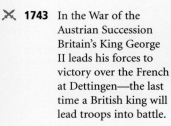
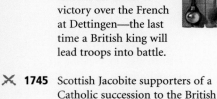

An early Celsius thermometer, dating from about 1790.

EUROPE

✕ **1743** In the War of the Austrian Succession Britain's King George II leads his forces to victory over the French at Dettingen—the last time a British king will lead troops into battle.

✕ **1745** Scottish Jacobite supporters of a Catholic succession to the British throne launch an ill-fated revolt led by the Young Pretender, Charles Edward Stuart (–1746).

📖 **1747** French author Denis Diderot begins work on his celebrated *Encyclopedia*, a compendium of knowledge from many fields.

👑 **1748** The Treaty of Aix-la-Chapelle ends the War of the Austrian Succession.

⊛ **1748** Excavations begin on the site of the rediscovered ancient city of Pompeii, Italy, buried by an eruption of Mt. Vesuvius in 79 A.D.

The Large Amphitheater in Pompeii, Italy, painted by Philipp Hackert in 1793.

AFRICA

👑 **1747** The West African Kingdom of Oyo comes completely under the control of the rival state of Dahomey.

WESTERN ASIA

✕ **1747** Nadir Shah of Persia is killed by one of his Afghan bodyguards; his death marks the beginning of Afghan independence.

👑 **1747** Ahmad Shah Durrani takes control of Afghanistan, which will become the greatest Islamic state of the late 18th century.

SOUTH & CENTRAL ASIA

✕ **1744** The English and French East India companies become involved in the Carnatic War.

✕ **1746** Joseph Dupleix, governor of the French Indies, captures the city of Madras (Chennai), the chief British base in the Carnatic.

✕ **1749** With the help of French allies Chanda Sahib defeats the nabob of Arcot and takes control of the Carnatic region.

EAST ASIA & OCEANIA

✕ **1743** George Anson, commander of the British warship *Centurion*, seizes over a million silver dollars and 500 pounds of bullion by capturing a Spanish galleon off the Philippines.

👑 **1745** Tokugawa Ieshige ousts Yoshimune as shogun of Japan; his reign will be marked by decline and growing corruption.

✕ **1747** The Chinese begin the pacification of Tibet with a campaign to subdue rebellions in the border regions (–1749).

1740–1750 A.D.

THE RISE OF PRUSSIA

IN THE 1500S PRUSSIA WAS A SMALL DUCHY *in the east Baltic region—a legacy of the Teutonic Knights military order, which had conquered the territory from pagan tribes in the mid 13th century. Its rise to prominence began in the early 17th century when it became part of the Duchy of Brandenburg under the dynamic leadership of the Hohenzollern Dynasty. Over the next 250 years Prussia emerged as the strongest German-speaking state, and it was under Prussian impetus that a united Germany would eventually come into being in 1871.*

▲ This flag was carried by a Prussian infantry regiment in the Seven Years' War. Prussia owed its rise to preeminence among the German states mainly to its military successes. The central role the army played in Prussian life also won the duchy a reputation for authoritarianism.

The foundations for Prussia's greatness were laid by the Great Elector of Brandenburg, Frederick William (1620–1688). Although nominally part of Brandenburg since 1618, the duchy effectively remained under Polish suzerainty until Frederick William, through war and guile, gained full sovereignty in 1660. Frederick William built up the military strength of the duchy, creating a standing army of 31,000 men—a sizable force for the time.

In 1701 Frederick William's successor Frederick I committed this force to support the Hapsburgs in the War of the Spanish Succession. In return Austria recognized his proclamation of the Kingdom of Prussia, with its capital in Berlin. But it was Frederick's son Frederick William I, ascending the throne in 1713, who stamped on Prussia the hallmark of militarism and absolute power that it was to bear for centuries to come. A well-organized system of conscription increased the army's strength to 83,000 men. Another key reform was the creation of an administrative "general directory" in 1722 that centralized the Prussian bureaucracy and forged the scattered Hohenzollern holdings into a unified state. Frederick William was popularly known as the "Soldier King" for his love of military drill, yet Prussia never went to war during his reign.

An Enlightened Despot

Alongside his military exploits, Frederick the Great was renowned as an "enlightened despot"—an absolute ruler who took a broad interest in contemporary culture and social reform. In 1745 he drafted his own designs for a grand new palace in the rococo style at Potsdam near Berlin. He called it Sans Souci ("Without cares"), and he played host within its sumptuous portals to leading writers and thinkers of the day, including the exiled French man of letters Voltaire.

Frederick himself was a competent composer and musician with a fondness for flute music; he also had ambitions as an author, although he chose to write in French rather than in German. Indeed, in his scathing 1780 essay *De la littérature allemande* ("On German Literature") he claimed his native language was only fit for "speaking to servants and horses."

Frederick II came to the throne on Frederick William's death in 1740. One of his first acts was to unleash the military might his father had built up, ordering an attack on Silesia that started the War of the Austrian Succession (1740–1748). Thus began a 46-year reign that saw Prussia double its territory, consolidating its position as a major European power. Frederick's expansionist strategy was not without risk; in the Seven Years' War, sparked when Prussia invaded Saxony, his capital of Berlin was occupied and burned by foreign troops, and Prussia only avoided total defeat when Russia changed sides. Yet the enduring strength of the king's rule, along with his active promotion of industry, commerce, and agriculture, amply earned him the title "Frederick the Great."

Following Frederick's death in 1786, Prussia fell under the lackluster rule of Frederick William II (to 1797) and then Frederick William III, under whom it struggled to contain the threat of Napoleon. Emerging finally on the winning side in the Napoleonic Wars, it would find itself well placed to become Europe's foremost power under its "Iron Chancellor," Bismarck.

▶ Germany in Frederick's day was a patchwork of small states, many of them still loosely linked within the Holy Roman Empire. Frederick substantially increased his territory through victories in the War of the Austrian Succession and the Seven Years' War.

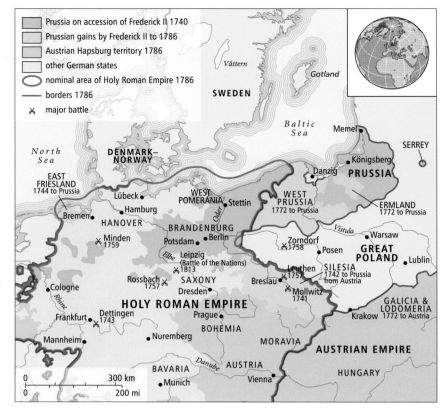

	Prussia on accession of Frederick II 1740
	Prussian gains by Frederick II to 1786
	Austrian Hapsburg territory 1786
	other German states
	nominal area of Holy Roman Empire 1786
	borders 1786
✕	major battle

👑 **1618** The duke of Brandenburg inherits the Duchy of Prussia with its capital at Königsberg (modern Kaliningrad, now a Russian enclave on the Baltic Sea).

✕ **1655** In the First Northern War Elector Frederick William of Brandenburg allies with Sweden to wrest control of Prussia from Poland, then switches allegiance (in return for full recognition of his sovereignty over Prussia) to help Poland expel the Swedes (–1660).

👑 **1685** Frederick William encourages Huguenots to settle in his realm after Louis XIV withdraws their protection; these French Protestants greatly enrich the commercial life of Prussia.

⊕ **1700** The Berlin Academy of Sciences is founded, with the philosopher Gottfried Wilhelm Leibniz as its first president.

👑 **1701** Elector Frederick III of Brandenburg proclaims himself Frederick I, "King in Prussia."

👑 **1713** Frederick William I ascends the throne; his reign lays the foundation of Prussia's future military and economic might through army, administrative, and financial reforms.

☀ **1732** Fleeing persecution, some 12,000 Protestants from Salzburg, Austria, are resettled in East Prussia.

👑 **1733** A cantonal system of recruitment is introduced whereby peasants from various regions are forcibly conscripted into local regiments.

👑 **1740** On assuming power, Frederick II introduces the principles of press freedom and freedom of worship in Prussia.

⊕ **1745** A canal is completed linking the Elbe and Oder rivers.

✕ **1756** Prussia precipitates the Seven Years' War with an attack on Saxony; Austria, France, and Russia take up arms against Prussia and England.

⊕ **1770** Frederick the Great undertakes agricultural reforms, including introducing the potato as a staple of the peasantry (–1780).

👑 **1772** In the First Partition of Poland Prussia acquires the region of West Prussia, linking the original duchies of Brandenburg and (East) Prussia into one large territory.

✕ **1813** At the Battle of the Nations outside Leipzig an alliance of Prussian and Russian forces wins a decisive victory over Napoleon. Prussia subsequently gains additional territories in Saxony and on the Rhine River at the end of the Napoleonic Wars.

AMERICAS

1750 Spain and Portugal sign the Treaty of Madrid, which confirms the boundaries of Brazil.

1752 Benjamin Franklin investigates the nature of electricity, including his famous experiment of flying a kite in a lightning storm.

1752 Iroquois territory south of the Ohio River is ceded to the British colony of Virginia under the Logstown Treaty.

1754 Clashes break out between French troops and American frontier settlers; the young George Washington, commanding an expeditionary force, suffers two defeats.

EUROPE

1754 The world's first iron rolling mill starts operations in Fareham, England.

1755 A massive earthquake destroys Lisbon, capital of Portugal, killing 30,000 people; the chief minister, the marquis of Pombal, rebuilds the city on a grid system.

Ornamental Sèvres porcelain vase decorated with hunting scenes.

1756 A national porcelain manufactory is founded at Sèvres, France.

1756 Prussian troops invade Saxony, which has allied with France, sparking the Seven Years' War; Prussia and England oppose Austria, France, Sweden, Russia, and other allies.

1757 A Bohemian army defeats Frederick the Great's Prussian forces at the Battle of Kolin (now in the Czech Republic).

AFRICA

1752 In the Sudan Sultan Abu al-Qasim of Darfur is killed resisting a Funj invasion force led by the sultan of Kordofan.

1756 The Seychelles Islands off the East African coast are claimed by the French for development by plantation owners and slave labor.

WESTERN ASIA

c.1750 As centralized Ottoman control declines, *derebeys* (local valley lords) become semiautonomous rulers in Anatolia.

1754 Ottoman Sultan Mahmud I dies and is succeeded by Osman III.

Ottoman Sultan Osman III, who reigned for only three years.

SOUTH & CENTRAL ASIA

1751 British forces under Sir Robert Clive win a major victory over the French and their ally Chanda Sahib at Arcot in the Carnatic.

1752 Ahmad Shah Durrani of Afghanistan besieges and takes the city of Lahore (in what is now Pakistan).

1752 The Marathas capture Khandesh and Berar (large regions of central India) from the nizam of Hyderabad.

1752 Clive forces the surrender of the French at Trichinopoly.

1754 French Governor Joseph Dupleix is recalled from India, leaving Britain in control of the south of the subcontinent.

1756 Siraj ud-Daulah, nabob of Bengal, takes Calcutta from the British; held overnight in a small dungeon (the "Black Hole of Calcutta"), 145 survivors allegedly suffocate.

EAST ASIA & OCEANIA

1751 The enlightened Japanese Shogun Yoshimune dies, six years after being deposed by Ieshige.

1751 Fresh Chinese forces invade Tibet, establishing a military protectorate and controlling the succession of the Dalai Lama.

1753 King Alaungpaya reestablishes a united Burma under the Konbaung dynasty and founds Rangoon (modern Yangon) as the new capital city (–1755).

👑 **1754** At the Albany Congress representatives of seven British colonies and chiefs of the Iroquois nations meet to plan a joint defense against the French; Benjamin Franklin's plan to unite the colonies is rejected by the colonial authorities.

✕ **1758** Fortunes ebb and flow in a series of military engagements. Prussian forces defeat the French at Krefeld and the Russians at Zorndorf; at Hochkirch an Austrian army overcomes the Prussians.

⊕ **1759** British engineer John Smeaton builds the Eddystone Lighthouse in the English Channel; his pioneering techniques are widely adopted around the world.

👑 **1758** France and Britain clash over control of Senegal, West Africa.

✕ **1755** The French and Indian War breaks out as British and French settlers vie for control of North America.

☀ **1759** The Jesuit order is expelled from Portugal and its colonies.

👑 **1759** King Ferdinand VI of Spain dies and is succeeded by Charles III.

📖 **1759** The French Enlightenment thinker Voltaire, exiled from his native land for his defense of political and religious tolerance, publishes his satirical fable *Candide*.

The French Enlightenment thinker Voltaire, portrayed at the age of 34.

✕ **1759** General James Wolfe defeats French troops under the marquis of Montcalm at the Plains of Abraham near Quebec, establishing British supremacy over Canada.

✕ **1759** The Prussian army suffers a heavy defeat at the hands of the Austrians and Russians at the Battle of Kunersdorf (now Kunowice, western Poland).

👑 **1759** The Khanate of Kokand (now Quqon in modern Uzbekistan) recognizes the sovereignty of China's Qing (Manchu) Dynasty.

No man did more to establish British rule in India than Robert Clive, seen here with the nabob of Bengal. Arriving in the country as a clerk with the East India Company, he rose to prominence by military victories against French and Indian forces. By 1764 he was governor general of Bengal, the state he had won for Britain seven years earlier. Later he was accused of corruption and, although ultimately vindicated, committed suicide in 1774.

✕ **1757** At the Battle of Plassey Clive's 3,000 troops are victorious over the huge army of Siraj ud-Daulah; Clive is aided by the treachery of the opposing general, Mir Jafar.

✕ **1758** In naval engagements off Pondicherry and Fort St. David French forces are defeated by the British Royal Navy (–1759).

✕ **1755** Under Manchu attack since the late 17th century, the Oirat Mongols of the Mongolian steppe are finally overcome after staging a failed revolt in Dzungaria.

✕ **1755** The Chinese invade and occupy Kashgaria (Chinese Turkistan) to quell an uprising by local Muslims (–1759).

👑 **1759** The Manchus consolidate all their newly conquered western territories into the military protectorate of Xinjiang.

AMERICAS

EUROPE

AFRICA

WESTERN ASIA

SOUTH & CENTRAL ASIA

EAST ASIA & OCEANIA

1750–1760 A.D.

311

THE SEVEN YEARS' WAR

BORN OF THE MUTUAL SUSPICION BETWEEN *the major European powers in the mid-18th century, the Seven Years' War was played out in a prolonged series of land battles and naval engagements across many different parts of the world. In Europe itself Austria and Prussia resumed hostilities over the disputed region of Silesia, while for Britain and France the European conflict grew out of intense colonial rivalries, particularly in North America and India.*

▲ French and British colonial forces meet at the Battle of Monongahela, an early clash in the French and Indian War—the arm of the Seven Years' War fought on the American continent. Fighting in America broke out in 1755, one year before the outbreak of war in continental Europe.

Just prior to the war new defensive pacts had redrawn the political map of Europe; this diplomatic revolution, which overturned previous alliances, saw Britain align itself with Prussia, while Austria joined forces with France and Russia (and later Sweden). Whether out of a wish to extend his empire or to launch a preemptive strike against the Austrian threat, Frederick the Great of Prussia started the war by sending troops to invade Saxony in August 1756. His forces made significant initial gains, overwhelming the Saxon army and taking many of its troops into the Prussian ranks; Prussian armies also consolidated their advantage in Bohemia.

Yet Prussia soon came to feel the full weight of the alliance ranged against it; Austria eventually drove its forces from Bohemia, while the French moved against Frederick's Hanoverian and British allies. Meanwhile Russia (whose ruler, the Empress Elizabeth, had long viewed Prussia's rise with alarm) overran East Prussia, and the Swedes invaded Pomerania.

Over the next three years the European war ebbed and flowed; many pitched battles were fought, with none proving decisive. Yet the wider conflict saw Britain make conclusive gains in its colonial struggle with France. In India British forces established supremacy on land and at sea, and the capture of Pondicherry in 1761 effectively ended French power in the subcontinent. In North America, despite early setbacks, superior naval power and supply lines enabled Britain to rout the French and their Huron allies, and by 1760 all of New France was in British hands. Nearer England, naval victories in 1759 off Lagos in Portugal and in Quiberon Bay (Brittany) destroyed French plans to invade Britain. A central

The Capture of Quebec

On September 13, 1759, a British fleet under the young General James Wolfe—although only 32 years old, he was already a veteran of the Jacobite Wars and the capture of Louisburg in Nova Scotia the previous year—sailed up the St. Lawrence River in Canada and landed 3,600 soldiers near the French stronghold of Quebec. In a daring operation the British troops scaled the rugged, undefended Heights of Abraham bordering the river and gained access to the Plains of Abraham, a favorable point from which to attack the city. The short battle that followed saw the British overrun the defenders. This key victory opened the way for the conquest of all of New France, as Canada east of the St. Lawrence was then known. Both the French commander Louis-Joseph de Montcalm and Wolfe himself (shown at right) were mortally wounded in the assault.

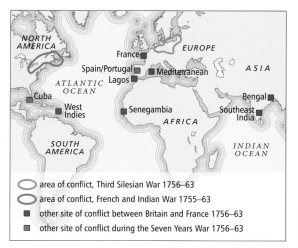

area of conflict, Third Silesian War 1756–63

area of conflict, French and Indian War 1755–63

■ other site of conflict between Britain and France 1756–63

■ other site of conflict during the Seven Years War 1756–63

◀ In some ways a precursor of the world wars of the 20th century, the Seven Years' War affected four continents as the European powers vied for colonial supremacy as well as mastery in Europe.

▼ In 1758 British forces take Louisburg, the French fort commanding the mouth of the St. Lawrence River.

III, an ardent admirer of Frederick, was assassinated only six months after coming to the throne, Catherine II did not renew hostilities. Austria and Prussia soon signed an armistice. Spain's late entry into the war to aid the French could not halt the tide toward peace.

The long conflict ended in 1763 with a peace settlement that confirmed Britain's gains in North America (including Florida, wrested from Spanish control). Frederick kept all his former territories and enhanced Prussia's reputation for military prowess, but at a high cost; some 180,000 Prussian troops and 33,000 civilians had perished.

figure in Britain's pursuit of its ambitions was its dynamic secretary of state, William Pitt the Elder.

In spite of suffering some major defeats, notably at Kunersdorf (Kunowice, Poland) in 1759, Frederick showed great resilience in countering the overwhelming military odds against him. Yet by the end of 1761 the Austrians and Russians were massing ominously on his borders, while the accession of a new British monarch, George III, in 1760 and Pitt's subsequent resignation as chief minister threatened to deprive Prussia of vital financial aid. However, a dramatic turnaround came in early 1762, when Elizabeth of Russia died. Although the new Czar Peter

👑 **1748** The Peace of Aix-la-Chapelle ends the War of the Austrian Succession; Prussia retains control of the former Hapsburg territory of Silesia.

⚔ **1755** In North America the French and Indian War breaks out between French and British colonists.

⚔ **1755** A British defeat at Monongahela is followed by victory at the Battle of Lake George in upstate New York.

👑 **1756** To safeguard his native Hanover, Britain's German-born King George II signs the Convention of Westminster with Prussia. In response France and Austria sign the First Treaty of Versailles.

⚔ **1756** Frederick the Great of Prussia invades Saxony, which has joined the Franco–Austrian coalition, so sparking the Seven Years' War.

⚔ **1757** Prussian forces suffer a heavy defeat at the hands of an Austrian army at the Battle of Kolin in Bohemia.

⚔ **1757** Troops of the British East India Company under General Robert Clive win a decisive victory over a combined Bengali and French force at the Battle of Plassey.

⚔ **1759** With General James Wolfe's victory on the Plains of Abraham outside Quebec French control of Canada is broken, and the French and Indian War comes to an end.

⚔ **1759** An English and Hanoverian army defeats a superior French force at the Battle of Minden.

👑 **1760** King George II dies; his grandson and successor George III takes a less hawkish line on the war.

⚔ **1761** The Family Compact between the Bourbon kings Louis XV of France and Charles III of Spain brings Spain into the war; Britain seizes the Spanish possessions of Florida, Havana in Cuba, and Manila in the Philippines (–1762).

👑 **1762** Under severe military pressure from Russian and Austrian forces Prussia is saved when Russia's Empress Elizabeth dies and is succeeded by Czar Peter III, an admirer of Frederick.

👑 **1762** After Peter III returns East Prussia to Frederick's control, he is overthrown by the Russian army and aristocracy, who put his wife on the throne as Catherine II ("the Great").

👑 **1763** The Seven Years' War ends with the signing of the treaties of Paris and Hubertsburg.

313

1760–1770 A.D.

AMERICAS

✕ **1762** In fighting linked to the Seven Years' War in Europe the British take Havana, Cuba, from Spain, and several West Indian islands from France.

👑 **1763** The Treaty of Paris brings the Seven Years' War to an end. All French territories in Canada and in America east of the Mississippi River are ceded to Britain, which also gains Florida from Spain.

✕ **1763** A Native American confederacy under the Ottawa leader Pontiac rises against the British; it unsuccessfully besieges Detroit.

👑 **1764** Britain's Parliament passes the Sugar Act, the first of a series of revenue-raising measures aimed at the American colonies.

EUROPE

👑 **1760** George II of England dies, to be succeeded by his grandson George III.

✕ **1762** War breaks out between Britain and Spain.

👑 **1762** Peter III of Russia ends hostilities with Prussia on disadvantageous terms. Angry nobles immediately help his wife seize power as Catherine II, "the Great."

Catherine the Great was a German princess who came to power in Russia in 1762 on the assassination of her husband, the feeble-minded Peter III. She proved an able ruler who substantially enlarged the lands she had inherited; in the course of her 34-year reign she won the Black Sea's northern coast from the Ottoman rulers of Turkey and much of Poland when that country was partitioned between neighboring powers. Her internal policies were less successful; she extended the powers of the nobility and worsened the condition of the serfs.

AFRICA

👑 **1762** Muhammad Abu Likaylik establishes his Hamadj Dynasty as the real rulers of the Sultanate of Funj in the Upper Nile Valley.

👑 **1766** Ngolo Darra seizes power in Segu, now the capital of an important Bambara state in what today is Mali.

👑 **1766** Muhammad ibn Uthman Dey takes charge in Algiers.

WESTERN ASIA

👑 **1761** The Ottoman Sultan Mustafa III signs a treaty of friendship with Prussia.

👑 **1763** With the death of Mustafa III's grand vizier, Raghib Pasha, the Ottoman Empire loses a highly effective administrator.

SOUTH & CENTRAL ASIA

✕ **1760** Chinese forces complete the conquest of the Tarim Basin region of Central Asia.

👑 **1761** The Muslim Haidar Ali takes advantage of confusion among members of the Maratha Confederacy to seize the throne of Mysore in southern India.

✕ **1761** Afghan leader Ahmad Shah Durrani routs a Maratha and Sikh force at Panipat outside Delhi.

✕ **1762** The Dutch attack the Kingdom of Kandy in Sri Lanka. They are defeated, but a second campaign three years later forces Kandy into line.

A European view of the Indian Muslim leader Haidar Ali.

EAST ASIA & OCEANIA

👑 **1760** The shogunate of Ieharu begins—a time of economic problems and social unrest in Japan.

✕ **1761** Dutch forces launch a punitive expedition to replace the Indonesian sultan of Siak.

✕ **1762** British take the Philippines from Spain in fighting linked to the Seven Years' War in Europe.

✳ **1765** Russian Lieutenant Ivan Sind begins a survey of the seas east of the Kamchatka Peninsula.

✕ **1766** China mounts a series of attacks on Burma (–1769).

✕ **1767** Burmese forces take control of the Kingdom of Ayutthaya in Thailand.

🌊 1765 The Stamp Act taxes American legal documents and newspapers. Angry settlers form the Sons of Liberty movement, forcing Britain to back down.

☀ 1767 Accused of fomenting rebellion among native peoples, the Jesuits are expelled from Spanish America.

⊕ 1769 A Spanish expedition leaves Baja California to establish missions farther north. Their first foundation is at San Diego.

🌊 1769 In the American colonies the Sons (and Daughters) of Liberty organize a consumer boycott of British products.

AMERICAS

📖 1762 In France Jean-Jacques Rousseau publishes *The Social Contract*.

🌊 1763 The Treaty of Paris ends the Seven Years' War.

🌊 1763 Augustus III of Poland dies, to be replaced by Catherine the Great's candidate for the Polish throne (and lover), Stanislaw II.

🌊 1763 The Peace of Hubertsburg brings peace between Prussia, Saxony, and Austria.

🌊 1768 Russia invades Ottoman-held Bulgaria.

Jean-Jacques Rousseau's hut at Ermenonville, France.

EUROPE

⚔ 1768 Ali Bey al-Kabir overthrows the Ottoman governor of Egypt.

⚔ 1768 A French fleet bombards Tunisian ports over that state's refusal to release Corsican ships taken by its corsairs.

⚔ 1769 Mawlay Muhammud of Morocco dislodges the Portuguese from their last colonial foothold on Africa's Atlantic coast.

AFRICA

🌊 1765 Saudi Emir Muhammad ibn Saud dies. His son Abd al-Aziz will continue to extend Saudi rule through the Arabian Peninsula.

🌊 1768 France's Baron de Tott is brought in to modernize the Ottoman army, especially its artillery.

⚔ 1768 Alarmed by Russian advances against Poland, the Ottoman Empire declares war on Russia.

WESTERN ASIA

⚔ 1762 The Mughal nabob of Bengal, Mir Kasim, rebels against the demands of the British East India Company.

⚔ 1764 Driven into exile, Mir Kasim gathers a Mughal alliance against the company, but the British defeat its forces at Buxar on the Ganges River.

🌊 1764 Ahmad Shah Durrani's forces withdraw from the Maratha lands, leaving a vacuum in which Mughal rule in India can at least nominally be restored.

⚔ 1767 The First Mysore War breaks out in southern India between the British and Haidar Ali (–1769).

⚔ 1769 Gurkhas conquer the Kathmandu Valley in Nepal.

SOUTH & CENTRAL ASIA

⊕ 1768 France's Louis-Antoine de Bougainville visits Tahiti and Samoa.

⊕ 1768 England's Captain James Cook sets out on his first voyage to the South Pacific.

French navigator Louis-Antoine de Bougainville.

⊕ 1769 Captain Cook circumnavigates New Zealand, charting the coasts. The islands, inhabited by several hundred thousand Maoris, had been known to Europeans since the Dutch navigator Abel Tasman first sighted them in 1642.

EAST ASIA & OCEANIA

1760–1770 A.D.

THE EAST INDIA TRADE

THE GREAT VOYAGES OF THE AGE OF ÐISCOVERY *had redrawn the map of the world, extending Europe's geographical and imaginative horizons. But the economic outlook was transformed too; vast fortunes could now be made in trade. Soon the Portuguese, who had opened the way to the east, were overtaken by the French, the Dutch, and the British, all of whom found a highly effective, arm's-length way of exploiting the resources of these distant regions—through merchant companies.*

▲ The Britsh, who issued this silver rupee in the name of their King Charles II, first established a presence in India at the port of Surat from 1612 on. In the 1660s Bombay came into British hands as part of a royal wedding settlement, and in 1672—the year when the coin was minted—it became the headquarters of the English East India Company.

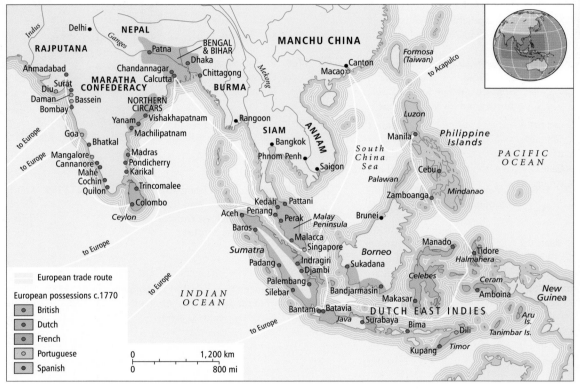

European trade route

European possessions c.1770
- British
- Dutch
- French
- Portuguese
- Spanish

0   1,200 km
0   800 mi

👑 **1619** The Dutch found a trading post at Batavia (now Jakarta) on the Indonesian island of Java.

👑 **1639** The British establish a base at Madras (modern Chennai) in southeastern India. Others will follow at Bombay (Mumbai) on the west coast in 1668 and at Calcutta (Kolkota) in1690.

👑 **1715** The British East India Company establishes a base at Canton (now Guangzhou), China.

⚔ **1757** Robert Clive's army defeats the French at the Battle of Plassey, breaking French power in India. Within four years Pondicherry will be taken.

👑 **1765** The Mughal Emperor Shah Alam grants Robert Clive and the East India Company the *diwani* (right to collect taxes) in Bengal, effectively conceding the province's government to them.

👑 **1769** Famine breaks out in Bengal, stripped of its resources under British rule. By 1770 three million people—half the population—will have died.

👑 **1773** Warren Hastings, the company's governor of Bengal, is appointed governor-general of India.

👑 **1775** Robert Clive commits suicide amid accusations of corruption and maladministration in Bengal.

▲ Shown in an 18th-century print, ships crowd the Hooghly River in Calcutta, the main British trading post on India's east coast and British India's capital from 1772 on. In the background stands Fort William, the stronghold around which the city grew up.

◀ Before the colonial era of the 19th century came a mercantile age when the European powers built up eastern trading empires. The British presence was strongest in India, the Spanish were dominant in the Philippines, and the Dutch in Ceylon and the East Indian spice islands.

The system was simple enough: Groups of merchant entrepreneurs were granted charters by a nation's rulers to open up overseas trade and to do whatever was needed to facilitate and protect it. In practice this meant the establishment of companies that quickly crossed the boundaries of what might normally be understood as commerce, and that behaved in many respects like sovereign states. Their functionaries bribed or bullied local rulers into providing sites for bases and deployed troops or warships to enforce the free flow of trade. In competition with each other they formed alliances and enmities with neighboring states, and intervened accordingly in local conflicts.

The first such business was Britain's East India Company, originally chartered by Elizabeth I in 1600. Trade grew slowly with Asia, Africa, and the Americas (Oceania did not yet figure in the European scheme). By the early 18th century tea, silk, porcelain, and other luxuries were being brought from China. Bases had also been set up in Thailand and Vietnam, and a network of contacts was established in the Spice Islands of Malaysia and Indonesia. In those regions, however, the company for a long time lost out to the Dutch, whose United East India Company (the *Vereenigde Oost-Indische Compagnie*, or V.O.C.) had been founded in 1602. The V.O.C.'s headquarters at Batavia (now Jakarta, Indonesia) were the center of a thriving commercial empire.

The wealth of India provided Britain with ample consolation. Here a toehold established in the early 17th century with the opening of posts at Surat in 1612, Madras (now Chennai) in 1639, Bombay (Mumbai) in 1668, and Calcutta (Kolkota) in 1690 grew beyond recognition over the ensuing 100 years. In some parts of the subcontinent the company took on the functions of government; in others it felt free to interfere at will. Initially a threat, its French equivalent, the *Compagnie des Indes*, was gradually squeezed out, losing its last major base with the capture of Pondicherry in 1761.

With power and wealth came temptation. There were ample opportunities for corruption, and bribery was rife among both local rulers and the officials who dealt with them. The rapacity of such men was partly blamed for the terrible effects of a famine that struck Bengal in 1769. British fortunes were lost alongside native lives at the time, and the ensuing scandal damaged the company, which came under increasing criticism through the early 19th century.

In 1857 native soldiers in the company's service unleashed the Indian Mutiny, a widescale revolt that finally convinced the British government to take direct charge of its most prized imperial possession. The establishment of a colonial regime finally brought the East India Company to an end. By that time an era had ended: The *Compagnie des Indes* had passed into history, while the Dutch government had long since stepped in to take over the administrative commitments of a V.O.C. increasingly pressured by the mounting power of the British.

🕮 **1785**   Warren Hastings returns to England to find himself impeached and facing a seven-year corruption trial.

🕮 **1799**   The V.O.C. goes into liquidation; its colonies are taken on directly by the Dutch government.

🕮 **1858**   A year after the Indian Mutiny Britain's Parliament passes the Government of India Act, which brings the subcontinent under the direct control of the crown.

Entrepôt of the Spice Islands

The V.O.C., or Dutch East India Company, had its headquarters at Batavia on the Indonesian island of Java (*right*). The Dutch first established a presence there in 1619, when the merchant adventurer Jan Pieterszoon Coen founded a settlement that in many respects resembled a Dutch town, complete with canals. From Batavia the V.O.C. spread its influence over the neighboring islands, where its presence was at first fiercely contested by local Islamic sultanates. Although the Dutch trading empire began to fade by the late 18th century, Batavia itself continued to thrive; it is now Indonesia's capital, Jakarta.

1770–1780 A.D.

AMERICAS

⚔ **1770** British troops shoot five people dead during a riot in Boston.

👑 **1773** Guatemala City becomes the capital of Guatemala after its predecessor, Antigua, is destroyed in an earthquake.

⚔ **1775** The Battle of Lexington sees the first exchange of fire in the American Revolutionary War.

A detail from a painting by George Caleb Bingham shows Daniel Boone escorting settlers through the Cumberland Gap.

EUROPE

👑 **1770** Fifteen-year-old Marie Antoinette, daughter of the Austrian Empress Maria Theresa, marries Louis, the heir to the French throne, in Paris.

⚙ **1771** More than 50,000 people die in a plague in Moscow.

👑 **1772** Russia, Prussia, and Austria agree to divide much of Poland between them in the First Partition of Poland.

⚙ **1773** Prussian scientist Wilhelm Scheele isolates hydrogen and oxygen (his findings are published in 1777).

☀ **1773** Pope Clement XIV dissolves the Jesuit order.

⚔ **1773** A Cossack soldier, Yemelyan Pugachev, declares himself to be Peter III, Catherine the Great's assassinated husband, and leads a popular uprising in southern Russia (–1775).

AFRICA

⚔ **1770** Dutch settlers from Cape Colony, South Africa, move east of Algoa Bay, coming into conflict with the African tribes of that region.

⚙ **1770** British explorer James Bruce reaches the source of the Blue Nile River in Ethiopia.

⚔ **1772** Ali Bey, ruler of Egypt since 1754, is defeated by an Ottoman army. He will die the following year.

WESTERN ASIA

⚔ **1770** An Ottoman fleet is defeated by the Russians at Chesme, off the coast of Anatolia.

👑 **1774** Abdul Hamid I becomes Ottoman sultan on the death of his brother Mustafa III, who has kept him prisoner for 43 years.

SOUTH & CENTRAL ASIA

👑 **1772** Civil war in the Maratha Kingdom on the death of Madhav Rao ends with his infant son Madhav Rao II on the throne and real power in the hands of the first minister, Nana Phadnis.

⚔ **1772** Haidar Ali, Muslim ruler of Mysore in central India, is defeated by the Marathas.

👑 **1773** Kabul becomes capital of Afghanistan in place of Kandahar.

EAST ASIA & OCEANIA

Captain James Cook, whose sextant is shown at left, played a crucial part in opening up Oceania to European settlement. In a first pioneering voyage from 1768 to 1771 he proved that New Zealand was an island and discovered the east coast of Australia, claiming it for Britain. On subsequent trips he probed Antarctica and discovered Hawaii and New Caledonia, but failed to find a passage from the Pacific to the Atlantic Ocean.

⚙ **1770** Explorer James Cook discovers the east coast of Australia and claims it for Great Britain.

⚙ **1773** James Cook becomes the first navigator to cross the Antarctic Circle (lying approximately 66.5° south of the equator).

✕ 1775 Frontiersman Daniel Boone marks out the Wilderness Road to Kentucky, repeatedly fighting off Native American resistance (–1778).

👑 1776 The Declaration of Independence is signed by representatives of the 13 colonies on July 4.

✕ 1777 The British are defeated at the Battle of Saratoga, New York; General Burgoyne surrenders.

✕ 1778 France declares war on Britain in support of the American cause.

✕ 1779 Spain declares war on Britain; it will retake western Florida and the Bahama Islands (–1783).

AMERICAS

👑 1774 Louis XVI becomes king of France on the death of his grandfather, Louis XV.

📖 1776 Publication of the 28-volume *Encyclopedia*, one of the great works of the Enlightenment, is completed in France.

👑 1778 France recognizes the independence of the United States in the Treaty of Alliance, signed in Paris.

⊕ 1779 The Iron Bridge, the first construction made entirely of cast iron, is built across the Severn River in Britain.

The Iron Bridge at Ironbridge, England.

EUROPE

👑 1777 The ruler of Morocco abolishes Christian slavery.

✕ 1778 The French regain control of the coastal region of Senegal.

AFRICA

👑 1774 The Ottomans sign the Treaty of Kuchuk-Kainarji to end the Russo–Turkish War.

The Vakil Bazaar in Shiraz, Iran, built by Karim Khan Zand.

✕ 1775 Persia's Shah Karim Khan Zand captures the port of Basra from the Ottomans (–1776).

👑 1779 Karim Khan Zand dies, leaving a disputed succession in Persia.

WESTERN ASIA

👑 1773 British colonial administrator Warren Hastings becomes governor general of the East India Company in India.

✕ 1778 Haidar Ali takes advantage of the war between Britain and France to attack the East India Company; he also renews his war against the Marathas (–1779).

SOUTH & CENTRAL ASIA

👑 1773 The British East India Company occupies a base at Balambangan, a small island off the northeast coast of Borneo (–1775).

✕ 1774 There is a major rebellion in Shandong, China.

👑 1774 Omai, a young Polynesian, is taken back to England on one of Cook's ships; he is presented to King George III and feted by London society (–1776).

✕ 1778 The Kingdom of Siam (Thailand) conquers Vientiane in Laos and makes it a subject state (–1779).

✕ 1779 On his third Pacific expedition James Cook is killed in a sudden violent dispute with a group of islanders in Hawaii.

EAST ASIA & OCEANIA

1770–1780 A.D.

THE AMERICAN REVOLUTIONARY WAR

IN THE 1770S ONE OF THE MOST DRAMATIC *and important events of modern world history took place: the rebellion of the 13 colonies of North America against rule by Great Britain and the subsequent creation of the United States of America as an independent republic. The colonies won their freedom after a war that saw setbacks and defeats but ended in British surrender in 1781. In the process a new nation was forged.*

▲ Benjamin Franklin drew this cartoon urging the American colonies to "Join, or Die" in 1754.

▶ The Revolutionary War was fought on the East Coast of the future United States.

By the late 18th century Britain was the most powerful colonial nation in the world. But its costly wars against the French had left it short of money, and it turned to its colonies, and especially to North America, for new sources of revenue. In 1765 the British Parliament imposed the Stamp Act on the 13 colonies. The measure caused outrage, and many colonists refused to pay the tax, adopting the slogan "No taxation without representation." More taxes and more protests followed, and in December 1773 a band of angry colonists, dressed as Native Americans, boarded a British ship and dumped its cargo of tea in Boston Harbor rather than pay the hated tea duty.

By now many Americans wanted to free themselves entirely from British rule. Hostility turned to war in April 1775 when rebel and British troops clashed at Lexington and Concord, Massachusetts. The first full battle of the Revolutionary War took place at Bunker Hill in June and was a defeat for the colonists. Two days earlier George Washington had been elected to command the Continental Army. The Declaration of Independence, proclaiming the separation of the 13 colonies from Britain, followed in July.

The war at first went badly for the United States. Washington scored a morale-boosting success at Trenton, New Jersey, in December 1776, but it was not until June 1777 that the Continental Army achieved its first major victory, against forces under General Burgoyne at Saratoga, New York. News of this success convinced France to enter the war on the side of the United States early in 1778, bringing much needed support. Washington and his army spent the severe winter of 1777 at Valley Forge, Pennsylvania, but managed to come through it intact. By now it was clear that the British lacked an effective strategy for winning the war. In 1781 their forces under Lord Cornwallis were besieged in Yorktown, Virginia. When a French fleet succeeded in cutting off supplies to his army, Cornwallis was forced to surrender, bringing the war to an end. The independence of the United States of America was formally recognized by the Treaty of Paris in 1783, and a new nation was born.

👑 **1765** The Stamp Act imposes direct taxation (on legal documents and newspapers) on the American colonies.

⚔ **1773** The Boston Tea Party is a violent protest by American colonists against the imposition of a tax on tea.

👑 **1774** The British Parliament passes the Coercive Acts to punish Massachusetts for the Boston Tea Party.

👑 **1774** The first Continental Congress meets in Philadelphia to protest the Coercive Acts, dubbed the "Intolerable Acts" by patriots.

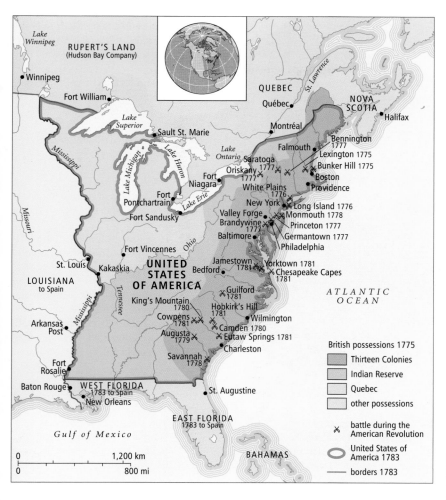

	British possessions 1775
	Thirteen Colonies
	Indian Reserve
	Quebec
	other possessions
✗	battle during the American Revolution
◯	United States of America 1783
—	borders 1783

We, the People

Once the war was ended, a great debate got under way as to how the United States should be governed. Representatives chosen to attend the Constitutional Convention, collectively known as the Framers of the Constitution, met in Philadelphia in 1787 to decide how much power should be given to the national government and how much freedom individual states should have to govern themselves. One vital task was to devise a system of checks and balances to prevent any part of the government from becoming too powerful; the executive arm was to be held to account by the legislature (the Senate and the House of Representatives) and the judiciary. With its opening words "We, the People" the U.S. Constitution—the first such known to history—triumphantly affirmed the principle of the popular will. Four years later the Bill of Rights, incorporating the first ten amendments to the Constitution, spelled out the rights of individual citizens against the power of the state, guaranteeing freedom of speech and of worship and the rights to a fair trial and to bear arms.

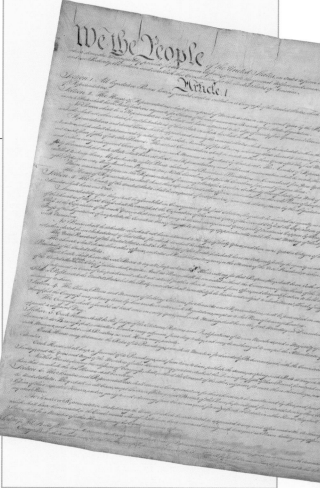

👑 **1775** George Washington is given command of the Continental Army.

✗ **1775** The rebels inflict heavy losses on the British at the Battle of Bunker Hill, the first full battle of the Revolutionary War.

👑 **1776** Washington crosses the Delaware River on Christmas night to seize Trenton.

✗ **1777** American forces suffer a setback at the Battle of Brandywine, Pennsylvania.

◀ Washington crosses the Delaware River to take Trenton, New Jersey, as shown in a painting by Emmanuel Gottlieb Leutze.

✗ **1777** Washington's army survives a bitter winter at Valley Forge and regroups (–1778).

✗ **1781** Yorktown falls, ending the Revolutionary War.

👑 **1783** The Treaty of Paris formally recognizes the independence of the United States of America.

👑 **1788** The U.S. Constitution comes into effect, having been ratified by the required nine states.

👑 **1791** The Bill of Rights, embodying the first ten amendments to the U.S. Constitution, is passed.

AMERICAS

✕ **1780** Inca nobleman Tupac Amarú II leads a revolt against Spanish colonial rule in Peru that is put down brutally (–1781).

👑 **1781** British forces in North America surrender at Yorktown, bringing the fighting in the American Revolutionary War to an end.

👑 **1782** Spanish settlers found Los Angeles.

✕ **1782** The British navy defeats the French at the Battle of the Saints in the West Indies, regaining control of the Caribbean Sea.

✕ **1782** George Washington creates the Badge of Military Merit to honor wounded soldiers; it is later renamed the Purple Heart.

👑 **1783** Britain formally recognizes the independence of the United States in the Treaty of Paris.

EUROPE

Shown here in a contemporary painting, the capture of the Bastille prison in 1789 was the opening act of the French Revolution. At the time when it was stormed by a Parisian mob, the fort held just seven prisoners, yet its symbolic role was vast: For two centuries past political detainees had been held there at the whim of the French king. The date of its fall, July 14, is still celebrated in France as a national holiday.

👑 **1780** Death of Maria Theresa, archduchess of Austria and Holy Roman empress.

👑 **1781** Holy Roman Emperor Joseph II abolishes serfdom throughout the empire.

✳ **1781** German-born British astronomer William Herschel discovers the planet Uranus; he originally calls it *Georgium Sidus* (George's Star) in honor of King George III.

AFRICA

👑 **1786** Sultan Abdul Hamid I sends troops to strengthen Ottoman control of Egypt.

👑 **1787** A British antislavery group acquires land in Sierra Leone on the west coast of Africa to found a colony for freed slaves.

👑 **1787** The Treaty of Paris returns Senegal to the British; they will hold it until 1790, when it passes back to France.

WESTERN ASIA

✕ **1784** By the Treaty of Constantinople the Ottomans agree to Russian annexation of the Crimea.

👑 **1784** Esfahan once more becomes the capital of Persia.

✕ **1787** The Second Russo–Turkish War breaks out (–1792).

SOUTH & CENTRAL ASIA

👑 **c.1780** Mahadji Sindhia extends Maratha power in the north of India and becomes the effective ruler of Delhi at the expense of the puppet Mughal emperor.

👑 **1782** Haidar Ali, sultan of Mysore, dies, to be succeeded by his son Tipu Sultan.

👑 **1785** Warren Hastings, British governor-general in India, returns home to face corruption charges.

👑 **1786** Charles Cornwallis, defeated commander of the British forces in the American Revolutionary War, becomes governor-general of the East India Company in India.

EAST ASIA & OCEANIA

✕ **1781** An Islamic revolt is suppressed in China's Gansu province; another will be put down in 1784.

👑 **1782** Rama I deposes Takson, first king of Siam (Thailand), in a coup; he goes on to found a new dynasty with Bangkok as his capital.

✳ **1783** A widespread famine kills more than 300,000 people in Japan (–1784).

☀ **1785** An edict is passed in Korea banning Catholicism.

👑 **1786** The British acquire the island of Penang (Malaysia) as a trading base and colony.

👑 **1786** Death of Ieharu, shogun of Japan since 1760.

👑 **1783** More than 30,000 British loyalists emigrate to Canada, settling mostly in New Brunswick and Ontario.

👑 **1784** The dollar becomes the U.S. monetary unit.

👑 **1787** Meeting in Philadelphia, the Constitutional Convention adopts the U.S. Constitution, which is later ratified by all 13 states (–1790).

👑 **1789** George Washington is elected first U.S. president.

An early U.S. dollar bill.

⊛ **1783** The Montgolfier brothers demonstrate their invention of a hot-air balloon to France's King Louis XVI at Versailles; the first manned balloon flight takes places over Paris later that year.

👑 **1783** The Russians take over the Crimea, deposing Shahin Girai, the last descendant of Genghis Khan, and found Sevastopol as their naval base on the Black Sea.

👑 **1786** Death of Frederick II the Great, king of Prussia since 1740; he is succeeded by his nephew Frederick William II.

📖 **1788** The *Times* newspaper is first published in London.

👑 **1789** Louis XVI of France summons the Estates-General for the first time since 1614; the Third Estate (made up of commoners) breaks away to form the National Assembly.

⚔ **1789** On July 14 the citizens of Paris storm the fortress–prison of the Bastille, regarded as the opening event of the French Revolution.

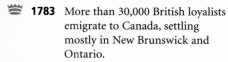

The Montgolfier brothers' balloon takes off from Paris.

👑 **1787** The U.S. government pays Morocco $10,000 to stop attacks on its shipping by privateers.

📖 **1789** Olaudah Equiano, a former slave, publishes his autobiography in Britain under the name of Gustavus Vassa.

👑 **1789** Selim III becomes Ottoman sultan on the death of his uncle Abdul Hamid I.

👑 **1789** Lotf Ali Khan becomes the last ruler of Iran's Zand Dynasty.

⚔ **1789** Tipu Sultan attacks Travancore, which is under British protection, starting a new war.

Tipu's Tiger: a celebrated mechanical toy, made for Tipu Sultan, featuring a tiger mauling a British officer.

⚔ **1787** Rice riots break out in Edo (modern Tokyo).

👑 **1788** The First Fleet of British settlers, including more than 700 convicts, lands at Botany Bay in Australia.

⚔ **1789** The crew of the *Bounty*, a British Royal Navy vessel, mutinies in the South Pacific and casts the commander, William Bligh, adrift with 18 men; he reaches Timor after a voyage of 4,000 miles (6,500 km) in an open boat.

AMERICAS

EUROPE

AFRICA

WESTERN ASIA

SOUTH & CENTRAL ASIA

EAST ASIA & OCEANIA

1780–1790 A.D.

EUROPEANS SETTLE AUSTRALIA

Long described as the "unknown land" (terra incognita) on early maps, Australia was the last continent on Earth to be discovered and colonized by Europeans. Its north and west coasts were first explored in the 17th century by Dutch sailors who called the shores they discovered New Holland. In 1770 an English navigator, Captain James Cook, discovered the continent's east coast and claimed it for Britain. The first settler fleet arrived just 18 years later.

◀ ▼ Captain Cook, seen below taking possession of New South Wales in the name of the British crown in 1770, did more than any other navigator to open up Australia to European settlement.

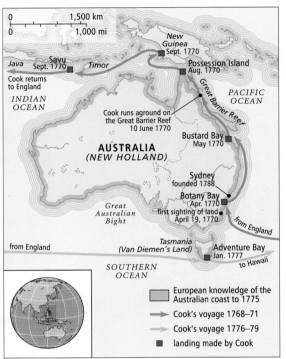

⚜ **1606** Willem Jansz, sailing from Bantam in Java, explores the northern coast of Australia west of Cape York Peninsula and calls the land New Holland.

⚜ **1616** Dutch sailor Dirk Hartog lands on an island on the west coast of Australia (now called Dirk Hartog Island).

⚜ **1642** Dutch sailor Abel Tasman discovers the island he names Van Diemen's Land (it will be renamed Tasmania in 1855) but does not come in sight of the Australian mainland.

⚜ **1770** Captain Cook discovers the east coast of Australia after sailing west from New Zealand; he explores its entire length of 3,000 miles (5,000 km) and makes a landfall at Botany Bay, near modern Sydney.

👑 **1788** The First Fleet of convicts arrives in Botany Bay on January 26, having left Portsmouth the previous May under the command of Captain Arthur Phillip, the colony's first governor.

👑 **1790** The Second Fleet reaches Port Jackson; of 1,000 convicts on board, more than a third die on the voyage or shortly after arrival.

👑 **1791** The Third Fleet arrives in Australia with the first group of Irish convicts on board.

✗ **1791** A group of convicts escape from Port Jackson and set out to walk to China (which they think lies somewhere to the north); they die of starvation.

👑 **1793** The first free settlers arrive in Australia. Numbering just 11 in all, they are granted free passage, land, and tools.

👑 **1794** The first political prisoners are transported to Australia.

Captain Cook, one of the greatest navigators who ever lived, explored the Pacific Ocean from Antarctica to Alaska on three expeditions between 1768 and 1779. It was on the first of these voyages that he first saw Australia, landing at Botany Bay not far from the modern city of Sydney. On returning to England, he reported that the place would be suitable for a settlement. Britain's jails were overflowing at the time—it was an age when people could be thrown in prison for as little as stealing a loaf of bread or a handkerchief—and the nation had become accustomed to sending as many as 1,000 convicts a year to penal settlements in Maryland and Virginia. But after the loss of the American colonies in 1783 this transportation stopped. So it was decided to start a new penal colony for convicts in Australia.

The First Fleet of 11 ships with more than 750 convicts on board—568 men, 191 women, and 19 children—arrived in Botany Bay in January 1788. The new arrivals nearly starved. The land proved far less fertile than had been hoped, their crops failed, and their livestock died or strayed. Fresh supplies were sent for from Cape Colony in South Africa, but they proved far from adequate to feed both the original settlers and the convicts carried on a second fleet, which arrived in 1790. The period was long remembered as "the starving time."

By the late 1790s Australia was receiving regular transports of convicts. They were mostly kept in Port Jackson, close to Botany Bay, although some were sent to Norfolk Island, a tiny dot in the Pacific some 900 miles (1,500 km) away to the east, or else to Van Diemen's Land (later Tasmania) several hundred miles to the south. They were put to work building roads and bridges or forced to provide unpaid labor on farms and landholdings. Treatment was harsh, with frequent floggings, and many tried to escape only to die in Australia's unforgiving outback. It was a cruel beginning for a new colony, and it left a bitter legacy of resentment long after Australia had become a place of hope and fulfillment for thousands of free immigrants from Europe in the 19th century.

◄ Cook entered Australian waters on two of his three great voyages of exploration. On the first he explored the east coast, claiming it for Britain. On his final voyage he touched land in Adventure Bay, Tasmania, in 1777.

A Brutal Persecution

If the convicts' fate was hard, that of Australia's original inhabitants, the Aborigines, was desperate. The Aborigines had already inhabited Australia for at least 60,000 years. Living in isolation from the rest of the world, they were nomadic hunter–gatherers who evolved a complex tribal culture that drew inspiration from the natural environment. Their unique rock art of paintings and engravings stretched back thousands of years and was sacred to the tribe, containing stories about a mythical "dreamtime" when the spiritual ancestors of the Aborigines brought the universe—rocks, rivers, desert, plants, animals, and humans—into being. The Europeans considered the Aborigines to be Stone Age people, little better than animals. Settlers stole their tribal lands and hunted them down. Persecution, warfare, and disease decimated their numbers. The worst atrocities were committed in Tasmania, where the Aborigine population was eradicated in a genocidal act of ethnic cleansing.

AMERICAS

👑 **1790** Philadelphia becomes the capital of the United States (–1800).

✳ **1790** Benjamin Franklin dies aged 84, having invented bifocal eyeglasses in the last year of his life.

👑 **1791** The U.S. Bill of Rights is ratified as the first 10 amendments to the Constitution.

👑 **1791** The Constitution Act, passed by the British Parliament, divides the province of Quebec into Upper and Lower Canada.

François Dominique Toussaint, who later adopted the name Toussaint–L'Ouverture ("The Opening"), was a patriot who led a slave uprising against the French planters of Haiti. He subsequently became virtual dictator of the island of Hispaniola (now shared between Haiti and the Dominican Republic), seeking to reconcile the different racial elements in its population. Although he paid lip service to the authority of France as the controlling colonial power, he ruled in practice as he saw fit. Such independence roused the hostility of Napoleon Bonaparte, who sent an army to bring the island to heel. Toussaint was treacherously seized at a peace parley and sent to France, where he died in prison in 1803.

EUROPE

Medical science took a major step forward in 1796 when the English physician Edward Jenner introduced the practice of vaccination. Jenner's technique involved innoculating patients with the cowpox virus to protect them from the more virulent smallpox—a procedure that aroused controversy at the time, as the cartoon at left indicates. Jenner devoted the rest of his life to promoting the cause of vaccination, which in time spread around the world, greatly reducing the mortality from smallpox and other lethal diseases.

📖 **1791** The Austrian composer Wolfgang Amadeus Mozart dies aged 35 and is buried in a pauper's grave.

⚔ **1792** France becomes a republic; the French Revolutionary War opens with French victories at Valmy (against the Prussians) and Jemappes (against the Austrians).

⚔ **1793** Louis XVI, deposed king of France, is guillotined by revolutionaries in Paris.

AFRICA

👑 **1792** Denmark becomes the first European country to ban the trade in African slaves.

👑 **1794** Morocco closes its frontiers to foreigners.

✳ **1795** Scottish explorer Mungo Park explores the course of the Niger River in central Africa.

WESTERN ASIA

👑 **1792** The Treaty of Jassy ends the Second Russo–Turkish War; the Ottomans regain some territory.

👑 **1793** Selim III tries to reform the Ottoman army on European lines, but is opposed by the janissaries.

⚔ **1794** Agha Muhammad Qajar becomes shah of Iran following the defeat and capture of Lotf Ali Khan.

SOUTH & CENTRAL ASIA

👑 **1792** Tipu Sultan of Mysore is defeated by British forces in the Third Anglo–Mysore War; his two sons are taken as hostages, and he loses half his territory.

👑 **1795** The Maratha ruler Madhav Rao II dies in an accident at the age of 21.

⚔ **1796** The British seize control of Ceylon (Sri Lanka) from the Dutch.

EAST ASIA & OCEANIA

👑 **1792** New Zealand's first white settlers (from Australia) land at the Bay of Islands.

👑 **1793** A British trade mission led by Lord Macartney fails to win any concessions from the Chinese emperor.

☀ **1795** The first Christian missionaries arrive in the Society and Marquesas islands of Polynesia to convert the islanders.

✕ **1791** Inspired by the ideals of the French Revolution, François Toussaint, a former slave, leads a successful uprising of slaves in Haiti (–1793).

👑 **1792** Columbus Day is celebrated for the first time in New York.

⊕ **1793** Eli Whitney develops the cotton gin, a mechanical device for removing seeds from cotton.

⊕ **1793** Explorer Alexander McKenzie crosses the Canadian Rockies and makes his way down the Fraser River to the Pacific Ocean.

✕ **1795** There are slave revolts in the Windward Islands and Jamaica (–1796).

👑 **1796** John Adams is elected the second president of the United States.

⊕ **1799** Eli Whitney mass-produces muskets for the U.S. Army using the assembly-line system.

The original cotton gin devised by Eli Whitney.

👑 **1795** Following an unsuccessful rising, Poland is divided among Russia, Prussia, and Austria; it will not regain its independence until 1919.

✕ **1795** France conquers the Netherlands, ruling it as the Batavian Republic.

⊕ **1796** An English doctor, Edward Jenner, develops a vaccination against smallpox.

✕ **1796** French general Napoleon Bonaparte wins a decisive battle against the Austrians at the Lodi Bridge in Italy.

👑 **1796** Death of Catherine the Great, empress of Russia; she is succeeded by her son, Paul I.

✕ **1798** Backed by a small French force, nationalist rebels in Ireland rise unsuccessfully against the British.

👑 **1799** Napoleon Bonaparte returns to France from Egypt to make himself first consul and effective ruler of the nation.

Wolfgang Amdadeus Mozart.

👑 **1795** In South Africa Cape Colony comes temporarily under British control.

✕ **1798** A French force under Bonaparte occupies Egypt but is defeated by the British at the Battle of the Nile.

👑 **1796** Agha Muhammad is formally crowned as the first of the Qajar Dynasty of Persian shahs.

✕ **1797** Agha Muhammad is assassinated and is succeeded as ruler of Persia by his nephew, Fath Ali Shah.

✕ **1798** The fourth Anglo–Mysore War breaks out between Tipu Sultan and British forces answering to a new governor general, the future marquis of Wellesley.

👑 **1799** Ranjit Singh establishes a Sikh state in Punjab.

✕ **1799** Tipu Sultan is killed when the British storm his capital at Seringapatam.

👑 **1796** Chinese Emperor Qianlong abdicates at the age of 84, having ruled since 1736.

✕ **1796** A major rebellion led by the Buddhist-inspired White Lotus Society breaks out in central China (–1804).

👑 **1799** Plagued by mounting debts, the Dutch East India Company goes into liquidation. Its surviving possessions are taken over by the Dutch state.

AMERICAS

EUROPE

AFRICA

WESTERN ASIA

SOUTH & CENTRAL ASIA

EAST ASIA & OCEANIA

1790–1800 A.D.

THE FRENCH REVOLUTION

▲ The sansculottes, or "men without breeches"—so called because they did not wear the knee breeches required in respectable society at the time—became the symbol of radical republicanism in France.

THE FRENCH REVOLUTION WAS A SEISMIC UPHEAVAL *in European history, setting off a chain of events that saw the end of the French monarchy and overturned French government and society. Welcomed by some and feared by others, it plunged the whole continent into political chaos and warfare, and led to the rise of Napoleon Bonaparte as ruler of France.*

The cost of France's support for the American colonies in their war against Britain was a heavy one that bankrupted the government. To raise new tax revenues, King Louis XVI was forced in 1789 to summon the Estates-General, France's representative assembly, which had not met since 1614. Soaring prices and food shortages fed the demand for political change, with the result that part of the Estates-General broke away to form the National Assembly, which began passing reformist legislation. When a rumor spread that the king's army was planning to close down the assembly, an angry crowd stormed the Bastille, a prison-fortress in Paris that was a hated symbol of royal tyranny.

This event is traditionally seen as the start of the revolution. The National Assembly adopted the slogan "Liberty, Equality, Fraternity," issued the Declaration of the Rights of Man, and passed a stream of reforming measures, abolishing serfdom, confiscating church property, and ending hereditary titles.

At first the National Assembly was prepared to work with the king, but Louis proved unwilling to cooperate with them. In 1791 he tried to flee the country with his unpopular wife, Marie Antoinette, but the pair were stopped and brought back to Paris. The National Convention, a new assembly elected in 1792, declared France a republic. After Austria declared war on France, the king and queen were accused of plotting to betray the nation and were executed in January 1793.

Now began the darkest period of the French Revolution, when Robespierre, leader of the radical Jacobin faction, seized control of the ruling Committee of Public Safety. During the Terror that followed, he took revenge on his opponents by having many of them guillotined. Robespierre's triumph was short-lived, and he was himself guillotined in 1794.

The convention then used military force to restore order, establishing a government of moderates called the Directory. The Directory was itself overthrown in

▶ A painting by J.J.F. Tassaert shows the coup staged on the night of July 27, 1794, when enemies of the Jabobin leader Robespierre seized and executed him and his closest political allies. Their action marked the end of the Terror, launched by Robespierre in the previous year in an attempt to sweep away all remaining vestiges of the old royalist regime.

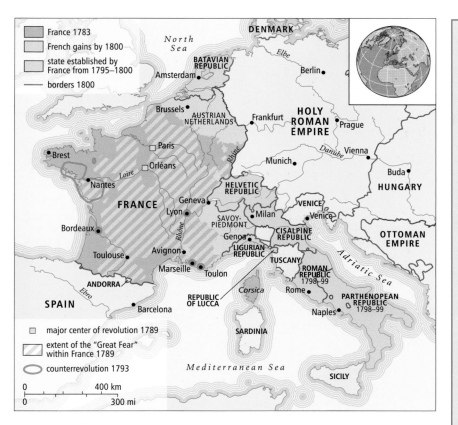

France 1783
French gains by 1800
state established by France from 1795–1800
— borders 1800

North Sea
DENMARK
Elbe
BATAVIAN REPUBLIC
Amsterdam
Berlin
Brussels
AUSTRIAN NETHERLANDS
Frankfurt
HOLY ROMAN EMPIRE
Prague
Paris
Loire
Rhine
Danube
Vienna
Brest
Orléans
Munich
Nantes
HELVETIC REPUBLIC
Buda
HUNGARY
FRANCE
Geneva
Lyon
SAVOY-PIEDMONT
Milan
VENICE
Venice
Bordeaux
Rhône
Genoa
CISALPINE REPUBLIC
OTTOMAN EMPIRE
Avignon
LIGURIAN REPUBLIC
Toulouse
Marseille
TUSCANY
Adriatic Sea
Toulon
ROMAN REPUBLIC 1798–99
ANDORRA
REPUBLIC OF LUCCA
Corsica
Rome
Ebro
SPAIN
Barcelona
PARTHENOPEAN REPUBLIC 1798–99
Naples

□ major center of revolution 1789
⬜ extent of the "Great Fear" within France 1789
⬭ counterrevolution 1793

SARDINIA
Mediterranean Sea
SICILY

0   400 km
0   300 mi

The Guillotine

The guillotine has entered popular myth as the symbol of the Terror in which the French Revolution culminated, responsible for sending thousands of aristocrats to their death in front of bloodthirsty Parisian mobs. Yet far from being a medieval instrument of torture, the guillotine was a creation of the Enlightenment, only introduced in 1791. Designed by the French physician Joseph Guillotin, it consisted of a sharp metal blade that descended rapidly between two wooden posts to behead its victim in an instant. In comparison to such earlier forms of capital punishment as decapitation with an axe, it was a fast and humane method of execution. The number of people guillotined in Paris during the revolution was around 2,600—a relatively small number compared with the 200,000 believed to have died in the civil wars and uprisings that accompanied the revolution, especially in the west and south of the country.

1799 in a coup led by Napoleon Bonaparte, a young general who had fought brilliant campaigns in Italy and Austria. Bonaparte now became first consul and ruler of the country. Although he remained dedicated to the spread of the revolution abroad, at home he created a military dictatorship.

▲ The revolution of 1789 centered on Paris and Orleans, although much of France was swept by the "Great Fear"—a panic fed by rumors of aristocratic reaction.

👑 **1789** The Third Estate—the section of the Estates-General composed of commoners—turns its back on the officially sanctioned parliament and instead sets up the National Assembly, with a pledge to draw up a new constitution.

✗ **1789** After the storming of the Bastille peasant uprisings spread across the country; the tricolor is adopted as the revolutionary flag.

👑 **1789** The National Assembly introduces a series of reforming measures and establishes equality before the law, freedom of the press, and religious toleration (–1791).

👑 **1791** Louis XVI tries to escape from Paris but is captured at Varennes.

👑 **1791** The king agrees to accept a new constitution.

👑 **1792** The moderate Girondist faction forms a government, but it is undermined by the radical Jacobins.

👑 **1792** The National Convention, elected by universal suffrage, is dominated by the Jacobins.

👑 **1793** The National Convention delegates power to the Committee of Public Safety, controlled by the Jacobin leader Robespierre; the Reign of Terror begins.

✗ **1793** Peasant guerrillas known as the Chouans lead a rising against the republican government in western France.

👑 **1793** The revolutionary calendar is adopted; it introduces a 10-day week, abolishes Sundays, and renames the months according to the seasons of the year.

👑 **1794** Robespierre is deposed and executed.

👑 **1795** The Directory—an executive of five members responsible to a bicameral legislative assembly—is established to rule France.

👑 **1799** The Brumaire coup overthrows the Directory and introduces the Consulate, with Napoleon Bonapare as first consul, sharing executive power with two others.

AMERICAS

📖 **1800** The U.S. Library of Congress is founded.

👑 **1800** John Adams becomes the first U.S. president to live in the Executive Mansion (renamed the White House in 1814).

⚙ **1800** German naturalist Alexander von Humboldt explores the Orinoco and Amazon rivers in South America (–1804).

A black-headed cacajo monkey, engraved from a sketch by Alexander von Humboldt.

👑 **1801** Thomas Jefferson succeeds John Adams as U.S. president after defeating Aaron Burr, who becomes vice president.

👑 **1803** Through the Louisiana Purchase the United States acquires from France an area including present-day Louisiana, Arkansas, Kansas, Oklahoma, Missouri, the Dakotas, Iowa, Nebraska, and parts of Montana and Wyoming.

EUROPE

⚔ **1800** Napoleon Bonaparte defeats the Austrian army at the Battle of Marengo in Italy (June) and at Hohenlinden in southern Germany (December).

⚙ **1800** Italian physicist Alessandro Volta invents the voltaic pile, the first chemical battery capable of storing electricity.

👑 **1801** The Act of Union that makes Ireland part of the United Kingdom of Great Britain and Ireland comes into effect on January 1; it will last until 1922.

⚔ **1801** Paul I, czar of Russia, is murdered by army officers trying to force him to abdicate.

⚙ **1804** The English inventor Richard Trevithick designs the first self-propelling steam engine.

⚔ **1804** Serbian national leader Kara George leads an uprising in Belgrade against Ottoman rule that spreads to the rest of Serbia.

AFRICA

👑 **1801** French troops withdraw from Egypt following defeat by the British.

⚔ **1801** U.S. ships attack Tripoli and Algiers on the North African coast in an attempt to end piracy in the Mediterranean (–1805).

☀ **1804** Islamic reformer Usman dan Fodio inspires an Islamic revival and *jihad* (holy war) in the Hausa kingdoms of northern Nigeria.

WESTERN ASIA

👑 **1800** Captain John Malcolm of the British East India Company visits Tehran in Iran to seek the support of the shah against the Russians.

☀ **1803** Islamic fundamentalists of the Wahhabi sect occupy the Hejaz in Arabia and seize the holy cities of Mecca and Medina (–1805).

⚔ **1804** Fath Ali Shah, a ruler of Iran's Qajar Dynasty, starts a war with Russia resulting from the Russian annexation of the Kingdom of Georgia.

SOUTH & CENTRAL ASIA

Ranjit Singh won the title of Lion of the Punjab for his victories over Afghans and Pathans, traditional scourges of northern India. The son of a Sikh tribal leader, he took Lahore in 1799 and proclaimed himself maharaja in 1801. Prevented by British power from expanding his kingdom eastward, he turned to the north, waging many victorious campaigns until his death in 1839.

👑 **c.1800** British traders in India begin to export opium to China.

👑 **1801** Ranjit Singh, founder of the Sikh Kingdom of the Punjab, declares himself maharaja ("great ruler") at the age of 21.

EAST ASIA & OCEANIA

☀ **1801** A wave of persecution against Catholics begins in Korea.

⚙ **1801** British naval captain Matthew Flinders circumnavigates the entire continent of Australia and charts its coastline (–1803).

👑 **1802** Nguyen Anh unifies Vietnam and makes Hué his capital.

AMERICAS

👑 **1804** Jean-Jacques Dessalines makes himself emperor of Haiti; he is assassinated two years later.

⚙ **1804** Meriwether Lewis and William Clark lead an overland expedition from the Missouri River across the Great Continental Divide to the Pacific Ocean and back (–1806).

⚙ **1806** Congress authorizes the Great National Pike, better known as the Cumberland Road, which will become the first federal highway (although construction will not begin until 1811).

👑 **1807** Congress passes an act prohibiting the importation of slaves into the United States, effective from January 1, 1808.

⚙ **1807** Robert Fulton starts the first commercial steamboat service in the world on the Hudson River between New York City and Albany.

👑 **1807** Former Vice President Aaron Burr is indicted for treason but acquitted.

EUROPE

model of Richard Trevithick's steam engine, the first to run on rails.

⚔ **1805** A British fleet under the command of Admiral Horatio Nelson defeats a combined French and Spanish fleet at the Battle of Trafalgar; Nelson himself is shot and killed.

⚔ **1805** Napoleon wins a decisive victory over the Austrians and Russians at the Battle of Austerlitz.

👑 **1806** Austrian Emperor Francis II gives up the title of Holy Roman emperor, so bringing the 1,000-year-old Holy Roman Empire to an end.

👑 **1807** Serfdom is abolished in Prussia.

⚔ **1807** Napoleon marches across Spain (allied with France at the time) to occupy Portugal.

AFRICA

👑 **1805** Muhammad Ali, an Albanian officer in Ottoman service, proclaims himself viceroy of Egypt.

👑 **1806** British forces reoccupy Cape Colony on the southern tip of Africa; they had earlier held the territory from 1795 to 1803.

👑 **1807** Britain ends its participation in the international slave trade.

WESTERN ASIA

⚔ **1805** Janissaries (crack Ottoman troops) take control of Aleppo, Syria.

⚔ **1807** Janissaries opposed to reform lead a revolt against Ottoman Sultan Selim III, who is deposed and replaced by his brother Mustafa IV.

Fath Ali Shah, second ruler of Persia's Qajar Dynasty, who reigned from 1797 to 1834.

SOUTH & CENTRAL ASIA

⚔ **1803** War breaks out between the British and the Maratha rulers of central India (–1805).

⚔ **1803** British forces occupy Delhi.

👑 **1803** Coastal Ceylon (Sri Lanka) is made a British colony.

EAST ASIA & OCEANIA

👑 **1803** The first penal colony is established on Van Diemen's Land (now Tasmania).

⚔ **1804** The White Lotus rebellion is brought to an end in China.

1800–1807 A.D.

1808–1815 A.D.

AMERICAS

🔱 **1808** Portugal's prince regent, the future King John VI, sets up a government in exile in Brazil.

⚔ **1810** Father Miguel Hidalgo leads an uprising in Mexico against Spanish rule; he is defeated and executed in 1811.

⚔ **1811** Paraguay declares its independence from Spain.

🔱 **1812** A Russian fur-trading colony is founded at Fort Ross on what will one day be the California coast.

🔱 **1812** Massachussetts governor Elbridge Gerry gives his name to gerrymandering—the practice of manipulating electoral boundaries for political ends.

⚔ **1812** The United States declares war on Britain (the War of 1812), citing as the cause the continued blockading of its ports and attacks on its commerce; U.S. forces invade Canada.

⚔ **1814** British troops burn Washington, D.C., during the War of 1812, which is ended by the Treaty of Ghent, signed in December.

EUROPE

⚔ **1808** An uprising against French troops in Madrid, Spain, is put down harshly; Napoleon goes on to invade and occupy the whole of Spain.

⚔ **1808** A British army lands in Portugal, beginning the Peninsular War against Napoleon (–1814).

Britain's prince regent, the future King George IV, dressed in ceremonial costume.

⚔ **1809** Andreas Hofer leads an uprising in the Tyrol region of Austria and northern Italy against the French.

🔱 **1809** Sweden cedes Finland to Russia after its defeat in the Finnish War.

📖 **1809** Death of Joseph Haydn, Austrian composer.

AFRICA

🔱 **1808** The British government takes responsibility for Sierra Leone, chosen by opponents of slavery as a colony to resettle freed slaves from North America and Jamaica.

🔱 **1810** Radama I becomes king of the state of Merina in the central highlands of Madagascar; he encourages the spread of mission schools.

🔱 **1814** Said ibn Sultan, ruler of Oman, strengthens Omani control over the Swahili coast of East Africa.

WESTERN ASIA

⚔ **1808** Selim III is assassinated during an uprising intended to restore him as sultan; his cousin Mahmud II takes the Ottoman throne.

⚔ **1811** Mahmud II sends Muhammad Ali Pasha, viceroy of Egypt, with an army to restore order in the Arabian Peninsula.

🔱 **1812** Jabir al-Sabah establishes a sheikhdom in Kuwait.

SOUTH & CENTRAL ASIA

A wooden figure of the Hawaiian war god carved for King Kamehameha I.

⚔ **1809** Ranjit Singh captures the town of Amritsar; he makes a treaty with the British fixing the eastern boundary of his Sikh kingdom at the Sutlej River.

🔱 **1809** Shoja Shah of Afghanistan signs a treaty with the British.

☀ **1813** Christian missionaries are allowed for the first time to seek converts in the British-ruled parts of India.

EAST ASIA & OCEANIA

⚔ **1810** Kamehameha I conquers rival chiefs to become the first king of the Hawaiian Islands.

⚔ **1811** The Dutch surrender Java to a British invasion force.

⚔ **1814** The Dutch regain control of Sumatra; Java will also be restored to them by treaty two years later.

📖 **1815** A British expedition explores the ancient Buddhist temple at Borobudur on Java.

The War of 1812 set the United States against Britain in a struggle linked to Europe's Napoleonic Wars. Much of the inconclusive fighting took place on the Canadian border. The chief U.S. victory took place in January 1815, two weeks after the war had officially ended, when forces under Andrew Jackson repulsed a British attempt to sieze New Orleans (left).

⚜ **1814** Guyana in South America is transferred from Dutch to British rule and is renamed British Guiana.

⚜ **1814** José Francia makes himself caudillo (dictator) of Paraguay, which had broken away from Argentina in the previous year.

AMERICAS

📖 **1810** Spanish artist Francisco de Goya starts work on *The Disasters of War*, a series of 82 prints recording the horrors of the Napoleonic occupation of Spain.

⚜ **1811** Britain's King George III is declared insane; his son becomes prince regent, marking the start of the Regency period (–1820).

⚔ **1812** Napoleon's army invades Russia and occupies Moscow, but the severe winter weather forces it to retreat (–1813).

⚜ **1814** Napoleon abdicates and is exiled to the Mediterranean island of Elba. Louis XVIII, younger son of Louis XVI, is restored as king of France.

⚜ **1814** The Congress of Vienna meets to decide the political future of Europe in the wake of Napoleon's defeat (–1815).

⚔ **1815** Escaping from Elba, Napoleon raises a new army in France only to be decisively defeated at the Battle of Waterloo.

EUROPE

⚜ **1814** Britain takes formal possession of Cape Colony (which it has occupied since 1806) and pays the Netherlands $20 million in compensation.

⚜ **c.1815** By this date the Mossi kingdoms of Yatenga and Wagadugu in Burkina Faso (central Africa) are in decline.

AFRICA

⚜ **1813** The Treaty of Gulistan brings an end to the war between Russia and Persia. Persia loses territory in the Caucasus region.

⚔ **1813** An Ottoman army retakes Belgrade from Kara George's Serbian nationalist forces.

WESTERN ASIA

📖 **1814** The first Indian museum for arts and natural sciences is established in Calcutta by the Asiatic Society of Bengal.

⚔ **1815** A border dispute causes British forces in India to go to war with the Gurkhas of Nepal.

SOUTH & CENTRAL ASIA

⊕ **1815** Mount Tambora, a volcano in Indonesia, erupts, killing more than 92,000 people; the explosion throws so much ash into the atmosphere that the following year will be known as "the year without a summer."

☀ **1815** The first Christian missionaries arrive in New Zealand.

A seated Buddha rests among stupas (circular shrines) at Borobudur on the island of Java (Indonesia).

EAST ASIA & OCEANIA

1808–1815 A.D.

NAPOLEON BONAPARTE

O NE MAN DOMINATED WORLD AFFAIRS *from 1800 to 1815 in an almost unprecedented manner: France's military leader and absolute ruler, Napoleon Bonaparte. Many people in Europe and America saw Napoleon as a hero who used his battlefield successes to spread the ideals of the French Revolution abroad; others detested him for his autocratic ways and the vast number of deaths his expansionist policies left in their wake. What is unchallenged is that he changed France, and the world, forever.*

▲ Taking advatage of the career opportunities opened by the French Revolution, Napoleon was a general by the age of 26 and supreme ruler of France four years later. His attempt to reshape Europe on revolutionary lines finally foundered by overstretching the nation's resources.

▶ At the height of his power in 1812 Napoleon dominated a European bloc larger even than Charlemagne's medieval Holy Roman Empire. While Napoleon himself was the driving force behind the entire enterprise, he put individual nations in the hands of trusted subordinates, several of them drawn from his own family.

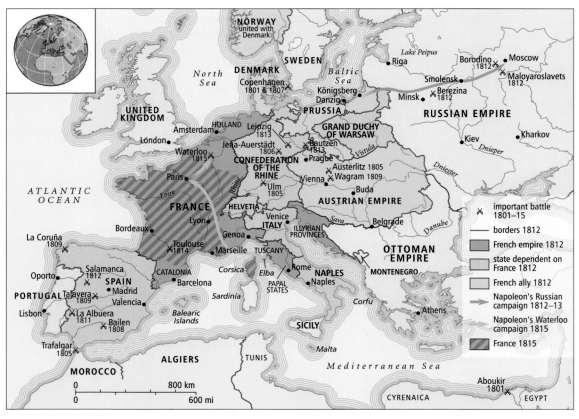

👑 **1793** Napoleon wins Toulon from the royalists and is made a brigadier general.

👑 **1795** Napoleon helps disperse a royalist mob in Paris and is given command of the army of the interior.

✕ **1796** Napoleon's victories in Italy and Austria win him glory and prestige (–1797).

👑 **1799** Napoleon becomes first consul.

👑 **1804** The Napoleonic Code is issued, reforming the laws of France; in the same year Napoleon crowns himself emperor of France in the presence of the pope.

✕ **1805** Napoleon defeats an Austrian and Russian army at the Battle of Austerlitz.

👑 **1808** Napoleon crowns his brother Joseph king of Spain.

✕ **1809** Napoleon defeats the Austrians at the Battle of Wagram.

👑 **1810** Napoleon divorces his wife Josephine Beauharnais in order to marry Marie-Louise, daughter of Francis I of Austria; a son is born in March 1811.

✕ **1812** Napoleon invades Russia but is forced to retreat.

👑 **1814** Napoleon abdicates and is exiled to the Mediterranean island of Elba.

Napoleon Bonaparte was born on the island of Corsica in 1769. His original name was Napoleone Buonaparte, and he spoke Italian until he was 10, when his family sent him to be educated at military schools in France. He graduated as a second lieutenant of artillery in 1785 at the age of 16.

Soon afterward France was plunged into the confusion of the French Revolution. Napoleon proved himself to be a soldier of genius in defense of its goals. He won victories in Italy and Austria that secured the safety of France and led him to see himself as a man of destiny. In 1799 he emerged from the coup that overthrew the ruling Directory as first consul and the most powerful man in France. He immediately set about restoring order to the nation, introducing wide-ranging reforms that established a highly centralized, efficient modern state with himself at its head. In 1804 he proclaimed himself emperor.

Napoleon continued to fight wars abroad, determined to build up France's power in Europe and the rest of the world. In 1805 he defeated the combined armies of Russia and Austria at the Battle of Austerlitz, one of his greatest victories. Unable to overcome the British at sea, he devised the Continental System—economic sanctions designed to exclude Britain from European trade. By 1808 he had made himself master of Europe from Spain to Poland. He redrew the map of the continent, placing members of his own family in positions of power: one brother became king of Spain, another king of Holland, and a third king of Westphalia, while his brother-in-law was made king of Naples.

In 1812 Napoleon sent an army to invade Russia, seeking to compel the czar to uphold the Continental System. The move overstretched his resources and paved the way for his downfall. Defeat in Russia left him greatly weakened, causing the other European powers to ally against him. In 1813 he was defeated at the Battle of Leipzig; in March 1814 the allies entered Paris. Napoleon abdicated and was exiled to the

Mediterranean island of Elba, but in less than a year he escaped and returned to France. His attempt to regain power failed when his armies were defeated at Waterloo in June 1815. This time he was exiled to the lonely island of St. Helena in the South Atlantic, from which there was no escape. He died there in 1821, still viewed by many in France as a national hero.

◀ Featuring Napoleon's favorite symbol, the eagle, this imperial coat of arms decorated the back of a throne offered to Bonaparte by the citizens of Strasbourg on the occasion of a state visit. As emperor, Napoleon shocked his radical supporters by creating an imperial nobility to replace the aristocracy of royalist days.

The Campaign of 1812

In June 1812 Napoleon invaded Russia with an army of more than 500,000 men. As they marched toward Moscow, the Russian forces fell back before them, burning the land as they went. Eventually, on September 7 the two armies met in battle at Borodino, just outside the Russian capital. There was terrible loss of life on both sides but no clear victor. A week later Napoleon advanced unopposed into Moscow, which was almost deserted. The defenders who had remained started fires, and soon the whole city was ablaze, leaving the French without food or shelter. Czar Alexander I refused Napoleon's offer of peace, and the emperor had no choice but to retreat. But his army had stayed in Moscow for five weeks, and by now winter was on the way. As the remnants of his forces retraced their route, thousands died of cold and starvation. Others were killed trying to cross the Berezina River. Fewer than 40,000 returned home.

⚔ **1815** Napoleon escapes from Elba and enters Paris in March, having raised a new army on the way. The "100 days" of revived Napoleonic rule end with the emperor's final defeat by British and Prussian forces at the Battle of Waterloo.

🏛 **1821** Napoleon dies in exile on St. Helena, a remote island in the Atlantic Ocean.

🏛 **1840** Napoleon's remains are returned to France to be reinterred in a marble tomb in Les Invalides, a mausoleum in Paris.

AMERICAS

1816 Argentina declares its independence from Spain.

1816 A slave revolt on the Caribbean island of Barbados is put down.

1818 The Stars and Stripes is adopted as the flag of the United States.

1818 The 49th Parallel is declared as the border between the United States and Canada.

EUROPE

1816 French physician René Laënnec invents the stethoscope, an instrument for listening to the heart and lungs.

1818 Mary Shelley publishes her novel *Frankenstein*, telling the story of a scientist who brings a monster to life.

1819 Eleven people are killed when cavalry soldiers charge a crowd of protesters in Manchester, England; the event becomes known as the Peterloo Massacre.

1820 Danish physicist Hans Christian Ørsted demonstrates that an electric current is able to deflect a magnetized compass needle.

1820 The Spanish army leads a revolution against the repressive government of King Ferdinand VII.

1821 Greece begins a war to win independence from the Ottoman Empire.

AFRICA

A brilliant but ruthless military leader, Shaka created a Zulu kingdom that took in all the Natal region of present-day South Africa. He created a formidable army of barefoot soldiers armed with long shields and stabbing spears, using it to exterminate neighboring tribes; the remnants were then incorporated into his empire. His triumphs destroyed the tribal structure of the surrounding region, creating widespread devastation and opening up the area to penetration by Boer colonists after his death.

1816 The French passenger ship *Medusa* runs aground off the coast of Senegal with great loss of life; the disaster causes a scandal in France and is the subject of a famous painting by French painter Theodore Géricault (1819).

WESTERN ASIA

1817 The Ottomans grant the Serbs limited self-government.

1819 British warships fire on ports along the Persian Gulf after a series of pirate attacks on British ships in the Indian Ocean.

1821 War breaks out again between Persia and the Ottoman Empire. Neither side makes lasting territorial gains (–1823).

SOUTH & CENTRAL ASIA

1816 The Gurkhas make peace with the British and agree on the frontier of Nepal, which now comes under British protection.

1817 British action against India's *pindari* (wandering bands of warriors) leads to outright war with the Marathas and their final defeat (–1818).

1819 Ranjit Singh conquers Kashmir.

EAST ASIA & OCEANIA

1816 A British trade mission led by Lord Amherst is expelled from China.

1817 Australia is officially named; earlier the island had been known as New Holland.

1818 The arrival of European settlers in New Zealand sparks a period of intertribal conflict among the indigenous Maori people known as the Musket Wars (–1835).

1819 A British trading station is founded at the southern tip of the Malay Peninsula; it will develop into the modern-day state of Singapore.

1820 Minh Manh becomes emperor of Vietnam and revives Confucianism, starting a wave of persecutions against Christians.

AMERICAS

⊕ **1818** The *Savannah* is the first steamship to cross the Atlantic.

👑 **1818** Spain cedes Florida to the United States.

✕ **1819** Simón Bolívar frees Colombia from Spanish control.

👑 **1821** Mexico wins independence from Spain.

✕ **1822** Forces loyal to Jean-Pierre Boyer of Haiti occupy Santo Domingo, uniting the island of Hispaniola under his rule.

EUROPE

The Greek War of Independence was marked by initial Greek successes followed by a successful Ottoman counterattack under Muhammad Ali that culminated in the retaking of Athens in 1827 (left). Foreign intervention saved the Greeks when a joint Russian, French, and British fleet defeated the Turkish navy at the Battle of Navarino soon after. Greek independence was confirmed at the London Conference in 1830.

⊕ **1822** Jean-Francois Champollion uses the Rosetta Stone, discovered by Napoleon's soldiers in Egypt, to decipher ancient Egyptian hieroglyphics (–1824).

⊕ **1822** English mathematician Charles Babbage builds a small prototype model of his "difference engine," or calculating machine, sometimes claimed as the world's first computer.

AFRICA

👑 **1816** Shaka becomes king of the Zulus and begins to expand Zulu power in southern Africa.

👑 **1817** Usman dan Fodio establishes the Sokoto Caliphate in the Hausa lands of northern Nigeria and southern Niger.

👑 **1818** Shehu Ahmad Lobbo establishes an Islamic state in Masina (present-day Mali) with its capital at Hamdallahi, literally "Praise to God" (–1821).

👑 **1820** British settlers begin to arrive in Cape Colony in great numbers.

✕ **1820** An Egyptian army led by Ishmail Pasha conquers Sudan on behalf of Muhammad Ali.

👑 **1822** The first group of freed slaves from the United States arrives to found the city of Monrovia in present-day Liberia, West Africa.

WESTERN ASIA

✕ **1822** A 30,000-strong Ottoman army invades Greece in an attempt to end the War of Independence.

SOUTH & CENTRAL ASIA

📖 **1819** The Ajanta Caves in central India are rediscovered: dating from the 2nd century A.D., they contain some of the finest examples of early Buddhist art in India.

EAST ASIA & OCEANIA

👑 **c.1820** The city of Nan Madol on Pohnpei in the Caroline Islands of Micronesia is abandoned; consisting of a series of artificial stone islets, it was the ceremonial center for the ruling chiefs of the Sandaleur Dynasty.

☀ **1820** The first Christian missionaries arrive in Hawaii and Tonga.

👑 **1821** Daoguang becomes emperor of China.

A carved porcelain Chinese brushpot from the reign of Daoguang.

1816–1822 A.D.

1823–1830 A.D.

AMERICAS

1823 U.S. President James Monroe recognizes the newly independent states of Latin America and warns against further European interference in the Americas (the Monroe Doctrine).

1824 The U.S. War Department sets up the Bureau of Indian Affairs, with Ely Parker of the Seneca Nation as its first director.

1824 After a tie in the electoral college the House of Representatives elects John Quincy Adams U.S. president over his rival Andrew Jackson. He will take office in 1825.

1825 The opening of the Erie Canal creates a 363-mile (584-km) waterway connecting the Great Lakes with the Atlantic Ocean.

1827 Joseph Smith, Jr., founder of the Church of Jesus Christ of Latter Day Saints, or Mormons, is given the golden plates of the Book of Mormon by the angel Moroni in a vision.

1827 The Baltimore & Ohio Railroad is chartered as the first commercial railroad to carry both passengers and freight. The first stretch of track will be opened in 1830.

EUROPE

1823 French troops invade Spain in support of Ferdinand VII, bringing the rebellion against his rule to an end.

1824 Charles X succeeds as king of France.

1824 First performance of Beethoven's ninth, and last, symphony; the great composer dies in 1827.

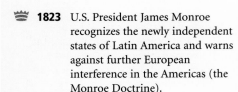

German composer Ludwig von Beethoven, painted by Ludwig Karl Stieler.

1825 The world's first railroad, the Stockton and Darlington Railway, opens in northern England. Regular passenger services begin five years later.

1825 The "Decembrists" —progressive army officers seeking to reform autocratic rule in Russia—stage an unsuccessful uprising.

AFRICA

1823 War breaks out between the British and the Ashanti Kingdom on the Gold Coast of West Africa (–1827).

1823 Muhammad Ali founds the city of Khartoum in Sudan.

1828 The Zulu leader Shaka, who is showing growing signs of insanity, is assassinated.

WESTERN ASIA

1826 Sultan Mahmud II crushes the last mutiny of the Janissaries in Istanbul, thus ending their power.

1827 The Ottoman navy is destroyed by a British, French, and Russian fleet at the Battle of Navarino.

1828 Mahmud II institutes a new western-style dress code, replacing the turban with the fez.

SOUTH & CENTRAL ASIA

1824 The British invade Burma (Myanmar) and capture Rangoon (–1826).

1826 Dost Mohammad becomes ruler of Afghanistan.

1826 In northern India Sayyid Ahmad of Bareli calls for a jihad (holy war) against the Sikhs.

EAST ASIA & OCEANIA

1823 Japanese artist Katsushika Hokusai, the greatest exponent of the school of *ukiyo-e* ("pictures of the floating world"), starts work on 36 views of Mt. Fuji (right).

1824 An Anglo-Dutch treaty confirms Britain as the dominant colonial power in Malaya and Singapore.

⊛ **1829** William Burt patents the first typewriter.

👑 **1829** Juan Manuel Rosas becomes caudillo (dictator) of Argentina.

👑 **1830** President Andrew Jackson authorizes the Indian Removal Act to resettle the five Native American tribes living east of the Mississippi River in territory set aside in the West.

As U.S. president from 1817 to 1825, James Monroe negotiated the Canadian boundary dispute with Britain and the takeover of Florida from Spain. He is best remembered now, though, for the Monroe Doctrine, warning the European powers from any further colonization in the Americas while also giving up any U.S. right to intervene in Europe. The doctrine was often invoked in later years, as this 1902 cartoon suggests.

AMERICAS

👑 **1826** John VI of Portugal dies. His eldest son Pedro, now emperor of Brazil, abdicates the Portuguese throne to his seven-year-old daughter, Maria II.

⊛ **1826** French inventor Joseph-Nicéphore Niepce takes the first successful permanent photograph.

👑 **1829** Turkey recognizes the Greeks' right to rule themselves (although full independence is not granted until 1832).

👑 **1830** In the July Revolution in France Charles X is forced to abdicate and is succeeded by the populist duke of Orleans, who rules as Louis Philippe.

✕ **1830** Belgium breaks away from the Netherlands and proclaims its independence.

✕ **1830** The Poles revolt against Russian rule (–1831).

DARLINGTON STATION.

The first rail locomotive to enter commercial service, kept on display in an English station.

✕ **1830** A French military force invades Algeria in North Africa, deposes the *dey* (ruler), and occupies the coastal towns.

EUROPE

AFRICA

👑 **1828** The Treaty of Turkmanchay ends the second Russo–Persian War, which broke out in 1826.

👑 **1828** Russia declares war on the Ottoman Empire, already embroiled with Greek rebels.

👑 **1829** Russia and Turkey make peace at the Treaty of Adrianople; Russia gains land on the Black Sea coast.

WESTERN ASIA

☀ **1828** Rammohan Roy, Indian religious reformer, founds the Brahmo Samaj (Society of God) to explore common ground between Hindu and western intellectual thought.

👑 **1829** The British in India take steps to end the Hindu custom of suttee (the burning of a widow on her husband's funeral pyre).

SOUTH & CENTRAL ASIA

✕ **1825** A revolt against Dutch rule on Java is put down with difficulty (–1830).

👑 **1826** Siam (Thailand) signs a commercial treaty with Great Britain.

✕ **1827** After Siamese troops devastate the Laotian city of Vientiane, control of northern Laos is divided between Thailand and Vietnam.

👑 **1828** The Dutch claim possession of the western half of New Guinea.

👑 **1829** The Swan River Colony is founded for free settlers at Perth in Western Australia.

EAST ASIA & OCEANIA

1823–1830 A.D.

THE LIBERATION OF LATIN AMERICA

▲ A rare combination of thinker and man of action, Simón Bolívar stood not just for the independence of Spain's American colonies but also for cooperation among the Spanish-speaking lands after independence. But his dreams of unity were shattered when Venezuela and Ecuador separated from Colombia in 1830.

IN THE EARLY 19TH CENTURY IT DID NOT TAKE LONG *for Latin America to follow the example of the United States and free itself from colonial rule. The torch of rebellion was lit in 1810, and within 14 years the whole of the Hispanic Empire from Mexico to Argentina had been broken up. In the same period Brazil declared its independence from Portugal.*

Simón Bolívar, the Liberator

Simón Bolívar stands alone in history as the only individual to have had a country, Bolivia, and a currency, the Venezuelan bolivar, named after him. He was born in 1783 to a wealthy family of Spanish descent in Caracas, Venezuela, but spent many years as a young man traveling in Europe, especially Italy and France, where he became an admirer of Napoleon. On his return to South America Bolívar threw his energies into the war against Spain. It took him 11 years to free Venezuela; he then went on to liberate Ecuador and to finally end Spanish resistance in Peru at the Battle of Ayacucho in December 1824. An inspiring leader of men in war, Bolivar dreamed of creating a federation of South American states, but his harsh style of rule once in power alienated many of his former supporters. By the time of his death in 1830 he had ceased to hold any real power, even in Colombia and Venezuela.

By the start of the 19th century the vast Spanish empire in America, stretching from southern California in the north to Chile in the south, was divided into five viceroyalties: New Spain (incorporating Mexico and Central America); New Granada (Venezuela, Colombia, and Ecuador); Peru (Peru and Bolivia); Rio de la Plata (Uruguay, Paraguay, and Argentina); and Chile. The Spanish colonists exported enormous quantities of gold and silver across the Atlantic Ocean from the mines of Mexico and Peru. They created large farming estates known as haciendas and ran them as absentee landlords, living in the coastal towns or returning to Europe for long periods while the Indian peoples were forced to work in the mines or as peons (landless laborers).

In the late 1700s, inspired by the success of the American Revolution and the French Revolution, independence movements began to develop in Latin America. Then, in 1808 Napoleon's army occupied Spain, and Napoleon's brother Joseph Bonaparte was made king, bringing fresh impetus to the demand for

---

1810 There are uprisings against Spanish rule in Mexico, Venezuela, Argentina, and Chile (–1811).

1811 Venezuela declares its independence from Spain (July 5).

1814 Bolívar is driven out of Venezuela by the Spanish and bases himself in Jamaica and Haiti while making repeated raids on the South American mainland.

1816 Argentina wins its independence from Spain.

1817 José de San Martín raises an army in Argentina and crosses the Andes to liberate Chile in partnership with Chilean revolutionary Bernardo O'Higgins.

1817 Bolívar returns to Venezuela, with a base in the Orinoco region.

1819 Bolívar assembles an army of 25,000, including many English and Irish mercenaries, to invade Colombia, where he wins the Battle of Boyacá.

1819 Bolivar proclaims the independent Republic of Colombia (December 17) and makes himself president.

1821 José de San Martín takes possession of Lima, Peru.

1821 Bolivar frees Venezuela from Spanish rule at the Battle of Carabobo (June 24).

1821 Mexico wins its independence from Spain.

1822 Pedro, crown prince of Portugal, declares Brazil's independence from Portugal, with himself as its emperor.

1822 Bolívar and General Antonio José de Sucre liberate Ecuador.

1822 Agustin Iturbide declares himself emperor of Mexico.

1824 Bolívar and de Sucre win the Battle of Ayacucho, defeating the last royalist army in Peru and completing the liberation of South America.

1825 Bolivia—previously part of the Spanish Viceroyalty of Peru—proclaims its independence, taking its name as a tribute to Bolívar.

change. Revolution first broke out in Mexico in 1810; but the uprising was quickly put down, and its leader, Miguel Hidalgo, was executed.

In 1811 Paraguay declared its independence, and Simón Bolívar began his fight to liberate Venezuela, his native land. By 1819 he had made himself president of the new Republic of Colombia, and two years later he expelled the Spanish from Venezuela as well. Meanwhile, another revolutionary leader, José de San Martín, first took part in the liberation of Argentina in 1816 and then led an army across the Andes to capture the Peruvian capital of Lima. By 1824, when Bolivar and General Antonio José de Sucre drove the Spanish out of the rest of Peru, all of Spain's empire in the Americas with the exception of the Caribbean islands of Cuba and Puerto Rico had won independence.

Liberation did not extend to everyone in Latin America, however. Power in the new states remained in the hands of people of Spanish descent. Beneath them were the mestizos (individuals of mixed European–Indian descent), and at the very bottom were the native Indians, who had virtually no rights, and the descendants of escaped African slaves. During the following decades there were frequent disagreements and border wars between the new states, many of which fell under the rule of caudillos, dictators who held power through their control of the army.

▶ At the height of his power in 1825 Bolívar governed an empire stretching from Venezuela to the Argentine–Bolivian border. Patagonia was never occupied by the Spanish.

Map legend:

- Spanish possessions lost 1810–25
- Spanish possessions 1830
- Portuguese possession lost 1822
- Republic of Greater Colombia 1819–30
- territory united with Mexico 1821–23
- 1818 date of separate statehood
- — borders 1830

scale varies in this projection

◀ The struggle to liberate the Spanish colonies in America was played out against the background of Spain's involvement in the Napoleonic Wars in Europe. At first Spain allied itself with France, provoking a British attack on Buenos Aires in 1806 (left). Two years later, when French troops occupied Spain, a bitter civil war broke out, leaving the home country in no position to send troops or money to help put down the colonial uprisings.

1831–1837 A.D.

AMERICAS

⚔ **1831** Nat Turner leads a slave revolt in Southampton, Virginia, that leaves 55 whites dead.

👑 **1831** Brazil's first emperor, Pedro I, abdicates and returns to Portugal to help his daughter Maria II regain her throne; he is succeeded by his son Pedro II.

The Alamo, a mission in San Antonio, Texas, played a famous part in the Texan rising against Spanish rule that broke out in 1835. Fewer than 200 defenders held out for 11 days against a Mexican army 3,000 strong; all were eventually killed, but the U.S. cause eventually prevailed.

EUROPE

✷ **1831** Traveling on the *Beagle*, a British naval vessel, the English naturalist Charles Darwin makes key discoveries that will lead him to formulate his groundbreaking theory of evolution (–1836).

👑 **1831** Leopold I becomes the first king of Belgium as the newly independent country becomes a constitutional monarchy.

⚔ **1831** The Polish diet (parliament) declares the nation's independence from Russia; Russian forces put down the revolt at the Battle of Ostrolenka.

👑 **1831** Exiled Italian patriot Giuseppe Mazzini founds the Young Italy independence movement, a model for radical reform groups throughout Europe.

👑 **1832** The Reform Act in Britain gives the vote to well-to-do men, doubling the electorate from 500,000 to 1 million.

👑 **1833** After a campaign by antislavery activist William Wilberforce, Britain passes a law abolishing slavery in the empire; it comes into effect on January 1, 1834.

AFRICA

👑 **1831** The French Foreign Legion is founded in Algeria.

⚔ **1831** Muhammad Ali, viceroy of Egypt, begins a revolt against his Turkish overlords that will see Egypt become an autonomous entity within the Ottoman Empire (his heirs will rule there until 1952).

👑 **1834** Said ibn Sultan, ruler of Oman, transfers his capital to Zanzibar off the East African coast, making it the center of a commercial empire built on cloves, ivory, and slaves.

WESTERN ASIA

The 1830s marked the start of the Great Trek, which saw thousands of Boers (Dutch settlers in South Africa) moving northward to escape English rule. Known as Voortrekkers, they soon came into conflict with the African peoples of the interior.

👑 **1832** Muhammad Ali wrests control of Syria from the Ottoman Empire.

👑 **1833** Austria, Prussia, and Russia agree to uphold the territorial integrity of the Ottoman Empire.

SOUTH & CENTRAL ASIA

⚔ **1834** Sikh forces under the command of Ranjit Singh take the key city of Peshawar on India's Northwest Frontier (now in Pakistan).

👑 **1835** English is adopted as the language of instruction throughout the areas of India controlled by the British.

👑 **1835** The ruler of Afghanistan, Dost Mohammad, proclaims himself emir and founds the Barakzai Dynasty.

EAST ASIA & OCEANIA

👑 **1834** The South Australia Act is passed in the British Parliament, allowing the establishment of a colony there.

👑 **1834** The British East India Company loses its monopoly on trade with China; the ensuing expansion of trade (especially in opium from British India) will create major friction with China's rulers.

👑 **1835** The city of Melbourne is founded in the Australian state of Victoria.

AMERICAS

⚔ **1831** A slave uprising hastens the end of slavery in Jamaica.

👑 **1834** The abolition of slavery in the British Empire emancipates almost 700,000 slaves in Britain's Caribbean colonies.

✹ **1835** In the United States Samuel Colt patents his revolving-breech pistol ("revolver").

⚔ **1836** Texas wins independence from Mexico in a war that ends at the Battle of San Jacinto; at the Alamo mission 188 defenders hold out against a Mexican army for 11 days before being overwhelmed.

⚔ **1836** The federation of Bolivia and Peru is proclaimed; Chile declares war on the new union, which only lasts for three years.

⚔ **1837** Two separate revolts, led by Louis Papineau in Lower Canada and William Mackenzie in Upper Canada, break out against British rule in Canada; both are put down.

EUROPE

👑 **1834** Under Prussia's leadership the Zollverein (customs union) is founded, embracing most German-speaking territories—an important step toward German unification.

⚔ **1834** Civil war erupts in Spain between Carlists (followers of Don Carlos) and the supporters of Isabella II over the disputed succession to the throne (–1839).

👑 **1836** In Britain the Chartists (backers of the People's Charter calling for the universal right to vote) found the first national movement representing working people.

📖 **1837** British novelist Charles Dickens starts works on *Oliver Twist* (–1839).

👑 **1837** Victoria becomes queen of Great Britain, beginning a reign that will last 64 years.

AFRICA

⚔ **1834** In the Sixth Xhosa War major clashes take place between Bantu warriors and English settlers in eastern Cape Colony (–1835).

👑 **1835** In southern Africa 10,000 Boers (Dutch settlers) protesting the abolition of slavery in Britain's Cape Colony begin the Great Trek north to the Zulu territory of Natal.

⚔ **1836** The Dutch Voortrekkers (as the participants in the Great Trek become known) defeat a force of 5,000 Ndebele warriors at the Battle of Vegkop.

WESTERN ASIA

👑 **1833** The Ottoman Empire and Russia sign the Treaty of Unkiar Skelessi, which closes access to the Black Sea to all but Russian warships in the event of war.

👑 **1833** The Turks recognize the independence of Egypt and relinquish control of Syria (and Aden in southern Arabia) to Muhammad Ali.

📖 **1837** Cuneiform script is deciphered by the scholar George Grotefend, leading to a new understanding of the ancient cultures of Mesopotamia (modern Iraq).

SOUTH & CENTRAL ASIA

The Afghan ruler Dost Mohammad and his son, as portrayed by a European artist.

EAST ASIA & OCEANIA

👑 **1837** Following the 44-year reign of Ienari, a new Japanese shogun, Ieyoshi, ascends the throne. He will open up Japan's ports to limited foreign trade.

✹ **1837** French explorer Dumont d'Urville starts a three-year Pacific voyage that will lead him to group the Oceanian islands as Melanesia, Micronesia, and Polynesia.

AMERICAS

1838 The confederation of the United Provinces of Central America breaks up as Rafael Carrera leads an Indian uprising in Guatemala, which declares independence the following year.

1839 The steamship *Sirius* reaches New York from London after 18 days, becoming the first vessel to cross the Atlantic Ocean solely on steam power.

1840 A report prepared by Canada's governor-general Lord Durham recommends the union of Upper and Lower Canada in a single state.

EUROPE

An 1845 photograph by William Henry Fox-Talbot shows the shed where he worked.

1838 The first railroad line in Russia links the czar's summer palace to St. Petersburg.

1839 In Britain William Henry Fox-Talbot demonstrates his "photogenic drawing" method of photography, while in France Louis Daguerre perfects the daguerrotype.

1840 The world's first postage stamp comes into circulation in Britain.

1840 Frederick William III of Prussia dies; his son and successor Frederick William IV promises changes but soon crushes liberal hopes for reform of the state.

1842 In Britain Parliament passes a law banning women from working below ground in the country's coal mines.

AFRICA

1838 As Britain's antislavery law comes into force, thousands of enslaved Africans are freed in Sierra Leone, beginning a southward exodus to their former homelands.

1838 British Methodists found a mission to aid Africans on the Gold Coast in West Africa.

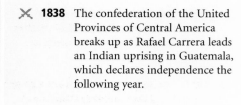

Covered wagons and field guns mark the site of the Battle of Blood River.

WESTERN ASIA

1839 Ottoman forces invade Syria but are routed by the Egyptians under Ibrahim Pasha at the Battle of Nizip (now in southern Turkey).

1839 Ottoman Sultan Mahmud II dies at a critical moment, with the weakened Ottoman Empire under threat of destruction.

1839 Under a new sultan, Abdul Mejid, the Ottoman Empire embarks on a program of reform known as the *tanzimat* ("reorganization").

SOUTH & CENTRAL ASIA

1838 To forestall Russia's southward expansion, British forces invade Afghanistan, beginning the first of the Afghan Wars; Emir Dost Mohammad is imprisoned.

1839 Death of Ranjit Singh, ruler of the Sikh Kingdom of the Punjab.

1839 The British install Shah Shuja, an unpopular puppet ruler, in Kabul.

1842 An uprising in Kabul forces the British to withdraw their troops.

EAST ASIA & OCEANIA

1839 As tensions rise over the import of opium into China, British colonial troops occupy Hong Kong.

1840 By the Treaty of Waitangi Britain undertakes to respect the Maoris' right to their own land in New Zealand; the treaty terms are soon violated by unregulated settlers.

Long a standard-bearer of civilization, China reached a low ebb in the 19th century. Foreign powers took advantage of its weakness, notably in two Opium Wars fought by Britain to protect the right of its merchants to import opium into China. Both conflicts ended with China forced to accept humiliating terms.

AMERICAS

⊕ **1842** In the United States Crawford Williamson Long performs the first operation using anesthetic (ether).

👑 **1844** The eastern part of the island of Hispaniola wins independence as Santo Domingo (now the Dominican Republic).

⊕ **1844** The inventor Samuel Morse transmits the first telegraph message, from Washington to Baltimore.

👑 **1845** The United States annexes Texas.

EUROPE

👑 **1843** In the wake of the Carlist War 13-year-old Isabella II is finally crowned queen of Spain; her reign is marked by instability.

✕ **1844** A weavers' uprising in Silesia (southern Poland) is brutally put down by Prussian troops.

👑 **1845** Potato blight causes a terrible famine in Ireland that will claim the lives of around a million people and drive many more into exile (–1851).

Ireland has suffered many famines, but few as terrible as the one that afflicted it from 1845 on, when potato blight devastated the crop the poor relied on for survival. In all, almost a million people died, and half as many again emigrated, mostly to the United States. Survivors blamed the British government for doing too little to mitigate the famine's effects, leaving a legacy of bitterness to haunt Anglo–Irish relations.

AFRICA

✕ **1838** At the Battle of Blood River in Natal Boer settlers crush a Zulu army resisting their advance, killing 3,000 warriors.

👑 **1840** Mzilikazi founds a new Ndebele state in what is now Zimbabwe.

👑 **1840** Kazembe IV, ruler of the central African territory of Kazembe, dies with his mineral-rich kingdom in the Luapula Valley at its height.

👑 **1840** The Boer repubic of Natal, founded by the Voortrekkers, is annnexed by the British and made part of Cape Colony (–1844).

👑 **1843** The British establish the colony of the Gambia in West Africa.

WESTERN ASIA

👑 **1840** By the Treaty of London Britain, Austria, Russia, and Prussia force Egypt's ruler Muhammad Ali to restore land to the Ottomans.

👑 **1841** Under the Straits Convention the leading European powers close the Bosporus and Dardanelles to foreign warships in time of peace.

👑 **1844** South Serbian nationalists led by Ilija Garasanin vow to resist Ottoman rule over the Balkan region.

SOUTH & CENTRAL ASIA

✕ **1842** The First Afghan War ends in a disastrous defeat for the colonial invaders; only 121 men survive the retreat from Kabul from an original force of over 16,000.

✕ **1843** The emirs of Sind and the Punjab refuse to cede sovereignty to the British East India Company; Charles Napier's army defeats them at the Battle of Hyderabad.

✕ **1845** The First Anglo–Sikh War breaks out when Sikh forces invade British territory across the Sutlej River.

EAST ASIA & OCEANIA

✕ **1840** Britain and China fight the First Opium War after Chinese authorities order the destruction of a large consignment of the drug (–1842).

👑 **1841** For helping the Sultan of Brunei quell piracy, Sir James Brooke is made raja of Sarawak in Borneo.

👑 **1842** The Treaty of Nanjing ending the First Opium War secures Britain trading privileges in China and cedes Hong Kong to Britain. It is the first of the so-called "Unequal Treaties," forced on an unwilling China by the western powers.

✕ **1843** Maoris kill white settlers in New Zealand at the Wairu River, beginning the First Maori War (–1847).

👑 **1844** China signs a treaty with the United States granting it similar trading rights to those obtained by Britain two years earlier.

1838–1845 A.D.

THE INDUSTRIAL REVOLUTION

FROM AROUND 1750 PROFOUND ECONOMIC *and social changes began in western Europe and North America that in time would radically affect people all over the world. Over the next 150 years mechanization and the growth of cities transformed these regions from agricultural commmunities to industrial societies. This period of change came to be known as the Industrial Revolution.*

Isambard Kingdom Brunel

Isambard Kingdom Brunel (left) was the greatest engineer of the industrial age. Born into an English engineering family, he was seriously injured in 1828 when a tunnel he and his father were excavating under the Thames River in London collapsed. He made his name in the 1830s, developing England's Great Western Railway. To carry the track, he devised bridges of pioneering design that enhanced his reputation for technical brilliance. Brunel then turned to building iron steamships that revolutionized sea travel, culminating in the massive *Great Eastern*. The ship, which could carry 4,000 passengers, was a technological triumph, but it turned out to be a commercial failure. Exhausted, Brunel died in 1859, just a year after its launch.

⚙ **1733** John Kay invents a mechanical device, the flying shuttle, that speeds up the weaving process.

⚙ **1764** Scottish engineer James Watt improves the steam engine by adding a separate condenser and by devising mechanisms that turn linear into circular motion for powering different machinery (–1774).

📖 **1776** The Scottish political economist Adam Smith publishes his influential work *The Wealth of Nations*. Smith advocates free trade and modern working practices, including the division of labor.

⚙ **1801** French inventor Joseph Jacquard develops a loom that can produce figured silk fabrics.

⚙ **1815** Scottish engineer John McAdam makes the first paved roads, using crushed stone.

⚙ **1825** The world's first commercial railroad opens to traffic, running between Stockton and Darlington in northern England.

⚙ **1827** France's Benoit Fourneyron develops the water turbine.

👑 **1833** Britain's Factory Act restricts the use of children in industry.

⚙ **1838** Isambard Kingdom Brunel's iron steamship *Great Western* becomes the first vessel to run regular transatlantic passenger services. The *Great Eastern* will follow 20 years later.

⚙ **1839** American inventor Charles Goodyear discovers how to vulcanize natural rubber, making the material much more durable.

👑 **1846** The repeal of the protectionist Corn Laws in Britain sees the beginning of the era of free trade between nations.

⚙ **1856** In England Henry Bessemer revolutionizes the manufacture of steel from iron ore, inventing a converter that rids molten pig iron of its impurities and produces cheap, carbon-tempered steel.

⚙ **1862** A machine gun is developed by the U.S. inventor Richard Gatling; 25 years later a much improved version devised by Hiram Maxim will come into widespread service.

The Industrial Revolution began in Britain, where plentiful coal and iron deposits, ready capital, and an empire hungry for exports created ideal conditions. The impetus came first from textiles; the manufacture of cotton and other fabrics, long a cottage industry, was transformed by the invention of mechanical means of spinning and weaving. The new machines were big and expensive, requiring workers to come together in large mills. With this centralizing of production communities changed from making many goods for local consumption to manufacturing a limited range of products for a wider market.

Mechanization also fostered the growth of heavy industry. Early in the 18th century the ironmaster Abraham Darby found a way of producing iron on a large scale, using coke in a blast furnace. Even more important for the huge increase in iron and steel output and in coal extraction later in the century was the supplanting of water power by steam power. The principle of the steam engine had been known since around 1700, and primitive beam engines had been built to pump water from mines; but it was only with James Watt's improvements to the basic design in the 1760s that steam power came of age. Watt and his collaborator, the industrialist Matthew Boulton, produced hundreds of efficient rotary motion engines to drive machinery in factories and mines.

The next step was to apply steam to locomotion. Britain's extensive canal system struggled to carry the ever greater flow of raw materials and goods. The first steam railroad was built to ferry coal from a mine to a waterway in northeastern England in 1825. Within decades the network had expanded enormously, carrying freight and passengers at previously unimagined speeds.

Britain's industrial monopoly was broken early in the 19th century as Belgium and France developed their textile, coal, iron, and arms industries. Even though Germany was still politically fragmented, industrialization began there from the 1840s on. Following unification in 1871, growth accelerated; by 1900 Germany had outstripped Britain in steel production and led the world in chemicals, including synthetic dyes, pharmaceuticals, fertilizers, and explosives. The United States started rather later than the European powers but experienced an extraordinary spurt of growth in the decades following the Civil War that saw it quickly catch up.

The social impact of the Industrial Revolution was also radical. The rural population of most of western Europe fell from 70 to under 10 percent between 1750 and 1914. The new city dwellers experienced overcrowding, poor housing and healthcare, and periodic unemployment. Measures were put in place to curb the worst forms of exploitation, such as child labor and excessive hours. But by the end of the century demands were growing for better political representation for working people, and organized labor in the form of labor unions and socialist parties was beginning to challenge the status quo.

▲ The early decades of the Industrial Revolution were marked by low pay and bad working conditions, like those experienced by these children moving coal in a mine. Child labor was finally restricted in Britain in 1833.

◀ James Nasmyth's revolutionary steam hammer was used from 1839 on to press machine parts at the Scottish engineer's foundry in Manchester, England.

⊕ **1865** Brunel's giant steamship *Great Eastern* lays the first transatlantic telegraph cable.

⊕ **1879** Thomas Alva Edison in the United States and Joseph Swan in England independently develop the electric light; within three years Edison is building power plants to provide electric lighting for homes.

⊕ **1885** German engineers Gottlieb Daimler and Karl Benz devise the internal combustion engine and build vehicles powered by it.

⊕ **1903** Orville and Wilbur Wright undertake the first succesful powered flight of a heavier-than-air machine at Kitty Hawk, North Carolina.

▲ major textile or silk producing area 1850
▓ heavy industrial or mining area 1850
— borders 1850

0 ——— 600 km
0 ——— 400 mi

◀ The Industrial Revolution developed in areas with good transport facilities and access to natural resources. Its early heartlands included Britain, Germany, and Belgium.

1846–1852 A.D.

AMERICAS

1846 Oregon Territory (Washington, Oregon, and Idaho, with part of British Columbia) is split between the United States and Canada, with the border at the 49th parallel.

1846 The U.S. Congress founds the Smithsonian Institution in Washington, D.C.

1846 Hostilities break out when the United States and Mexico fail to reach agreement on the purchase of New Mexico; Mexican forces are routed at the battles of Palo Alto and Resaca.

An African–American miner in the California gold rush.

EUROPE

1846 A Polish revolt against foreign overlords is suppressed; the Republic of Cracow (in existence since 1815) is dissolved and the territory granted to Austria.

1846 In Britain the Corn Laws, which imposed a high import duty on foreign grain, are repealed—a significant victory for free trade.

1847 Famine in Ireland drives over 200,000 people to emigrate in a single year, mainly to America.

1848 The German political thinkers Karl Marx and Friedrich Engels publish the *Communist Manifesto*, a blueprint for socialist revolution by the working classes.

1848 Prodemocracy uprisings take place in many countries across Europe, including Italy, France, Germany, Austria, and Hungary (–1849). In France King Louis Philippe hands over power to the Second Republic.

1849 Italian revolutionary Giuseppe Garibaldi helps found the Roman Republic; when French troops restore Pope Pius IX to power, Garibaldi flees to America.

1849 Frederick William IV of Prussia spurns the offer of the National Assembly in Frankfurt to be the constitutional monarch of a unified Germany; nascent democracies are crushed throughout Europe.

AFRICA

1847 Liberia becomes a free and independent republic.

1848 Muhammad Ali's son Ibrahim Pasha dies in Cairo 40 days after taking over as viceroy of Egypt.

1848 Now firmly under the colonial control of France, the North African state of Algeria is split into three "departments" (administrative divisions).

1849 The French found Libreville in Gabon (equatorial West Africa) as a home for freed slaves.

WESTERN ASIA

1848 Nasr al-Din becomes shah of Persia, beginning a 48-year reign in which he will introduce some western ideas to his kingdom.

1849 Russian forces occupy the Ottoman Danubian principalities of Walachia and Moldavia, which have risen in revolt.

1850 The Bab, an Islamic mystic, is executed for heresy in Persia. His followers are ruthlessly persecuted and eventually expelled (–1864).

SOUTH & CENTRAL ASIA

1846 Forces of the British East India Company defeat the Sikhs at Aliwal and Sobraon; the Treaty of Lahore brings the First Anglo–Sikh War to a close.

1848 The Second Anglo–Sikh War begins; the British defeat the Sikhs at Chillianwalla and Gujarat, and annex Punjab and Sind by treaty (1849).

1851 Rama IV succeeds Rama III as king of Siam (Thailand); the new ruler orders the building of canals and roads, and undertakes administrative reforms.

EAST ASIA & OCEANIA

1848 In Australia the explorer Ludwig Leichhardt, who has already probed Queensland and the Northern Territory in 1844–1845, disappears while attempting an east–west crossing of the continent.

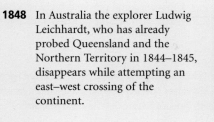

Lasting 14 years and costing 20 million lives, the Taiping rebellion devastated China. Led by a visionary who claimed to be Jesus Christ's younger brother, the revolt, which promised egalitarian social reform, only collapsed with the fall of the rebel capital of Nanjing (left) in 1864.

AMERICAS

👑 **1848** The Mexican War ends with the United States gaining all lands north of the Rio Grande—California, Arizona, and New Mexico.

⚙️ **1848** Thousands of prospectors swarm to the California gold rush.

👑 **1850** California joins the United States as the 31st state.

👑 **1850** The Fugitive Slave Act requires all states to return slaves to their former masters, increasing tension between the northern and southern states.

⚙️ **1851** U.S. inventor Isaac Singer patents the continuous-stitch sewing machine.

📖 **1852** Harriet Beecher Stowe publishes her antislavery masterpiece *Uncle Tom's Cabin*.

EUROPE

1848 has gone down in European history as the Year of Revolutions. The first broke out in Paris, and copycat revolts followed in Italy, many German states, and across the Austrian Empire, including Vienna (left). The risings, inspired partly by growing nationalism and partly by middle-class frustration at aristocratic rule, all eventually collapsed in the face of popular alarm at the forces of disorder they unleashed.

⚙️ **1851** In London the Great Exhibition showcases the manufactured goods of an industrializing world.

👑 **1851** Emperor Franz Josef I suspends the Austrian constitution and imposes martial law across the Austro-Hungarian Empire.

👑 **1851** Louis Napoleon, president of France's Second Republic, stages a coup, creating the Second Empire, with himself as Emperor Napoleon III, in 1852.

AFRICA

👑 **c.1850** The powerful Zanzibari merchant Tippu Tib leads caravans trading in ivory and slaves into the interior of East Africa, creating a personal empire in the eastern Congo region.

⚔️ **1851** British ships lay siege to Lagos in Nigeria in an effort to end the extensive trade in slaves that takes place there.

👑 **1852** Boer settlers found the republic of Transvaal to the northeast of South Africa; Britain recognizes its sovereignty at the Sand River Convention.

WESTERN ASIA

☀️ **1852** The Bab's successor, taking the name of Baha Ulla ("Splendor of God"), founds the Baha'i faith as a variant form of Babism.

SOUTH & CENTRAL ASIA

⚔️ **1852** The Second Anglo-Burmese War breaks out. British forces besiege the capital, Rangoon.

The Aphonphimok Prasat, a disrobing pavilion in the Grand Palace complex in Bangkok, built on the orders of Rama IV.

EAST ASIA & OCEANIA

⚔️ **1850** The Taiping Rebellion breaks out in southern China. Lasting 14 years, this insurrection led by Hong Xiuquan is a major challenge to the authority of the ruling Qing (Manchu) Dynasty.

👑 **1850** The first Chinese immigrants to the United States leave Canton to settle in New York, founding Chinatown; thousands more will follow, mainly to labor on the U.S. transcontinental railroads.

⚙️ **1851** In Australia extensive gold deposits are discovered at Bathurst, New South Wales.

👑 **1852** Britain passes the New Zealand Constitution Act, formalizing the colonial settlement of the country.

1846–1852 A.D.

1853–1860 A.D.

AMERICAS

1854 The Kansas–Nebraska Act destroys the 1820 Missouri Compromise over slavery; bitter fighting breaks out in Kansas between opponents of slavery (Free Soilers) and its supporters.

1854 Through the Gadsden Purchase the U.S. government buys parts of southern Arizona and New Mexico for $10 million in order to facilitate the construction of a southern railroad to the Pacific coast.

Elisha Otis's safety elevator encouraged the development of high-rise buildings.

EUROPE

1856 British inventor Henry Bessemer introduces a process (named after him) for making steel more cheaply and efficiently.

1858 France's Emperor Napoleon III survives an assassination attempt and orders a crackdown on all opponents of his autocratic rule.

1859 The German National Union is founded to lobby for a unified Germany.

AFRICA

1853 Britain grants Cape Colony its own legislative assembly.

1854 In South Africa Britain cedes all territory north of the Orange River to the Boer republics.

1855 Ferdinand de Lesseps is contracted to build the Suez Canal linking the Mediterranean to the Red Sea.

WESTERN ASIA

The Crimean War saw Britain and France make an alliance to prevent further Russian expansion at the expense of the declining Ottoman Empire. The campaign was marked by high loss of life from disease and from futile but heroic actions like the famed Charge of the Light Brigade (left). The war was a setback for Russia, which sued for peace in 1856.

1853 Russia again occupies Walachia and Moldavia; its ships destroy a Turkish Black Sea fleet at Sinope.

1854 The Crimean War breaks out in response to Russian expansion in the Black Sea. Meeting their 1841 treaty obligation, Britain and France invade the Crimean Peninsula of southern Russia.

SOUTH & CENTRAL ASIA

1853 The Second Anglo–Burmese War ends, leaving Britain in control of Pegu (lower Burma). Mindon Min, the new Burmese ruler, develops Mandalay as his new capital.

1853 Britain annexes the Maratha principality of Nagpur in the Deccan region of central India.

1856 Oudh in northern India is annexed by the British.

1856 Persian forces occupy the city of Herat in northwestern Afghanistan, sparking hostilities with Britain.

EAST ASIA & OCEANIA

1853 U.S. Commodore Matthew Perry arrives at Edo Bay, near modern Tokyo, with a fleet of "black ships." By the threat of force he secures an agreement for trade and friendship with imperial Japan.

1854 Taiping rebels overrun Nanjing and make it the center of resistance to Manchu rule.

Commodore Perry as caricatured by a Japanese artist of the time.

1854 Commodore Perry returns to Japan to sign the Treaty of Kanagawa, opening the ports of Hakodate and Shimoda to foreign commerce.

1855 The Miao rebellion against China's Manchu rulers breaks out in the southern province of Guizhou (−1857).

AMERICAS

⊕ **1857** U.S. inventor Elisha Otis installs the first safety elevator in a building in New York City.

〰 **1857** Irish immigrants found the Irish Republican Brotherhood in New York; its supporters ("Fenians") support violence to further Irish independence from Britain (–1858).

〰 **1858** Britain's Queen Victoria selects Ottawa as the capital of Canada.

〰 **1859** Oregon is admitted to the Union as the 33rd state.

✕ **1859** U.S. abolitionist John Brown raids the armory at Harper's Ferry, Virginia, to arm a slave revolt; he is captured and hanged.

〰 **1860** Abraham Lincoln is elected as 16th president of the United States on a platform opposing the expansion of slavery. His election paves the way for the ensuing secession of the southern slave-owning states from the Union.

EUROPE

〰 **1859** Napoleon III secretly agrees to support Sardinia–Piedmont in its struggle to win Italian independence from Austria.

✕ **1859** With French backing the Piedmontese army fights the Austrians to a draw at the Battle of Solferino, leaving 30,000 dead.

✕ **1860** Italian nationalist leader Giuseppe Garibaldi and his "Thousand Redshirts" win control of Sicily and southern Italy.

AFRICA

⊕ **1856** In Egypt a railroad line links Cairo to the Mediterranean port of Alexandria.

〰 **1856** Death of Said ibn Sultan, ruler of Zanazibar and founder of an East African trading empire.

✕ **1859** Spain conquers Tetuán in Morocco—its first modern colonial venture in Africa.

WESTERN ASIA

⊕ **1855** British nurse Florence Nightingale introduces pioneering standards of sanitation and hygiene into the military hospital at Scutari (Istanbul), saving many lives.

✕ **1856** After a 322-day siege the key Russian fortress town of Sevastopol in the Crimea falls to British and French forces.

〰 **1856** The Congress of Paris brings the Crimean War to an end. Russia makes concessions in the Balkans, Turkey's independence is guaranteed, and the Black Sea is proclaimed a neutral zone.

Florence Nightingale inspects a ward of her hospital at Scutari in the Crimea.

SOUTH & CENTRAL ASIA

〰 **1857** Shah Nasr al-Din of Persia recognizes the independence of Afghanistan.

✕ **1857** The Indian Mutiny against British rule erupts, sparked by rumors that new Indian Army rifle cartridges are greased with pork or beef fat, taboo to Muslim and Hindu troops respectively.

〰 **1858** In the wake of the suppression of the Indian Mutiny the Government of India Act transfers sovereignty over the subcontinent from the East India Company to the British crown.

EAST ASIA & OCEANIA

〰 **1856** In Australia the island of Tasmania, formerly a penal colony, is granted self-government.

✕ **1856** The Second Opium War erupts between Britain and China over the opium trade; British warships besiege Canton and destroy an attacking Chinese fleet (–1857).

〰 **1859** Formerly part of New South Wales, Queensland is made a separate state within Australia.

✕ **1859** A Franco–Spanish naval force occupies Saigon, marking the start of the French annexation of Cochin China (southern Vietnam) as the nucleus of the future colony of Indochina.

✕ **1860** An Anglo–French expeditionary force occupies Beijing and destroys the summer palace of the Chinese emperors outside the capital in retaliation for the seizure of envoys under a flag of truce.

1853–1860 A.D.

COLONIALISM

TO SECURE FRESH SOURCES OF *raw materials and to open up new markets for the manufactured goods that began to pour from their factories as the Industrial Revolution gathered pace, European powers sought to expand their existing overseas colonies and win new ones. Having long since established trading empires in Asia and the Americas, they increasingly took on the role of rulers as well as merchants, seeking to impose western standards on distant lands.*

▲ In an archetypal colonial scene Indian villagers report their problems to a visiting district commissioner—the local representative of the British Raj (ruling power).

After the loss of its colonies in North America and the final defeat of Napoleon I in 1815, Britain sought to strengthen its empire and to expand trading opportunities in Asia. In 1819 the colonial administrator Sir Stamford Raffles established the free port of Singapore, which stood at a key point to control trade throughout the region. From 1824 to 1826, following an accord with the Dutch and the founding of the Straits Settlements, Britain consolidated its hold over the Malayan Peninsula. At the same time, British forces from India responding to an invasion of Bengal attacked the neighboring Kingdom of Burma, swiftly overrunning the country's coastal regions. By the mid 1880s the whole country had been annexed to India.

There was soon a booming trade in cotton goods, manufactured in India or increasingly in Britain itself, which were shipped through Singapore to Southeast Asia and China. But a more lucrative trade in another Indian product, opium, caused the outbreak of war between Britain and China in 1840. When China's imperial government ordered the confiscation of the drug, Britain responded with military force. At the end of a one-sided conflict Britain gained the crown colony of Hong Kong, another important East Asian base, which only reverted to Chinese rule in 1997.

In Africa the British colonization of the Cape of Good Hope as Cape Colony began with the founding of a naval base at Simonstown in 1809. In 1835 the original Dutch settlers, protesting a recent British ban

---

1815   At the end of the Napoleonic Wars one-fifth of the world's population is already under the control of the British Empire.

1819   British administrator Sir Stamford Raffles founds the free port of Singapore on the Malaysian Peninsula, which grows into an important trading center.

1824   In the First Anglo–Burmese War the British seize control of the coastal provinces of Arakan and Tenasserim, expanding their empire eastward from Bengal in India (–1826).

1830   The French under King Louis Philippe begin their colonization of Africa by occupying Algeria. The Foreign Legion is founded from international recruits to serve in Africa (–1831).

1835   Dutch settlers in South Africa undertake the Great Trek. After defeating the Zulus at the Battle of Blood River, they found the Republic of Natal (–1838).

1838   The First Afghan War breaks out as British forces invade Afghanistan to prevent the southward spread of the Russian Empire from threatening India (–1842).

1852   Britain annexes the Pegu region of southern Burma during the Second Anglo-Burmese War, leaving Burma a landlocked state (–1853).

1854   France extends and consolidates its hold over Senegal, the center of a growing West African empire.

1857   After quelling the Indian Mutiny, the British transfer control of government of the subcontinent from the East India Company directly to the crown (–1858).

1859   Under their ambitious Emperor Napoleon III the French capture the city of Saigon in Cochin China (Vietnam), beginning their creation of the colony of Indochina.

1859   Spain overruns the Moroccan region of Tetuán, establishing a presence in North Africa that will lead to the establishment of Spanish Morocco in 1912

1863   Napoleon III of France attempts to build an overseas empire in Mexico; the United States pressures French troops to withdraw (–1867).

c.1870   The discovery of valuable minerals (principally gold and diamonds) in southern Africa precipitates the "Scramble for Africa."

The Indian Mutiny

Known in India as the First National War of Independence, the Indian Mutiny broke out in May 1857 among sepoys—Indian troops in British service—stationed in the north of the country. Sparked by rumors that new rifle cartridges from England were smeared with beef or pork fat, respectively taboo to Hindus and Muslims, the uprising was also fueled by nationalist resentment at colonial rule. Quickly gaining support, the rebels captured the capital, Delhi, and besieged outpost garrisons at Lucknow and Kanpur. The revolt was quelled only by the intervention of large-scale reinforcements in mid-1858. India's last Mughal ruler, used by the mutineers as a figurehead, was deposed by the British authorities in the wake of the rebellion. Atrocities hardened attitudes on both sides; Europeans were mercilessly slaughtered in Meerut, while captured mutineers were blown to pieces to discourage native soldiers from further rebellion.

on slave labor, left to travel upcountry on the "Great Trek," in time founding the Boer republics of the Transvaal and Orange Free State. Tension between the two white settler communities was to erupt later in the century in the bitterly fought Anglo–Boer Wars.

France lacked Britain's stability, experiencing revolutions in 1830 and 1848, yet it also embarked on colonization, seizing Algeria, a former Ottoman possession, in 1830. The capital, Algiers, fell after three weeks, but the French were harried by the resistance forces of Abd-el-Kader for a further 15 years. Eager for access to markets in Southeast Asia, France sent an expeditionary force in 1858 to take Saigon. Four years later the emperor of Annam was forced to sign a treaty ceding control of eastern Cochin China (so called to distinguish it from the Cochin region of India) to the foreigners, and over the next two decades the French protectorate was extended to all of Vietnam and neighboring Cambodia.

Yet there were failures too. Emperor Napoleon III overplayed his hand disastrously when he tried to take control of Mexico in 1863. Despite being embroiled in civil war, the United States soon forced the French to abandon the venture, and the unfortunate puppet emperor they had installed, Austria's Archduke Maximilian I, was deposed and executed. Faced with the anticolonial resolve of the Monroe Doctrine, the European powers would make no further attempts to colonize the Americas.

◀ The largest and most widespread colonial empire in the mid-19th century was Britain's, which straddled the world from Canada to Australia. Spain's once-great Latin American empire had been wiped out, leaving the nation with only the Caribbean islands of Cuba and Puerto Rico. The Dutch had retained their East Indian possessions, while the French, who had lost to the British in India and Canada, had expanded into Africa with the occupation of Algeria.

353

1861–1867 A.D.

AMERICAS

1861 The American Civil War breaks out when Confederate forces shell Fort Sumter, South Carolina.

1863 Abraham Lincoln issues the Emancipation Proclamation, declaring all slaves in rebel states to be free.

1863 French forces occupy Mexico City, proclaiming Maximilian of Austria emperor; he is formally inaugurated in 1864.

1865 The first transatlantic telegraph cable is successfully laid (–1866).

1865 The War of the Triple Alliance sets Paraguay against Argentina, Brazil, and Uruguay. The bloodiest war in Latin American history, it will cost Paraguay 300,000 dead—60 percent of its population at the time (–1870).

EUROPE

1861 In the wake of Garibaldi's victories in the south the Kingdom of Italy is proclaimed with Victor Emmanuel, king of Piedmont, as its ruler.

1861 Czar Alexander II emancipates Russia's serfs, initiating a series of reforms that includes the setting up of zemstvos (self-governing local councils) three years later.

1862 French author Victor Hugo writes *Les Misérables*.

1862 Otto von Bismarck becomes premier and foreign minister of Prussia.

1863 Polish nationalists stage an unsuccessful insurrection against Russian rule (–1864).

1864 Prussia and Austria go to war with Denmark, which is forced to cede the disputed territory of Schleswig–Holstein to Prussia.

1864 French scientist Louis Pasteur introduces the pasteurization process, initially for wine.

1864 The Red Cross is established by the first Geneva Convention, establishing the principle that battlefield medical facilities are neutral.

1865 Austrian monk Gregor Mendel publishes his findings on cross-breeding, initiating the science of genetics (but the significance of his work will not be appreciated for another 35 years).

Laboratory equipment used by Louis Pasteur on display in a French museum.

AFRICA

1861 British forces annex the region around Lagos as a British colony.

1862 The United States recognizes 15-year-old Liberia as an independent republic.

1863 Ismail, the new khedive (ruler) of Egypt, embarks on an ambitious program of modernization.

WESTERN ASIA

1861 Abdul Aziz becomes Ottoman sultan on the death of Abdul Mejid. His reign sees the empire opened up to western influences.

1866 Abdul Aziz sends troops to Crete to quell an insurrection against Ottoman rule (–1868).

1867 Abdul Aziz visits the Great Exhibition in Paris, becoming the first Ottoman sultan to travel to Europe.

SOUTH & CENTRAL ASIA

1862 India experiences an economic boom thanks to the increased demand for cotton caused by the American Civil War (–1866).

1863 Civil war breaks out in Afghanistan on the death of its ruler, Dost Mohammad (–1870).

1865 Russian forces drive into central Asia, conquering Tashkent, which will become the capital of Russian Turkistan two years later.

EAST ASIA & OCEANIA

1862 The French establish a protectorate in Cochin China.

1863 Muslim rebellions break out in China's Gansu, Qinghai, and Shanxi provinces.

1864 The western powers bombard Kagashima and Shimonoseki in Japan in response to attacks on their nationals.

1864 Australia starts importing kanaka (native) laborers from the Solomon Islands to work on Queensland sugar plantations.

✗ **1865** Confederate forces under Robert E. Lee formally surrender at Appomattox Court House; the American Civil War comes to an end soon after.

✗ **1865** President Lincoln is assassinated.

👑 **1866** Reconstruction gets under way in the southern U.S. states.

✗ **1867** Maximilian I of Mexico is executed after France withdraws support for his regime.

👑 **1867** Russia sells Alaska to the United States for $7.2 million.

👑 **1867** The British North America Act brings Ontario, Quebec, New Brunswick, and Nova Scotia together in the federal Dominion of Canada.

AMERICAS

📖 **1865** Russian author Leo Tolstoy publishes the first part of his great novel *War and Peace* (–1869).

✗ **1866** Prussia defeats its former ally Austria in the Seven Weeks' War.

👑 **1867** Austria becomes Austria-Hungary with the establishment of the Dual Monarchy; already emperor of Austria, Francis Joseph I is now crowned king of Hungary in Budapest.

✗ **1867** In Italy Garibaldi launches the March on Rome but is defeated and taken prisoner by French and papal troops.

📖 **1867** The German political philosopher Karl Marx publishes the first volume of *Das Kapital* ("Capital").

No man did more to shape Europe in the late 19th century than Germany's "Iron Chancellor," Otto von Bismarck. As chief minister of Prussia from 1862, he built up the army, then allied with Austria to defeat Denmark, winning Schleswig–Holstein from the Danes. Two years later, in 1866, he went to war with his former Austrian allies, winning a decisive victory in the Seven Weeks' War. His greatest triumph came with the defeat of Napoleon III's France in the Franco–Prussian War of 1870, after which he united most of the German states in a German Second Empire (*Reich*) with William I of Prussia as its emperor.

EUROPE

✗ **1863** British forces fail to suppress Ashanti raiders attacking the Gold Coast (modern Ghana).

☀ **1866** Scottish explorer–missionary David Livingstone begins his final expedition to Africa.

⊛ **1867** Diamonds are discovered in South Africa.

AFRICA

WESTERN ASIA

⊛ **1865** A telegraph service is opened between India and Europe.

Workers lay a section of the Indo–European telegraph cable off Fao in the Persian Gulf.

SOUTH & CENTRAL ASIA

✗ **1864** The Taiping Rebellion is finally put down in China with the capture of Nanjing.

👑 **1865** New Zealand's capital moves from Auckland to Wellington.

👑 **1867** The transportation of convicts from Britain to penal settlements in Australia comes to an end.

👑 **1867** Japan's last shogun resigns, bringing almost 700 years of feudal military government to an end.

EAST ASIA & OCEANIA

1861–1867 A.D.

THE AMERICAN CIVIL WAR

I N THE MID-19TH CENTURY THE UNITED STATES TORE ITSELF APART *in a brutal civil war. The principal issue dividing the two sides was slavery, a central part of the economy in the nation's Southern states but deeply unpopular in the North. When Abraham Lincoln won the presidential election of 1860 on an antislavery ticket, 11 Southern states rebelled, joining together to form the Confederate States of America. The conflict that followed lasted four years and cost the nation 162,000 dead.*

▲ A Union soldier leads a charge on Confederate lines in the course of the American Civil War. Advances in rifle technology meant that infantry casualties were regularly high.

▶ Artillerymen from Connecticut pose beside a battery of gigantic mortars employed in the siege of Yorktown, Virginia, in 1862.

✕ **1854** Violence erupts between pro- and antislavery factions in Kansas, newly opened to settlement.

👑 **1857** In the Dred Scott case the U.S. Supreme Court decides that descendants of slaves are not entitled to the protection of the U.S. Constitution.

✕ **1859** Antislavery militants led by John Brown raid a government arsenal at Harper's Ferry (now in West Virginia). Brown is captured and hanged.

👑 **1860** Abraham Lincoln is elected the 16th president of the United States.

👑 **1860** South Carolina becomes the first state to secede from the Union. Ten other states will follow its example over the next five months (–1861).

👑 **1861** The Secessionist states draw up plans to establish the Confederate States of America, with their own government, constitution, and congress.

✕ **1861** Confederate forces fire the first shots of the civil war by bombarding the Union outpost at Fort Sumter in Charleston Harbor, South Carolina.

✕ **1861** Confederate forces win an early victory at the encounter known in the South as Manassas and in the North as the First Battle of Bull Run.

✕ **1862** On the western front Union forces under Ulysses S. Grant win a bloody victory at the Battle of Shiloh.

✕ **1862** Union forces capture New Orleans, the South's most important port.

✕ **1862** Confederate forces advancing into Maryland are driven back at the Battle of Antietam (known to Confederates as Sharpsburg).

👑 **1862** President Lincoln announces his intention to free all slaves in Confederate territories unless the rebel states agree to return to the Union. This Emancipation Proclamation formally comes into force on January 1, 1863.

✕ **1863** Another Confederate incursion into the north ends in defeat at the Battle of Gettysburg.

✕ **1863** The Confederate stronghold of Vicksburg on the Mississippi River falls after a short siege.

Fighting broke out in 1861 and was at first concentrated mainly on two fronts. One centered around the border state of Virginia, where Confederate forces initially gained ground, pressing into Union territory in 1861 and again in 1863. The second front was in the Mississippi Valley, which cut through the Southern heartlands. Here Union General Ulysses S. Grant made deep inroads into Confederate territory, splitting the Southern states in two by 1863.

Although the war was hard fought, the contest was always an unequal one. The North was prosperous and urban, home to well over 20 million people and much of the nation's industrial might. In contrast, the poorer agricultural South had just 9 million inhabitants, 4 million of them slaves. Eventually the North's superior manpower proved decisive, and by early 1865 the Confederate forces were forced to accept surrender.

The great achievement of the Union victory was the abolition of slavery across the United States. Yet the cost was heavy. Nearly one Confederate soldier in four was dead, and much of the South was in ruins. Even the slaves who had nominally won their freedom found in practice that there was little for them to do but go on working for their old masters as sharecroppers, often on terms that were barely better than they had known before. The Civil War left wounds that would take a century or more to heal.

▶ The border states and the South bore the brunt of the fighting in the Civil War. The Confederates' deepest incursion into Union territory was the 1863 campaign that ended at Gettysburg.

Abraham Lincoln

Abraham Lincoln is remembered now as the preserver of the Union, even though at the time of his election as 16th president Southern secessionists accused him of being its destroyer. Born into poverty in a Kentucky log cabin, he was largely self-educated, first rising to prominence in the 1840s as a lawyer in Springfield, Illinois. In his early political career Lincoln was a moderate abolitionist, prepared to accept the continuation of slavery in the Southern states but opposed to its extension to the new lands of the West. Even so, his views were sufficiently marked to bring about immediate confrontation with the South when he took office in 1861. By 1862 he had embraced the policy of emancipation (freedom) for all slaves. His conduct of the war was marked by an unflinching drive to win but also by a lack of rancor toward defeated opponents. His assassination by an embittered Southerner at the war's end caused a national outburst of grief.

⚔ **1864** Union General William T. Sherman leads a Union army through Confederate Georgia, capturing Atlanta and spreading devastation in his wake.

⚔ **1865** The Confederate capital of Richmond falls to Union forces.

⚔ **1865** The Confederate commander Robert E. Lee surrenders to his Union counterpart Ulysses S. Grant at Appomattox Court House, Viriginia.

👑 **1865** Five days after Lee's surrender President Lincoln is shot in a Washington, D.C., theater by John Wilkes Booth, a Southern sympathizer; Lincoln dies the following day (April 15).

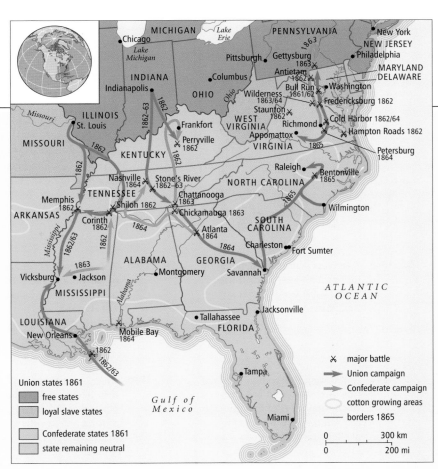

Union states 1861
- ▮ free states
- ▮ loyal slave states

- ▮ Confederate states 1861
- ▮ state remaining neutral

- ⚔ major battle
- ➡ Union campaign
- ➡ Confederate campaign
- ◯ cotton growing areas
- — borders 1865

0   300 km
0   200 mi

AMERICAS

👑 **1868** U.S. President Andrew Johnson survives impeachment by radicals angered by his obstructive attitude to Reconstruction.

👑 **1868** A new amendment to the U.S. Constitution (the Fourteenth) grants citizenship to freed slaves.

⚔ **1868** Carlos Manuel de Céspedes leads a rebellion against Spanish rule in Cuba, inaugurating what will become known as the Ten Years' War.

EUROPE

👑 **1868** A revolution in Spain establishes constitutional monarchy and liberal democratic rule.

⚔ **1870** The Franco–Prussian War breaks out; Prussian forces invade France, defeat the French army at Sedan, and lay siege to Paris. Emperor Napoleon III is taken prisoner, bringing the Second Empire to an end.

The Franco-Prussian War saw France and a newly unified Germany confronting one another for domination of northern Europe. The contest proved onesided when Bismarck's Prussian army defeated Napoleon III's forces at Sedan and went on to besiege Paris. In the ensuing peace settlement France lost the provinces of Alsace and Lorraine, leaving a legacy of bitterness in Franco-German relations that endured well into the 20th century.

AFRICA

⚔ **1868** A British military force frees diplomats held prisoner by Emperor Theodore II of Ethiopia. Theodore commits suicide.

✳ **1869** The Suez Canal opens.

👑 **1871** The Fante Confederation of Akan peoples is discouraged by the British, who see it as a threat to their hegemony on Africa's Gold Coast.

📖 **1871** Henry Morton Stanley of the *New York Herald* tracks down the British missionary and explorer David Livingstone, missing in the East African bush for several years and feared dead.

WESTERN ASIA

A Western caricature of Turkish statesman Midhat Pasha.

👑 **1869** The Ottoman army is reorganized along Prussian lines.

👑 **1869** Midhat Pasha becomes the Ottoman governor of Baghdad: his three-year administration will be a time of rapid and radical modernization (–1872).

👑 **1870** By the Treaty of London the Ottoman Empire is forced to accept Russia's right to build a Black Sea fleet.

👑 **1870** Sa'ud ibn Faisal deposes his brother Abdallah to rule as emir in Saudi Arabia.

SOUTH & CENTRAL ASIA

👑 **1868** Two years after being deposed by his half-brothers, Shir Ali Khan reestablishes himself as ruler of Afghanistan.

⚔ **1868** Russia conquers the khanates of Samarkand and Bukhara in central Asia (modern Uzbekistan).

👑 **1869** Lord Mayo succeeds Lord Lawrence as viceroy of India. His brief term in office will transform the Raj's chaotic finances.

EAST ASIA & OCEANIA

👑 **1868** In the Meiji Restoration imperial rule is reintroduced in Japan when supporters of the Emperor Mutsuhito overthrow the forces of the Tokugawa Shogunate.

⚔ **1870** Angry crowds in Tianjin, a city near Beijing, kill French diplomats and missionaries amid a rising tide of antiwestern feeling in China.

👑 **1871** U.S. naval forces strive unsuccessfully to open Korea up to foreign trade.

✺ **1869** Teams constructing the Central Pacific and Union Pacific railroads meet at Promontory Point, Utah: the entire North American continent is now crossed by a single railroad.

✗ **1869** French settlers and French-speaking native tribes in what is now Manitoba rise up against the Canadian Confederation in the Red River Rebellion. (–1870)

👑 **1872** Mexico's reforming President Benito Juárez dies: a succession struggle ensues.

👑 **1873** A financial crash on Wall Street rocks the U.S. economy.

👑 **AMERICAS**

👑 **1870** The annexation of the Papal States means that Italian reunification is almost complete; only the Vatican Palace and its immediate environs remain outside the new nation.

👑 **1871** Germany's Chancellor Otto von Bismarck declares Germany unified under William I, formerly king of Prussia but now emperor of the Second Reich.

✗ **1871** Paris surrenders to the Prussians. Angry radicals respond by establishing the Commune, a workers' republic suppressed after several weeks of vicious fighting.

👑 **1871** The Treaty of Frankfurt brings the Franco-Prussian War to an end. The French give up the disputed provinces of Alsace and Lorraine to Germany.

👑 **1872** The secret ballot is introduced for elections in Britain.

👑 **1873** William I of Germany, Francis Joseph of Austria, and Alexander II of Russia form the League of the Three Emperors, intended to maintain a common front against Ottoman Turkey.

EUROPE

✗ **1873** The Second Ashanti War breaks out when British settlers on the coast of Ghana refuse to hand an escaped slave back to the inland Ashanti people; it will end in the burning of Kumasi, the Ashanti capital (–1874).

👑 **1873** Accession of Moulay al-Hassan as sultan of Morocco. His modernizing instincts will bring him into conflict with conservative clerics.

Welsh newsman H.M.Stanley meets David Livingstone at Ujiji in East Africa.

AFRICA

✗ **1871** A program of Ottoman expansion in Arabia begins with the conquest of Hasa in the Gulf Coast region. Sheikh Abdallah al-Sabah of neighboring Kuwait also accepts Ottoman overlordship.

👑 **1871** Mirza Husayn, chief minister of Persia, inaugurates a large-scale modernization program but falls foul of conservative factions and is forced out of office (–1873).

✗ **1872** Ottoman forces conquer Arabia's Red Sea coast, as well as large parts of Yemen to the south.

✺ **1872** Persia grants the entrepreneur Paul von Reuter a 70-year monopoly to develop modernized transportation, industry, mining, and other facilities in return for regular payments to the state. The concession is later annulled.

WESTERN ASIA

✗ **1872** Lord Mayo is assassinated by a convict during a visit to the Andaman Islands prison colony.

👑 **1873** Russia annexes the khanate of Khiva (Uzbekistan).

👑 **1873** The British Raj is reformed to allow more Indian participation at local level.

SOUTH & CENTRAL ASIA

✗ **1872** Vientiane, Laos, is sacked by Chinese brigands—mostly deserters from the imperial armies or refugees from civil conflict.

👑 **1872** European settlers finally prevail over New Zealand's indigenous people to end the Maori Wars.

👑 **1873** Siam's young King Chulalongkorn initiates a program of reform.

✗ **1873** French adventurer François Garnier leads an expedition that takes Hanoi in northern Vietnam.

EAST ASIA & OCEANIA

1868–1873 A.D.

THE AGE OF INVENTION

THE LIVES OF ORDINARY PEOPLE IN THE WEST *were transformed more radically by technology in the 19th century than they had been in the preceding thousand years. In 1800 most people still lived in the countryside, rising at dawn and going to bed soon after dark by the light of oil lamps and candles. By 1900 railroads crisscrossed the land, the telegraph had been developed, and electricity was harnessed for everyday use in applications ranging from lighting the home to washing clothes.*

▲ Electric power was the force that did most to change people's lives, and by the late 19th century the United States was the world leader in electrical development. It owed its position largely to inventor Thomas Edison, who patented 225 separate devices between 1879 and 1882, including the carbon filament lamp shown above.

The 19th century saw science come out of the laboratories and technology emerge from the mills and mines. Just as steam power revolutionized industry early in the century, so electric power did the same later for everyday life. Electricity was at first little more than a scientific curiosity, its properties demonstrated to wondering gentlefolk at fashionable public lectures. In time, however, its practical applications began to be explored, a process in which British scientist Michael Faraday's discoveries were to prove far-reaching. His work on electromagnetism led to the invention of the electric motor and the transformer, complementary mechanisms from which many later developments would flow.

As the century went on, technological progress developed momentum as fresh inventors built on the work of their predecessors. For example, France's Louis Thimmonier developed the first-ever sewing machine in 1830, but it was left to the American inventor Elias Howe to devise the first practical model for domestic use 15 years later. Samuel Morse conceived the idea of the telegraph in 1832. He and other pioneers then worked on the concept for the next 12 years, producing a series of refinements to improve the system, and by 1866 a telegraph cable had been laid across the Atlantic Ocean. Thomas Edison produced the first practical lightbulb in 1879, although others had produced earlier experimental

models. The Scots-born inventor Alexander Graham Bell is credited with the invention of the telephone, although refinements made by Edison were essential to the finished product.

Cumulatively the seperate breakthroughs by individuals of genius made the 19th century the age of invention: By its later decades their discoveries were

Stephenson's *Rocket*

On September 15, 1830, the world's first regular passenger rail service opened in northern England. The inauguration of the Manchester to Liverpool Railway was marked by tragedy when a leading English statesman, William Huskisson, was killed when he fell under a train. Even so, the advantages of the iron way were plain to see, and the day proved a triumph for the *Rocket*, the steam locomotive devised by British engineer George Stephenson that powered the train. Chosen against stiff opposition at the previous year's Rainhill Trials, it raced along, cheered to the skies by festive crowds. Exuberant though they were, they could scarcely guess the importance of what they were witnessing: The railroad would have implications for just about every area of life. Not only would it allow bulk transportation and mass tourism, with all they entailed for economic and cultural life; it would also radically alter people's sense of space and social geography.

✳ **1804** Englishman Richard Trevithick invents a working steam locomotive, but the first really successful one will be George Stephenson's *Rocket*, tested in 1829.

✳ **1821** British scientist Michael Faraday invents the electric motor.

✳ **1830** France's Louis Thimmonier invents the first known sewing machine.

✳ **1831** Faraday develops the electric transformer and dynamo.

✳ **1832** U.S. painter Samuel Morse starts work on the electric telegraph; six years later he perfects his famous code, and 12 years later the first telegraph line is established.

✳ **1834** An early refrigerator is invented by Jacob Perkins.

▲ In 1831 British scientist Michael Faraday helped bring on the electrical era by demonstrating the principle of magnetic induction, using equipment like the electromagnet shown above.

transforming the conditions of daily life. The first, ether-based refrigerator was made by Jacob Perkins in 1834; by the end of the century refrigerated storage and transport were a fact of life. Charles Goodyear's discovery of "vulcanized" rubber (made more resilient by cooking it with sulfur) meant relatively little to the general public in 1839, but it had an effect once John Boyd Dunlop made a practical pneumatic tire in 1889. Dunlop's discovery itself would only come into

its own once, by a similarly gradual process of improvement, the modern motor industry was born.

By 1900 railroads had shrunk traveling times dramatically: It took days rather than weeks or months to cross from coast to coast in the United States. Messages could be sent between continents by telegraph, people could speak by telephone from one city to another, sound had been recorded, and electricity was starting to illuminate workplaces and homes. Automobiles were becoming faster and more available, and the Wright Brothers were already contemplating the next great leap forward by thinking about the possibility of powered flight.

▲ The railroad era that got under way with George Stephenson's *Rocket* saw most of Europe crisscrossed with track by 1870. The United States also experienced a railroad boom in the wake of the Civil War; the first transcontinental link was completed in 1869.

⊕ **1845** U.S. inventor Elias Howe creates the first successful domestic sewing machine.

⊕ **1850** The world's first underwater telegraph cable links Calais, on the coast of France, to Dover, England.

⊕ **1858** Hamilton Smith devises the first rotary washing machine.

⊕ **1876** Alexander Graham Bell invents the telephone; Thomas Edison's addition of a vibrating-diaphragm microphone the following year will improve its performance dramatically.

⊕ **1877** German engineer Niklaus Otto invents what is generally considered to be the prototype for all subsequent internal combustion engines.

⊕ **1879** Thomas Edison captures the world's first recorded sound on his phonograph.

⊕ **1885** Working independently, German engineers Karl Benz and Gottlieb Daimler develop the first functional automobiles.

⊕ **1889** John Boyd Dunlop develops a successful pneumatic tire.

⊕ **1898** Rudolf Diesel produces the engine that will be named after him.

AMERICAS

A Remington No.1 typewriter of c.1876.

1874 The first commercially produced typewriter, the Remington, is introduced.

1876 Sitting Bull's Sioux defeat General George Custer's U.S. forces at the Battle of the Little Big Horn.

1876 The Molly Maguires workers' movement in the Pennsylvania coalfield is broken by the execution of 10 of its ringleaders.

1876 Inventor Alexander Graham Bell patents the telephone.

EUROPE

1874 The first Impressionist exhibition is held in France. Claude Monet's painting *Impression: Sunrise* gives the group its name, which is originally intended as a criticism.

1875 Rebellion breaks out in Bosnia against Ottoman rule.

1876 The Constitution of 1876 restores the Spanish monarchy.

*Claude Monet's painting **Impression: Sunrise**.*

AFRICA

1875 Britain buys the Ottoman Empire's share in the Suez Canal, becoming the majority owner.

1876 An Anglo–French commission takes financial charge of a bankrupt Egypt.

1877 Britain annexes Transvaal, South Africa, held at the time by the Dutch-descended Boers.

1879 French forces start an expansionist push across West Africa by moving east from Senegal into the Niger Valley.

1879 The Zulu War breaks out in South Africa; British forces suffer a crushing defeat at Isandhlwana.

WESTERN ASIA

1874 A financial crisis leaves the Ottoman state bankrupt, leading to confusion and disorder in the empire (–1875).

1875 Abdallah ibn Faisal deposes his usurping brother Sa'ud to reclaim the throne of Saudi Arabia.

1876 Murad V seizes power as Ottoman sultan in a coup d'état, deposing his autocratic uncle Abdul Aziz.

1876 Murad is declared insane following a breakdown. Abdul Hamid II becomes sultan in his place. In deference to western criticism he gives the Ottoman Empire its first written constitution.

SOUTH & CENTRAL ASIA

1874 Famine and agrarian unrest bring turmoil to Bengal; the British viceroy Lord Northbrook wins respect for his skillful and humane handling of the situation.

1876 Russia seizes Kokand in eastern Uzbekistan. The khan of Kalat (in modern Pakistan) cedes Quetta to the British, who hope to use the city as a bulwark against further Russian expansion.

1876 Famine breaks out in India's Deccan region: By 1878, 5 million lives will have been lost.

1877 Britain's Queen Victoria assumes the title of empress of India.

EAST ASIA & OCEANIA

1874 The Second Treaty of Saigon apparently cements France's hold over Vietnam, but the emperor proves reluctant to honor its terms, and conflict continues.

A Chinese portrait of the dowager Empress Cixi.

1875 China's Emperor Tongzhi dies without an heir, to be succeeeded by his cousin Dezong, still a small boy. His uncle Prince Gong is his official regent, but real power rests with the dowager (widowed) Empress Cixi.

AMERICAS

👑 **1876** In the revolution of Tuxtepec General Porfirio Díaz seizes power in Mexico in a coup. His hold on power will be endorsed by electors the following year.

⚔ **1877** Large-scale labor unrest breaks out in the United States, with railroad strikes and riots.

⊕ **1877** Thomas Alva Edison develops the phonograph, the first device for playing recorded music.

⚔ **1879** The War of the Pacific breaks out as conflict flares between Chile on the one side and Peru and Bolivia on the other; Chile will emerge victorious (–1884).

⚔ **1879** In Argentina's War of the Desert General Julio Roca attacks the native peoples of the Pampas, opening land as far as the Río Negro for settlement (–1880).

👑 **1880** Ferdinand de Lesseps, builder of the Suez Canal, forms a company to build the Panama Canal.

EUROPE

⚔ **1876** A Bulgarian uprising against Ottoman rule is savagely put down.

📖 **1876** Composer Richard Wagner produces the complete *Ring* cycle of operas for the first time.

⚔ **1877** Russia intervenes in the Balkans in support of local Slavs (Serbs and Montenegrins) rising against Ottoman rule. Britain and Austria ally to oppose Russian expansion in the region.

👑 **1878** A show of allied strength compels Russia to back down. The Berlin peace conference confirms the independence of Serbia, Romania, and Montenegro; Austria occupies Bosnia.

AFRICA

⚔ **1880** The First Boer War breaks out when Transvaal's Boers declare themselves independent of Britain.

The Zulu War set British troops and Africans fighting under British colors (left) against Cetshwayo's Zulu nation. After going down to defeat at Isandhlwana, the British forces won the upper hand; Cetshwayo was captured, and his capital was burned.

WESTERN ASIA

⚔ **1878** Badly defeated in the Russo–Turkish War, Abdul Hamid II is forced to surrender most of the Ottoman Empire's European possessions under the Treaty of San Stefano. At home he suspends the constitution and takes dictatorial power.

👑 **1880** The sheikh of Bahrain surrenders his right to determine foreign policy in return for protection from Britain, starting a trend among the sheikhdoms of the Persian Gulf.

⚔ **1880** The Kurds revolt under Shaykh Ubaydallah. The rising is suppressed by joint Ottoman and Persian forces.

SOUTH & CENTRAL ASIA

⚔ **1878** Alarmed by Shir Ali Khan's overtures to Russia, Britain starts the Second Afghan War. Shir Ali abdicates in favor of his son Yaqub Khan, but Afghanistan is conquered in 1879.

👑 **1880** Britain deposes Yaqub Khan and places Shir Ali's more tractable nephew Abd al-Rahman Khan in power in Afghanistan.

👑 **1880** Lord Ripon, a liberal committed to local self-government, is appointed British viceroy of India.

EAST ASIA & OCEANIA

⚔ **1875** An uprising in the Malay states against British rule is firmly put down.

👑 **1876** New Zealand, formerly six separate provinces, becomes a united dominion of the British Empire.

👑 **1876** Japan imposes the Treaty of Kanghwa on Korea, which undertakes to open itself to trade and diplomatic contacts.

⚔ **1877** The Satsuma Rebellion breaks out in Japan as a defiant last stand of the samurai class, now marginalized by the introduction of conscription for commoners.

👑 **1880** Korea and the United States sign a Treaty of Amity and Commerce.

1874–1880 A.D.

AMERICAS

1881 James Garfield is assassinated after less than a year as U.S. president.

1881 Argentina and Chile resolve a long and bitter border dispute over the division of previously unclaimed Patagonia. Argentina gains the eastern half of Tierra del Fuego, Chile the west.

1882 The Chinese Exclusion Act severely restricts Chinese immigration into the United States. Follow-up legislation will effectively end the flow of Asian immigrants.

EUROPE

1881 Reforming Russian Czar Alexander II is assassinated by revolutionaries. He is succeeded by his reactionary son Alexander III.

1881 The Kingdom of Romania is proclaimed.

An early Daimler wire-wheel car.

1882 In the Phoenix Park Murders Britain's chief secretary for Ireland and his undersecretary are assassinated in Dublin by Fenian radicals.

AFRICA

1881 French forces occupy Tunisia, nominally still part of the Ottoman Empire but in practice largely independent.

1881 In the First Boer War Boer forces win the Battle of Majuba Hill. Under the ensuing Treaty of Pretoria Britain concedes autonomy to Transvaal.

1882 British forces occupy Egypt at the request of its Ottoman governor Tawfik Pasha, who has been threatened with a coup by his own officers.

1884 Britain's General Charles Gordon and his army are besieged in Khartoum, Sudan, by supporters of Muhammad Ahmad, self-styled Mahdi, or Muslim Messiah.

1885 Khartoum falls to the Mahdi's troops, and General Gordon is killed.

1885 Leopold II of Belgium is recognized as ruler of the Congo Free State: Millions will die in the brutal colonization process that follows.

WESTERN ASIA

1881 Sultan Abdul Hamid issues the Decree of Maharrem, establishing a Public Debt Administration designed to bring Ottoman finances under control.

1882 The first wave of Jewish settlement starts in Ottoman Palestine. Some 30,000 people will arrive in the course of the next three decades.

1886 Shah Nasr al-Din invites the Islamic visionary Jamal al-Din, known as al-Afghani, to Persia, but he soon becomes a destabilizing presence.

SOUTH & CENTRAL ASIA

1882 British viceroy Lord Ripon's Rent Commission recommends a series of reforms to tenancy laws in India, offering greater protection for peasants and their families.

1882 The Indian Education Commission is established by Lord Ripon to find ways of extending educational opportunities for Indian children.

EAST ASIA & OCEANIA

1884 By the Treaty of Hué France establishes protectorates in Annam and Tonkin (the central and northern parts of modern Vietnam).

A miner seeking his fortune in the Australian gold rush stands by the entrance to a shaft.

1885 China and Japan sign the Convention of Tianjin, stipulating that each will remove its forces from Korea.

1885 A gold rush begins at Kimberley, Western Australia.

The Statue of Liberty, designed by French sculptor F.A. Bartholdi.

AMERICAS

⚔ **1883** Chile prevails in the War of the Pacific, winning territory from Peru and Bolivia's coastal lands.

⊕ **1885** The Canadian Pacific Railway is completed.

⊕ **1886** New York's Statue of Liberty, a gift from the French people, is dedicated by President Cleveland.

⚔ **1886** Apache Chief Geronimo surrenders to U.S. forces.

EUROPE

👑 **1882** Germany, Austro–Hungary, and Italy join together in the Triple Alliance.

👑 **1884** At the Berlin Conference European powers divide Africa up into spheres of influence.

⊕ **1885** German engineers Gottlieb Daimler and Karl Benz both produce working motor cars.

👑 **1886** William Gladstone's Irish Home Rule Bill fails in the British Parliament, leaving the prime minister's Liberal Party divided.

👑 **1887** The National Union of Women's Suffrage Societies is founded in Britain to advance the cause of votes for women.

AFRICA

⊕ **1886** Gold is discovered in Transvaal and diamonds on Boer territory at Kimberley, confirming Britain's resolve to add these territories to its South African possessions.

👑 **1887** Britain offers to withdraw from Egypt but reserves the right to remain if the peace of the country is under threat.

An early clash between western forces and militant Islam took place in the Sudan in the 1880s. A Nubian named Muhammad Ahmad proclaimed himself the Mahdi, a Muslim Messiah sent to prepare the world for the last days. In 1885 his forces captured Khartoum, killing Britain's General Gordon (right), who had been sent to evacuate Egyptian troops from the area. The Mahdi himself died five months later, probably of typhus, and the rebellion he had inspired was bloodily put down by British forces in the following decade.

WESTERN ASIA

☀ **1887** The Henchak, a revolutionary socialist group, is established by Armenian exiles in Geneva, Switzerland, causing tension to mount in the Ottoman Empire.

SOUTH & CENTRAL ASIA

👑 **1882** Explorer Kishen Singh returns to India, having completed a secret four-year survey of eastern Tibet and the western Gobi Desert on behalf of the British.

👑 **1884** Lord Ripon leaves India after a viceregency that has delighted indigenous Indians but appalled the Anglo-Indian ruling class.

👑 **1885** The Indian National Congress is formed to campaign for independence from Britain.

EAST ASIA & OCEANIA

👑 **1885** Germany and Britain occupy the eastern parts of New Guinea not already under British or Dutch control.

⚔ **1886** The Third Anglo-Burmese War (begun in 1885) concludes in a British victory. Burma is in future to be administered as a part of British India, and its capital is moved from Mandalay to the port of Rangoon.

👑 **1887** China recognizes Portugal's right to administer the trading settlement of Macao.

👑 **1887** The United States acquires the naval base at Pearl Harbor, Hawaii.

1881–1887 A.D.

THE SCRAMBLE FOR AFRICA

▲ A Yoruba craftsman in Nigeria made this carving of Britain's Queen Victoria in the late 19th century. The European colonization of Africa brought about a monumental clash of cultures between peoples with little or no knowledge of each others' ways.

BEFORE THE 1870S THE INTERIOR *of Africa had largely escaped the attention of the outside world. Parts of the continent were already well known to foreigners; the coasts had long been exploited by European and Arab merchants, while the North African coastlands had been part of the Mediterranean world since Roman times. In the mid-19th century, however, explorers penetrated to the heart of what Europeans called the "Dark Continent." Their discoveries stirred the interest of the colonial powers, which were soon competing for sovereignty and mineral rights in the newly opened lands.*

In the 17th and 18th centuries Europe had known West Africa's coasts as a source of slaves and South Africa's Cape of Good Hope as a convenient staging post for ships en route to India. With the 19th century the situation changed radically: For all its incalculable humanitarian benefits, the abolition of the slave trade brought chaos to those African kingdoms that had built power and prosperity around the trade. The leading European nations—Britain and France in particular—offered individual states protection against their local enemies, gaining footholds of trade and political influence for themselves. Farther south British expansion into the Cape hinterland dislodged the region's Dutch-descended Boer farmers, forcing them to make their Great Trek through lands recently destabilized by the expansion of Shaka's Zulu kingdom into the territory of Transvaal.

A series of explorers were meanwhile helping open up Africa to exploitation, even though that was rarely the intention behind their efforts. Early in the century a Scot, Mungo Park, traveled up the Niger River; in its mid years the missionary David Livingstone penetrated to the heart of the continent; while from 1857 on, two Englishmen, Richard Burton and John Hanning Speke, investigated the Great Lakes region, searching for the source of the White Nile.

Whatever the explorers' own motives, the mapping of a region often preceded a colonial claim. By the 1870s opportunistic entrepreneurs in European capitals were studying opportunities for trade and profit in a continent most never even visited. King Leopold II of Belgium took a leading role; as president of the International African Association, he would build up a private kingdom in the Congo Basin

---

1805 Scottish explorer Mungo Park dies while tracing the course of the Niger River.

1807 Britain abolishes the slave trade.

1835 The Great Trek takes the Boers (settlers of Dutch origin) from Cape Colony on Africa's southern tip overland into the interior of the continent, crossing the Orange and Vaal rivers into the Transvaal.

1841 Scottish missionary David Livingstone heads north from the Cape on a decade-long trek across the Kalahari Desert to the Zambezi River, opening a pathway into central Africa.

1858 British explorers John Hanning Speke and Richard Burton reach Lake Tanganyika.

1862 Speke identifies Lake Victoria as the source of the White Nile.

1867 The first major diamond find in Cape Colony is made at Hopetown.

1868 French colonists establish a protectorate in Ivory Coast.

1876 Leopold II of Belgium establishes the International African Association with a view to undertaking colonial projects.

1881 The French occupy Tunisia.

1882 British forces occupy Egypt.

1884 The Berlin Conference addresses conflicting colonial claims to African territory by European powers.

1885 Germany annexes East Africa (now Tanzania). Leopold II of Belgium sets up the Congo Free State.

1885 Muslim followers of the Mahdi take Khartoum, Sudan. The killing of General Gordon causes patriotic outrage in Britain.

1890 Zanzibar becomes a British protectorate.

1895 The territory of the British South Africa Company in what is now Zimbabwe and Zambia is named Rhodesia in Cecil Rhodes's honor.

1896 An Italian attempt to seize control of Ethiopia is defeated at the Battle of Adowa.

1899 The Second Boer War breaks out between British and Boer settlers in southern Africa.

that would in time become notorious for its brutal exploitation of native labor.

By the 1880s the unclaimed lands of Africa had become pawns in a complicated struggle for national prestige played out by most of the major European powers. Britain and France were at first the main players; British dreams of a north–south empire stretching "from the Cape to Cairo" clashed with French ambitions for a band of colonies reaching from the Atlantic to the Indian Ocean. From 1878 on Germany made its voice heard, establishing protectorates in Togo and Cameroon as well as in East and Southwest Africa. Italy laid claim to Somaliland and Eritrea, but its plans to take over Ethiopia also were crushed when its army went down to defeat at Adowa in 1896.

By that time much of the continent, with the exception of Ethiopia and Liberia, had been parceled out among European governments that had little knowledge or understanding of the African populations they presumed to rule. As the name suggests, the Scramble for Africa was largely unplanned and opportunistic; its legacy was a continent whose traditional societies were disrupted in pursuit of interests that were not their own.

▼ The years between 1880 and the outbreak of the First World War in 1914 transformed the map of Africa into a patchwork of European colonies. Only Ethiopia, which drove back an Italian incursion in 1896, and Liberia, originally established with U.S. aid as a home for freed slaves, managed to resist the tide of foreign domination.

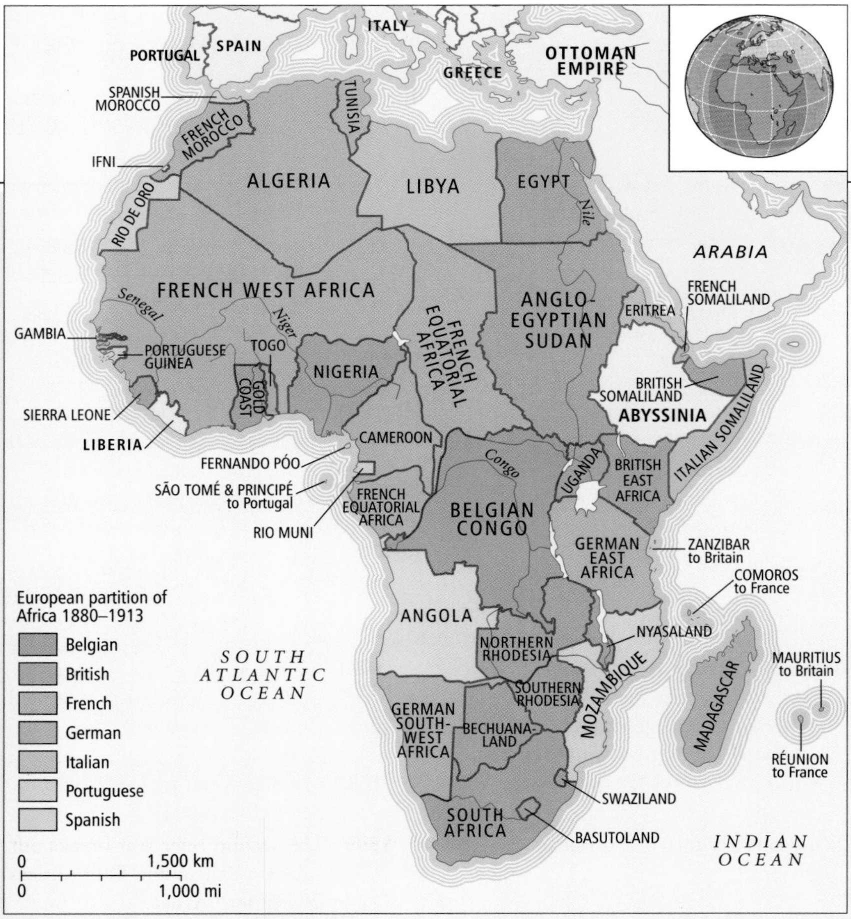

Cecil Rhodes, Empire-Builder

No individual embraced the colonization of Africa more ambitiously than Britain's Cecil Rhodes, shown in the cartoon above as a colossus bestriding the continent from the Cape of Good Hope to Cairo in Egypt. Rhodes traveled to South Africa as a teenager and stayed to make his fortune; at one time his firm controlled more than 90 percent of the world's production of diamonds. He used his immense wealth to build political influence, buying up newspapers and using them to promote his imperialist views. In 1885 he was instrumental in persuading the British government to establish a protectorate in Bechuanaland, north of Cape Colony; four years later he founded the British South Africa Company, winning for it a charter granting the company the right to exploit the vast tract of land later named Rhodesia in his honor. In 1890 he became prime minister of Cape Colony, devoting much of his energies to his long-held goal of bringing the independent Boer republics of Transvaal and the Orange Free State under British rule in a united, white-ruled South Africa. The Boers took up arms to resist his plans, and the result was the Second Boer War. Although British forces eventually prevailed, Rhodes did not live to see their triumph, dying in 1902, two months before the conflict ended.

European partition of Africa 1880–1913

- Belgian
- British
- French
- German
- Italian
- Portuguese
- Spanish

Map labels: PORTUGAL, SPAIN, ITALY, GREECE, OTTOMAN EMPIRE, SPANISH MOROCCO, FRENCH MOROCCO, IFNI, TUNISIA, RIO DE ORO, ALGERIA, LIBYA, EGYPT, ARABIA, Nile, Senegal, FRENCH WEST AFRICA, Niger, FRENCH EQUATORIAL AFRICA, ANGLO-EGYPTIAN SUDAN, ERITREA, FRENCH SOMALILAND, GAMBIA, PORTUGUESE GUINEA, TOGO, NIGERIA, GOLD COAST, SIERRA LEONE, LIBERIA, CAMEROON, FERNANDO PÓO, SÃO TOMÉ & PRINCIPÉ to Portugal, RIO MUNI, FRENCH EQUATORIAL AFRICA, Congo, BELGIAN CONGO, UGANDA, BRITISH EAST AFRICA, BRITISH SOMALILAND, ABYSSINIA, ITALIAN SOMALILAND, GERMAN EAST AFRICA, ZANZIBAR to Britain, COMOROS to France, ANGOLA, NYASALAND, NORTHERN RHODESIA, SOUTHERN RHODESIA, MOZAMBIQUE, MADAGASCAR, MAURITIUS to Britain, GERMAN SOUTH-WEST AFRICA, BECHUANALAND, RÉUNION to France, SWAZILAND, SOUTH AFRICA, BASUTOLAND, SOUTH ATLANTIC OCEAN, INDIAN OCEAN

0 — 1,500 km
0 — 1,000 mi

1888–1893 A.D.

A memorial stone commemorates
Sioux dead at Wounded Knee.

AMERICAS

1889 Emperor Pedro II of Brazil is forced to abdicate: the country becomes a republic.

1889 Ferdinand de Lesseps's Panama Canal scheme collapses.

1889 Oklahoma is opened up for settlement.

1890 Sioux refugees are massacred at Wounded Knee, South Dakota, by U.S. cavalrymen.

EUROPE

1888 Germany's Emperor Frederick III dies and is succeeded by William II.

1889 Scottish inventor John Boyd Dunlop develops the pneumatic tyre.

1889 Charles Stewart Parnell, leader of the Irish nationalist cause in the British parliament, is brought down by revelations of an adulterous love affair.

1889 The Eiffel Tower is built in Paris.

1890 William II dismisses Germany's longtime chancellor, Otto von Bismarck.

1893 Having been passed by the British House of Commons, Gladstone's Second Irish Home Rule Bill is blocked in Parliament's upper chamber, the House of Lords.

1893 Scottish socialist Keir Hardie founds Britain's Independent Labour Party; as the Labour Party, it will become one of the nation's two main political parties (the other being the Conservatives).

AFRICA

1889 Ethiopia's new ruler, Menelik II, signs the Treaty of Ucciali with Italy; the Italians will interpret the pact as a license to establish a colonial protectorate.

1889 France establishes a protectorate in Ivory Coast; the territory will be made an outright colony four years later.

1889 Cecil Rhodes's British South Africa Company is granted a charter to exploit territories to the north of Cape Colony.

WESTERN ASIA

1888 The Young Turk movement gets under way in Ottoman Turkey; army officers and intellectuals meet secretly to oppose Sultan Abdul Hamid's despotism.

1889 Abdallah ibn Faisal dies; al-Rahman ibn Faisal succeeds him as emir of Saudi Arabia.

1889 Abdul Hamid welcomes Emperor William II to Istanbul for a state visit, cementing the growing friendship between the Ottoman Empire and Germany.

SOUTH & CENTRAL ASIA

1888 Lord Lansdowne succeeds Lord Dufferin as viceroy of India; his term of office will be a time of relative peace, prosperity, and cautious political reform.

1888 The Himalayan Kingdom of Sikkim becomes a British protectorate; its boundary with Tibet is clearly demarcated for the first time.

1891 War breaks out after British diplomats visiting Manipur in the Himalayan foothills are killed. The ringleaders are executed, and the small kingdom is absorbed into the province of Assam.

EAST ASIA & OCEANIA

1889 Japan's New Constitution establishes a bicameral (two-chamber) diet or parliament but restricts its powers severely. The emperor will be the true ruler of the new Japan.

1890 New Zealand holds its first general election based on full male suffrage, electing a Liberal–Labor government that will hold power for more than 20 years.

1891 French painter Paul Gauguin settles in Tahiti in search of fresh artistic inspiration.

1892 Gold is discovered at Kalgoorlie, Western Australia.

1893 France establishes a protectorate in Laos.

🌊 **1891** Led by naval officer Captain Jorge Montt, conservative elements in Chile seize power from liberal President José Manuel Balmaceda.

⊕ **1892** Boll weevils attack the cotton crop in the American South.

✕ **1892** Pitched battles break out between striking workers and owners' men at the Homestead Steelworks, Pittsburgh. The eventual outcome is a demoralizing defeat for organized labor.

🌊 **1892** Ida B. Wells begins her campaign against lynching in the American South.

🌊 **1893** The failure of a number of major railroad companies causes panic on Wall Street and plunges the U.S. economy into a four-year depression (−1897).

AMERICAS

A pro-Dreyfus cartoon shows the French Republic in the grip of brutish militarism. The Dreyfus Affair, in which a Jewish army officer was sent to the Devil's Island prison camp on trumped-up charges for a crime he did not commit, split French public opinion down the middle. Liberals such as the writer Émile Zola charged the anti-Dreyfusards with anti-Semitism and contempt for truth and justice, while opponents of Dreyfus in turn accused the liberals of a lack of patriotism and disrespect for the army.

🌊 **1893** French army officer Alfred Dreyfus is wrongfully accused of treason in a case that will divide France for over a decade. Convicted by courtmartial in 1894, he will not be finally vindicated until 1906.

EUROPE

🌊 **1890** Britain takes possession of Zanzibar, giving Germany the Frisian island of Helgoland in exchange.

🌊 **1890** Cecil Rhodes becomes prime minister of South Africa's Cape Colony.

🌊 **1891** A British protectorate is established in Nyasaland (now Malawi).

AFRICA

☀ **1891** Jamal al-Din al-Afghani is deported from Iran, the shah having tired of his persistent criticisms of his government.

✕ **1891** Muhammad ibn Rashid, ruler of Jabal Shammar, defeats Saudi forces and puts the royal family to flight, bringing to an end the second Saudi state.

WESTERN ASIA

🌊 **1892** The Indian Councils Act grants greater powers to local government in British India.

🌊 **1893** The Durand Line marks the border between India and Afghanistan.

SOUTH & CENTRAL ASIA

🌊 **1893** New Zealand becomes the first country in the world to give women the right to vote in national elections.

🌊 **1893** The Hawaiian monarchy is overthrown in a U.S.-backed coup: The Republic of Hawaii will be proclaimed the next year.

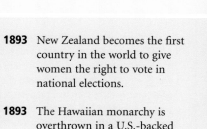

Two Tahitian Women on the Beach, *painted by the French expatriate artist Paul Gauguin.*

EAST ASIA & OCEANIA

1888–1893 A.D.

1900–1906 A.D.

AMERICAS

⬤ **1900** Republican William McKinley is reelected president of the United States, defeating radical challenger William Jennings Bryan for a second time.

⬤ **1901** President McKinley is assassinated by an anarchist. Vice-President Theodore Roosevelt succeeds him.

⬤ **1902** The British, German, and Italian navies act jointly to blockade Venezuelan ports over unpaid government debt.

EUROPE

⬤ **1901** Britain's Queen Victoria dies, and is succeeded by her son Edward VII.

⬤ **1903** In Britain Emmeline Pankhurst forms the Women's Social and Political Union to campaign for women's suffrage (the right to vote). Its supporters are known as suffragettes.

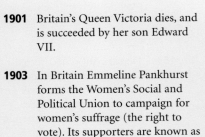

⬤ **1903** Russia's Social Democratic Party splits between the minority Mensheviks and the majority (and more extreme) Bolsheviks.

⬤ **1904** Britain and France ally themselves in the Entente Cordiale ("Friendly Understanding").

English suffragette leader Emmeline Pankhurst addresses a crowd in 1908.

AFRICA

✕ **1900** In the Second Boer War British armies relieve besieged British forces at Kimberley, Ladysmith, and Mafeking, South Africa.

✕ **1901** Ashanti in northern Nigeria is annexed to Britain's Gold Coast colony (later Ghana).

✕ **1903** Britain completes the conquest of northern Nigeria, ruling the region as a protectorate through the existing Sokoto Caliphate.

⬤ **1904** Belgium appoints a commission to investigate oppression in the Congo Free State.

✕ **1904** The German authorities in South West Africa (now Namibia) suppress the Herero people, killing three-quarters of the population (–1907).

WESTERN ASIA

⬤ **1901** The Zionist leader Theodor Herzl meets with Ottoman Sultan Abdul Hamid II, hoping to persuade him to grant land in Palestine for a Jewish state.

⬤ **1901** Iran grants a 60-year monopoly on oil-exploitation rights through most of the country to William Knox D'Arcy, a British citizen.

⬤ **1902** Abd al-Aziz ibn Sa'ud returns from exile to take Riyadh, creating the third Saudi state while still nominally acknowledging the ultimate authority of the Ottoman sultan.

SOUTH & CENTRAL ASIA

✕ **1904** Britain sends a force to Tibet on the pretext of protecting the country from Russian interference and compels Tibet to open its borders to foreign trade.

⬤ **1905** Britain's viceroy in India, Lord Curzon, divides Bengal into a largely Hindu Western Bengal and a mainly Muslim Eastern Bengal and Assam.

⬤ **1906** An Anglo-Chinese convention recognizes Chinese sovereignty over Tibet.

EAST ASIA & OCEANIA

✕ **1900** The Boxer Rebellion breaks out in China, marked by attacks on foreigners and their embassies. An international force including U.S., British, Russian, French, and Japanese contingents is brought in to put the rising down.

✕ **1900** Russian forces take control of Manchuria from China.

⬤ **1901** An administration is set up in the U.S.-run Philippines. The United States backs the conservative Federal Party as popular resistance continues despite the capture of the rebel leader Emilio Aguinaldo.

⬤ **1901** Various British colonies come together to form the Commonwealth of Australia.

As this cartoon showing the Japanese emperor ta[…] the Russian bear suggests, Japan's victory over Ru[…] in the Russo–Japanese War of 1904–1905 represe[…] a significant shift in the global balance of power. […] the first time in more than two centuries a Europe[…] power was humiliatingly defeated by an Asian na[…] Japan's success was a sign that the colonial order […] the 19th century might be coming to an end. It al[…] encouraged militarism in Japan's ruling elite.

AMERICAS

✕ **1902** Colombia's War of the Thousand Days comes to an end, with 100,000 people killed.

👑 **1903** When the French Panama Canal Company goes bust, the United States buys the lease of the Canal Zone and supports Panama's secession from Colombia as an independent nation.

✕ **1904** Civil war breaks out in Uruguay between the landowning Blancos and the urban, liberal Colorados.

⊕ **1906** An earthquake and ensuing fire devastate San Francisco.

EUROPE

👑 **1905** Norway breaks away from union with Sweden, choosing Prince Carl of Denmark to reign as King Haakon VII.

✕ **1905** In St. Petersburg the czar's troops fire on demonstrating workers on Bloody Sunday, triggering a wider uprising. To quell the unrest, Nicholas II concedes limited reforms, including the establishment of an elected assembly, the duma.

👑 **1906** The first Labour Party members are elected to the British Parliament.

👑 **1906** Russia's duma meets for the first time, only to be quickly dissolved by the czar, who considers it too radical.

AFRICA

👑 **1906** By the Treaty of Algeciras European powers agree to recognize the claims of France and Spain to rule Morocco.

Beginning in 1899, the Second Boer War set farmers of Dutch origin (left) living in southern Africa against the British. It was an unequal contest that the British Army was always likely to win. Yet the Boers fought so well that the Treaty of Vereeniging, which ended the war in 1902, won them substantial concessions.

WESTERN ASIA

✕ **1903** Rioting stirred by resentment at foreign influence breaks out in the Iranian cities of Esfahan and Yazd, with violence directed against members of the Baha'i faith.

✕ **1904** A force sent to bolster Ottoman authority is defeated by Abd al-Aziz ibn Sa'ud, further boosting Saudi prestige in Arabia.

👑 **1906** In response to growing unrest, Shah Muzaffar ud-Din is forced to concede a constitution in Iran. A *majlis*, or constituent assembly, is established.

SOUTH & CENTRAL ASIA

👑 **1906** The Simla Deputation, a body of leading Muslims, calls on the new viceroy of India, Lord Minto, to improve the status of India's Muslim minority.

👑 **1906** The All India Muslim League is founded as a mouthpiece for India's Islamic community

EAST ASIA & OCEANIA

✕ **1902** The Philippines insurrection is suppressed, but smaller scale resistance continues.

👑 **1902** Japan allies with Britain to resist Russian expansion in East Asia.

✕ **1904** The Russo–Japanese War breaks out.

✕ **1905** Japanese forces gain control of Manchuria and defeat the Russian Pacific fleet in the naval Battle of Tsushima.

👑 **1905** The Treaty of Portsmouth ends the Russo–Japanese War. Japan gains northern Sakhalin and is given a free hand to establish a protectorate in Korea.

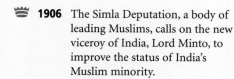

1900–1906 A.D.

371

AMERICAS

Members of the NAACP march in protest against lynchings.

1907 Industrial unrest sweeps Chile.

1910 The National Association for the Advancement of Colored People (NAACP) is founded to campaign for the rights of African–Americans.

1910 The Mexican Revolution breaks out when Francisco Madero is elected president but denied office. The dictatorship of Porfirio Díaz, who originally came to power in 1877, is subsequently overthrown (in 1911), and Madero installed in power.

EUROPE

1907 The Triple Entente among Britain, France, and Russia comes together to counter the Triple Alliance already formed by Germany, Austria-Hungary, and Italy.

1908 Crete takes advantage of Ottoman troubles to declare union with Greece.

1908 Bulgaria declares its independence from the Ottoman Empire.

1909 French aviator Louis Blériot makes the first powered flight across the English Channel.

1910 Revolution in Portugal: The monarchy is brought down and a republic proclaimed.

1910 George V ascends the British throne at a time when the British Empire is at its peak.

Louis Blériot arrives in England after completing the first cross-Channel flight.

AFRICA

1908 Belgium takes direct charge of the administration of the Congo Free State, which is renamed Belgian Congo.

1910 South Africa gains autonomy as an independent dominion of the British Empire. Afrikaner leader Louis Botha is elected prime minister in white-only elections.

1911 The Agadir Incident sees France and Germany squaring up over rival colonial claims to influence in Morocco.

WESTERN ASIA

1908 Young Turks stage a revolution in Ottoman Turkey, seeking to establish a constitutional government while keeping Sultan Abdul Hamid II as head of state.

1909 In Persia supporters of constitutional government depose Shah Muhammad Ali and place his young son Ahmad on the Iranian throne, with a regent.

1909 After the failure of a counter-revolutionary coup, Ottoman Sultan Abdul Hamid II is deposed to make way for his more malleable brother Mehmed V.

SOUTH & CENTRAL ASIA

1909 The Indian Councils Act concedes increased representation to native Indians in local government, but the growing nationalist movement is unimpressed.

1910 Lord Hardinge is appointed viceroy in India. One of his first moves (in 1911) will be to annul the partition of Bengal, a decision greeted triumphantly by Hindus.

1911 The purpose-built city of New Delhi becomes India's capital.

EAST ASIA & OCEANIA

1907 Japanese moves to disband the Korean army cause a widespread revolt against Japanese rule.

1908 China's Emperor Dezong dies, followed days later by Dowager Empress Cixi, the power behind the throne for 30 years. Power passes to the boy-emperor Puyi.

1910 Japan annexes Korea. Over 20,000 Koreans have died in the three-year fight for independence.

1911 Sun Yat-sen leads a full-scale nationalist revolution in China. The following year Emperor Puyi abdicates, and the Republic of China is established.

1913 Reformer Francis Harrison is appointed U.S. governor of the Philippines. He advocates independence for the islands and places Filipinos in positions of responsibility in the administration.

👑 **1911** The Triangle Shirtwaist fire, in the New York City factory of that name, kills 146 mainly female immigrant garment workers, highlighting bad working conditions in "sweatshops" at this time.

👑 **1912** Theodore Roosevelt breaks with the Republicans to lead his own Progressive Party.

⚔ **1912** U.S. forces invade Nicaragua. The country will remain under U.S. occupation for 20 years.

👑 **1912** The Democrat challenger Woodrow Wilson wins the U.S. presidential election.

⚔ **1913** Mexico's President Madero is deposed and murdered by members of the military; General Victoriano Huerta takes power.

AMERICAS

⚔ **1912** The First Balkan War breaks out when Bulgaria, Greece, Serbia, and Montenegro join forces to win their independence from Ottoman Turkey, along with that of a new nation, Albania (–1913).

👑 **1913** The Home Rule Bill granting limited independence to Ireland is passed by Britain's House of Commons but rejected by the House of Lords.

Britain's King George V, shown in these patriotic vignettes with his wife Mary.

⚔ **1913** The Second Balkan War breaks out. Serbia, Greece, Romania, and Turkey now unite against Bulgaria, which has set itself against Serbian claims to Macedonia. Bulgaria is beaten and the region repartitioned.

EUROPE

⚔ **1911** Italy sends a force to occupy Tripoli, Libya.

👑 **1912** Using local unrest as a pretext, France imposes a protectorate on southern Morocco; the northern third of the country becomes a protectorate of Spain.

👑 **1913** The Native Land Act ratifies the existing segregation of races in South Africa, with black African farmers confined to the more marginal lands.

AFRICA

⚔ **1911** The Ottoman Empire wages war unsuccessfully on Italy to protest the Italian annexation of Tripoli, an Ottoman territory in North Africa (–1912).

⚔ **1913** Young Turks led by Enver Pasha stage a coup against the sultan's ministers following Ottoman reverses in the First Balkan War.

WESTERN ASIA

👑 **1912** Tibet and Mongolia both take advantage of the revolution in China to reclaim their independence, expelling Chinese officials.

👑 **1913** Yuan Shikhai, newly elected president of the Chinese Republic, acknowledges the independence of Tibet and the autonomy of Outer Mongolia.

SOUTH & CENTRAL ASIA

👑 **1913** Elected president of the Chinese Republic, Yuan Shikhai suspends the constitution and expels Sun Yat-sen's Kuomintang nationalists from the assembly.

The Chinese army, some of whose troops are seen marching at left, gave its support to nationalist forces opposing the national government in 1911. The last Manchu emperor, six-year-old Puyi, gave up the throne, ending more than 2,000 years of imperial rule.

EAST ASIA & OCEANIA

1907–1913 A.D.

THE TRANSPORTATION REVOLUTION

THE FIRST WORKABLE INTERNAL COMBUSTION *engine was built as early as 1876; the first powered airplane took off in the early years of the new century, in 1903. Their inventors are well known, but other transportation revolutionaries whose entrepreneurship was as remarkable as their engineering remain largely unsung. The impact of their innovations would be felt far beyond the realm of travel, with implications for every aspect of modern life.*

▲ Commuters—one masked against smog—flood from a Tokyo subway train. Mass transportation was largely a creation of the 20th century.

On December 17, 1903, Orville Wright became airborne over Kitty Hawk, North Carolina. His flight lasted only seconds and took him no more than 120 feet (36 m), but its importance was immediately apparent. To have built a powered flying machine fulfilled a dream that had haunted the collective imagination for centuries: Was there any future challenge human ingenuity could not meet?

Less immediately apparent was the eventual global impact of air travel, although there were clues in the fast-expanding influence of the automobile. The achievements of the early motor engineers may have

been less spectacular than the Wright brothers' feat, but their effect on the age was more profound. Many years would pass before air travel became cheap enought for mass transportation, but the auto transformed the United States as early as the 1920s.

Without the internal combustion engine such developments would have been impossible, yet the transport revolution was not just a product of advances in engineering technology. At least as important were innovations in industrial organization. Henry Ford pioneered assembly-line manufacturing techniques that allowed quality and quantity to come

---

1876 Nicolaus Otto designs the world's first practicable internal combustion engine.

1885 Karl Benz, another German engineer, produces an improved model, while Otto's student Gottlieb Daimler develops the prototype for the modern auto engine.

1900 Germany's Count Ferdinand von Zeppelin designs a rigid airship powered by an internal combustion engine. Within a decade "zeppelins" are making scheduled passenger flights.

1903 The Wright Brothers, Wilbur and Orville, make the first manned, powered flight in a heavier-than-air craft at Kitty Hawk, North Carolina. Orville is the pilot, covering a distance of 120 ft (36 m).

1907 An Italian-built Itala wins a 10,000-mile (16,000-km) auto race from Beijing to Paris.

1908 Henry Ford introduces the assembly line for the manufacture of cars. His new Model T retails at under $1,000—an automobile for the middle classes.

1911 Airmail is established in England, India, and the United States.

1913 Ford's new factory at Highland Park, Michigan, marks the coming of age of mass production: By 1914 it is producing Model Ts at a rate of one every 40 seconds.

1914 World War I breaks out in Europe. The next four years' hostilities will see aircraft mobilized for bombing, reconnaissance, message-carrying, and other roles.

1919 The first transatlantic passenger flights are made.

1927 Charles Lindbergh makes the first solo transatlantic flight in *The Spirit of St. Louis.*

1927 Production of the Model T Ford ceases. Some 16 million have been built over 19 years.

1928 British aviation engineer Frank Whittle conceives the idea of the jet engine. It will take him nine years to produce a working model.

1937 The highly-publicized *Hindenburg* disaster, in which the German airship bursts into flames at its U.S. moorings killing 36 passengers, effectively brings the age of airship travel to an end.

1939 U.S. engineer Igor Sikorsky invents the modern helicopter.

1964 The first Japanese bullet train enters service between Tokyo and Osaka, traveling at speeds of up to 125 m.p.h. (200 km/h).

1970 The Boeing 747 wide-bodied passenger plane comes into service. Such "jumbo jets" will help reduce the cost of flying.

together for the first time. There was a revolution in marketing, too. The spread of car ownership in North America was significantly boosted by fresh advertising techniques making sophisticated use of new media such as mass-market newspapers and radio. The falling prices associated with mass production did much to make automobiles more affordable, but newly devised credit-purchase plans also helped spread the costs. Thousands of families were soon able to own a car: The sense of empowerment the acquisition gave them was remarkable.

Thanks both to its industrial and commercial might and to its vast extent, the United States quickly became the first truly motorized society. Auto ownership increased rapidly after World War I, boosted by better roads and also by more practical design; in the course of the 1920s the open-top bodies originally favored largely gave way to models with roofs. By the 1930s North America possessed 85 percent of the global stock of motor vehicles.

Following World War II, however, car ownership also spread rapidly in other developed economies. In 1958 there were 119 million cars in use around the globe; by 1974 the figure had soared to 303 million, and in 1991 it reached 591 million.

Air travel made its mark rather more slowly; the technological challenges to be surmounted to get large numbers of people airborne were greater, and for a time dirigible airships competed with airplanes for passenger traffic. In the years following World War II, however, aviation too became a form of international mass transportation, dramatically reducing long-haul journey times in a world that was increasingly being talked of as a "global village."

▲ Wilbur Wright flies a glider biplane that he designed with his brother Orville at Kitty Hawk, North Carolina, in 1902. Having attached an engine to the plane, the brothers would make the first powered flight at the same location in the following year.

Factory of the Future

In 1913 Henry Ford opened a purpose-built factory at Highland Park, Detroit. Its most immediately striking feature was its sheer size. Ford saw that everything, from steel to working space, was cheaper bought in bulk. More radical, however, was the assembly line he had devised. Each vehicle under construction moved slowly through the plant, parts being added in strict order by designated workers performing the same repetitive task on each new chassis as it passed. Labor was plentiful and therefore cheap: Workers had to be trained in their single, designated tasks but did not need the all-around experience and expertise of earlier master craftsmen. Between the economies of scale Ford's gigantic plant achieved and the advantages of mass production, his manufacturing methods drove finished prices inexorably down. Eventually a Model T would retail at around $300, a sum even modestly prosperous Americans could afford.

AMERICAS

1914 The Panama Canal is opened, although frequent landslides will limit its usefulness in its early years.

1917 An earthqake destroys Guatemala City and opens the floodgates of opposition to the U.S.-backed regime of Manuel Estrada Cabrera.

1917 The United States declares war on Germany. In all, some 2 million U.S. soldiers will travel to Europe to fight in World War I; 115,000 will be killed (–1918).

EUROPE

1914 Archduke Franz Ferdinand, heir to the Austro-Hungarian throne, is shot dead by a Bosnian nationalist in Sarajevo.

1914 World War I begins, setting the Central Powers—Germany, Italy, and Austria-Hungary—against Britain, France, and Russia.

1916 In Ireland the Easter Rising against British rule is suppressed by British troops.

1916 British and German warships duel inconclusively in the Battle of Jutland, the major naval engagement of World War I.

1917 Following battlefield defeat, Russia undergoes two separate revolutions. The first (in March) brings czarist rule to an end and establishes democratic government; the second, in November, brings the Bolsheviks to power.

World War I led to the collapse of two empires (the Ottoman and the Austro-Hungarian) and helped end czarist rule in Russia. It also left 10 million combatants dead. Casualty rates were particularly high among infantrymen like these British troops seen going "over the top" at the Somme in 1916.

AFRICA

1914 British and German troops fight one another in Tanganyika. South Africa occupies German Southwest Africa (Namibia).

1916 Prince Ras Tafari seizes power in Ethiopia, toppling Emperor Lij Eyasu to rule as regent and imperial heir.

1919 Britain exiles Egyptian nationalist leaders, sparking an uprising that is put down by force.

WESTERN ASIA

1914 When war breaks out in Europe, the Ottoman Empire allies with Germany and the Central Powers.

1915 British and ANZAC (Australia and New Zealand Army Corps) troops land at Gallipoli in the Dardanelles but are beaten back by Ottoman forces.

1915 Mass deportations of Armenians from eastern Turkey, intended to reduce the risk of rebellion, result in up to 1.5 million deaths.

SOUTH & CENTRAL ASIA

1915 Mohandas "Mahatma" Gandhi takes up the struggle for Indian independence.

1916 Czarist forces put down an uprising in Uzbekistan against food shortages and poor conditions, killing thousands.

1918 Soviet forces take Turkestan, triggering widespread (but uncoordinated) *basmachi* ("bandit") resistance by tribesmen across Central Asia.

EAST ASIA & OCEANIA

1914 A Constitutional Compact proclaimed in China confirms the dictatorial powers of Yuan Shikhai.

1914 Japan joins the European allies in declaring war on Germany. It opens hostilities by occupying the islands of Micronesia, previously a German colony.

1914 Malaya is taken under British control.

1915 Yuan Shikhai announces his intention to rule China as a new emperor but dies (in 1916) before the imperial system can be restored.

♛ **1919** President Woodrow Wilson's 14 Points peace plan is adopted at the Versailles Conference ending World War I, but the U.S. Congress rejects the treaty and refuses to join the League of Nations (–1920).

♛ **1918** British women over the age of 30 win the right to vote.

♛ **1918** World War I ends in the defeat of Germany and its allies. The Austro-Hungarian Empire breaks up, and two new nations emerge: an independent Poland and the Kingdom of Serbs, Croats, and Slovenes (the future Yugoslavia).

♛ **1919** The Treaty of Versailles imposes harsh peace terms on Germany, including the restoration of Alsace and Lorraine to France.

♛ **1919** Britain takes over Tanganyika (Tanzania); German forces withdraw to Mozambique.

⚔ **1916** Sharif Husein leads an Arab uprising against Ottoman rule. With British help Aqaba, Baghdad, and Damascus are captured (–1918).

Yuan Shikhai, who became president of China following the revolution of 1911.

♛ **1919** The Volstead Act (coming into force in 1920) bans alcohol and introduces the Prohibition era.

Vladimir Lenin led the Bolsheviks to power in Russia in November 1917.

♛ **1919** Upper Volta (now Burkina Faso) gains autonomy from French Sudan (Mali); Cameroon is split into French and British halves.

♛ **1917** In the Balfour Declaration Britain's foreign secretary declares his country's support for the establishment of a "national home for the Jewish people in Palestine."

♛ **1919** The British government passes the Rowlatt Acts, giving the authorities in India far-reaching emergency powers to tackle seditious activity.

⚔ **1919** Nationalist discontent at the Paris Peace Conference's decision to restore German concessions in China finds expression in the Fourth of May Movement, sparking violent student protests in Beijing.

⚔ **1919** Peasant guerrilla leader Emiliano Zapata is treacherously killed amid continuing civil strife and disorder in the Mexican Republic.

♛ **1919** The League of Nations is established as a forum for the resolution of future international disputes.

⚔ **1919** The Spartacists—German communists—stage an unsuccessful uprising in Berlin. In Hungary communists temporarily seize power under Béla Kun.

⚔ **1919** Civil war breaks out in Russia between the communist Red Army and counterrevolutionary Whites.

♛ **1919** The Second Pan-African Congress holds meetings in London, Paris, and Lisbon.

♛ **1918** The Ottoman authorities sue for peace at the end of World War I. Military defeat leads to the disintegration of the Ottoman Empire.

⚔ **1919** British troops open fire on demonstrators in Amritsar, India, killing 379 unarmed protesters.

♛ **1919** Ho Chi Minh founds the Indochinese Communist Party in the part of French Indochina that will eventually regain its independence as Vietnam.

AMERICAS

EUROPE

AFRICA

WESTERN ASIA

SOUTH & CENTRAL ASIA

EAST ASIA & OCEANIA

1914–1919 A.D.

377

1920–1926 A.D.

AMERICAS

✕ **1920** Mexican generals proclaim the Republic of Sonora, going on to defeat President Carranza and to force the surrender of the revolutionary leader Pancho Villa.

👑 **1920** The Nineteenth Amendment gives U.S. women the vote.

👑 **1921** Republican Warren Harding is sworn in as 29th president of the United States. One of his first significant steps is to raise customs barriers against European trade.

👑 **1921** The Immigration Act (further tightened in 1924) limits the number of foreign nationals who can enter the United States.

EUROPE

✕ **1920** Admiral Nikolaus Horthy leads a counterrevolution in Hungary.

✕ **1921** The communist Red Army finally overcomes its White opponents in the civil war that has divided Russia since 1918.

👑 **1921** Britain concedes autonomy to the Irish Free State, excluding six Ulster counties with a predominantly Protestant population; they remain part of the United Kingdom under the name of Northern Ireland.

✕ **1922** The Union of Soviet Socialist Republics (USSR) is set up; Soviet troops occupy Ukraine.

✕ **1922** Fascist leader Benito Mussolini leads the March on Rome, taking power as Italy's prime minister.

AFRICA

✕ **1921** Spain seeks to extend its territories around Tangiers inland into the upland Rif region, sparking an uprising that also affects French Morocco.

👑 **1922** Muhammad Abd el-Krim, leader of the Rif Rebellion against French and Spanish rule, establishes the Rif Republic (–1926).

👑 **1922** Britain grants Egypt independence under King Fuad I but retains control over defense and foreign policy, the Suez Canal, and the administration of Sudan.

WESTERN ASIA

Shown here in the traditional clothing he later rejected for Western dress, Mustafa Kemal did more than anyone to create modern Turkey out of the ruins of the Ottoman Empire. From 1919 on he organized resistance to the nation's dismemberment, then oversaw the abolition of the sultanate and the establishment of a secular republic. He served as Turkey's president from 1923 until his death in 1938, winning from his countrymen the honorary title of Atatürk ("father of the Turks").

✕ **1920** Greece attempts to divide Turkey in keeping with the terms of the Treaty of Sèvres, but Mustafa Kemal leads a successful resistance (–1922).

👑 **1922** Following the breakup of the Ottoman Empire, the League of Nations mandates Britain to govern Palestine and France to rule Syria and Lebanon.

SOUTH & CENTRAL ASIA

👑 **1920** The map of Central Asia is redrawn as areas in the former empire of the Russian czars are re-created as autonomous soviet socialist republics (ASSRs) of the Soviet Union.

👑 **1920** Gandhi's policy of nonviolent civil disobedience toward the British authorities is adopted by the Indian National Congress.

👑 **1922** Gandhi is arrested by the British on charges of sedition: He will spend the next two years in prison.

EAST ASIA & OCEANIA

👑 **1921** In Guangzhou (Canton) the warlords ruling much of northern China pledge to destroy the Kuomintang (nationalist) state; in Shanghai the Chinese Communist Party is formed.

👑 **1923** Sun Yat-sen reaches an agreement with the Chinese Communist Party: Kuomintang nationalists will fight alongside communists to free a reunited China from the warlords.

👑 **1925** Sun Yat-sen dies; he is succeeded as head of the Kuomintang by Chiang Kai-shek.

✕ **1926** Chiang Kai-shek launches the Northern Expedition against the warlords.

AMERICAS

♨ **1923** Republican Calvin Coolidge succeeds as U.S. president on the sudden death of Warren Harding.

This falcon collar was one of the treasures found in Tutankhamen's tomb in 1922.

♨ **1924** The Coolidge administration is rocked by the Teapot Dome scandal, which forces the resignation of Secretary of the Interior Albert Fall.

♨ **1924** Native Americans are granted full U.S. citizenship.

EUROPE

♨ **1923** Hyperinflation devastates the German economy. French troops occupy the coal-mining Rühr region in response to the nation's failure to keep up with the war-reparation payments dictated by the Versailles peace treaty.

♨ **1924** Led by Prime Minister Ramsey MacDonald, the Labour Party comes to power in Britain for the first time.

♨ **1924** Lenin dies, unleashing a prolonged power struggle in the Soviet Union.

♨ **1925** Mussolini proclaims himself Il Duce ("The Leader") of a Fascist Italy.

AFRICA

📖 **1922** Pharaoh Tutankhamen's tomb is unearthed in Egypt.

♨ **1923** White colonists in Southern Rhodesia gain autonomy within the British Empire.

♨ **1923** Abyssinia (Ethiopia) is recognized as an independent state by the League of Nations.

♨ **1924** The Universal League for the Defense of the Black Race is founded in Paris by exiles from French West Africa. It will play a vital role in the growth of African independence movements.

WESTERN ASIA

♨ **1923** Kemal establishes a republic in Turkey with its capital at Ankara. Extensive measures are taken to westernize and secularize what had been a traditional Muslim society. The new nation receives international recognition in the Treaty of Lausanne.

✕ **1925** Having taken Mecca in the previous year, Saudi forces complete the conquest of Arabian territories previously ruled by Husein's Hashemite Dynasty.

♨ **1925** Iran's ruling assembly, the *majlis*, winds up the Qajar Dynasty, deposing Ahmad Shah and electing Reza Khan as first shah of the Pahlavi Dynasty.

✕ **1925** Druze tribesmen rise unsuccessfully against the French in Syria's Great Revolt.

✕ **1925** A revolt by Kurds in eastern Turkey is quickly put down, but Kemal takes advantage of the crisis to assume far-reaching emergency powers.

SOUTH & CENTRAL ASIA

♨ **1924** Soviet Central Asia is further redefined as smaller entities are subsumed into four socialist republics: Kazakhstan, Kirgizia, Turkmenistan, and Uzbekistan.

♨ **1924** The Mongolian People's Republic is founded; it will not be recognized by neighboring China for another 21 years.

EAST ASIA & OCEANIA

For 24 years until his final defeat by Mao Zedong's Communists, Chiang Kai-shek struggled for control of China. His Nationalist forces (left) battled warlords, leftists, and the Japanese before their eventual evacuation to Taiwan in 1949.

♨ **1926** Japan's Emperor Yoshihito dies. He is succeeded by his son Hirohito, who will reign until 1989.

1920–1926 A.D.

379

AMERICAS

Warner Bros. Supreme Triumph
AL JOLSON
THE JAZZ SINGER

Although not the first film to feature recorded sound, The Jazz Singer *marked the commercial breakthrough of "the talkies."*

❋ **1927** Al Jolson's *The Jazz Singer* inaugurates the era of "talking pictures" in the cinema.

❋ **1927** Charles Lindbergh makes the first nonstop solo flight across the Atlantic, flying from New York to Paris in his monoplane *The Spirit of St. Louis.*

♕ **1929** Republican Herbert Hoover becomes U.S. president.

♕ **1929** The Wall Street Crash: American shares lose more than $40 billion in value in a single month. The crash contributes to the beginning of the Great Depression of the 1930s.

✕ **1930** Revolution in Brazil brings dictatorial powers to Getúlio Vargas.

EUROPE

♕ **1927** Stalin emerges as the dominant figure in the collective leadership now ruling the Soviet Union.

❋ **1928** British scientist Alexander Fleming discovers penicillin.

♕ **1929** The Kingdom of Serbs, Croats, and Slovenes is renamed Yugoslavia.

♕ **1929** Stalin confirms his position as ruler of the Soviet Union by forcing his chief rival, Leon Trotsky, into exile. He launches the first five-year plan, aimed at modernizing the Soviet economy.

Against the will of his predecessor Lenin, Joseph Stalin emerged from the infighting after Lenin's death as the sole ruler of the Soviet Union. He crushed all opposition, launching a reign of terror to protect his dictatorship.

AFRICA

♕ **1928** In Egypt Hassan al-Banna founds the Muslim Brotherhood, an Islamic revivalist organization.

♕ **1929** The Riotous Assemblies Act is passed by the South African parliament to suppress protests by the country's black majority.

♕ **1930** Ras Tafari is crowned as Emperor Haile Selassie I of Ethiopia.

WESTERN ASIA

♕ **1928** On Mustafa Kemal's orders Latin script replaces Arabic for writing the Turkish language.

♕ **1928** France sets up an assembly in Syria but suspends it when it votes to end French rule.

✕ **1929** Fighting between Jews and Arabs in Palestine claims 250 lives.

SOUTH & CENTRAL ASIA

♕ **1929** Tajikistan—previously treated as part of Uzbekistan—becomes a separate Soviet republic.

♕ **1930** Leading Indian opposition to a salt tax, Mahatma Gandhi heads a march to the seashore at Dandi. He is arrested and imprisoned.

♕ **1931** The new viceroy of India, Lord Irwin, issues the Irwin Declaration, promising India a future role as a self-governing dominion of the British Empire.

EAST ASIA & OCEANIA

✕ **1927** Having defeated China's northern warlords, Chiang Kai-shek establishes a new capital at Nanking and orders a massacre of communists, his former allies.

♕ **1927** Ahmed Sukarno forms the Nationalist Party of Indonesia (NPI) to press for independence. His arrest by the Dutch colonial authorities two years later will cause widespread unrest

♕ **1928** Forced into flight by Chiang Kai-shek's purge, Chinese communist leaders Mao Zedong and Zhou Enlai succeed in establishing a Soviet-style statelet in Jiangxi, southern China.

✕ **1931** Japanese troops occupy Manchuria in northern China.

AMERICAS

✹ **1931** The Empire State Building in New York City becomes the world's tallest building.

✗ **1932** Outbreak of the Chaco War between Bolivia and Paraguay, fought for possession of the disputed Northern Chaco region. Paraguay will emerge victorious three years later.

👑 **1932** In the United States the Great Depression is at its worst, with more than 15 million workers unemployed.

The Great Depression of the 1930s began in the United States but cast its shadow worldwide. The Wall Street Crash of 1929 led to an enduring financial crisis; eventually about half of U.S. banks failed. Lack of funds puts millions of people out of work; in 1932 alone nearly 20,000 businesses went bankrupt. Unemployed workers obtained what help they could from charity-run soup kitchens (left).

EUROPE

👑 **1930** Hitler's Nazis (National Socialists) run second in elections to the Reichstag (Germany's parliament), winning 107 seats.

👑 **1931** King Alfonso XIII leaves Spain as his country declares itself a republic.

👑 **1932** Stalin's attempt to impose the collectivization of agriculture produces famine in Ukraine.

👑 **1932** António Salazar comes to power in Portugal. His Estado Novo ("New State") dictatorship will rule the nation for the next 36 years.

✹ **1932** English physicists John Cockroft and Ernest Walton first split the atom. In the same year James Chadwick discovers the neutron.

AFRICA

👑 **1930** The Land Apportionment Act sets aside the most productive half of Southern Rhodesia's land for white farmers.

👑 **1932** Upper Volta is subsumed into Côte d'Ivoire (Ivory Coast) in French West Africa.

WESTERN ASIA

👑 **1932** Iraq gains its independence under King Faisal I, but Britain retains a military presence in the country.

👑 **1932** King Saud's Kingdom of the Hejaz is renamed the Kingdom of Saudi Arabia.

✹ **1932** Oil is discovered in Bahrain.

SOUTH & CENTRAL ASIA

👑 **1932** Imprisoned again, Gandhi goes on hunger strike on behalf of India's lowcaste untouchables.

EAST ASIA & OCEANIA

👑 **1932** A military coup in Siam ends 150 years of absolute monarchy: King Prajadhipok is forced to accept a constitution.

✹ **1932** Sydney Harbor Bridge is completed in Australia.

Seen here under construction in 1930, Sydney Harbor Bridge had the largest single-arch span in the world when it was completed two years later.

1927–1932 A.D.

THE MASS MEDIA

THE RAPID GROWTH OF THE MASS MEDIA IN THE *20th century was in its way every bit as dramatic as the diffusion of printing 400 years earlier. The development of radio, television, and the movies created new audiences for entertainment and information. Advertisers were quick to grasp the power of these new means of communication in reaching out to a public of millions, and from the marriage of art and commerce the modern consumer society was born.*

▲ A rocket lands on a bemused Moon in a scene from one of the earliest fantasy films, George Méliès's *A Trip to the Moon* (1902). The first film shown to a paying public was exhibited in 1895; by the 1920s stars like Charlie Chaplin and Mary Pickford were famous around the world.

The early history of mass entertainment in the United States owes much to the inventive genius of Thomas Edison. He produced the first successful silent motion pictures, while his most famous invention, the phonograph, helped spread the popularity of ragtime, jazz, and blues music in the early decades of the 20th century. Piano sales fell as people listened to the latest sounds of Bessie Smith and Louis Armstrong on their wind-up gramophones.

Yet it was radio, which entered U.S. homes as a popular form of entertainment in the 1920s, that brought the greatest changes to people's lives. Sales of radios soared from a total of $60 million in 1922 to $426 million in 1929 as families tuned in to a diverse schedule of musical variety shows, comedies, and quizzes. Live broadcasts of baseball games and boxing bouts turned professional sports into a national obsession. At the same time, on-air commercials boosted the demand for new goods and products such as cars, refrigerators, and washing machines, and the soap opera was born when detergent companies began sponsoring serial dramas on radio.

Early experiments with television began in the 1900s, but it was not until the late 1920s that practical ways of transmitting television pictures were developed. By the mid-1930s RCA was transmitting television programs from Radio City, New York, and its regular broadcasting service was launched in 1939. But only around 200 TV sets were owned at this time

---

✳ **1895** The Lumière brothers open the world's first cinema in Paris, France.

✳ **1901** Italian radio pioneer Guglielmo Marconi transmits a radio signal across the Atlantic.

📖 **1903** Thomas Edison produces *The Great Train Robbery*, the first American commercial silent movie.

✳ **1920** The first radio news broadcast is made by Station 8MK in Detroit, Michigan.

✳ **1926** John Logie Baird gives the first practical demonstration of a television system in London, England.

📖 **1927** The first commercially successful talking film, *The Jazz Singer*, is released.

✳ **1928** Russian-born electronics pioneer Vladimir Zworykin patents the use of the cathode ray tube in televisions.

📖 **1935** *The Hit Parade* is aired for the first time on U.S. radio.

📖 **1938** Orson Welles's realistic radio production of a science-fiction story, *The War of the Worlds*, causes panic among American audiences.

♛ **1947** The Voice of America begins to transmit radio broadcasts into the Soviet Union.

♛ **1952** The first political advertisements appear on U.S. television during the presidential election contest between Dwight Eisenhower and Adlai Stevenson.

✳ **1952** The world's first pocket transistor radio is introduced.

✳ **1954** The first U.S. color television set goes on sale at a price of $1,175.

The Golden Age of Hollywood

In the early 1900s the home of the movie industry was New York, but by 1915 it had moved to Hollywood, whose clear California skies proved more suitable for filming than the uncertain climate of the East Coast. By the 1930s the cinema had outstripped all other forms of mass entertainment in popularity. In the anxious years of the Depression and World War II the world of the movies and the glamorous lifestyle of their stars offered audiences a heady mix of sophistication, passion, comedy, and swashbuckling adventure. The Hollywood studios at this time were making about 400 movies a year, watched by 90 million Americans a week. Hollywood's allure reached an early peak in 1939, the year in which two of the top-grossing films of all time, *The Wizard of Oz* and *Gone with the Wind* (right), reached the screens.

◀ A jubilant crowd in Washington D.C. holds up headlines proclaiming the end of World War I in 1918. News became a commodity with the spread of mass-circulation newspapers early in the 20th century.

worldwide, and television did not take off in a big way until the late 1940s and 1950s, when sets became cheaper, and programs such as *I Love Lucy* and *The Ed Sullivan Show* won large audiences nationwide.

News coverage was also radically affected by the new media. Advances in printing technology speeded up the flow of news to newspapers; but as the century went on, their monopoly on reporting current events fell, first to radio news broadcasts and then also to television and the Internet.

By the 1960s television was a major influence on American life. Broadcasts from Vietnam and images of the bodies of slain U.S. soldiers being brought home in body bags had a powerful effect in swinging public opinion against the war. More than 600 million people worldwide watched the first moon landing live on TV on July 20, 1969. From that time on world events, wherever they occurred, would be played out under the gaze of television cameras. A new age in global awareness had dawned.

⊕ **1962** Communications satellite *Telstar* relays the first live television transmissions around the world.

⊕ **1971** The first Internet e-mail is sent by computer engineer Ray Tomlinson.

⊕ **1989** Timothy Berners-Lee develops the worldwide web (–1991).

◀ Worldwide syndication turned some early TV personalities into international celebrities. Comedienne Lucille Ball became one of the world's best-known faces thanks to the global success of the sitcom *I Love Lucy* (left).

AMERICAS

✳ **1933** The Golden Gate Bridge is built in San Francisco Bay (–1937).

👑 **1933** Prohibition ends.

✳ **1934** After drought in the Midwest many farmers leave the "Dust Bowl."

👑 **1934** Lázaro Cárdenas becomes president of Mexico, introducing a program of social reform.

✳ **1935** Wallace Carothers develops nylon, a synthetic polymer, for Dupont; the first nylon product, a toothbrush, goes on sale in 1938.

👑 **1935** The Chaco War between Paraguay and Bolivia ends; the greater part of the disputed territory goes to Paraguay, but Bolivia gains access to the sea via the Paraguay River.

✳ **1936** The Hoover Dam is completed on the Colorado River.

EUROPE

👑 **1933** Adolf Hitler becomes chancellor of Germany; he assumes dictatorial powers and outlaws all political parties except the Nazi Party.

👑 **1934** Joseph Stalin eliminates political enemies in the Soviet Union; many are found guilty of invented crimes in "show trials" and shot, while millions more are deported to labor camps (gulags).

Adolf Hitler's Nazi Party came to power in Germany against a backdrop of economic breakdown and lingering bitterness over the nation's defeat in World War I. Although the party was voted in democratically, it rapidly set about outlawing democracy, taking all the reins of authority, both constitutional and judicial, into its own hands. Thereafter it based its actions on a racist ideology, an aggressive foreign policy at the expense of Germany's neighbors, and a totalitarian internal regime that subjected all citizens' individual interests to the greater good of the Nazi state.

AFRICA

👑 **1934** Libya is formed from the union of the two Italian colonies of Tripoli and Cyrenaica.

⚔ **1935** An Italian army invades Abyssinia (Ethiopia).

⚔ **1936** Emperor Haile Selassie goes into exile as Italy makes Abyssinia part of its African empire (–1941).

WESTERN ASIA

👑 **1934** Women win the right to vote in Turkey.

👑 **1935** Persia is renamed Iran.

👑 **1935** Mustafa Kemal is given the title Kemal Atatürk ("Father of the Turks") by the Turkish national assembly.

⚔ **1936** British occupation authorities limit future Jewish immigration to Palestine following violent clashes with Arabs (–1939).

SOUTH & CENTRAL ASIA

👑 **1933** Mahatma Gandhi goes on hunger strike for Indian independence.

👑 **1935** The British Parliament passes the Government of India Act, introducing elected provincial governments in India.

👑 **1936** The National Congress Party scores convincingly in the first elections held under the terms of the Government of India Act (–1937).

EAST ASIA & OCEANIA

A woodcut by Li Hua symbolizes the agony of the Chinese people subjected to invasion by Japan.

👑 **1933** Japan withdraws from the League of Nations.

✳ **1933** The Nissan Motor Company is founded in Tokyo, Japan.

👑 **1934** The Japanese install Puyi, the last emperor of China, as emperor of a newly created puppet state in Manchuria under the name of Kang De.

⊕ **1939** Albert Einstein writes to President Roosevelt suggesting the United States should study the feasibility of a program to develop the atomic bomb.

Originally called Boulder Dam, the Hoover Dam was renamed in 1947 for the president who ordered its construction.

⚔ **1936** The Spanish Civil War breaks out between right-wing forces led by General Francisco Franco and the leftist Popular Front government. It will end in victory for Franco's forces (–1939).

📖 **1937** Pablo Picasso paints *Guernica* to protest the bombing of the Basque town of that name in the Spanish Civil War.

⚔ **1938** German troops take over Austria (March) and the Sudetenland region of Czechoslovakia (September).

⊕ **1938** German physicists Otto Hahn, Lise Meitner, and Fritz Strassman create nuclear fission (–1939).

⚔ **1939** The first Nazi concentration camp is established at Dachau in Germany.

👑 **1939** (March) The Axis powers—Italy and Germany—sign a formal treaty of cooperation, the "Pact of Steel."

👑 **1939** (August) Hitler and Stalin sign the German–Soviet Nonaggression Pact.

⚔ **1939** (September) Germany invades Poland; Britain and France declare war on Germany, beginning World War II.

👑 **1936** In South Africa black citizens win the right to vote, but only for white politicians.

⊕ **1938** A live coelacanth is caught off South Africa. The fish had been thought extinct for 60 million years.

👑 **1937** Turkey, Iraq, Iran, and Afghanistan sign a nonaggression pact establishing the Oriental Entente.

⊕ **1938** Oil reserves are discovered in Saudi Arabia.

👑 **1938** Death of Kemal Atatürk.

👑 **1938** A meeting between Gandhi and Ali Jinnah, leader of the Muslim League, fails to settle growing differences between the leaders of the Congress Party and India's Muslims.

Muhammad Ali Jinnah, leader of India's Muslim League, addresses a party convention in New Delhi.

⚔ **1934** Chinese communists break out from their enclave at Jiangxi, where they have been surrounded by Chiang Kai-shek's Kuomintang nationalist forces, and undertake the Long March to Yan'an in Shaanxi Province, where they regroup (–1935).

👑 **1935** Mao Zedong becomes leader of the Chinese Communist Party.

👑 **1936** Japan signs the Anti-Comintern Pact with Germany against Soviet Russia.

⚔ **1937** Japan invades China, bombing the Kuomintang-held cities of Shanghai and Nanking, and killing thousands of civilians. The ensuing Sino-Japanese War will last for eight years (–1945).

👑 **1939** The Kingdom of Siam is renamed Thailand.

AMERICAS

EUROPE

AFRICA

WESTERN ASIA

SOUTH & CENTRAL ASIA

EAST ASIA & OCEANIA

1933–1939 A.D.

1940–1945 A.D.

AMERICAS

👑 **1941** At a secret meeting off the coast of Newfoundland President Roosevelt and British leader Winston Churchill set out the terms of the Atlantic Charter for the future of postwar Europe.

✳ **1942** A team led by Italian physicist Enrico Fermi sets off the first controlled, self-sustaining nuclear chain reaction at Stagg Field, University of Chicago.

👑 **1945** President Roosevelt dies in office less than six months after becoming the only U.S. president in history to be reelected to a fourth term.

EUROPE

✕ **1940** (April–June) Germany invades and occupies Denmark, Norway, the Netherlands, and France.

✕ **1940** (June) French General Charles de Gaulle escapes to England and founds the Free French movement.

✕ **1940** (September) German planes bomb England in the Blitz (–1942).

✕ **1941** Germany invades the Soviet Union; the Germans advance to Moscow by December but are forced back by the cold weather.

✕ **1942** The Nazis adopt the "final solution," a genocide campaign aimed at the total extermination of the Jews; mass deportations to the death camps follow.

A Star of David of the type all Jews over age six were forced to wear in Nazi-occpied territories.

✕ **1942** Defeat at Stalingrad, Russia, ends further German expansion in the east (–1943).

✕ **1943** (May) The Nazis suppress a Jewish uprising in the Warsaw ghetto in Poland.

✕ **1943** (June) Allied forces land in Italy.

✕ **1943** (July-August) The Battle of Kursk, the biggest tank battle in history, ends in a narrow victory for the Soviet army and leads to the collapse of the German offensive in Russia.

AFRICA

✕ **1940** An Italian attempt to invade Egypt from Libya is driven back by British and Australian forces.

✕ **1941** Italy surrenders its East African empire (Ethiopia, Eritrea, and Somaliland).

WESTERN ASIA

✕ **1941** A joint British–Soviet force invades and occupies Iran, which is sympathetic to Germany (–1942).

👑 **1943** Lebanon gains independence from France.

👑 **1945** The Arab League is founded with seven initial members; it aims to speak for all Arab nations.

SOUTH & CENTRAL ASIA

👑 **1940** The Muslim League, meeting at Lahore, demands that those regions in which Muslims are the majority population should become independent states within India.

✕ **1942** Japanese troops advancing through Burma (Myanmar) reach the border with India.

👑 **1943** Indian nationalist leader Subhas Chandra Bose, fighting against the British in Burma, announces the formation of a Provisional Government of Free India.

EAST ASIA & OCEANIA

✕ **1940** Japan occupies French Indochina, the Philippines, the Dutch East Indies, Malaya, and Singapore, which falls in February 1942.

✕ **1941** The Japanese navy launches a surprise attack on the U.S. fleet in Pearl Harbor, Hawaii.

The Japanese attack on Pearl Harbor on December 7, 1941, killed over 2,000 people and sank 29 ships.

✕ **1942** U.S. forces begin to make significant gains in the war against Japan after defeating the Japanese fleet at the Battle of Midway (June) and landing on Guadalcanal in the Solomon Islands (August).

👑 **1944** (July) Hideki Tojo resigns as prime minister of Japan as U.S. forces continues to make gains in the Pacific.

⊛ **1945** The first atomic bomb is detonated in the desert near Los Alamos, New Mexico, by scientists working on the Manhattan Project.

〰 **1945** Mass demonstrations on behalf of jailed populist Argentinian leader Juan Perón bring about his release and propel him into the presidency (in 1946).

〰 **1945** The United Nations charter, drawn up at the Dumbarton Oaks Conference in Washington, D.C., in 1944, is signed at the San Francisco Conference.

World War II saw the United States allied with the democratic nations of Western Europe and with the Soviet Union against Hitler's Germany, Mussolini's Italy, and the militarist government of Japan. In the west victory in North Africa in 1943 was followed by the liberation of Italy (1943–1944) and the post-D-Day drive through France into Germany (1944–1945). The war in the Pacific theater was marked by initial gains by Japan, whose forces were gradually driven back by troops such as the Marines shown planting the U.S. flag on Iwo Jima in February 1945 (right).

✕ **1944** On D-Day (June 6) Allied troops commanded by General Dwight D. Eisenhower land in Normandy, France, at the start of the campaign to liberate Europe.

✕ **1945** Hitler commits suicide as the Soviet Red Army approaches Berlin.

〰 **1945** Germany surrenders on May 7, ending the war in Europe; the next day, May 8, is celebrated as VE (Victory in Europe) Day.

✕ **1941** The German Afrika Korps regains land in North Africa until checked at El Alamein (1942).

✕ **1942** An Anglo–American force under General Dwight D. Eisenhower invades French North Africa.

✕ **1943** Axis resistance in North Africa comes to an end by mid-May.

✕ **1945** Jewish militant groups resume attacks against British military targets in Palestine.

〰 **1944** Gandhi launches the "Quit India" campaign, demanding Britain's immediate withdrawal; he is arrested and held in prison for two years.

〰 **1945** Britain releases Indian nationalist leaders from prison.

✕ **1944** (December) The Japanese use kamikaze pilots at the Battle of Leyte Gulf in the Philippines, the largest naval battle in history and a major U.S. victory.

✕ **1945** One month after atomic bombs are dropped on Hiroshima and Nagasaki, U.S. General Douglas MacArthur and Admiral Chester Nimitz accept the surrender of Japan on board USS *Missouri*.

The dropping of atomic bombs on the Japanese cities of Hiroshima and Nagasaki in August 1945 introduced a new era of mass destruction on a potentially devastating scale. The awesome power of the weapons raised the specter of widespread annihilation, fundamentally changing the nature of war.

AMERICAS

EUROPE

AFRICA

WESTERN ASIA

SOUTH & CENTRAL ASIA

EAST ASIA & OCEANIA

1940–1945 A.D.

AMERICAS

🔱 **1947** President Harry S. Truman commits the United States to support free peoples in the struggle against communist totalitarianism (the "Truman Doctrine"); immediate aid is given to Greece and Turkey.

🔱 **1947** Secretary of State George Marshall announces a plan to help Europe rebuild its war-shattered economies (the Marshall Plan).

Chuck Yeager pilots the record-breaking Bell X-1.

✳ **1947** Chuck Yeager becomes the first man to break the sound barrier, flying a Bell X-1.

EUROPE

🔱 **1946** Italy becomes a republic after a referendum decides in favor of abolishing the monarchy.

🔱 **1948** Britain's Labour Government introduces a free, tax-financed National Health Service.

🔱 **1949** Two separate states are formed in Germany: the democratic Federal Republic of Germany (West Germany) and the communist People's Republic of Germany (East Germany).

⚔ **1949** The civil war (since 1944) between communists and monarchists in Greece ends in victory for the monarchists.

✳ **1949** The Soviet Union tests its first atomic bomb.

AFRICA

🔱 **1948** The Afrikaner-dominated National Party wins power in South Africa.

🔱 **1949** The National Party introduces apartheid, separating white from black South Africans, who are deprived of democratic rights.

⚔ **1952** The Mau Mau uprising against British colonial rule in Kenya leads to a state of emergency (–1956).

WESTERN ASIA

On May 14, 1948, David Ben-Gurion proclaimed the creation of Israel (left). The Jewish state was bitterly opposed by Palestinian Arabs, who received military support from Syria, Jordan, Egypt, and Lebanon. Israel won the ensuing war, substantially enlarging its territory but creating an enduring refugee problem

🔱 **1946** Syria and Transjordan win independence, respectively, from France and Britain.

⚔ **1946** Jewish militants plant a bomb in the King David Hotel in Jerusalem, killing 91 people.

SOUTH & CENTRAL ASIA

🔱 **1946** Jawaharlal Nehru is elected leader of the Congress Party in India as independence talks resume.

⚔ **1946** Growing violence between Hindus and Muslims increases pressure on the British to create a separate Muslim state (Pakistan).

🔱 **1947** India and Pakistan separate. Violence mars partition; 14 million people move between the two countries, and at least half a million are killed en route.

EAST ASIA & OCEANIA

🔱 **1946** Women are given the vote in Japan.

🔱 **1946** The Republic of the Philippines is formally inaugurated as an independent nation.

✳ **1946** The United States begins nuclear weapons testing off Bikini Atoll in the Pacific Ocean.

🔱 **1946** Japan's new constitution transfers sovereignty from the emperor to the people.

🔱 **1948** Separate states are established in North and South Korea.

🔱 **1948** Hyperinflation in China weakens the Kuomintang government, boosting support for the nationalists' communist rivals.

🔱 **1949** The Netherlands recognizes the independence of Indonesia after a three-year war.

🔱 **1949** Chinese communist leader Mao Zedong declares the establishment of the People's Republic of China.

🔱 **1949** Chiang Kai-shek relocates China's Kuomintang government to the island of Taiwan (–1950).

⚔ **1950** The Korean War begins between the communist North, aided by Chinese forces, and the South, backed by a U.S.-led United Nations force (–1953).

♒ **1947** Congress's investigations into communist influence in the movie industry lead to the imprisonment of ten Hollywood screenwriters and directors who have refused to cooperate with the House Un-American Activities Committee.

♒ **1948** The Organization of American States is formed to promote regional peace and security.

♒ **1950** Senator Joseph McCarthy's claims of communist infiltration in the U.S. State Department start a wave of anticommunist hysteria.

♒ **1952** The United Nations Building is completed in New York City.

AMERICAS

♒ **1949** The North Atlantic Treaty Organization (NATO) is set up to defend Europe and North America from the threat of Soviet aggression.

♒ **1951** France, West Germany, Italy, the Netherlands, Belgium, and Luxembourg form the European Coal and Steel Community, the prototype of the European Union.

Nazi war criminals on trial at Nuremberg, Germany; 12 are sentenced to death in 1946.

EUROPE

♒ **1952** A group of army officers in Egypt overthrows the monarchy and establishes a republic.

♒ **1952** With UN approval Ethiopia takes over the neighboring state of Eritrea.

AFRICA

♒ **1947** The UN approves a plan to divide Palestine into a Jewish and an Arab state.

♒ **1948** The Jewish state of Israel declares itself an independent nation.

⚔ **1948** The first Arab–Israeli war leaves Israel with extended borders; more than 1 million Palestinians flee Israel in the aftermath of the war, while more than 250,000 Holocaust survivors arrive in Israel from Europe (–1949).

♒ **1949** Transjordan annexes the West Bank and renames itself the Hashemite Kingdom of Jordan.

WESTERN ASIA

⚔ **1948** Mahatma Gandhi is murdered by a Hindu extremist.

♒ **1948** Ceylon (Sri Lanka) wins independence from Britain.

⚔ **1948** India and Pakistan go to war over the frontier state of Kashmir (–1949).

⚔ **1950** Chinese troops invade Tibet.

SOUTH & CENTRAL ASIA

Mao Zedong, leader of China's communists, proclaims the birth of the People's Republic of China on October 1, 1949. Communists and nationalists had vied for power in China since the 1920s, although their contest was temporarily suspended during the Japanese occupation of the country from 1937 to 1945. When civil war broke out again following Japan's defeat in World War II, the communists unexpectedly prevailed, forcing Chiang Kai-shek's nationalist forces to seek refuge on the island of Taiwan.

♒ **1952** Japan officially regains its independence as the postwar U.S. occupation comes to an end.

✴ **1952** The United States explodes a hydrogen bomb at Eniwetok Atoll in the Pacific.

EAST ASIA & OCEANIA

1946–1952 A.D.

THE END OF EUROPE'S EMPIRES

A sailor joins Jamaicans celebrating their country's independence from Britain in the streets of the capital, Kingston, in August 1962.

AFTER 1945 THE COLONIAL POWERS *of Europe faced growing opposition to their rule. Nationalist pressures within the colonies to shed the old ties of empire won international backing from the United States and the United Nations, whose charter, adopted in 1945, recognized the right of all nations to choose their own government. The path to independence was violent and divisive for many countries, but by 1975 nearly all the former colonies of Asia, Africa, and the Caribbean had become fully self-governing.*

Between 1940 and 1945 most of the colonies in mainland and island Southeast Asia were occupied by Japan. At the end of the war European rubber planters, tea growers, traders, and administrators returned to their colonial possessions, expecting to pick up the threads of empire as they had been before the war. Instead, they encountered well-armed and organized nationalist movements, many of them communist inspired, that were determined to fight for self-rule. By 1949 the Dutch had been forced to abandon the Dutch East Indies, which became the independent nation of Indonesia. The French pulled

out of Vietnam and the rest of Indochina after a humiliating defeat at Dien Bien Phu in 1954, paving the way for a civil war between the communist north and noncommunist south of the country that escalated into the Vietnam War of the 1960s and 1970s. In Malaya British-backed forces became involved in a long struggle against the communists before the nation finally won independence in 1957.

Britain was the largest imperial power in 1945. Although it handed over control in southern Asia by 1948, granting independence to India, Pakistan, and Sri Lanka, it did not give up its colonies in other parts

▶ The decolonization process got under way in Asia at the end of World War II, notably with the granting of independence to India and Pakistan. By the 1950s the first African countries were also winning their freedom. The "wind of change," said by Britain's Prime Minister Harold Macmillan in 1960 to be sweeping the continent, subsequently became a gale: In the course of the decade more than 20 nations won the right to self-determination, leaving only a handful of territories still under colonial rule.

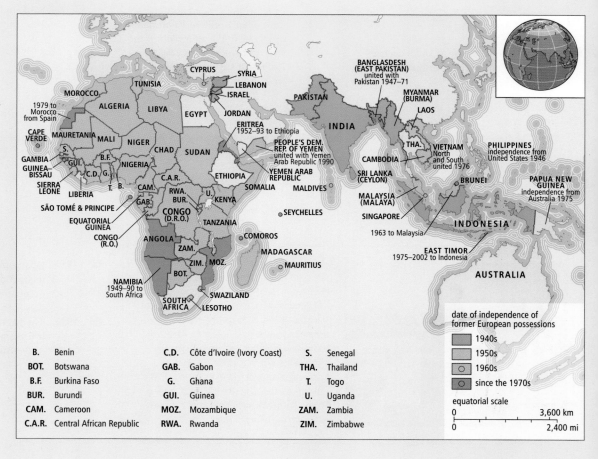

B.	Benin	C.D.	Côte d'Ivoire (Ivory Coast)	S.	Senegal
BOT.	Botswana	GAB.	Gabon	THA.	Thailand
B.F.	Burkina Faso	G.	Ghana	T.	Togo
BUR.	Burundi	GUI.	Guinea	U.	Uganda
CAM.	Cameroon	MOZ.	Mozambique	ZAM.	Zambia
C.A.R.	Central African Republic	RWA.	Rwanda	ZIM.	Zimbabwe

date of independence of former European possessions
- 1940s
- 1950s
- 1960s
- since the 1970s

equatorial scale
0 — 3,600 km
0 — 2,400 mi

of the world so readily. Yet by the late 1950s it was obvious that the days of empire were over. In the 20 years after 1957, 34 new independent nations were created in the former British colonies of West and East Africa, the Caribbean, and the Pacific. In most the transition to self-rule was relatively peaceful. But the white settler community of Southern Rhodesia refused to hand power to the black majority, starting a conflict that lasted until 1980, when the country finally gained independence as Zimbabwe.

In French Algeria nationalist forces determined on self-rule launched a bitterly fought insurgency that plunged the French government into crisis in the late 1950s. Algeria eventually won its independence in 1962. Long nationalist wars were also fought in the Portuguese colonies of Angola and Mozambique, and the years of civil strife that followed the independence of the two countries in 1975 left them among the world's poorest nations. They were not alone in their deprivation, however: Most of the new countries of Africa lacked infrastructure and investment, and in the years following independence much of the continent experienced internal violence, dictatorship, poverty, and mounting debt—the harsh legacy of a century or more of colonial exploitation.

The Agony of Partition

In British-ruled India the nationalist struggle, led by Mahatma Gandhi, was well advanced by the outbreak of World War II in 1939. The war delayed progress, but in 1945 the British government began to prepare for the handover of power. In August 1947 India became two separate independent states: India, which was predominantly Hindu, and Pakistan, mainly Muslim. The partition was accompanied by terrible violence. Between 12 and 14 million people were made homeless as Hindus living on the Pakistani side of the new frontier fled to India, and Muslims journeyed the other way. There were mass killings too; historians estimate that between 500,000 and 1 million people were massacred as sectarian hatred reached heights not witnessed before in the subcontinent.

🏛 **1946** French forces return to Indochina, newly liberated from Japanese control.

🏛 **1946** The Philippines become independent of the United States.

🏛 **1947** The independent states of India and Pakistan come into being.

🏛 **1948** Ceylon (Sri Lanka) and Burma (Myanmar) gain their independence from Britain.

🏛 **1951** Libya becomes the first colonial state in Africa to gain full independence.

✕ **1954** The French are defeated at the Battle of Dien Bien Phu in North Vietnam and withdraw from colonial rule in Indochina.

🏛 **1960** France's former colonies in Africa win independence, with the exception of Algeria.

🏛 **1962** Jamaica and Trinidad are the first British colonies in the Caribbean to gain full independence.

🏛 **1962** In Africa Algeria finally wins independence from France.

🏛 **1965** British settlers in Southern Rhodesia declare unilateral independence rather than accept black majority rule.

🏛 **1970** The British Pacific islands of Tonga and Fiji become independent.

🏛 **1975** Portugal withdraws from its colonies in Africa.

✕ **1976** Indonesia forcibly takes control of East Timor a year after its independence from Portugal.

🏛 **1980** Following a lengthy guerrilla war, the white government of Southern Rhodesia accepts majority rule, and the nation becomes legally independent as Zimbabwe.

🏛 **1990** Namibia (formerly Southwest Africa) is the last colony in Africa to gain independence.

◀ In comapny with his wife Winnie, Nelson Mandela celebrates his release from jail in 1990. Mandela, who had been imprisoned by the apartheid regime 27 years previously, subsequently negotiated an end to white-minority rule in South Africa and in 1994 became the country's first black president.

AMERICAS

1953 Dwight D. Eisenhower is inaugurated as U.S. president in succession to Harry S. Truman.

1953 Jonas Salk succeeds in developing a vaccine against polio.

1955 A military coup in Argentina deposes Juan Perón.

1955 In Montgomery, Alabama, Rosa Parks is arrested for violating race laws after refusing to give up her bus seat to a white man.

1956 Cuban revolutionary Fidel Castro launches a guerrilla campaign to overthrow the dictatorship of Fulgencio Batista.

1956 "In God We Trust" is adopted as the U.S. national motto.

EUROPE

1953 In Cambridge, England, James D. Watson of the United States and the English scientist Francis Crick announce the discovery of the chemical structure of DNA.

1953 On the death of Joseph Stalin Nikita Khrushchev becomes leader of the Soviet Union.

Francis Crick (right) and James D. Watson exhibit a partial model of a DNA molecule.

1955 The Allies end their postwar occupation of West Germany and Austria; West Germany joins NATO.

1955 The Soviet-dominated countries of Eastern Europe form the Warsaw Pact in opposition to NATO.

1956 The Soviet Union sends tanks into Hungary to put down an anticommunist uprising.

AFRICA

1954 Rebels organized by the F.L.N. (National Liberation Front) launch a war of independence against French rule in Algeria.

1956 Egypt's leader, Gamal Abdel Nasser, nationalizes the Suez Canal; in the ensuing Suez Crisis Britain and France send troops to Egypt, but international opinion forces them to withdraw.

1957 Ghana (formerly the Gold Coast) is the first British colony in Africa to gain independence.

1960 In Egypt construction starts on the Aswan High Dam (–1970).

1960 South African police fire on antiapartheid demonstrators in the black township of Sharpeville, killing 69 people.

WESTERN ASIA

1953 A CIA-backed coup in Iran deposes Mohammed Mossadegh's nationalist government and reinstates Reza Pahlavi as shah.

1956 During the Suez Crisis Israel invades the Sinai Peninsula.

1958 Iraq becomes a republic after the monarchy is overthrown in a military coup.

SOUTH & CENTRAL ASIA

1953 In the Himalayan Mountains New Zealander Edmund Hillary and Nepalese climber Tenzing Norgay complete the first successful ascent of the world's highest peak, Mount Everest.

1956 Pakistan becomes the first Islamic republic.

1958 Ayub Khan establishes a military dictatorship in Pakistan.

1958 The army takes power in Burma (Myanmar), independent from Britain since 1948.

1959 Ceylon's prime minister, Solomon Bandaranaike, is assassinated.

EAST ASIA & OCEANIA

1953 The Korean War ends; North and South Korea remain divided along the ceasefire line of the 38th parallel.

1954 Vietnam is divided between communist North Vietnam, ruled from Hanoi, and the noncommunist South, with its capital at Saigon.

1955 A meeting of newly independent African and Asian states at Bandung, Indonesia, commits itself to anticolonialism and neutrality between East and West.

👑 **1957** The governor of Arkansas calls out the National Guard to prevent black students from enrolling in high school in Little Rock.

⚙ **1958** The National Aeronautics and Space Administration (NASA) is created to lead the U.S. government's space program.

⚔ **1959** Fidel Castro overthrows the Batista dictatorship and turns Cuba into a socialist state.

⚙ **1960** The U.S. Food and Drug Administration approves the sale of a birth-control pill.

AMERICAS

👑 **1957** The European Economic Community (EEC), later the European Union (EU), is created by the Treaty of Rome.

⚙ **1957** The Soviet Union launches Sputnik I, the first artificial satellite; the Space Race begins.

👑 **1958** Summoned back to power from retirement, General de Gaulle founds France's Fifth Republic.

The European Economic Community brought together nations that had been bitter rivals in the past and created the framework for a peaceful future. It had its roots in the European Coal and Steel Community, founded in 1951. At first there were just six members—West Germany, France, Italy, Belgium, the Netherlands, and Luxembourg. The organization, which changed its name to the European Community in 1967 and to the European Union in 1993, had 12 members by 1986 (see flag, left) and 25 following a further round of enlargement in 2004.

EUROPE

The war waged from 1954 to 1962 against the French authorities in Algeria was the bloodiest of all the anticolonial struggles of the decades after World War II. Algerian nationalist demands for independence were bitterly resisted by long-established French settlers and the army. Summoned from retirement to address the crisis, France's wartime hero General de Gaulle finally negotiated a settlement that, following a 1962 referendum, created an independent Algeria.

⚔ **1960** The province of Katanga attempts to break away from the newly independent Republic of Congo, starting a bitter civil war.

👑 **1960** The independent state of Somalia is created from the former colonies of British and Italian Somaliland.

Completed in 1970, the Aswan High Dam brought Egypt's annual Nile flood under human control.

👑 **1958** Syria and Egypt form the United Arab Republic (–1961).

👑 **1960** Nazi fugitive Adolf Eichmann is captured by Israeli agents and flown to Israel to stand trial for wartime atrocities against Jews.

AFRICA

WESTERN ASIA

👑 **1959** Fleeing Chinese communist rule, the Dalai Lama, the spiritual and political leader of Tibet, seeks asylum in India, where he establishes a government in exile.

👑 **1960** Sirimavo Bandaranaike, widow of the assassinated prime minister of Ceylon (Sri Lanka), becomes the world's first elected female head of government.

SOUTH & CENTRAL ASIA

👑 **1958** In China Mao Zedong initiates the Great Leap Forward—a three-year plan for accelerated economic development that ends in disaster following bad harvests.

⚔ **1959** Communist troops begin to infiltrate South Vietnam along the Ho Chi Minh Trail—a concealed forest route from North Vietnam.

⚙ **1959** An international treaty recognizes Antarctica as a scientific preserve and bans military activity there.

EAST ASIA & OCEANIA

1953–1960 A.D.

THE COLD WAR

▲ A communist-era poster solicits volunteers for the Red Army. At the end of World War II the armed forces of the Soviet Union were the largest in the world, with some 5 million soldiers under arms.

IN 1947, WHEN COMMUNISM WAS ON THE ADVANCE *in Europe and Asia, President Harry S. Truman pledged U.S. support for the free peoples of the world resisting subjugation by another power. The U.S. policy of containment embodied in the Truman Doctrine lay at the heart of the Cold War, the period of hostility between the United States and the Soviet Union and their respective allies that dominated international politics in the latter half of the 20th century.*

The Berlin Wall

At the end of World War II Berlin lay within the Soviet-occupied zone of Germany, but the city itself was divided into four sectors. East Berlin was controlled by the Soviets and West Berlin by three of the other wartime Allies—the United States, Britain, and France. Access between East and West Berlin was sealed off after communism was imposed in East Germany, but a steady stream of refugees found their way surreptitiously to the western sector. It was a dangerous and desperate measure; people caught fleeing were shot on sight. From August 1961 the East Germans closed off the escape routes altogether by building a barrier of concrete and barbed wire that ran through the heart of the city. The Berlin Wall remained the most powerful symbol of the Cold War era until November 1989, when the East German government suddenly opened its borders to the west. A jubilant crowd attacked the hated wall with pickaxes and crowbars, and it came down almost overnight.

1946 British Premier Winston Churchill uses the phrase "Iron Curtain" in a speech at Fulton, Missouri.

1947 The governments of Eastern Europe (Poland, Czechoslovakia, Hungary, Romania, and Bulgaria) come under growing Soviet influence.

1948 The Soviets blockade West Berlin in an attempt to expel the other Allied Powers; only a huge airlift of supplies from the West saves West Berlin from starvation (–1949).

1955 West Germany joins NATO; the Warsaw Pact is formed.

1960 Soviet missiles shoot down a U.S. U2 spy plane flying over the USSR; the pilot, Gary Powers, is captured and tried for espionage.

1962 In the Cuban Missile Crisis the world faces the threat of nuclear war until the Soviet Union withdraws its missiles from Cuba.

1972 U.S. President Richard M. Nixon and Soviet Premier Leonid Brezhnev sign the first Strategic Arms Limitation Treaty between the United States and the Soviet Union.

1975 At Helsinki, Finland, the Soviet Union promises to respect human rights in return for Western recognition of postwar boundaries in Eastern Europe.

1979 The Soviet invasion of Afghanistan worsens relations with the West; the United States boycotts the Moscow Olympic Games the following year.

1983 President Reagan announces the Strategic Defensive Initiative (the "Star Wars" program) to develop a defensive shield against incoming nuclear missiles.

1985 Mikhail Gorbachev comes to power in the Soviet Union, inaugurating a new policy of *glasnost* (openness) and *perestroika* (reconstruction).

1987 The United States and Soviet Union agree to limit intermediate nuclear weapons.

1989 The Berlin Wall comes down.

1991 The collapse of the Soviet regime in Russia marks the end of the Cold War.

The Soviet Union suffered terrible losses in World War II, and in the wake of Germany's eventual defeat its leader, Joseph Stalin, determined to create a buffer zone against future invasion from the west. He sought to do so by imposing one-party communist rule in the countries Soviet forces had liberated in Eastern Europe. Stalin went on to close the borders of the Soviet-zone nations, erecting what came to be known symbolically as the Iron Curtain. The creation of a communist state in the eastern half of Germany in 1949 was stark confirmation of a Soviet-dominated bloc in Eastern Europe. In the same year the Soviet Union first developed an atomic bomb.

To counter the growing threat of Soviet aggression, the United States and Western powers formed the North Atlantic Treaty Organization (NATO). When democratic West Germany joined NATO in 1955, the Soviet Union responded by setting up the Warsaw Pact, a military alliance of Soviet-dominated states. The Soviet Union also gave military and financial backing to many of the independence movements active around the world at the time in order to build up a sphere of influence to challenge that of the United States.

Over the next decades the superpowers stockpiled more and more nuclear weapons. By the 1960s each had enough to annihilate the other several times over,

a situation known as "mutually assured destruction," or MAD. The Cold War came closest to turning hot in 1962, when Soviet missiles were installed in Cuba, on America's doorstep. President Kennedy ordered their removal. For a time the world seemed poised on the brink of nuclear war until a U.S. naval blockade forced the Soviets to back down. The incident alarmed both sides enough for the two to agree to halt further nuclear tests. In 1969, in a further effort to reduce international tension, talks to limit strategic arms got under way. But relations between the two superpowers, blowing sometimes warm, sometimes cold, continued to dominate international politics throughout the 1970s and 1980s.

Eventually the economic dynamism of the United States decisively tipped the balance of power. While the Soviet economies stagnated in corruption and inefficiency, American prosperity went from strength to strength. Soviet planners came to realize that they could not match U.S. expenditures on defense or on technological advancement, and that a radical change of course was necessary. Their first hesitant steps to open up Soviet society unleashed a pent-up wave of dissent in the oppressed nations of the Soviet bloc. The sudden collapse of communism in Eastern Europe in 1989 finally sounded the deathknell of the old Soviet system and brought the Cold War to a close.

▲ U.S. President Ronald Reagan meets Soviet Premier Mikhail Gorbachev at a summit meeting in 1985. The pair oversaw a time of détente, or a thaw in relations, as the Cold War finally wound down.

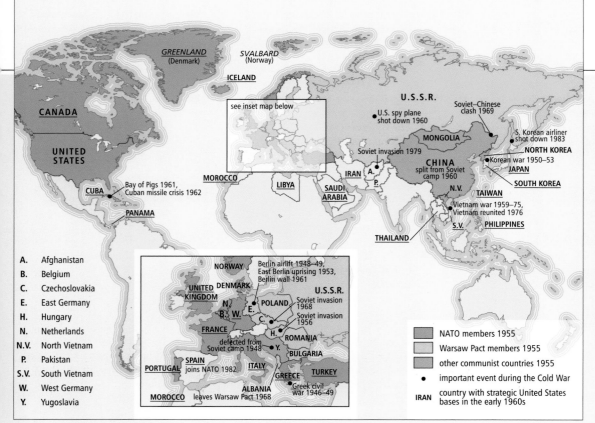

◀ The Cold War divided much of Europe and Asia into two hostile camps—on the one hand, the democratic nations allied in the North Atlantic Treaty Organization (NATO), and on the other, the Soviet-bloc members of the Warsaw Pact. The situation was complicated by the presence of communist powers that were hostile to the Soviet Union, notably China, Mongolia, and Yugoslavia, all of which were fearful of Russian dominance.

1961–1967 A.D.

AMERICAS

1961 John F. Kennedy is inaugurated as the 35th U.S. president.

1961 The U.S.-backed Bay of Pigs invasion of Cuba ends in failure.

1961 Freedom Riders challenging segregation laws on interstate transport are attacked by angry mobs in Alabama and Mississippi.

1963 Martin Luther King delivers his "I have a dream" speech at the Lincoln Memorial during a civil rights march on Washington, D.C.

1963 President John F. Kennedy is assassinated in Dallas, Texas, and is succeeded by Vice President Lyndon B. Johnson.

1964 The Civil Rights Act opposing racial discrimination goes into law in the United States.

1965 Militant black leader Malcolm X is assassinated in New York City.

President Kennedy in Dallas shortly before his assassination.

EUROPE

1961 Soviet cosmonaut Yuri Gagarin becomes the first man in space.

1961 Russian ballet star Rudolf Nureyev requests asylum in France while performing with the Kirov Ballet.

1961 The nonaligned movement comes into being at a conference in Belgrade, Yugoslavia, hosted by President Tito.

1963 During a visit to Berlin U.S. President Kennedy emphasizes his support for the people of West Berlin, stating, "*Ich bin ein Berliner*" ("I am a citizen of Berlin").

AFRICA

1961 UN Secretary–General Dag Hammarskjöld is killed in an air crash while on a peace mission to Katanga, a secessionist region of the Congo.

1961 Independence wars begin in the Portuguese colonies of Angola and Mozambique.

1962 Algeria gains independence from France, with Ben Bella as its first prime minister (later president).

1963 The Organization of African Unity (OAU) is established in Addis Ababa, Ethiopia.

1964 Nelson Mandela is sentenced to life imprisonment in South Africa for sabotage and treason.

WESTERN ASIA

1961 In Israel former Nazi leader Adolf Eichmann is sentenced to death for crimes against humanity; he is hanged the following year.

1961 Kuwait becomes independent.

1964 The Palestine Liberation Organization (PLO) is founded.

1964 The Islamic cleric Ayatollah Khomeini is exiled from Iran for his criticism of the shah.

SOUTH & CENTRAL ASIA

1961 The Portuguese colony of Goa is united with the state of India.

1962 Chinese troops occupy the Aksai Chin region of Kashmir, provoking hostilities with India.

1962 General Ne Win seizes power in Burma (Myanmar) and imposes military rule.

1964 Jawaharlal Nehru, prime minister of India since independence, dies in office.

1965 Hindi becomes the official language of India.

1965 India and Pakistan go to war for a second time over Kashmir.

EAST ASIA & OCEANIA

1962 U.S. military advisers are sent to assist the South Vietnam government in its struggle against communist North Vietnam.

1963 China publicly criticizes the Soviet Union as a diplomatic rift opens up between the two principal communist powers.

1963 The Federation of Malaysia is set up, incorporating Malaya, North Borneo, Sabah, and Sarawak.

☗ **1967** Guerrilla leader Che Guevara is captured and killed in Bolivia.

☗ **1967** During a visit to Montreal, Canada, French President Charles de Gaulle declares his support for Quebec independence.

☗ **1967** Tens of thousands march in Washington, D.C., to protest the Vietnam War.

The civil rights movement of the early 1960s transformed the face of the United States. Demonstrators led by figures like Martin Luther King (seen center, left, leading a protest march in Washington in 1963) fought to end segregation in the Deep South and to fight discrimination throughout the nation. The drive for equal rights culminated in the Civil Rights Act of 1964 and the Voting Rights Act of 1965, which together gave federal agencies extra powers to enforce equal treatment of the races.

AMERICAS

☗ **1964** Premier Nikita Khrushchev is ousted from power in the Soviet Union.

☗ **1966** France withdraws from NATO.

⊛ **1967** British astronomers Antony Hewish and Jocelyn Bell discover pulsars.

EUROPE

☗ **1966** Kwame Nkrumah, first prime minister of Ghana, is overthrown while on a visit to Beijing.

☗ **1966** President Hendrik Verwoerd, a principal architect of apartheid, is assassinated in South Africa.

⚔ **1967** Civil war splits Nigeria when the eastern province of Biafra attempts to break away (–1970).

⊛ **1967** South African surgeon Christiaan Barnard carries out the first human heart-transplant operation.

A soldier on service in the Biafran War.

AFRICA

⚔ **1967** Israel defeats its Arab neighbors in the Six-Day War, occupying the West Bank, Gaza Strip, Sinai Peninsula, and Golan Heights.

WESTERN ASIA

Indira Gandhi was part of a political dynasty: Both her father and her son Rajiv served, as she did, as India's prime minister. She served two terms in office before she was killed in 1984 by members of her Sikh bodyguard, angry that she had sent troops into the Golden Temple of Amritsar.

☗ **1966** Indira Gandhi, the daughter of India's first prime minister Jawaharlal Nehru, is herself elected prime minister.

SOUTH & CENTRAL ASIA

⚔ **1964** An alleged torpedo attack on two U.S. destroyers in the Gulf of Tonkin leads to U.S. entry into the Vietnam conflict.

⚔ **1965** The war in Vietnam escalates as U.S. bombing of North Vietnam begins.

☗ **1965** Singapore declares its independence from Malaysia.

☗ **1966** Mao Zedong launches the Cultural Revolution in China (–1968).

⊛ **1967** China explodes its first hydrogen bomb.

EAST ASIA & OCEANIA

1961–1967 A.D.

1968–1974 A.D.

AMERICAS

🜲 **1968** U.S. civil rights leader Martin Luther King is assassinated.

🜲 **1968** Democratic presidential hopeful Robert Kennedy, brother of murdered President John F. Kennedy, is shot dead after a campaign rally in Los Angeles.

✵ **1969** Astronauts Neil Armstrong and Buzz Aldrin of the Apollo 11 mission become the first men to walk on the surface of the moon.

✵ **1970** The Boeing 747, the world's first wide-bodied airliner, enters service across the Atlantic.

🜲 **1970** As opposition to the Vietnam War gains momentum in the United States, four student protestors are shot dead by the National Guard on the campus of Kent State University, Ohio.

EUROPE

🜲 **1968** Student unrest spreads across Europe, protesting the Vietnam War and local grievances; students' and workers' strikes almost topple the French government.

🜲 **1968** Alexander Dubcek's Czech government institutes the Prague Spring of liberal reforms, quickly crushed by Warsaw Pact troops.

✵ **1969** The Anglo-French Concorde supersonic airliner makes its maiden flight.

✕ **1969** In Northern Ireland violence between the majority Protestant community and demonstrators demanding enhanced civil rights for the Catholic minority sparks a 30-year period of "Troubles."

🜲 **1970** Riots in Poland force the resignation of Communist Party head Wladyslaw Gomulka.

🜲 **1971** Women win the right to vote in Switzerland, the last European country to introduce universal suffrage.

AFRICA

🜲 **1969** Colonel Muammar al-Gadhafi overthrows the monarchy and proclaims himself Libya's leader.

✕ **1970** Biafra surrenders to Nigerian forces, giving up its three-year struggle for independence.

🜲 **1971** President Mobutu renames the Congo Zaire.

WESTERN ASIA

✕ **1970** Civil war breaks out in Jordan when King Hussain expels guerrillas of the Palestine Liberation Organization, based in the country since their defeat by Israel in the 1967 Six Days' War.

✕ **1972** Three militants of the Japanese Red Army Faction carry out a machine-gun and grenade attack on the concourse of Lod Airport, Israel, killing 24 people.

✕ **1973** Egyptian, Syrian, Iraqi, and Jordanian forces launch a surprise attack on Israel while it celebrates the Yom Kippur religious festival; after initial setbacks the Israelis repel the invading armies.

SOUTH & CENTRAL ASIA

✕ **1971** East Pakistan rebels against being united with West Pakistan, 1,000 miles (1,600 km) away. East Pakistan wins independence as Bangladesh (−1972).

EAST ASIA & OCEANIA

The Vietnam War grew out of a civil conflict between the two halves of Vietnam established after the French withdrawal in 1954. Guerrillas from the communist North sought to subvert noncommunist South Vietnam, leading to the large-scale intervention of U.S. forces from 1964 on. Some 56,000 U.S. soldiers and 3 million Vietnamese died before the last troops were withdrawn in 1973. Two years later North Vietnamese forces entered the Southern capital of Saigon, reuniting the country under communist rule.

✕ **1973** With CIA help right-wing military forces under General Augusto Pinochet overthrow the elected Marxist regime in Chile; its leader, Salvador Allende, commits suicide.

👑 **1973** The former dictator of Argentina, Juan Perón, returns after 18 years in exile. Aged 77, he resumes the presidency as head of the Justicialista Party but dies the following year; his second wife, Isabel, will succeed him in power.

👑 **1974** U.S. President Richard M. Nixon resigns under threat of impeachment for authorizing illegal bugging of his political opponents at the Watergate complex in Washington, D.C.

AMERICAS

✕ **1972** At the Munich Olympics in Germany Palestinian terrorists from the Black September group kill two Israeli athletes and take nine others hostage; a bungled police rescue attempt results in their deaths.

The Concorde supersonic jet airliner remained in service until 2004.

👑 **1973** Britain, Denmark, and Ireland join the European Economic Community, increasing the membership from six to nine countries.

👑 **1974** A bloodless military coup in Portugal, led by General Antonio de Spinola, brings more than 40 years of dictatorship to an end.

EUROPE

👑 **1971** Idi Amin seizes power in Uganda, establishing one of Africa's most brutal dictatorships (–1979).

👑 **1974** President Habib Bourguiba of Tunisia is declared president for life.

👑 **1974** Ethiopia's long-term Emperor Haile Selassie I is deposed in a communist-led military coup.

AFRICA

👑 **1973** An international oil crisis takes hold as Arab oil producers curtail supplies to Western nations that supported Israel in the Yom Kippur War; the price of crude oil increases fourfold (–1974).

✕ **1974** To forestall a move by Greek Cypriots toward union (*enosis*) with Greece, Turkish troops invade northern Cyprus (mainly inhabited by Turkish Cypriots) and partition the island.

👑 **1974** The Arab League recognizes the PLO as the representsative body of the Palestinian people; PLO chairman Yasser Arafat addresses the UN General Assembly.

WESTERN ASIA

👑 **1972** Independent since 1948, Ceylon becomes a republic and changes its name to Sri Lanka.

👑 **1974** Floods and a devastating famine grip the fledgling state of Bangladesh, claiming hundreds of thousands of lives.

⊕ **1974** India announces that it has successfully tested its first atomic bomb, becoming the sixth nation to join the "nuclear club."

SOUTH & CENTRAL ASIA

✕ **1968** Vietcong insurgents launch the Tet offensive against South Vietnam, almost capturing the capital, Saigon, before being driven back.

👑 **1970** Fiji and Tonga win independence within the British Commonwealth.

👑 **1972** The South Pacific Forum is established to promote regional cooperation.

U.S. President Nixon visits the Great Wall of China.

✕ **1972** The United States begins unilateral withdrawal of its troops from Vietnam under President Nixon's "Peace with Honor" disengagement plan.

👑 **1972** President Nixon flies to Beijing to meet Premier Zhou Enlai, beginning a new era of rapprochement between the United States and communist China.

EAST ASIA & OCEANIA

FIRST STEPS IN SPACE

▲ U.S. astronaut Buzz Aldrin steps onto the moon's surface on July 21, 1969. Neil Armstrong, his companion in the Apollo 11 lunar module, had preceded him a few minutes earlier, making the two the first humans to set foot on the moon.

THE IDEA OF VENTURING BEYOND THE BOUNDS *of Earth has long fired peoples' imaginations. The French writer Jules Verne described a fictional voyage to the moon as early as 1865, while England's H.G. Wells published* The War of the Worlds *in 1898. But science fiction became scientific fact in the late 1950s, as the United States and the Soviet Union competed against one another to take the lead in probing beyond the Earth's atmosphere. Within decades numerous missions had investigated most of the planets of the solar system, and some had traveled far beyond into deep space.*

Using the expertise of former German scientists who had developed sophisticated rocketry during World War II, the emerging superpowers built ever more powerful rockets, initially as ICBMs (intercontinental ballitic missiles) to carry their nuclear warheads and then from the late 1950s onward as space launch vehicles. The "Space Race" got under way in earnest in 1957 when, to the alarm of U.S. policymakers, the Soviet Union put the small Sputnik 1 satellite into orbit. Four years later the Russians scored another notable first by sending the first man into space.

American tethered "walks" outside space capsules caught the public attention in the mid-1960s, but the United States' long-term ambition announced by President John F. Kennedy was to put the first man on the moon. This goal was realized on July 20, 1969, by the Apollo 11 mission—an event watched live on television by millions of people around the globe. In all, ten U.S. astronauts walked on the moon before the Apollo program was abandoned in 1972. Meanwhile the Soviet Union concentrated its efforts on unmanned probes to Venus.

In the 1970s and 1980s both countries constructed space stations: The Soviet Salyut 1 was launched in 1971 and America's Skylab two years later. Salyut was replaced by the larger Mir, which had a permanent crew, in 1986. By then a new era of space exploration had begun when in 1981 the United States embarked

---

❋ **1903** Russian physicist Konstantin Tsiolkovsky publishes *A Rocket into Cosmic Space*, in which he produces designs for multistage rockets and predicts exploration of the solar system.

❋ **1919** In *A Method of Reaching Extreme Altitudes* U.S. rocket pioneer Robert Goddard describes a project for a space probe to the moon.

✕ **1944** Scientists in Nazi Germany led by Wernher Von Braun develop the V2 rocket as a long-range weapon against the Allies.

❋ **1957** The world's first satellite, the 185-lb (84-kg) Sputnik 1, is launched by the Soviet Union; it orbits the Earth for 57 days, transmitting a radio signal.

❋ **1958** After several launch failures the first successful U.S. space probe is Explorer I, which discovers the Van Allen radiation belts around the Earth.

♛ **1961** U.S. President John F. Kennedy announces his country's intention of landing a man on the moon before the end of the decade.

❋ **1961** The first man in space is Soviet cosmonaut Yuri Gagarin, who makes a single orbit of the Earth in Vostok 1 before a successful reentry.

❋ **1962** Astronaut John Glenn becomes the first American in space, piloting his Friendship 7 capsule around the Earth.

❋ **1962** The U.S. Telstar 1, the first active communications satellite, goes operational, transmitting TV signals and telephone messages.

▲ Soviet cosmonaut Yuri Gagarin became the first space traveler when his craft Vostok I circled the Earth 188 miles (302 km) up in 1961.

❋ **1963** The Soviet Vostok 6 mission puts the first woman into space, cosmonaut Valentina Tereshkova.

❋ **1969** The Apollo 11 lunar module lands on the surface of the moon on July 21. Neil Armstrong and Buzz Aldrin become the first humans to set foot on extraterrestrial terrain.

on the space shuttle program, deploying reusable launch vehicles. The most notable shuttle mission took place in 1990 to launch the Hubble Space Telescope, which has provided clear images of distant galaxies. In addition, several deep space probes set off on long-term missions; almost 30 years after its launch Pioneer 10 was over 7 billion miles distant when it reestablished contact with Earth in 2001.

Heavy military and commercial funding sustained the huge cost of programs in the heyday of space exploration. One ambitious but ultimately unsuccessful venture was the U.S. plan known as the Strategic Defense Initiative (popularly called "Star Wars"), which sought to position laser-equipped satellites in space to target and destroy incoming nuclear missiles. The end of the Cold War saw state support for space programs greatly diminish, even though spy satellites continued to play an essential role in military surveillance. Yet pioneering work continues to be undertaken, and numerous satellites have been launched by the United States and Russia (and lately by China and the European Space Agency) to monitor weather, survey Earth's mineral resources, and further telecommunications.

◀ The Earth as seen from the space shuttle *Columbia* on a 1995 mission. Such images provided a new perspective on the planet, emphasizing its fragility as an island of life in space.

⊛ **1972** The final moon mission takes place when Apollo 17 takes off from Cape Kennedy.

⊛ **1981** The first reusable spacecraft, NASA's *Columbia* space shuttle, is launched.

⊛ **1983** The Pioneer 10 space probe (launched in 1972) becomes the first spacecraft to leave Earth's solar system, journeying on into deep space.

⊛ **1986** The space shuttle *Challenger* explodes shortly after blastoff, killing all seven astronauts aboard.

⊛ **2003** The *Columbia* space shuttle breaks up on reentry over Texas, and all its crew perish.

The Saturn V Rocket

One key to the success of the U.S. Apollo program was the power and reliability of the rocketry employed. The largest operational launch vehicle ever built, the Saturn V rocket was developed by a team led by the German scientist Wernher Von Braun. Standing 363 feet (110 m) tall (60 ft/18m higher than the Statue of Liberty), these huge, three-stage rockets were equipped with five engines on each of their first two stages, generating some 7.5 million lb (3.4 million kg) of thrust. Only with such power at its disposal—used for a total of just 20 minutes—was NASA able to launch the heavy lunar module payloads beyond Earth's gravitational pull. A comparable Soviet rocket was a failure, and their moon program was abandoned. In all, 13 Saturn V rockets were launched without mishap. The enormous Vertical Assembly Building in which the stages were put together, one of the world's largest, still stands at Kennedy Space Center, Florida.

1975–1981 A.D.

AMERICAS

1976 Democratic candidate Jimmy Carter is elected 39th U.S. president.

1976 In Argentina a bloodless coup topples Juan Perón's widow Isabel from power and brings in martial law.

1978 In Jonestown, Guyana, 914 members of a religious cult run by the Reverend Jim Jones (including 260 children) commit suicide by taking poison.

1979 The United States experiences its worst nuclear accident to date when a reactor core at the Three Mile Island plant in Pennsylvania comes close to meltdown.

EUROPE

1975 General Francisco Franco, dictator of Spain since 1939, dies. The monarchy is restored under his chosen successor, Juan Carlos, grandson of Spain's last king, who sets about reintroducing democratic politics.

1977 Czech dissidents found the prodemocracy Charter 77 reform movement, one of the first organizations to openly challenge communist authority.

Members of the Solidarity union demonstrate in Warsaw.

AFRICA

1975 Portugal grants its African colonies of Angola and Mozambique independence; civil war immediately breaks out in Angola.

1976 King Hassan II of Morocco invades the Western Sahara. His troops are opposed by Polisario Front guerrillas supported by Algeria (–1992).

1976 Protests against the apartheid South African regime break out in the black township of Soweto, near Johannesburg; police kill 176 demonstrators.

WESTERN ASIA

1975 Civil war breaks out in Lebanon between Christian Falangist militias and Muslim forces supported by PLO guerrillas (–1991).

1978 Israeli forces intervene in the Lebanese civil war, bombarding the ports of Tyre and Sidon; a UN peacekeeping force is established in southern Lebanon to prevent insurgency against Israel.

1979 Egypt and Israel conclude the Camp David accord, a peace deal that brings an Israeli withdrawl from the Sinai Peninsula and promises autonomy to the Palestinian occupants of the West Bank.

SOUTH & CENTRAL ASIA

1975 Mujibur Rahman, Bangladesh's premier since independence, is deposed and murdered in a coup.

1975 India undergoes a crisis when a court calls for the resignation of premier Indira Gandhi; rejecting the demand, she assumes repressive special powers.

1977 A coalition of opposition parties led by Moraji Desai defeats Indira Gandhi's Congress Party in the Indian elections.

1979 Amid growing civil unrest and economic instability Shah Reza Pahlavi, who has ruled Iran since 1941, is forced to step down; the Muslim religious leader Ayatollah Ruhollah Khomeini returns from exile to set up an Islamic state.

EAST ASIA & OCEANIA

Pol Pot's Khmer Rouge regime launched a ruthless campaign of agrarian socialism in Cambodia (renamed Democratic Kampuchea). Most of the urban population was resettled in rural forced-labor camps. People whose loyalty was suspect—in practice, much of the middle class—were ruthlessly exterminated in unmarked killing fields (left). One-fifth of the population may have died in this way.

1975 North Vietnamese troops enter the South Vietnamese capital of Saigon, reuniting the country under communist rule.

1975 The Khmer Rouge gain control of Cambodia, launching a purge of the professional class that will kill between one and three million people (–1978).

👑 **1979** Nicaraguan dictator Anastasio Somoza is overthrown after a sustained guerrilla campaign by left-wing Sandinista rebels.

👑 **1980** Former Hollywood actor Ronald Reagan defeats Jimmy Carter in the race for the White House; Carter's reelection chances are seriously damaged by the disastrous failure of a mission to rescue U.S. hostages held in Iran.

⊛ **1981** The space shuttle *Columbia* embarks on its maiden mission from Cape Kennedy, Florida.

⊛ **1981** The first cases of AIDS (acquired immune deficiency syndrome) are diagnosed in the United States.

👑 **1979** Margaret Thatcher leads the Conservative Party to electoral victory, becoming Britain's first woman prime minister (–1990).

👑 **1980** President Tito of Yugoslavia dies.

👑 **1980** Polish workers led by Lech Walesa establish the independent Solidarity trade union; the organization will play a pioneering role in the downfall of communism in Eastern Europe.

👑 **1981** John Paul II (pope since 1978) is seriously injured by a gunman in St. Peter's Square, Rome.

✕ **1977** War breaks out between Somalia and Ethiopia over the disputed Ogaden region; Ethiopia, with Cuban and Russian aid, overruns the region the following year.

👑 **1979** Uganda's dictator Idi Amin is driven into exile.

👑 **1980** Zimbabwe gains its independence under Robert Mugabe.

👑 **1981** President Anwar el-Sadat of Egypt is assassinated by Islamic extremists opposed to the Camp David peace accord with Israel.

👑 **1980** A military coup suspends democracy in Turkey.

✕ **1980** The Iran–Iraq War develops from a border dispute between the two nations; it will last for eight years and costs over a million lives.

✕ **1981** Iraq's attempt to acquire nuclear power is thwarted when Israeli warplanes destroy a reactor under construction at Osirak.

The Iranian Revolution of 1979 marked an important swing against westernization in the Islamic world. Muhammad Reza Pahlavi, who had ruled Iran with U.S. support since 1941, was forced into exile in favor of Ayatollah Ruhollah Khomeini, a radical Shiite scholar who had earlier been exiled by the shah. Under Khomeini's influence the new regime introduced strict Islamic law and favored Muslim tradition over modernization.

👑 **1979** Radical Iranian students overrun the U.S. embassy in Tehran, taking 66 staff hostage and demanding the shah's extradition from the United States.

✕ **1979** Soviet forces invade Afghanistan; they will become bogged down in a nine-year guerrilla war.

✕ **1975** Following the collapse of Portuguese colonial rule, East Timor declares independence but is quickly invaded by neighboring Indonesia (–1976).

⊛ **1976** In the worst recorded earthquake disaster in history 655,000 people are killed in Tangshan, northeastern China.

👑 **1976** Mao Zedong, China's leader since 1949, dies. In a sign that the nation is moving away from Maoism, the Gang of Four—a group of intellectuals who were leaders of the Cultural Revolution, among them Mao's wife—are arrested. Put on trial in 1980, they will be sentenced to lengthy jail terms.

✕ **1979** Vietnamese troops invade Cambodia, deposing Pol Pot; the defeated Khmer Rouge regime will undertake a guerrilla war against the new regime (–1992).

AMERICAS

EUROPE

AFRICA

WESTERN ASIA

SOUTH & CENTRAL ASIA

EAST ASIA & OCEANIA

1975–1981 A.D.

1982–1988 A.D.

AMERICAS

1982 Argentina and Britain go to war over sovereignty of the Falkland Islands (Malvinas) and South Georgia; the British forces prevail.

1983 U.S. Marines are sent to Grenada to reverse a leftist military coup.

1986 The space shuttle *Challenger* explodes on takeoff from Cape Kennedy, killing all seven crew.

1986 Pilots Dick Rutan and Jeana Yeager fly their experimental airplane *Voyager* nonstop around the world without refueling; the flight takes nine days.

1987 On Black Monday (October 19) stockmarkets in New York and then around the world experience a major crash, wiping billions of dollars off the value of shares.

EUROPE

The Cold War rapidly started to thaw after Mikhail Gorbachev came to power in the Soviet Union in 1985. He and U.S. President Ronald Reagan (left) embarked on a policy of détente that culminated in 1987 in an arms control treaty, the first to reduce existing stockpiles. Gorbachev's attempts to liberalize Soviet society released a pent-up pressure for change that ended by bringing down the communist system both in the Soviet Union itself and in its Eastern Bloc satellites.

1983 Buoyed by success in the Falklands War, Britain's Prime Minister Margaret Thatcher wins a landslide general election victory.

1985 Mikhail Gorbachev comes to power in the Soviet Union on the death of Konstantin Chernenko; Gorbachev adopts a reformist agenda based on *glasnost* (openness) and *perestroika* (reconstruction).

AFRICA

1984 A major famine strikes Ethiopia and Sudan in East Africa, claiming around 100,000 lives.

1985 Live Aid rock concerts, held in Philadelphia, London, Moscow, and Sydney, raise $60 million for African famine victims.

1986 Tripoli is attacked by U.S. warplanes flying from British bases in retaliation for Libyan leader Colonel Gadhafi's support for international terrorism.

WESTERN ASIA

1982 Israel sends troops into Lebanon, starting an occupation that lasts three years (–1985).

1982 Hundreds of unarmed Palestinians are killed when Israeli-backed Falangist militia attack the Sabra and Chatila camps in West Beirut.

1983 Suicide bombers drive truck bombs into the compounds of peacekeeping troops in Beirut, killing 241 U.S. marines and 58 French paratroopers.

1985 Palestinian terrorists hijack the Italian cruise ship *Achille Lauro*, killing one passenger.

1987 The Palestinian *intifada* ("uprising") against the Israeli occupation of the West Bank and Gaza gets underway.

SOUTH & CENTRAL ASIA

1983 On his return to the Philippines to fight for democracy, opposition leader Benigno Aquino is shot by an assailant at Manila airport; the government is suspected of having a part in the assassination.

1984 Indian troops storm the Golden Temple, a Sikh holy site at Amritsar, where armed militants seeking an independent Punjab ("Khalistan") have taken refuge; over 700 rebels are killed.

1984 Four months after the Golden Temple assault India's premier, Indira Gandhi, is assassinated by members of her Sikh bodyguard in revenge.

EAST ASIA & OCEANIA

1983 Premier Deng Xiaoping of China introduces economic reforms that will transform China's largely agricultural economy.

1983 The Labour Party under Prime Minister Bob Hawke is returned to power in the Australian general election.

1983 A Soviet fighter shoots down a South Korean Boeing 747 airliner that has strayed into Russian airspace, killing all 269 on board.

The space shuttle Challenger *explodes on takeoff from Cape Kennedy, Florida.*

🔱 **1987** The United States and the Soviet Union sign their first ever nuclear arms reduction treaty, covering the two countries' medium- and short-range arsenals.

🔱 **1988** Vice President George Bush is elected 41st president of the United States.

🔱 **1988** The United States and Canada sign a comprehensive free trade agreement, becoming effective on January 1, 1989.

AMERICAS

🔱 **1986** Spain and Portugal join the European Community, bringing the membership to 12 countries (Greece having joined in 1981).

🔱 **1987** Margaret Thatcher leads the Conservative Party to a third successive victory, the first such achievement in 20th-century British politics.

✕ **1988** A U.S. airliner is destroyed by a terrorist bomb over the Scottish town of Lockerbie, killing 270 people; a Libyan agent will eventually be convicted of the outrage.

⊕ **1986** A nuclear reactor at Chernobyl in Ukraine explodes, killing 300 people and exposing large areas of Europe to radiation.

EUROPE

🔱 **1987** An accord between rival leaders Robert Mugabe (ZANU-PF) and Joshua Nkomo (ZAPU) to amalgamate their parties makes Zimbabwe a one-party state.

Live Aid stars raise money for African famine victims at London's Wembley Stadium.

AFRICA

🔱 **1988** A UN resolution brings the eight-year conflict between Iran and Iraq to an end.

✕ **1988** Iraqi forces use chemical weapons against the Kurdish town of Halabja, killing 4,000 civilians.

WESTERN ASIA

⊕ **1984** An accident at the Union Carbide chemical plant in Bhopal, northern India, releases a cloud of poisonous gas that kills almost 4,000 people and permanently blinds many others.

🔱 **1986** President Ferdinand Marcos of the Philippines is deposed by a "people power" movement led by Corazon Aquino, widow of Benigno Aquino.

🔱 **1988** Benazir Bhutto, daughter of the executed Pakistani leader Zulfikar Ali Bhutto, becomes the country's prime minister (–1990).

SOUTH & CENTRAL ASIA

🔱 **1985** French agents in New Zealand blow up the *Rainbow Warrior*, a Greenpeace vessel protesting French nuclear tests in the Pacific.

🔱 **1986** Martial law, first imposed in 1949, is finally lifted in Taiwan.

✕ **1987** Two military coups are staged on the Pacific island of Fiji.

EAST ASIA & OCEANIA

1982–1988 A.D.

THE COMPUTER AGE

STARTING AS A MACHINE THAT STORED *data or performed mathematical calculations, the computer has become an indispensable tool of the modern age that can process information for myriad different purposes. Present in most factories, offices, shops, and colleges, as well as in a majority of homes in the developed world, computers have revolutionized the way people work and play.*

▲ An early IBM personal computer illustrates the classic trinity of box, keyboard, and monitor, which (with the addition of a printer) introduced millions of people to home computing in the last two decades of the 20th century.

Developed in the 19th century, the precursors of modern computers were punched-card mechanical devices that could store and process data. One of the pioneers of this technology was the U.S. statistician Herman Hollerith, whose company later grew into IBM. Yet the development of the digital computer as we know it today had to await the invention of electronic components such as thermionic tubes and transistors. The early electronic machines, developed from the latter part of World War II on, were large and expensive, and remained the preserve of major business corporations and government departments. These mainframe computers carried out large-scale clerical and administrative tasks such as payroll processing and census analysis.

▲ Colossus, developed in England in World War II to help break German military codes, was the world's first electronic computer.

---

* **1801** French inventor Joseph-Marie Jacquard mechanizes weaving by making a loom controlled by a system of punched cards that lower and raise threads in the right sequence.

* **1822** English mathematician Charles Babbage creates his "difference engine" to calculate complex logarithms; his associate Ada Lovelace writes a program for his proposed "analytical engine," a prototype of the digital computer.

* **1890** Herman Hollerith uses an electrically driven punched-card reader to process the results of the U.S. census.

* **1931** U.S. inventor Vannevar Bush builds the first analog computing machine to use electronic components.

* **1943** The first fully electronic computer, Colossus 1, is developed at Bletchley Park, England; it is used to decipher German military codes.

* **1946** U.S. engineers J. Presper Eckert and John Mauchly complete ENIAC, the first general-purpose computer. They go on to develop UNIVAC, the first commercial digital computer using stored programs, which goes into use in 1951.

* **1965** Texas Instruments develop the first pocket calculator, the Pocketronic (marketed by Canon from 1970).

* **1971** The U.S. corporation Intel produces the world's first microprocessor, the 4004.

* **1975** Micro Instrumentation and Telemetry Systems (MITS) produces its pioneering home computer kit, the Altair 8800, which can be bought by mail order.

* **1976** The world's first supercomputer, the Cray 1, is built for use at the Los Alamos nuclear laboratory in New Mexico.

* **1976** Bill Gates and Paul Allen found Microsoft, a software producer that comes to dominate the market in operating systems and applications programs for personal computers.

* **1977** Apple Computer of California, run by Steven Jobs and Steve Wozniak, introduces the first mass-market personal computer in assembled form (the Apple II).

* **1981** IBM introduces its Personal Computer (PC).

* **1984** Apple introduces the Macintosh ("Mac"), a revolutionary personal computer that employs a mouse, icons, and the desktop graphical user interface.

* **1991** The worldwide web is made freely available, revolutionizing the flow of information on the Internet.

* **2000** A virus known as "I Love You," spreading via e-mail, affects millions of computers worldwide.

The information technology (IT) revolution that saw computer use and ownership spread dramatically began with the advent of the microprocessor, a complex silicon chip that could operate around a million times faster than the first vacuum tube computers. The tiny size and weight of this component enabled the development of the microcomputer for individual use. The personal computer (PC) was introduced by IBM in 1981. Smaller companies entered a rapidly expanding market, offering cheaper "clone" machines that could run first the MS-DOS disk-operating system and then, from 1985 on, Windows, both of them devised for the PC by Microsoft. Another household name, Apple Computer Inc., pioneered its own Mac operating system and graphical user interface. Growth in this area has been enormous; while just 25,000 enthusiasts had home computers in the United States in 1977, by 2001, 178 million American homes were equipped with a PC or Mac.

As software programs in fields such as games or desktop publishing have become more sophisticated, so processor speed and hard-drive storage size have increased. Another major factor driving personal computing has been the popularity of e-mail and the worldwide web (see box below). These channels of information and communication are used by millions

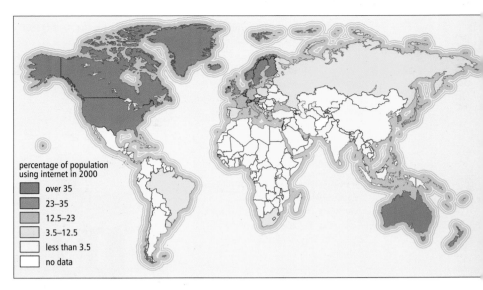

percentage of population using internet in 2000
- over 35
- 23–35
- 12.5–23
- 3.5–12.5
- less than 3.5
- no data

worldwide daily and have transformed the way people do business and spend their leisure time.

At the opposite end of the modern computing spectrum supercomputers performing vast numbers of calculations per second are employed to analyze complex systems. Research fields in which these massively powerful machines are used include weather forecasting, nuclear physics, and astronomy.

▲ By the turn of the millennium Internet use was most firmly entrenched in North America, parts of Europe, Japan, South Korea, Australia, and New Zealand.

The Worldwide Web

The worldwide web is a service that enables computer users to exchange information through servers attached to a network of networks (the Internet). It was developed in the late 1980s by a British physicist, Timothy Berners-Lee, who wanted to create a system for researchers to share documents and view each others' databases. With the growth in personal computer ownership the web took on a commercial dimension soon after it became freely available in 1991, with Internet service providers (ISPs) linking individual users to the Internet for a fee. The web is now home to millions of pages covering every conceivable subject, as well as countless companies conducting e-business online. People access it not just from their homes and offices but also from workstations in public libraries and in internet cafés like the one in Amsterdam seen at right.

1989–1994 A.D.

AMERICAS

1989 Paraguayan dictator Alfredo Stroessner is ousted in a military coup after 34 years in power.

1989 In the worst oil spill in U.S. history the tanker *Exxon Valdez* runs aground in Prince William Sound, Alaska, with devastating consequences for marine life.

1989 U.S. troops are sent to Panama to topple its dictator, General Manuel Noriega, who is accused of drug trafficking and money laundering.

1990 The Human Genome Project is launched with biologist James D. Watson at its helm; the base sequence of the human genome will be plotted by 2003.

1990 General Pinochet steps down as military ruler of Chile, restoring civilian rule after 17 years.

EUROPE

1989 Across Europe the communist regimes of Soviet satellite countries (Czechoslovakia, East Germany, Poland) collapse as their citizens demand democratic reform.

1989 In Romania communist dictator Nicolae Ceaucescu is deposed and executed.

Demonstrators in Germany's capital celebrate the destruction in 1989 of the Berlin Wall.

1990 Boris Yeltsin becomes the first freely elected president of Russia.

1990 Unrest breaks out in some Soviet republics; Lithuania declares its independence, and Russian troops kill nationalist protestors in Tbilisi, Georgia.

1990 East and West Germany are reunited after 45 years of division.

AFRICA

1990 After 27 years in jail veteran South African antiapartheid leader Nelson Mandela is freed from detention, vowing to continue the struggle for black majority rule.

1991 Kenneth Kaunda, leader of Zambia since its independence in 1964, is defeated by Frederick Chiluba in a landslide election victory.

WESTERN ASIA

1989 Ayatollah Khomeini of Iran issues a death sentence (*fatwa*) against British writer Salman Rushdie, whose novel *The Satanic Verses* is thought to insult Islam.

1990 Over 1,400 Muslims die in a stampede during the annual pilgrimage (*hajj*) to Mecca.

1990 Iraq invades the neighboring state of Kuwait; a UN resolution demands Iraqi withdrawal.

1991 A U.S.-led coalition of forces under a UN mandate undertakes to liberate Kuwait; Iraqi forces crumble in the ensuing Gulf War.

1993 Israeli Premier Yitzhak Rabin and Palestinian leader Yasser Arafat sign a U.S.-brokered peace deal; the PLO and Israel recognize each other's legitimacy.

SOUTH & CENTRAL ASIA

1989 Soviet troops withdraw from Afghanistan having failed to pacify the *mujaheddin* Islamic resistance.

1990 Benazir Bhutto is relieved of her post as prime minister of Pakistan after being accused of corruption.

1991 A cyclone sweeps across Bangladesh, killing some 135,000 people and leaving millions homeless.

EAST ASIA & OCEANIA

1989 Emperor Hirohito of Japan dies after 62 years on the throne; he is succeeded by Crown Prince Akihito.

Students in Tiananmen Square, Beijing, call for democratic reform.

1989 Chinese students occupy Tiananmen Square in Beijing for two months, demanding democratic reforms; the protest is crushed by the army and militia.

⊛ **1990** The Hubble Space Telescope is launched from the space shuttle *Discovery*, although a flaw in its mirrors initially impairs its performance (repaired 1993).

🏛 **1993** Bill Clinton becomes the 42nd U.S. president.

Saturn as seen from the Hubble Space Telescope.

🏛 **1993** In the first Islamic terror bombing in the United States an explosion rocks the World Trade Center in New York.

🏛 **1994** The North American Free Trade Agreement (NAFTA) links the United States, Canada, and Mexico in an enlarged free-trade zone.

AMERICAS

🏛 **1990** Margaret Thatcher quits as British prime minister after 11 years.

🏛 **1991** The Soviet Union and the Warsaw Pact are both formally dissolved.

✕ **1991** The Yugoslav federation starts to disintegrate as Slovenia and Croatia declare independence; Serbian forces attack Bosnia when it too votes to break away.

🏛 **1993** Czechoslovakia separates into two states, the Czech Republic and Slovakia, after a peaceful plebiscite approves this "Velvet Revolution."

🏛 **1993** Nations of the European Community (now renamed the European Union) sign the Maastricht Treaty, committing them to a program of ever closer union.

🏛 **1993** An attempted coup in Moscow is put down after President Boris Yeltsin rallies troops loyal to the reformist regime.

⊛ **1994** The Channel Tunnel is opened, linking Britain and France.

EUROPE

✕ **1992** A UN peacekeeping mission to Somalia ends in conflict between U.S. forces and troops loyal to warlord General Aideed (–1995).

✕ **1994** In the central African state of Rwanda interethnic violence between the majority Hutu population and the minority Tutsis claims over 1 million lives.

🏛 **1994** In South Africa's first multiracial elections the African National Congress wins a decisive victory, and Nelson Mandela is elected as the country's new president.

AFRICA

The Gulf War was fought to expel Iraqi forces from Kuwait. A U.S.-led multinational coalition quickly established air supremacy, attacking Iraqi ground troops who could find no shelter in the desert terrain. The war ended with Kuwait liberated, Iraq's leader Saddam Hussein still in power, and up to 100,000 Iraqi soldiers dead.

🏛 **1994** Israel and the neighboring Arab Kingdom of Jordan sign a peace treaty, formally ending 46 years of hostility.

WESTERN ASIA

🏛 **1991** Former Indian Prime Minister Rajiv Gandhi is assassinated by a Tamil extremist.

☀ **1992** Hindu militants destroy a 16th-century mosque on an ancient Hindu holy site at Ayodhya in India; more than 1,000 die in the ensuing Hindu–Muslim rioting.

✕ **1994** Russian troops invade the Central Asian republic of Chechnya, where Muslim separatists are campaigning for independence; heavy casualties result.

SOUTH & CENTRAL ASIA

🏛 **1990** Democracy campaigner Aung San Suu Kyi wins Myanmar's general election; the ruling military junta declares the result void and places her under house arrest.

🏛 **1991** Mount Pinatubo on the Philippine island of Luzon erupts; 200 people are killed, and a wide area is devastated by lava and volcanic ash.

EAST ASIA & OCEANIA

1989–1994 A.D.

1995–2005 A.D.

AMERICAS

1995 The Southern Cone Common Market (Mercosur) comes into effect following an agreement made four years earlier to create a free-trade area among Argentina, Brazil, Paraguay, and Uruguay.

1995 A truck bomb planted by right-wing extremists destroys a federal building in Oklahoma City, killing 168 people.

1996 Bill Clinton is reelected, the first Democrat president to win a second term since 1936.

1999 A Senate trial acquits President Clinton of perjury and obstruction of justice.

EUROPE

1995 The Dayton Peace Accord brings the bloody civil war in Bosnia to an end; the state is divided between a Muslim–Croat federation and a Bosnian Serb republic.

1997 Conservative rule in Great Britain ends after 18 years when the Labour Party under its young leader Tony Blair wins a landslide general election victory.

1997 Researchers at the University of Edinburgh, Scotland, create the first cloned animal, a lamb named Dolly; she will live for only six years, affected by premature aging and disease.

1998 Voters in Northern Ireland and the Irish Republic endorse the Good Friday Agreement, bringing the prospect of peace after 30 years of paramilitary violence.

1998 Serbian paramilitaries ravage the Yugoslav province of Kosovo, conducting ethnic cleansing against the Albanian populace, but withdraw after NATO orders airstrikes against Serbia (–1999).

2000 Serbia's President Slobodan Milosevic is ousted in a popular uprising; he will later be indicted for war crimes and put on trial by an international court.

AFRICA

1995 Genocidal violence between Hutu and Tutsi tribesmen spreads from Rwanda to neighboring Burundi, where a huge refugee population has taken shelter.

1995 In Zaire, central Africa, an outbreak of the deadly Ebola virus, which has no cure, claims 244 lives.

1997 Zaire's tyrannical ruler Mobutu Sese Seko is overthrown by rebel forces under Laurent Kabila. The country is later renamed the Democratic Republic of Congo.

WESTERN ASIA

1995 Israeli Prime Minister Yitzhak Rabin is assassinated by an extreme nationalist opposed to his policy of dialogue with the Palestinians.

1995 The Palestine National Authority, led by Yasser Arafat, takes control of the West Bank and Gaza.

1997 Reformist Mohammed Khatami is elected president of Iran.

1999 King Hussein of Jordan dies and is succeeded by his son Abdullah.

SOUTH & CENTRAL ASIA

1996 The Taliban, hard-line Muslim fundamentalists, overrun the Afghan capital Kabul, taking control of Afghanistan after two years of fighting.

1997 Burmese democracy leader Aung San Suu Kyi is released from six years' house arrest by the ruling military junta.

Taliban fighters pose with their weapons in the Afghan mountains.

EAST ASIA & OCEANIA

British leaders formally return sovereignty over Hong Kong to China in 1997.

1995 Despite international protests, France resumes nuclear weapons testing at Muroroa Atoll in French Polynesia.

1995 The Japanese port of Kobé suffers extensive damage in a major earthquake; 6,000 people die.

1995 Members of the Aum Shinri Kyo cult release nerve gas on the Tokyo subway, killing 12 and injuring 5,000 people.

👑 **2000**   Republican George W. Bush emerges the winner in a tight and disputed U.S. presidential election. He is reelected in 2004.

⚔️ **2001**   On September 11 Islamic terrorists fly airliners into the World Trade Center in New York City and the Pentagon in Washington, D.C.; a fourth plane crashes in Pennsylvania. Around 2,750 people die in the attacks.

⚔️ **2001**   The United States leads an invasion of Afghanistan, whose government is accused of harboring terrorists.

⚔️ **2003**   The United States launches an invasion of Iraq.

👑 **2004**   Ten new countries join the European Union, bringing the total membership to 25.

☀️ **2005**   Pope John Paul II dies after 26 years as head of the Roman Catholic church.

Serbia's attempts to hold Yugoslavia together under its own leadership suffered a crippling blow in 1995 when NATO launched air strikes on Serb positions. Late that year Serbia, Croatia, and Bosnia–Herzegovina accepted a U.S.-sponsored peace plan. Violence broke out again in 1998 in largely Muslim Kosovo.

AMERICAS

EUROPE

⚔️ **1998**   The Islamist terror group al-Qaeda bombs U.S. embassies in Kenya and Tanzania, killing over 200 people.

👑 **1999**   The African National Congress consolidates its power with an increased majority in South Africa's second universal-suffrage election.

⚔️ **2003**   Unrest breaks out in the Darfur region of Sudan, where government troops and their allies kill some 180,000 people and displace two million (–2005).

AFRICA

👑 **1999**   A major earthquake in northern Turkey claims 17,000 lives.

👑 **2000**   Israel ends its occupation of southern Lebanon.

👑 **2004**   Yasser Arafat dies and is replaced by Mahmoud Abbas, who renews negotiations with Israel.

👑 **2005**   Iraqis vote in their first election since the downfall of the dictator Saddam Hussein, overthrown during the 2003 U.S. invasion. Kurdish leader Jalal Talabani becomes president of Iraq.

WESTERN ASIA

☀️ **1997**   Humanitarian worker and Nobel Peace Prize winner Mother Teresa of Calcutta dies in India, aged 87.

Mother Teresa visits a Calcutta orphanage.

👑 **1998**   The government of Pakistan is overthrown in a military coup; General Pervez Musharraf becomes head of state.

👑 **2001**   Pakistan is a major ally in the U.S. invasion of Afghanistan.

SOUTH & CENTRAL ASIA

👑 **1997**   Hong Kong reverts to Chinese rule after 155 years of British sovereignty.

👑 **1999**   East Timor votes for independence from Indonesia; after much violence it will achieve its goal in 2002.

👑 **2000**   The first-ever meeting takes place between the leaders of North and South Korea.

👑 **2002**   Islamic terrorists bomb nightclubs in Bali, Indonesia, killing around 200 people.

👑 **2004**   An earthquake beneath the Indian Ocean triggers a tsunami that kills approximately 310,000 people in Indonesia, Thailand, Sri Lanka, India, and other countries ringing the ocean.

EAST ASIA & OCEANIA

1995–2005 A.D.

FACTS AT A GLANCE: PREHISTORY

Achaemenid Dynasty
The ruling dynasty of Persia from c.700 to 330 B.C. Under the Achaemenids Persia became the center of a huge empire stretching from India in the east to Libya in the west.

Adena Culture
A group of North American hunter-gatherer communities that settled in the Ohio River valley from c.1000 B.C. The culture was at its peak from c.700 to 100 B.C.; finds from sites include copper jewelry and decorated human skulls.

Aeolia
Ancient name for the coastal region of northwest Asia Minor, including the island of Lesbos, which was settled by Hellenic (Greek) peoples from c.850 B.C.

Akhetaten
The city built in around 1348 B.C. by Akhenaten to replace Thebes as the capital of New Kingdom Egypt. Akhetaten was devoted to the cult of the *aten*, or sun's disk, whereas Thebes was the stronghold of the high priests of the old religion. Akhetaten was abandoned not long after Akhenaten's death, when the old faith was restored. Today the site is known as Tell el-Amarna.

Akkadians
A people speaking a Semitic language who inhabited a region to the north of Sumer in the mid-3rd millennium B.C. They rose to prominence from c.2350 B.C. under a charismatic ruler, Sargon the Great, who made their capital city, Akkad, the center of a significant (if short-lived) empire.

Alaca Höyük
A royal burial site of the early Bronze Age in central Turkey. In each small, roofed tomb the body was placed centrally, knees drawn up to the stomach, and accompanied by rich gifts in bronze and precious metals.

Al Mina
Trading post established by the Greek city-state of Euboea around 800 B.C. at the mouth of the Orontes River in what is now eastern Turkey. Al Mina provided contacts not only with local traders but also with merchants from central and eastern Anatolia and Mesopotamia.

Arameans
A Semitic people who moved east from the Syrian desert to occupy the northern reaches of the Euphrates River. By the 11th century B.C. they were encroaching on Assyrian territory in southern Anatolia and northern Arabia. The Arameans were conquered by the Assyrians in the 9th century B.C., but their Aramaic language survived to become the common tongue of West Asia for the next thousand years.

Archaic Period (Egypt)
The period from c.3100 to 2575 B.C. when Egypt's scattered chiefdoms were brought under the rule of a unified state but the full pharaonic traditions of the Old Kingdom had yet to emerge.

Archaic Period (Greece)
Starting around 750 B.C., the time in which Greek civilization began to emerge from the relative economic, political, and cultural stagnation of the "Dark Age."

Ark of the Covenant
In Jewish tradition the container that God ordered Moses to build in order to house the stones inscribed with the Ten Commandments; its precise specifications are given in Exodus 25:1–22.

Aryans
Warlike peoples believed to have originated on the Eurasian steppes (grassland) who swept across the Persian plateau and into northern India sometime after 2000 B.C. Other Aryan groups are thought to have headed for China and Europe. The Aryan language is believed to have been the ancestor of all the various Indo-European tongues, including Sanskrit.

Assyrians
A warlike people from northern Mesopotamia who dominated West Asia from the 14th to the late 7th centuries B.C. At its peak in the 8th century the Assyrian empire stretched over most of the lands of the Fertile Crescent.

astrologer
A person who studies the relative position of the planets and stars in the belief that they influence events on Earth. The idea that the movements of the heavenly bodies affect human lives was first developed by the Babylonians.

Babylon
The main city of ancient Mesopotamia, located on the Euphrates River and first settled c. 3000 B.C. It was the capital of two successive empires separated by almost 1,000 years: the Old Babylonian Empire (c.1750–1595 B.C.) and the Neo-Babylonian Empire (c.600–539 B.C.).

Ban Kao Culture
Named after a site in southern Thailand, this distinctive Neolithic culture created remarkably accomplished pottery, stone tools, and jewelry. Its influence extended well down the Malay Peninsula.

Beaker People
People thought to have been of Iberian origin who spread out over Europe in the 3rd millennium B.C. Their sites are identified by distinctive earthenware beakers, which were placed in burial chambers to hold a drink for the dead on their last journey.

Brahmanas
Written at the start of the 8th century B.C. in India, these texts are interpretive commentaries on the Vedas, explaining the content of the hymns and the rituals they prescribe.

Bronze Age
A period of technological development between the Stone Age and the Iron Age during which bronze was commonly used to make weapons and tools. It began in West Asia in the 4th millennium B.C.

Canaan
A region of western Asia between the Mediterranean and Dead Seas. The home of various Canaanite city-states in the 2nd millennium B.C., it was conquered c.1200 B.C. by the Israelites, who regarded it as the land promised by God to their founding father Abraham.

Carthage
The Phoenicians' most famous colony, established c.814 B.C. on the coast of North Africa near present-day Tunis. It became an important commercial center, controlling a trading empire stretching to southern Spain and the western Mediterranean islands. By the time it was destroyed by the Romans in 146 B.C., its population had grown to more than half a million.

Celts
People speaking related Celtic languages who spread out from Central Europe c.1000 B.C. to inhabit parts of France, Germany, Iberia (Spain and Portugal), and the British Isles. Celtic languages survive in Brittany, Ireland, Wales, and Scotland.

Chaldeans
A Semitic people inhabiting a region of ancient Babylonia. The Chaldeans became dominant in the region, establishing a Babylonian dynasty from 626 to 539 B.C.

Chavín Culture
The first great culture of ancient Peru, named for the Andean town of Chavín de Huantar where its first artifacts were excavated in 1919. Chavín-style temple complexes featured flat-topped pyramids, central plazas, and huge stone relief carvings. The culture flourished for almost 1,000 years, from c.1200 to 300 B.C.

Chinchorro Culture
A culture based in a few fishing villages on what is now the Peru–Chile border that practiced mummification of the dead as early as c.5000 B.C., about 2,500 years before the Egyptians started mummifying bodies.

Chorreran Culture
A culture based in Ecuador from 1200 to 300 B.C., marked by a distinctive style of pottery.

cuneiform
A form of writing using wedge-shaped marks (*cuneus* being Latin for "wedge") developed by the Sumerians about 3000 B.C. Cuneiform characters were impressed in wet clay or wax with the pointed end of a reed.

Cyclades
A group of islands in the Aegean Sea between Greece and Turkey, the Cyclades are famous for abstract sculpted figures crafted during the 3rd millennium B.C. They were produced from a local marble that split easily, which meant that the sculptors concentrated on producing essential forms rather than details.

diaspora
A dispersion or spreading; specifically the dispersal of Jews around the world after the Babylonian and Roman conquests of Palestine.

dolmen
A prehistoric burial chamber consisting of a stone slab laid on two or more upright stones. Dolmens are most numerous in northwest Europe but are also found in North Africa and as far east as Japan.

domestication
The process of bringing wild plants and animals under human control. At first humans domesticated certain plants and animals to secure a reliable food source. Later they bred animals such as the horse and ass as beasts of burden.

Dorians
Nomadic herdsmen and raiders believed to have wandered westward into Greece from Asia Minor (modern Turkey) in the 11th Century B.C. The Dorians spread death and destruction in their path, but also brought with them knowledge of ironworking.

Dorset Culture
Culture that spread across the American Arctic in the 8th century B.C., based around the hunting of walruses, seals, and other sea mammals. With its exquisite little figures, frequently human, and its razor-sharp harpoon heads and blades, it represented a clear artistic and technological advance on the "small tools" tradition it replaced.

Elamites
People of a kingdom based in western Iran that conquered the Sumerian city of Ur in c.1950 B.C. and later exerted influence on the rulers of Babylon and Assyria.

Etruscan League
A loose economic and religious league formed among 12 Etruscan city-states in the 6th century B.C. It may have been modeled on similar confederations in Greece.

Etruscans
Inhabitants of Etruria, the dominant civilization in Italy between 800 and 300 B.C. The Etruscan city-states were eventually conquered by the Romans, who adopted many features of Etruscan civilization.

Exodus
The escape of the Jews led by Moses from exile in pharaonic Egypt, as described in the biblical Book of Exodus. Egyptian sources make no reference to the event, which may have taken place in the reign of the pharaoh Merneptah (c.1224–1214 B.C.).

Fertile Crescent
A semicircle of formerly fertile land stretching across West Asia from Israel through what is now Lebanon and Syria and then down the length of Mesopotamia to the Persian Gulf. Settled agriculture and the world's earliest civilizations developed in the region.

Gauls
Celtic-speaking peoples who inhabited France and Belgium in Roman times. Although divided into different tribes, the Gauls shared a common religion controlled by priests, called druids, who came from noble families.

Great Pyramid
The largest Egyptian pyramid, with a height of 480 feet (146 m) and smooth sides angled at 52° to the horizontal. Built at Giza as the tomb of King Khufu in around 2550 B.C., it is the only one of the Seven Wonders of the Ancient World to have survived to the present day.

Hallstatt Culture
An Iron Age culture of the ancient Celts, named after the town in Austria where its remains were first identified in the mid-19th century near ancient salt mines. Its influence was strongest in the lands around the headwaters of the Danube River.

Harappa
A large city and commercial center of the Indus Civilization in the Punjab region of present-day Pakistan. Like Mohenjo-Daro, it was laid out on a grid pattern with standardized, brick-built housing.

Hattusas
The Hittite capital, located in the mountains of central Anatolia, near the modern village of Boghazköy. Even in ruins it remains impressive, proclaiming the power—and the unabashed militarism—of its founders.

Hebrew
An Israelite, or the descendant of one of a group of northern Semitic peoples including the Israelites; also the language of the ancient Hebrews and any of various later forms of this language.

hegemon
The name given in ancient Greece to a leader who dominated or had authority over other rulers within a region; the most powerful figure within a confederation.

hieroglyphics
A system of writing used by the ancient Egyptians and based at first on the pictorial representation of things; soon, however, a phonetic (sound-based) element evolved to supplement these images, giving it greater flexibility.

Hittites
A warlike people of uncertain origin who established a state in central Anatolia in the mid-16th century B.C. and went on to extend their dominion through much of the Middle East. Hittite military success owed much to their skilled use of three-man war chariots. They remained a force in the region for almost 500 years, only to be wiped off the map by unknown assailants around the year 1200 B.C.

hominids
Extinct ancestors of humans that evolved from African apes between 12 and 2.5 million years ago. Several different hominid species have been identified. Their main humanlike features were two-legged walking, increased brain size, and the use of tools.

Homo erectus
"Upright man," a species of early human that lived in Africa, Asia, and Europe between about 1.8 and 0.5 million years ago. *Homo erectus* used axes and were the first humans to make and control fire.

Homo sapiens
"Wise man," the species name given to modern humans, who first emerged in Africa about 160,000 years ago.

413

hunter-gatherers
People who live off the land in small nomadic groups, feeding themselves by hunting game and gathering nuts, berries, seeds, and other plant foods. All humans lived as hunter-gatherers in the centuries before the development of agriculture; a few small hunter-gatherer groups still survive to this day.

Hyksos
Middle Eastern immigrants to Egypt who built a power base in the Nile Delta around their capital at Avaris. Eventually (in c.1640 B.C.) they gained control of Lower Egypt, while also forcing the Egyptian rulers of Upper Egypt to pay them tribute. The time of their ascendancy is known as the Second Intermediate Period.

ice age
Any of several periods of severe global cooling, the last of which ended about 10,000 years ago. During the coldest phases of the ice age ice sheets spread as far south as New England.

Indus Valley Civilization
The first great Indian civilization, which covered about 500,000 square miles (1.3 million sq km) of territory along and around the Indus Valley.

Ionians
Migrants from mainland Greece who colonized the southern Aegean coast of Asia Minor (today's Turkey) and its offshore islands, many passing through the growing port of Athens as they fled the advance of overland invaders from the north.

irrigation
Artificial watering of dry agricultural areas by means of dams and channels.

Israelite
Member of an ethnic group claiming descent from Jacob, a Hebrew; also, in a more limited sense, a citizen of the northern kingdom of Israel (c.925–721 B.C.).

Jebusites
A people of unknown origin (possibly refugees from the crumbling Hittite Empire) who occupied the citadel of Zion before King David and his Jews seized it for their capital around 1000 B.C.

Kadesh, Battle of
A hard-fought and mutually draining encounter between Ramses II's Egyptian forces and Muwatallis's Hittites in c.1285 B.C. Both sides claimed victory, but signed a nonaggression pact in the battle's aftermath.

Knossos

The majestic palace complex on the coast of Crete around which the Minoan culture centered. The palace's mazelike basement inspired the legend of the Labyrinth and its attendant Minotaur (half-man and half-bull), but was probably used for storing produce.

Kush
An independent African kingdom on the Nile River that emerged from the Egyptian province of Nubia in the 10th century B.C. In the 8th century B.C. under King Kashta it extended its rule into Egypt, providing that country with its 25th dynasty of pharaohs. The Kushites were strongly influenced by Egyptian customs, worshiping Egyptian gods and burying their kings in stone pyramids.

La Galgada
A temple mound built c.2300 B.C. by communal labor in northern Peru. The temple contained small rooms with central fireplaces where offerings to the gods were burned.

Lagash
A Sumerian city-state that emerged as a major power in southern Mesopotamia around 2500 B.C. Much of our knowledge of Sumerian society, religion, and politics comes from thousands of inscribed clay tablets found at Lagash.

Lapita Culture
A Stone Age Oceanian culture characterized above all by its richly decorative pottery, made from c.1300 B.C. on. The Lapita people were great ocean voyagers, and anthropologists have used finds of Lapita pottery to track the colonization of the islands of eastern Melanesia and Polynesia.

La Venta
Ceremonial center in the Tabasco region of Mexico that became the focus of the Olmec Culture after the destruction of San Lorenzo.

Longshan Culture
A Chinese culture based in large, fortified villages that spread out from the lower and middle Yellow River valley c.2500–1950 B.C. Famous for its refined black pottery, Longshan culture also produced the first known bronze artifacts in China.

Lothal
A major port of the Indus Civilization, located in what is now the Indian state of Gujarat. Lothal was an important trade link between India and Mesopotamia.

Lucy
The name given to the 3.5 million-year-old fossil remains of a female hominid discovered in 1974 in Ethiopia. The structure of Lucy's skeleton, assigned to the species *Australopithecus afarensis*, indicated that she could walk upright.

lugal
A Sumerian word, literally meaning "great man," that came to mean "king." We know the names of some Sumerian *lugals* from a surviving king list, a semifactual record of Sumerian rulers from c.3000 to 1800 B.C.

lur
A prehistoric Scandinavian wind instrument, possibly used for ceremonial purposes and also in battle to rally troops and frighten the enemy.

Lydia
A wealthy kingdom in western Asia Minor (Turkey) that flourished in the 7th and 6th centuries B.C. The first state to use coined money, Lydia was conquered by the Persians in 547 B.C.

Magadha
A Hindu state that dominated the Ganges Delta region of eastern India in the 6th century B.C.

Mahabharata
Indian epic poem describing the dynastic power struggles of a line of Aryan rulers in northern India, possibly in the 10th century B.C. The work of many different hands, it was probably written down around 300 B.C.–100 A.D., although it contains material passed down orally (by word of mouth) from much earlier times.

Maya
A native people of southeastern Mexico and Central America. Mayan civilization reached its height around 300–900 A.D. but its roots can be traced back to as early as 1500 B.C.

Medes
An Indo-European people who allied with Babylon to conquer Assyria in 612 B.C., bringing to an end the days of Assyrian greatness. The Medes went on to establish a short-lived empire but were themselves subjugated by Persia in 550 B.C.

Megiddo
City in what is now northern Israel that was taken after a seven-month siege by Pharaoh Thutmose III in c.1456 B.C. The Egyptian victory destroyed a coalition of Canaanite princes recognizing the overlordship of Mitanni and opened the way for the expansion of Egyptian power into Syria.

Memphis
The earliest capital of a united Egypt, founded by King Menes c.2950 B.C.

Mesopotamia
An ancient Greek name meaning "between the rivers," applied to the fertile land between the

Tigris and Euphrates rivers in southern Iraq. Here the Sumerians, Babylonians, and Assyrians established their civilizations.

Middle Kingdom
The second main period of Egyptian prosperity and power, lasting from c.2040 to 1640 B.C., when the pharaohs of the 11th–13th Dynasties restored unified rule to Egypt and further centralized government, while also extending the amount of cultivable land in the Nile Valley and expanding southward into Nubia.

Minoan Culture
The artistically dazzling culture that flourished on the eastern Mediterranean island of Crete in the 2nd and 3rd millennia B.C. The high point of Minoan culture was reached in the so-called "palace" era between c.2000 and 1450 B.C., when luxurious dwellings were built for the island's rulers at Knossos and other centers.

Mittani
A kingdom in northern Mesopotamia that grew in power through the mid-16th century B.C., first turning back an expansionist Egypt and then allying with the pharaohs against the Hittites. It then fell into decline, and by the end of the 14th century B.C. its lands had been divided between the Hittite and Assyrian empires.

Mohenjo-Daro
A large city of the Indus Valley Civilization on the Indus River in present-day Pakistan. Dating from around 2500 B.C., the city was laid out on a grid pattern, with main roads up to 30 feet (9 m) across and sidestreets up to 10 feet (3 m) wide.

mortuary cult
The worship of the dead—especially dead kings—as divine protectors of the living. In Egypt such devotion inspired the construction of the pyramids and the practice of mummification.

Mount Thera
A volcano on the island of Santorini in the southern Aegean whose eruption in the mid-15th century B.C. brought about the destruction of the cities of Minoan Crete.

Mycenae
A fortified city near the coast of the Pelepponesian Peninsula in southern Greece that became the center of a Bronze Age civilization that flourished c.1600–1250 B.C. Mycenaean Greeks conquered Minoan Crete and besieged Troy.

Naqada
One of the earliest towns to develop in ancient Egypt and the site where evidence of a prepharaonic society was first unearthed in the late 19th century. Its name is now often applied to the culture of Egypt's late predynastic period, in the 4th millennium B.C.

Neanderthals
A race of early humans whose remains were first identified in the Neander Valley, Germany. The Neanderthals lived in Europe and West Asia in the last ice age, from around 120,000 to 28,000 years ago. Their last traces have been found in the Iberian Peninsula; after that they either died out or, possibly, merged into the main *Homo sapiens* population.

Neolithic
Adjective referring to the New Stone Age, the final period of the Stone Age, starting c.10,000 years ago, in which hunter-gatherers learned to domesticate plant and animal species and started settling down to an agricultural way of life.

New Kingdom
The period from c.1550 to 1070 B.C. when Egypt was ruled by the pharaohs of the 18th to 20th dynasties. A time of prosperity, territorial expansion, and ambitious building projects, the New Kingdom period is widely regarded as the high point of ancient Egyptian civilization.

Nile Delta
The broad, marshy plain across which the Nile fans out in innumerable smaller channels as it reaches the Mediterranean Sea. The pharaohs ruled this area as part of Lower Egypt.

Nubia
A region of Africa directly beyond Egypt's southern border, centered on the Nile Valley and roughly corresponding with modern Sudan. Nubia's fate was always closely linked with that of Egypt: At times it was conquered and pillaged by the pharaohs' armies, at others it was seen either as an important trading partner or as a military threat. The kingdom of Kush, which rose to power in Nubia in the 10th century B.C., eventually provided Egypt with a dynasty of Nubian pharaohs.

Odyssey
Homer's famous epic poem describing the adventures that befell the Greek hero Odysseus on his long journey home from the Trojan War.

Old Kingdom
The first great age of Egyptian civilization, usually dated c.2575–2125 B.C. and taking in the reigns of the 4th to 8th dynasties of pharaohs; some authorities, however, also include the first three dynasties of Early Dynastic pharaohs, pushing its origins back to c.2950 B.C. The Old Kingdom was a time of stability that laid the seeds for 3,000 years of ancient Egyptian culture; today it is particularly remembered as the Age of the Pyramids.

Olmecs
A people who flourished c.1250–200 B.C. in southern Mexico and parts of Guatemala, Honduras, and Costa Rica, and who were responsible for the first great culture of the Central American region. Olmec culture is famous particularly for its ceremonial centers and for its colossal stone heads.

Olympic Games
First held in 776 B.C., the ancient (like the modern) Olympic Games were held every four years, in their case at Olympia in the Peloponnese. The games brought together champion athletes from Greece's scattered city-states to compete in running, wrestling, and other athletic events.

papyrus
A type of paper made by the ancient Egyptians from the crushed stems of the papyrus reed.

Persians
A people of ancient Iran who established an empire in southwest Asia under Cyrus the Great, conquering first the Medes to their north then the Neo-Babylonian Empire to their east.

pharaoh
The title given to the rulers of ancient Egypt. Pharaohs were worshiped as gods and were responsible for maintaining *maat*—good order.

Phoenicians
Seafaring traders from the coast of present-day Lebanon who set up trading colonies around the Mediterranean as early as 1000 B.C.

Phrygia
Ancient country of west-central Asia Minor that rose to prominence from c.1200 B.C., when settlers from eastern Europe moved in to occupy territories formerly belonging to the collapsed Hittite realm.

Phung Nyugen
A Neolithic culture that flourished from c.4,000 years ago in northern Vietnam; by 1500 B.C. it had evolved into the Dong Dau Bronze Age culture.

pictograph
A picture used in early writing to represent an object.

polis
The origin of the modern word "politics," it was the independent city-state that became characteristic of classical Greece. Although city-states sometimes fell under the control of tyrants, they also often acted as testing grounds for the concept of democracy; even though democratic rights were invariably limited, their citizens still seem to have felt involved and empowered.

Polynesians

Seafaring people who probably originated in Southeast Asia and the East Indies and whose progess was marked by the spread of the Lapita culture. Notable for their navigational skills and double-hulled dugout canoes, they settled Samoa and Tonga by c.1000 B.C.

Poverty Point Culture

A transitional phase between the Archaic (hunter-gatherer) and Formative (settled agricultural) stages of development among the native peoples of the American South. Taking its name from an archaeological site in Louisiana, where the earliest known earthworks in North America were found, its influence eventually extended to sites from Florida to Arkansas.

radiometric dating

A method of measuring the passage of time by means of the rate of decay of radioactive elements.

Rig-Veda

The world's oldest sacred text. A compilation of 1,028 Hindu hymns grouped into ten books, it started to take shape from c.1500 B.C. and was probably given its final shape c.900 B.C.

Romans

A tribe of shepherds living in the hills of west-central Italy before they founded the city of Rome in the 8th century B.C., the Romans would in time go on to conquer much of the known world.

San Lorenzo

A ceremonial center in southern Mexico where the beginnings of Olmec civilization are found. Perched on a clay platform 150 feet (45 m) high, symmetrical earth banks clustered around rectanguar courtyards that were decorated with colossal stone heads (probably portraits of Olmec leaders) and carved basalt slabs.

Sanskrit

The common language of culture in Aryan India and the ancestor of many modern Indian tongues; in its pure form it is studied by scholars of the classical Hindu texts.

scribe

A man skilled in writing—a key figure in many ancient societies. Chronicles kept by scribes gave a state its historical self-image; their recordkeeping ensured its economic effectiveness.

Scythians

Nomadic tribespeople from Central Asia who were skilled horsemen and archers. Scythian leaders were buried in tombs with gold jewelry and horse sacrifices.

Sea Peoples

Raiders who caused disruption throughout the eastern Mediterranean region toward the end of the 2nd millennium B.C. They left no direct legacy, but their activities affected all the great West Asian civilizations of the age.

Second Intermediate Period

The period from c.1640 to 1550 B.C. in which a succession of Asiatic Hyksos rulers held power in Lower Egypt. Unified rule was eventually restored by Ahmose, the ruler of Upper Egypt, and the pharaohs of the ensuing New Kingdom.

Semitic

The language group of various southwest Asian peoples, including the Babylonians, Assyrians, and Hebrews. Semitic peoples founded the religions of Judaism, Christianity, and Islam.

Shang Dynasty

The earliest Chinese dynasty for which there is direct archaeological evidence. Traditionally dated from 1766 to 1027 B.C., it held sway over much of northern China. Its rulers were buried in deep pits accompanied by many human sacifices.

Skara Brae

A prehistoric settlement on the Orkney Islands, Scotland. Occupied until about 2500 B.C., the settlement is well preserved because the houses were sunk into the ground and were built entirely of stone, including the furniture.

Sparta

Ancient Greek city-state in the southern Peloponnese. Sparta's formidable fighting forces became legendary; all eligible adult males were trained as soldiers.

Spring and Autumn Period

A troubled period (722–481 B.C.) of Chinese history during which the Zhou kingdom began to fragment into semiindependent states that vied with each other for power.

Step Pyramid

The earliest form of Egyptian pyramid, consisting of up to six stages, each smaller than the one below and probably representing a stairway to the heavens. The only surviving step pyramid, and probably the only one to be completed, was built for the pharaoh Djoser in around 2650 B.C. Unlike the somewhat similar ziggurats of the Sumerians, a step pyramid was built as a royal tomb rather than as a temple.

Stone Age

The period of prehistory during which people relied on stone to make tools and weaponry, the skills of metalworking being as yet undiscovered.

Stonehenge

A circular stone monument on Salisbury Plain, Wiltshire, England. Used probably as a ritual center and possibly also as an astronomical observatory, Stonehenge was built in stages over more than a thousand years, starting in around 2800 B.C. Some of the stone blocks added in the later stages weighed as much as 50 tons.

Sumerians

People of the world's earliest civilization, which was established c.3500 B.C. in the fertile land between the Tigris and Euphrates rivers in the south of present-day Iraq.

Troy

The city famously fought over in Homer's *Iliad*. The probable site of Troy has been identified on the western coast of what is now Turkey, close to the Dardanelles Strait.

Tyre

A Mediterranean port in modern-day southern Lebanon, Tyre was a major seaport of the Phoenician empire, famous for its silk and purple "Tyrian" dye.

Ugarit

A prosperous city-state on the coast of Syria from as early as 1500 B.C., Ugarit is remembered today mainly for the discovery of tablets on which an early form of alphabetic writing is inscribed. Ugarit may in fact have been the birthplace of the alphabet.

Upanishads

Any of some 250 Hindu sacred texts written in Sanskrit, the ancient language of India. Forming a secret doctrine, the *Upanishads* aimed to provide a mystical path to discovering truth and also introduced the idea of reincarnation.

Ur

A Sumerian city-state founded around 2900 B.C., which remained an important center under the Babylonians and Assyrians. Excavations in the early 20th century revealed a huge ziggurat and a royal cemetery containing treasures of gold, silver, and precious stones.

Urartu

First mentioned by Assyrian scribes c.1260 B.C., Urartu was a kingdom in the mountains of eastern Anatolia (modern Turkey) to the north of Assyria. In the 9th century B.C. Urartu was a real threat to the Assyrians, but its power was broken by Sargon II in c.714 B.C.

Uruk
The earliest Sumerian city, founded around 4000 B.C., Uruk has yielded some of the earliest examples of writing in the form of hundreds of inscribed clay tablets dating to about 3300 B.C.

Valley of the Kings
A secluded valley across the Nile River from the Egyptian capital of Thebes where pharaohs of the New Kingdom period chose to site their tombs. By electing to be buried in this remote spot, they hoped to avoid the attentions of tomb robbers.

Veda
Literally "books of knowledge," a series of sacred poems dating back to India's Aryan period and probably composed from c.1500 to 900 B.C. The hymns set out the ordering principles not only of Hinduism but of Aryan society in general.

Villanova Culture
An Iron Age culture named for a small town near Bologna, Italy, that flourished between 900 and 700 B.C. Skilled metalworkers, the Villanovans may have contributed to early Etruscan civilization.

Woodland Period
The time around 2000 B.C. when hunter-gatherers in the forests of eastern North America began to turn to agriculture: Modern scholars see the change as a gradual transition rather than a "Neolithic Revolution."

Xia Dynasty
The legendary first dynasty of China, dated c.2200–1766 B.C. Archaeological evidence suggests that the Xia rulers, if they existed, may have formed part of the Longshan Culture.

Zapotecs
Central American people who dominated an area of southern Mexico centered on the Oaxaca Valley to the west of the Mayan lands for around 1,000 years. In c.800 B.C. they developed the first hieroglyphic script yet found in the Americas.

Zhou Dynasty
The most enduring dynasty in Chinese history, which claimed to rule by the "Mandate of Heaven." In its heyday as the Western Zhou it built up political unification, but its power disintegrated during the ensuing Eastern Zhou period. It was finally overthrown in 221 B.C. by the Qin Dynasty.

ziggurat
A form of temple invented by the Sumerians and adopted by the Babylonians and other peoples of Mesopotamia. It was a stepped structure, each stage smaller than the one below, with a shrine built on the summit.

Zoroastrianism
An Iranian religion that views existence as an unending struggle between good and evil; the great creator, Ahura Mazda, is symbolized by fire. Though largely displaced by Islam, the creed survives today among the Parsi community centered in western India.

FACTS AT A GLANCE: THE CLASSICAL AGE

acropolis
Literally "high city," the fortified citadel of a Greek city-state.

Adena Culture
A group of North American hunter–gatherer communities that settled in the Ohio River valley from about 1000 B.C. The culture was at its peak from approximately 700 to 100 B.C.; finds from sites include copper jewelry and decorated human skulls.

Alans
A nomadic tribe that established itself in southeast Russia in the first three centuries A.D. Under pressure from other nomads one group of Alans moved west to Spain.

Anasazi Culture
A farming and hunter–gatherer culture in the North American Southwest. Early Anasazi lived in houses sunk into the ground around larger buildings that may have been used as religious centers.

Anatolia
The Asiatic part of Turkey, known in Roman times as Asia Minor.

Anglo-Saxons
Germanic peoples (Angles, Saxons, and Jutes) who migrated to Britain from Germany and Denmark from about 450 A.D. on and established a number of kingdoms there. In time the Anglo-Saxons became known as the English.

Armenia
An ancient country occupying the mountainous region of western Asia between the Black Sea and the Caspian Sea, Armenia became allied to the Roman Empire in 69 B.C. In 303 A.D. it became the first country to adopt Christianity as a state religion.

Aryans
Nomadic pastoralists from Central Asia who migrated into the Indian subcontinent around 1500 B.C. They introduced Sanskrit, the language of the earliest Hindu scriptures.

Asia Minor
The Asiatic part of present-day Turkey, also known as Anatolia.

Axum
A powerful trading kingdom in northeastern Ethiopia. From the 1st century A.D. up to the Byzantine era Axum traded with Greeks, Romans, Arabs, and Indians.

Bactria
Ancient country in what is now northern Afghanistan. Part of the Persian Empire in 500 B.C.,

it was conquered by Alexander the Great in 328 B.C. On his death it became part of the Hellenistic Seleucid Kingdom until about 250 B.C.

Ban Chiang Culture
A farming culture in northeast Thailand. By about 300 B.C. the Ban Chiang people were producing printed textiles and pottery that was often painted with images of humans, animals, and insects.

barbarian
Term used by the Romans to denote all peoples living outside the frontiers of the Roman Empire, but in particular the Germanic-speaking peoples settled on its northern frontiers.

basilica
A Roman public building used as law courts or offices. The building consisted of a large hall flanked by columns with an aisle on each side; the design was adopted by early Christians for their churches.

Basketmaker Culture
A society of the early Anasazi Culture that had no pottery but used baskets and other woven artifacts.

bodhisattva
A person who by his or her good deeds is free to enter the state of perfect serenity called *nirvana* but who, out of compassion for all living things, remains in the world to work for the salvation of others.

Caria
An ancient region on the coast of southwest Asia Minor that was an independent kingdom under King Mausolus (c.377–353 B.C.).

Carthage
A great maritime trading city founded by the Phoenicians near modern Tunis on Africa's north coast. Destroyed by the Romans during the Punic Wars, Carthage was rebuilt as a Roman colony in 45 B.C.

catacomb
A network of underground burial chambers.

Catholic
A member of the Christian church recognizing the authority of the pope in Rome.

Celts
Iron Age peoples of Europe sharing a common culture and related languages, called *keltoi* by the Greeks and Gauls by the Romans. From the 5th century B.C. on, bands of Celts invaded Greece and Italy. Others migrated into western Europe as far as Spain and the British Isles.

Champa
Also known as Lin-yi Champa. Kingdom founded about 192 A.D. on the central and southern Vietnamese coast. Its language, culture, and religion were shaped mainly by trade with Hindu India.

Chavín de Huantar
Site in northern Peru that was an important cult center from about 900 to 200 B.C. It has given its name to the Chavín style of art, featuring carved mythical creatures combining feline, serpent, bird, and human characteristics.

Cisalpine Gaul
The section of the Roman province of Gaul that lay south of the Alps.

city-state
A self-governing city controlling a surrounding area of land, large or small. In ancient Greece a city-state was called a *polis*, from which the English word "politics" derives.

Colosseum
The largest amphitheater in Rome, 615 feet (187 m) long and 160 feet (49 m) high. It could even be flooded for mock sea battles.

consul
One of two annually elected officials who exercised supreme civil and military authority during the Roman Republic. After the establishment of the empire the office became purely honorary.

Dacia
A kingdom north of Rome's Danube frontier in modern Romania. Conquered by the Romans in 106 A.D., Dacia remained a province until 272, when it was abandoned to the invading Goths.

diaspora
The dispersal of the Jews following the Roman sack of Jerusalem in 70 A.D. and the crushing of the Jewish revolt of 135.

Ephthalite Huns
Also known as the White Huns. A branch of the Huns who overran much of the Sassanian Empire of Persia in the 4th to the 6th centuries A.D. and helped bring about the downfall of the Gupta Dynasty in northern India in about 510.

Etruscans
An advanced civilization in Etruria (northern and central Italy) that dominated early Rome. Rome shook off Etruscan rule in 509 B.C., and Etruria was eventually absorbed into the Roman Empire.

Franks
A Germanic people who settled in what is now

the Netherlands in the 3rd century B.C. After the fall of the Western Roman Empire the Frankish kings gradually conquered most of Gaul. France is named for them.

Funan

A trading kingdom in what is now Cambodia and southern Vietnam. Funan grew rich on the profits of the seaborne trade between India and China from the 2nd to the 6th centuries A.D.

Galatia

A state in Asia Minor founded in the 3rd century B.C. by Celtic settlers. It became a Roman province in 25 B.C.

Gaul

The region approximating to present-day France and Belgium lived in by the Celts. The Romans gradually conquered all of Gaul between 225 and 51 B.C.

Great Wall of China

A continuous defensive barrier built along China's northern border to protect the settled Chinese people from raiding nomads. About 25 feet (8 m) tall, it is a brick-faced structure of earth and stone with carefully sited watchtowers.

Gupta Dynasty

The dynasty founded by Chandragupta I, king of Magadha, that ruled an empire in northern India from the 4th to 6th centuries A.D. Hindu culture flourished under the Guptas.

Hadrian's Wall

A defensive stone barrier built by Hadrian to protect Roman Britain from the tribes of the north.

Han Dynasty

Chinese dynasty that ruled (with one short interval) from 206 B.C. to 220 A.D. Under the Han rulers science and technology made remarkable advances.

Hellenistic Period

The period lasting from the death of Alexander the Great in 323 B.C. to the Roman conquest of Egypt in 30 B.C., during which Greek culture was the dominant influence in the eastern Mediterranean and western Asia.

Hinduism

The dominant religion and culture of India since ancient times. A complex system of beliefs and customs, Hinduism includes the worship of many gods and a belief in rebirth.

Hohokam Culture

A farming culture centered on the Gila River in present-day Arizona. To water their fields, the Hohokams dug 300 miles (500 km) of canals.

Hopewell Culture

A farming culture of eastern North America. From about 100 B.C. the Hopewell constructed massive earthworks as ritual centers.

Huns

Nomadic peoples from Central Asia, one group of whom (known as the Black Huns) migrated to eastern Europe around 370 A.D. and established a kingdom in present-day Hungary. Legendary for their violence, they disappeared from history after the death of their leader Attila in 453. *See also* Ephthalite Huns.

Ionia

Ancient name for the central west coast of Asia Minor, including some islands of the eastern Aegean Sea. Ionia was named for the Ionians, Greek-speaking peoples who migrated to the region from mainland Greece from the 11th to 9th centuries B.C.

Izapa Culture

A culture associated with Izapa, an archaeological site near Chiapas, Mexico. Its inhabitants may have transmitted the Olmec calendar and religious beliefs to the Maya.

Jainism

A religion founded in India by the 6th century B.C.; it teaches the necessity of self-denial in order to obtain spiritual liberation and urges sympathy and compassion for all forms of life.

Jin Dynasty

Also known as the Western Jin. Shortlived Chinese dynasty set up by Wudi in 265 A.D.

Juan-Juan

An alliance of Central Asian nomads that controlled the northern frontier of China from the early 5th to mid 6th century A.D. They included the Avars, who later harassed eastern Europe.

Judea

Roman province in the southern part of ancient Palestine, formerly the Jewish kingdom of Judah.

Julian calendar

A calendar introduced in 45 B.C. by Julius Caesar. It had 12 months rather than the previous ten; the additional months, July and August, were named for Caesar and Augustus, respectively.

Kalinga

An ancient region on the east coast of India in the present-day state of Orissa.

Koguryo

The earliest Korean state. Arising in the 1st century A.D., it was strongly influenced by Chinese culture.

Buddhism was introduced in 372. It was conquered by the neighboring state of Silla in 668.

Kushans

A wealthy dynasty of kings (mid 1st–4th centuries A.D.) who ruled an empire in Afghanistan and northern India that controlled trade along the Silk Road.

Lapita Culture

Ancient Pacific culture named for an archaeological site in New Caledonia. The Lapita people probably came from Southeast Asia, bringing with them domesticated animals and a type of pottery incised with geometric patterns.

La Tène Culture

Iron Age culture associated with the Celts, which takes its name from a prehistoric settlement in Switzerland. The characteristic La Tène art style developed around 450 B.C. and made use of lively animal motifs and intricate geometrical patterns.

Macedon

Mountainous kingdom in northern Greece bordering the Aegean Sea. It rose to importance in the 4th century B.C. under Philip II, father of Alexander the Great.

Magadha

One of the 16 kingdoms of northern India mentioned in classical Hindu writings. It was located on the middle Ganges River and formed the heartland of the Mauryan Empire.

Mahayana

A school of Buddhism that teaches that the highest ideal is for individuals to work for the salvation of others (*see* bodhisattva).

Masada

A rock fortress high above the Dead Sea in Judea where the Jews made their last stand in their revolt against the Romans. After the Romans captured the stronghold in 73 A.D., the defenders committed suicide rather than fall into their hands.

Mauretania

The "land of the Moors," covering coastal Morocco and Algeria. In 44 A.D. the Emperor Claudius divided it into two Roman provinces, but large parts of the country remained under Moorish chieftains.

Mauryan Dynasty

The first north Indian dynasty to extend its rule into central and eastern India. The Mauryan Empire (c.321–180 B.C.) was created by Chandragupta Maurya and enlarged by his son Bindusara and grandson Ashoka.

Maya

Amerindian people of southern Mexico, Guatemala, and Honduras. The Maya of the Classic Period (c.250–800 A.D.) are noted for their stepped pyramids, carved monuments, and knowledge of astronomy. They used a hieroglyphic form of writing.

Meroë

Nubian kingdom from about 590 B.C. to 350 A.D. Egyptian influence was strong: The kings and queens of Meroë were buried in pyramids, and inscriptions were carved in a hieroglyphic script, as yet undeciphered.

Moche Culture

The culture associated with the Moche River valley in coastal northern Peru, which flourished from about the 1st to 8th century A.D. The Moche people built ceremonial centers with platform mounds; one of them, the Pyramid of the Sun, is the largest such mound in South America.

Monte Albán

Capital of the Zapotec people, in Mexico's Oaxaca region. Founded around 500 B.C., Monte Albán was the dominant regional center for over 1,000 years.

Nabataea

A kingdom that expanded along the caravan routes radiating from the city of Petra, in modern Jordan. It became the Roman province of Arabia in 106 A.D.

Nazca Culture

A culture that flourished in the southern deserts of Peru from about 370 B.C. to 700 A.D., famed for creating large designs in the desert gravel that sometimes extended for miles. Seen most easily from the air, their purpose remains unknown.

Neoplatonism

A philosophy that sees everything on Earth as a reflection of an eternal divine reality. It developed in the late Roman Empire and remained influential throughout the Middle Ages.

Nicaea, Council of

The first general council, or gathering, of the Christian church, called by Constantine in 325 A.D. to establish a shared set of beliefs.

Nok Culture

An Iron Age culture that flourished in Nigeria from about 500 B.C. to 200 A.D. Its art is characterized by terracotta sculptures of people and animals.

Nubia

The region to the south of Egypt on the Nile River, roughly equivalent to modern Sudan. The ancient Egyptians called it Kush.

Numidia

The country of the Numidae, covering an area in the north of present-day Algeria and western Tunisia. It became a Roman province in 46 B.C.

Ostrogoths

A Germanic people living in the area around the Black Sea who were conquered and displaced by the Huns in about 372 A.D. Under their leader Theodoric (c. 455–526), they moved into Italy in 488 and established a kingdom there that lasted until 555.

paganism

Belief in many gods.

Palmyra

An ancient oasis city in the Syrian desert that prospered from its position on the caravan route from the Mediterranean to the Persian Gulf. It became part of the Roman Empire in 18 A.D.

Parthians

A nomadic people from Central Asia who ruled Persia (modern Iran) and Mesopotamia (Iraq) from about 247 B.C. to 226 A.D. The Romans captured the Parthian capital in 115 A.D., but they never succeeded in totally subduing the region.

patricians

A class of Roman citizens descended from the oldest noble families. In early republican times they alone could enter the Senate or hold other high offices.

Peloponnesian Wars

Two series of conflicts (457–445 and 431–404 B.C.) between the city-states of Sparta and Athens, fought mostly in the Peloponnese, the southern peninsula of mainland Greece.

Pergamon

Ancient Greek city near the modern Turkish town of Bergama. An ally and then possession of Rome, it became a center of Greek art and culture.

Persepolis

The chief royal residence and capital of the Achaemenid Dynasty of Persia, famed throughout the ancient world for its opulent splendor.

Persian Empire

The empire in western Asia created by Cyrus the Great (550–529 A.D.) of the Achaemenid Dynasty. At its height it extended from the Mediterranean Sea to the Indus Valley. It lasted until 331 B.C., when it was conquered by Alexander the Great.

Phoenicians

Seafaring traders, originally from Lebanon, who established a vast commercial empire with its main center at Carthage. The Roman word for Phoenician was *Punicus*, as in Punic War.

plebeians

A class of Roman citizens composed of traders and small farmers. The plebeians had their own assembly, but its resolutions became legally binding on the whole population only after 287 B.C.

Pope

The title given to the bishops of Rome who, claiming descent from St. Peter, from the third century on asserted their leadership of the Christian church.

Ptolemaic Dynasty

The dynasty of pharaohs of Macedonian descent who ruled Egypt from 323 to 30 B.C. The last of the Ptolemies was Queen Cleopatra.

Punic Wars

Three wars fought between Rome and Carthage. The conflict began as a dispute over Sicily but became a protracted struggle for control of the whole Mediterranean.

Puranas

Sacred Hindu writings dealing with ancient times and events.

Qin

A Chinese state that unified China in 221 B.C., giving its name to the whole country and to the dynasty that ruled it for the next 15 years.

Ramayana

Indian epic poem of about 300 B.C. in which the hero Rama and his friend Hanuman strive to recover Rama's wife Sita from the demon king Ravana.

Saba

An ancient country, known as Sheba in the Bible, roughly equivalent to present-day Yemen in southwest Arabia. Saba's wealth was based on its control of the caravan trade in incense, aromatic resins valued throughout the ancient world for use in religious ceremonies and as a component of perfumes and cosmetics.

Sakas

Nomads from Central Asia who invaded Afghanistan and eastern Persia from about 170–130 B.C. and established a kingdom in northwestern India around 94 B.C.

Samnites

An ancient people of central Italy who were conquered by the Romans in a series of wars between 343 and 290 B.C.

Sanskrit
The dominant classical language of India and the sacred language of Hinduism.

Sassanians
Also known as Sassanids. Dynasty of Persian kings (224–651 A.D.) named after Sassan, grandfather of Ardashir I, the first Sassanian ruler.

Scythians
Nomads from Central Asia who migrated into the region north of the Black Sea during the 8th and 7th centuries B.C. They traded with the Greeks and were conquered by Philip II of Macedon in 339 B.C.

Seleucid Dynasty
The dynasty founded by Seleucus I that ruled much of Asia Minor, Mesopotamia, and Syria during the Hellenistic period from 321 to 64 B.C.

Senate
Rome's governing council. In early republican times the Senate was composed of about 80 patricians. At the end of the republic there were about 600 senators, drawn from all classes of society. Under imperial rule the Senate's powers were greatly reduced.

Shu
The westernmost of the three kingdoms of China after the fall of the Han Dynasty in 220 A.D. The other two were Wei and Wu.

Silk Road
Ancient overland trade route extending for roughly 4,000 miles (6,400 km) between China and Europe.

Social War
A three-year uprising by Rome's Italian allies, who demanded full Roman citizenship. In 88 B.C. Rome agreed to their demands. The creation of new Roman communities led to the development of urban centers throughout Italy.

Sogdiana
A northeastern province of the Persian Empire (in present-day Uzbekistan) conquered by Alexander the Great between 329 and 327 B.C.

Sohano Period
A cultural period (c.200 B.C.–600 A.D.) in the Pacific characterized by pottery with geometric decoration. It probably developed from the Lapita Culture.

stele
A stone monument (plural stelae) carved with sculptured images or inscriptions, usually commemorating a ruler's achievements.

Suevi
One of a number of Germanic peoples displaced by the Huns. They established a kingdom in Spain in 409 A.D. that was later absorbed into the Visigoth Kingdom.

Talmud
The most important work of post-Biblical Jewish literature, containing Jewish law and tradition.

Theravada
A school of Buddhism that emphasizes the meditative way of life as the way for individuals to attain *nirvana*.

Thrace
A country formed of parts of modern Greece, Bulgaria, and European Turkey. Conquered by Philip of Macedon in 342 B.C., it was later incorporated into the Roman Empire.

Tiahuanaco
A city close to Lake Titicaca in Bolivia that was the center of an Andean empire from about 300 to 700 A.D.

Toba
Nomads who conquered northern China in 386 A.D. and established a dynasty in the state of Wei.

tribune
An official elected by the plebeians to protect their interests. When the position was created in 494 B.C., two tribunes were elected annually; later this number was increased to ten.

Trojans
People of Troy, an ancient city thought to have occupied a site at Hisarlik, close to the mouth of the Dardanelles strait in modern Turkey. According to the Greek poet Homer, Troy was destroyed by the Greeks after a long siege.

Teotihuacán
Ancient city in the Valley of Mexico about 30 miles (50 km) north of Mexico City. At its height (c.300–600 A.D.) it had a population of around 150,000 and covered a larger area than ancient Rome.

Twelve Tables
The first Roman code of laws, inscribed on stone in 451 B.C. Until the end of the republic schoolboys had to learn them by heart.

Vandals
A Germanic people who invaded the Roman Empire between 406 and 409 A.D. and settled in Spain. In 429 they reached North Africa and established a kingdom there from which they attacked Rome in 455. The Vandal Kingdom survived until 534.

Visigoths
A Germanic people, related to the Ostrogoths, who invaded the Roman Empire in the 4th century and founded a kingdom in southern France and Spain.

Warring States Period
Period of Chinese history from 481–221 B.C., when the authority of the Zhou emperors was in disarray and power was in the hands of a few major states almost constantly at war with one another.

Wei
The northernmost, as well as the richest and most populous, of the three kingdoms of China after the collapse of the Han Dynasty in 200 A.D.

Wu
In the south of China one of the three kingdoms of China after the collapse of the Han Dynasty.

Xiongnu
A Central Asian tribe of nomads who posed a constant threat to the Chinese Empire. The Xiongnu were probably the Huns who invaded the Roman Empire in the 5th century A.D.

Yamato Kings
The rulers of the Yamato Plain on Honshu Island, who gradually extended their authority throughout the whole of Japan between the 4th and 8th centuries A.D. They were strongly influenced by Chinese culture.

Yayoi Culture
Japan's first rice-farming and metalworking culture. Mirrors and coins at Yayoi sites indicate that Japan at the time had contacts with Han China.

Yellow Turbans
Chinese rebels, mainly poor peasants, who began a two-year revolt against Han corruption in 184 A.D. They were led by three magicians.

Zapotecs
A people of ancient Mexico living in the Oaxaca Valley region. They developed the earliest script in the Americas around 800 B.C., and their most important center was at Monte Albán, which flourished between 400 B.C. and 700 A.D.

Zhou Dynasty
China's longest-lasting imperial dynasty, which held power from 1122 to 256 B.C.

421

FACTS AT A GLANCE: EARLY MIDDLE AGES

Abbasid Dynasty
The dynasty of caliphs that controlled most of the Islamic world from 750 to 1258 from their capital at Baghdad, Iraq. They claimed descent from Abbas, the uncle of Muhammad.

Almagest
The most influential work on astronomy of the Middle Ages. Written in Greek by the Egyptian astronomer Ptolemy (c.90–168 A.D.), it was translated into Arabic as *Al-Majisti* ("Great Work"). Medieval Latin translations reproduced the title as *Almagesti*.

Althing
The parliament of Iceland (the word is Icelandic for "general assembly"). The oldest parliament in the world, it was established in 930 and met each summer as both legislature and court on the Thingvellir Plain, northeast of Reykjavik.

Amida sect
Populist Buddhist sect that preached salvation in paradise for all who worshiped a monk named Amitabha who had attained Buddhahood. The cult, which developed in China in the 6th century, spread to Korea and then to Japan, where it formed the basis of the later Pure Land sect.

Anasazi Culture
An agrarian civilization of the American Southwest that, having first emerged as the "Basketmaker Culture" around the 2nd century B.C., reached its apex around 800 A.D. in the adobe-built towns of the Pueblo Period.

Anglo-Saxons
Germanic peoples (Angles, Saxons, and Jutes) who migrated to Britain from Germany and Denmark c.450 A.D. and established a number of kingdoms there. In time the Anglo-Saxons became known as the English.

Annam
A state located in what is now northern Vietnam that was conquered in about 214 B.C. by the Chinese, who named it An-Am, "Peaceful South." Independent from 939, Annam was incorporated into Vietnam in 1946.

Avars
Nomads from Central Asia who migrated westward in the 6th century A.D. into the region of Hungary previously occupied by the Huns. They were defeated by Charlemagne in 796.

Bantu
A people originating in West Africa who migrated slowly to the south and east between around 200 and 650 A.D., carrying with them the skills of settled agriculture and ironworking and a common language.

Benedictine Order
Order of monks and nuns founded by the Italian St. Benedict in the 6th century. Benedictines had a strong influence on learning in medieval Europe.

Berbers
The original inhabitants of North Africa, occupying the area west of Egypt as far as the Atlantic coast. Their lands were colonized by the Phoenicians and the Romans in ancient times, and were invaded by the Arabs in the 7th century A.D. After some resistance they converted to Islam.

Bulgars
Central Asian nomads, the Bulgars joined the westward push of peoples from this region in the 7th century. They ended up in the Balkans, first as invaders and then as mercenary soldiers employed by the Byzantine Empire.

Byzantium
City founded as a Greek colony on the European side of the Bosphorus on a site now occupied by part of Istanbul. Renamed Constantinople in 330 A.D., it became first the eastern capital of the Roman Empire then sole capital of the Byzantine Empire. The name "Byzantium" is also sometimes applied to the Byzantine Empire itself.

caliph
Derived from the Arabic *khalifah*, or "representative," this title was conferred on those rulers of the Muslim world in whom the authority of the Prophet as Allah's voice on Earth was believed to be perpetuated.

Capetian Dynasty
French dynasty founded by Hugo Capet in 987 that ruled until 1328, when it was succeeded by the House of Valois.

Carolingian Dynasty
The dynasty of Frankish kings descended from Pepin of Landen (died 640 A.D.), who became mayor of the palace to the Merovingian King Chlothar II. The greatest of the Carolingians was Charlemagne, or Charles the Great, who was crowned emperor in 800. The dynasty derives its name from Carolus, the Latin form of Charles.

Chalukya Dynasty
Southern Indian dynasty that ruled in the Deccan region, with interruptions, from 535 to 1200 A.D. The Chalukyas' imperial heyday came in the reign of Pulakesin II (608–42). Their spectacular capital, Badami, was remarkable for its temples, their spires and pinnacles cut directly from the rock.

Champa
With its capital near what is now Da Nang, this Hindu kingdom founded by Indian traders dominated central Vietnam from its foundation in about 200 A.D. right through to the start of the 2nd millennium.

Chenla
A state that emerged among the Khmer people of Cambodia in about 400 A.D. By about 550 it had united all the Khmer people in a single empire and had grown strong enough to overthrow the neighboring state of Funan, based in the Mekong River Valley. It was at its height around 700 but began to decline shortly afterward.

Chimú Culture
South American civilization that flourished on the coast of Peru from the 11th to the 15th centuries, when it was conquered by the Incas. As well as producing fine work in gold and pottery, the Chimú built aqueducts and possibly developed a system of writing by painting patterns on beans.

Chola Dynasty
Southern Indian dynasty that came to the fore in about 850 A.D., when Vijayalaya seized the city of Tanjore. Their empire extended overseas to include parts of modern Malaysia and Indonesia, but declined from the mid 11th century.

Colchis
An ancient country on the Black Sea (part of today's Republic of Georgia). According to Greek legend, it was the land of the Golden Fleece sought by Jason and the Argonauts.

Confucianism
The doctrine derived from the teachings of the celebrated Chinese administrator and philosopher Confucius (551–479 B.C.), known in China as Kongfuzi. In later times Confucianism, which emphasized learning, respect, and good conduct, became a state religion in China.

Copts
Members of the Coptic Church, a branch of Christianity founded in Egypt in the 5th century that still survives today. The Copts were Monophysites and were frequently persecuted as heretics.

Danegeld
A tax paid to Viking raiders or occupation forces by peoples eager to avert attacks. In England it was imposed from 991 A.D. by Anglo-Saxon kings to raise the money to pay tribute to the Viking invaders of England.

Danelaw
Area of north and east England granted to Danish Vikings in the 9th century. The Danelaw survived as a separate territory until 954, and its settlers had a lasting influence on local language and culture.

dendrochronology
Analysis of the annual growth of tree rings to date past events. Variations in climate year by year produce distinctive rings.

Dravidians
The original inhabitants of southern India, the Dravidians were marginalized by the expansion of Aryan and later Muslim civilizations from the north.

Eastern Roman Empire
Eastern half of the Roman Empire, with its capital at Constantinople, whose founder, Emperor Constantine, divided the empire at his death in 337 A.D. While the Western Empire collapsed in 476, the Eastern Empire survived to become the Greek-speaking Byzantine Empire.

Ephthalite Huns
Also known as the White Huns. A branch of the Huns who overran much of the Sassanian Empire of Persia in the 4th to 6th centuries A.D. and helped bring about the downfall of the Gupta Dynasty in northern India in about 455.

Fatimid Dynasty
Muslim Shiite dynasty founded in Tunisia in 909 by Ubayd Allah, who claimed descent from the Prophet Muhammad's daughter Fatima and her husband Ali. In 969 the Fatimids conquered Egypt, founding the city of Cairo as their capital. The dynasty survived until 1171.

feudal system
Medieval European social and economic system characterized by the granting of land in return for political and military service to an overlord.

Franks
A Germanic people who settled east of the Rhine River in what is now the Netherlands in the 3rd century B.C. After the fall of the Western Roman Empire the Frankish kings gradually conquered most of Gaul (France), Italy, and Germany, creating an empire that lasted from the 6th to the 9th century. France is named for them.

Frisians
A Germanic people who occupied the coast and offshore islands of a region approximating to the present-day Netherlands and part of north Germany. They were conquered and converted to Christianity by Charlemagne in 784.

Fujiwara
The ruling clan in Japan from 858 to 1185. During that period the office of emperor became merely ceremonial, while real power was exercised by Fujiwara chancellors and regents.

Funan
A trading kingdom in what is now Cambodia and southwestern Vietnam that grew rich on the profits from the seaborne trade between India and China. It was overthrown by Chenla in about 550.

glyph
A unit of the symbolic script carved in stone by the Mayans. Glyphs were used to represent both words and numbers.

Greek fire
An inflammable substance used as a weapon by the Byzantines. Its formula (a state secret) has not survived, but it probably involved combinations of naphtha, sulfur, petroleum, bitumen, and other chemicals. Greek fire was used either as a missile hurled from a catapult or as a flamethrower.

Gupta Dynasty
The dynasty founded by Chandragupta I, ruler of Magadha, that came to control an empire in northern India from the 4th to 6th centuries A.D. Hindu culture flourished under the Guptas.

Gurjara Dynasty
Nomads of Central Asian origin who migrated into the Indian subcontinent in the 4th and 5th centuries A.D., the Gurjaras established a ruling dynasty in the region of Rajasthan in northern India in about 550. The Gurjara–Pratihara Dynasty, which united much of north India in the 8th century, may have been descended from them.

hajj
The pilgrimage to Mecca that every Muslim is obliged to undertake, if at all possible, at least once in the course of his or her lifetime.

Heian Period
The period of Japanese history from 794 to 1192, beginning with the shifting of the nation's capital from Nara to Heian (modern Kyoto). The era came to be seen as a golden age of peace, prosperity, and national self-confidence during which the country at last broke free from the cultural domination of China.

hijra
Also known as the Hejira. The "migration" of Muhammad and his followers from Mecca to the city of Medina, 250 miles (400 km) to the north on the Arabian Peninsula. It took place in 622 A.D., which has since been Year 1 in Islamic chronology.

Holy Roman emperor
A title bestowed by the pope from medieval times on a leading central European ruler, thought of as the chief secular champion of the Christian cause. The first Holy Roman emperor was the Frankish Emperor Charlemagne, crowned in the year 800; the title was finally abolished by Napoleon Bonaparte in 1806.

Huari Culture
Culture that flourished in the Andean region of Peru from the 6th to 9th centuries. It centered on the city of Huari in the Ayacucho Valley, which covered almost 2 square miles (5 sq. km) and may have housed 70,000 people.

Huns
Nomadic peoples from Central Asia, one group of whom (known as the Black Huns) migrated to eastern Europe in about 370 A.D. and established a kingdom in present-day Hungary. Legendary for their violence, they disappeared from history after the death of their leader Attila in 453. *See also* Ephthalite Huns.

Iconoclast Controversy
Religious conflict that split the Byzantine Empire in the 8th and 9th centuries, when a succession of emperors sought to forbid the veneration of icons (holy images) on the grounds that it contravened the biblical injunction against the worship of graven images. The iconoclasts (icon destroyers) eventually lost the argument in 843, when icons were restored to imperial favor.

Igbo
People of the eastern Niger Delta lands who developed an advanced Iron Age culture centered on Igbo-Ukwu, which was probably a royal site. The Igbo used local iron ores and imported copper to make fine swords and bronze ornaments.

Kanem
Central African state established in about 800 A.D. by nomadic herders who settled down to pursue a more agricultural lifestyle. By the 11th century it had become a major trans-Saharan trading center.

Khitans
Horse-riding nomads related to the Mongols who, in the 10th century A.D., established an empire centered on Beijing and administered on semi-Chinese lines.

Khmer Empire
Established in the 6th century A.D. in what are now Cambodia and Laos, the Khmer Empire reached its height in the 10th to 12th centuries, when its capital was Angkor Wat.

kofun
Massive burial mounds found in Japan and dating from about the 4th to 6th centuries A.D. They are known as "keyhole tombs" for their shape.

Koguryo
The earliest Korean state, founded in the 1st century A.D. and strongly influenced by Chinese culture. Koguryo was conquered by the neighboring state of Silla in 668.

Koran
The holy text of Islam. Believed to have been divinely dictated to the Prophet Muhammad in the form of long poems, or *shuras*, it was brought together in book form in about 650 A.D. by the Caliph Uthman.

Lombards
A Germanic people who established a kingdom in northern Italy from 568 to 774.

Macedonian Dynasty
Byzantine dynasty founded in 867 by Emperor Basil I. The early Macedonian emperors regained territories lost to Muslim rulers, expanded trade, and fostered a revival of learning. After a period of decline the dynasty ended in 1081.

Maghreb
Also spelled Maghrib. The western part of Islamic North Africa covered by the modern states of Libya, Tunisia, Algeria, Morocco, and Mauritania.

Magyars
People originating in northeastern Europe who gradually migrated south to found the Kingdom of Hungary in the late 9th century.

Mayan long count
In the complex calculations of the Mayan calendar, the reckoning of long periods of time in terms of *baktuns*, each equivalent to 144,000 days (approximately 400 years). History was measured in cycles of 13 baktuns; the current cycle, starting in 3114 B.C., ends in 2012.

Merovingian Dynasty
The dynasty of Frankish kings that ruled the kingdom founded by Clovis from 481 until 751, when they were supplanted by the Carolingians.

Mesopotamia
The ancient Greek name, meaning "between the rivers," for the fertile land between the Tigris and Euphrates rivers in southern Iraq. Here the Sumerians, Babylonians, and Assyrians established their civilizations.

Mississippian Culture
The successor to the Hopewell Culture, this tradition emerged along the Mississippi Valley in the 9th century: It organized agriculture on an unprecedented scale and constructed large and elaborate flat-topped burial mounds.

Moche Culture
The culture associated with the Moche River valley in coastal northern Peru, which flourished from about the 1st to 8th century A.D. The Moche people built ceremonial centers with platform mounds; one of them, the Pyramid of the Sun, is among the largest in the Americas.

monasticism
An austere way of life followed by groups of men or women living in a religious community. Many religions practice monasticism, including Buddhism and Christianity. Monasticism developed in the early Christian church in the 3rd and 4th centuries.

Monophysite sect
Christians who believed that the person of Jesus Christ remained wholly divine even when he took human form (orthodox teaching holds that Jesus has two natures: human and divine).

Moravia
An area along the Morava River, a tributary of the Danube, that was settled by Slavs in the 6th century. The Moravians subsequently swore allegiance to the Franks.

Nara
The first imperial capital of Japan, from 710 to 784, and an early center of Japanese Buddhism.

Nestorian sect
A Christian sect that stressed the separateness of Jesus's two natures, human and divine. The doctrine was propounded by the Syrian ecclesiast Nestorius, patriarch of Constantinople from 428 to 431, when he was condemned as a heretic. To escape persecution, many of his followers emigrated to Iraq, Syria, and Persia.

Normans
Descendants of the Norsemen who in the 10th century settled in northern France and adopted French language and culture, while retaining their aggressive Viking energy. The Normans conquered England, Scotland, parts of Wales and Ireland, southern Italy, Sicily, and Malta.

Northern Zhou Dynasty
Dynasty that seized power in western Wei (the northernmost kingdom of China) in 557 and expanded its power base into eastern Wei and southwest China. In 581 the Northern Zhou were overthrown by one of their generals, Yang Jian, who reunited China and founded the Sui Dynasty.

Nubia
The region to the south of Egypt on the Nile River, roughly equivalent to modern Sudan.

Olmecs
A people who flourished from about 1250 to 200 B.C. in southern Mexico and neighboring regions and who were responsible for the first great culture of the central American region. Olmec influence lingered on in the Mayan and other cultures for many centuries.

Orthodox church
Also known as the Eastern Orthodox church. The branch of the Christian church recognized throughout the Greek-speaking world of the eastern Mediterranean. Its spiritual head was, and is, the patriarch (archbishop) of Constantinople. The Slavs of eastern Europe and the Russians subsequently became part of the Orthodox church.

Ostrogoths
A Germanic people living in the area north of the Black Sea who were conquered and displaced by the Huns in about 370 A.D. Under their leader Theodoric (c.455–526) they moved into Italy in 488 and established a kingdom that lasted until 555.

pagoda
A religious monument introduced with Buddhism into China and other Southeast Asian countries. Derived from the Indian stupa—a pinnacled dome housing Buddhist relics—Chinese pagodas are multistoried buildings whose design was based on existing watchtowers.

Pala Dynasty
Founded by Gopala in 750, but brought to prominence by his son Dharmapala (770–810), this dynasty built a formidable empire in Bengal and Bihar, in northern India.

papacy
The ruling body of the Catholic church, headed by the pope (the bishop of Rome). In the Middle Ages the pope was recognized as the undisputed head of the church in the west and also had considerable political power as the ruler of the Papal States.

Polynesians
Seafaring people who probably originated in Southeast Asia and the East Indies, and whose progess was marked by the spread of the Lapita Culture. Notable for their navigational skills and double-hulled dugout canoes, they settled Samoa and Tonga by about 1000 B.C. and spread out across other Pacific islands in the course of the next two millennia.

pre-Columbian
Adjective used to describe objects, cultures, and peoples of the Americas predating the arrival of the explorer Christopher Columbus in 1492.

Pueblo Culture
A culture in southwestern North America characterized by large apartment settlements centered on a ceremonial building called a kiva. The first pueblos were built in about 900 A.D.; by the year 1000 many of them consisted of 200 rooms or more.

Romanesque
A style of architecture found throughout western Europe from the 8th to 12th centuries, marked by rounded arches and vaulted ceilings supported on solid piers. Arches, doors, and windows frequently have incised decorations.

Rus
The first Russian state, which was founded by Swedish Vikings in the 9th century centered on the towns of Novgorod and Kiev. The word may derive from the Finnish name for Sweden, *Ruotsi*.

Sassanian Dynasty
Dynasty of Persian kings (224–651 A.D.) named after Sassan, grandfather of Ardashir I, the first Sassanian ruler.

Saxons
Germanic people inhabiting the Baltic coast of north Germany. In the late 8th century they resisted for 32 years Charlemagne's campaigns to absorb them into the Frankish Empire, but were eventually conquered and converted to Christianity in 785. Saxony, their homeland, later became a powerful medieval duchy.

Seljuk Turks
Nomadic fighters from Central Asia, the Seljuks became Muslims on arrival in West Asia around the 10th century. They went on to found an empire, reinvigorating an enfeebled Sunni Islam.

Shiites
Muslims of the Shia-i Ali, the "Party of Ali," claiming allegiance to Muhammad's son-in-law and to those imams believed to be his spiritual successors.

Slav
Originally from Central Asia, the Slavs settled in eastern and southeastern Europe during the 2nd and 3rd millennia B.C. Modern Slavs include Russians, Ukrainians, Poles, Czechs, Slovaks, Serbs, Croats, Slovenes, Macedonians, and Bulgars.

Song Dynasty
One of China's greatest dynasties (960–1279), whose rulers presided over a remarkable flowering of art and literature. The Song period also saw the invention of movable type for printing and gunpowder for use in weapons.

Srivijaya
Maritime empire that dominated much of the Malay–Indonesian archipelago from the 6th to the 14th centuries. Influenced by India and largely Buddhist, it also blended indigenous traditions.

stupa
Dome-shaped Buddhist monument representing the universe and usually containing relics of the Buddha or of a Buddhist saint.

Taika Reform
A series of measures announced by Emperor Kotuku in 646 that were intended to remodel Japanese society along Chinese lines, in the process transferring power from local lords to the emperor himself.

Tang Dynasty
A line of emperors inaugurated by Gaozu in 618 that presided over a time of immense power and prosperity for China, as well as a golden age of literature, art, and ideas. The dynasty ended with Ai Zong's overthrow in 907.

themes
Military districts of the Byzantine Empire. Each theme was governed by a general and settled by soldiers who, in return for land and tax exemptions, performed military service for the emperor.

Tiahuanaco
The capital of a civilization established on the southern shores of Lake Titicaca in the Bolivian Andes Mountains. Founded in about 500 A.D., the city reached the height of its influence in the late 1st millennium A.D.

Toltecs
The people who ruled central Mexico from the 9th to the 12th centuries A.D. Expert builders and metalworkers, their capital was at Tula, north of present-day Mexico City.

Uighurs
Warlike nomads from Central Asia, the Uighurs invaded both China and Tibet in the 8th century, and were soon pushing westward, building an empire that anticipated that of Genghis Khan.

Umayyad Dynasty
The successors of Umar, who ruled the Islamic world as caliphs after the Prophet Muhammad's death; their legitimacy long challenged, they were overthrown by the Shiite Abbasids in 750.

Vandals
A Germanic people who invaded the Roman Empire in 406–409 A.D. and settled in Spain. In 429 they reached North Africa and established a kingdom there, from which they attacked Rome in 455. The Vandal Kingdom survived until 534.

Varangians
Swedish Vikings who founded Rus and opened up trading routes to Byzantium and the Arab lands. The name may come from an Old Norse word meaning "men of the pledge," or confederates.

Vedas
Literally "books of knowledge," a series of sacred poems dating back to India's Aryan period and probably composed from about 1500 to 900 B.C. The hymns set out the ordering principles not only of Hinduism but of Aryan society in general.

Vinland
Norse name for the area of North America, probably on the Newfoundland coast, that the Viking adventurer Leif Eriksson visited in about the year 1000 A.D.

Visigoths
A Germanic people related to the Ostrogoths who invaded the Roman Empire in 376 A.D. and founded a kingdom in southwestern France and Spain.

Wei
The northernmost, as well as the richest and most populous, of the three kingdoms into which China was divided after the collapse of the Han Dynasty in 200 A.D. The other two were Shu and Wu.

Yamato kings
The rulers of the Yamato Plain on the island of Honshu who gradually extended their authority throughout the whole of Japan between the 4th and 8th centuries A.D. They were strongly influenced by Chinese culture.

Zapotecs
A people of ancient Mexico, living in the Oaxaca Valley, who developed the earliest script in the Americas. Their most important center was at Monte Albán, which flourished between 400 B.C. and 700 A.D.

Zoroastrianism
Religion founded by Zoroaster (also known as Zarathustra), a Persian prophet of the 6th century B.C., which sees the world and history in terms of a struggle between the forces of good and evil. It is still practiced by a few communities in Iran and by the Parsis of western India.

FACTS AT A GLANCE: HIGH MIDDLE AGES

Adena Culture
A group of North American hunter-gatherer communities that settled in the Ohio Valley from about 1000 B.C. The culture was at its peak from c.700-100 B.C.; finds from sites include copper jewelry and decorated human skulls.

Albigensians
The name given to members of the Cathar sect living in southern France in the 12th and 13th centuries. As Cathars, they believed that matter is evil and that Christ did not really undergo birth or death. A papal crusade against them was supported by the French king and northern nobles. It led in the first decades of the 13th century to their eradication and the destruction of the rich culture of the lands where they flourished.

Almohad Dynasty
A Moroccan religious movement, the al-Muwahhidun were angered at what they saw as the increasing decadence of Islam. Seizing power in 1130, they ruled until 1269, extending their influence through much of the Maghrib and into al-Andalus (southern Spain).

Almoravid Dynasty
A Berber dynasty that established a religious and military empire in North Africa in the 11th century and extended its rule over Muslim Spain.

Anasazi Culture
An agrarian civilization of the American Southwest that, having first emerged as the "Basketmaker Culture" around the 2nd century B.C., reached its apex around 700 A.D. in the adobe-built towns of the Pueblo Period.

Andalusia, Kingdom of
Known in Arabic as al-Andalus, this Islamic state in southern Spain lasted from 711 to 1492, by which time it was much reduced in extent and influence. It reached a height of prosperity and cultural richness around the 11th century.

Angkor
The ancient capital of the Khmer Empire in northwestern Cambodia, whose ruins date mainly from the 10th to 12th centuries.

antipope
A rival put up as pope in opposition to the official papacy in Rome by a ruler who felt the church's choice would be hostile to his own interests. Frederick I Barbarossa's 1159 appointment, Adrian IV, was just one example of many from the medieval period.

artesian well
A well in which water rises to the surface through a borehole from an underground reservoir, or aquifer, under natural pressure. The name comes from the first known artesian well, drilled by monks at Artois, France, in the 12th century.

Assassins
European name for a Shiite Muslim sect founded in the 11th century by Hasan-i Sabbah, a fanatical opponent of Sunni Islam. The Assassins used murder as a political weapon—hence the English word "assassination."

atabeg
A Turkish military governor. As the Seljuk Empire broke up, atabegs such as Zangi of Mosul set themselves up as independent rulers.

Ayubbid Dynasty
The line of sultans founded by Saladin when he seized power in Egypt in 1171. They ruled not only Egypt itself but also much of West Asia until the dynasty's collapse in 1250.

Ayutthaya
A powerful kingdom of central Thailand that flourished between the 14th and the 18th centuries. Its capital city of the same name is about 55 miles (90 km) north of Bangkok, the modern capital of Thailand.

Aztecs
Mesoamerican people who built an empire in the Valley of Mexico in the course of the 15th century. Their origins are uncertain: They are believed to have arrived from the north, probably around the year 1200. They built their capital, Tenochtitlán, on the present site of Mexico City.

bailey
The space within the outer walls of a castle, usually including an exercise yard, stables, storerooms, and living quarters for the garrison.

Balts
Peoples of northern Europe living beside the Baltic Sea in the region of present-day Lithuania, Latvia, and Estonia.

Benin
West African kingdom founded during the 13th century by a ruler known as the oba. By the 16th century Benin's territory covered a region between the Niger River delta and what is now the Nigerian capital, Lagos.

Bohemia
A medieval kingdom corresponding very roughly with what is now the Czech Republic (although the easternmost region of that country, Moravia, was then a separate state).

Bulgars
Central Asian nomads, the Bulgars joined the westward push from this region in the 7th century. They ended up in the Balkan region of southeast Europe, first as invaders and then as mercenary soldiers employed by the Byzantine Empire.

Buyid Dynasty
Also known as the Buwayhid Dynasty. Shiite Muslim dynasty originating in Persia that occupied Baghdad, capital of the Sunni Abbasid Dynasty, in 945. The Buyids ruled in the name of the Abbasid caliph until they were expelled by the Seljuk Turks in 1055.

Byzantine Empire
The successor to the Eastern Roman Empire, with its capital at Constantinople (present-day Istanbul).

Cahokia
Mississippi Culture town located in Illinois. By the end of the 11th century Cahokia was home to as many as 25,000 people, but the population began to decline after 1200, and by the 1400s the site had been abandoned.

calligraphy
The art of handwriting, practiced in all literate civilizations but regarded in China and Japan as one of the greatest of the visual arts.

camera obscura
A box with a tiny hole for projecting the inverted image of the scene outside onto a screen inside.

Canyon de Chelly
A canyon in northeastern Arizona formed where a narrow stream has cut deep into the plateau. The Ancestral Pueblo people built dwellings at the base of the red sandstone cliffs and in caves on the canyon sides. Canyon de Chelly is now a national monument.

Castile
Former kingdom in northern Spain that derived its name from the large number of castles built on its frontier with the Moors. In 1230 it was permanently united with the kingdom of Léon.

Chichimecs
A nomadic people from northern Mexico who are thought to have destroyed the Toltec capital of Tula around 1175.

Children's Crusade
Mass movement that in 1212 led up to 30,000 Christian children from France and northern Europe to set off on a fruitless quest to liberate the biblical Holy Land from Islamic control. Most disappeared without trace.

Chimú
A powerful, urban-based civilization that flourished on the arid coastal strip of northern Peru from about 1200. Its capital, Chan Chan, may have had as many as 200,000 inhabitants. Toward 1400 the Chimú were incorporated into the expanding empire of the Incas.

chivalry
The code of behavior embodying the ideals of gallantry by which knights in medieval Europe were expected to live. The word derives from the French *chevalier*, meaning "horse soldier."

Chola Dynasty
Southern Indian dynasty that came to the fore in 850 A.D. when Vijayalaya seized the city of Tanjore. Their empire extended overseas to include parts of modern Malaysia and Indonesia, but declined from the 12th century on.

Cistercian Order
A monastic order founded by Robert de Molesme at Cîteaux, France, in 1098. It followed a strict rule of work and prayer. The charismatic churchman St. Bernard of Clairvaux helped promote the order, and by the end of 12th century there were more than 500 Cistercian monasteries throughout Europe.

Concordat of Worms
A peace agreement to end the contest between the pope and the German emperor over lay investiture made in 1122 at Worms, a town on the Rhine River in Germany that was an important bishopric in medieval times.

Coptic Church
A branch of Christianity founded in Egypt in the 5th century that still survives there today.

Crusades
A series of Christian military expeditions sent by the pope and led by kings and princes to win back the biblical Holy Land from the Muslims. Crusades also took place against the Muslims in Spain and the pagan Balts and Slavs of northern Europe.

Dalmatia
Eastern Adriatic region covering present-day Croatia, Bosnia, Herzegovina, and Montenegro.

Deccan Plateau
A raised area of largely level country occupying much of central and southern India, including inland areas of the modern states of Andhra Pradesh, Kamataka, Kerala, and Tamil Nadu. It is bordered to east and west by mountains—the Western and Eastern Ghats respectively; to the north it falls away toward the northern plains.

Delhi Sultanate
The Muslim kingdom established in northern India by Muhammad Ghuri when he captured Delhi in 1193. Under his successors it would expand to rule much of the subcontinent. Surviving Ghenghis Khan's 1222 invasion in a weakened state, the sultanate was finally destroyed by the onslaught of Tamerlane's forces in 1398.

Domesday Book
A survey of property in England carried out in 1086 by royal officials on the instructions of William the Conqueror for taxation purposes and to discover the value of crown lands. The *Domesday Book* is still preserved today in two volumes in the Public Record Office, London.

Dominican Order
An order of friars (wandering monks) founded by St. Dominic (c.1170–1221). Rather than minister to the poor like the Franciscans, however, their mission was to spread the orthodox Catholic word among pagans, Muslims, and errant Christian sects.

dowager
A widow holding a title and authority received from her deceased husband.

Druze
A religious sect whose members believe that the Fatimid caliph al-Hakim (996–1021) is God. Founded in Egypt in the 11th century, the sect fled to Palestine to avoid persecution. Most of its members now live in Syria, Lebanon, and Israel.

duchy
A feudal estate granted by an emperor or king to a duke, the highest rank of noble.

earl
Originally a Danish underking. When England unified under a single king in the 10th century, the earls still held extensive powers within their territories, known as earldoms. The Normans broke up the earldoms but kept the title of earl as the equivalent of their own rank of count.

ecclesiastical
Adjective relating to the organization and administration of the Christian church rather than its spiritual or moral teachings.

excommunication
A judgment issued by the pope or a bishop banning an individual from participating in the rites of the Catholic church for a limited or indefinite period.

Fatimid Dynasty
Muslim Shiite dynasty founded in Tunisia in 909 by Ubayd Allah, who claimed descent from the prophet Muhammad's daughter Fatima and her husband Ali. In 969 the Fatimids conquered Egypt, founding the city of Cairo as their capital. The dynasty survived until 1171.

fief
A feudal estate (land holding) granted to a vassal (tenant) by a sovereign lord such as a king or duke.

Franciscan Order
A religious order founded by St. Francis of Assisi (c.1181–1226) whose members were friars, living among the people as wandering beggars, rather than monks cloistered in settled and often wealthy monasteries. The Franciscans were often known as the Gray Friars, from the color of their cowls.

Franks
A Germanic people who settled east of the Rhine River in what are now the Netherlands in the 3rd century B.C. After the fall of the Western Roman Empire the Frankish kings gradually conquered most of Gaul (France), Italy, and Germany, creating an empire that lasted from the 6th to the 9th century. France is named for them.

Fujiwara Clan
The ruling clan in Japan from 858 to 1185. During that period the office of emperor became merely ceremonial, while real power was exercised by Fujiwara chancellors and regents.

Ghana, Empire of
Not to be confused with today's West African country, the Empire of Ghana was established farther north in an area that includes parts of present-day Mali, Senegal, and Mauritania. There the Soninke people built a realm that flourished between the 5th and 13th centuries on the trade in gold with North Africa.

Golden Horde
Western portion of the Mongol Empire, covering most of Russia. Also known as the Kipchak Khanate, it was founded in the mid 13th century by Genghis Khan's grandson, Batu.

Gothic style
The architectural style associated with the great cathedrals of medieval Europe and characterized by soaring spires and vaulted roofs, extravagantly sculpted stonework (including grotesque gargoyles), and spectacular stained-glass windows. Gothic architects and craftsmen sought through their works to impress the glory of God and the church on a population that remained largely illiterate.

427

Great Zimbabwe

A stone-built fortified settlement on the Harare Plateau in the country that now bears its name, built around 1200 as capital of a wealthy and powerful southern African empire with trading contacts as far afield as China.

Hanseatic League

Association of German trading cities and merchant groups that flourished in the 13th and 14th centuries. The league monopolized trade in the Baltic region and established commercial bases from Novgorod to London.

Hausa

A people living in scattered communities along West Africa's Niger River who came together to form larger states around 1200. Each state specialized in economic activities ranging from textiles to slave trading; competition between them eventually gave way to chronic conflict.

Heian

The period of Japanese history from the foundation of Heian (later named Kyoto) as the Japanese capital in 794 to the end of the 12th century. It was a golden age of Japanese literature and of a leisured court culture.

Hohenstaufen Dynasty

A family of princes who ruled Germany and northern Italy as Holy Roman emperors from 1138 to 1254. The Hohenstaufens were also known as Waiblingers, from their castle of Waiblingen in Germany, while their principal rvials for the imperial title were the influential Welf family. In Italy the two names became corrupted into Guelphs and Ghibellines—titles that came to identify the rival parties of the pope and emperor respectively in the wars of the 13th century.

Hojo Clan

Warrior clan that came to dominate Japan for a century after the decline of the Minomoto line of shoguns in the early 13th century.

Hoyasala Dynasty

A family of rulers from the Western Ghats, the mountains between India's Deccan Plateau and southwestern ("Malabar") coast. From the 11th century they carved out a significant empire at the expense of the declining Chalukya Dynasty.

Ife Culture

Early culture of the Yoruba people, established in the 13th century in the city and kingdom of Ife in present-day Nigeria. Ife Culture is characterized by naturalistic sculptures made of bronze or wood.

Ifriqiya

A medieval North African province, roughly corresponding to modern Tunisia, that gave its name to the continent of Africa. In 1230 the governor of Ifriqiya renamed the country after its new capital, Tunis.

Inca

Name of the ruling dynasty that built an empire centered on Cuzco in southern Peru in the 15th century. The term also served as the title of the ruling emperor. The first Inca emperor was Manco Capac, who came to the throne in about 1200 A.D.

Inquisition

Roman Catholic court set up in 1233 to suppress heresy (religious dissent). At first punishment was by excommunication; later inquisitors used fines, imprisonment, torture, and execution.

insei

Literally "cloister government," a system that enabled emperors of 12th-century Japan to escape the influence of the powerful Fujiwara Clan by nominally abdicating while continuing to exercise power through their young sons, whom they installed on the throne.

Investiture Contest

A dispute between the Catholic church and state in the 11th and 12th centuries over the right claimed by many rulers to appoint clergymen. In 1075 Pope Gregory VII forbade all lay (nonchurch) investiture, provoking a clash with the Holy Roman Emperor Henry IV.

Islam

Literally meaning "surrender" to God's will, the faith based on the teachings of the Prophet Muhammad in 7th-century Arabia and subsequently spread through military expansion and trade through much of West Asia and beyond. Its followers are known as Muslims.

Jainism

A religion founded in India by the 6th century B.C, Jainism teaches the necessity of self-denial in order to obtain liberation of the soul and urges sympathy and compassion for all forms of life.

jihad

Derived from the Arabic term for "strive" or "fight," this word may refer simply to a moral or spiritual struggle but is also used to describe the waging of a holy war on the enemies of Islam.

Jin Dynasty

Two dynasties of this name have held power in China. One briefly united the nation under Emperor Wudi and his successors from 265 to 316 A.D.; the other controlled eastern Manchuria, northern China, and part of Mongolia from 1127 to 1234.

junk

Southeast Asian wooden sailing vessel, distinguished by a broad, flat prow, little or no keel, high masts with sails braced by battens, a high poop deck at the rear, and a deep rudder.

Jurchen

A people of Manchuria who invaded northern China in 1127, expelling the Song Dynasty, whose ruler and government fled south. The Jurchen established their own Jin Dynasty, which ruled from 1127 to 1234, when it fell to the Mongols.

Kamakura Period

The period between 1185 and 1333 when, after decades of civil conflict, Japan was united under the rule of the shoguns of the Minamoto family, whose capital was at Kamakura.

Kante Dynasty

The royal house under whose rule West Africa's Soso Kingdom reached its greatest extent and influence between 1180 and 1230. Its most famous king, Sumanguru, reigned in the early years of the 13th century.

Khalji Dynasty

An Afghan Turkish family that won power when Firuz Khalji toppled the last slave sultan of Delhi in 1290. The dynasty reigned until 1320, when Sultan Mubarak was assassinated in a coup engineered by his chief minister, Khusrau Khan.

khan

Meaning "ruler" or "prince," the title held by the Mongol conqueror Genghis and his successors. The word also came to be used by non-Mongol rulers in China, Central Asia, and Turkey.

Khitans

Horse-riding nomads related to the Mongols who in the 10th century A.D., established an empire centered on Beijing and administered on semi-Chinese lines.

Khmer Empire

Established in the 6th century A.D. in what are now Cambodia and Laos, the Khmer Empire reached its height in the 10th to 12th centuries, when its capital was Angkor.

Khurasan

Region of central Iran that in medieval times was often invaded by nomadic peoples from Central Asia. During the 11th century Khurasan was controlled first by Mahmud of Ghazni and then by the Seljuk Turks.

Kievan Russia

The early Russian state, founded in the 9th century and centered on Kiev in present-day Ukraine.

Kilwa
Situated on a small island off what is now Tanzania, this city was for many centuries one of the main trading centers of East Africa's Swahili Coast. Established in the 10th century by Arab traders, it was taken over around 1200 by settlers from Shiraz in Iran.

knight
A mounted soldier in the service of a lord. According to the code of chivalry, knights were inducted into their rank, often on the field of battle, after serving in the lord's household as a page and then a squire.

kKnights Hospitaller
Members of a religious military order established to defend the Latin Kingdom of Jerusalem in the 12th century.

Latin Empire
The empire established by the armies of the Fourth Crusade in Asia Minor and Greece after they sacked Constantinople in 1204 and expelled the Byzantine emperor. It lasted until 1261, when the Byzantine Greeks recaptured their lost lands.

lay
Relating to the laity or followers of a religion, as distinguished from its clergy.

lay investiture
The practice, common in the early Middle Ages, whereby kings and princes were able to appoint churchmen such as bishops and abbots to office. When Pope Gregory VII tried to end lay investiture, claiming the right for the church alone, the Holy Roman Emperor Henry IV and his successors saw it as an attack on imperial power. The resulting struggle became known as the Investiture Contest.

Léon
Christian kingdom in central Spain founded in 913. Léon was permanently united with the kingdom of Castile in 1230.

Lombard League
An association of north Italian cities established in 1164 to resist the power of the Holy Roman Empire.

Lombards
Also known as Langobards ("long beards"); a Germanic people who established a kingdom in Italy from 568 to 774.

longboat
The typical boat used by the Vikings—a narrow, shallow-draft, seagoing vessel, usually with a high curving bow and sternpost, propelled by a single sail and oars.

longhouse
A communal dwelling of the Northern Iroquoian farming peoples of North America. Longhouses were occupied by several families and had three or more hearths; they stood in village clusters within a palisade.

lost-wax technique
A method of casting metal objects by which a wax model is enclosed in clay, leaving a hole in the bottom of the casing. When the whole is baked, the wax melts and runs away, leaving a hard clay mould in which the metal object is then cast.

madrasa
An Islamic educational institution. The madrasa system was pioneered by the 11th-century Seljuk vizir Nizam al-Mulk as a way of countering Shiite propaganda.

Magna Carta
A charter signed by King John of England in 1215 in which he agreed to respect the rights and privileges of his feudal barons.

mahdi
Meaning in Arabic "restorer of the faith," this title—implying the coming of a messiah who will establish the reign of justice on earth—has been assumed by many Muslim leaders through history.

Mamelukes
Originally descended from freed Turkish slaves, the Mamelukes were a military elite who seized power in Egypt in 1250, establishing a sultanate that lasted until 1571.

Manchuria
A region in east Asia that today forms the northeastern part of China. It was the homeland of the Jin Dynasty, which seized part of China from the Song, and of the Manchu, who provided China's last imperial dynasty from 1644 to 1911.

Manding
Mande-speaking peoples who established states in West Africa in the 13th century.

Maya
Amerindian people of the Yucatán Peninsula and southern Mexico, Guatemala, and Honduras. The Maya of the Classic Period (c.250–800 A.D.) are noted for their stepped pyramids, carved monuments, and knowledge of astronomy. They used a pictographic form of writing.

Mesoamerica
Literally "Middle America"; the term used by historians of the pre-Columbian era to indicate the part of the Americas that lies between what are now the north of Mexico and Panama.

Minamoto Clan
A powerful warrior clan of medieval Japan whose chieftains assumed the title of shogun—literally, "commander of the imperial guard"— in the late 12th century, in effect making them the nation's true rulers.

minaret
One of the towers outside a mosque from which Muslims are summoned to prayer five times a day by the chanting call of the muezzin. A great mosque may have as many as six minarets.

Mogollon Culture
A civilization that flourished around a thousand years ago in the uplands along what is now the border between Arizona and New Mexico. The Mogollon were increasingly influenced by their Anasazi neighbors, the two cultures finally becoming indistinguishable.

Mongols
A loose association of nomadic herdsmen and raiders originating in the grasslands of eastern Siberia. Under Ghenghiz Khan and his successors they created the largest land empire ever seen.

mosque
From the Arabic *masjid*, "place of prostration," the name given to a Muslim place of worship. Basically a large hall or arena with steps or a platform from which the Friday sermon is preached, a mosque typically has an arched mihrab or wall-niche indicating the direction of Mecca, Muhammad's birthplace, which Muslims must face while praying.

motte
A hill or mound, either natural or artificial, on which a medieval castle keep was built

muezzin
The official of a mosque whose task it is to issue the five-times-daily call to prayer from a minaret.

Navarre
Medieval kingdom comprising the Spanish province of Navarre and an adjoining area of southwestern France. Its Christian rulers resisted conquest by the Moors, retaining their independence until 1284, when Navarre became French as part of a marriage alliance.

Neo-Confucianism
A revival of Confucian philosophy in Song Dynasty China. Its followers believed that the universe resulted from an interplay between the realm of principle (which might be termed "laws") and the realm of matter and energy.

nomad
A person who has no settled home but lives

on the move, whether as a hunter-gatherer or a pastoralist or herder, moving livestock from place to place in search of the best possible pasturage.

Norse

Term applied to Scandinavian Vikings—Danes, Swedes, and Norwegians—who from the 8th to the 11th centuries raided and settled in Britain, Ireland, France, Russia, Iceland, Greenland, and other lands.

Novgorod

The original capital of Russia, founded in 862. After the capital moved to Kiev, Novgorod continued to flourish as a commercial center with a monopoly on the Russian fur trade.

Orthodox church

Also known as the Eastern Orthodox church. The branch of the Christian church recognized throughout the Greek-speaking world of the eastern Mediterranean. Its spiritual head was, and is, the patriarch (bishop) of Constantinople. The Slavs of eastern Europe and the Russians subsequently became part of the Orthodox church.

Outremer

A name meaning "land overseas" used particularly by Norman and French crusaders to describe the Crusader States established in Palestine and Syria.

overlordship

A system of rule in which every man owes fealty (loyalty and obedience) to the man immediately above him in a hierarchy topped by a king or emperor.

Pagan

A city on the Irrawaddy River in Myanmar that was the capital of a powerful Buddhist empire from the 9th to the 13th century.

Pala Dynasty

Founded by Gopala in 750, but brought to its height by his son Dharmapala (770–810), this dynasty built a formidable empire in Bengal and Bihar in northern India.

patriarchate

The office (or time in office) of a patriarch, the title of the leaders of the Eastern Orthodox church and the Coptic church.

pit hut

The standard dwelling for the Mogollon Culture: a circular pit a yard (1 m) or more deep, roofed over with a frame of logs, covered by reeds and twigs, and sealed off with mud.

Plantagenet Dynasty

A line of English rulers descended from the French nobleman Geoffrey Le Bel, Count of Anjou, who was said to have worn a *planta genista*, or "sprig of broom," in his cap. His son Henry II became king of England in 1154, and his descendants remained in power until the 15th century.

Prussians

A Slavic people living on the Baltic coast of what is now Poland who were converted to Christianity by the Teutonic Knights; they gave their name to the later state of Prussia.

Pueblo Culture

A culture in southwestern North America characterized by large apartment settlements centered on a ceremonial building called a kiva. The first pueblos were built in about 700 A.D.; by the year 1000 many of them consisted of 200 rooms or more.

Punjab

One of the northernmost districts of India, bordering what is now Pakistan, and the first area to fall before the advance of Mahmud of Ghazni's Islamic forces in the 11th century.

Pure Land School (Jodoshu)

School of Japanese Buddhism founded in the late 12th century by Honen, which taught that devotion to amida ("infinite light") was the best possible route to salvation and was open to everyone.

Pyu

A Tibeto–Burman people who established a number of city-kingdoms in the Irrawaddy Valley of northern Myanmar in the 1st millennium A.D. The Pyu states were destroyed in about 835 by Nanchao.

Ramayana

Indian epic poem, written in about 300 B.C., in which the hero Rama and his friend Hanuman strive to recover Rama's wife Sita, abducted by the demon king Ravana.

Roman Catholic church

The Western or Latin Christian church, headed by the pope, the bishop of Rome. Today, the Roman Catholic church is the largest Christian community, with a membership of about 1 billion believers.

romance

In the Middle Ages a tale of chivalry and knightly valor marked by the hero's reverent adoration for a fair but often unattainable lady. The courtly romances drew on a common stock of source

material, especially the legends associated with King Arthur, a semilegendary British ruler of the Dark Ages.

Rum

A corruption of "Rome"; the Islamic name for Anatolia (today's Asiatic Turkey), which had been a province of the Roman Empire. In the late 11th century Rum broke away from the Seljuk Empire to become an independent sultanate.

Saladin

The name westerners have given to Salah al-Din al-Ayubbi (1138–93), an Iraqi Kurd who rose to prominence in the service of the Zangid Dynasty then ruling Syria and Egypt as the emir's viceroy in Egypt. In 1171 he seized power in his own name, restoring Sunnism as Islam's dominant strain. He defeated the European crusaders at Hattin (1187).

Salado Culture

A culture that emerged in the upper valleys of the Salt and Gila rivers in eastern Arizona around the start of the 12th century, blending influences from the Mogollon, Hohokam, and Anasazi traditions.

samurai

The hereditary class of warriors that dominated Japanese society from the 12th to the 19th century. Samurai lived by the code of bushido ("the way of the warrior"), which prized above all things skill with weapons, especially the sword and the bow, physical fitness, and courage in battle.

secular

Nonreligious; for example, a secular state is one in whose government priests or other spiritual leaders play no part.

Seljuk Turks

A Turkic tribe or clan who migrated west from Central Asia to found, in the 11th century, an empire covering Anatolia (present-day Asiatic Turkey) and much of Iran and Syria.

Sena Dynasty

A line of kings who brought much of what is now Bangladesh under their rule in the second half of the 12th century. Their kingdom was swallowed up after 1202 by the Delhi Sultanate.

Shahnama

Literally "The Book of Kings"; the Persian national epic, written by the poet Firdausi (c.935–1020). The poem recounts the history of Iran from the earliest times to the Muslim Arab conquests of the 7th century.

sheriff

Originally "shire reeve"; an official delegated by Anglo-Saxon earls from the 11th century on to administer England's shires (or counties, as they are now called). The office was retained by the Normans, who also introduced the sheriff system to Wales and Scotland.

Shiites
Muslims of the Shia-i Ali, the "Party of Ali," claiming allegiance to Muhammad's son-in-law, and to those imams believed to be his spiritual successors.

shogun
Literally "commander of the imperial guard," the title came from 1192 on to be used by the leader of Japan's ruling warrior family. For almost seven centuries the shoguns were the true rulers of Japan, leaving the country's emperors to occupy themselves primarily with ceremonial duties.

Song Dynasty
One of China's greatest dynasties, whose rulers presided over economic growth and a flowering of art and literature. The Song period (960–1279) also saw the invention of movable type for printing and of gunpowder for use in weapons.

Soso
A West African trading kingdom that from the late 12th century came first to rival and then briefly to dominate its northern neighbor, the Kingdom of Ghana, until both were overshadowed by the influence of Almohad Morocco in the 13th century.

Srivijaya
Maritime empire that dominated much of the Malay–Indonesian archipelago from the 6th to the 14th centuries. Influenced by India and largely Buddhist, it also blended indigenous traditions.

Sufi
A Muslim mystic who attempts, through intense meditation or a trance state brought on by repetitive prayer, music, or (in the case of the "whirling dervishes") dance, to transcend worldly concerns and find spiritual enlightenment.

sultan
Taken from the Arabic word for "power" or "authority," this title is often loosely applied to any Muslim ruler but is associated especially with the emperors of the Ottoman Dynasty.

Sunni
A member of the largest sect of Islam, which believes that the first three caliphs were rightful successors to Muhammad and that religious guidance should come from the Koran and other scriptures, not from a human authority.

Taira Clan
The warrior clan that emerged by the mid 12th century as the main power in a strife-torn Japan

only to be displaced by the Minamoto after Yoritomo's victory in the Gempei War (1180–85).

Tarascans
An ancient Mesoamerican people whose descendants still live in the state of Michoacán in northwestern Mexico. Their language is unrelated to any other native Mexican language.

temple mountain
A Hindu temple built in the form of a pyramid symbolizing Mount Meru, the mythical home of the gods.

Teutonic Knights
Members of a German Christian military order founded in 1190 in Palestine, who wore white robes with black crosses. From 1228 they waged crusades against the pagan Prussians and Balts of northeastern Europe, and subsequently controlled Prussia until the 16th century.

theologian
Someone who studies religious questions such as the nature of God and his relations with humans and the universe.

Thule Culture
A culture that developed among the Inuit people along the Arctic coast of North Alaska about 900 A.D. and spread rapidly eastward to reach Greenland by the 12th century. The Thule Inuit hunted whales and used kayaks (skin-covered boats) and dog-drawn sleds for transportation.

Toltecs
The people who ruled central Mexico from the 9th to the 12th century A.D. Expert builders and metalworkers, their capital was at Tula, north of present-day Mexico City.

Trebizond, Kingdom of
A city on the southeastern coast of the Black Sea that broke off from Byzantium just before the sacking of Constantinople by crusaders in 1204.

troubadour
A singer who composed and sang chansons d'amor (songs about themes of love and courtship) at aristocratic courts from the 11th to the 13th centuries, especially in the south of France.

Uighurs
A Turkic nomadic people from the Asian steppe who, having invaded China and Tibet in the 8th century, pushed westward into what are now Uzbekistan, Kazakhstan, and Kirghizistan in the centuries that followed.

vassal
A person who placed himself under the protection of a feudal lord by swearing loyalty and promising

to fight on his lord's behalf in return for land.

Vatican
The city-sized complex of churches, palaces, and offices in Rome, Italy, that is the home of the pope and headquarters of the Roman Catholic church.

Vikings
Scandinavian sea warriors who raided and settled in the rest of Europe from the 8th to 11th centuries.

vizier
The chief minister of the Seljuk Empire. Nowadays an administrative official in some Muslim countries.

Welfs
A German family who became dukes of Bavaria in the 11th century. Their supporters in Italy became known as Guelphs.

Wessex
An Anglo-Saxon kingdom founded in the 5th or 6th century A.D. in western England, which established supremacy over much of England under its best-known ruler, Alfred the Great.

Xiaxia
Also known as Hsia-Hsia. Kingdom of the Tibetan-speaking Tangut tribes that was established in the 11th century and flourished until conquered by Genghiz Khan in the early 13th century.

Yadava Dynasty
A line of kings whose territories lay in the northern part of India's Deccan Plateau.

Zagwe Dynasty
A line of Christian kings ruling in upland Ethiopia from 1137 to 1270. Their empire included modern Eritrea as well as parts of what is now Somalia; it is famed for its sunken churches hewn directly out of the bedrock.

Angevin Dynasty
Named for their origins in Anjou, France, the Angevins formed two distinct dynasties. The first, including the early Plantagenet kings (Henry II, Richard I, and John), ruled not only England but France. The second, expelled from Anjou, reigned in southern Italy from 1266 to 1442, despite losing Sicily in the Sicilian Vespers revolt of 1282.

Aragon, Kingdom of
Kingdom centered on the northeastern Spanish region of that name but in medieval times extending far wider to include the Spanish regions of Catalonia and Valencia and also Italian territories including Naples, Sardinia, and Sicily.

Bahri Dynasty
The first of two distinct lines of Mameluke rulers, originally Turkic slave-soldiers, the Bahri sultans held sway in Cairo from 1250 to 1382. They took their name from the location of their barracks, at al-Bahr beside the Nile River.

Cilicia, Kingdom of
Christian kingdom in southeastern Turkey, sometimes known as Lesser Armenia (Armenia proper lay to the north, between the Black and Caspian seas). It fell to the Mameluke rulers of Egypt in 1375.

Circassians
The people of Circassia, a northwestern district of the Caucasus region between the Black and Caspian seas. The name is also given to the rulers of the Mameluke Burji Dynasty, who originated in the region.

classical style
An art style drawing its inspiration from the culture of ancient Greece and Rome that flourished in western Europe during the Renaissance period from the 14th to 16th centuries.

daimyo
In Japan local warlords who seized power during the Onin War (1467–1477). They ruled the surrounding countryside from strongly defended castles and built up personal armies of loyal samurai warriors, whom they rewarded with landed estates.

Delhi Sultanate
The Muslim kingdom established in northern India by Muhammad Ghuri when he captured Delhi in 1193. Under his successors it would expand to rule much of the subcontinent.

Dominican Order
An order of friars (wandering monks) founded by St. Dominic (c.1170–1221). Rather than minister to the poor like the Franciscans, their mission was to spread the orthodox Catholic word among pagans, Muslims, and errant Christian sects.

Falasha
Ethiopian Jews who claim descent from the biblical King Solomon and Queen of Sheba but whose ancestors were probably converted by Jews who lived in southern Arabia around the start of the Christian era.

Flemish
The word used for the distinctive linguistic, cultural, and ethnic makeup of the people of Flanders.

Franciscan Order
A religious order founded by St. Francis of Assisi (c.1181–1226) whose members were friars, living among the people as wandering beggars rather than monks cloistered in settled (and often wealthy) monasteries. The Franciscans were sometimes known as the Gray Friars from the color of their cowls (the hoods of their robes).

fresco
From the Italian word for "fresh," a method of painting with water-based colors directly onto freshly applied plaster. The artwork thus dries along with the plaster to become an integral part of the finished wall or ceiling.

Gascony
An area of southwestern France that, regarded as a separate and semiindependent territory, was claimed by both French and English kings. It was fought over several times between the 11th and 15th centuries.

Georgia, Kingdom of
A Christian kingdom in the Caucasus Mountains that was conquered by Genghis Khan in 1221 and turned into a Mongol tributary state. Timur the Lame invaded it at least six times.

ghazi
An Islamic warrior dedicated to spreading the faith through jihad (holy war).

Granada, Emirate of
Muslim kingdom in southern Spain, the last to hold out against the Christian reconquest of the peninsula. Its rulers built the Alhambra Palace in the city of Grenada as their main residence.

Great Schism
Split in the Catholic church from 1378 until 1417 that saw rival popes claiming supremacy. The schism did lasting damage to the church.

Guanche
The original inhabitants of the Canary Islands, situated in the Atlantic Ocean off the coast of northwest Africa.

Hohenstaufen Dynasty
A family of princes who ruled Germany and northern Italy as Holy Roman emperors from 1138 to 1254.

Hundred Years' War
A lengthy conflict between the rulers of England and France, fought primarily over the English kings' dynastic claims to large areas of French territory. The war actually lasted for 116 years, from 1337 to 1453, interspersed with periods of truce; by its end all the English territories in France had been lost with the exception of Calais, held until 1558.

Hussites
Followers of the Bohemian (Czech) church reformer Jan Hus, who was burned at the stake for heresy in 1415. The Hussites were Bohemian nationalists, equally opposed to the influence of the papacy and the Holy Roman emperor.

incunabulum (plural: incunabula)
Any book printed in Europe before 1501.

Iroquois
Native American people based in the Great Lake and Eastern Woodland regions of North America, where they formed a confederation of five main tribes. The Iroquois lived in fortified villages; the men hunted, and the women grew crops.

Jagiellonian Dynasty
Important ruling family of eastern Europe from the 14th to 16th centuries, founded by Jagiello (1351–1434), who became grand duke of Lithuania in 1377. In 1386 he married Queen Jadwiga of Poland to become King Vladislav II, thus uniting the crowns of Lithuania and Poland.

janissary
The personal bodyguard of the Ottoman sultan (from the Turkish *yeniçeri*, meaning "new force"), recruited from the Christian boys drafted to the sultan's court under the devshirme system.

Jenné-Jeno
Founded in around 200 B.C., this West African city controlled the north–south trans-Saharan trade throughout the first millennium A.D. It was eventually supplanted by the Kingdom of Ghana and then by Kanem.

Khmer
People of Southeast Asia centered on what is now Cambodia. In the 6th century A.D. they established

an empire in Cambodia and Laos that reached its height in the 10th to 12th centuries, when its capital was Angkor.

Kongo
Bantu-speaking kingdom south of the Congo River in central Africa. It survived until 1665, when it broke up following military defeat at the hands of the Portuguese.

Lan Xang
Buddhist kingdom of the Lao people of Southeast Asia. Before establishing their realm, they were under the rule of the Khmer kings of Angkor Wat.

Lithuania, Kingdom of
The last pagan kingdom in Europe, which finally converted to Christianity in 1387 after agreeing to unite with Poland.

Lodi Dynasty
An Afghan dynasty that ruled from Delhi in northern India from 1451 until 1526.

Low Countries
The area of western Europe now covered by the Netherlands, Belgium, and Luxembourg; they are literally "low," large areas actually lying only inches above sea level.

Majapahit
A Javanese Hindu kingdom established in the late 13th century that embarked on an aggressive campaign of expansion in the mid-14th century. By the 1360s the Majapahit Empire included most of modern Indonesia and Malaya.

Makurra, Kingdom of
Also spelled Mukurra. The largest of the three states to emerge in Nubia after the collapse of Meroë in 350 A.D. (the other two were Nobatia – conquered by Makurra in the 8th century—and Alwa). Christianity was introduced into Makurra in the 6th century. After the Arab incursions of the 7th century its people came under great pressure to convert to Islam. Makurra was finally conquered by the Arabs in the 14th century.

Manding Empire
An alternative name for the Empire of Mali that emphasizes its Mande roots.

Maoris
Polynesian people who settled the previously uninhabited islands of New Zealand from the 9th century on.

Marinid Dynasty
Members of a minor Moroccan tribe that came to prominence in 1248 when it captured the city of

Fez and established a capital there. The Marinids became rulers of Morocco by taking Marrakesh and overthrowing the Almohads in 1269.

mausoleum
An elaborate building designed to house the tomb of a famous individual.

Maya
Amerindian people of the Yucatán Peninsula and adjoining areas of southern Mexico, Guatemala, and Honduras. The Maya of the Classic Period (c.250–800 A.D.) are noted for their stepped pyramids, carved monuments, and knowledge of astronomy. They used a pictographic form of writing.

miracle play
Performed by amateur players at holy festivals, miracle plays were popular entertainments in medieval Europe. They depicted the miraculous works of Christ in the gospels or similar scenes from the lives of the saints.

Morea
A province of southern Greece, located on the Peloponnese Peninsula, that was the last surviving remnant of the Byzantine Empire after the fall of Constantinople in 1453. It finally fell to the Ottomans in 1460.

movable type
In printing, small rectangular blocks, usually made of metal but sometimes of wood, each bearing a raised letter or other character.

Mughal Empire
The empire established by the Mughals, Islamic successors of Timur the Lame who conquered northern India in 1526 and subsequently extended their rule over much of the subcontinent.

Mughal School
An Indian school of painting best known for its miniatures—exquisitely executed small works. It flourished under the Mughal Dynasty.

Muromachi Period
The period of Japanese history from 1338 to 1573 when the country was effectively ruled by the Ashikaga shoguns. It takes its name from the Muromachi district of Kyoto, the then capital, where the shoguns took up residence from 1392.

Muscovy
State centered on Moscow in what is now western Russia that first became established in the 13th century. After the Mongol and Ottoman conquests it became an isolated bulwark of Christianity, following the Eastern Orthodox branch of the faith.

Mwenemutapa
A state on the Zambezi River in southeastern Africa that dominated the gold trade of the region after the decline of Great Zimbabwe.

Nahuatl
The language of a number of native peoples in what is now central Mexico, including the Aztecs. Varieties of Nahuatl are still widely in use today.

Nanchao
A state in what is today southern China, in the area between the Mekong and Chang (Yangtze) rivers. It was powerful from the 9th century to 1253, when the Mongols overran and destroyed it.

Naples, Kingdom of
Realm in the southern part of Italy that was united with the island of Sicily from 1140 to 1268 under various dynasties of kings.

Neo-Confucianism
A revival of Confucian philosophy in Song Dynasty China. Its advocates believed that the universe resulted from an interplay between the realm of principle (which we might call "laws") and the realm of matter and energy.

New World
The Western Hemisphere, especially the continental landmasses of North and South America. The term was first used in the 16th century to distinguish the newly discovered lands of Europe's age of exploration from the "Old World" of Europe and Asia.

Nicaea, Kingdom of
Byzantine kingdom based at Nicaea (modern Iznik, Turkey). It was established by Theodore I Lascaris as a sort of Byzantium-in-exile after western crusaders conquered Constantinople in 1204.

Noh theater
Highly stylized form of theatrical performance that developed in Japan in the 14th century. It involved masks, elaborate costumes, music, dance, and mime.

Otomi
A Nahuatl-speaking people who in the course of the 12th and 13th centuries built an empire in central Mexico.

Ottoman Dynasty
Line of Muslim rulers named after Osman or Uthman, a Turkic tribal leader who came to prominence in eastern Anatolia in 1281. From the 14th century on the Ottomans built a great empire in Western Asia and the eastern Mediterranean that endured until 1919.

Oyrat Mongols
A tribal confederacy of Mongols (also known as Kalmyks) who frequently attacked China's northern frontier during early Ming Dynasty times.

pandemic
An epidemic stretching over a wide geographical area, usually affecting many different countries.

Peasants' Revolt
An uprising in England in 1381, led by Wat Tyler, in protest at low wages and the imposition of the Poll Tax. The rebels marched on London, where they beheaded the archbishop and the king's treasurer before being persuaded to disperse by promises of reform. The promises were not kept, and their leaders were subsequently killed.

pictograph
A picture used in early forms of writing to represent an object.

Poll Tax
A tax levied by England's King Richard II in 1377, 1378, and again in 1380 on every man and woman in his kingdom. The money was intended to support English troops fighting in the Hundred Years' War.

Prester John
A legendary Christian prince believed by medieval Europeans to be the ruler of a mythical African empire, sometimes associated with Ethiopia.

quarantine
A state of enforced isolation imposed on people suspected of carrying a dangerous disease and intended to prevent them from spreading it.

Red Turbans
Chinese rebels opposed to the Mongol rulers of the Yuan Dynasty, so called because of the distinctive red headdresses they wore in battle. Their leader, Zhu Yuanzhang, went on to found the Ming Dynasty.

Renaissance
A revival of classical (Greek and Latin) learning that started in Italy in the 14th century and eventually spread across Europe. The intellectual ferment stimulated a great age of creativity and innovation in the arts.

Serbia, Kingdom of
Long a Byzantine province, Serbia became an independent kingdom under Stefan Nemanja (1168). His Nemanjene successors made Serbia the dominant power in the Balkans, culminating in the reign of Stefan Dusan (1331–1355).

shogun
Literally meaning "commander of the imperial guard," the title that from 1192 on was used by the leader of Japan's ruling warrior family.

Sicilian Vespers
The uprising of the people of Sicily against the rule of France's Angevin Dynasty in 1282. After massacring French settlers on the island, they invited the Aragonese ruler Peter III to take charge.

Sicily, Kingdom of
This kingdom, comprising not only the island of Sicily but much of southern Italy besides, was established when French Norman invaders ousted Byzantine and Arab traders from key coastal settlements in the 12th century.

slave sultan
One of a line of rulers of the Delhi Sultanate in northern India, beginning with Qutbuddin in 1206, who were so called because both Qutbuddin and several of his successors had been born as slaves and won renown and power as soldiers.

Song Dynasty
One of China's great dynasties whose rulers presided over economic growth and a flowering of art and literature. The Song period (960–1279) also saw the invention of movable type for printing and of gunpowder for use in weapons.

Songhai Empire
A trading empire centered on the city of Gao in what is now northwestern Nigeria. Long overshadowed by the power of Mali to the west, it emerged to eclipse Mali in the 15th century.

Soso
A West African trading kingdom that from the late 12th century came first to rival and then briefly to dominate its northern neighbor, the Kingdom of Ghana. Both were eventually overshadowed by the Empire of Mali in the 13th century.

Srivijaya
Maritime empire that dominated much of the Malay–Indonesian archipelago from the 6th to the 13th centuries. Influenced by India and largely Buddhist, it also blended indigenous traditions.

Statute of Labourers
A government measure passed in England in 1351 in the wake of the Black Death. At a time when labor had become scarce, it aimed to prevent laborers from using their new bargaining power to demand higher wages. The discontent it caused was one of the factors behind the Peasants' Revolt.

Sukhothai
The kingdom that arose around the ancient Buddhist shrine-city of that name in northern Thailand when refugees from Nanchao fled there after Kublai Khan's 1253 invasion. It remained a regional power through the 13th and 14th centuries.

Tamil
The language and culture of the peoples of southern India. The 7th century saw a renaissance in Tamil music, art, and poetry.

Tarascans
An ancient Mesoamerican people whose descendants still live in the state of Michoacán in western Mexico. Their language is unrelated to any other native Mexican language.

Tatar
The name given to the peoples of the Golden Horde, the descendants of mixed Turkic–Mongolian ancestry of the Mongol army of Genghis Khan that carved out a substantial khanate in Russia in the 13th century. The Russians continued to pay large amounts of tribute to the Golden Horde until 1480.

Tepanecs
The dominant people in Central Mexico when the Aztecs arrived in the region at the end of the 13th century. Their overthrow in 1428 provided the Aztecs with the core of their future empire.

Teutonic Knights
Members of a German Christian military order founded in 1190 in Palestine, who wore white robes with black crosses. From 1226 they conducted crusades against the pagan Prussians and Balts of northeastern Europe, subsequently controlling Prussia until the 16th century.

Theravada
A school of Buddhism that emphasizes the meditative way of life as the path for individuals to attain *nirvana* (release from suffering).

Transoxiana
The region east of the Oxus (Amu Darya) River in modern-day Uzbekistan where Timur the Lame was born. He subsequently made it the center of his empire and turned its capital, Samarkand, into one of the great cities of his day.

Tuaregs
Camel-driving nomads of the Sahara Desert who made a living by raiding and increasingly trading between the sedentary peoples of North Africa's Mediterranean coast and the empires of sub-Saharan Africa.

Tudor Dynasty
The royal family of England from 1485 to 1603, named for a Welsh nobleman, Owen Tudor, whose grandson became the first Tudor king, Henry VII. The two best-known Tudor monarchs were Henry VIII (1509–1547) and Elizabeth I (1558–1603).

Tughluq Dynasty
The line of rulers established in the Delhi Sultanate when in 1320 Ghiyasuddin—a member of the Turkic Tughluq clan—took power from the Khalji Dynasty, destroyed by internal dissension. The Tughluq Dynasty remained in power until 1412.

Turkmen
Tent-dwelling pastoral nomads living east of the Caspian Sea along the borders of Afghanistan and Iran.

Valois, House of
A dynasty that succeeded to the throne of France in 1328 and ruled until 1589. The first century of Valois rule was dominated by the Hundred Years' War with England.

Vijayanagar
Powerful Hindu kingdom of southern India that flourished from the mid-14th to the 16th century.

Vikings
Scandinavian sea warriors who raided and traded with the rest of Europe from the 8th to the 11th century. Many of them settled outside Scandinavia.

Wallachia
Medieval principality of eastern Europe (now in southern Romania) that was conquered by the Ottoman Turks in 1387.

Wars of the Roses
Civil wars in England from 1455 to 1485, fought between rival dynasties competing for the throne. Supporters of the Lancastrian claimants wore a badge showing a red rose, while the Yorkists' badge was a white rose.

woodblock printing
Method of printing by which a design carved in relief into a woodblock is transferred to a sheet of paper.

woodcut
Print made from a carved woodblock.

Yuan Dynasty
Mongol dynasty that ruled China from 1279 to 1368 after Kublai Khan overthrew the previous Song Dynasty.

Zagwe Dynasty
A line of Christian kings ruling in upland Ethiopia from about 1125 to 1270. Their empire included modern Eritrea as well as parts of what is now Somalia; it is famed for its sunken churches hewn directly out of the bedrock.

Zapotecs
A people of ancient Mexico living in the Oaxaca Valley who developed the earliest script in the Americas. Their most important center was at Monte Albán, which flourished between 400 B.C. and 700 A.D.

Zaria, Emirate of
The name given to the state of Zazzau after its rulers converted to Islam in the 13th century. From about 1300 it assumed an increasingly dominant position among the Hausa states.

Zazzau
The southernmost of the seven Hausa states that sprang up at the start of the 2nd millennium in what are now northern Nigeria, Ghana, Niger, and Togo. Under Muslim rule Zazzau would be renamed the Emirate of Zaria.

Zen
Form of Buddhism introduced into Japan from China in the 12th century. Zen teaches that everyone has the potential to achieve enlightenment through methods such as meditation; the sect has influenced many aspects of Japanese culture, including the tea ceremony.

Zianid Dynasty
A line of Islamic rulers in Morocco who, having dominated the Maghreb (western North Africa) through the 12th century, were thereafter increasingly squeezed by the ascendant power of the Marinid sultans.

FACTS AT A GLANCE: EARLY MODERN WORLD

absolutism
A system of government in which the authority of the ruler is total, with no one to account to and no restraining checks and balances.

Aceh
Northeastern region of the island of Sumatra in Indonesia. The first Muslim stronghold in Southeast Asia, it reached a political zenith under Sultan Iskander Muda (1607–1636). Aceh fiercely resisted Portuguese and later Dutch intervention.

alchemy
Medieval pseudoscience that claimed to be able to transform base metals into precious metals, notably gold; it was supplanted by the rise of the science of chemistry in the 18th century.

Anabaptists
Members of a radical Protestant sect in Germany who believed in adult baptism and the complete separation of church and state; they were frequently persecuted for their extreme views.

Anatolia
The Asiatic part of Turkey, known in Roman times as Asia Minor.

Anglican
Anything relating to the Church of England or a member of that church.

archbishopric
The center of an ecclesiastical province in the Christian church, presided over by an archbishop.

Armada
The Spanish word for a military fleet. Specifically, it refers to the fleet of 130 warships carrying almost 20,000 soldiers sent by Philip II of Spain in 1588 to invade England.

audiencia
In Spanish America a tribunal responsible to the Spanish crown that first supervised and then supplanted the authority of the conquistadors in governing the newly conquered territories.

Barbary States
Nominally provinces of the Ottoman Empire, these states in what are now Libya, Tunisia, Algeria, and Morocco were ruled by the Barbarossa brothers and by successive generations of corsairs.

bastion
A projecting part of a fortification, built out from the wall.

Bidar
Now located in the southern Indian state of Karnataka, Bidar was originally the capital of the Bahmani Kingdom. Under the Barid Shahi Dynasty it was the home of one of the five Muslim Deccani Sultanates until its annexation by the Mughals in 1657.

Bourbon Dynasty
The line of French kings founded by King Henry IV (ruled 1589–1610). The Bourbons were deposed during the French Revolution but restored to the throne in 1814. The last Bourbon king of France was Louis Philippe (reigned 1830–1848).

boyar
A member of the landowning group of Russian aristocrats whose power was broken by Czar Ivan the Terrible in 1565.

buccaneer
An English, Dutch, or French adventurer who preyed on Spanish shipping in the Caribbean and off South America. Buccaneers had no official government commission.

Burma, Kingdom of
State founded by King Anawratha at Pagan in 1044 that unified all Burma; it was overthrown by the Mongols in 1287. Burma was later reunified by the Toungou Dynasty from 1539 on.

Byzantine Empire
The successor to the Eastern Roman Empire, with its capital at Constantinople (present-day Istanbul).

Calvinist
A follower of the strict Protestant doctrines preached by the reformer John Calvin of Geneva. Calvinists believe that people's fate is divinely preordained at birth.

Church of England
Independent branch of the Christian church that came into being in 1534 following the English King Henry VIII's break with Rome in order to obtain a divorce from Catherine of Aragon. Elizabeth I confirmed its status as a Protestant episcopalian church (one having bishops).

colonialism
A system by which strong states exercise administrative control over weaker ones, supposedly in the best interests of the colonized states' subjects.

Council of Trent
General council of the Roman Catholic church that met at Trent, a town in the foothills of the Alp, in three sessions, from 1545 to 1563. It redefined Catholic teaching and is regarded as one of the starting points for the Counter Reformation.

Counter Reformation
A reform movement that got underway in the Roman Catholic church from the mid-16th century in response to the challenge presented by the Protestant Reformation.

czar
The title of the ruler of Russia, derived from the Roman imperial title "caesar." It was adopted by Ivan IV the Terrible in 1547 and was used by his successors until the Russian monarchy was abolished in 1917.

Dai Viet
Also known as Annam. A state located in what is now northern Vietnam that was conquered in about 214 B.C. by the Chinese, who named it An-Am, "Peaceful South." Independent from 939, Dai Viet was incorporated into Vietnam in 1946.

Deccani Sultanates
Group of five Muslim states on the Deccan Plateau of central India: Bijapur, Ahmadnagar, Golconda, Berar, and Bidar. Created from the breakup of the Bahmani Kingdom from 1490 on, they succumbed to Mughal expansion in the 17th century.

Diet of Worms
An assembly of the princes of the Holy Roman empire held at the city of Worms in Germany in 1521 in the presence of the Emperor Charles V, at which Martin Luther was invited to withdraw his demands for reform of the Roman Catholic church. On refusing to do so, he was banished, and an edict was issued condemning his writings.

Din-I Ilahi
Literally "divine faith." New religion established by the Mughal Emperor Akbar (reigned 1555–1605) after disputes with orthodox Muslim leaders who criticized his relaxed attitude toward other faiths.

Dutch War of Independence
The war fought by the seven northern provinces of the Spanish Netherlands (the United Provinces) against Spanish rule. The uprising began in 1567; independence was achieved by 1609 but not formally recognized by Spain until 1648.

encomienda
A system of forced labor in Spanish America by which native peoples were made to work lands assigned to individual conquistadors in return for protection and instruction in the Christian faith.

Funj
Sultanate in what is now Sudan, founded by Amara Dunkas in 1504. It came to dominate the trans-Saharan trade in gold.

alendar
The calendar introduced by Pope Gregory XIII in 1582, still in use today, to correct errors in the Julian calendar it replaced. Mistakes had arisen because the average Julian year of 365 and a quarter days was 11 minutes and 10 seconds longer than the solar year.

Guinea Company
The company licensed by Portugal in the 1480s to exploit the resources of Guinea and West Africa, particularly the trade in slaves bound for Brazil. In 1588 the English licensed their own Guinea Company.

harquebus
An early type of portable gun supported on a tripod or on a forked rest that was braced against the shoulder. Sometimes spelled "arquebus."

Hispanic
Of Spanish culture or origin.

Hispaniola
Large Caribbean island, now divided between the states of Haiti and the Dominican Republic. In the 16th century it was the center of Spanish colonial power in the region.

Holy League
An alliance organized in 1511 by Pope Julius II to drive the armies of France out of northern Italy. It included Spain, Venice, the Holy Roman Empire, and England.

Huguenots
French Protestants of the 16th and 17th centuries. The derivation of the name is uncertain.

humanist
A person embracing humanism, a worldview popularized during the Renaissance that made human beings rather than God the focus of intellectual attention.

Hussite Wars
Religious wars that set followers of the Bohemian (Czech) church reformer Jan Hus, burned at the stake for heresy in 1415, against the forces of the Holy Roman emperors and the Catholic church. The Hussites were Bohemian nationalists, equally hostile to secular and ecclesiastical authorities.

indulgence
Paper granting absolution for sins, thereby shortening the time a sinner spent in purgatory. The sale of indulgences by representatives of the medieval Catholic church was one of the abuses most criticized by Protestant reformers.

Jesuit
A member of the Society of Jesus.

Julian calendar
A calendar introduced in 45 B.C. by Julius Caesar. It had 12 months rather than the previous ten; the additional months, July and August, were named for the emperors Caesar and Augustus.

Kaaba
A small, cubic temple of bricks draped in black silk housing a sacred stone (presumably a meteorite) that fell from the heavens in ancient times. Built according to tradition by Ibrahim (Abraham) and his son Ishmael in Mecca, the Kaaba is the central shrine of Islam.

Kandy, Kingdom of
Independent monarchy in Sri Lanka that emerged at the end of the 15th century. After withstanding incursions by the Portuguese and Dutch, it was the last Sinhalese kingdom to fall to a colonial power when conquered by the British in 1818.

khanate
The name given to a realm ruled by a khan, the title taken by the Mongol conqueror Genghis and his successors on assuming power. The word also eventually came to be used by non-Mongol rulers in China, Central Asia, and Turkey.

Kongo, Kingdom of
Bantu-speaking kingdom south of the Congo River in central Africa. It survived until 1665, when it broke up following defeat by the Portuguese.

Kotte, Kingdom of
Sinhalese kingdom based in southwestern Sri Lanka. At its height in the 15th century it briefly unified all the island, but was weakened by the separation of Jafna and Kandy in 1477 and was subjugated by the Portuguese in the 16th century.

Laws of the Indies
Generally, the body of laws by which the Spanish crown governed its colonies in the Americas. More specifically, the term is applied to the New Laws passed in 1542 to bring the colonies more closely under royal control, often seen as bringing the conquistador era to an end.

League of Cambrai
A military alliance, named for the town in northern France where its terms were agreed, made between the pope, the Holy Roman emperor, and the kings of France and Aragon in 1508.

Livonia
A region on the east coast of the Baltic Sea, equivalent to most of present-day Latvia and Estonia, which was ruled by the crusading order of Teutonic Knights from the 13th to the 16th century, when it was divided between Poland and Sweden after the Livonian War with Russia (1558–1582).

Lutheranism
Branch of Protestantism that follows the teachings and principles of the German theologian Martin Luther (1483–1546).

Mahabharata
Indian epic poem describing the dynastic power struggles of a line of Aryan rulers in northern India, possibly in the 10th century B.C.

Mannerism
A style of 16th-century art and architecture (c.1530–1590) that was characterized by unusual effects of scale, light, and perspective, the contortion of natural forms, and the use of bright, harsh colors.

matchlock
An early mechanism for firing a gun. It consisted of a lighted wick (the match) fixed to a pivoting arm, which was lowered into the flashpan to ignite the powder-charge when the marksman depressed the trigger. Also the name for the gun itself.

mausoleum
An elaborate building designed to house the tomb of a famous individual.

Mecca
The city in western Arabia where the Prophet Muhammad was born in the 6th century A.D., but sacred long before that time thanks to the presence of the sacred stone known as the Kaaba.

Ming Dynasty
The last indigenous Chinese dynasty, founded by Zhu Yuanzhang, who reconquered China from the Mongol Yuan Dynasty in 1368. It was finally supplanted by the Manchu (Qing) dynasty in 1644.

Moriscos
After the fall in 1492 of Granada, the last Muslim stronghold in Spain, the name given to Spanish Muslims who chose Christian baptism rather than exile and to their descendants.

Muscat
A seaport on the Gulf of Oman in the far southeast of the Arabian Peninsula that was hotly fought over by Portuguese and Ottoman forces through the 16th century.

Muscovy
State centered on Moscow in western Russia and first established in the 13th century. After the

437

Mongol and Ottoman conquests it became an isolated bulwark of Christianity, following the Orthodox branch of the faith.

Naples, Kingdom of
Medieval kingdom that, with Sicily, came under Spanish control after 1503.

New Spain
The name given to the northern part of Spain's colonial empire on the American mainland. Founded by Hernán Cortés following the conquest of the Aztecs, it eventually stretched north into what is now the southern United States and south to Honduras and El Salvador.

Northwest Passage
Sea passage from the Atlantic to the Pacific Ocean around the north coast of Canada, long sought unsuccessfully by explorers until finally traversed by the Norwegian Roald Amundsen from 1903 to 1906.

papal bull
An edict issued by the pope (from the Latin *bulla*, meaning "seal").

Protestant
Any of the churches or their members that broke with the Roman Catholic church in the course of the Reformation. Protestants originally took their name from the "Protestation" by supporters of Martin Luther against the decision made at the Diet of Speyer in 1529 to reaffirm the edict of the Diet of Worms against Luther's teachings.

Puritan
A Christian of strict Protestant persuasion who opposed the role of bishops in the church hierarchy and sought a simple and plain form of worship.

Rajputs
Hindu landowning class of northwest India (Rajputana, later Rajasthan). Rising to prominence from the 9th century and reaching their height in the early 16th, they ruled such cities as Jodhpur and Jaipur. Akbar allowed them independence within the Mughal Empire, and they subsequently ruled as autonomous princes under the British Raj.

recantation
The withdrawal of a former belief or opinion, usually with a public confession of error.

Reformation
The 16th-century religious movement that began with the demand by Luther, Zwingli, and others for the reform of abuses within the Roman Catholic church. The Reformation led to the founding of the Protestant churches and the political division of Europe along religious lines.

regent
A person who governs a kingdom or other domain in place of the sovereign, who may be too young to rule, absent, or incapacitated (for instance, by mental illness).

Safavid Dynasty
Beginning with Esmail I in 1501, this Persian dynasty came to rule over not only Iran but also Armenia, Georgia, and parts of Uzbekistan, Turkmenistan, Azerbaijan, and Afghanistan. Esmail's support for the Shiite branch of Islam had a profound impact on the region's subsequent history.

St. Bartholomew's Day Massacre
The bloodiest event of the French Wars of Religion, when in 1572 Catholics slaughtered thousands of French Protestants.

Schmalkaldic League
A defensive alliance formed by a number of Protestant princes and cities of the Holy Roman Empire in 1531 to defend themselves from attack by the Emperor Charles V. It was named for the town of Schmalkalden in Germany.

Scholasticism
The rigid system of teaching in the medieval "schools" or universities of western Europe, which held that all philosophical speculation should be directed to a better understanding of Christian theology.

shah
The title assumed by the rulers of Persia

Sharifian Dynasty
An alternative name for Morocco's Saadi Dynasty and its successor, drawing on the fact that their rulers claimed descent from Muhammad through the Prophet's daughter Fatima. (Such descendants are known by the Arabic word *sharif*, "illustrious one.") The Saadi Dynasty is correctly the First Sharifian Dynasty. Quarrels within the family led to the replacement of the Saadi by the Second Sharifian or Alawi Dynasty, which took over in 1660 and rules to this day.

Sher Shah Sur
Also called Sher Khan (c.1486–1545). Afghan emperor of northern India who, after serving the first Mughal ruler Babur, seized power from his successor Humayun, proclaiming himself ruler of Delhi in 1540. His administrative reforms were adopted and extended by Akbar the Great.

shogun
Literally "commander of the imperial guard," the title given from 1192 on to the leader of Japan's ruling warrior family. For almost seven centuries

the shoguns were the true rulers of Japan, leaving the country's emperors to occupy themselves primarily with ceremonial duties.

Shona
A collection of communities dwelling in the grasslands of southeast Africa and united by both language and a pastoralist (herding) lifestyle. A succession of Shona states grew rich and powerful by exploiting the region's gold and ivory.

Sinan
The greatest architect of the Ottoman era. Born to Greek Christian parents in 1489, Sinan was taken in boyhood as a janissary or slave soldier of the sultan. He showed a flair for military engineering and then for architecture; by 1539 he was the official architect of Suleiman I.

Sistine Chapel
A chapel in the Vatican built in the late 15th century by Pope Sixtus IV; its many Renaissance artworks include a painted ceiling and fresco of the Last Judgment by Michelangelo.

Sitavaka, Kingdom of
State in southwestern Sri Lanka that arose c.1521 after the decline of the Kingdom of Kotte. Its rulers struggled in vain to expel the Portuguese from the island; the ruling dynasty came to an end in 1594.

Society of Jesus
A religious order of priests founded by the Spanish mystic and former soldier Ignatius Loyola (1491–1556) to fight heresy. It played an important part in the Counter Reformation.

Songhai Empire
A trading empire centered on the city of Gao in what is now northwestern Nigeria. It emerged to eclipse Mali in the 15th century.

Spice Islands
Former name of the Molucca archipelago of eastern Indonesia, famous for the production of spices, especially nutmeg, mace, and cloves.

Stockholm Bloodbath
The mass execution of Swedish nobles in 1520 by Danish forces under King Christian II. The massacre had the effect of hardening Swedish resistance to the Union of Kalmar.

supernova
A giant star that suddenly increases very greatly in brightness because of an explosion ejecting most of its mass.

Swahili
Deriving from the Arabic *sahil* or "coast," Swahili is the language still spoken down much of Africa's

eastern seaboard. It is a Bantu-based tongue into which innumerable Arabic words have been absorbed through centuries of commercial and cultural contact.

synod
A church council or ecclesiastical court.

Taklamakan Desert
Extensive arid region of Central Asia occupying the greater part of the Tarim Basin between the Tien Shan and Kunlun mountain ranges. It was home to the khanates of Turfan and Kashgar after c.1500.

tea ceremony
An important household ritual in Japan in which tea prepared in special utensils is offered to guests in a set order. Tea drinking was introduced to Japan by Zen monks, who drank it to keep awake while meditating. The tea ceremony later spread outside the monasteries, becoming an occasion for friends to gather and discuss aesthetics.

Toungou Dynasty
Dynasty that unified Burma from 1539 on after the capture of the Mon capital Pegu. Its greatest rulers, Tabinshweti and Bayinnaung, subdued the Shans as well as the Mons. The realm lost ground to neighboring powers in the 17th century when Burma fragmented into a multitude of smaller states.

Treaty of Amasya
An agreement in 1555 between Ottoman Turkey and Safavid Iran that recognized Ottoman suzerainty over Iraq. By ending mutual hostilities between the two powers, it enabled both to attain their full magnificence.

Treaty of Cateau-Cambrésis
The treaty between France and Spain that in 1559 recognized Italy as an area of Spanish influence.

Treaty of Granada
A treaty signed in 1500 between King Louis XII of France and the Spanish monarch Ferdinand II of Aragon in which the two powers agree to divide the Kingdom of Naples between them.

Treaty of Saragossa
Agreement made in 1529 between Spain and Portugal to revise the Treaty of Tordesillas—which in 1494 had drawn the boundaries between the overseas conquests of the countries—in favor of Spain.

Treaty of Tordesillas
Treaty made between Spain and Portugal in 1494 to resolve disputes over the two nations' rival claims to newly discovered lands in the Americas. The treaty proposed a line 370 leagues (1,150

miles) west of Cape Verde; all lands to the west of it were to belong to Spain, all to the east to Portugal.

Tumed Mongols
Branch of the Khalka Mongols inhabiting eastern Mongolia. Under their leader Altan Khan (1507–1582) they became dominant over the western Oirat Mongols and captured the former Great Khanate capital at Karakorum; Tumed influence declined after Altan Khan's death.

Union of Kalmar
The union of Denmark, Sweden, and Norway under one crown, formed in 1397. Swedish nobles came to resent having a king residing in Copenhagen, Denmark, and broke away several times. Finally, in 1523 Gustav I Vasa, a Swedish nobleman, led a successful uprising against Denmark and was elected king of Sweden, thus ending the union.

Union of Lublin
The union of Poland with the Grand Duchy of Lithuania that in 1569 created a single kingdom headed by a king jointly elected by the nobles of Poland and Lithuania.

Union of Utrecht
Defensive alliance of the seven northern provinces of the Netherlands against Spain. The union became the foundation of the Dutch Republic.

usurper
Someone who seizes a kingdom or political power unlawfully.

Uzbeks
Nomadic pastoralists (herders) of Turkic origin inhabiting the steppes of Central Asia, in particular the area now known as Uzbekistan. In the 16th century their raids represented a real threat to the rising power of Safavid Persia.

Vatican
The palace and official residence of the pope in Rome.

Venice, Republic of
An independent republic ruled by a doge or chief magistrate from the port of Venice on the Adriatic coast of northeast Italy. A major sea power from the 13th to the 16th century through its control of trade with West Asia, Venice ruled islands and ports in the eastern Mediterranean as well as part of the Italian mainland (the Veneto).

viceroy
Literally "vice (or deputy) king," a viceroy rules a province or conquered territory on behalf of his sovereign.

Vijayanagar
Powerful Hindu kingdom of southern India that flourished from the mid-14th to the 16th century.

vizier
The chief minister of the Seljuk Empire; used loosely, the term was later applied to the chief administrative official in many Muslim countries.

wheel lock
A later refinement of the matchlock that substituted a flint and spring-loaded wheel for the lighted wick. When the trigger was pulled, the flint struck the wheel to make a spark that ignited the powder charge.

White Sheep Turkmen
A federation of Turkmen tribes in eastern Anatolia, northern Iraq, and western Iran, formed in the 14th century in rivalry with the Black Sheep Turkmen farther south. It was forced into retreat by the expansion of Safavid Persia in the 16th century.

Xavier, St. Francis
Spanish Jesuit missionary who introduced Christianity to India (Goa) from 1542 to 1545 and to Japan from 1548 to 1551, when he visited the then-capital Kyoto and Kagoshima.

Xhosa
A predominantly pastoralist (herding) people living in the southeast of what is now South Africa. At the start of the 16th century they were comparative newcomers, having migrated into the region from the north not long before.

Zeydis
A breakaway sect of Shiite Muslims for whom the succession of sacred teachers, or imams, should have come down through Zeyd ibn Ali, great grandson of Ali, Muhammad's cousin, whom Shiites see as Muhammad's spiritual heir.

Acadia
Province on Canada's Atlantic coast settled by France from 1632 but contested by the British, who called the region Nova Scotia (New Scotland). The British eventually secured the territory in the 18th century, deporting many of its French-speaking inhabitants to Louisiana, whose Cajun population derives its name from the word "Acadian."

Angola
Portuguese colony established in lands south of the Congo River that had previously been a hunting ground for Kongo slavers who sold their captives to the Portuguese. By 1576, however, Portugal had its own coastal foothold at Luanda. The Dutch coveted the colony, seizing it briefly in the 1640s.

Ashanti
After decades of war among the various Akan peoples, the Ashanti gained the ascendancy on Africa's Gold Coast. By 1700 their empire was the region's superpower, trading gold and slaves for the firearms that ensured its continuing dominance.

Assam
Independent state founded by the Ahom kings in the 13th century. After warring with Muslim Bengal in the 17th century, it was overrun by Burma from 1817 to 1822 and came under the control of the British Raj from 1826 on.

Azerbaijan
Territory on the western shore of the Caspian Sea. Conquered by Safavid Persia in the 1520s, it was contested by the Ottomans from the 1590s, but by 1618 the Safavids had regained possession.

Batavia
City on the northwestern coast of Java, Indonesia, known today as Jakarta. It was named by the Dutch when they seized it in 1619, making it the headquarters of the Dutch East India Company.

Bengal
Region in northeastern India annexed by the Mughal Empire in 1576. After the English founded Calcutta, Bengal came under the control of the East India Company. It is now divided between Bangladesh and the Indian state of West Bengal.

Bhutan, Kingdom of
Ancient kingdom in the eastern Himalayas long ruled by a spiritual figurehead, the Dharma Raja. Overrun by Manchu China from 1720 on, it increasingly came under the influence of the British Raj in India and was partly annexed in 1865.

Bishops' War
A rebellion (1639–1640) in Scotland following the decision of King Charles I of England and Scotland to impose bishops on the Presbyterian church.

Body of Liberties
Compendium of laws created in Massachusetts Bay Colony in 1641 and often seen as a forerunner of the American Bill of Rights. The measures guaranteed limited religious toleration and the right to petition the government while banning "inhumane, barbarous, or cruel" punishments.

Brandenburg–Prussia
A state in northern Europe formed when the Hohenzollern family, hereditary electors (princes) of Brandenburg, acquired eastern Prussia through inheritance in 1618. Frederick William, the Great Elector (1620–1688), extended its boundaries even further by military conquest.

canonization
The process by which the Catholic church declares an individual to have been a saint.

cardinal
A high official of the Catholic church belonging to the Sacred College, from among whose number the pope is elected.

Carolina Colony
Colony established in North and South Carolina by settlers from Virginia in the mid-17th century and governed in the name of the British King Charles II (who gave the Latin version of his name, Carolus, to the territory).

Catalan Revolt
A revolt (1640-1659) in Catalonia in northeastern Spain against the government of Olivares, chief minister of King Philip IV. The leaders of the revolt declared their independence from Spain and placed themselves under French protection.

charter
A legal document issued by a ruler or government conferring rights and privileges or establishing a constitution.

Commonwealth
The period of republican government in England from the execution of King Charles I in 1649 until 1660, when his son Charles II was restored to the throne.

Copernican system
The theory that the sun is the center of the solar system and that the planets orbit around it, first outlined by the Polish astronomer Nicolaus Kopernik (Copernicus) in 1543.

Cossacks
Bands of warlike adventurers renowned for their horsemanship and courage, probably descended from peasants who had escaped serfdom to settle on the southern frontiers of Russia in the 14th century. They took part in the conquest of Siberia and were later recruited by the czars to form cavalry regiments in the Russian army.

Defenestration of Prague
Defenestration is the act of throwing someone out of a window. In 1618 Protestant nobles threw two imperial councillors from an upper window of Prague Castle and then elected the Protestant Frederick V of the Palatinate as king of Bohemia in place of the Catholic Holy Roman Emperor Ferdinand II—an act of rebellion that marked the start of the Thirty Years' War.

Dejima
An artificial island in Nagasaki harbor, Japan, to which Dutch merchants were confined (all other traders having been expelled) by order of Shogun Iemitsu after the Shimabara rebellion of 1637 and the subsequent persecution of Christians.

Denkyera, Kingdom of
Kingdom that arose among the Akan peoples of what is now southwest Ghana in the early 17th century.

divine right of kings
The belief that hereditary monarchs derive their authority to rule their subjects directly from God, from which it follows that rebellion against kings is disobedience to the will of God.

dowry
Goods, money, or land that a woman brings to her husband on marriage.

East India Company (Dutch)
Known in the Netherlands as the United East India Company (Vereenigde Oost-Indische Compagnie, or VOC), the Dutch East India Company was established in 1602 to exploit commerce with the East Indies. Headquartered at Batavia (modern Jakarta) on the Indonesian island of Java, it negotiated with (and sometimes fought against) local rulers, creating a virtual monopoly of the spice trade. The company fell into decline in the 18th century and went into liquidation in 1799.

East India Company (English)
English chartered company established in 1600, holding a trading monopoly on all commerce with the Indian subcontinent. It traded with the Mughal Empire and was engaged in a long struggle for supremacy with its French counterpart. It increasingly became an instrument of colonial

administration until its sovereignty over India was finally transferred to the British crown in 1858 in the wake of the Indian Mutiny.

East India Company (French)
Trading organization founded in 1644 as a competitor to its Dutch and English counterparts. Establishing bases at Chandernagore and Pondicherry, its governor-general Joseph-François Dupleix vied unsuccessfully for power in India with the British in the mid 18th century. The company was dissolved in 1769.

Edict of Nantes
Order signed by King Henry IV of France in 1598 at Nantes, a city on the Loire River in western France, guaranteeing freedom of worship to Protestants. It marked the end of the French Wars of Religion, but was revoked by Louis XIV in 1685.

Edict of Restitution
An edict of the Holy Roman Emperor Ferdinand II, issued in 1629, decreeing that confiscated church property should be returned to whoever had possession of it in 1555—a measure aimed at recovering Catholic land lost to Protestants.

factory
A trading post of the English East India Company. The first was established at Surat in Gujarat, western India, in 1608.

False Messiah
Any of a number of pretenders who have claimed to be the Messiah, or "anointed one," of Jewish tradition, sent by God to deliver humanity from the dominion of death and sin.

First Northern War
A war (1655–1660) in which Sweden invaded Poland with the help of Brandenburg-Prussia. Fear of Swedish expansion subsequently led Russia, Denmark, and the Holy Roman Empire to intervene, and few gains were made.

French and Indian Wars
A series of wars fought between 1689 and 1763 by British and French settlers in North America, together with their respective local allies. The separate phases are known as King William's War (1689–1697); Queen Anne's War (1702–1713); King George's War (1744–1748); and the American part of the Seven Years' War, usually known as the French and Indian War (1755–1763).

Fronde
A series of civil wars in France from 1648 to 1653, waged by the nobility against the government of Cardinal Mazarin, chief minister during the minority of King Louis XIV.

Georgia
Country on the northeastern shore of the Black Sea. Under Safavid domination through much of the 16th century, it was taken by the Ottomans in the 1590s but restored by 1618.

Gold Coast
A region of coastal West Africa roughly corresponding with modern Ghana. Named for its abundant gold reserves, it was rich in other minerals too, most notably copper and iron, and also became a center for the slave trade.

grand vizier
Title given to the Ottoman government officer in overall charge of the entire empire. Although he was generally a slave by birth or upbringing, his power often matched the sultan's.

Great Khanate
The largest and most easterly of the four Mongol khanates arising after the death of Genghis Khan. Initially covering much of modern China and Korea, it was ruled from Karakorum.

haiku
Japanese poetic form of 17 syllables (in three lines, with five, seven, and five syllables respectively). Popular in the Tokugawa period, its chief exponent was Matsuo Basho (1644–94).

Holy League
A military alliance between Catholic Spain, Venice, and the Papacy that had the aim of expelling the Ottomans from Europe.

Houses of Parliament
The legislature, or lawmaking assembly, of England since medieval times, comprising the House of Lords (nobility) and the House of Commons; also the building in London where they meet.

Iroquois Confederacy
League of five Iroquois-speaking peoples—the Mohawk, Oneida, Onondaga, Cayuga, and Seneca—who in the early 17th century inhabited much of modern New York state.

Jamestown
The site in what is now Virginia of the first enduring British settlement in North America, established by an expedition sent out from England in 1607.

kaolin
A fine white clay mineral used in the manufacture of hard- and soft-paste porcelain and bone china.

Karelia
A region of northeastern Europe whose inhabitants are Finnish-speaking. Formerly an independent medieval state, it came under Swedish rule in the 17th century and was later ruled by Russia from 1721 to 1917, when it was divided between Finland and the Soviet Union.

Khalsa Brotherhood
Community instituted in 1699 by the tenth Sikh guru Goband Singh as a race of warrior saints ready to die for the faith. The outward signs of membership are the so-called "five Ks": *kangha* (comb), *kacch* (cotton undershorts), *kirpan* (dagger), *kara* (steel bracelet), and *kesh* (uncut hair).

King James Bible
The English translation of the Bible published in 1611 on the orders of King James I; also known as the Authorized Version.

King William's War
The first conflict of the French and Indian Wars fought between British and French settlers in North America. Fighting broke out in connection with the European War of the League of Augsburg, in which France and Britain were enemies. The principal action of the war was the taking of Port Royal in Nova Scotia by the British in 1690.

Kokand, Khanate of
Islamic state in the western Ferghana Valley of Central Asia, founded in the early 16th century by the Uzbeks; it developed as a major trade center, with the city of Kokand as its capital from 1740. It was the last major khanate to fall to Russian expansion, in 1876.

Long Parliament
The English Parliament that was summoned by King Charles I in November 1640 and remained legally in being until it voted for its own dissolution in 1660.

lord protector
The title taken by Oliver Cromwell when he took charge of the government of England at the urging of the army in 1653, and which on his death in 1658 passed briefly to his son Richard Cromwell. This period of English history is known as the Protectorate.

Luba, Kingdom of
State in the upper Lomami Valley of eastern Angola that came to rule an empire of over 60,000 square miles (150,000 sq. km). The Luba claimed descent from divine ancestors, and their kings, deified at death, exercised a powerful hold over their subjects.

Lunda Empire
The Lunda Kingdom emerged in the 1670s in what

is now eastern Angola to the west of Luba, which Lunda eventually eclipsed thanks to the wealth generated by the trade in copper and in slaves.

Matamba, Kingdom of
A state in the interior of what is now Angola whose rulers resisted European domination long after the coastal kingdoms had fallen in the 17th century, successfully playing off the Portuguese against the Dutch.

Mataram, Sultanate of
Kingdom in south–central Java that grew quickly under its first ruler, Sultan Agung (1613–1645), but came increasingly into conflict with the Dutch settlement at Batavia. It declined under subsequent rulers and was divided in 1755.

mausoleum
An elaborate building designed to house the tomb of a famous individual.

Mayflower Compact
An agreement drawn up on the *Mayflower*—the ship that brought the Pilgrims to New England in 1620—concerning the future government of the colony. It committed the settlers to self-government in accordance with the will of the majority.

mercenary
A soldier who fights under the colors of a state other than his own for pay.

Ming Dynasty
The last indigenous Chinese dynasty (1368–1644), founded by Zhu Yuanzhang, who reconquered much territory from the Mongols (Yuan). It was supplanted by the Manchu (Qing) Dynasty.

Molucca Islands
Group of islands in eastern Indonesia including Ceram, Ternate, and Amboina. As major producers of nutmeg, cloves, and mace, these "Spice Islands" were the focus of European trade and colonization from the early 16th century on. When the Dutch seized the Moluccas between 1595 and 1662, they gained a monopoly on the spice trade.

National Covenant
A covenant signed in 1638 by Scots opposed to the religious policies of King Charles I and in support of the Presbyterian church.

Navigation Acts
A series of protectionist laws passed by the British Parliament from 1651 to 1696 with the aim of boosting Britain's share of overseas trade by insisting that all imports had to be carried in British ships or in those of the country of origin.

New Amsterdam
The name given to New York City from 1626 to 1664, when it was occupied by Dutch settlers as the capital of the colony of New Netherland.

New England Confederation
Alliance of the colonies of Massachusetts Bay, Connecticut, New Haven, and Plymouth forged in 1643 for purposes of defense. Each colony kept its own independence in internal matters but agreed to consult on matters concerning "mutual safety and welfare." The confederation, which played an important part in coordinating the settlers' efforts in King Philip's War, was dissolved in 1684.

New France
Name given to the extensive territories in North America explored and settled by French colonists in the 16th to 18th centuries. At its peak in the early 18th century New France stretched from the Gulf of St. Lawrence to the Great Lakes and down the Mississippi Valley to the Gulf of Mexico.

New Model Army
An army created by Oliver Cromwell in 1644 to fight for Parliament against the king in the English Civil War. Well-trained and highly disciplined, it was a major force in defeating the Royalists, and it later had a political role under the Commonwealth and Protectorate.

New Netherland
Short-lived colony established along the Hudson River from 1621 on by the Dutch West India Company. The territory was taken over by the English in 1664, who divided it between the colonies of New York and New Jersey.

New Sweden
Short-lived Swedish colony on the Delaware River, comprising parts of modern Pennsylvania, New Jersey, and Delaware. Established by the New Sweden Company in 1638, it was overrun by Dutch settlers under Peter Stuyvesant in 1655.

Northwest Passage
Sea passage from the Atlantic to the Pacific Ocean around the north coast of Canada, long sought unsuccessfully by explorers until finally traversed by the Norwegian Roald Amundsen from 1903 to 1906.

Parliamentarian
A supporter of Parliament in the English Civil War; sometimes also called a Roundhead.

Parthenon
The temple of the goddess Athene on the Acropolis in Athens, which was built in the 5th century B.C.

pasha
The respectful title given to a vizier, senior military officer, or provincial governor under the Ottoman Empire. He often had considerable freedom of action on the ground.

Pequots
Algonquian-speaking Native American people inhabiting the northeastern coast of Connecticut in the early 17th century. They came into conflict with English settlers and were defeated in the Pequot War of 1637.

Pilgrims
Name given to the English settlers who founded Plymouth Colony in Massachusetts in 1620.

Plymouth Company
A joint-stock company chartered in 1606 by King James I of England to found colonies in America between the latitudes of 38° and 45°N (in modern terms, from southern Maryland to the Canadian border). A colony established at the mouth of the Kennebec River in what is now Maine failed, and in 1620 the company was reorganized as the Plymouth Council for New England.

Powhatan Confederacy
Alliance of Native American tribes under the leadership of Powhatan, established in coastal Virginia when the Jamestown colonists arrived in 1607. Relations with the newcomers were uneasy and broke into open violence in 1622, when Powhatan's successor organized a large-scale attack on the colony.

Presbyterian
A member of a church, such as the Presbyterian Church of Scotland, that is governed by elders of equal rank (presbyters) rather than by bishops and priests. The first Presbyterian church was established in Geneva, Switzerland, by the reformer John Calvin in 1541.

Protestant Union
An alliance of German Protestant rulers and cities formed in 1608 to defend their lands and rights against the Holy Roman emperor's attempts to reestablish Catholicism.

Puritan
A Christian of strict Protestant persuasion who opposed the role of bishops in the church hierarchy and sought a simple and plain form of worship.

Qing Dynasty
Final Chinese imperial dynasty (1644–1912); its zenith was under Kangxi and Qianlong (1654–1792), when China reached its greatest territorial extent, stretching from Turkistan in the west to the island of Taiwan in the east.

Quakers
Members of the Society of Friends.

Rajputs
Hindu landowning class of northwest India (Rajputana, later Rajasthan). Rising to prominence from the 9th century and reaching their height in the early 16th, they ruled such cities as Jodhpur and Jaipur.

rationalism
Reliance on reason and experience rather than faith or superstition as the means of explaining the world and discovering knowledge.

republican
Someone who believes that power should be held by the people or their elected representatives, not by a monarch ruling with an aristocracy.

Restoration
The reestablishment of the monarchy in England with the assumption of power by King Charles II, son of the deposed Charles I, in 1660.

Rhenish Palatinate
A state on the Rhine River in Germany ruled by a hereditary ruler called the prince palatine. The princes of the Palatinate were the leaders of the Protestant movement in Germany before and during the Thirty Years' War.

Romanov Dynasty
The dynasty that ruled Russia from the accession of Michael Romanov in 1613 until the overthrow of the last czar, Nicholas II, in 1917.

Royalist
A supporter of Charles I in the English Civil War.

Royal Society
The oldest, and still the leading, scientific society in Britain, which received its charter from King Charles II in 1662.

shah
Persian for "king." Originally the title of the kings of Persia, it also came to be used by the rulers of other countries in South and Central Asia

Society of Friends
A Christian sect founded in England in the mid-17th century. Its beliefs include nonviolence, the rejection of set forms of worship, and simplicity of dress and speech. Its members are known as Quakers.

States-General
The legislative assembly of the Dutch Republic.

Stuart Dynasty
The royal house of Scotland from 1371 and of England from the accession of James VI of Scotland to the English throne in 1603 until 1714.

Sufi
A Muslim mystic who attempts, through intense meditation or a trance state brought on by repetitive prayer, music, or (in the case of the "whirling dervishes") dance, to transcend worldly concerns and find spiritual enlightenment.

Swiss Confederation
League of Swiss cantons (states) that came together to defeat their Hapsburg overlords in the 14th and 15th centuries.

Taj Mahal
Marble mausoleum in Agra, northern India, built by the Mughal Emperor Shah Jahan as a monument to his dead wife Mumtaz Mahal.

theocracy
Government by a priesthood. In theocratic states adherence to the tenets of a faith determines the political and legal system. Tibet under the Dalai Lama was a theocracy from the 1640s until its annexation by China in the 1950s.

Time of Troubles
A period of intense unrest in Russia (1598–1613) marked by peasant and Cossack revolts, foreign invasion, and civil war. It ended with the election of Michael Romanov as czar.

Triple Alliance
An alliance forged in 1668 between the Dutch Republic, England, and, Sweden to wage the War of Devolution against France.

Turkmen
Tent-dwelling pastoral nomads living east of the Caspian Sea along the borders of Afghanistan and Iran.

United Provinces
The seven allied provinces—Friesland, Gelderland, Groningen, Holland, Overijseel, Utrecht, and Zeeland—that made up the Dutch Republic.

Uzbeks
Nomadic pastoralists (herders) of Turkic origin inhabiting the steppes of Central Asia, in particular the area now known as Uzbekistan.

Van Diemen's Land
Former name of the island of Tasmania off Australia's southern coast. Originally named by the Dutch explorer Abel Tasman for his patron Anthony van Diemen, the governor of Batavia, it was given its present name in 1855.

Versailles
A vast palace built for King Louis XIV southwest of Paris, one of the glories of French classical architecture. From 1682 Louis spent most of his time at Versailles and expected his nobles to spend much of the year there too.

Virgin of Guadalupe
Seen in a vision by a native Mexican in 1531, Our Lady of Guadalupe became the focus of a Catholic cult that made her shrine in central Mexico the most important pilgrimage site in Latin America.

Wampanoag
Algonquian-speaking Native American people inhabiting the coastal areas of Massachusetts at the time of arrival of the first English colonists. The Wampanoag never recovered from defeat by the settlers in King Philip's War (1675–1676).

War of the League of Augsburg
The war (1689–1697) between Louis XIV of France and the League of Augsburg, an alliance first formed in 1686 and consisting of Emperor Leopold I, Spain, Sweden, and Bavaria, later joined by Britain, the Dutch Republic, and Savoy.

West India Company (Dutch)
Company chartered by the States-General (parliament) of the Dutch Republic in 1621 to exploit trade with the Americas. It had extensive operations in Brazil (finally lost to the Portuguese in 1654) and in coastal North America, where its lands were taken over by the British in 1664. Its achievements included the founding of New Amsterdam—today's New York City.

William of Orange
Stadtholder (chief magistrate) of the Netherlands who married Mary, the daughter of King James II of England. When James's pro-Catholic policies alienated his Protestant subjects, a group of prominent politicians invited William to land in England in 1688 and depose the king. William was crowned joint monarch with Mary as King William III of Britain in February 1689.

Zanzibar, Sultanate of
The Muslim state established by the rulers of Oman after they captured the island of Zanzibar, just off the African coast, from the Portuguese in 1698. Their victory put an end to Portugal's 200-year presence in East Africa and restored the old order on the Swahili Coast.

Zunghar Mongols
Leading tribe of the Oirat Mongols that tried but failed to unite the Mongols against the Manchus. Oirat forces under their leader Galdan were crushed by the Manchus in 1696.

Acadia
Province on Canada's Atlantic coast settled by France from 1632 but contested by Britain, which called the region Nova Scotia (New Scotland). The British eventually secured the territory in the 18th century, deporting many of its French-speaking inhabitants to Louisiana, whose Cajun population derives its name from the word "Acadian."

Act of Union
Act of Parliament that in 1707 established the parliamentary and political union of England and Scotland as Great Britain. The English and Scottish crowns had been united since 1603.

American Revolution
The war fought between 1776 and 1783 by inhabitants of the 13 colonies on the Atlantic seaboard of North America to win independence from Great Britain. Their victory created the United States.

Anglo-Mysore Wars
Four wars fought by the Mysore sultans Haidar Ali and his son Tipu Sahib against forces of the British East India Company. The first (1767–1769) brought gains to Mysore, but in subsequent conflicts (1778–1784, 1789–1792, 1798–1799), the British steadily got the upper hand, capturing Mysore's capital Seringapatam in 1799.

Ashanti
After decades of war between the various Akan peoples the Ashanti gained ascendancy on Africa's Gold Coast. By 1700 their empire was the region's superpower, trading gold and slaves for the firearms that ensured its continuing dominance.

Bastille
A medieval fortress in Paris that was used as a royal prison in the 18th century.

Batavia
City on the northwestern coast of Java, Indonesia, known today as Jakarta. It was named by the Dutch when they took it in 1619, making it the headquarters of the Dutch East India Company.

Batavian Republic
The name given to the Netherlands by the French after they conquered it in 1795.

Benin
West African kingdom founded in the 13th century by a ruler known as the oba. By the 16th century Benin covered a region between the Niger Delta and what is now the Nigerian city of Lagos.

bey
Title taken by the governor of a province under the Ottoman Empire.

Bill of Rights
The name given to the first ten amendments to the U.S. Constitution, adopted in 1791 and designed to protect the rights of the individual against the state.

Botany Bay
Inlet of the Tasman Sea south of Sydney, Australia, where in 1770 the English seafarer Captain James Cook became the first European to make a landing on the continent. It was the site of the first penal settlement, which was soon moved to the more favorable harbor at Port Jackson (Sydney).

Brandenburg
German state ruled by the Hohenzollern family from the 15th century on that became the nucleus of the Kingdom of Prussia, established in 1701.

Brumaire coup
The coup that overthrew the Directory government of France in 1799 and saw the appointment of Napoleon Bonaparte as first consul. It was named for the month in the French Revolutionary calendar when it took place; Brumaire (October–November) means "foggy."

cabinet
In Britain a committee of senior ministers, chosen from the majority party in Parliament, that manages the affairs of the country.

cantonal
Relating to a canton, an administrative subdivision of some European countries.

Coercive Acts
A series of acts passed by the British Parliament in 1774 to punish American colonists for resistance to British rule, notably in the Boston Tea Party.

Constitution Act
Act of the British Parliament that in 1791 divided the then province of Quebec between a mainly English-speaking Upper Canada (now part of Ontario) and, to the north, a mostly French-speaking Lower Canada (eastern Quebec).

Constitutional Convention
The federal convention called in Philadelphia in 1787 to draw up the U.S. Constitution. The document came into effect in March 1789, having been ratified by the required nine states (the ninth was New Hampshire).

Continental Army
The army set up in 1775 by the Continental Congress representing the 13 colonies opposed to British rule in North America. George Washington was appointed commander-in-chief.

corsair
A pirate from one of the Barbary States of the North African coast who preyed on Christian shipping with the backing of the Ottoman Empire.

Cossacks
Bands of warlike adventurers renowned for their horsemanship and courage, probably descended from peasants who had escaped serfdom to settle on the southern frontiers of Russia in the 14th century. They took part in the conquest of Siberia and were later recruited by the czars to form cavalry regiments in the Russian army.

creole
A term originally used in Latin America to describe native-born offspring of European settlers as opposed to first-generation immigrants from Europe. More loosely the term is also now used to describe people of mixed race.

Dahomey, Kingdom of
West African state corresponding with modern Benin. Dahomey never acquired an empire, but from the 17th century on its rulers grew rich by raiding their neighbors to seize slaves for sale to European traders.

Darfur, Sultanate of
Kingdom in the western part of what is now the Sudan. An Islamic sultanate from 1603, it endured until 1875, although weakened in the mid-18th century by internal dissension and wars with neighbors.

Declaration of Independence
The statement adopted by representatives of the 13 American colonies on July 4, 1776, proclaiming separation from Great Britain and the foundation of an independent republic.

deist
An Enlightenment term for someone who, rejecting belief in God as revealed in the Bible, held instead that there is a supreme being who is the source of natural law but does not intervene in the affairs of the world.

derebeys
Literally "valley lords"; hereditary local rulers in Anatolia who, although nominally under Ottoman authority, often went very much their own way.

Directory
The French Revolutionary government set up in 1795, made up of two councils and an executive of five members. Its aim was to prevent power falling again into the hands of one man, as it had done under Robespierre during the Reign of Terror.

Druse
Member of a Muslim sect that broke away from Shiite Islam in the 11th century. The Druse's close-knit and independent communities in the mountains of Lebanon were largely left to their own devices under Ottoman rule.

elector
A German prince having the right to take part in the election of the Holy Roman emperor.

emir
This Arabic title originally denoted a descendant of Muhammad through his daughter Fatima but came to be applied to any important commander.

empiricism
The theory, stimulated by the rise of experimental science, that all knowledge is derived from the experience of the senses; it was developed by such Enlightenment thinkers as John Locke and David Hume.

Encyclopedia, The
A 28-volume reference work, published between 1751 and 1776 by a group of French scholars under the direction of Jean d'Alembert and Denis Diderot, that promoted the ideas of the Enlightenment.

enlightened despot
A term used to describe 18th-century European monarchs such as Catherine the Great of Russia and Frederick the Great of Prussia who were influenced by the intellectual ideas of the Enlightenment while retaining absolute control of government.

Enlightenment
The intellectual movement of 18th-century Europe that believed in reason as the key to human knowledge and progress, and was hostile to religious intolerance and superstition. The criticism of absolute government developed by proponents of the Enlightenment fueled revolutionary ideas in France and the United States.

Family Compact
An agreement forged in 1761 between the Bourbon kings of France and Spain, together with the rulers of Bourbon lands in Italy, that brought Spain into the Seven Years' War against Britain.

First Fleet
The first shipment of convicts sent from Britain to Australia. Its arrival in Botany Bay in January 1788 marked the start of the European settlement of Australia.

flying shuttle
An invention by John Kay that allowed a weaver to propel a shuttle (the device holding the yarn) through a width of cloth on a loom with only one hand. By speeding the process of weaving and increasing productivity, it played a key part in the mechanization of the textile industry in Britain.

French and Indian War
The name generally given to the Anglo-French conflict in North America between 1755 and 1763, the last of a series of clashes beginning in the previous century that are collectively known as the French and Indian Wars.

Ghilzai
An Afghan tribe of Pathan (Pushtun) origin, based in Kandahar. After the assassination of the Persian ruler Nadir Shah in 1747 they and the Abdalis established a united Afghan state under the leadership of the warlord Ahmad Shah Durrani.

Gibraltar
A naval base on a narrow, rocky peninsula near the southern tip of Spain, of strategic importance for control of the western Mediterranean. Captured by the British in 1704 and formally ceded to them in 1713, it remains a British dependency.

Girondists
Members of the moderate republican party that held power in revolutionary France from 1792 to 1793. Their name refers to the fact that the party leaders came from the department of the Gironde in southwestern France.

gouache
A water-based paint that, unlike regular watercolors, has white pigment or glue added to give a bolder, more solid, less translucent effect.

Great Northern War
War fought from 1700 to 1721 in northern Europe between Charles XII of Sweden and a coalition led by Peter the Great of Russia; the war confirmed Russia as the leading power in the Baltic region.

Gurkhas
Warriors from the hill tribes of Nepal. After fiercely resisting British encroachment in the early 19th century, they were incorporated from 1860 on into the British army, where they still form an elite unit.

hacienda
The name given in Spanish America to the large, privately owned estates into which much of the land was divided.

Hanoverian Dynasty
Line of British monarchs descended from the elector (hereditary ruler) of Hanover, who became George I of Great Britain in 1714. The last Hanoverian monarch was Queen Victoria (d. 1901).

Hohenzollern Dynasty
The family of the electors of Brandenburg who became kings of Prussia from 1701 to 1871 and emperors of Germany from 1871 to 1918.

Illuminati
Members of a secret society founded in 1776 in Bavaria, southern Germany, to spread Enlightenment ideas; it was hostile to the Catholic church, especially the Jesuits.

Jacobins
Members of a French revolutionary club founded in 1789, which took its name from the former Jacobin convent in Paris where they held their first meetings. The Jacobins overthrew the moderate Girondists in 1793.

Jacobites
Supporters of the deposed King James II and his heirs, especially among the Catholic clans of Scotland, who launched rebellions in 1715 and 1745 to restore the Stuart Dynasty to the thrones of Scotland and England.

Javanese Wars of Succession
A series of wars fought between rival claimants to the throne of the Javanese sultanate of Mataram, under the rule of Sultan Agung (1613–1646) a strong sultanate that challenged Dutch intervention on the island. Mataram was subsequently torn apart by internal feuding; it was divided between the Dutch principalities of Surakarta and Jogjakarta in 1755.

Kashgaria
Key trading state in Central Asia on the major caravan routes into the Ferghana Valley. Originally under Chinese control, it fell to the Mongols in 1219, was sacked by Timur the Lame in the late 14th century, and came under the rule of the Chinese Qing dynasty from 1755 onward.

King George's War
One of the French and Indian Wars, fought between French and British settlers from 1744 to 1748 as the North American component of Europe's War of the Austrian Succession.

Kordofan, Sultanate of
Islamic kingdom in what is now central Sudan. From the mid-17th century it came partly under the rule of the Funj Sultanate of Sennar—a conquest that was completed during the 1750s.

Luang Prabang
A Laotian–Thai kingdom on the Mekong River in northwest Laos that seceded from Lan Xang when the kingdom came under Vietnamese rule in 1707. Luang Prabang itself fell under French rule as part of the Indochinese Union in 1893.

Louisburg
A French fortress on the southern coast of Cape Breton Island, Canada, that was captured by British forces in 1748 and again, definitively, ten years later.

Loyalists
The name applied to colonists in the American Revolution who remained loyal to Britain. Many subsequently settled in Canada, while others returned to Britain.

Maputo
Now the capital of modern Mozambique, a site that formerly served as a trading post used by several European countries. In the late18th century it became a Portuguese colony, and the city was named Lourenço Marques.

marine chronometer
An instrument that measures time accurately at sea in spite of a ship's movement or variations in temperature, humidity, and air pressure. With an accurate chronometer ship's captains could determine their longitude at sea.

Mississippi Company
French mercantile company with a monopoly on trade with France's American colonies west of the Mississippi River. It collapsed spectacularly in 1720.

Mons
Inhabitants of Lower Burma around the Irrawaddy Delta. The Mon Kingdom, based around the city of Pegu, was overrun by the rulers of the Toungou Dynasty in 1539. They in turn conquered the Toungou in 1752, but lost their independence to the northern Konbaung Dynasty soon after.

Muradid Dynasty
Ruling dynasty of Tunisia founded by Murad Bey, who, appointed Ottoman governor of Tunis in 1612, established an all-but-independent state in the province.

Mysore, Sultanate of
Muslim state in southern India estabished after the overthrow of the Hindu Vijayanagar Kingdom in

1565. Mysore became a major regional power under Haidar Ali, who usurped the throne in 1761.

Natchez
Native American people who in the18th century inhabited an area of Mississippi around the city now named after them. They clashed with French settlers, who defeated and displaced them.

National Assembly
The elected assembly set up at the start of the French Revolution in 1789 after the Third Estate of commoners withdrew from the Estates General.

nawab
Title given to Muslim princes in India.

nizam
Title adopted by the Muslim rulers of Hyderabad in south-central India; it was first used by the Mughal Viceroy Asaf Jah Nizam al-Mulk in 1724.

Oirat Mongols
People from western Mongolia around Ulan Bator. Mongols who did not claim descent from Genghis Khan, they began to encroach on Xinjiang and Tibet in the 15th and 16th centuries, challenging the rule of the Chinese Ming Dynasty. They were overwhelmed by the Manchus in 1755.

Old World, The
The world known to Europeans before the discovery of the "New World" of the Americas—in other words Europe, Asia, and northern Africa.

Oman, Sultanate of
A sheikhdom of southern Arabia whose rulers first threw the Portuguese out of Muscat, their stronghold on the Persian Gulf (1650), then took over their East African possessions, including Zanzibar and Mombasa (1698).

Osei Tutu
Ruler of the Ashanti from about 1680 to 1717, Osei Tutu liberated his people from the domination of Denkyira then led them to regional dominance on Africa's Gold Coast.

Ottawa
Algonquian-speaking Native American people who lived along the Ottawa River at the time of European penetration of North America. They allied with French settlers against the Iroquois.

Ottoman Dynasty
Named for Uthman, a Turkic tribal leader who came to prominence in eastern Asia Minor in 1281, a line of rulers who built a great and enduring empire in western Asia and the eastern Mediterranean from the 14th century on.

Oudh, Kingdom of
Former kingdom now forming part of the northeast Indian state of Uttar Pradesh. Muslim-ruled from the 12th century, it came under British control with the agreement of the Mughals in 1756 and was fully incorporated into British India in 1856.

Oyo, Kingdom of
A state in the interior of what is now western Nigeria whose warrior elite grew wealthy from the proceeds of the slave trade: they raided settlements in the surrounding countryside and traded their captives with visiting merchants on the coast.

Park, Mungo
Scottish explorer (1771–1806) who in 1795 set out to explore the Niger River, thought at the time to be a tributary of the Gambia—hence his departure up that river from the West African coast. Succeeding in reaching the Niger, he was taken prisoner by a local chief but escaped to safety.

Partitions of Poland
The division of Poland among Prussia, Russia, and Austria, depriving it of its independent statehood. There were three partitions of Polish territory, in 1772, 1793, and 1795.

pasha
The respectful title given to a vizier, senior military officer, or provincial governor under the Ottoman Empire. Pashas often had considerable freedom of action.

Pawnee
Native American people of the Great Plains who in the 18th century inhabited the Kansas–Nebraska region.

penal colony
Settlements established by the British authorities first in the Americas and then in Australia to which convicts found guilty of serious crimes were deported for punishment by hard labor. About 10 percent of all transportees were kept in penal colonies, which were established at such sites as Port Jackson (Sydney) and remote Norfolk Island.

peon
In Spanish America a landless agricultural laborer.

Peru, Viceroyalty of
One of the great administrative divisions of colonial Spanish America, ruled from Lima by a viceroy and comprising modern-day Peru and northern Chile. Prior to the creation of a separate Viceroyalty of New Granada in 1717, it incorporated all of Spain's American possessions south of the Isthmus of Panama except for the Venezuelan coast.

Piedmont
The name given to the alluvial plateau stretching along the eastern flank of the Appalachian mountain chain in North America.

Pomerania
A region on either side of the mouth of the Oder River on the south coast of the Baltic Sea, now on the border between modern Germany and Poland. A medieval duchy, it later became part of Brandenburg–Prussia but was much disputed. In 1648 western Pomerania was ceded to Sweden.

Pompeii
An ancient city in Italy buried for centuries beneath layers of lava and ash following a volcanic eruption in 79 A.D. until excavated from 1748 on.

Pontiac
Ottawa chief who led an uprising against British colonial forces in North America that broke out shortly after the conclusion of the French and Indian War in 1763.

Pragmatic Sanction
An edict passed by Emperor Charles VI of Austria in 1717 making provision for his daughter Maria Theresa to succeed to all the hereditary Hapsburg territories in Europe should he die without a son.

prime minister
The executive head of government in Britain (and in other countries with a parliamentary system), who is usually the leader of the largest party in Parliament. Robert Walpole (1676–1745) is regarded as the first British prime minister.

privateer
A pirate licensed by a government to attack and prey on the shipping of its enemies, as the Barbary Corsairs were by the Ottoman Turks.

Protestant
Any of the churches or their members that broke with the Catholic church in the Reformation. Protestants originally took their name from the "protestation" by the supporters of Martin Luther against the decision made at the Diet of Speyer (1529) to reaffirm the edict of the Diet of Worms against Luther's teachings.

Punjab
One of the northernmost districts of India, bordering what is now Pakistan. It was the first area to fall before the advance of Mahmud of Ghazni's Islamic forces in the 11th century.

Reign of Terror
The most violent period of the French Revolution, from mid 1793 to July 1794, during which the Jacobins are thought to have murdered more than 40,000 people in Paris and elsewhere.

rococo style
A style of decoration popular in early 18th-century Europe characterized by light colors—pale pinks, greens, and blues—and the use of ornate scrollwork and shell motifs.

Qajar Dynasty
Dynasty established in Persia (Iran) in 1794, when, after years of unrest, the last Zand ruler, Lotf Ali Khan, was overthrown by Agha Mohammad Khan Qajar. It would reign until 1925.

Qing Dynasty
Final Chinese imperial dynasty (1644–1912); its zenith was under Kangxi and Qianlong (1654–1792), when China reached its greatest territorial extent, stretching from Turkistan in the west to the island of Taiwan in the east.

Qosot Mongols
One of the four constituent tribes of the Oirat Mongols; their leader, Gushri Khan, helped the fifth Dalai Lama attain power in Tibet by overthrowing the king of Tsang in 1642.

Quakers
Members of the Society of Friends, a Christian sect founded in England in the mid-17th century. Its beliefs include nonviolence, the rejection of set forms of worship, and simplicity of dress and speech.

Queen Anne's War
One of the French and Indian Wars that set French and English settlers of North America against one another in the 17th and 18th centuries. Fought from 1702 to 1713, it was the American component of Europe's War of the Spanish Succession.

Rio de la Plata, Viceroyalty of
Administrative division of Spain's South American empire, separated from the Viceroyalty of Peru in 1776, that comprised Argentina, Paraguay, Bolivia, and southern Chile. Its capital was Buenos Aires.

Rohilkhand, Kingdom of
Area of northern India in the modern state of Uttar Pradesh that was ruled by the Rohillas from 1721 until 1774, when it was overrun by the British and the nawab of Oudh.

Rohillas
Afghan people who spread south in the early 18th century to take control of the north Indian region of Rohilkhand.

Royal African Company
Also known as the British Africa Company. Originally chartered by the English crown in 1663 as the Company of Royal Adventurers of England to trade with Africa, the company had a monopoly on the trade in slaves between West Africa and America's English colonies—a privilege fiercely contested by independent traders in the 1720s.

rupee
The standard monetary unit of countries of the Indian subcontinent.

Russian Orthodox church
Russian branch of the Orthodox church, the form of Christianity recognized throughout the eastern Mediterranean world.

Russo-Turkish Wars
A series of conflicts fought from the 17th to the 19th centuries in which an expansionist Russia attempted to increase its Balkan territories at the expense of the Ottoman Empire: the war of 1768–1774 brought major gains for Russia.

Safavid Dynasty
Beginning with Esmail I in 1501, this Persian dynasty ruled over not only Iran but also Armenia, Georgia, and parts of Uzbekistan, Turkmenistan, Azerbaijan, and Afghanistan. Esmail's commitment to the minority Shiite branch of Islam had a profound impact on the region's subsequent history.

Saudi Dynasty
Line of local Arabian rulers established in the 15th century by Muhammad ibn Saud with its capital at Riyadh. In the mid-18th century they embraced Wahhabism and embarked on a program of expansion.

Segu
Trading city on the upper Niger River in modern Mali populated by Bambara-speaking people; it became the center of a powerful kingdom under the leadership of Mamari Kubali (1712–1755).

serf
A laborer who was not free to move from the land on which he or she worked.

Saxony
A duchy, later a kingdom, on the Elbe River in eastern Germany that was ruled by an elector.

sextant
Navigational instrument used to determine a ship's latitude; devised independently by British and American inventors around 1730, it works by sighting a heavenly body through a telescope and measuring its angle above the horizon.

Siak, Sultanate of
Originally part of the Sultanate of Malacca–Johore on the Malaysian Peninsula, Siak developed out of internal feuding in 1723 as a separate state. The sultanate accepted Dutch authority in 1858.

Siam, Kingdom of
Successor state in Thailand to the Kingdom of Ayutthaya (1351–1767) after the city of Ayutthaya itself was overrun by the Burmese. The capital was subsequently moved to Thon Buri (1767–1782) and then to Bangkok.

Sierra Leone
Country of coastal West Africa that from 1787 was the site of Freetown, a British colony for repatriated and shipwrecked slaves. It was run by the British Sierra Leone Company from 1791 to 1808, when it became an official crown colony.

Silesia
A region of central Europe, now in southwest Poland, that was the cause of several wars between Prussia and Austria in the 18th century.

Sons of Liberty
In the American Revolution secret groups that sprang up in the late 1760s to organize resistance to the Stamp Act.

South Sea Bubble
The crash that in 1720 followed a speculative boom in the shares of the South Sea Company, set up to trade with Spanish America. The financial crisis that followed threatened the stability of the British government.

Stamp Act
Measure passed by the British Parliament in 1765 in an attempt to recoup some of the expense of administering the American colonies. In future all newspapers, legal documents, and other official papers were to bear a revenue stamp. The discontent the act caused on the grounds of "No taxation without representation" helped create the resistance that bred the American Revolution.

sultan
Taken from the Arabic word for "power" or "authority," this title is often loosely applied to any Muslim ruler but is associated especially with the emperors of the Ottoman Dynasty.

Table of Ranks
Introduced by Peter the Great of Russia in 1722 as a reforming measure to modernize the Russian state, the Table of Ranks listed 14 parallel ranks for officers and officials in the army, civil service, and court. Although modified by later czars, it remained in force until 1917.

Third Estate
The lowest of the three estates, or assemblies, of the French Estates-General, representing commoners (that is, middle-class townspeople and rural gentry). The First Estate represented the nobility and the Second Estate the clergy.

transportation
A legal sentence of banishment from England, initially to North America and later to Australia. Some 162,000 people were transported between 1788 and 1868.

Treaty of Alliance
A treaty signed in 1778 between France and the United States in which they agreed to aid each other in the event of a British attack on either. By bringing France into the American Revolution, it tipped the scales in favor of the United States. The treaty was annulled in 1799.

Vientiane
The capital of the Lao kingdom of Lan Xang from the mid-16th century. The Kingdom of Vientiane came into being when the southern Laotian states seceded from Vietnamese-dominated Lan Xang in 1707. Coming under Siamese control in 1778, the city became the seat of French rule in Indochina from 1899 onward.

Wahhabis
Followers of Muhammad 'Abd al-Wahhab (1703–1787), whose highly conservative interpretation of Islam became closely associated with the rule of the House of Saud in Arabia.

War of Jenkins's Ear
Maritime war fought in the Caribbean between Britain and Spain from 1739 to 1741. The background to the conflict was commercial rivalry between the two nations, and more specifically the British desire for a bigger share of Spanish-American trade. War fever was stirred by the claim of a Captain Robert Jenkins that Spanish coastguards had cut off one of his ears.

War of the Austrian Succession
War fought from 1740 to 1748 that arose from the refusal of Prussia, France, and Spain to accept Maria Theresa's right to succeed to the Hapsburg dominions on the death of her father, Emperor Charles VI of Austria. Most of Europe's major powers were drawn into the conflict. At the end of the war Austria kept almost all its territories except for Silesia, which was seized by Frederick the Great of Prussia.

War of the Polish Succession
War fought from 1733 to 1735 over the right of Elector Frederick Augustus I of Saxony to succeed to the throne of Poland. His claim was backed by Austria and Russia but opposed by France and Spain. The powers eventually agreed to recognize him as king, and the chief result of the war was to increase Russian influence in Poland. The Treaty of Vienna ending the war was not finally ratified until 1738.

War of the Spanish Succession
War fought from 1701 to 1713 over the succession to the Spanish throne on the death of the childless Charles II, the last Hapsburg king of Spain. The war was fought throughout Europe and spread to the colonies. It was ended by the Treaty of Utrecht (1713), which confirmed the Bourbon succession in Spain.

White Lotus Society
A secret Chinese society tracing its origins to the 4th century A.D. that preached the coming of the Buddha. Vowing to restore the Ming Dynasty by overthrowing the Qing (Manchu), it launched a major rebellion at the end of the 18th century.

Zand Dynasty
Dynasty of rulers in Persia (Iran), effectively established by Karim Khan Zand in the 1750s, although he ruled through the figurehead of the infant Safavid Esmail III. His six successors from 1779 were increasingly beleaguered, and in 1794 the Zands were supplanted by the Qajar shahs.

Zunghar Mongols
Leading tribe of the Oirat Mongols that tried but failed to unite the Mongols against the Manchus. Zunghar forces under their leader Galdan were crushed by the Manchus at Jao Modo in 1696.